SOLDIER

SOLDIER

The Life of Colin Powell

Karen DeYoung

ALFRED A. KNOPF NEW YORK 2006

THIS IS A BORZOI BOOK
PUBLISHED BY ALFRED A. KNOPF

Copyright © 2006 by Karen DeYoung

All rights reserved. Published in the United States by Alfred A. Knopf, a division of Random House, Inc., New York, and in Canada by Random House of Canada Limited, Toronto.

www.aaknopf.com

Excerpted material from *My American Journey* by Colin Powell, copyright © 1995 by Colin L. Powell, is reproduced courtesy of Random House, Inc. and the author.

Library of Congress Cataloging-in-Publication Data

DeYoung, Karen, [date]
Soldier : the life of Colin Powell / Karen DeYoung.—1st ed.
p. cm.
Includes bibliographical references and index.
ISBN 1-4000-4170-8 (alk. paper)
1. Powell, Colin L.   2. Statesmen—United States—Biography.
3. United States. Dept. of State—Biography.   4. Generals—
United States—Biography.   5. African American generals—
Biography.   6. United States. Army—Biography.   7. Powell,
Colin L.—Childhood and youth.   8. Powell, Colin L.—Family.
9. Powell family.   I. Title.
E840.P64D49 2006
973.931092—dc22   2006045288
[B]

Manufactured in the United States of America

First Edition

For my wonderful father,
Bill De Young

SOLDIER

1

I will never not be a soldier.

—Colin L. Powell

At precisely 5 p.m. on September 19, 2005, students and faculty bustling along the shaded sidewalks of the National War College stopped and stood at silent attention as the notes from a solitary bugle drifted by on a late-summer breeze. The crisp cadences of the ceremonial Retreat, signaling the official end of the day, were a quotidian reminder that this bucolic campus beside the Potomac River in Washington, D.C. was no ordinary seat of higher learning. Located inside a military installation, Fort Lesley J. McNair, it was surrounded by high redbrick walls and protected by armed guards at every gate.

Despite its bellicose name, the War College had been established at the end of World War II as an institution devoted as much to the avoidance of war as to its practice. Its students were drawn from among the most promising midlevel officers in the armed forces but also from the Department of State, in recognition of diplomacy's critical role in keeping the nation secure. Warriors and diplomats studied side by side, learning about each other and from the great strategists in both their fields.

On this warm September evening, the college was celebrating its sixtieth anniversary with a speech by its most distinguished graduate, retired general and former Secretary of State Colin Luther Powell. As the last bugle note sounded, those on their way to Powell's 5:30 address resumed their journey toward Roosevelt Hall, an imposing, neoclassical administration and classroom building on the waterfront.

The summer of 2005 was also an anniversary for Powell himself. It marked exactly thirty years since he had arrived on campus as a thirty-eight-year-old lieutenant colonel in the Army Infantry. At the time, the New York City–born son of Jamaican immigrants was already well on his way to a brilliant career, with two tours in Vietnam, a stint in the Pentagon and a prestigious White House fellowship under his belt. If he fulfilled the promise that more senior officers saw in him, he could expect to retire after thirty-five years of service with two or more general's stars on his shoulders. He would be one of only a handful of black officers to have risen to such heights.

Powell ultimately soared beyond even his own dreams, becoming national security adviser to one president and chairman of the Joint Chiefs of Staff, the military's highest office, under two more. He brought the U.S. military through the end of the Cold War and guided it to victory in the Persian Gulf War in 1991. By the time he retired from the Army in 1993, he was a national icon of wise leadership—"the most trusted man in America," according to opinion polls—and his face and inspiring life story were known throughout the world.

When President-elect George W. Bush selected Powell as his secretary of state in December 2000, it was hailed as a stroke of genius. With Powell as the nation's most senior Cabinet officer and fourth in the line of succession to the presidency, America's foreign policy would be in good hands. For Powell himself, it was the culmination of a lifetime of achievement, the seamless melding of soldier and statesman that the National War College had been established to create.

Since leaving the State Department in January 2005 after Bush's election to a second term, Powell had traveled the lecture circuit making paid speeches on leadership and U.S. foreign policy to corporate boards and industry conventions. He never spoke about the specific circumstances of his resignation as secretary of state except to say, when asked, that Cabinet reshuffles were normal at the end of a four-year mandate and his departure had been a "mutual decision" between him and the president. He artfully brushed aside inquiries about the many published accounts of deep ideological schisms that had rent Bush's national security team and the private humiliations he had reportedly endured at the hands of powerful colleagues.

Audiences often asked about his public role in promoting and defending what many considered to be the most ill-advised act of Bush's presidency: the March 2003 invasion of Iraq. Powell had thrown his considerable personal and professional reputation behind the administration's charges that Iraq possessed chemical, biological and perhaps even nuclear weapons and posed an imminent threat to the United States. In a crucial speech to the United Nations Security Council six weeks before the invasion was launched, he had convinced many skeptical Americans that the threat posed by Iraqi dictator Saddam Hussein was real.

But the war had gone sour almost from the moment U.S. troops rolled triumphantly into Baghdad two months later. A full-blown insurgency had erupted against the occupation forces, Iraq had become a killing field for American soldiers and after two and a half years there was still no end in sight. Powell's credibility had been seriously undermined when the threatening weapons he cited as the main justification for invasion turned out not to exist.

No one in his legions of admirers wanted to believe that Powell had been duped by the White House—or, worse yet, that he had knowingly betrayed the nation's trust. Many assumed that he had privately argued against such a clearly misguided adventure and been overruled. But if that was the case, why had such a proud and accomplished man continued to lend the administration his wisdom and expertise—not to mention his credibility?

In fact, Powell had never advised against the Iraq invasion, although he had warned Bush of the difficulties and counseled patience. But the larger mystery of his tenure as secretary of state remained. For four years, over Iraq and a host of other foreign policy issues, he had found himself entrenched in regular combat with conservative ideologues—including the vice president and the secretary of defense. Though he had scored some victories, the rumored humiliations had been real. He had been purposely cut out of major foreign policy decisions more than once, and his advice had often gone unheeded or been only grudgingly accepted by the president. Why hadn't he resigned?

The easy answer had the virtue of truth: soldiers didn't quit when they disagreed with the decisions of their commanders. The fact that he had been out of uniform since 1993 was irrelevant to Powell; he would be a soldier until he drew his last breath. But there were other, less easily explained reasons, tangled up in the complicated human core where a man's deepest beliefs about himself and the world around him reside.

After four long years, Powell had anticipated the end of his service and sometimes even longed for it. He had never directly told the president but thought he had made clear to him during the summer of 2004 that he did not intend to stay beyond the next presidential inauguration on January 20, 2005. But when the end of his tenure came, and because of the way it came, his satisfaction at having done his duty was tinged with anger and disappointment.

As the November 2 election approached, gossip and media speculation about a potential second Bush term centered on the likelihood of Cabinet changes. With Iraq in chaos, some thought that Defense Secretary Donald

Rumsfeld was a leading candidate for departure. Others were doubtful—getting rid of Rumsfeld meant acknowledging that mistakes had been made.

Many thought the president might ask the secretary of state to reenlist, at least temporarily. Powell was still the most popular member of his team, far more popular than the president himself. Moreover, a number of foreign policy balls were in the air: the Palestinian-Israeli peace process, which Powell had shepherded for years, was at a critical juncture, and crucial elections for an interim Iraqi government were scheduled for the end of January. Senior Powell aides, long aware of his determination to leave, had recently become convinced that the secretary anticipated an invitation to stay. They were equally certain that he intended to accept, especially if Rumsfeld would be gone.

On Thursday, November 4, two days after winning 51 percent of the vote against Democratic challenger Senator John F. Kerry, Bush told reporters at a White House news conference that he was heading to Camp David, the presidential retreat in the hills of western Maryland. Over a three-day weekend with National Security Adviser Condoleezza Rice and White House Chief of Staff Andrew Card, Jr., he said he intended to "begin the process of thinking about the Cabinet and the White House staff." That afternoon, Card told Cabinet members in a conference call that the president would not ask for the pro forma resignation letters customarily offered at the end of a first term.

When he returned the following Monday, Bush's first announcement was that Card would be staying in his job. On Tuesday, the White House announced two resignations: Secretary of Commerce Donald Evans, a personal friend of Bush who wanted to move back to his home state of Texas, and Attorney General John Ashcroft. The president's legal counsel, Alberto Gonzales, was named as Ashcroft's replacement.

On Wednesday, November 10, Powell received a telephone call from the White House at his State Department office. The caller was not Bush but Card, and he got right to the point. "The president would like to make a change," he said, using a time-honored formulation that avoided the words "resign" or "fire." Card noted briskly that there had been some discussion of having Powell remain until after the January 30 Iraqi elections, but that the president had decided to take care of all Cabinet changes sooner rather than later. Bush wanted Powell's resignation letter dated Friday, November 12, Card said, although the White House expected him to stay at the State Department until his successor could be confirmed by the Senate.

The president himself made no contact with Powell. For two days, the only person at the State Department Powell told about Card's call was his deputy and friend of decades, Richard Armitage. He typed his resignation letter himself on his home computer. (The White House later pointed out a typo and sent it back to be redone.)

Some who had departed high government positions under similar circumstances had used their letters as emotional postcards. When then–Treasury Secretary Paul O'Neill was told at the end of 2002 that the president wanted to "make some changes" in his economic team (O'Neill's call came from Vice President Dick Cheney), he composed four terse and bitter sentences. But Powell was loath to reveal either surprise or insult. He used the letter to claim the decision to resign as his own.

"Dear Mr. President:" he wrote. "As we have discussed in recent months, I believe that now that the election is over the time has come for me to step down as Secretary of State…effective at your pleasure." He was pleased, Powell said, to "have been part of a team that launched the Global War Against Terror, liberated the Afghan and Iraqi people, brought the attention of the world to the problem of proliferation, reaffirmed our alliances, adjusted to the Post–Cold War world and undertook major initiatives to deal with the problem of poverty and disease in the developing world. In these and in so many other areas, your leadership was the driving force of our success."

Powell signed the letter "Very respectfully," the phrase used by every Army recruit and officer when writing formally to a superior. As instructed, he handed it to Card at the White House on Friday. That evening, he informed Grant Green and Marc Grossman, his undersecretaries of management and policy, and his own chief of staff, Lawrence Wilkerson, although he kept from them the details of Card's call.

Form and style, in Powell's view, were almost as important as substance; presentation could make or break any initiative. After his inelegant dismissal as secretary of state—typical of the peremptory manner in which the Bush White House did business—he wanted at least to control the way his departure was announced. Over the weekend, he put together a plan: he would inform his inner-office staff at exactly 8:20 a.m. on Monday, November 15. He would tell his other senior aides at their regular 8:30 staff meeting. At 10:15, he would send an e-mail to his friends and extended family. He called Card and told him he expected the White House would then publicly announce his resignation.

At midmorning Monday, the White House released five separate statements under Bush's name, reporting the resignations of the secretaries of agriculture, energy, education, and state and the head of the Republican National Committee. Each statement was three paragraphs long and titled "President Thanks [official's name]." When White House spokesman Scott McClellan briefed the media shortly after noon, all but one of the resignation questions were about Powell. Had Bush tried to persuade him to stay? Had Powell offered? If so, had the president turned him down? McClellan avoided a direct answer. "I think you saw from Secretary Powell's letter that this is a discussion that they've had for some months now, or over recent months at least. And Secretary Powell made a decision for his own reasons that this was now the time to leave."

At 1 p.m., Powell made his way to the press briefing room on the State Department's second floor. It had been a "great honor and privilege to have been once again given the opportunity to serve my nation," he told reporters in an opening statement designed to preempt the kinds of questions that had peppered McClellan. "It has always been my intention that I would serve one term," and after he and the president had had "good and fulsome discussions on it, we came to the mutual agreement that it would be appropriate for me to leave at this time."

But did he offer to stay? a reporter asked. Or "did the president just choose to say, let's do the letter now?"

"I made no offer," Powell replied. "We had pretty much come to our mutual agreement without anybody having to make any offer, counteroffers, anything like that. We knew where we were heading."

The next morning, Bush nominated Condoleezza Rice to replace Powell as secretary of state.

Powell's departure topped the week's news from Washington, and the inevitable reviews of his four years as the nation's chief diplomat were mixed. He was hailed as a man of honor and stature who would be hard for Bush to replace. But he was also criticized widely for failing to live up to his potential. Powell was a "good soldier" who ultimately prized "loyalty over leadership," wrote *The New York Times* editorial page, no admirer of the Bush administration. "There were moments in his tenure when Mr. Powell could have resigned over principle. But he soldiered on, leaving when it was safe and convenient for his boss." On the political right, long-standing critics bade him good riddance.

Powell was outraged when *The Washington Post* reported that he had arrived at the White House for a meeting with Bush on November 12, the day he dropped off his resignation letter, with "a list of conditions under which he would be willing to stay." Powell had been with Bush that day, but only in the context of the president's meeting with visiting British Prime Minister Tony Blair. There had been no list of demands; there had been no conversation at all with the White House, beyond Card, about his departure. "Anybody who knows me," he said afterward, "knows that I never would have gone to the President of the United States with a set of demands as to what it [would] take to keep me." He was offended by the very idea.

Powell saw Bush regularly over the next two months, passing through the Oval Office for official meetings on a variety of subjects that took place as if nothing had transpired. Eventually, the White House contacted Wilkerson to schedule what it described as a "farewell call" with the president being arranged for each departing Cabinet secretary. Set for January 6, Powell's appointment was later rescheduled for January 13, one week before the second-term inauguration. As the date approached, Card's office asked the State Department to provide "talking points" to prepare the president for the meeting.

For Wilkerson, the request was the last straw from a White House he saw as incapable of showing either respect or common courtesy. "There was no way we were going to provide talking points," he later recalled. "If the President of the United States couldn't have his principal Cabinet officer call on him after four years in office and think of something to say, it was a disgrace. I even hung up on one of them." When the White House persisted, Wilkerson said bitterly, he decided to make something up. "We gave them something like 'China, India-Pakistan.' "

Seeing the meeting scheduled on his calendar, Powell asked his staff about its purpose. They told him they assumed it was a good-bye photo opportunity with Bush, suggesting that perhaps he should bring his family. "We've got a houseful of pictures," Powell replied dryly. Was he supposed to talk to the president? Or was the president supposed to talk to him? "Am I supposed to say: 'This is what I think? Or what?' " Nothing, he was told. It was just a "farewell call."

The appointed time found Powell already at the White House for a routine meeting; when it concluded, he lingered in the Oval Office as the others left the room. As Powell later remembered it, Bush seemed puzzled and called after his departing chief of staff, "Where you going, Andy?"

"Mr. President, I think this is supposed to be our farewell call," Powell prompted.

"Is that why Condi ain't here?" Over four years, Rice had almost always been present when Powell met with the president.

That was probably the reason, Powell replied. Card walked back inside,

and the three men sat down. Powell had already decided to use the opportunity—likely his last as secretary of state—to unload.

The war in Iraq was going south, he said after a few moments of small
talk, and the president had little time left to turn it around. The administration's hope was that the upcoming election would change the dynamics
on the ground and the Iraqi people would finally be ready and able to
begin standing up to the insurgents on their own. But the administration
had entertained such hopes before over the past two years—when it had
set up a new legal framework for Iraq, when it had first turned a modicum
of government power over to handpicked Iraqis and when ousted dictator
Saddam Hussein had been captured—and they had been dashed every
time. There would be a window of about two months after the election "to
start to see progress," he told Bush. "If by the first of April this insurgency
is not starting to ameliorate in some way, then I think you really have a
problem."

Elections, and talking about democracy, were unlikely to stop the
insurgency, he said. Only the fledgling Iraqi Army could do that, and it
was unclear whether it would ever succeed. Its competence was not just a
matter of training, Powell said; it was a question of whether the troops
believed in what they were fighting for. They were no different from
American soldiers, who fought because they believed in their institutions
and in their country, and their civilian and military leaders. And when
that belief vanished, as it had in Vietnam, the going got tough.

Closer to home, Powell continued, Bush needed to begin his new term
by paying serious attention to the poisoned relations between his State
and Defense departments. Senior officials in Rumsfeld's office at the Pentagon were actively and dangerously undermining the president's diplomacy, he said, mentioning several by name. Bush replied that every
administration had similar problems and recalled the legendary battles
between Secretary of State George Shultz and Defense Secretary Caspar
Weinberger in President Ronald Reagan's administration. Powell assured
him that he had been there, as Weinberger's chief military aide and later
as Reagan's national security adviser, and that what was happening now
was something altogether different.

Powell's last-minute intervention appeared to have little impact on the
president. The session ended with a cordial handshake, and the secretary
returned to the State Department. "That was really strange," he reported
to Wilkerson. "The President didn't know why I was there."

Eight months later, as Powell strode into the plush, red-curtained and
-carpeted Roosevelt Hall auditorium at the National War College, the

applause from a sea of military uniforms was appreciative but muted. At his civilian speeches, audiences usually stood and cheered the moment he walked onstage. But this was family. It was almost as if he had just returned to them from a faraway battle whose outcome was uncertain and they weren't quite sure how to receive him.

He began, as all good speakers do, with a personal note and a laugh, naming the more prominent members of his own War College class of 1976. Some of them were in the audience, he said, noting approvingly that they had "all walked in under their own power." At age sixty-eight, Powell retained his military bearing and still had a full head of hair, albeit more gray than black.

He recalled his time at the college as a turning point in his career and in his perspective, from a midlevel officer's inward-looking institutional gaze to a future leader's appreciation of the wider world. "That's where you are today," Powell told the students in the audience. "It's time to come outside...and look at all that is out there...the opportunities and the risks. It is time to...understand the role of diplomacy and understand politics—yes, dirty, nasty politics."

He outlined some of the ways the world had changed over the three decades since he was a War College student and told stories about his encounters with the high and the mighty during a long career in the corridors of power. Relaxed and without a text, using his hands easily for emphasis, he wove together the past and the future, the personal and the political. When he concluded after nearly half an hour, the audience rose to its feet, and the applause was loud and long.

Powell invited questions, and after a few softballs a young man in a dark suit stood and said he was from the State Department. Was it true, he asked, that Powell had disagreed about the timing of the Iraq invasion? Was that his only point of disagreement over the war? Had he ever considered resigning?

Powell replied by rote with a familiar chronology: the recalcitrance of Saddam Hussein after he was defeated in the Persian Gulf War of 1991; Saddam's subsequent refusal to verify the United Nations–mandated destruction of his weapons systems; the failure of international economic sanctions to force him to change his ways; and the inefficiency and expense of American air patrols designed to keep him in check. After Afghanistan-based al-Qaeda terrorists struck New York and Washington on September 11, 2001, some members of the president's national security team had argued that immediate retaliation should be directed at Iraq. Powell had thought that Afghanistan should be the target, he said, and Bush had agreed with him. Later, when pressure for an invasion of

Iraq had grown, Powell had proposed trying diplomacy at the United Nations before resorting to war, and again the president had agreed.

He had told Bush at the time that "if diplomacy doesn't work, the military option will still be there," Powell said, and he had always known that "someday a choice might come." When the moment arrived and Bush decided to go to war, "I supported him. I can't go on a long patrol and then say 'never mind.' "

No, he concluded. He had "never thought of resigning."

2

What a island! What a people! Man an woman, old an young Jusa pack dem bag an baggage An tun history upside dung!

—Louise Bennett

Early in the twentieth century, around the time of the First World War, Alice McKoy left her husband and her home on a sugar plantation at the isolated western tip of the island of Jamaica. Her abandonment of Edwin McKoy, a plantation overseer and the father of her nine children, was scandalous behavior for the time and place, although some believed Edwin's fondness for rum had given her ample reason to leave. But those who knew her well said Alice was a feisty woman—a *tartar* in the local patois—who simply wanted more out of life than what the humid savannas of Westmoreland Parish, or the whole of Jamaica, had to offer. Although she would return to live there many years later, not long before she died, she left Jamaica with no intention of coming back soon.

Alice's journey began in the waning days of a massive, decades-long migration from the islands of the Caribbean. Like tens of thousands before her, she made her way south to Panama, where there was work on the newly opened shipping canal across the narrow isthmus between North and South America, and then to New York City. In 1923, Alice sent for her twenty-two-year-old daughter. Her name, a combination of down-to-earth plainness and light-as-air whimsy, was Maud Ariel, although everyone she knew called her Arie.

Like Arie McKoy, young Luther Theophilus Powell came from a family of nine children. But while Arie's father could afford to send her to high school and a secretarial course, Luther's formal education had ended early. He worked in a general store owned by family friends not far from the small Jamaican village where he was born.

Luther's parents, Aubrey and Rosena Powell, were subsistence farmers who scratched out a living on a small plot of land near the island's south-ern coast, where the rolling topography was unfit for sugar. The village, called Top Hill, was little more than a few small shops and a church along a rutted dirt road; most of its population lived scattered along narrow paths of rust-colored earth that bled into the surrounding fields of wild, shoulder-high guinea grass. At the end of each path was a tiny house and a dirt yard that served as kitchen, dining room and parlor. Indoor plumb-ing was nonexistent, and electricity was still more than half a century away. Life in Top Hill revolved around work, extended families and the Church of England. The Powells ate what they could grow and raised a handful of goats and sheep that foraged in the tall grass.

Luther was getting by, but Jamaica held little future for him, and in the early spring of 1920 he appeared at his parents' home to announce that he had earned enough money to buy a steamship ticket to the United States. His youngest sister, Ernie, remembered the day well into her ninth decade of life. "He didn't tarry long. He came here, got his things together and left." He arrived in Philadelphia aboard a United Fruit vessel carry-ing Jamaican bananas on April 26, 1920, a month after his twenty-second birthday.

In his sepia-colored passport photograph, Luther Powell is sitting straight and stiff in a high-backed wicker chair that evokes the tropics. He is clean-shaven and dressed in a stylish, wide-lapel suit, his tie neatly held in place with a round stickpin, and although he is attempting to look stern his eyes are wide and anxious. In her own passport photo, Arie McKoy is seated in a nearly identical chair. Her body is turned slightly sideways, but she is facing the camera. Her head is tipped a bit, and her hair is smoothly combed to the side and fastened with a small barrette. The hint of a smile is playing on her shapely lips.

Among the nearly 3.4 million immigrants who flooded the United States in the postwar years between 1918 and 1924, fewer than 58,000 were Negroes. Uniformly classified by the U.S. Bureau of Immigration as "Africans (black)," virtually none of them had come from Africa, and their colors ranged from ebony to near porcelain. Most were West Indians, and unlike the many newcomers who had fled lives of hardship in Europe, few thought of themselves as poor or irrevocably torn from the land of their birth. Long after Luther and Arie had met and married, started a family and become U.S. citizens—he in 1936 and she in 1940—they still consid-ered themselves Jamaicans. They never spoke ill of their lives on the island or gave any high-sounding reasons for why they had left. Although the McKoys were better off in Jamaica than the Powells, neither family had wanted for the basics. Education and opportunity were available within limits; they had freely practiced their religion and brought it with them intact to the United States.

When Luther and Arie arrived, America was already beginning to roll up the welcome mat for all but a narrow slice of immigrants. Beyond the small minority of "Africans," a growing number of the newcomers were considered "nonwhite"—including Spaniards, Italians, Russians, Greeks and Jews—and their arrival had spawned the pseudoscientific definition of a true "American race" that was largely restricted to those with the whitest skin who had arrived earlier, from Britain, Scandinavia or Germany. Government commissions concluded that certain races were "unassimilable" and that dilution of the existing population would lead to cultural and intellectual degeneration. The entrance of Asian immigrants had been severely restricted since the late 1880s; the new landing of southern and eastern Europeans led to the imposition of increasingly convoluted physical and mental tests for admission.

A literacy test imposed by Congress in 1917 required aspiring U.S. entrants to read a specified passage of thirty to forty words, "printed in plain legible type." The text in use in the early 1920s was taken from the Bible's Seventh Psalm: "He hath also prepared for him the instruments of death; he ordaineth his arrows against the persecutors. Behold, he travaileth with iniquity and hath conceived mischief, and brought forth falsehood. He made a pit, and digged it, and is fallen into the ditch which he made." Some criticized the passage as too complicated, with too many words not in common use. But whereas many Europeans faltered, West Indians—virtually all English-speaking products of the British colonial education system, many with high school diplomas or beyond—passed with ease. In 1923, the year Arie McKoy landed in New York, 98.6 percent of all incoming "African" immigrants could read and write.

Immigration regulations recognized no nuance in the category, noting that " 'African (black)' refers to the African Negro, whether coming from Cuba or other islands of the West Indies, North or South America, Europe or Africa. Any alien with admixtures of blood of the African Negro should be classified under this heading." Yet surprisingly little official interest was shown in restricting the entry of West Indians. In part, this was because they passed all the intelligence tests and their small numbers and gravitation toward a few northeastern cities allowed them to slip largely under the racial radar. Most important, in the convoluted bureaucracy of the day, their British passports trumped their color. On paper at least, they were already members of the "American race," and it would be years before racial purists set out to rectify the mistake.

Arie arrived at Ellis Island, the immigration gateway to New York, on May 2, 1923, aboard the SS *Turrialba*. Sick from the weeklong journey from Kingston via the Cayman Islands and vowing she would never make another trip by sea, she nevertheless told immigration officials she had no intention of residing in the United States and would return to Jamaica after three months. For reasons lost to history, they listed her occupation as "nurse." They confirmed that she was neither insane nor an anarchist and that she possessed $50 in cash. Whether or not she originally intended just a visit, she quickly settled into Alice's Harlem apartment at 30 West 134th Street and the warm embrace of New York's growing Jamaican community. Fully a quarter of the city's Negro population was Caribbean-born by the 1920s, and Harlem was their neighborhood of choice.

It was the height of the Harlem Renaissance—the outpouring of Negro literature, music and political expression between the end of World War I and the Great Depression—and West Indians were in the thick of it. The Jamaican activist Marcus Garvey had started a New York branch of his Universal Negro Improvement Association, the largest organized Negro mass movement of its time. The Jamaican poet Claude McKay wrote of the beauty of the city streets, the ugliness of American racism and an immigrant's longing for the islands of "bananas ripe and green...and dewy dawns, and mystical blue skies in benediction over nun-like hills." Eric Walrond, from British Guiana by way of Panama, chronicled the Caribbean diaspora in journalism and short stories. The vaudevillian Bert Wheeler, from Antigua, played regularly at Harlem's Lafayette Theatre and was the only Negro ever to appear as a Ziegfeld Follies headliner. Robert L. Douglas, from Saint Kitts, began the Harlem Renaissance Big Five, one of the most successful basketball teams of the era. The team played in the Renaissance Casino ballroom, where finely dressed West Indians also gathered for formal events.

Much about their new home was disquieting to the islanders. Harlem in the 1920s was in transition from a majority white to a majority Negro community. Whites still controlled much of the commerce and property, and few Negroes owned their own homes. Nonwhite women could not try on clothing at Blumstein's, the leading department store on 125th Street, Harlem's main crosstown drag. Negroes were restricted to balcony seating in most of the movie theaters and weren't allowed at all in most of the local restaurants.

The institutionalized racial discrimination and strict color line imposed in the United States must have puzzled light-skinned Alice and Arie McKoy more than most West Indians, since at home they were considered all but white.

The Jamaica they had left had its own informal racial pecking order, but it was far more complex and flexible than what they found in New York. As in the United States, Negroes had first come to the West Indies as slaves, brought from Africa in staggering numbers during the eighteenth century to harvest sugar on the plantations that covered the small island outposts of Britain's colonial empire. By the time the British Parliament outlawed the slave trade in 1805, 750,000 Africans had passed through or been deposited in tiny Jamaica, 155 miles long and 46 miles across at its widest point. It was nearly twice the number that arrived in the United States, before and after its independence from Britain, until the Civil War ended slavery there in 1865.

The sheer magnitude of the slave shipments, along with the small population of whites and blanket British emancipation in 1833, eventually launched the Caribbean Africans on a different path from that of their brethren in North America. Slave descendants became property owners and local government officials, and the lingering disadvantages of a dark hue could be trumped by income, level of schooling and ability to "act British." The bottom social and economic rungs still tended to be occupied by the darkest Jamaicans and light skin was aesthetically favored, but racial identity became negotiable.

Jamaicans tended to attribute the state of affairs they found in the United States to a lack of ambition on the part of American Negroes, and they did not hide their disdain. Many of them had been on their way up the economic ladder at home and saw no reason to be shunted back downward in this opportunity-rich new country. They were vocally proud of the fact that their ancestors had been released from slavery decades before the Americans and never tired of noting that they were the majority race back home. They found black Americans' elation over small racial triumphs demeaning—Bruce Llewellyn, the son of Luther Powell's cousin, Nessa, remembered his mother rolling her eyes at oft-told stories of dancing in the streets of Harlem when Samuel J. Battle became New York City's first Negro police officer in 1914. In Jamaica, she would sniff, all of the officers were Negroes, as were the police chief and the commissioner.

The West Indians set themselves apart from American Negroes in ways both conscious and unconscious. While they gave their labor and lives to their new country, their hearts belonged to the islands and to the

British manners that were the mark of status back home. "She was thoroughly British in her ideas, her manners and her plans for her daughters," Shirley Chisholm, who in 1968 became the first black woman elected to the U.S. Congress, recalled of her Barbadian mother. The Brooklyn-born Chisholm, whose father was from British Guiana, had been packed off at age three to live with her grandmother in Barbados, where she could get a good British education. Most British West Indians had been raised in the staid Church of England and found little in common with what they saw as "displays of emotionalism that border on hysteria" in the soulful American Negro forms of worship. To Jamaicans, church meant ornate robes and incense, formality and the oratory of the English service.

Jamaicans felt superior to American blacks and acted like it. "West Indians of color do not have their activities, social, occupational and otherwise, determined by their race," the Jamaican-born journalist W. A. Domingo archly explained in a 1925 article published in a prominent New York journal of sociology. "They do not suffer from the local anesthesia of custom and pride which makes otherwise intolerable situations bearable." Success in America was quickly defined as staying away from the natives, lest their perceived lethargy and very real lack of status rub off.

American Negroes returned the islanders' scorn in full measure, calling them "Jewmaicans" for the emphasis they placed on hard work and education and their failure to appreciate the harsh history and reality of American racism. Although the immigrants themselves could easily tell the difference between a Jamaican and a Trinidadian, to many Americans of color they were all "monkey-chasers"—undifferentiated tropicals with haughty airs who talked funny, dressed strangely and were annoyingly clannish. "When a monkey-chaser dies," went a song popular among American Negroes in New York, just dump him in the Harlem River "and he'll float back to Jamaica."

Rejecting and rejected by their fellow "Africans," the West Indians stuck close together inside their families and churches. They formed innumerable social organizations restricted to their own kind and often even looked to their former colonial master to protect their interests. They formed the British Colonial Society in Harlem, with the blessing of the resident British consul, to provide assistance to the newcomers and "combat prejudice of southern blacks."

While the islanders' affectations of superiority irritated American Negroes, they drew scant interest from a white majority that paid little attention to their British manners and careful delineations of class and education. The newcomers quickly learned that skin color was their most salient attribute in the United States. University graduate or illiterate, West Virginian or West Indian, fair-skinned or brown or deepest black—all Negroes were considered inferior to whites in every way.

Many of the Caribbean émigrés possessed both education and professional skills but found few opportunities to use them in New York. Even in trades open to Negroes, unions were protective of jobs. The islanders' self-assertiveness often compelled them to fight anew battles American Negroes had given up on long ago, and in rare instances they won. It was Caribbean women who integrated New York's garment industry "by their determination, sometimes reinforced by a dexterous use of their hatpins." According to stories long retold by their descendants, the women simply ignored the sign on the door that read "No blacks need apply."

Alice McKoy was part of the garment worker assault; after beginning her life in New York as a maid, she was eventually hired as a seamstress. But what had been advancement for Alice was a step backward for her daughter, who arrived hoping to use her education and secretarial skills. No such opportunity was available to nonwhites, and Arie, too, went to work in a garment factory.

Part of a minority within a minority, Alice and Arie still lived as much in Jamaica as in New York, surrounded by West Indian friends and increasing numbers of arriving relatives bound by common experiences and memories of home. They gathered frequently to dance to island music and feast on rice and peas and curried goat washed down with Jamaican rum. Those who had space in their Harlem apartments earned extra dollars taking in new arrivals. There were few Americans of any color in their world.

Luther Powell had not lingered long in Philadelphia. He traveled first to Connecticut, where he worked as a gardener on the estates of the rich and in a brass factory, and then to New York, where he found a job as a building superintendent. Finally, Luther, too, made his way to the garment industry in the stockroom of a manufacturer of suits and women's coats. According to one family history, Luther was one of Alice's many boarders, and it was in her apartment that he first met Arie and began courting her. Other family members later insisted that the two had met in Pelham Bay Park in the Bronx, where Jamaicans often gathered for weekend picnics.

Short in stature, slender and a natty dresser, Luther had an upright demeanor and an outgoing, optimistic nature. He was devoted to the Episcopal Church, the American equivalent of his beloved Church of England. He liked to read the newspapers and talk about current affairs, and on the rare occasion when he couldn't discern a fellow Jamaican by sight, the lilt of the island accent was invitation enough to start a conversation. In an oft-told family story, Luther was walking past Macy's department store on Thirty-fourth Street one day when he overheard the cadence of Jamaica in the voices of two young women. Within minutes of introducing himself and determining that they were visitors to New York and unmarried, he began to extol the virtues of two of his nephews back home. University educated and well employed, they would be good catches, he said, offering up their names. Here, the story usually went straight to the punch line. One of the girls, recognizing a nephew's name as that of a coworker in Kingston, the Jamaican capital, sought him out after returning home. "Your uncle in New York wants to know why you can't find a girl to get married," she chided. They wed several years later.

Arie was a bustler, always doing something useful. Where Luther saw everyone as a potential partner for conversation or a drop of rum, she was reserved among strangers. He was a dreamer; she was a worrier, and those who didn't know her well found her aloof. Years after her death, her son still pictured her at home, wearing an apron, "always in motion, cooking, washing, ironing, sewing, after working all day downtown." She was small, barely topping five feet, "with a beautiful face, soft brown eyes ... and ... a melting smile."

After they married in 1929, Luther and Arie set up housekeeping with Alice in a spacious apartment on Harlem's Broadhurst Avenue, amid relatives and friends from the islands. Their first child was born in 1931, a daughter they named Marilyn, and despite the advancing Depression Arie quit her job to stay home. Alice continued working through President Franklin Delano Roosevelt's Works Progress Administration, although she swore the family to secrecy over this acceptance of government "welfare."

By the time the extended family moved into a new apartment on Morningside Avenue, just below Columbia University, Alice's youngest child, Arie's sister Laurice, had joined them from Jamaica. On April 5, 1937, Arie gave birth to a son. She and Luther decided to call him Colin, a nice English name that Luther had seen on a shipping label in the warehouse that morning.

Colin's arrival was one of several reasons to celebrate that spring. Just a month after his birth, more than five thousand West Indians packed

Harlem's regal Rockland Palace for a coronation ball honoring Britain's—
and Jamaica's—new King George VI and Queen Elizabeth. The event
was sponsored jointly by the British Consulate and St. Ambrose Episcopal
Parish, with the price of admission listed in British currency: three
shillings, one penny and two farthings. The ballroom was decorated with
the Union Jack and colonial flags, and the guests sang "The Star-Spangled
Banner" only after they finished "God Save the King."

For immigrant families from the Caribbean, the Bronx was the next step
up from Harlem, and in the early 1940s the extended Powell family relocated to the Bronx neighborhood of Hunts Point. A blunt stub of land
extending from the southeast corner of the borough into the East River,
Hunts Point teemed with low-rise, turn-of-the-century brick buildings
whose roomy apartments were filled with a mix of Jewish, Italian and
West Indian immigrants. Inside their homes and in the churches and syn-
agogues where they spent their day of rest, the newcomers continued the
traditions of eastern Europe, the Mediterranean and the Caribbean. But
in the schools and on the streets that served as playgrounds, their children
were thrown together in a polyglot jumble of cultures and colors and
became Americans.

Luther and Arie settled with Alice into a third-story walk-up with four
bedrooms at 952 Kelly Street. Arie's uncle rented an apartment down the
street and her sister, Laurice, wed a serviceman and set up her own home
nearby. Luther's younger sister Beryl had arrived from Jamaica in 1924,
and she and an assortment of cousins lived in close proximity. Little happened in the life of any family member, whether in New York or Jamaica,
that wasn't quickly relayed in the steady flow of letters between Arie and
her sisters back home. It was the women who kept the ties and traditions
intact, and life among the Powells during the years bracketed by the Second World War and the Korean War was an unchanging calendar of family gatherings for every holiday and milestone, with tables filled with
home-cooked Jamaican food as the rum flowed freely and calypso music
poured from the record player.

Nearly every household on Kelly Street and the surrounding blocks
had a family member in the military, and many of them had more than
one. Colin's best friend, Gene Norman, whose parents had emigrated
from the Virgin Islands, had four uncles in the service, and Laurice's husband, Vic, was with the Army's 4th Armored Division in Europe. Young
boys in the neighborhood were obsessed with World War II, tracking
troop movements on maps pinned to their bedroom walls and waging liv-

ing room battles with toy soldiers. They played war in the street, dressed in odds and ends of military gear from the local surplus store and gathered on Saturdays to watch newsreels of the real thing at the Tiffany Theater around the corner. They knew the names of the big ships and military units, who was fighting in the Pacific and who was in Europe. Colin's friends took to saying his name with a long "O," after Captain Colin P. Kelly, the young B-17 pilot who had become America's first hero of the war when he bombed a Japanese battleship and crashed to his death in the Philippines three days after Pearl Harbor. Powell started introducing himself as "Coh-lin," although at home he remained "Cah-lin," the way the British pronounced it.

Colin was mesmerized by battlefields half a world away, but his own boyhood world was snug and self-contained. Its limits were defined by the direct line of sight of his parents, aunts and uncles from their Kelly Street windows, later extending to the distance he and Gene Norman could ride their bikes on a Saturday afternoon. St. Margaret's Episcopal Church, the elementary school P.S. 39, the junior high P.S. 52, and Morris High, the oldest public high school in the Bronx, were all within easy walking distance.

As far as the Powell children knew, America was populated almost entirely by Jews, Italians and West Indians—most of them Jamaicans. There were few American Negroes in their neighborhood—none of them among Marilyn's and Colin's closest friends. They were only vaguely aware that there were places beyond Hunts Point where people were defined solely by the color of their skin. Colin's friend Gene, two years older and more experienced, regaled him with stories from a family trip to Virginia, where there were different water fountains labeled "white" and "colored" and whole neighborhoods he and his family had not been allowed to enter. Returning black servicemen talked about their experiences at training camps "down South." But it was as if they had all traveled to another planet; those kinds of restrictions didn't apply in the South Bronx, and the Powell children had little exposure to them.

Nobody they knew was rich, but no one was really poor, either. As soon as Colin entered school, Arie was back in the garment district sewing on buttons and trim. Luther had advanced in the shipping department at Gaines, the clothing manufacturer on Manhattan's Thirty-seventh Street where he worked, and his employee discount kept the whole family in new clothes. Marilyn and Colin were the best-dressed children on the block, and the visit of any family member from Jamaica always included an outfitting trip to Gaines.

To his friends, Colin's father seemed a man of some importance—invariably dressed in coat and tie, with a dark hat and well-shined shoes—but always with time to give serious consideration to what a young boy had to say. His mother tended to act as if doom were just around the corner, but there was always food on the table, nice furniture in the apartment and a little money for extras. Colin's most precious possession was his chrome-fendered Columbia bike, the deluxe model with white-walled balloon tires, a motorcycle-like "tank" and tassels streaming from the handlebars. Marilyn took piano lessons and played each week at Sunday school. In the early 1950s, Luther bought his first car, a 1946 Pontiac, which he parked proudly outside the apartment with such slow care that it became a running joke on the block.

To their own children, Luther and Arie seemed less sweethearts than partners, joined in the business of keeping an extended family together, safeguarding its traditions and raising successful progeny with secure futures. The McKoy daughters were all *tartars* like their mother, and it was Arie who organized and fretted and pushed her children to excel, making them read at night and teaching them to do math problems in their heads. Luther was the one who brought home presents and invited everyone, from the garbage collectors to the man who delivered the heating oil, to come inside for rum or coffee and a chat.

The Jamaicans loved their adopted country, but they joked among themselves that they were "lousy citizens," keeping the customs of the islands and retaining their reverence for Great Britain. The Powells and every other West Indian family they knew gathered around the radio in the wee hours of June 2, 1953, to listen to the live broadcast of Queen Elizabeth II's coronation. Yet in a uniquely American way, they believed fervently in the strength of their own bootstraps and their right to all that the United States had to offer in exchange for their hard work. Powell family politics were New Deal Democratic, and a wartime portrait of President Roosevelt—the American flag and U.S. Capitol in the background—always occupied pride of place on the living room wall. Luther had men working under him at Gaines and considered himself "management," but Arie was a proud member of the International Ladies Garment Workers Union. They both studied the new Social Security Act with care.

Five years older than Colin and always at the top of her class, Marilyn was the brains of the family and the apple of her father's eye. Colin was a mediocre student, and his parents worried about his future. Arie and her sisters filled their letters with competitive bragging about their children, and Colin's mother was acutely conscious of her son's scholastic short-comings. Alice's second-born, Ethlyn, had a job at the post office in the town of Balaclava back home and had married a man who worked for the railroad. Their four boys—one of them, Vernon, nearly the same age as Colin—were all reportedly doing well in their studies.

Colin made up for his less-than-perfect grades with good behavior. He wasn't one to go looking for trouble; if it found him, he tended to walk, maybe even run, the other way. By junior high school, some of the neighborhood boys had started to experiment with drugs, but Colin and his friends feared the wrath of their parents far more than the disdain of the streets and stayed away. The repository of their clan's dreams and ambitions, the Powell children understood that bringing shame upon the family was the worst imaginable sin, and even when they were out on their own they always felt the weight of Arie sitting on one shoulder and Luther on the other. After one of his rare youthful misadventures—the procurement of a few bottles of beer with friends playing hooky from church camp—Colin escaped punishment by being the first to stand up and confess when they were caught.

He was the youngest of his gang on Kelly Street, and he knew the others thought he was a bit of a mama's boy. He could swing a broom handle bat well enough, fly a kite and pitch pennies, but he was never a great athlete. Colin enjoyed a joke as well as the next kid, and his distinctive, braying laugh was a familiar sound on the block. But he had a remarkable ability to shift gears abruptly from play to duty. When one of his parents leaned out the window in the evening to call him home from a game of stickball, Colin never sighed or pleaded for more time like the rest of the boys—he stopped what he was doing and headed for the front door. Luther and Arie never lectured; they seemed able to instill values in their children through a sort of moral osmosis. Long after Marilyn was married and struggling with her own two daughters, she still couldn't figure out how they'd done it.

It was at church that Colin most pleased his parents. St. Margaret's was High Church with all the trimmings; inside its sturdy walls, the priests wore vestments the royal family would envy. Services were formal affairs, with ceremonial processions and ritual chants as parishioners knelt and crossed themselves. To the Jamaicans who made up nearly the entire St. Margaret's congregation, anything less was simply not church. The Powells had their own family pew. Luther was a senior warden, Arie headed the altar guild and Colin was an acolyte, tending the altar and spreading incense during services.

The high point of the religious year came on Easter Sunday, when Colin would stand to one side as the children of the congregation came forward for confirmation. The bishop placed his hand on each head to ask for the Lord's protection, and a great "Amen" arose from the pews. When Colin became a teenager, the parish priest elevated him to subdeacon, and the experience of standing in priestly robes at the altar on Christmas Eve, chanting the epistle by candlelight as incense floated through the over-heated air, became a treasured memory.

Marilyn was less in awe of the church, especially since all of its impor-tant roles were reserved for males. She had little use for incense and thought that Colin was as much enthralled with the pageantry and cos-tumes as he was imbued with the Holy Spirit. Her attention soon focused on higher education, but after more than a year of commuting an hour and a half each way to Brooklyn College by subway, she was eager to find a smaller campus where she could feel a part of real student life. When she entered the state teachers' college in Buffalo, 460 miles from home, there were only two other Negro students enrolled.

Vivacious and always popular, Marilyn quickly found a steady boyfriend and soon announced that she was in love and wanted to marry him. Norman Berns was a Lutheran from Buffalo, and his religion was only slightly less shocking to her parents than the fact that he was an American Caucasian. As far as her family knew, Marilyn had never even been out with a non-Jamaican. Norman's parents said they'd always hoped he would marry a Lutheran, a lament that Marilyn initially took as code for racial disapproval. Luther was concerned that his beloved daugh-ter would be hurt. He told them to wait a year, warning Norman that "We've never had a divorce in this family." But after the entire Powell family drove north to visit the Bernses in Buffalo, he pronounced himself satisfied, and in August 1953, he sprung for a wedding party at the finest venue in the Bronx, the Concourse Plaza Hotel on the Grand Concourse.

By the time Colin graduated from Morris High, most of his friends were gone from the neighborhood. Gene Norman had joined the Marines after a year of college and others had volunteered or were drafted to fight in the Korean War. Despite his mediocre grades, it was unthinkable to Luther and Arie that Colin would follow them into the garment industry or try to turn his summer job unloading trucks for a local retailer into a career. He was eligible to attend City College of New York, which admit-ted virtually any city resident with a high school diploma in exchange for a $10 fee. Founded in 1847, its mission was "to provide children of the poor and new immigrants the higher education that could give them access to the American dream."

After consulting her sisters, Arie decreed that Colin would study engineering, a popular field that in the 1950s seemed to assure a steady income and, not incidentally, was the one that two of her sister Ethlyn's boys, Vernon and Roy Meikle, had chosen. Marilyn worried that her parents expected too much of her little brother. Still two months shy of his seventeenth birthday, he was sweet and unsophisticated, and she thought he knew too little of the world outside the neighborhood to succeed on a big urban campus. But on a frigid February morning in 1954, Colin took two city buses from the Bronx to Harlem and walked another fifteen blocks to the CCNY campus at 141st Street and Convent Avenue.

An essay for his first assignment in freshman civil engineering, written in a crabbed, sixteen-year-old hand, reflected both his naive rectitude and his lack of scholarship. Asked to describe himself and his ambitions, he began with a promise to "speak straight-forward and honestly" and a plea for exemption from "any imposition put on me because of dangling participles, incomplete sentences etc."

> I consider myself a fairly nice decent person. I am easy to get along with and am able to make friends easily. I have a pretty big shoulder and anyone is welcome to cry on it. I am not two-faced and do not like anybody who is. I have known people who are two-faced and they don't seem able to get along well with anyone. If I like a person I will stick by him all the way: even give him my last dollar, but then again I ... would not ask a friend for his last dollar. Well so much for me, I'd better stop before I start showing my conceit.
>
> I had wanted to go to an out of town college but I was not sure of my ability to secure a degree ... so I decided to come to C.C.N.Y. rather than spending hundreds of dollars of my parents money finding out what I wanted to be. C.C.N.Y. was recommended to me by my high school principal, who graduated from C.C.N.Y.... and science teachers also informed me that it had an excellent engineering course.
>
> In college I hope to, first and foremost, receive an education which will help me in my future endeavors. I also hope to meet in school people who I can count among my close friends for the rest of my life. I hope to learn how to get along and work with other people and also to learn how to become self-sufficient.

When I first entered C.C.N.Y. I was awed by the great com-
plexity of the school as well as all the people I met coming and
going. At first I felt alone, but I know that in time I will be part
of that vast crowd looking out over the new entering freshmen.

Years later, Powell offered a different assessment of his early goals in
an article he wrote for the City College alumni magazine: "I went to college for a single reason. My parents expected it. I don't recall having had
any great urge to get a higher education. I don't even remember con-
sciously thinking the matter through."

He lasted in his chosen field through the first semester and into summer school, plodding painfully through pre-engineering courses and
finally hitting a wall when confronted with a mechanical drawing class
that seemed far beyond his abilities. Dropping out was unthinkable, so he
changed his major to geology, a subject about which he was equally clue-
less but one in which the course work seemed manageable. Luther, who
had gotten used to bragging about Colin's prospects as an engineer,
couldn't fathom "my son, the geologist"; Arie was crestfallen and worried
about what her sisters would think. A family meeting ensued, with much
discussion over what kind of work a degree in geology would qualify a
young man for, with what income and pension. At the end of the day, they
managed grudgingly to convince themselves that college was college and
that was all that mattered.

Marilyn had also been right about her brother's social prospects. Colin
went to a few school dances but nothing seemed to click, and the long
daily commute took up much of his free time. He didn't seem to belong
fully anywhere. At school, life was a confusing whirl. In the neighborhood, he became known as the "college kid," an affectionate tease that
only underscored his separation from the block.

Kelly Street itself, whose every concrete stoop and rooftop he knew as
intimately as his own skin, was about to disappear from his life. The
neighborhood had been changing with a new wave of migrants, many of
them Puerto Ricans and American Negroes displaced by urban renewal
in Manhattan. The immigrants of thirty and forty years earlier who had
once found their Hunts Point apartments so spacious began to look for
houses to buy, with their own patch of earth, in quieter parts of the city.
Laurice moved farther north in the Bronx to a duplex with a basement, a
backyard and a garage, and others from the neighborhood went all the
way to Queens, a borough they had once considered distant suburbia.
Luther and Arie had talked for years about owning their own house, especially at Christmas dinners, when they opened the dining table they usu-

ally kept pushed against the wall. Once they set up the chairs and got all the guests seated, it took up the entire living room.

Money for a down payment was their biggest obstacle, and the prospect of mortgage debt made them nervous. A solution finally came with the usual Jamaican mix of the sacred and the secular. Luther and his sister Beryl were regular gamblers, betting a dime or a quarter with a bookie in the local numbers game nearly every day. As he sat in church one Sunday, Luther saw a number on a listing of hymnal pages posted on the wall. Convinced he had seen the same number in a dream, he and Beryl scraped together a $25 bet. They hit it big, and the $11,000 payout was delivered to the apartment that night in small bills by a faceless man carrying a suitcase.

It took several years to find their dream home—two bedrooms, a postage-stamp yard and a driveway—on Elmira Avenue in the southeastern Queens neighborhood of Hollis. The Powells bought the house for $17,500 from a Jewish family, but the new neighborhood was not the melting pot that Kelly Street had been. Queens was already becoming like much of the rest of the country, where ethnicity and skin color erected invisible walls. Most Jews were on their way out of Hollis; nearly all of its middle-class residents were what the white majority now referred to as "colored."

CCNY was a hotbed of liberalism, even communism, during the 1950s. Paradoxically, it was also home to one of the country's largest contingents of the Reserve Officer Training Corps, the campus-based Army training program that produced more officers than the service's own academy up the Hudson River at West Point. To receive a Reserve Army commission at the end of the four-year program, students in ROTC took a series of elective military courses along with their academic curriculum and attended six weeks of summer camp at a Regular Army base.

Colin had noticed the ROTC students during his first term as he trod glumly to engineering classes. What attracted him more than anything else was their uniforms. The young cadets looked sharp in their dark brown shirts and ties and gleaming brass buckles. Compared to his solitary, stumbling progress through college, they seemed to belong to something and to know where they were going. Many of them happened to be majoring in geology, and when Colin returned to campus in the fall of 1954, it didn't take much thought for him to walk into the nondescript building that housed the ROTC drill hall and sign up.

He was issued a hand-me-down uniform on the first day. When he wore it home from school, the younger kids on the block teased him, and Luther and Arie were more perplexed than ever at the path his college career was taking. But as he stood at attention that night in front of his bedroom mirror with his shoes shined, tie knotted and hat with the ROTC leaf and emblem nestled firmly on his head, he no longer saw a directionless young man lost on a big campus. There was no trace of the mama's boy, the mediocre student or the lackluster athlete. Standing before him was a soldier.

By the time the fall term was over, ROTC had filled the voids in Colin's college life. Churchlike in its traditions and rituals, it provided a structure with well-defined goals and a ready-made group of friends. Most young men at the time joined ROTC to ensure that they would serve their two years of required military service as officers. But to Colin, the future mattered far less than finding a niche in the present. To his amazement, he was courted that fall by three of the military societies that were the ROTC equivalent of fraternities on campus, and he eventually settled on the Pershing Rifles, a group known for its fancy rifle drills. The synchronized routines of marching and weapon handling rivaled the most intricate dance choreography, and the drill competitions held at universities across the country were the ROTC equivalent of intercollegiate athletics. The PR drill team at CCNY was considered one of the best.

Outside the campus walls, 1954 was a year of tumultuous events that would profoundly affect the world, the United States and the life of Colin Powell. French colonial forces withdrew from Indochina after losing the battle of Dien Bien Phu to Communist-led Vietnamese nationalists, leading President Dwight D. Eisenhower to warn of countries succumbing to Communist domination like "falling domino[es]." The U.S. Supreme Court ruled that separate public schools for black and white children were inherently unequal and violated the Fourteenth Amendment, lighting the long fuse of racial turmoil that would rock the country for the next two decades. The Soviet Union and the subjugated countries of Eastern Europe formed the Warsaw Pact and drew the Iron Curtain closed. In Washington, D.C., Senator Joseph McCarthy of Wisconsin convened hearings to determine whether the U.S. Army was "soft" on communism.

Colin was oblivious to most of it. The ROTC drill hall had become his second home, and the PR members were the brothers he had never had. They partied and chased girls together and he found in the endless drills and crisp military lessons the discipline, ambition and camaraderie that had been lacking in his student life. The sense of loyalty and belonging reminded Colin of his extended family, and there was nothing about it he did not love. As he muddled through his academic courses, barely maintaining a C average, he soared in his ROTC studies and training and developed a special expertise in solo rifle-twirling that put him in the spotlight. He eventually became a drillmaster and commander of the entire company.

Colin found he liked leading others and had a talent for the delicate balancing act required to win the respect and affection of those he led while demanding their high performance. He started a mental list of leadership qualities: A leader had to set an example and keep up standards. If he wanted his troops to drill an extra hour, he had to show he could do it with them. If his shoes weren't shined so he could see his face in them, the cadets would see little reason to shine their own. A leader had to be prepared to make tough decisions for the good of the group, even at the expense of a temporary loss of their affection. A leader had to be a little more serious than those he commanded and maintain a psychological distance from them.

By his last two years at CCNY, he was spending less and less time at the house in Queens. He was at the drill hall most Saturdays, practicing routines, polishing shoes and brass and hanging out with the guys. He also had met a girl, a fellow commuter on the subway, although Arie repeatedly wondered aloud why he couldn't find someone from Jamaica. Despite his parents' dismay at his increasing involvement in the military, his sister Marilyn was relieved that he had found a niche that suited him, with structure and a social life, along with the pageantry and formality he loved.

Most of Colin's ROTC friends were, like him, native New Yorkers and the sons or grandsons of immigrants. In one of the first official Army forms he filled out, his list of "Relatives Living in a Foreign Country" ran to two single-spaced pages of Jamaican names. Although Colin and Ronnie Brooks, the tall, trim son of a Harlem Baptist preacher, were the only Negroes for much of his time in the Pershing Rifles, he never perceived that their color held them back or was an issue to the rest of the cadets. Between the two of them, they held every PR leadership position and won every competitive honor.

Colin had spent his first two college summers mopping floors and picking up other jobs at the local Coca-Cola and Pepsi bottling plants. ROTC cadets were required to spend six weeks training at an Army base between their third and fourth years, and the summer of 1957 found twenty-year-old Colin on a Greyhound bus headed for Fort Bragg in

Fayetteville, North Carolina. He saw his first trip to the American South as a great adventure, but Luther, who knew only slightly more than his son about life in the land of Jim Crow, was concerned enough to ask the priest at St. Margaret's to find some black Episcopalians near the post to watch out for him. His father's anxiety ultimately seemed silly, since the cadets barely left the base, and Colin was unaware of any racial animosity as they studied Army manuals, trained on the rifle range and learned how to set up camouflage and roadblocks.

At the end of the course he was awarded a set of pens, mounted on a marble base with a plaque designating him the best cadet in his company. He placed second best overall in the camp, an honor that left him bursting with pride until a white supply sergeant told him, as they were turning in their gear and preparing to leave for home, that his color was the only reason he hadn't won first place. Colin wasn't sure how to respond, so he said nothing.

On November 8, 1957, early in his senior year, he applied for appointment as a second lieutenant and signed up for the standard two years of duty required of every ROTC graduate at the time. He listed three service choices—Military Police, Corps of Engineers and Signal Corps—drawn more from thin air than from any specific career ambitions. As his time of active duty approached, Luther and Arie convinced themselves that the Army was only a temporary diversion from their son's pursuit of a "real" profession. Every young man had to do his time in the military, but no one they knew wanted to make a career of it, and they assumed he would come to his senses after his brief obligatory service.

The ROTC commanding officer at City College, Colonel Harold C. Brookhart, had taken a special interest in his model cadet and worked to give Colin every advantage. Brookhart recommended Colin as one of fourteen "Distinguished Military Graduates" in the ROTC class of 1958, an honor that meant he would be eligible for a Regular Army commission. Much to Colin's delight, it also obligated him to three years of active duty, rather than two in the activated Army Reserve. Shortly before graduation, Brookhart sent him to spend a three-day weekend at West Point, where Brookhart's son was a cadet in the class of '58. When Colin returned, Brookhart called him into the drill hall to ask how the trip had gone and to give him some advice as he headed for basic training at Fort Benning, Georgia.

"You'll do well," Brookhart told him, but things would be different from college in Georgia and in the Army. "You may not like what you see, but you have to be prepared to compromise. You have to try not to upstage or overturn... you need to go along." By way of warning, Brookhart pointed to Benjamin O. Davis, Jr., the first Negro to attend West Point in the twentieth century and a member of Brookhart's class of 1936. Davis spent four years at the academy rejecting repeated entreaties to leave despite the fact that his white classmates refused to speak to him. He was given no roommate and ate his meals alone. At Fort Benning, his first assignment, his West Point classmates continued to shun him for trying to "buck the system."

At the time, Colin appreciated what he thought was good advice, similar to what his parents had taught him about not looking for trouble. Only years later did he realize, with belated offense, that Brookhart had been warning him to be "a good Negro."

Colin received his Reserve commission—to be quickly followed by active duty—on June 10, 1958. The day was memorable not only for the thrill of taking the oath to "support and defend" the country against all enemies and to "obey the orders of the President of the United States," but also for the chance to wear a new, tailor-made uniform for the first time after years of ROTC hand-me-downs. Each prospective new officer received a $300 uniform allowance, and together with the $600 his father had given him from a savings account started when Colin was a child, it was more than enough for a complete outfit from the best military tailor in the city. The next afternoon was graduation, and Arie had to send a cousin to drag him out of a nearby tavern, the PR hangout, where the new officers had resumed a party from the night before. His parents watched proudly as their groggy, hungover son was awarded his B.S. degree in geology and listened to a commencement speech by Jonas Salk—another New York–born son of immigrants and CCNY graduate—who had recently discovered a vaccine for polio.

A few days later, Colin boarded a bus for Georgia. "Do your three years," Arie told him. "Come home, we'll get a job. We'll be all right."

Fort Benning, like many military bases in the South, was named after a Confederate general. The bachelor officers' quarters, in a quadrangle of Depression-era buildings at the center of the base, were Spartan: single rooms with a washbasin and communal showers. During the eight weeks of Infantry Officer Basic Course, Colin's 184-member class spent most of its time learning how to organize and deploy the platoon-size units that would be their first commands and how to use a radio and a compass and fill out military forms. They marched, did calisthenics and ran obstacle courses in the muggy Georgia heat. Colin thought it was wonderful and graduated eighth in his class.

He was accepted into both the Ranger and Airborne schools and signed up for another three months of marching through the mountains of north Georgia and southern Tennessee and slogging through swampland at a Ranger camp near Eglin Air Force Base in the Florida panhandle. Every Infantry officer worth his salt wanted to be a Ranger, the Army's rapid-deployment commandos, and Airborne Rangers were the Infantry elite. The Airborne course was only three weeks—the first spent being shouted at and learning to fall correctly, the second jumping off the 250-foot training towers that dominated the Benning landscape, the third diving out the door of a sluggish military transport aircraft. Colin had been in an airplane only once before in his life—a New York Air National Guard C-46 that had carried him to an ROTC drill competition in Nebraska—and after two days and five queasy jumps he didn't care if he ever parachuted again.

The important thing was that he left Fort Benning in the early fall of 1958 wearing the black-and-gold Ranger tab and Airborne wings. The courses had been all about endurance, carrying out tasks under pressure and keeping your cool, and he had passed them with flying colors. He was lean and fit and full of self-confidence. After spending Christmas leave at home, he was to take up his first assignment, holding the line against Soviet communism with the Army's 3rd Armored Division in West Germany.

Despite Colonel Brookhart's warning and Luther's ongoing fears, nothing amiss had happened to Colin in the Deep South. Inside the Fort Benning walls, he lived in a white world that allowed well-behaved Negroes to participate. If any of his white fellow officers had problems with his presence there, they chose not to mention it or he chose not to notice. Off post, he knew what the rules were. He could not visit the bars and restaurants frequented by his white friends or sit at the lunch counter at Woolworth's. If he passed an attractive white woman on the streets of Columbus, he averted his eyes. He bought an old Nash Rambler and used it to travel to the few decent restaurants in the Negro part of town. Southern houses of worship were strictly segregated, and at the Ranger training camp in north Georgia, his commander arranged for a white enlisted man to drive him some distance away on Sunday mornings, to a Baptist church in Gainesville where he sang Gospel songs and swayed along with the black congregation.

Nearly four decades later, Powell recalled those days as a time of emotion suppressed through force of will and a determined focus on whatever achievement was available to him. "I wanted, above all, to succeed at my Army career," he wrote in his 1995 memoirs.

I did not intend to give way to self-destructive rage, no matter how provoked. If people in the South insisted on living by crazy rules, then I would play the hand dealt me for now. If I was to be confined to one end of the playing field, then I was going to be a star on that part of the field. Nothing that happened off-post, none of the indignities, none of the injustices, was going to inhibit my performance. I was not going to let myself become emotionally crippled because I could not play on the whole field. I did not feel inferior, and I was not going to let anybody make me believe I was.

3

The way for a young man to rise, is to improve himself every way he can, never suspecting that any body wishes to hinder him.

—Abraham Lincoln

In those early years, I was looked at as a black lieutenant. . . . And I just said to myself, ". . . Before this is through, I'm going to be the best lieutenant you ever saw. You will not categorize me as the best black lieutenant you ever saw."

—Colin L. Powell

A heavy snow blanketed the southern half of West Germany when Second Lieutenant Colin Luther Powell arrived in Frankfurt on a frigid night in mid-January 1959. Assigned to the Third Armored Division, 48th Infantry, he was headed to a base in Gelnhausen, some forty miles from the East German border. He had only a vague idea of what he was supposed to do when he got there, but there was no better posting than central Europe for an ambitious young officer. It was where the action was, on the front lines of a Cold War that seemed to be nearing the boiling point. Just beyond the Vogelsberg Mountains, twenty Soviet divisions and six thousand tanks were poised to barrel through the Hessian Corridor, a gap in the highlands that had been the historic invasion route during a millennium of European wars. Over the past two years, the Soviet Union had tightened its hold on the East, fortifying its borders, squeezing the United States and its allies to withdraw from a divided Berlin and crushing a nascent rebellion in Hungary. At home, America was in a rising panic over a perceived "missile gap" with the Russians, and President Eisenhower was fighting a losing battle against calls for bigger defense budgets and more sophisticated weapons.

Powell had spent a restive Christmas at Luther and Arie's, eager to leave and get his career under way. Upon arrival in Gelnhausen, he was assigned a two-room apartment in the bachelor officers' quarters and his first field command, a platoon of forty soldiers in Company B of the 2nd Armored Rifle Battalion. His job was to train and exercise them to fit into the overall mission of the division—to "give the Reds their first bloody nose," as the head of the U.S. Seventh Army put it, should Communist tanks roll across the border. As his charges shivered to attention that first bone-chilling morning, Powell was struck by how much they reminded him of the neighborhood boys he had grown up with in the Bronx. Most were the same age as he, or even a bit older, and he struggled with the impulse to befriend them before remembering what he had been taught at Fort Benning: Take care of your troops, but keep your distance.

When they weren't practicing how to march and shoot or polishing boots and buckles, they were sitting in jeeps and armored vehicles, staring at the collectivized farms beyond the ten yards of scorched earth the Soviets had cleared along their side of the border. Shortly after his arrival, Powell and his platoon were given a mission of high responsibility: guarding the division's most prized possession, the 280 mm "Atomic Cannon." The biggest artillery piece in the Army, it was 84 feet long and weighed 85 tons once the two locomotive-sized tractors required to move it were attached to the front and back.

The gun owed its existence to the ongoing Cold War turf battles among the service branches, specifically to the Army's demand for a nuclear weapons capability to match that of the Navy and the Air Force. The United States considered itself undermanned and underequipped compared to Soviet ground forces in Europe, and the nuclear-tipped shells, with their range of only eighteen miles, were to be the first wave of America's nuclear-based strategy of "massive retaliation" designed to overcome the Communists' numerical superiority in men and machines. The cannon was awe-inspiring but entirely impractical, too heavy to airlift and impossible to hide from the Soviets. Deactivated after less than a decade, it would come to symbolize for Powell, more than thirty years later at the height of his military career, a whole class of weapons the Army could well do without. The weapon itself was almost as ridiculous as its mission: firing a tactical nuclear weapon from the middle of one German field into another.

Enthusiastic and sharp, Powell quickly became the go-to guy for special assignments and he thrived on being singled out. While other lieutenants continued field-training their platoons, he moved from guarding the Atomic Cannon to being selected as company adjutant and leading the battalion pistol team to the division championship. There was no one better at military spit and polish; he could see his own reflection in his shoes and his uniform was so well starched he needed a broom handle to separate his pants legs before putting them on. His Pershing Rifle skills gave him an important edge over the West Pointers at the pomp and ceremony the Army loved. For the last two months of his tour, not long after his promotion to first lieutenant, Powell was assigned a captain's slot as company commander. His climb through the ranks was more rapid than that of some of his contemporaries, and he paid close attention to the lesson the Army system was designed to teach young lieutenants: to respond to the professional and personal needs of the young soldiers below him even as he pleased the more senior officers above.

But though Powell was singled out for responsibility repeatedly, many of the early assessments written by his commanders showed an officer still finding his way. The printed evaluation forms almost always elicited a torrent of positive adjectives for even the most pedestrian of officers, but there were subtle gradations of good whose true meaning required translation skills unique to the Department of the Army. Among the many superlatives in use, "excellent" amounted to only the faintest of praise and could stop a rising career in its tracks. In mid-May 1959, Powell's captain described his performance as "superior." While better than "excellent," it still fell short of "outstanding" or "exceptional," and his evaluator noted indifferently that "Lt. Powell is an aggressive, dependable and conscientious officer who takes pride in his professional ability." Five months later, raters wrote of his "high moral standards" and "neat appearance," while cautioning that he "appears to lack force."

It wasn't until his second year of duty that his efforts began to pay off on paper, where it counted. "Lt. Powell is one of the most outstanding young Lieutenants I have seen," effused his battalion commander in December 1960. "He is an original thinker, and his ideas are good. He is a driver and accepts responsibility willingly. He expresses his opinions quietly and convincingly. If his recommendation is not accepted, then he cheerfully and promptly executes the decision. He is calm and unexcitable. He is well liked by both superiors and subordinates. He has high standards and he demands and gets high standards." On the question of "promotional potential," he was singled out as "one of the few exceptional officers who should be considered for more rapid promotion than his contemporaries."

"For black GIs, especially those out of the South, Germany was a breath of freedom," Powell later reflected. "They could go where they wanted, eat where they wanted, and date whom they wanted, just like other people."

During his time in Gelnhausen, there were never more than a half-dozen Negro officers in the brigade, and usually no more than three at any one time. If they spent too much time together, grouping at the officers' club bar or talking at a party, more often than not a white superior would come by and jokingly tell them to scatter, lest a surprise attack wipe them all out at once. Even if they had wanted to, they were too few to form a cohesive minority. But their goal in the Army of the 1950s was not to stand out. It was to fit in—and none was better at fitting in than Powell.

One of his friends among the officers was First Lieutenant Isaac B. Smith, an artilleryman. Ike Smith was a sharecropper's son from deeply segregated Louisiana who had grown up in a town where black men stepped off the sidewalk when a white person wanted to pass. Like nearly all Negro officers in the Army, Smith was an ROTC graduate of an all-black school in the South—in his case, Southern University in Baton Rouge—and he still found it difficult not to say "Yes, Sir" to a white sergeant. Before joining the military, he had never eaten at the same table or spent a social moment with a white person.

Smith outranked Powell and chewed him out a few times just to show he could do it. But unlike the contempt that many in the next generation of black soldiers would display toward those who excelled at assimilation, Smith and the others saw Powell as a "knight in shining armor" to emulate. "We were not about separation," Smith later recalled. "We were more concerned about adapting to the environment we were in; we wanted to be accepted. That was far more difficult for me to do than Colin." The light-skinned second lieutenant from the Bronx had none of the subservient manner that a lifetime of second-class citizenship had imprinted upon the others. He spoke without the accent or vernacular of the Negro South that whites often found unintelligible and equated with ignorance. Somehow, his family's Jamaican lilt and the phonological peculiarities of the Bronx had combined to produce a speech pattern that betrayed no race or region. The other Negro officers often felt tongue-tied around whites and unsure of their social skills or status, but Powell always appeared to know the right thing to say and do. While they tried to avoid being singled out, he sought it.

Powell seemed to get along with everyone. Like the other bachelors, he dated the schoolteachers on post and spent his share of evenings at the officers' club bar. But unlike many of them, Powell "scraped ice" off his car most mornings—a popular expression meaning that he was rarely among those who kept their vehicles warm carousing through the cold West German nights until dawn. Many evenings, he would turn up uninvited for dinner at the home of a buddy in the married quarters.

As he began to be noticed by superior officers, his contemporaries— black and white—assumed that his color won him special attention. But they rarely seemed to begrudge the achievements of a man who clearly worked hard and made the most of the opportunities he was offered. The Army was under pressure to demonstrate its lack of bias; if blacks looked up to him, whites who had never known a Negro before the Army were pleasantly surprised that they could almost forget about color in his presence. Lieutenant Powell, an efficiency report in early 1959 noted approvingly, was able to "converse with excellent diction."

Twenty-one years old and naive of the more ignoble ways of the world, Powell had been largely untouched by the many years of racial turmoil in the armed forces that had preceded his own happy introduction to Army life and, to some extent, still existed. The military that he entered in 1958 had only recently achieved the desegregation that President Harry S. Truman had ordered a decade earlier. The last all-black Army unit in Europe had finally been integrated less than five years before Powell's arrival, and it was not unheard of for white soldiers still to balk at serving under black officers.

Negroes had fought in significant numbers in every war since the American Revolution, although George Washington, the commander of the colonial army, had allowed them to enlist only when he heard the British were offering freedom to any slave who agreed to fight with the Redcoats. After the Revolution, they were again barred from serving until the next conflict came along, setting a pattern of peacetime prohibition lifted only for the manpower demands of war—of prejudice versus pragmatism—that would endure well beyond the next century. During the Civil War, 180,000 free blacks and former slaves fought in segregated Northern units for half the pay and with 40 percent higher casualties than their white contemporaries. After that war, Congress established the first permanent Negro regiments—two cavalry and two infantry, with white officers in command—to show its gratitude and to help fight new battles against the Indians who were impeding the white nation's westward expansion.

Two hundred thousand black soldiers served in France during World War I, all of them in segregated units and most as laborers. They were not encouraged to stay after victory was won. In the late 1930s, in response to growing agitation by civil rights leaders whose focus at the time was on numbers rather than conditions of service, the Army adopted a quota system guaranteeing a one-in-ten ratio of blacks to whites in uniform, the same proportion as in the general population. But "they are not permitted to serve in the air corps, the coast artillery corps, the tank corps, the engineer corps, the chemical warfare service, the field artillery, the signal or any of the other special services," R. L. Vann, the crusading editor of *The Pittsburgh Courier,* one of the largest-circulation black newspapers in the country, complained in 1938. "They serve only in the infantry, cavalry, and to a small extent in the quartermaster and medical corps, and many of those supposedly combatant troops are assigned to duty as servants at Army service schools. In the Navy they are rigidly restricted to service as mess attendants." By 1940 there were only 5,000 Negroes in the Army, all serving in segregated units; of five black officers, three were chaplains.

World War II approached amid rising concern that the military was undermanned. When Congress enacted the first peacetime draft in 1940, it prohibited racial discrimination in selecting and training for the armed forces. The measure bypassed the whole issue of segregation, and the Army interpreted it to mean that Negroes were welcome as long as they were restricted to separate units and trained in segregated facilities. By effectively institutionalizing two separate armies—one for whites and one for blacks at every level from training to deployment—the new law had the perverse effect of actually increasing segregation in some less racist parts of the country.

Once the war began, Negro enlistment increased so dramatically that all segregated Negro units were filled to capacity by early 1942 and the War Department limited black induction to only those cases that were "obviously in the best interest of the service." But the overflow continued even after the war, and by 1946 the quota system had been overtaken. The Army was distressed to learn that 16 percent of all enlisted men were Negroes, all of them separately trained and housed in facilities that were splitting at the seams. In response, it changed enlistment qualifications for blacks, increasing the required score on the General Classification Test to 99 while leaving it at 70 for whites. Once recruiting had been "confined to Negroes with high learning ability," the War Department reported a year later, the proportion of Negroes dropped to 13 percent.

Efforts to evaluate the Negro soldier's wartime role—spurred by revulsion at Nazi racism and shameful episodes of postwar discrimination against black veterans—sparked a series of studies recommending increased service opportunities for nonwhites while still stopping short of calling for desegregation. But by the middle of 1947, President Harry Truman had detected a deeper change in the public mood, along with the possibility that black votes could help salvage his own fading chances for reelection.

The Republicans also had their eye on black votes, and their party platform, adopted at the July 1948 convention in Philadelphia that nominated Thomas E. Dewey as their presidential candidate, opposed "the idea of racial segregation in the armed services." When the Democratic Convention convened three weeks later, also in Philadelphia, to nominate Truman for reelection, the party's liberal wing went even further pushing through a plank that vowed to integrate the military, protect blacks' voting rights, guarantee equality in the civil service and make lynching a federal crime. Truman decided to call the Republicans' bluff and announced he would reconvene the GOP-controlled Congress, already in its summer recess, to vote on civil rights legislation, "which they say they are for." Not all Democrats were pleased, and the infuriated southern wing of the party walked out of the convention, formed its own Dixiecrat Party and nominated South Carolina Governor Strom Thurmond, an ardent segregationist, as its presidential candidate.

Truman had little chance of winning a congressional vote on civil rights, so his top advisers focused on the one area in which he could act without legislative approval and would likely encounter the least opposition from the Democratic electorate: his role as commander in chief of the armed forces. When the special session opened on July 26, he issued Executive Order 9981, declaring that it was "the policy of the President that there shall be equality of treatment and opportunity for all persons in the armed services without regard to race, color, religion or national origin." In November, Truman won more than two thirds of the black vote, a higher percentage than his Democratic predecessor, Franklin Roosevelt, had ever attained. Black turnout in crucial states such as Ohio and Illinois was seen as decisive in securing his reelection.

Most Negroes in the military experienced Truman's order the same way Julius Becton did. The Philadelphia-born Becton, who much later would play an important role in Powell's rise within the Army, had caught the tail end of World War II as a nineteen-year-old second lieutenant in an all-black unit in the Pacific. By 1948, he was serving in the Army Reserves while on a football scholarship at Pennsylvania's Muhlenberg College. At Reserve training camp at Aberdeen Proving Ground in Maryland that summer, his white commander assembled the unit and read them the desegregation order, then looked them in the eye and announced, "As long as I'm here, there'll be no change."

It wasn't until the manpower demands of war once again forced the military's hand that the Army began to genuinely cooperate. By the height of the Korean War in early 1951, large numbers of black troops were whiling away their time in Japan because white units would not accept them. Desperately in need of trained replacements and morally opposed to segregation, General Matthew B. Ridgway, commander in the Far East, formally asked the Department of the Army to take action to fully integrate all forces in his theater of operations.

Becton had returned to active duty in Korea and was heading an all-black platoon when his white battalion commander received news that replacements were on the way, along with instructions that they were to be put where they were needed and not separated by color. The first non-Negro soldier to arrive at Becton's platoon was a Mexican American. "Don't let anything happen to that guy," Becton instructed his sergeant.

When he returned to stateside duty after the war, Becton was put in charge of an all-black support unit assigned to trash pickup, at Camp Edwards near Boston. But as time went on, it became clear that Korea had finally knocked the props out from under segregation. Despite the fears of field commanders, racial discord in integrated units during the war had been minimal, and after-action studies concluded that desegregation had had no detrimental effect—and some positive influence—on the Army's overall fighting capability. U.S. installations in Europe were the last to change; it was there that the Army's final segregated unit, an engineer battalion, was integrated in April 1954.

As much as he loved Army life in Gelnhausen, Powell was homesick. He declined an offer to extend his tour in Europe and headed back to the United States near the end of 1960. He had not seen his family since a home leave eighteen months earlier, when he had stormed out of the house after his father had firmly rejected his plan to marry his longtime girlfriend, arguing that it was the wrong time and she was the wrong girl for him—and for the Powell family. As if to prove his maturity and separation from his parents, Colin registered to vote that fall, although he left blank the space indicating party affiliation.

He had little knowledge of the electoral issues of the day, and an extended conversation with one of his Gelnhausen commanders had convinced him that proper Army officers stayed as far away from politics as possible. "Military officers have to be nonpolitical," Captain William C. Louisell, Jr., had said over cigarettes in the orderly room one day. "And the only way to be nonpolitical is the way I do it. I don't vote. Never voted for anyone. Never will vote for anyone." Powell thought refusing to vote altogether was carrying the idea a bit too far and cast his ballot for John F. Kennedy in the 1960 presidential election. But he decided that as long as he was in the military he would split his tickets between Democrats and Republicans.

After a brief visit home to his parents in Queens, Powell reported to his next assignment, at Fort Devens, Massachusetts, where he was to serve as the liaison officer for the battalion chief of operations and training. Luther and Arie had retained some hope that their son's time in uniform was only temporary, and they were thunderstruck when he reenlisted at the end of his three-year commitment in the summer of 1961. Leaving the Army had never entered his mind. "I did not know anything but soldiering," he later wrote. "What was I going to do, work with my father in the garment district? As a geology major, go drilling for oil in Oklahoma? The country was in a recession; if I stayed in the Army, I would soon be earning $360 a month." But his primary motivation was that he loved what he was doing.

The Army clearly loved him, too, and by this time the superlatives needed little translation. "I consider Lt. Powell to be the most outstanding officer of his comparable grade and experience that I have encountered in this organization," his Fort Devens commander wrote. Mature "far beyond his age and experience," with "keen insight and professional knowledge," Powell was an officer who "time and time again has gone beyond what was normally expected of him." Tapped to fill a captain's slot in an office job, he earned the same high marks behind a desk as he had in the field. When his promotion to captain finally came in mid-1962, even Luther puffed up with pride and began to think that perhaps there was something to be said for a military career.

Although Luther had not raised the subject again, Colin and his girlfriend had drifted apart during their year and a half of separation since his father had discouraged their marriage. He was at loose ends at Fort Devens one weekend in the fall of 1961 when an Army buddy, a young black man from Queens named Michael Heningburg, asked him to come along on a visit to Boston. Heningburg had a date and wanted Colin to escort her roommate along with them. Powell had never been on a blind date and nearly backed out when he heard the young woman was from Alabama, a place he couldn't imagine had much to offer a man from the urban North.

Her name was Alma Johnson, and she was furious that her roommate had committed her for the evening without asking. She, too, had little interest in blind dates, and even less in soldiers. A graduate of Nashville's Fisk University, one of the nation's leading predominantly black institutions, she was working for the Boston Guild for the Hard of Hearing giving hearing tests out of a mobile van while she pursued a graduate degree in audiology at Emerson College. From a straitlaced family of educators and pillars of Birmingham's black middle class—her father and uncle were high school principals, and her mother, among many other upright activities, was a leader in the Negro Girl Scouts—Alma had escaped to Boston from a life of white gloves and tea. She had an active social life, and the men she went out with were players, most of them several years older than she and described disparagingly by her mother as traveling salesmen or worse. As far as relationships were concerned, Alma was aiming for dash and glamour.

When the appointed evening came, she decided to express her irritation by wearing a beige dress that clung tightly to her ninety-eight-pound figure and piling on extra makeup, making it clear that she was a woman who was far too sophisticated for either a blind date or a soldier. As tall, gangly Colin Powell walked through the door of her apartment, dressed in civilian clothes with his hair cropped close and his cheeks rosy from the cold, her first thought was "Who is this baby?" He was several months older than she but looked like a teenager, and she was instantly embarrassed by her own appearance. After the introductions, she quickly excused herself, returning a few minutes later with her face scrubbed and an outfit that was so conservative he later asked her why she dressed like a librarian.

"We took the girls out to a club in the Dorchester section," Powell recalled. "We had a few drinks, listened to music, and talked. After almost exclusive exposure to girls with New Yawky voices, I was much taken by the soft-spoken Southerner. And Alma did talk, most of the evening, while I listened entranced. At one point, she put a question to me natural enough in that era of compulsory military service: How much time did I have left in the Army?" When he told her he was in for life, "she looked at me as if I were an exotic specimen." They parted at the end of the evening, and he called her the next day to ask her out again.

Alma thought he was the nicest man she had ever met, and they began spending their weekends together—years later, her mother would remark to an aunt that she hadn't known Alma had so much sense as to hold on to him. He would drive to Boston in his blue Volkswagen or she would take the bus to Fort Devens, where they would usually spend their evenings at supper or drinks and dancing with other couples on post. Most of Colin's friends were young married couples with children, many of them white, and to Alma's pleasant surprise color seemed a nonissue in his circle. Just before Christmas, as she was leaving to visit her sister in Nashville, he asked if she would stop in Queens for the traditional Powell family New Year's Eve party on her way back to Boston.

The holiday event loomed as a crucial test for both sides. As usual, the basement family room on Elmira Avenue was packed with relatives and friends, mounds of food and the sounds of calypso streaming from an old 78 rpm record player. People of all ages were dancing, and everybody was talking at once without losing a step—mostly about Alma, whose imminent arrival was clearly the focus of the evening. Colin was nearly twenty-five, and the family thought it was high time he married, but the Jamaicans had already chalked up several possible negatives about his new, mysterious girlfriend. She wasn't West Indian. She wasn't from New York. And she was an American black—with all that implied about clashing cultures—whose skin might be too dark for their concept of beauty and breeding.

When Alma walked down the basement stairs, Colin's sister Marilyn thought she was the prettiest woman she had ever seen. Slender, with high cheekbones and fine features, she had green eyes and skin the color of richly creamed coffee. She moved through the crowd with a quiet grace that belied her intimidation at the din of a Powell party and the frank visual assessments of various middle-aged female relatives. After she had been embraced by Luther and Arie, she was stalked by Luther's sister Beryl, the self-appointed judge of all strangers in their midst. "Aunt Beryl had no children of her own and compensated by doting on her nephews and nieces, of which I was the chosen, her 'Col-Col,' " Powell later recalled. "Beryl planted herself next to Alma and eyed her up and down, wordlessly. The guests pretended to keep partying but watched Aunt Beryl out of the corners of their eyes." Every time Alma turned around, Beryl was there, "her face scrunched in skepticism." Finally she wandered off to voice her approval to the others. "The courtship could proceed, even if the poor child was not Jamaican."

Once Alma got used to the competing conversations and sideways glances, the dancing and laughter in the Powell basement were a revelation to her. Her parents never gave parties like that; in fact, they never gave parties at all.

Far from the sleepy military backwater of Fort Devens, the Cold War was escalating. The border between the two Germanys was more heavily fortified than ever, and another anti-Communist front had been opened halfway around the world in Vietnam, a place Powell had never even heard of.

It had been eight years since the French defeat at Dien Bien Phu ended a century of colonial occupation. An international conference held in Geneva in 1954 had temporarily partitioned Vietnam into two military zones, with the French retreating to the south and then leaving altogether while the Communist-dominated nationalists regrouped in the north, pending elections and reunification. The elections had never taken place. Instead, Vietnam had remained divided and the United States had thrown its support behind Ngo Dinh Diem, an anti-Communist aristocrat who had declared himself president of a southern Republic of Vietnam after a "nationwide" referendum of questionable legitimacy. Diem's Army of the Republic of Viet Nam (ARVN) was engaged in a low-intensity war with the National Liberation Front, the nationalist guerrillas the Americans called Viet Cong, for Vietnamese Communists. Diem and his American backers believed that the Viet Cong were a wholly owned subsidiary of the northern Communists, who themselves were seen as little more than pawns of the Soviet Union and the newly ascendant Communist government of China.

The Eisenhower administration had made an early determination that the ARVN could defeat the guerrillas on its own with U.S. training, equipment and intelligence. At the very least, U.S. aid would keep South Vietnam out of Communist control; ideally it would propel the country toward reunification on the Western side of the Cold War ledger. President Eisenhower was willing to provide assistance—more than a billion dollars in aid by the time he left office in 1961—but saw no need for significant U.S. military involvement in the new South Vietnamese republic. When the French withdrew in 1954, the U.S. presence there had consisted of a 342-man Military Assistance Advisory Group, or MAAG. The level remained fairly constant throughout the 1950s. A small U.S. Special Forces team, operating from Okinawa, had begun training Vietnamese Army commandos in 1957, and in 1960 more than two dozen Special Forces instructors were sent to South Vietnam to set up a permanent training program.

Kennedy's election the same year marked the beginning of an abrupt change in U.S. policy. In a meeting with his top advisers a week after his January 1961 inauguration, the new American president was told that the Diem government was close to defeat and a Communist victory would not only constitute "a major blow to U.S. prestige and influence" but would also leave the rest of Southeast Asia "easy pickings for our enemy." By spring, Kennedy had authorized an additional 500 U.S. military personnel—including 400 Special Forces and two Army helicopter companies, with pilots and maintenance crews—to train and assist the ARVN. The military also initiated a crash program at the Fort Bragg Special Forces School to instruct U.S. Regular Army officers in counterinsurgency operations and deploy them as advisers to ARVN units on the ground.

Once the dam was broken, the number of U.S. military personnel in South Vietnam grew rapidly, and by the end of 1961 the MAAG presence, not including Special Forces, had reached 2,067. That number had more than doubled by the summer of 1962, when Powell received his orders for six weeks of training at Fort Bragg and onward deployment to Vietnam by the end of the year.

Arie was horrified by the news that her son was headed to a shadowy war halfway around the world, and Alma made it clear that she was not pleased. She and Colin had been dating steadily and exclusively for the past eight months. Alma's mother, Mildred, had met Colin on a trip to New York in February and had had dinner in Queens with Luther and Arie. But her father, R. C. Johnson, barely knew Colin existed. Although both her parents were concerned that she had not yet found a husband, she was fairly certain her father would disapprove of either a West Indian or a soldier and would completely reject the combination in one man. It was a moot point as far as Colin was concerned, since marriage was far from his mind and he had no intention of spending any time in Birmingham. Hoping to convey his enthusiasm for his new assignment face-to-face, he drove to Boston to see Alma. They would write to each other, he told her.

"No, we won't," she replied. "I'm too old to be a pen pal." If that was what he was offering, they might as well end it now; she could not guarantee she would still be around when he came back.

He drove back to Fort Devens in a funk and lay awake that night pondering. He had never been much of a romantic, and the Army had already taught him that calm analysis would produce a far better result than raw emotion. He did the calculus: Alma was kind, thoughtful, smart and beautiful. She was a good cook and a great dancer. His parents approved of her, and he liked her mother. She loved him, and he loved her. If she had said they ought to wait and see how they felt when he came home after a year, that would have been fine with him. But she had given him what amounted to an ultimatum. By morning, he had made his decision. He drove back to Boston and told her, "Here's what we're going to do. We're getting married in two weeks. Call your folks and tell them." He didn't believe in engagement rings, he said. The money could be better spent on a refrigerator or other things they needed to set up housekeeping.

The ceremony was scheduled for Saturday, August 25, at Birmingham's First Congregational Church, with a reception at the Johnson home. Alma's sister, Barbara, would be her maid of honor, and Ronnie Brooks, Colin's Pershing Rifles friend, would serve as his best man. Colin had a three-day pass from Fort Devens; once he was finally released from his service there in the fall, they would travel together to Fort Bragg.

The Powell family had given Alma its highest accolade: "You fit in so well. We keep forgetting you're not one of us." Luther was pleased but reluctant to attend the wedding—he and Arie had never traveled south of New Jersey, and for all he knew, they would all be killed once they set foot below the Mason-Dixon Line. And what about Marilyn's white husband, Norman? They would be staying in an all-black part of Birmingham. Would a white man married to a black woman be even more at risk than they were? Would Birmingham Negroes drag Norm out of the car and beat him?

In the end, they all headed south together, Luther included, but they drove straight through for fear of stopping. Alma had arranged for the Powells to stay in the home of family friends, and Luther and Arie were more than a little intimidated at the seemingly opulent lives of Birmingham's black elite, starting with their host's airy instructions to leave their bags for the maid to carry inside. Alma's black South, with its college degrees and manicured lawns, was a far cry from what they knew of American Negroes. The church wedding and a reception at the Johnsons' went as planned the next day, although the Powells were somewhat surprised that there was no alcohol or music at Alma's parents' house. The reception guests simply filed in the door, greeted the two families, got their piece of cake, and moved on and out.

Nothing happened in Birmingham to justify Luther's fears, but as they started the trip back north on Sunday morning, Norman, Marilyn and the senior Powells agreed that they had all felt uneasy during their brief southern sojourn and were glad to be going home. Once Colin and Alma came back north, the Powells held their own reception in the basement family room in Queens, where the rum flowed and they danced and talked until nearly dawn. Compared to the subdued Johnson fete, Colin noted, "the Powell party was a cultural one-eighty."

Two months later, their worldly possessions jammed into the back of his Volkswagen, Colin and his pregnant wife were on their way to Fort Bragg. There was no on-base married housing for temporary, Vietnam-bound trainees; they planned to rent a furnished house or apartment in nearby Fayetteville for the length of the six-week adviser course. When Colin left for Vietnam, Alma would move in with her parents in Birmingham and await the birth of their first child.

After a frustrating day of house hunting, the Powells concluded that there were no middle-class rental accommodations available for blacks in Fayetteville. All Army posts were well integrated by the mid-1950s, but military desegregation meant nothing when black soldiers ventured outside the gates, particularly in the South. At dinner that night at the home of Joseph Schwar, a friend from Gelnhausen now based at Fort Bragg, Colin's anger rose as he related their experience with local real estate agents.

"You talk to people on the phone," and everything's fine, he said. "Then you walk in and they see you're black, and then immediately they've got a section of town that they're going to take you to." Among the several offerings had been an empty shack in the middle of an overgrown field that had been turned into a trash dump.

They had run out of options, they told the Schwars, and had decided that Alma would go on to Birmingham while Colin stayed alone in bachelor quarters on post. Schwar and his wife, Pat, immediately offered them a room in their Army duplex. Alma had visited the bathroom upstairs and knew that the five Schwars were already distributed among three tiny bedrooms. But Joe and Pat were adamant—the two older boys could move into the baby's room, and Colin and Alma could take their bunk beds.

They became an instant extended family. But the comfort they all felt inside the duplex vanished, at least for Alma, once they walked out the front door. There were few places she and Pat could go together off post—Alma was not allowed to try on clothes at Fayetteville department stores, and they couldn't sit down for coffee at the lunch counters. The Powells and the Schwars couldn't go out to a movie together unless they wanted to sit in separate sections of the theater, they couldn't play minia-ture golf, go bowling, or enjoy any of the other modest entertainments the town had to offer. Pat's South Philadelphia temper erupted every time she thought of it. But to Alma, it was just the way things always had been.

4

I see these things, still I am a slave/When banners flaunt and bugles blow/Content to fill a soldier's grave/For reasons I shall never know.

—Charles Trueman "Buck" Lanham

Powell was anxious to get to Vietnam, and his regret at leaving his new wife and missing the birth of his first child was as fleeting as the shadow of a solitary cloud in a sun-filled sky. He and Alma spent the first few weeks of December 1962 getting her settled into her parents' new home in the northern Birmingham suburb of Tarrant City. After they trimmed the Christmas tree and exchanged early gifts, Powell made his way to the airport alone. Public displays of emotion made him uneasy, and he had asked Alma not to come. By Christmas Eve, he was sitting in the officers' club at Clark Air Base in the Philippines, waiting for the next day's Military Air Command flight to Saigon.

He was eager for real combat—the Army in Germany was a placeholder, guarding the static line that separated America's team from its opponents in a game that never moved. In Southeast Asia, the ball was in play. Saving Vietnam from communism, he believed, was "the finest thing we could do for our families, our country, and freedom-loving people everywhere."

As Powell headed toward South Vietnam at the end of 1962, the number of U.S. military personnel there had grown to more than 11,000. Although it ranked far below the continuing standoff in Berlin and a Soviet-backed revolution in Cuba on Washington's priority list, enthusiasm for the effort was high. Robert McNamara, Kennedy's defense secretary, kept a full statistical account of ARVN battle wins and losses down to each Viet Cong reported killed and every enemy weapon seized, and his trend lines indicated that the Communist-backed insurgency would be defeated by 1965.

All of the uniformed Americans in South Vietnam were called "advisers," although most served as clerks, drivers, mechanics and administrators supervising the incoming aid and supporting those closer to the front lines. There were Special Forces in secret camps around the country, aircraft pilots and crews, and about 1,000 Army advisers actually assigned to ARVN headquarters and combat units in the field. One of 291 officers and noncoms attached to Vietnamese infantry battalions at the beginning of 1963, Powell was assigned to the 400-man 2nd Battalion, 3rd Infantry Regiment of ARVN's 1st Division in Quang Tri. The northernmost province of South Vietnam, Quang Tri bordered the Seventeenth Parallel, which divided the country in two. The battalion's mission was to rout insurgents from the A Shau Valley, a remote region of mountainous forest along the Laotian border.

Although they were the point men of U.S. policy, few ARVN field advisers had qualifications any more compelling than achievement of rank, attendance at the regular Army schools and low-level command tours such as Powell's in Gelnhausen. The weeks of Special Forces training they were given at Fort Bragg were of limited utility—a once-over in Vietnamese language and culture and instruction in jungle ambush tactics, hand-to-hand combat, psychological operations and civic action. Some of the advisers were allowed an extra month of training at the service's language school in Monterey, California, but not Powell. Although he was told he would be working with an interpreter once he arrived, none ever showed up.

On paper, the field advisers were little more than an armed version of the civilian Peace Corps that Kennedy had established in 1961 to bring American know-how and goodwill to friendly nations in the developing world. Warned that they had "no command jurisdiction" over their assigned ARVN units and were prohibited from engaging in combat, they were to serve as mentors and exemplars of U.S. military discipline, knowledge and can-do spirit. Deployed in two- or three-man teams per ARVN battalion, they were also to serve as an on-the-ground "network" to provide U.S. policy makers with regular reports about both the Viet Cong's and ARVN's performance and plans.

The Army had already invested considerable training of a different sort in these men; they had been taught to command and control their troops within a rigid structure based on obedience to authority and unit cohesion. This assignment was different. Far from command and authority, they were told to establish relationships with the Vietnamese based on persuasion, suggestion and avoidance of offense. Alton Sheek, a lieutenant eventually teamed with Powell in Quang Tri Province, thought of the adviser instruction as "untraining," and it required a significant psychological adjustment to the mind-set of the young Army officers.

Since they could not give orders, advisers were told to tactfully "plant" ideas with Vietnamese commanders, always letting the locals take credit for success. In addition to discreetly proffered advice, their mere presence would signal the strength of U.S. backing for South Vietnam's struggle and provide a model for proper military behavior in everything from respectful relations with civilians to personal hygiene, good posture, punctuality and weapons maintenance—all areas where the Americans had found the South Vietnamese forces wanting. Athletic events were recommended as a way to ingratiate themselves and build unit spirit, and the advisers were told to teach American games to the Vietnamese while learning some of the local sports.

Encouraged to "show an interest in Vietnamese customs, language, history and people," advisers were warned not to "flaunt your higher standard of living" or boast of U.S. superiority. A list of cultural taboos cautioned against tapping a Vietnamese on the shoulder, touching the head of a Vietnamese or cutting one's fingernails or toenails at night. They were not to "summon a Vietnamese by shouting, whistling or waving." Shaking hands was encouraged, but they should "refrain from 'back-slapping' " since "almost without exception, Vietnamese feel this to be a personal affront." Patience was a prime virtue. "Never expect the job to be done at the snap of a finger—and don't snap your finger."

Most ARVN soldiers were said to be illiterate, and "there is a marked difference between Vietnamese and Americans with respect to physical stamina." While the Vietnamese reportedly admired honesty, they were said not to practice it very much themselves. "They are given, at times, to brutality and high emotionalism," the Army advised. "Also, they are credulous and will believe almost anything. That is why Communist propaganda can gain such headway."

December was Saigon's springtime, the coolest month of the southern Vietnamese dry season. Powell arrived on Christmas Day, 1962, and was bused to the Rex Hotel, which had been taken over by the U.S. Army for office space and officer billets. From its rooftop bar, the city below was a riot of color and noise punctuated by the backfire of ARVN jeeps. Small men in broad straw hats pedaled bicycle cabs as white-uniformed traffic policemen whistled directions. There was little sense of imminent danger, although the military bus windows had been strung with chicken wire to repel tossed grenades. The road into Saigon from Ton Son Nhat Airport passed by row upon row of simple white crosses at the vast French military cemetery, where the gates were inscribed with the dedication *a tous ceux qui sont tombés sous ses drapeaux.* Field kits issued to new arrivals included two sets of jungle fatigues, rubber-soled canvas and leather boots, a helmet and a medical/survival kit with salt and malaria tablets, bandages and antibiotics, waterproof matches, a knife and a fishing line with hooks. An Army doctor warned them against drinking untreated water, and an enthusiastic major general delivered a rousing pep talk on the importance of their mission.

Bored with the preparations and ready for action, Powell was finally cleared on January 2 for departure to Quang Tri, capital of the province with the same name. As his small military cargo plane lifted off from Ton Son Nhat, he was unaware that local ARVN units and their American advisers were streaming from Saigon in the opposite direction toward the village of Ap Bac, fifty miles south in the Mekong River Delta. In what was about to become the bloodiest and most costly battle since the Americans had arrived in Vietnam—and an ominous contradiction of Washington's early optimistic analyses—government troops backed by artillery, armor and helicopters were about to be defeated there by a Viet Cong force they outnumbered four to one.

"When the battlefield was searched," an Army historian later recorded, "only three enemy bodies were found. Reports from the field attempted to declare this controversial battle a victory for the South Vietnamese. It was not." The ARVN dead numbered sixty-one; three American advisers were killed and five U.S. helicopters carrying South Vietnamese troops were shot down. On January 7, five days after the battle, a front-page article in *The Washington Post* quoted U.S. officers as charging that ARVN soldiers had refused direct orders to advance into Ap Bac and that their American adviser, an Army captain, "was killed while out front pleading with them to attack."

As Powell raced enthusiastically into the conflict that would play a major role in defining his life and career, Alma reluctantly faced a different kind of war, one that her husband barely knew existed and felt little empathy for. After a decade of sporadic escalation, America's domestic struggle for civil rights was about to explode on the streets of Birmingham.

Her return to her parents' home felt like a step backward to a place Alma had gladly escaped years before. Surrounded by her mother's carefully tended gardens, the big house was like a tomb compared to her vibrant cosmopolitan life in Boston. Her father, R. C. Johnson, was an imposing figure and part of the establishment side of a black community in Birmingham that was deeply divided over how to respond to the demands for equal rights that were sweeping the nation. While black student groups and local firebrands railed against the segregated status quo, conservative black clerics, business leaders and educators opted for accommodation with the white political structure and shied away from confrontation with its notorious police commissioner, Eugene T. "Bull" Connor.

Birmingham called itself "The Magic City," a symbol of robust southern industry, and blacks' resentment had yet to boil over as it had in so many other cities. But for all its reluctance to fight back, Birmingham's black community had not been spared the more violent manifestations of American racism. A bus full of Freedom Riders, traveling from Washington, D.C. to New Orleans to protest the segregation of interstate transport facilities, had been set upon and beaten by a white mob at Birmingham's Trailways station on Mother's Day 1961. Connor's police were nowhere to be found; he claimed they had taken the holiday off. Later that year, the city government responded to a federal court order to desegregate Birmingham's sixty-seven public parks, thirty-eight playgrounds, eight swimming pools and four golf courses by firing park employees and posting "No Trespassing" signs. When white taxpayers complained and demanded access, Mayor Art Hanes responded, "I don't think any of you want a nigger mayor or a nigger police chief... but I tell you that's what'll happen if we play dead on this park integration."

Dozens of Birmingham's Negro churches and homes had been bombed over the past decade; no one had ever been charged with the crimes. Alma's own mother had been confronted by the Ku Klux Klan while camping outside the city with a group of women, some of them white, on a training retreat for Girl Scout counselors. Awakened in her tent by noises outside, Mildred Johnson had walked through the trees to the white women's tent and found it surrounded by robed Klansmen, who warned they had all better clear out once the sun rose.

A month after Alma's return, George C. Wallace took office as Alabama's governor. In his inaugural speech, he promised "segregation forever" and action against the "fat, well-fed whimperers" who proposed "the false doctrine of communistic amalgamation" of the races.

To Martin Luther King, Jr., leader of the nationwide nonviolent civil rights movement, Birmingham was ripe for testing. A significant breakthrough there would demonstrate to the hard-core South that segregation's days were truly numbered. In early January 1963, King began planning a public showdown with Connor, joining forces with local activists who had long despaired at mobilizing the Negro citizens making up more than a third of the city's population. But after a springtime campaign of lunch counter sit-ins and demonstrations made little progress, King and local movement leaders decided to take a bold gamble. They exhorted Birmingham's black children—still barred from whites-only public schools nearly a decade after the U.S. Supreme Court had ordered nationwide desegregation—to join peaceful marches from their churches through the city's downtown. In scenes that came to symbolize the brutality of white southern resistance for much of the world, Connor met them with fire hoses, police dogs and mass arrests.

R. C. Johnson traveled downtown every day to the all-black Parker High School, where he was the principal, but he wanted no part of the marches. Alma's father believed that education and discipline were the keys to the future of black Americans—on that issue, at least, he and Luther Powell agreed. Johnson and Alma's uncle George Bell, the principal at Ullman, Birmingham's newly opened second black high school, were appalled at what they saw as the cynical endangerment of the children, and when activist volunteers drove up to Parker to ferry the students to the churches, Johnson tried to bar the high school doors. The students trampled the chain-link fence to get out. John Wesley Rice, Jr., the Ullman guidance counselor, would not even consider allowing his eight-year-old daughter, Condoleezza, to participate in the children's protest, although he took her to watch the upheaval from a distance.

The turbulence was concentrated downtown, but anxiety reached black communities in every corner of Birmingham. Johnson had always had trouble sleeping, and now he sat watch into the wee hours in the darkened house with a shotgun in his lap. He made Alma and her infant son stay as far away from the windows as possible, sometimes sending them to spend the night in the safety of the basement. While hanging her newborn's diapers on the clothesline one day, Alma ran from the sound of gunshots outside a neighbor's house and the screech of a car speeding away.

Michael Kevin Powell had arrived early on March 23, 1963, nearly seven months to the day after Colin and Alma's wedding. When the pains started, Alma's doctor had sent her to the hospital to confirm his diagnosis of false labor. Her parents had dropped her off and returned to the vegetable garden they were planting at the new house. But the labor had been real, and when she gave birth that evening she was alone. Alma and Colin had agreed that when it happened she would mail him the news and a photograph in an envelope marked "Baby Letter" in big letters, and he had alerted the nearest military mail drop, in the northern South Vietnamese city of Hue, to be on the lookout. But for weeks after sending the letter she heard nothing back. After stories of Birmingham's eruption hit the national news, Luther and Arie called to urge her to bring the baby to safety in New York, saying they thought it was what Colin would want. She assured them that she and Michael would be just fine.

With its jails bursting with hymn-singing children, its economy paralyzed by the unrest and the nation recoiling in horror at televised scenes of police brutality, white Birmingham finally capitulated. But agreement by city leaders to start desegregating public facilities and businesses only further enraged the Klan and other racist groups, and the approaching summer brought a new bombing campaign. One of the first attacks gutted the march organizers' headquarters at the black-owned A. G. Gaston Motel. The only place in town where blacks could find decent accommodations, it was where Alma and Colin had spent their wedding night.

Major George Price, the newly arrived regiment-level adviser at Quang Tri, found Alma's "Baby Letter" gathering dust in a pile of undelivered mail more than a month after Alma had sent it from Birmingham. By then Powell knew about the birth—a letter from his mother had mentioned in passing how happy she and Luther were about the baby—but he had no details and no direct word from his wife. Price was a Mississippi-born football player and ROTC graduate from South Carolina State University, an imposing black man whose booming voice ran in the family—his older sister was the opera star Leontyne Price—and he lost no time ordering immediate delivery of the specially marked missive. An L-19 observation plane was sent to fly over the battalion's remote operations area, and Powell and the Vietnamese soldiers watched as it dropped a small box attached to a big yellow handkerchief that billowed to the ground. Inside were a batch of candy and the envelope with Alma's letter and Michael's first picture.

"The Vietnamese crowded around, clucking and smiling," Powell later wrote. "I let them see the photo. Then it went into my breast pocket and stayed there." As the plane disappeared, Lieutenant Sheek, the only other American on the ground for miles in any direction, patted Powell's back and watched in sympathy as the jubilation on the captain's face turned to frustration when he realized how long it would be before he could hold his son.

After arriving in Quang Tri in early January, Powell had spent weeks waiting for the weather to clear before joining the South Vietnamese

troops in the mountains. Dry season in Saigon was monsoon season farther north, and a steady rain had grounded helicopters and delayed his
arrival at the battalion's makeshift base in the valley. The A Shau camp
was little more than a metal airstrip stamped into the cleared jungle
ground, with an "earth-and-wood fortress ringed by pillboxes" that Powell would later recall had "a French Foreign Legion quality, *Beau Geste*
without the sand." The small outpost seemed to have been placed in the
most defenseless position possible, at the bottom of tall, wooded hills
where even a rolled boulder would have flattened the thatched, dirt-
floored huts.

After he was introduced to his Vietnamese counterpart, Battalion
Commander Captain Vo Cong Hieu, they engaged in a colloquy that
years later formed the tragicomic core of Powell's mental library of Vietnam tales. When he asked why the outpost had been so vulnerably
located, Hieu assured him in broken English that it was necessary to perform the "very important" mission of protecting the airstrip. Why was the
airstrip in that particular place? Because, Hieu said, it was needed to supply the outpost. "I would spend nearly twenty years, one way or another,
grappling with our experience in this country," Powell later wrote. "And
over all that time, Vietnam rarely made much more sense than Captain
Hieu's circular reasoning on that January day in 1963."

The battalion's task, set by Saigon and Washington, was to interdict
supplies and personnel traveling south to the Viet Cong from North Vietnam. The valley was considered an integral part of the Ho Chi Minh
Trail, the lengthy logistical and infiltration route that meandered along
the Laotian border. Quang Tri Province itself was judged nearly devoid
of resident Viet Cong—with inexplicable certitude, official U.S. analysts
that year put the number at 240. On weeks-long excursions from the
A Shau base camp, the battalion walked single file through the narrow valley, traversing the mountainsides whose tall trees blocked most of the sun
but little of the rain and climbing across vines as thick as a man's wrist as
they searched for the enemy supply line and invited inevitable attacks.

After months of patrolling, they had yet to see a single Viet Cong guerrilla, alive or dead. But their invisible enemy had made its presence
known time and time again. A sudden crack of rifle fire that seemed to
come from everywhere and nowhere at once would echo through the forest, and an ARVN soldier would drop. The sound would send the battalion crashing through the trees, trying in vain to find the source of the fire.
The ambushes usually targeted the head of the mile-long column, far
from the midpoint where Powell positioned himself in keeping with his

status as an adviser and noncombatant. Most came in the morning, after the noise of preparing their evening bivouac had broadcast their overnight location to anyone listening in the forest. All the Viet Cong had to do was wait until the sun was up and the battalion spread out and began to march again. After a morning attack, Powell felt he could let his guard down and relax for the rest of the afternoon.

The ARVN dead and wounded were carried on litters to clearings on higher ground where an evacuation helicopter could land. The aircraft would touch down for mere seconds to load the bodies, and the pilots—sometimes Vietnamese, sometimes U.S. Marines—provided rare contact with the outside world during that season's long march through the forest. This remote part of the republic was not the center of the war. That was farther south, where the highlands slid into broad plains and the Mekong Delta and finally down to where the South China Sea met the Gulf of Thailand. There, the ARVN and the Viet Cong often fought face-to-face.

Powell's superior officers seemed pleased with his service, praising him in writing for "perform[ing] his duties as a Battalion Senior Advisor in an outstanding manner and demonstrat[ing] personal qualities that clearly distinguish him from his contemporaries." While in the valley, they said, his battalion "was conducting a continuous operation against the Viet Cong," and Powell had "aided materially" in its "combat effectiveness."

Whatever illusions the U.S. military was operating under about its achievements in the A Shau Valley and the performance of Captain Powell, Powell himself felt little sense of accomplishment. As the ambushes continued, he could never persuade the Vietnamese to split the column into shorter, parallel lines that would provide a more diffuse target, and he made little progress in getting the soldiers to operate more stealthily in their nightly camps in the forest. They seemed incapable of following his instructions on quick and proper unloading of a supply helicopter. There was nowhere to train, and even his upright American posture suffered as he tried to blend in with the short-statured Asians. His major operational success came when he procured a handful of armored vests for the point squad at the head of the column and convinced the soldiers that wearing them was worth the hot discomfort. As instructed, he kept careful daily notes in the pocket-sized green notebook the Army had issued. Many of the penciled entries began with the word "Rain" and ended with the number of casualties they had suffered.

After the first soldier from the battalion was killed just days into their initial foray from the A Shau base camp, Powell had spent a restless night in the forest full of lonely fear and doubt about what in the hell he was doing there. But by the next morning, with the skies clear and a sliver of sun hitting his face, his natural optimism returned and it was easy to believe once again that his presence in a mountainous forest at the seeming edge of the earth was an integral part of a worthy strategic objective. He awoke feeling "oddly invigorated. Someone else was dead, but not me, a sense of elation, I was to learn, common to men in the wake of battle, even as they mourn dead comrades. Somehow, the world did not look so frightening in the light of day. This awareness—that things will look better in the morning—was to get me through many a dark night." Within an hour of packing up and starting off, the battalion was ambushed again.

Life had improved somewhat when Lieutenant Sheek joined them in March as they constructed a new base camp farther up the valley at Be Luong, part of a line of rudimentary compounds established to give at least an illusion of control over enemy supply routes. Blond and sturdy, Sheek had been in these forests before, as an adviser to an ARVN field artillery unit near the demilitarized zone at the North Vietnam border the previous year. When he had opted to stay after the artillery contingent was pulled back, he had been assigned to Powell's infantry battalion. To his amazement, the Vietnamese actually seemed to like and respect the tall, slender black captain. In Sheek's experience, the South Vietnamese soldiers and their officers always smiled cooperatively at the advisers tagging along with them, only to laugh behind their backs and ignore their suggestions. They had been at war long before the Americans got there and would likely be at it long after the Americans left. Who knew whether anything was ever actually accomplished? But Powell's easygoing manner genuinely engaged them. If the United States was ever going to succeed here, it would require Vietnamese support, Sheek thought, and Powell clearly had it.

At the base camp or living rough on their treks through the mountain forest, Powell and Sheek slept where the Vietnamese slept and ate what the Vietnamese ate: rice with pieces of the live animals they brought with them to slaughter and cook, rice alone when the animals ran out, and sometimes just whatever they could scavenge when the helicopter resupply was delayed. Once when the monsoons were particularly heavy, they survived on tapioca root for days; another time they gnawed on corncobs. In the evenings, the Americans would entertain themselves and the Vietnamese by singing every song whose words they could remember and some they made up. Sheek considered himself a hick, brought up in rural North Carolina in a hardscrabble family whose tastes ran to country and western. Powell, by contrast, seemed to him fine and cultured, an urban man whose repertoire ranged from calypso to Broadway musicals, some of which he had actually seen on stage. Sheek had never seen a musical in his life.

"Colin had an air about him," Sheek later recalled. "He was very much in control of things and knowledgeable. And he had a way of making you feel accepted." The subject of race rarely came up between them, except when Powell kidded Sheek about how his whiteness made him a better target for the Viet Cong. Night after night they talked, sharing their life stories and, when they were extraordinarily lucky, finishing a batch of homemade chocolate chip cookies that had somehow made its way to them from Alma's oven. Their anticipation of the resupply helicopter every two weeks was "almost sexual," and they counted the days until the arrival of a new supply of cigarettes and the dog-eared paperbacks that made the rounds of the isolated encampments.

The mountain villages they occasionally came across on their long marches were always empty; resident Montagnard tribesmen had either been ousted and sent down to the coastal towns by a previous ARVN patrol or were hiding unseen until the soldiers went away. Destroying property that might prove useful to the enemy was a major part of their mission, and the battalion burned the flimsy huts and destroyed whatever food crops they found, chopping them down with machetes or using hand-sprayed herbicide. The destruction of Vietnamese homes and livelihoods would later be harshly criticized as the war became more unpopular at home. At the time, Powell considered it "counterinsurgency at the cutting edge."

In faraway Saigon, the U.S. military leadership seemed to be overseeing a different war than the one Powell was witnessing in the field. In January 1963, MACV, the new Military Assistance Command Vietnam, which had incorporated the MAAG, reported that ARVN troops throughout the northern region were engaged in "deep raids and attacks into remote VC [Viet Cong] areas" and were "wresting the initiative" from enemy units. "Provided trend continues, progress toward positively defeating the VC will accelerate." Just as encouraging as action in the field was the stepped-up intelligence they were supposedly receiving from the population. "Once fearful or in favor of the Viet Cong, very little information came from the people," MACV reported. "Today Viet Cong movement has been extremely limited by the constant reporting by a population growing progressively more loyal" to the South Vietnamese government.

Powell's contact up the chain of command ended in Hue, and he doubtless never saw the MACV assessment of the I Corps zone, which included Quang Tri Province. But the idea of "deep raids" against the Viet Cong in the A Shau Valley was laughable. His entire 400-man battalion could be stopped in its tracks by a single VC sniper who melted away unseen. "There was no front, no ground gained or lost," he later wrote in his memoirs, "just endless, bloody slogging along a trail leading nowhere." It seemed equally doubtful that the sullen civilians whose homes and crops were destroyed, and who were forcibly removed from their villages to live in fenced and guarded encampments under Diem's "Strategic Hamlets" program, were a reliable source of intelligence.

In the A Shau Valley, each of the 2nd Battalion's encounters with the enemy differed in its details but rarely in its outcome. One day in February, they had just finished loading the dead and wounded from the previous day's ambush into an evacuation helicopter when unseen Viet Cong opened fire from the trees. ARVN soldiers guarding the perimeter of the landing zone fired back, and a Marine gunner on the rising helicopter mistakenly fired at the soldiers, killing two and tearing the hand off another.

Another day lodged itself forever in Sheek's memory. "We were walking single file on a trail through the underbrush, probably 10 to 15 feet high. At one point, the whole battalion, one line across, crossed an open field going from one tree-covered area to another, and I thought to myself, 'How dumb that you'd walk across an open field single file.' How dumb. We got hit. I had a medic in front of me who had his calf blown away. Another guy was shot right between the eyes." Forced to make their retreat at night, they carried the dead and wounded through waist-deep water to reach a landing zone.

On May 18, five months after Powell's arrival, he recorded the battalion's first confirmed enemy casualty in his notebook. "For once," he later recalled, "our point squad spotted the VC before they spotted us. For once, we did the ambushing. We nailed them. A hail of fire dropped several VC, and the rest fled. We approached gingerly. One man lay motionless on the ground, the first dead Viet Cong that I could definitely confirm we had killed." Lying on his back, eyes staring blankly at the tree canopy, the guerrilla was dressed in traditional black pajamas with rubber sandals on his feet. "I felt nothing, certainly not sympathy. I had seen too much death and suffering on our side to care anything about what happened on theirs." They left him lying on the ground.

In late July, the battalion was ordered to take a break and began a several-day march toward one of the Special Forces camps that dotted the region.

As Powell walked along in the single-file line of troops, careful to position his feet in the same place as the man before him, he misstepped and came down hard on the sharpened point of a *punji* stick buried in a shallow hole, a Viet Cong booby trap that had been covered with dung to cause the maximum possible damage. The point grazed the thick rubber sole of his boot, pierced the canvas at the instep and went straight through his foot. By the time they reached the camp several hours later, he could barely walk and was evacuated by helicopter for medical care in Hue.

The telegrams sent separately to Alma and his parents were stamped "Casualty Message." While informing them that Powell had been injured as "the result of hostile action," it noted that he was "not repeat not seriously injured," a reassurance Luther discounted as he kept the news from Arie, much to her later fury. But the wound was enough to end Powell's march through the valley, and he was reassigned to the 1st ARVN Division headquarters in Hue under the command of George Price, who had been newly promoted to division G-3, the operations and planning adviser.

Powell felt he had done his job as an American "presence." Troops in his South Vietnamese battalion trusted and respected him, and he considered Captain Hieu a friend. But while the ARVN soldiers were brave and committed, they were hard to train and were fighting against an ephemeral enemy that played by a different set of rules. Nothing Powell had seen or experienced led him to believe his side was winning, and his doubts only increased at division headquarters. Desk jockeys there totted up meaningless statistics and wrote reports that rarely reflected the surreal nature of his battalion's blind trek.

The Army continued to praise him, often for successes he didn't recognize. A lieutenant colonel in Hue wrote glowingly for Powell's file that the captain had developed a "vigorous and comprehensive program to improve the [battalion's] combat effectiveness." The camp whose construction he had supervised at Be Luong was "of inestimable value in this counterinsurgency effort." Special note was made of Powell's "assistance rendered in the planning and the conduct of a crop destruction operation. This program was executed only after extremely careful planning and coordination," an apparent reference to their crude hacking down of Montagnard foodstuffs.

By that point, he just wanted to go home. For an adviser returned from the field, the headquarters at Hue was a tableau of everything that was already clearly wrong with the Vietnam effort. As intelligence analysts plotted and assessed their own version of the war, American pilots strutted around wearing reflector sunglasses and comparing the size of the ornate hunting knives and combat-useless revolvers strapped to their hips. Senior ARVN officers did their own strutting, wearing silken flight scarves and colorful jumpsuits that became more outlandish as they rose in rank. Special Forces soldiers strode arrogantly through the base with tough expressions on their stubbled faces. Hue was Powell's "first experience of elite people in elite units, who almost always get in elite trouble if you don't watch it."

The American advisers had been warned against involvement in Vietnamese politics and told that "it is your military obligation to support the incumbent government just as you do your own. This is U.S. national policy." Out in the field, they were oblivious to both Vietnamese and U.S. politics, but at headquarters it was hard to ignore the problems of the Diem government. Diem was a Catholic, part of the minority converted by the French, and he had long repressed the majority Buddhists, particularly in Hue. As his unpopularity grew, the Kennedy administration, despite its own pledge "to support the incumbent government," began thinking about alternatives. In August, Diem placed Hue under martial law; Powell and the rest of the American troops stationed there were confined to their quarters lest they become involved in the turmoil and tagged with the same public opprobrium as the ARVN soldiers.

However troubling the political situation, Washington was nonetheless convinced that the military campaign against the Viet Cong was progressing steadily toward its goal of ending "direct military involvement of U.S. personnel in the Vietnam insurgency" by the end of 1965. At a May 1963 conference with U.S. military commanders in Honolulu, McNamara had ordered MACV to begin planning for the withdrawal of 1,000 American soldiers by the end of that year as a demonstration of the gradual transfer of training and other U.S.-performed functions to the Vietnamese. The withdrawal plans set off alarm bells in some U.S. government quarters and concern that a drawdown would attract attention to the fact that the Kennedy administration had already misled the public about deployments to Vietnam, claiming a 12,000-troop presence when the number had already reached 15,000. The unintended result, the U.S. Embassy in Saigon warned, could be a front-page story reading "U.S. in the last few months has quietly boosted troop strength in Vietnam." More attuned to political realities on the ground, the embassy proposed that any withdrawal announcement be postponed indefinitely, reasoning that "any such announcement now could be distorted to look like U.S. disengagement and thus of faltering support for the GVN [Government of Vietnam] at a critical moment. This, in turn, could be exploited by both the Buddhists and the Viet Cong."

Further repression against the Buddhists and a failed coup attempt against Diem led to an extensive policy review in Washington, and in late September Kennedy sent McNamara and General Maxwell D. Taylor, the chairman of the Joint Chiefs of Staff, to assess the situation. Their visit, from September 26 to October 2, was emblematic of "the great difficulty encountered by high level fact-finding missions and conferences in getting at the 'facts' of a complex policy problem like Vietnam in a short time," the "Pentagon Papers," the Defense Department's historical review of Vietnam policy begun in 1968, later noted dryly.

Part of their itinerary took McNamara and Taylor to Hue, where George Price, Powell's superior officer, was among their official briefers. "They asked us about how secure the area was," Price recalled. "I said, 'Sir, I'm not trying to be ridiculous, but I would say it's about as secure as Birmingham, Alabama.' And that was right after they'd blown up the church with the kids in it."

In the months after the children's marches in the spring of 1963, the course of desegregation in Birmingham had been one step forward and two steps back. The city government had appointed a 153-member Community Affairs Committee to make good on its pledge to end segregation, but it had named only 28 blacks to the panel and given none of them a seat on the all-important steering group. In July, segregation ordinances governing public accommodations had been repealed and most previously all-white restaurants were desegregated without significant incident, although at Woolworth's, the lunch counter waitress ran away when black customers were seated.

In August, King held a March on Washington to declare victory, drawing 250,000 people who spread from the foot of the Lincoln Memorial to the far reaches of the National Mall. His "I Have a Dream" speech became as famous as the iconic photographs of children running from fire hoses and police the previous May. But by September, the mood in Birmingham had turned ugly again. As local public schools opened for the year, Wallace sent state troopers to prevent the entry of black children. When a federal court ordered the troopers to stand down, the governor called out the state National Guard to surround the schools. Kennedy responded on September 10 by federalizing the Guard.

Five days later, on September 15, a massive explosion shattered the peace of Sunday-morning worship services around the city. An estimated fifteen sticks of dynamite had been placed in the basement of the Six-teenth Street Baptist Church; the blast killed four black girls in the base-ment bathroom and wounded dozens more. To the young Condoleezza Rice, worshiping at another church only a few blocks away, the explosion sounded "almost like a train coming." The Johnson family was also at a different church that morning, but Alma knew the Sixteenth Street build-ing well. She had been in that basement, where the children gathered for Sunday school and the air smelled of damp concrete. Soon after the blast, the streets around the church filled with a crowd of angry blacks and police gunshots began to fill the air. As Alma, her mother and her aunt drove through a black neighborhood, rushing to get home, a man approached them. They had better find another route, he said, lest resi-dents mistake their fair skin for white and stone their car.

Upon their return from South Vietnam, McNamara and General Taylor went immediately to brief Kennedy at a special meeting of his National Security Council. Their lengthy report largely reaffirmed pre-trip views that the republic was in the midst of a political crisis but indicated that the military campaign was going well; particularly well, Taylor noted, in the northern part of the country. McNamara had already issued orders to speed up planning for the withdrawal of U.S. troops, starting with the symbolic 1,000-man drawdown before the end of the year.

A White House announcement after the briefing noted that although the political situation remained "serious," the military campaign "has made progress and is sound in principle." Major U.S. assistance would be "needed only until the insurgency has been suppressed or until the national security forces of the Government of South Viet-Nam are capa-ble of suppressing it." By the end of the year, the White House said, train-ing for ARVN forces "should have progressed to the point where 1,000 U.S. military personnel assigned to South Viet-Nam can be withdrawn." On October 11, Kennedy ordered the initial drawdown.

Not everyone in the U.S. government agreed with the McNamara-Taylor assessment, and there were suspicions that the optimistic progress report "actually cloaked a situation that was not only bleak, but deterio-rating." In an evaluation circulated among government agencies on Octo-ber 22, the State Department's Bureau of Intelligence and Research (INR) recalculated some of the statistics and concluded that trends actu-ally indicated a steady erosion of the military situation over the past sev-eral months. But rather than raising high-level doubts, distribution of the report brought an extended turf battle over which Cabinet department had the right to make military assessments and ultimately elicited a written apology from Secretary of State Dean Rusk to McNamara.

For Powell, implementation of the 1,000-man withdrawal meant early release from his scheduled yearlong tour in Vietnam, and by November 1, he found himself in Saigon on his way home. Field officers hated trips to the capital—it was "where all those rear-echelon wimps hung out" and no infantryman worth his salt wanted to spend time there. But on the day he arrived it seemed for once that there was more action in the city than outside. ARVN troops, dressed in full battle gear and piled into military trucks, were racing around town, closing roads and blocking access to the airport. Tanks rolled through the streets firing on government buildings, and there were reports that some ARVN commanders had been relieved of their duties and taken prisoner by others.

Just after 2 p.m., all U.S. active-duty soldiers were restricted to their bases, and at 5:30 an announcement over the American Armed Forces Radio ordered all U.S. dependents and non-official personnel to get off the streets. Just before 6:30, a plane flying over the city dropped leaflets announcing that "the day the people have been waiting for is here" and that a military government had been established. Artillery rounds smashed into the Presidential Palace at nine that night, but it wasn't until the next morning that Diem and his brother, Ngo Dinh Nhu, were cornered and killed. In the afternoon, the Americans sent an Army captain over to examine the two bodies and verify the .45-caliber bullet holes. In Washington, Kennedy quickly ordered full support for the new government.

As he waited for his departure flight the first week in November, Powell walked through Saigon snapping scrapbook pictures of the smashed palace and empty streets under the new military regime. "At age 26," he wrote in his memoirs, "I had no penetrating political insights into what was happening. I thought like a soldier who knew his perimeter, and not much more. To me, the coup was just another baffling facet of this strange land." Flying out of Ton Son Nhat, he felt little satisfaction with his own mission but remained a believer in the rightness of his country's involvement in Vietnam. "The ends were justified, even if the means were flawed...the mission was simply bigger and tougher than we had anticipated." They were never going to succeed without a drastic change in strategy and commitment, he had told one of the intelligence analysts before departing Hue. "It'll take half a million men."

Powell's *punji* stick wound had earned him a Purple Heart and a

Bronze Star. All of his ratings in Vietnam had been the highest possible, with recommendations for advanced schooling and rapid promotion. His new stateside assignment, back at Fort Benning for the Infantry Officer Advanced Course, would put him on a trajectory for early promotion to major.

The reduction in force that cut short Powell's tour would eventually be revealed as little more than a public relations effort. "At the end of 1963," military historians assessed less than a year later, "previous consideration of the progress of the war changed as the new military government became established.... On paper the war had seemed to be progressing well but in actuality [it] was being lost." By the spring of 1964, political and military downturns led to a complete U.S. reevaluation, and "national policy shifted from pullout to buildup."

5

In war more than elsewhere things do not turn out as we expect. Nearby they do not appear as they did from a distance.

—Carl von Clausewitz

In the summer of 1964, twenty-seven-year-old Colin Powell committed his first public political act, slapping a red-and-blue "LBJ" sticker on the rear bumper of his Volkswagen. Thrust into the White House as the nation reeled from the assassination of John Kennedy barely six months earlier, President Lyndon Baines Johnson had quickly achieved a milestone that had eluded Kennedy: passage of a federal Civil Rights Act.

Somewhat to his own surprise, Powell had begun speaking out on civil rights since his return to Fort Benning. He still wouldn't dream of attending a rally or marching in the street or picketing a polling site—that was out of bounds for men in uniform in any case. And while he found Martin Luther King inspiring, he was put off by what he saw as the rantings of the new breed of more confrontational black activists. Powell had long been oblivious to most race-based injustices and shrugged off those he couldn't ignore. Yet he now found himself explaining to his fellow student officers the absurdity of "property rights" as justification for keeping blacks from eating, sleeping and living in proximity to whites.

It was "property rights" that kept him, early in 1964, from finding a place for Alma and the baby to live with him off post in the city of Columbus, Georgia, adjacent to Fort Benning. The Powells ended up in a rental house across the state line in the black neighborhood of Phenix City, Alabama, while he sat in a temporary assignment waiting for the Infantry Officer Advanced Course to begin. That spring, a local Columbus drive-in exercised its "property rights" by refusing to serve him a hamburger—an incident that sent him screeching out of the parking lot in a rare public display of fury.

In her letters to Vietnam, Alma had spared him many of the details of Birmingham's convulsive year, but as he began to understand the events of 1963, he grew uneasy living in a southern city. Relief came late in the summer, when he became eligible for married quarters and relocated his small family inside the Army's sheltering walls. "For me, the real world began at the post," he later wrote. "I regarded military installations in the South as healthy cells in an otherwise sick body."

Few Army officers came from schools such as Harvard or MIT, where equality was at least preached if not always practiced. Military demographics were heavily concentrated in the South, and many of Powell's white classmates were stridently opposed to the new civil rights law. In the officers' club and mess hall or standing in the hall for a smoke break between classes, he found himself explaining just what "property rights" meant to a black man who dreaded trips outside his own neighborhood for fear he couldn't find a decent place to eat or would be turned away from a public bathroom—or worse. A road trip through the South was a special form of torture for people of his race.

He would never be a polemicist or a firebrand on race or any other subject, but he knew that everything about him was a challenge to race-based inequality—he was smart and attractive and a decorated warrior who had excelled at every challenge the Army put before him. The discussions were a useful opportunity to develop his growing skills of persuasion.

The Advanced Course—ten months of instruction on tactics, leadership and weapons programs—was the next step up the ladder for junior officers who hoped to make the military a career. Powell found the classes easy and graduated first in his group of 200 and third in the entire class of 400 men. His teachers were so taken with his aptitude and manner that upon completion of the course they recommended he become an instructor himself. Although he would soon be promoted to major, he had limited service experience and no academic training. But his remarkable capacity to work long hours at full speed and his ability to quickly digest and concisely translate massive amounts of data had attracted notice. He had a widely appreciated sense of humor, and he wasn't one of the "spring butts" peppered through every class—the overeager youngsters who hopped to their feet with an answer to every question. Always prepared and poised, his style was more to wait until asked and then bowl over the instructors with succinct accuracy. Respectful of superiors and able to project both authority and accessibility to juniors, Powell was developing a presence.

The three-week course for new instructors would become the single most valuable learning experience of his life. The Army applied classic drill technique to the subtle art of public speaking, teaching them "how to move before a class, use our hands, adopt an authoritative tone, hold center stage, project ourselves, and transmit what was inside our heads into someone else's." Graded on everything from how well they manipulated a pointer and told a warm-up joke to the agility with which they handled unanticipated questions, they were made to repeat a speech as many times as it took to reach the end without saying "um" or "uh."

As an instructor, Powell was an unqualified success. He had never struck his Army friends as the warrior type; his leadership potential was far more apparent when he had a pointer in his hand rather than a gun. "I used to kid him about being an adviser in Vietnam," recalled Steve Pawlik, a fellow Fort Benning instructor. "He was misassigned as an infantryman; he's not a killer by nature. He's a mediator."

After a succession of short-lived governments failed to halt Saigon's downward political and military spiral, the first regular American combat units were deployed in the spring of 1965. The proxy fight between South Vietnamese soldiers and Viet Cong guerrillas had become a direct Cold War confrontation between the United States and North Vietnam. By the beginning of 1966, U.S. troop levels had reached 200,000, a figure that would double before another year had passed. The U.S. strategy became one of attrition: to inflict the heaviest possible losses on the enemy in the belief that it would eventually give up.

With few exceptions, Army officers graduating from Fort Benning courses in the mid-1960s were bound for the war; Powell saw many of his buddies from ROTC and Germany pass through Georgia on their way to Southeast Asia. His teaching assignment had only temporarily delayed what he knew was an inevitable second Vietnam tour, and as it drew to an end in the spring of 1967, he warned Alma that they should be ready for new orders.

Just as Vietnam had become a different war, Powell was a different man from the cocky young lieutenant who had headed eagerly to Saigon in December 1962. He had come home to a wife he barely knew and a son who didn't know him at all and had spent the next four and a half years building his family. Their second child, a daughter they named Linda, was born in April 1965. In accordance with the custom of the times, he hadn't witnessed the birth—when Alma's labor pains started, he dropped her off at the base hospital on his way to class. But he was determined to give

Linda the early paternal attention his son had missed out on, and this time it would be harder to leave.

As he awaited new orders in the spring of 1967, Powell was given a further reprieve that would keep him out of the war for nearly another year: an appointment to the Command and General Staff College at Fort Leavenworth, Kansas. The course would teach him to supply, move and prepare for combat a division of ten to fifteen thousand men or more.

In recognition of their growing family, the Powells purchased a new 1967 Chevy Bel Air for the drive to Kansas. The journey across the South and into the Great Plains was the first of countless grueling family treks from one posting to another over the years to come, with the car stuffed with necessities to tide them over until their household shipment arrived, Alma calmly riding shotgun and the kids squabbling in the backseat. Powell loved to drive, but he was a single-minded demon on the road. As adults, the Powell children could count on the fingers of one hand the tourist detours on those moves and the few vacations they had taken as a family—once to Disney World and another time to a Wyoming ranch that belonged to someone their father worked for in Washington. What they remembered most were motorized forced marches, punctuated by fast-food pit stops and grudging bathroom breaks as their father sang along with the car radio.

Alma found she liked the small-town life at Leavenworth, where an Army friend helped them find a two-bedroom garden apartment rental in an off-post complex filled with the families of Colin's classmates. They had little furniture and ate their first home-cooked meal atop a footlocker, but there was a community swimming pool on the corner and a safe cul-de-sac where the children could play. The complex was filled with young married couples, most with children, all making about the same pay and with near-identical military experiences and aspirations. With the military scrambling to supply officers for Vietnam, the Command College had doubled its usual class size to more than 1,300.

In June 1968, Powell graduated second in his class, a pleasing result but an unaccustomed fall from first place that he blamed on one question on his final exam—and an answer that would gnaw at him for years. It was a war-fighting hypothetical, asking for a command decision in the face of an enemy attack. Powell recommended a tactical defense, withholding a counterattack until there was more information about the enemy's strength and position. When the instructor nicked his grade, he berated himself for not coming up with a bolder response. But as he turned it over again and again in his mind, he became convinced that he had been right in choosing caution and information gathering over quick offensive action, particularly when human lives were involved.

He eventually came to see the incident as a window into a core aspect of his personality—a reluctance to rush ahead until the lay of the land was clear. Powell knew his military history well; there were countless examples of brazen acts that had led to crushing defeats. But he also knew that caution could be a vice as well as a virtue. As he rose to jobs of higher responsibility and visibility, he carried with him a three-by-five card that he slid under the glass top of his ever-larger desks. It read, "Avoid Conservatism."

While Powell was hunkering down to family life and his studies, the nation outside the gates of Fort Leavenworth was undergoing profound changes. Heartfelt student debates over "property rights" seemed quaint in the face of the black power militants who had seized the initiative from nonviolent civil rights leaders. From Harlem in 1964 to Los Angeles in 1965 and Newark and Detroit in 1967, riot and destruction swept the country. After Martin Luther King's assassination by a white gunman in the spring of 1968, whole blocks of Washington, D.C. were burned to the ground. At the same time, the antiwar movement, begun with student "teach-ins" in 1965, had expanded along with the U.S. deployments to South Vietnam. The once-separate streams of protest now often flowed together, finding common cause in what they saw as an immoral war that was draining national resources and being fought largely by those too poor or unconnected to evade it.

Powell and many other black officers at Fort Leavenworth viewed the upheaval as if through the far end of a telescope, with detachment that bordered on disdain for those who burned their own cities and disgust for antiwar demonstrators. The officers were not white, but they didn't feel fully black if "black" meant torching their own communities and punching a defiant fist toward the sky. Insulated and integrated, the part of America they lived in was one where they could not only succeed but excel, and they had little inclination to disrupt it. "We were not eager to see the country burned down," Powell later wrote. "We were doing well in it."

There were many signs, however, that the war in Vietnam was faltering. Powell had already lost several friends killed in combat. Media coverage had turned increasingly negative as troop deployments and the number of American casualties rose hand in hand. Leavenworth wives with husbands in Vietnam were sometimes treated rudely off post—some were even threatened—and the war was a subject they discussed only among themselves. Even Robert McNamara, the perpetually optimistic defense secretary, had resigned in the fall of 1967 after expressing public doubts about the war. By the following spring, the United States' goal had shifted from military victory to a negotiated settlement. Demonized and depressed, President Johnson announced he would suspend a sustained bombing campaign against North Vietnam and would not seek reelection. In November, Richard Nixon won the presidency on the promise of "peace with honor."

As Powell received his orders to return to Vietnam in mid-1968, an internal Defense Department report, titled "Alternate Strategies," offered a starkly negative assessment of what had been accomplished in the years since he had marched through the South Vietnamese highlands searching in vain for Viet Cong. "We know that despite a massive influx of 500,000 [U.S.] troops, 1.2 million tons of bombs a year, 400,000 attack sorties per year, 200,000 enemy KIA [killed in action] in three years, 20,000 US KIA, etc., our control of the countryside and the defense of the urban areas is now essentially at pre–August 1965 levels." But the war was far from over; 1968 would become its bloodiest year, with 16,592 more American dead.

In early July 1968, Powell drove his family to Birmingham, where Alma's sister, with two small children of her own and in the midst of a divorce, had found a small house near their parents' for the women to share. Before he left, Colin gave Alma an envelope with instructions to open it in the event of his death and told her he wanted to be buried in Arlington National Cemetery, across the Potomac River from Washington, D.C. They had a farewell dinner at the Parliament House, Birmingham's finest restaurant. It had been off limits to blacks at the time of their last goodbye; they were still the only nonwhites in the dining room, and the black cooks and busboys peeked out at them from the kitchen.

The next morning, July 21, Colin allowed Alma to drive him to the airport, although they said their farewell in the parking lot and he walked into the terminal alone. A week later he had arrived at his new assignment, once again to the far north of South Vietnam.

Five years earlier, South Vietnam's five northern provinces—the U.S. military's I Corps Tactical Zone—had been considered a combat backwater with few indigenous Viet Cong. Now the region was one of the deadliest for American forces, with huge swathes of territory under the control of the North Vietnamese and their southern allies and most of the rest contested at best. Three divisions—two Marine and one Army—were concentrated on the coast at Da Nang and Chu Lai and at the inland combat base at Khe Sanh, just fourteen miles south of the demilitarized zone.

The Army component of I Corps was the 23rd Division, cobbled together out of three disparate brigades in September 1967 and named the Americal, after a division deactivated at the end of World War II. The 20,000-man Americal was based at Chu Lai in Quang Ngai Province at the southern end of the zone. A half-hour helicopter ride to the south and slightly inland lay Powell's new assignment, as a battalion executive officer at a base near the village of Duc Pho.

Carved out of the rolling red piedmont between the South China Sea and the western highlands, the Duc Pho base was a muddy, sprawling encampment of tents, ammunition dumps, sandbags, watchtowers and a busy airstrip lined with helicopters. The administrative headquarters of the 3rd Battalion, 1st Infantry, 11th Infantry Brigade, it was the depot through which the battalion's combat troops at firebases and landing zones farther inland were rotated and supplied with food, ammunition and mail, and where the bodies of American dead and wounded were processed. Powell's job was to manage the two-way flow.

Face-to-face ground combat was relatively rare in the Americal operations zone, where every village was assumed to be infiltrated by Viet Cong. Most American soldiers in the area felt the same frustrations that Powell had experienced five years earlier in the nearby A Shau Valley—an unreadable civilian population, territory that was never really conquered, and an enemy that was everywhere and nowhere and seemed to have an unending supply of replacement troops. The A Shau had now been largely abandoned to the enemy. Those patrolling in the field lived on a knife edge of constant anxiety. There were extraordinary acts of American bravery, but most combat troops never got a chance to identify, let alone shoot, their attackers. The majority of Americal casualties were caused by snipers, mines and booby traps.

To an officer recently arrived from the college atmosphere at Fort Leavenworth, where shoes were shined and trousers creased and battle command was practiced with pencil and paper, America's war-fighting machine in the northern reaches of South Vietnam seemed marked by an indiscipline that was alternately morose and arrogant. It was visible in the discarded machinery that lay rusting around the firebases; in the scribbled and often incomplete headquarters records; in the sweat-stained, rumpled uniforms of enlistees and draftees alike; in the beads, bracelets and headbands that violated all uniform regulations; and in the marijuana smoke that wafted through the American camps.

It was not the kind of high-profile assignment Powell had been hoping for, but he took it up with his usual gusto, ordering the firebases cleaned up and the records brought up to date in categories from vaccinations to body counts. He made sure the troops in the field were supplied with bullets and beer and readied the battalion for its annual inspection. There were mines to be cleared and casualties to be retrieved—"recently healthy young American boys, now stacked like cordwood" on the floor of doorless UH-1 helicopters on flights that Powell sometimes rode along on from the landing zones back to Duc Pho. Life on the base itself was not without significant risk. Mortar attacks were a daily occurrence, and all of the many Vietnamese who came into and out of the camp were suspected of having enemy sympathies.

The Americal Division commander, Major General Charles M. Gettys, was a World War II combat veteran with a gruff voice and a carnivorous grin, a devout Roman Catholic who attended Mass on base every morning. Gettys was an old-school officer who had little interest in the niceties or modern theories of personnel management and trusted his staff and field commanders to do what was required in any situation. He was known for quickly sizing up others and making decisions, as he had done when selecting Captain Ronald Tumelson as his personal aide.

"He said, 'I've got three questions for you,' " Tumelson later recalled.

" 'Can you read a map?' Yes, sir.

" 'Can you run the radio in the helicopter?' I've never done it, sir, but I can learn.

" 'Can you keep me supplied in Scotch?' I said yes, sir, I will find a way to do that. He said, 'Good. Come to work for me tomorrow.' "

Tumelson poured the general's whiskey, accompanied him on his trips around the southern reaches of the I Corps zone that were the Americal's operations area and kept him apprised of things worth knowing that might fall beneath his radar. A month after Gettys assumed command, Tumelson suggested that the general might want to reconsider his recent choice of a senior officer to temporarily take over division planning and operations while they waited for the permanent G-3 to be released from combat. The man Gettys had selected was disliked by those below him and incapable of pleasing those above, including the many MACV generals from Saigon and civilian VIPs from Washington who cycled regularly through Chu Lai for briefings on one of the hottest regions of the war.

Gettys dismissed Tumelson without comment, but at his staff meeting the next morning, he announced he had changed his mind and had a new temporary G-3 in mind. Two days later, Major Colin Powell was summoned to Chu Lai and installed in the job.

Powell had crossed Gettys's screen a few weeks earlier. Reading an article in a months-old issue of the *Army Times* circulating through headquarters, he remarked to Tumelson that the number two Command College graduate pictured in a front-page story about the Fort Leavenworth school was the battalion executive officer he had just met on a visit to Duc Pho.

Powell became acting G-3 on September 28, 1968. The move into a slot normally reserved for a lieutenant colonel, from the administration of a 950-man battalion to war planning for a 20,000-man division with artillery and a fleet of 450 helicopters, was an unforeseen but welcome leap.

Chu Lai had grown in just a few years from a small Marine landing zone to a massive complex with 6,000 Vietnamese employees, a major evacuation hospital, clubs for officers and enlisted men, daily and biweekly newspapers, tennis and basketball courts and an eighteen-hole miniature golf course set up on a concrete slab near the beach. But despite these tenuous comforts of home, with troops continually rotating in and out and the regular thud of mortars the war never seemed far away.

There were other dangers that had little to do with the Vietnamese. Just before Powell arrived at division headquarters, a group of black soldiers had begun marauding through the complex at night, robbing and often beating up other soldiers, usually whites. During one such spree, the intended victim had reached inside his footlocker, pulled out an M-16 and unleashed a full magazine on the intruders in his tent. Military authorities judged the shooting to be self-defense but transferred the man out of the division the next day.

It was far from an isolated event. "Racial incidents and disturbance have become a serious and explosive problem," the division reported at the end of October 1968. "Investigations reveal that marijuana or alcohol are [*sic*] almost always involved to some degree.... Assaults, accidental and/or intentional loss of life have increased during this reporting period."

Barely a year earlier, the military—and American society in general— had taken satisfaction in the presence of substantial numbers of African Americans among the troops and the perceived racial harmony they represented. "More than anything, the performance of the Negro G.I. under fire reaffirms the success—and diversity—of the American experiment," *Time* noted in a May 26, 1967, cover story titled "The Negro in Vietnam." The magazine reported that black soldiers had no interest in, and some animosity toward, the raging black power movement at home.

But King's assassination in April 1968 seemed to have shattered the veneer of racial calm. Cooperation on the battlefield was rarely in doubt, but rear areas often became self-segregated camps where the frustrations and fears of the war, the increasing lack of discipline, and anger and resentment over what was happening at home combined in a cauldron of hostility. Wallace Terry, the black correspondent who written about the troops for *Time* in 1967, found an entirely different breed of African-American soldier in Vietnam on a later visit. The eager young man who had been proud to fight in an integrated military had largely disappeared, he wrote, replaced by angry blacks who denounced the war as a fight against a dark-skinned people and saw their principal battle as taking place in the civil rights struggle at home.

The percentage of blacks in Vietnam and their proportion of the total number of deaths averaged about 12.5 percent for the totality of the conflict (although black casualties rose above 20 percent during 1968–69). But black officers such as Powell were still a relative rarity, totaling only three out of every hundred in the Army by the end of the war.

Powell had seen the dual tensions of combat and race up close during his two months at Duc Pho, where he regularly moved the cot inside his officer's tent to avoid possible attacks from his own compatriots. But his office work at division headquarters kept him somewhat apart from both. He was not given to deep introspection, and while he sometimes wondered about the way the war was being fought, he did not doubt the overall wisdom of trying to save Vietnam from communism. What he later called "the career lobe" of his brain was in high gear, and he concentrated on his personal success. To the extent he thought about it at all, he tended to see the disintegration of morale and lack of discipline—with or without the racial component—as the result of structural and management problems within the massive and increasingly unwieldy military force.

Combat units in Vietnam were constant revolving doors. Officers rotated back to the rear after brief battlefield commands, and soldiers, many of them draftees on one-year tours, had no vested interest in either the war or the armed forces. Most frontline troops served in companies where the casualty and replacement rates made next to impossible the bonding, brotherhood and respect for leadership that Powell saw as the glue that held the Army together. Men who had neither trained nor fought together were thrown into units with neither pride nor purpose—the haphazard assembly of the Americal out of three random brigades and its stepchild existence as an Army division under Marine Corps command was a prime example. Bases such as Duc Pho "contained dozens of new men waiting to be sent out to the field and short-timers waiting to go home," Powell later wrote. "For both groups, the unifying force of a shared mission and shared danger did not exist. Racial friction took its place."

The Army needed to prove to itself and to Washington that the war was achieving something, and in the absence of territory conquered and retained or a decrease in attacks, it began judging success by other means. The most extreme of these was the body count, the number of enemy dead that would become exaggerated beyond the belief of any rational observer as military units engaged in what Powell later called "a macabre statistical competition" that pitted "companies against companies, battalions against battalions, brigades against brigades. Good commanders scored high body counts. And good commanders got promoted."

But body counts were just the beginning. Between November 1968 and January 1969, the Americal meticulously reported, its psychological operations unit had "disseminated 131,335,000 leaflets," broadcast "more than 1,200 hours of air, ground and waterborn [sic]" propaganda appeals over loudspeakers, and shown 795 movies to 77,852 Vietnamese. Eleven bridges, one temple and seven dispensaries had been built and four sets of playground equipment erected.

In a humanitarian drive at Chu Lai, troops contributed 17,385 bars of soap to be given to Vietnamese civilians. Throughout the Americal zone, thirty-three of sixty "strategic hamlets"—the encampments into which rural Vietnamese were involuntarily relocated to prevent their contact with the Viet Cong—were listed as "pacified." The rest were considered "contested," and although every soldier in the field knew differently, none was deemed under enemy sway. During the same period, the division reported, its air unit had expended five million rounds of 7.62 mm ammunition from helicopter miniguns and 50,000 40 mm rounds, while losing only twelve aircraft and eight crew members.

Space was always tight in the commanding general's helicopter, and it was especially crowded on the afternoon of Saturday, November 16, 1968. Gettys had received word that U.S. forces had captured a North Vietnamese Army base camp in the hills west of Chu Lai that was so sophisticated it had two-story buildings on site, and the general rounded up his senior aides to fly out to see it. There were nine people aboard for the hourlong flight: Gettys; three crew members and a door gunner; Tumelson, who was two weeks short of ending his tour and had brought along the young captain designated to replace him as Gettys's aide; Colonel Jack Treadwell, the division chief of staff and a World War II Medal of Honor winner; and Powell, seated near the door next to Tumelson on a cramped bench. As usual, Gettys refused to wear the radio headset that allowed communications over the engine roar, and he was shouting and scribbling notes to Tumelson as they approached the landing zone.

Tumelson later recalled that he had radioed ahead to tell the troops they were coming. "I knew approximately where we were and approximately where they were, and told them to 'pop smoke'—throw out a smoke grenade" as the helicopter approached a small landing zone hacked out of the triple-canopy forest. The color of the smoke, agreed upon in advance, would assure the pilot that friendly forces awaited them and show him which way the wind was blowing as he began the delicate landing maneuver—a vertical drop into a round hole whose diameter extended only a few feet beyond the circulating rotor blade.

The pilot aborted his first try, as the nose tilted too far down and the rotor blew the colored smoke in every direction. On the second attempt, the smoke still obscured the clearing and the crew chief yelled that the tail rotor was coming too close to the trees. As the pilot leveled the aircraft, it hovered for a moment about three stories off the ground before suddenly being swiped by a crosswind. They all heard the whacks of the rotor hitting the surrounding trees. Tumelson reached for the radio squawk button to tell the pilot to abort again, but the helicopter began to drop like a runaway elevator. Powell assumed the crash position—head down, arms wrapped around his knees. The aircraft smashed halfway on its side on the forest floor, and smoke filled the cabin. Powell, the gunner, and crew chief, and Getty's new aide tore off their seat belts, jumped out and began to run, following standard procedure in expectation of a fire. When they realized the others were still inside, they ran back, and while the gunner pulled out the unconscious pilot, Powell dragged first Gettys and then Treadwell out of the helicopter and into the woods.

Tumelson was trapped. Folded over, his head wedged between the radio console and the transmission that had fallen from the ceiling, he appeared dead. Despite having what was later determined to be a broken ankle, Powell went back again and climbed inside to retrieve the body. As he pulled on the twisted metal, Tumelson began to groan.

Word that the commanding general's helicopter had crashed quickly reached battalion headquarters, setting off a whirlwind of activity down the line as rescue helicopters were dispatched and urgent messages sent to Saigon and Washington. With no place for the rescue craft to land, the injured were winched up over the trees into evacuation helicopters and transported back to the Chu Lai hospital.

Powell's ankle was put in a cast and he was sent back to his quarters. Gettys, with a dislocated shoulder, insisted on returning to duty the next day, while Treadwell was hospitalized with a deep gash on his head and then confined to quarters for another week. Tumelson was sewn up and shipped home after a few days. An artery in his neck had been severed, Gettys later told him, although bleeding had apparently been cut off by the pressure of his bent posture and dislodged helmet until Powell pulled him out and it began to spurt. "What Gettys told me was the only reason I was alive was that Powell reached in, pinched off the artery where I was bleeding and held it until he got me out of the bird," Tumelson recalled. He never saw Powell again to thank him.

That night, Powell argued that his injuries were not serious and asked that a next-of-kin notification not be sent to his parents and Alma. The request was denied on the grounds that a helicopter crash involving such a high-profile passenger would likely result in publicity about the incident at home.

Spending the weekend with her parents, Alma and the children were getting ready for church on Sunday morning when the telephone rang with the message that a telegram was waiting. Her father drove her to the telegraph office to pick it up, waiting in the car as she walked inside with trepidation. After she read that Colin had not been seriously injured, he offered the consolation that "At least you don't have to go home and tell your children they don't have a father." But it was weeks before she received a letter from Colin assuring her that he was all right. An identical telegram had been sent to his parents in Queens, and this time Luther shared it with Arie. But his previous assessment that she could not take the news that her only son had been injured appeared to be borne out. Whether it was serious or not, word of Colin's injury seemed to his sister, Marilyn, to age their mother overnight.

Two weeks after the crash, Powell's temporary assignment as division G-3 ended when the permanently assigned lieutenant colonel arrived in Chu Lai, and Powell stepped down to become his deputy. On December 3, Gettys awarded him the Soldier's Medal, the Army's highest award for noncombat heroism. "With complete disregard for his own safety and while injured himself," the commendation read, "Major Powell returned several times to the smoldering aircraft which was in danger of bursting into flames. In one instance he had to break away part of the wreckage in order to get to a trapped individual. Through his efforts all personnel were saved."

As the American presence in Vietnam plateaued at 536,100 troops, 1968 became the worst year of the war by nearly every yardstick, with 1969 a close second. Nearly half of the more than 58,000 Americans killed in the conflict died during those two years, along with tens if not hundreds of thousands of Vietnamese. President Nixon, elected on a pledge to end the war, began the pullout even as the military draft continued. As an ever-larger number of Americans turned against the conflict, Washington saw the biggest protest demonstrations in its history and many homecoming soldiers found themselves shunned as war criminals. Among the troops still in Vietnam, events occurred during 1968 that would long affect the American psyche and tarnish the military for a generation. Few who served during that period were left untouched.

On December 9, a week after Powell stepped down as G-3, Americal headquarters received an internal memo from Saigon. Addressed to the division adjutant general, Lieutenant Colonel Bernard L. J. Callahan, it requested information to help the MACV commander, General Creighton Abrams, respond to a letter sent to him by a recently departed division soldier, Tom Glen of the 11th Brigade. Glen's eight-page, handwritten letter, dated November 27, 1968, and dropped into the military mail system with an Arizona return address as he was leaving Vietnam, was an anguished and disturbing indictment of the treatment of Vietnamese civilians and military captives by American soldiers. "Far beyond merely dismissing the Vietnamese as 'Slopes' or 'Gooks,' " Glen wrote, "in both deed and thought too many American soldiers seem to discount their very humanity." He wrote of psychological and physical humiliation, beatings and indiscriminate shooting at civilians and the unjustified destruction of their homes.

"Severe beatings and torture at knife point are the usual means" of questioning captive suspects, "and on occasion aroused scout dogs have been used to terrify prisoners." Such actions not only violated the Geneva Conventions on treatment of prisoners, Glen said, they violated the very soul of America. "If this conflict is to be resolved favorably, we must seek

and obtain the aid of the Vietnamese people; yet American soldiers themselves make obtaining this more difficult, and perhaps more significantly
practice here the intolerance which is so divisive of our country."

Glen offered no specifics—no dates, names or places—but wrote that
he had witnessed such activity "not only in my own unit, but also in others we have worked with, and I fear, it is universal. If this is indeed the
case, it is a problem which cannot be overlooked, but can, through a more
firm implementation of the codes of MACV and the Geneva Convention,
perhaps be eradicated."

Callahan distributed the Glen letter to a half dozen senior Americal
officers with a cover memo asking each to provide "information upon
which to base a reply" within two days. The longest response came from
Lieutenant Colonel Albert L. Russell, who commanded Glen's battalion.
In two typewritten pages outlining the "conduct of war" briefings every
incoming soldier was required to attend, Russell described Glen as "a fine
soldier and a hard worker," intelligent and well liked by his fellow troops.
But no one who had worked with Glen over the past year, Russell wrote,
remembered him having come into contact with prisoners of war or
remarking on their treatment. The battalion had an open-door policy, and
all members were encouraged to bring problems and suggestions to his
attention; it was unfortunate that Glen had not followed the chain of
command. "That he should write a letter, charging violations coached
[sic] in vague generalities after he had rotated makes his charges suspect
and casts doubt on the moral courage he must possess to weather the
onslaughts against the idealistic convictions he purportedly advocates."

The division assistant chief of staff for civil affairs wrote Callahan that
he had no specific information regarding Glen's claims. Although isolated
instances of the treatment described undoubtedly occurred, he said, he
doubted that Glen had seen such things himself and also raised the "chain
of command" issue. In similar responses, the division staff judge advocate
and inspector general wrote that they had no specific information regarding Glen or his charges.

The G-3 had also been sent a copy of Callahan's memo, and it is
unclear why Powell responded instead of Lieutenant Colonel Richard D.
Lawrence, the new operations officer whose deputy he had become. In
four numbered paragraphs, Powell wrote that "although there may be isolated cases of mistreatment of civilians and [prisoners] this by no means
reflects the general attitude throughout the division. In direct refutation
of this portrayal is the fact that relations between Americal soldiers and
the Vietnamese people are excellent. The Vietnamese people are truly

appreciative of the many civil improvement projects that have been undertaken by Americal units and the direct interest that Americal soldiers have taken in their welfare and the improvement of their standard of living." All incoming soldiers were instructed on treatment of Vietnamese civilians, Powell wrote. It was "unfortunate that SP4 Glen does not specify incidents or individuals concerned so that an investigation might be conducted. It is also unfortunate that SP4 Glen did not bring these allegations to his immediate superiors or the IG prior to the end of his tour."

The official response to Glen was written by Abrams's chief of staff in Saigon, Brigadier General Howard H. Cooksey, who made many of the same points raised by the Americal staff officers. After voicing appreciation for Glen's "articulate expression," Cooksey agreed that the attitudes of some soldiers amounted to racism that "cannot be eradicated by any Geneva Convention or MACV Directive." Such attitudes had to be distinguished from "overt acts," he wrote, and the latter "are not merely dismissed as unfortunate; on the contrary, they are not tolerated." But anyone who witnessed a war crime, especially if he failed to report it to his superiors, was not "absolved of responsibility for that crime merely because he did not actively participate in it." It would be terrible to believe that the activity Glen described was typical of American soldiers, Cooksey wrote. "That such attitudes are 'frequent' is an assessment that I cannot share."

The military heard nothing more from Glen. A week after Cooksey's response, as part of its ongoing effort to "bring about a better understanding of a part of Western culture," the Americal held a series of Christmas parties at Chu Lai. Soldiers donated their own money to buy candy for the Vietnamese children in the surrounding area and distributed twelve thousand toys shipped from the United States through Da Nang. For the soldiers' own celebration, Bob Hope appeared at Chu Lai as part of a 1968 Christmas tour that included the film star and singer Ann-Margret; Les Brown and his band; and the Golddiggers, a dancing group of miniskirted, go-go-booted young women who had appeared on Dean Martin's television show.

In March, Gettys recommended Powell for early promotion to lieutenant colonel, and Powell was awarded the Legion of Merit for "exceptionally outstanding conduct in the performance of meritorious service to the United States." Before leaving for Vietnam the previous year, Powell had applied for time off after his tour to return to civilian school, and the Army had approved it. He had already taken the Graduate Record Exam and scored 1140 out of 1600—enough for admission to a master's degree program—and was awaiting a response to his application to George Washington University in Washington, D.C. Vietnam was almost behind him, but questions about mistreatment of the Vietnamese, and the military's response to them, would soon resurface both for the Army and for Powell.

Just before lunchtime on May 23, 1969, Lieutenant Colonel William D. Sheehan of the MACV inspector general's office placed a reel-to-reel tape recorder on Powell's desk and turned it on. He was in Chu Lai, Sheehan said, as part of an inquiry concerning certain events that had taken place between March 1 and March 20, 1968, "in the general vicinity of grid coordinates BS 7178" and involving an American unit called Task Force Barker. Asked if he knew of any operations on those dates, Powell replied that he had not arrived in Vietnam until July 1968 but was aware that the task force had been operating as part of a "composite force targeted against enemy units in the area." It was known as the Batangan Peninsula, a spit of land jutting into the South China Sea north of Quang Ngai City. Asked to refer to the G-3 records—the Division Tactical Operations Center logs—from the specified period, Powell said they reflected a number of enemy contacts, the most significant being "a combat assault into a hot LZ [landing zone]" by several task force companies on March 16. At Sheehan's request, he read aloud the entry describing a series of encounters that had resulted in twenty-one Viet Cong dead, several Vietnamese detained for questioning and two American soldiers wounded by a booby trap.

Asked if the journal entry included anything that "reflects the fact that the indigenous personnel in BS 7178 were advised to evacuate the area," Powell said he saw nothing to that effect. Sheehan asked if there was any more information, Powell said no and the lieutenant colonel ended the interview. He never mentioned what the inquiry was about and advised Powell not to discuss it with anyone.

It would be six months before Powell and the rest of the world knew the subject of the interview, one of a number Sheehan conducted with the Americal during the same period. In a widely published article in mid-November 1969, the freelance reporter Seymour Hersh described the slaughter of hundreds of unarmed Vietnamese women, children and elderly by Americal soldiers on March 16, 1968, in the hamlet of My Lai on the Batangan Peninsula. By the time of his article, Hersh wrote, the commander of one 11th Brigade company in My Lai that day, Lieutenant William Calley, had already been charged with murder.

A secret Department of the Army investigation into the incident had begun seven months before Hersh's article—a month before Sheehan's interview with Powell—in response to yet another troubling message from an 11th Brigade veteran, Ron Ridenhour. Unlike Glen's earlier letter, Ridenhour's March 29, 1969, account included names, dates and a horrifically specific story that he had pieced together from soldiers who had been present on that morning a year earlier in the Batangan village the Americal troops called "Pinkville." Writing to several members of Congress he had selected for their public concern about the war, Ridenhour said he had not been present and could not verify for certain what had happened in Pinkville, "but I am convinced that it was something very black indeed."

He wrote of infants being shot out of their mothers' arms by American soldiers, old men killed where they stood and women raped and murdered. Dozens of civilians had been thrown into ditches and mowed down with automatic rifle fire. Contrary to the official reports of the operation filed at the time, there had been no firefight. Instead, everyone in the hamlet and an adjoining village—perhaps hundreds of people—had been killed in a savage rampage that had continued for hours. Some of the troops had even stopped to eat lunch and then continued killing. Ridenhour, who had left Vietnam at the end of 1968, four months before sending his letter, concluded with a plea for action: "I remain irrevocably persuaded that if you and I do truly believe in the principles of justice and the equality of every man, however humble, before the law, that form the very backbone that this country is founded on, then we must press forward a widespread and public investigation of this matter with all our combined efforts."

Congress demanded answers, and the Army began an immediate inquiry. But the investigation was far from public and, at least in its initial stages, hardly widespread. At its beginning, it had amounted to a continuation of a cover-up that had begun the day of the massacre itself.

There had, in fact, been several real-time reports of what had actually happened in My Lai. A helicopter pilot who had flown over at least part of the slaughter while it was occurring had reported it immediately. Within weeks, a local Vietnamese official had written the Army about allegations concerning "the killing of 450 civilians including children and women by American troops" in My Lai and the surrounding area. A Viet Cong pamphlet that appeared in the region, titled "The American Devils Divulge Their True Form," described an operation in which "the American enemies went crazy. They used machine guns and every kind of weapons to kill 500 people who had empty hands," including "many pregnant women ... [and] some families in which all members were killed."

As a result of these reports, Colonel Oran K. Henderson, the 11th Brigade commander at the time, had been asked to investigate. Five weeks after the massacre, following what he called an "informal" inquiry, Henderson dismissed the allegations as baseless. In a written report, he concluded that a total of 128 Viet Cong had been killed in extended firefights in My Lai on the day in question and that 20 noncombatants had "inadvertently" died when they were caught between the opposing forces. Henderson made no reference to the helicopter pilot's eyewitness assertions and suggested that the stories told by the local Vietnamese were "obviously a Viet Cong propaganda move to discredit the United States." He proposed that a counterpropaganda campaign be waged. Henderson's report was duly filed away, and that summer, an article lauding the March 16 "victory" in the Batangan Peninsula appeared in the Americal magazine *Southern Cross*. American troops had killed 128 Viet Cong in the incident, the article said, and the 11th Brigade was awarded a special commendation for the battle.

After receiving congressional inquiries about Ridenhour's letter in the spring of 1969, the Army first asked for information from Saigon headquarters. Colonel Howard K. Whitaker of the MACV inspector general's office spent three days in Chu Lai in mid-April and interviewed, among many others, division G-3 Lieutenant Colonel Lawrence, Powell's direct superior. Lawrence, according to Whitaker's April 17 report, "provided G-3 logs pertaining to TF Barker including OP orders, tactical plans and after action reports," a more extensive readout than Powell was asked for by Sheehan two months later. In a report of his investigation, Whitaker essentially repeated Henderson's conclusions of a year earlier. My Lai, he noted, was "a VC stronghold" and the after-action reports by the companies involved claimed heavy enemy losses during the March 16, 1968, operation, with 128 killed. Adding additional details, Whitaker wrote that "the civilian population supporting the VC in the area numbered approximately 200," which "created a problem in population control and medical care of those civilians caught in fires of opposing forces." U.S. military units had assisted "civilians leaving the area and in caring for and/or evacuating the wounded."

Whitaker concluded from "all available documents" that Ridenhour had "grossly exaggerated the military action in question" and that there was no evidence to substantiate his allegations. All of the individuals named in Ridenhour's letter had long since returned to the United States, he said, suggesting that the Army try to find them there if it wished to continue the investigation.

After receiving Whitaker's report, the Army convened a comprehensive board of inquiry in Washington under Lieutenant General William Peers. Sheehan's interview of Powell in Chu Lai in May 1969 was part of that effort. The Peers report was completed and delivered to Army Chief of Staff General William Westmoreland, Abrams's predecessor as MACV commander, on March 14, 1970 (although it would not be released publicly until nearly five years later). It concluded that there had been no firefight that morning in My Lai and no evacuation or medical care for civilians. Instead, as Ridenhour had claimed, American troops had conducted a massacre of unarmed civilians in which "the precise number of Vietnamese killed cannot be determined but was at least 175 and may exceed 400." The Vietnamese, who years later erected an official memorial, put the total at 504.

Although others were charged, only Lieutenant Calley, the company commander, was ever convicted for the My Lai crimes. His sentence of life in prison was met with widespread disapproval by a public divided between those who thought he was a scapegoat for more senior responsible officers and those who thought the conviction would undercut the troops still in Vietnam. Two days after the verdict, President Nixon ordered Calley restricted to house arrest while appeals were heard; in 1974 his sentence was reduced to twenty years, and after spending three and a half years at home, Calley was paroled.

Tom Glen's letter did not surface publicly from the vast Vietnam archives until decades later, just as Powell began to contemplate becoming a candidate in the 1996 presidential election. The letter was accurately construed as an early, pre-Ridenhour alert about American atrocities that had been brushed off by Army leaders. As the presidential race got under way and Powell's career came under microscopic examination, some commentators added together Powell's involvement in the Glen reply and the fact that he had been interviewed in the wake of the Ridenhour allegations to conclude, at least by implication, that he had played a role in the My Lai cover-up.

In retrospect, it seemed clear that My Lai was one of the incidents involving the 11th Brigade that Glen had heard about. In the days and weeks following the massacre, word that something terrible had happened in "Pinkville" was widely circulated in the Americal; Tumelson, who was in the division at the time, recalled having been shown pictures by one of the participants. Gossip about that incident and other, less celebrated American assaults on civilians was so widespread that it was unlikely that Powell, who arrived in Vietnam four months after My Lai, was completely unaware of it. Yet when he and other officers at Americal headquarters had been asked in December 1968 to provide information to help MACV formulate an answer to Glen, all had responded with uniform denials of abuse and defensive reminders of Glen's failure to observe the chain of command or make his allegations in a timely manner. However vague Glen's charges were, no real effort was made to investigate them in Chu Lai, Saigon or Washington, and no one from the Army had ever contacted Glen to ask for more information.

Even if they had no specific knowledge of My Lai, all of the officers asked to contribute to the Glen response had reason to believe that relations between American soldiers and Vietnamese civilians were strained at best. Beyond the candy and toys at Christmas and the new schools and bridges, vast numbers of Vietnamese citizens had been removed from their villages and herded into "secure" hamlets while their homes were burned to the ground and their livestock and crops were killed, all in the name of "pacification." By 1968, an estimated 70 percent of all the villages in Quang Ngai Province had been destroyed by the ARVN and American troops to prevent enemy infiltration, and there was widespread animosity toward both, even among those with no sympathy for the Viet Cong. For the troops of the Americal, who were rarely involved in firefights but were regularly targeted by snipers and maimed by booby traps and land mines, it was easy to believe that every Vietnamese was a potential insurgent.

Powell's "direct refutation" of Glen's report and description of the "excellent" relationship between "Americal soldiers and the Vietnamese people" were clearly what the Army wanted itself and the country to believe. But judging by his own post-Vietnam descriptions, Powell himself did not believe it. When he was asked just two years after his return from Vietnam to provide a sworn statement in the 1971 case of Brigadier General John W. Donaldson, a former 11th Brigade commander who was charged with separate war crimes in the Batangan Peninsula, Powell said that "For the most part, the local population was unsympathetic if not actually hostile to US/GVN [Government of Vietnam] efforts. Willingly or unwillingly, they shielded enemy troops and thereby made their detection and identification very difficult."

Donaldson was accused of shooting indiscriminately at unarmed Vietnamese civilians from his command helicopter. In his statement, Powell noted that the hilly terrain and limited ability of ground troops to cover the vast region made helicopters valuable surveillance tools. "The general technique used was to locate military-age males (MAM) from the air and to pick them up for an identity check and questioning." When a MAM was spotted, the helicopter would descend, circle and order the Vietnamese to stop for interrogation, a risky endeavor that often resulted in helicopter occupants being shot by snipers. "On many occasions," Powell said, "MAMs surprised in this manner either immediately opened fire or attempted to evade. If fire was received, fire was immediately returned by the helicopter in accordance with rules of engagement. If the individual attempted to evade without firing, it was up to the judgment of the senior occupant of the aircraft" whether to shoot him. "To the best of my knowledge, there was no specific set of rules covering this specific circumstance." The technique was particularly valuable in the area of 11th Brigade operations, he said, which was rife with "hostiles who attempted to camouflage themselves into the general population." The charges against Donaldson were eventually dropped.

In response to a question about My Lai in a 1990 interview, Powell said that much of Quang Ngai Province during the late 1960s had been "lousy Indian country. I don't mean to be ethnically or politically unconscious, but it was awful. There were nothing but VC in there. I'm not excusing what happened, but when you went in there, you were fighting everybody." It was the kind of environment, he felt, that required troops with the best training, the best leaders and the most discipline—all of which, he said, had been lacking at My Lai.

If his first tour in Vietnam had been a trying but noble effort to help contain Communist expansion, Powell saw his second deployment more than five years later largely as something to be endured. He was well aware that much of what he did contributed little if anything to defeating a North Vietnamese Army that was clearly fighting a different war than the Americans were. Every afternoon at division headquarters, he laid out the "H & I"—harassing and interdicting—coordinates for that night's artillery fire, based on intelligence that everyone involved knew was imprecise at best. The artillery batteries would fire into the jungle until dawn, never knowing what, if anything, they hit. Like so many other things in Vietnam, they did it so they could tell headquarters they had done it, so that their commanders would know they were doing *something*. In Powell's mind, there was never any objective for the war less vague than causing the enemy to pay too high a price to continue. But the enemy, it turned out, was willing to pay a far higher price than the Americans were.

Powell was like many other young officers who saw the irrationality and futility of the effort on a daily basis, and the experience would later play a major role in his own command decisions at the highest level. But whether they felt it was not their place—or were simply happy to punch a ticket necessary for promotion, escape alive and forget Vietnam—few of them tried to do anything about it. Beyond what he witnessed in the Americal, it would be some time before Powell grasped the larger failings of a military effort that, he later wrote, had "lost touch with reality" and become complicit in its own undoing. The reluctance of midlevel and senior officers who knew better—himself included—to acknowledge the truth and speak it to those in power had indirectly given license to those below them to violate their own training and consciences.

During and forever after the Vietnam War, Powell found it difficult to criticize the troops themselves, many of them young, inexperienced soldiers who walked into combat zones with little faith in their cause, under ill-prepared or even incompetent leadership. In the Americal, combat commanders were shuffled so quickly and casualty rates were so high that the traditional practice of rotating entire units in and out of combat was often abandoned as individual soldiers were sent to the frontline like substitutes in a football game. The absence of unit cohesion and the erosion of standards for leadership and training, in Powell's hindsight view, had been directly responsible for the breakdown in morale, discipline and professional judgment that had allowed My Lai to happen.

He had "witnessed as much bravery in Vietnam as I expect to see in any war," Powell later wrote. Ultimately, he was proud of his service and the way "American soldiers answered the call in a war so poorly conceived, conducted, and explained by their country's leaders."

6

Learn who's who; develop a stable of contacts; always be responsive to a stranger; never put a guy off; become an expert in something and a generalist in everything.

—Colin L. Powell

With his military haircut and tucked-in shirt, John Saur felt like an alien at George Washington University in the fall of 1969. The antiwar movement was at full boil, and GWU, just blocks from the White House and the State Department, was a hotbed of student protest in the nation's capital. The shouts of demonstrators echoed regularly along the narrow campus streets, and the acrid scent of tear gas lingered in the air. Many of the low-rise university buildings bore battle scars—smashed doors and windows covered with plywood and graffiti that screamed "NLF yes, USA no," a salute to the Viet Cong's National Liberation Front.

As he sat down for his first class in the graduate business school, Saur couldn't help but notice that one of the other new students seemed even more out of place than he did. Sitting calmly erect among the scruffy blue jeans and ersatz combat jackets was an Army major in full uniform, his chest studded with medals and ribbons. "This guy," Saur thought with admiration, "has a lot of nerve."

However confident he appeared, Powell's stomach was churning. It wasn't the fact that many of his fellow students hated what he represented that set his nerves on edge; he was accustomed to physical separateness and had learned to use his minority status—as a black, a military officer or whatever other form it took—to get his competitive juices flowing. What worried him about graduate school was that for the first time in his life, he felt his skills might be inadequate for the challenge at hand. Most of the active-duty military officers who attended graduate school enrolled in international affairs programs. But Powell, in what now seemed a perverse insistence on doing something different, had registered for an MBA, the subject area that seemed to offer him the least potential for success. After scanning his mediocre CCNY transcripts and noting that he had flunked calculus, his campus adviser had already suggested he might want to rethink his plans.

A week into their first term, Saur looked up in the library to see the tall Army major approaching him with a smile and an outstretched hand. "I'm Colin Powell and I notice we're in all the same classes. I was wondering if you'd like to be study partners." Saur, a Notre Dame graduate who had just completed an enlisted tour in the Navy, figured Powell had looked at his haircut and picked him out as a veteran. They embarked on a study relationship that paid off for both: Saur maintained a 3.6 grade point average, and Powell, to his and his adviser's amazement, would finish the two-year program with As in every course but one (a B in Digital Computation). What Saur would later remember most vividly about him was his total control—invariably prepared for class, with an answer for every question, Powell seemed to radiate an unflappable competence and to effortlessly dominate whatever situation he encountered.

After a study session, they would often sit in the crowded student union, surrounded by undergraduate buzz, and chat about their lives and families. Powell talked about the Vietnam War, but usually only in the abstract. He was adamant in his support of the draft—provided it was administered fairly—which he thought resulted in a better force than an all-volunteer military. By drawing in men who would return to civilian life, it helped ensure that careerism and unthinking deference to authority—the virtue and the vice of professional soldiers—would not skew military decision making. Like many Army officers of the day, Powell also feared that an end to the draft would mark the final estrangement between the military and the citizens it existed to serve.

Saur told him he was wasting his time in the military; with Powell's skills and smarts, he could rise higher in the world and make a lot more money on the outside. Powell disagreed and said he doubted that the business world was as ready as the Army to offer real opportunities to blacks. "I would be window dressing in a corporation to a certain point, and then I would hit a ceiling."

Until he packed away his uniform and allowed his normally close-cropped hair to grow into the slightest hint of an Afro, Powell continued to draw stares and antiwar insults on campus. To Saur, he always seemed coolly impervious. "One evening, we were sitting there amid all these hippies, and a guy came up and started haranguing Colin about the war, calling him a 'mindless military robot' and making fun of his uniform."

Powell stared at the student in bemused silence, twirling the cigar that he usually carried on campus but never lit, and when the rant was over he swept his gaze slowly around the room. "It was full of kids just like this guy—long hair, jeans, wire-rim glasses, old fatigue jackets. Then Colin looked the young man up and down and said, 'Who do you say is in uniform?' And the kid just sputtered for a minute and walked away."

The GWU campus could be hostile territory for an Army officer, but Woodbridge, Virginia, where Colin and Alma set up housekeeping, was safely behind friendly lines. After seven years of marriage and the birth of two children, they had finally purchased their first house, in a neighborhood packed with middle-class families—many of them military—looking for low prices and good schools. It was far from their dream home—a friend had sent Alma pictures of the area before Colin came home from Vietnam, and she had tossed them aside as hopelessly suburban and lacking character. But though she had saved a considerable portion of Colin's salary while he was overseas, real estate closer to the city was out of the question. Twenty miles from the capital, they could afford—just barely— the five bedrooms they wanted. The house was depressingly empty; they needed everything from furniture to clothes and spent their first weekend shopping at a discount warehouse. Alma's parents tried to help with money they had gleaned from cashing in a burial insurance policy purchased for her in childhood, but Colin resented the $600 gift from his in-laws. It was the last time they accepted funds from either of their parents.

The Johnsons were less worried about Alma and Colin's finances than they were about life for a black family in lily-white suburban Virginia. Alma had been in Woodbridge before—it was the highway town where they had tried and failed to find a gas station bathroom they were allowed to use on the drive south from Boston to Fort Bragg in 1962. But most of the capital area's main military installations—Fort Myers, Andrews Air Force Base, Arlington National Cemetery and the Pentagon itself—were in Virginia, across the Potomac River from Washington, and military families tended to gravitate southward toward picket-fence communities along the road to Richmond.

Michael and Linda entered the local elementary school as the only black children in their classes. Alma had converted to her husband's Episcopal faith two years earlier in a ceremony in Fort Leavenworth's nineteenth-century chapel, and after the Powells settled into their new house on DeSoto Court, she called the local Episcopal church to say they were interested in joining. "By the way, we're black," she told the minister in an offhand tone that concealed her wariness. "I'm not," he responded. "But if it doesn't make any difference to you, it doesn't make any difference to me." It seemed an equally good omen that the church was named St. Margaret's, the same as the one where Colin had worshiped as a child.

Despite Alma's fears, the Powells prospered in Woodbridge. In May 1970, their third child was born, a daughter they named Annemarie after Alma's high school drama teacher. As his father had before him, Powell became a deacon at St. Margaret's. He had also inherited Luther's love of wagering and took over as head of the parish poker club. Intrigued by a neighbor who spent his spare time tinkering with cars, Powell bought a Chevrolet manual and began spending his weekends in the garage developing what would become a lifelong hobby. The more complicated his life became over the years, the more soothing he found the unchanging logic of wires and valves. An engine problem always had a satisfying solution if you took the time to find it.

General William Westmoreland, the Army chief of staff, was handed the final version of the Peers Commission report on My Lai nearly two years to the day after the March 1968 events on the Batangan Peninsula. Beyond concluding that American soldiers had committed "acts of murder, rape, sodomy, maiming and assault on noncombatants and the mistreatment and killing of detainees," the report outlined failures of leadership throughout the Americal chain of command. Soldiers had been allowed to develop a "permissive" attitude toward treatment of the Vietnamese and lacked knowledge of their own rights and responsibilities when confronted with what they thought were possibly illegal orders. In the days and weeks after the massacre, senior officers had turned a deaf ear to widespread reports of war crimes, and some had actively participated in a cover-up.

In response to the report, Westmoreland ordered the Army War College to conduct a study of the overall state of "discipline, integrity, morality, ethics, and professionalism" in the service. His directive made no mention of Vietnam and referred only vaguely to "several unfavorable events" in recent years. "By no means do I believe that the Army as an institution is in moral crisis," he wrote. The task was assigned to two lieutenant colonels, Walt Ulmer and Mike Malone, who spent ten weeks interviewing more than 450 junior and midlevel officers.

In a July briefing on their "Study on Military Professionalism" for the senior Army leadership in Westmoreland's Pentagon conference room, Ulmer and Malone reported that the service was drowning in just the sort of moral and leadership crisis Westmoreland had denied existed. Vietnam, they said, was not the cause but an effect of conditions inside an Army whose leaders had lost their way. Senior officers were obsessed with promotion and tended to ignore anything that might impede their own careers, including questions raised by their juniors. The Army ideal, they explained, was "characterized by individual integrity, mutual trust and confidence, unselfish motivation, technical competence and an unconstrained flow of information." The reality for most soldiers was "an ambitious, transitory commander—marginally skilled in the complexities of his duties—engulfed in producing statistical results, fearful of personal failure, too busy to talk with or listen to his subordinates, and determined to submit acceptably optimistic reports which reflect faultless completion of a variety of tasks at the expense of the sweat and frustration of his subordinates." In conclusion, they recommended that the Army consider a wholesale revision in officer training, assignment, evaluation and promotion systems; the elimination of the six-month combat commands that amounted to "ticket punching" for the upwardly mobile; and the establishment of a new code of officer conduct.

When the two lieutenant colonels finished their presentation, Westmoreland looked around at his colleagues with a stunned expression and muttered, "I just can't believe that." The next day, Ulmer and Malone were told that Westmoreland had decided their findings were "too explosive to release at that time" and should remain closely held within the military.

Years would pass before the War College study saw the light of day. But its conclusions quickly spread by word of mouth, and within days officers throughout the Army were intimately familiar with its results. "The worst part of it was that nobody could deny it," Powell later reflected. "We all knew it was true."

Many officers had come home devastated by their experiences in Vietnam. Some blamed the politicians in Washington or the media, while others sympathized with or even joined the antiwar movement. Among Powell's contemporaries, a significant number spent years grappling with whether they should resign rather than continue to serve a system they felt was so manifestly broken.

Powell himself never experienced the gut-wrenching doubts that caused some to reconsider their careers in the military. Although he had responded with extraordinary bravery when confronted with physical risk, he had ascended to a different stratum of military life when he left the battalion at Duc Pho for Gettys's American headquarters. And to a

career officer with a strong belief in decorum, the strident, scruffy protesters who surrounded him on the George Washington campus were
easy to dismiss.

Powell saw the failures of Vietnam as institutional, not personal. "I had
no ghosts requiring exorcism," he told an interviewer years later. "I went
as a professional soldier and served twice as a professional soldier....
Most Americans who went to Vietnam came out and went back to life
without having ghosts chasing them. Some had difficulties, and I feel for
those who had difficulty." He saw no point in rehashing the experience;
he never watched any of the dozens of movies made about Vietnam after
the war.

He blamed the Army leadership but reserved special scorn for "the
way our political leaders supplied the manpower for that war. The policies—determining who would be drafted and who would be deferred,
who would serve and who would escape, who would die and who would
live—were an anti-democratic disgrace" for which he would never forgive them. With words that would seem ironic years later, when he served
in the administration of a president who had sat out the war in the Texas
Air National Guard, Powell wrote that he was especially angry that "raw
class discrimination" had allowed so many of the sons of the rich and
powerful to avoid the conflict they supported. The unfair administration
of the draft and the refusal of Presidents Johnson and Nixon to call up the
Reserves and the National Guard had allowed too many white, well-off
Americans to ignore the war being waged in their name. He saw the Ohio
National Guard's killing of four Kent State University students during an
antiwar demonstration in May 1970 as the ultimate irony: the weekend
soldiers who were off limits for use defending their country abroad were
available to shoot its young at home.

As another wave of massive demonstrations swept through Washington in
the spring of 1971, Powell watched from the sidelines. On April 22, John F.
Kerry, a former naval officer decorated for his Vietnam service, testified
against the war before the Senate Foreign Relations Committee as veterans and mothers of slain soldiers marched to Arlington National Cemetery. Two days later, Powell followed hundreds of thousands of protesters
walking along Pennsylvania Avenue from the White House to the U.S.
Capitol. Standing off to the side, he watched hundreds of Vietnam veterans fling their medals and ribbons at the Capitol building.

He understood the bitterness they felt but could never join the
protests. "I still believed in an America where medals ought to be a source

of pride, not shame, where the uniform should be respected, not reviled, and where the armed forces were an honorable part of the nation, not a foreign body to be rejected by it." To Powell, the Army was not something you could cast aside when it disappointed you. Instead, like a family, it should band closer together in times of trouble. He thought of those who quit the service in protest as slightly inferior beings, although never as lowly as those who had used money or connections or unmerited draft deferments to weasel their way out of the war in the first place. "At a very unpleasant time, when the country turned away from the Army, we did not get out," he recalled years later. "We stuck it out and we fixed it."

As he worked to complete his master's thesis—"The Impact of Separate Pricing on Computer Users and the Data Processing Industry"—and headed toward graduation, Powell was offered a chance to do something constructive about the parlous state of the Army. Promoted to lieutenant colonel while at school, his next military assignment was on the Pentagon staff of the assistant vice chief of staff, or "A-Vice," Lieutenant General William DePuy, a man of high stature and some controversy within the service. A World War II veteran, DePuy had led the 1st Infantry Division in Vietnam, where he was credited with refining the high-casualty search-and-destroy tactics that were the basis of Army operations under West-moreland. He was notorious for firing battalion commanders he deemed incompetent or insufficiently aggressive.

DePuy had returned from Vietnam as the special assistant for counterinsurgency to the Joint Chiefs of Staff. In March 1968, after a visit to South Vietnam on behalf of the White House, he had briefed President Johnson on the discouraging war situation, a presentation that administration hawks later blamed for "poisoning the well" and contributing to Johnson's announcement two days later that he would not seek reelection (DePuy himself later said he didn't think that Johnson, who was drinking a Coke and playing with his grandchild during the briefing, had paid much attention to him). The following year, DePuy was appointed A-Vice, a position that had been largely co-opted by Defense Secretary McNamara as part of his effort to establish an informational channel inside the services behind the backs of the Joint Chiefs.

With McNamara gone, DePuy used the office to reassert the "authority and responsibility which had been taken away [from the Army chief] ... during the McNamara regime and for a long period thereafter" and as a brain trust for internal Army reform. His analyses and planning ultimately led the Pentagon to cut the size of the force in half, from 1.6

million in 1969 to 800,000 in mid-1973, when the Vietnam withdrawal was completed. A new, more centralized promotion system was designed to eliminate the prevailing "buddy system," and the unwieldy Continental Armies, the service's U.S.-based command, was reorganized and separated into a Forces Command (FORSCOM) for the troops and a Training and Doctrine Command (TRADOC) to run the various Army schools and serve as a think tank. Under DePuy's direction, the Army battle doctrine was updated for the first time since the Korean War.

With DePuy, Powell was introduced to the elevated world of the military high command and exposed to some of the Army's best and brightest thinkers. One of his assignments was to accompany the general on his trips to Army posts around the country to explain the reforms. DePuy rarely read from a prepared text, relying instead on a series of slides to structure his extemporaneous remarks—a briefing technique that Powell would later adopt with great success. Powell's own skills at organizing and communicating were noted in the Army's inner sanctum, and his reviews were glowing. Major General Herbert J. McChrystal, Jr., the head of the planning office that formed the analytical core of the reform effort, judged Powell's potential "unlimited" and recommended that his career be "carefully monitored to provide assignments of increasing responsibility and opportunity."

Despite the post-Vietnam improvements, the Army's highest echelons remained the ultimate old boys' network, a cloistered society in which whom you knew was often as valuable as what you knew. Black officers often felt at a particular disadvantage, isolated not only because of residual racism and their small numbers but because most had come to the service from segregated civilian lives. They had their own walk and talk, and both were considered foreign to an institution built on conformity to the majority culture. Powell recognized that he was lucky—his walk, talk and light skin were soothing to whites. "I don't shove it in their face," he once remarked. "I don't bring any stereotypes or threatening visage to their presence. Some black people do. Two, I can overcome any stereotypes or reservations they have, because I perform well. Third thing is, I ain't that black."

He had already been in close and profitable proximity to a number of prominent "old boys." But his first stint at the Pentagon also introduced him to a loose and still small network of midlevel and senior black officers who were determined to forge their own support structure and help nurture those coming after them. As he walked along a Pentagon corridor one day, Powell was accosted by Colonel Robert B. Burke, a stocky, distinguished-looking black man who asked, "How come you haven't checked in yet?" Burke instructed Powell to be at his house at 8 p.m. the following Saturday and to bring his wife.

Few in the network of black officers had had Powell's early career breaks; most were older and had reached their professional peak. In addition to providing a sympathetic ear and solid advice to their juniors, they focused on ROTC programs, the traditional path into the Army for black officers. By the early 1970s, ROTC was rapidly disappearing from universities in much of the country, an indication of the low esteem in which the military was held. The antiwar demonstrations that resulted in the shootings at Kent State had begun when students there set fire to the ROTC headquarters on campus, and while most programs were dying quieter deaths, they were dying all the same. At CCNY, where the cadet class had soared to 1,400 during Powell's era, enrollment had dropped to 81 by 1972, the year in which the university administration shut the program down. It was only in the South that the ROTC tradition remained relatively strong, especially at the nearly two dozen historically black colleges and universities known collectively as the HBCUs.

The Army had begun a conscious effort to expand its programs at the HBCUs in an attempt to serve the dual purpose of keeping ROTC alive and increasing the still paltry number of African-American officers in an institution whose proportion of black enlisted men and draftees had expanded rapidly. Many of the southern black graduates found themselves in the same predicament as Powell's Gelnhausen friend Ike Smith, who had traveled from a Louisiana sharecropper's shack to an ROTC program at an all-black Louisiana university and then straight into the white man's Army. Although Smith had overcome his perceived cultural shortcomings and eventually reached the rank of major general—and the Army itself had undergone profound changes since he and Powell had served in Gelnhausen—many black ROTC graduates still faced significant cultural obstacles. Large numbers flunked out of their first active-duty training school.

The black officers called themselves "The Rocks," after Brigadier General Roscoe C. "Rock" Cartwright, who had begun his career in the segregated Army as a World War II draftee and become the third African American to reach general officer rank. In groups of three or four, The Rocks offered their services to the presidents and military science professors of HBCUs to talk to students about "what was expected of them" in the Army, explained Julius Becton, one of the most senior black officers in the service. "What we wanted to do was to go to these kids before they came into the Army and explain some of these pitfalls and explain why it's important. Once you get out of school and get into a basic course, no one is going to be there to tell you to sit down and do your homework. Or get in before midnight. Or don't go catting off downtown. That's a discipline you have to have for yourself." To the senior officers from the generation before him, Powell was a paragon. "Colin was not threatening. He did not have the zoot suit attitude, the bebopping attitude," Becton recalled. "He was trained and educated in New York."

Nearly a decade after Colin and Alma had moved in with Joseph Schwar and his wife at Fort Bragg, the Powells were able to return the favor. Schwar had completed a Vietnam tour with the Special Forces, gone to graduate school and received a new assignment in the Army chief of staff's office at the Pentagon. Powell's Woodbridge house was big enough to temporarily accommodate the Schwars and their four children, along with the five Powells and several dogs, while they looked for a more permanent place to live.

The two men were impressed by the turns each other's career had taken—they had both ended up close to the seat of Army power, even if they were still far from occupying it. But it became clear to Schwar that one of them, at least, was about to move closer when Powell confided that his Infantry bosses were pressuring him to apply for something called a White House Fellowship. Pleased to be singled out, Powell was nonetheless concerned about making yet another diversion from the traditional route up the military ladder: the command of troops. He had been at the Pentagon for only six months, and the fellowship, beginning the following September, would take him out of the mix for another full year. "On the one hand, it's going to take me away from the Army," he told Schwar. "On the other hand, it's the Army hierarchy that's telling me to do it. And if I don't do it, what am I going to do?"

Initiated by the Johnson administration in 1964, the fellowship program was recognized as a career enhancer for up-and-coming young men, most of them civilians (only 10 women were among the 120 fellows in the program's first seven years). Candidates were nominated by business and academic leaders, although the only formal criteria were that applicants be between the ages of twenty-three and thirty-five, hold U.S. citizenship, and demonstrate good character, leadership qualities and the "promise of future development." Federal employees were barred from applying, but an exception had been made for military officers.

The service chiefs were eager to give promising young officers a taste of the upper echelons of civilian power and, not incidentally, to create a cadre of future uniformed leaders with high-level political contacts. Nominations for the fellowships were hotly contested among the service branches, and the competition extended down to the internal branch specialties. His Infantry bosses judged correctly that Powell—an honors graduate of every military school he had attended, a decorated combat veteran with a master's degree in business and a minority to boot—was a winning choice. Schwar thought that Powell's color only enhanced his attractiveness, evidence of both how far the Army had come on racial issues and how far it still had to go.

With Schwar's help, Powell filled out the eight-page application and solicited personal recommendations from General Gettys and his George Washington University adviser. He asked George Price, his commanding officer during his first Vietnam tour and now a colonel in the adjutant general's office at the Pentagon, to put in a good word for him and composed a three-hundred-word essay on why the fellowship would benefit both him and the government. His education and military experience had given him a good understanding of both theory and practical reality, Powell wrote. "In particular, I feel that I have an affinity for dealing with people and people-related problems." As the fellowship enhanced his own familiarity with national issues and how the government worked, he felt his presence would help build bridges between the military and the White House. "During the past few years a gap has developed between the military services and the larger society of which they are a part. My association with such a distinguished group of leading young Americans may help to narrow that gap."

At thirty-five, Powell was the oldest of the sixteen men and one woman selected from more than 1,500 applicants for the 1972–73 fellowship class. As the program approached its September start date, each fellow was asked to choose employment preferences from a list of White House and Cabinet offices. Luis Nogales, a twenty-five-year-old Chicano leader and assistant to the president of Stanford University in California—one of three minorities in the group together with Powell and another young black man—listed five preferences. He emphasized in a handwritten note on the bottom of the form that he was not interested in an offer he had received from Vice President Spiro Agnew's office; it was an election year, and he was a Democrat. Nogales finally ended up at the Interior Department, where he interpreted Secretary Rogers Morton's offer to send him to Micronesia to do a governance study as a way to get rid of him. Finally, he landed in a job in the office of an Interior undersecretary, a Stanford alumnus.

Powell was similarly discouraged after his first few months as a fellow. He had interviewed at the Department of Housing and Urban Development and at the FBI, but both seemed to be a stretch for his experience and newly minted expertise in business and budgets. After a brief conversation with Frank Carlucci, a career Foreign Service officer who was the deputy to Office of Management and Budget Director Caspar W. Weinberger, he chose OMB, the White House agency that oversaw the budgets of executive branch departments. But Powell's initial assignments were dull and bureaucratic, and his cubicle in an office building outside the White House was both physically and psychologically far removed from the locus of power.

His fellowship year finally took off in February 1973, after Weinberger and Carlucci were replaced by defense industry executive Roy Ash and his deputy, Fred Malek, a special assistant to President Nixon who was well on his way to becoming a major player in the Republican Party. Malek had been on the fellowship selection committee, and Powell immediately sent a note of congratulations that also allowed him to remind the new boss of his presence in the bowels of the budget office. Within days, Powell had been moved from the outer fringes of OMB to a seat outside Malek's door as special assistant to the deputy director.

He quickly learned that Malek cared little for the budget process except as part of a much larger agenda of extending direct White House control into the far corners of the executive branch bureaucracy. Malek was known as Nixon's "hatchet man," and Powell became the operative's operative, controlling access to Malek and transmitting his edicts to trembling agency heads. Saying he was calling for Fred Malek, Powell later recalled, was like being "a mob fixer asking for payment."

An important part of the fellows' year was exposure to movers and shakers outside their assigned jobs, and among others they were addressed by Supreme Court Justice Thurgood Marshall and feminist leader Gloria Steinem. Steinem had just founded *Ms.* magazine and revealed that she had had an abortion, scandalizing one half of the nation while thrilling the other. The fellows witnessed a space launch in Florida, had a photo opportunity with President Nixon in the Oval Office and lunched at the Pentagon with Defense Secretary Elliot Richardson. They spoke with the CBS television star reporter Dan Rather—the journalist wore two bracelets engraved with the names of prisoners of war in Vietnam and spoke disparagingly of Nixon—and they traveled to Atlanta to meet with Georgia Governor Jimmy Carter, a politician whose intelligence and mastery of issues so impressed Powell that he cast his absentee presidential ballot for Carter more than three years later.

The fellowship also included foreign travel, although deciding where to go had been problematic in years past. Before a scheduled visit to the Soviet Union in 1971, Anatoly Dobrynin, the Soviet ambassador to Washington, had labeled all five military members of that year's fellows class "criminals" because of their Vietnam service. They had been left behind in Helsinki while the civilians in the group continued on to Moscow. By January 1973, when the American troop withdrawal from Vietnam was nearly complete, the three Air Force and two Army officers in Powell's class were allowed to enter the Soviet Union, although under conditions that often seemed a parody of East-versus-West spycraft.

Surrounded by KGB agents who made little effort to disguise their identities, locked inside their hotel at night and confined to a single rail-car during a three-day trip across Siberia, they were alternately bored and awed by what they were allowed to see. Powell dressed in civilian clothes with an American flag pin on his lapel and wore a gray karakul hat he bought in a Siberian market. But the Soviets seemed as interested in his color as they were in his military status. Powell and his fellow minority member, Nogales, were constant targets of attention from the attractive female interpreter assigned to them—just the kind of undercover spy the CIA had warned them about in a briefing before the trip.

"The first several days, there were philosophical conversations about communism and capitalism," Nogales later recalled. "Then it was about how minorities were mistreated in the United States. The third topic of conversation was about sex, and how she wanted to be with us." On their last night in Moscow, the fellows were taken to see a ballet. "Somehow, she arranged to sit between Colin and me, and during the whole performance, she kept working both our legs. We both had a sense of humor about it, but we both knew it was serious business." They were disappointed when the CIA declined to debrief them upon their return.

Two subjects were of paramount interest to the Nixon White House as the fellowship year drew to a close in the summer of 1973. The ongoing Senate hearings on the Watergate scandal vied for the front pages with the administration's attempts to simultaneously juggle two foreign policy balls—its historic "opening" to China and a nascent détente with the Soviet Union—amid rising mutual suspicion between the two Communist behemoths. The Vietnam War had ended slowly and messily, and Henry Kissinger, Nixon's national security adviser and soon-to-be secretary of state, saw the normalization of relations with Peking as key to both Nixon's legacy and his own. But Powell was less than enthusiastic when the White House arranged a three-week trip to China in July. He was well into preparations for his next military assignment as a battalion commander in South Korea, and the thought of being away from Alma and the children on the eve of a yearlong overseas deployment did not sit well with any of them.

By the end of the China tour the fellows were fed up with staged visits to industrial plants, happy peasants and opulent dinners where their government hosts kept their glasses filled to the brim with the local firewater. When it wasn't raining, un-air-conditioned China was oppressively hot. But the White House was well pleased with this latest step toward normalization. Brent Scowcroft, an Air Force brigadier general who was Kissinger's deputy at the White House, wrote to Defense Secretary James Schlesinger (Elliot Richardson had resigned over Watergate some months earlier) of the particular importance of the five military fellows on the trip. Not only did the officers have "a unique opportunity to learn first-hand about China...the United States has benefited by their important contribution to better understanding between our two countries."

Luis Nogales judged that at the beginning of the yearlong fellowship, the group had been evenly divided between Democrats and Republicans. But it was "tough to resist" the proximity to power, and at the end he was fairly certain that all but he and another two or three Democrats had switched sides. He could never quite tell where Powell came down. "What I remember about him was that he was altogether a regular guy and not full of himself." Many of the fellows were too young to have had solid careers and had been assigned little more than internlike busywork for the year. But Powell, the oldest of the group, seemed to the others to have held a real job at OMB.

Powell later recalled his initial reluctance to apply for the fellowship as "the error of a greenhorn.... In all the schools of political science, in all the courses in public administration throughout the country, there could be nothing comparable to this education." He had been introduced to powerful figures who would become career patrons and had learned his first lessons in bare-knuckle politics and bureaucratic maneuvering at the feet of a master, Fred Malek. He was one of the few active-duty military officers to have traveled extensively behind the Iron Curtain in both the Soviet Union and China, and he had supped with the famous and the powerful.

Both Malek and Roy Ash sent letters of praise to Powell's military bosses. "I needed someone familiar with the ins and outs of the organization whom I could rely on to act for me and who could get things done," Malek wrote to Secretary of the Army Howard H. Calloway. "Colin was a perfect choice." He had asked Powell to stay on, "but it was his decision to finish the Fellowship year as planned and return to the Army." Malek closed with a civilian version of the Army's highest accolade, recommending that Powell's "career path be carefully charted to provide opportunities for rapid progression and increasing responsibility." At the bottom of a pro forma letter of acknowledgment, Calloway wrote in longhand, "The Army agrees with your evaluation. We think Col. Powell is a superb officer!"

As far as his family in New York was concerned, the fellowship had opened the door wide to unlimited future greatness for their boy from the Bronx. He had been at the White House, and it was only a matter of time until he would return. Joe Schwar, too, felt that Powell's career had taken a sharp upswing and he had begun to step out ahead of his military contemporaries. "Colin Powell to most of these people was a sheet of paper" going into the fellowship, Schwar reasoned. But he had been given an opportunity to sell himself, and he had made the most of it. "I think at the outset it was just another assignment to him. But he would have had to have been deaf, dumb and blind not to recognize that when you start to hobnob and rub elbows with guys like Frank Carlucci and Caspar Weinberger," other opportunities would begin to appear.

7

I got into the Army and I stayed. I kept getting promoted.
I kept waiting for that to be it, when they'd say no more.
They didn't.

—Colin L. Powell

On a steamy August morning in 1974, five senior Army officers gathered
in a conference room in a nondescript office building leased by the Pentagon in suburban Virginia. They were members of the selection board of
the Senior Service Colleges, gathered to make appointments from among
eligible colonels and lieutenant colonels to the military's five institutions
of higher learning: the Army, Navy and Air Force War Colleges, the
Industrial College of the Armed Forces and the National War College.
Attendance at one of the schools was a prerequisite for any officer who
hoped eventually to make general.

Stacked on the table before them were individual officers' files filled
with efficiency reports, commendations and other personnel notes. Over
the next several hours, each member separately rated the candidates on a
scale from one to six, with six being the highest. When they compared
scores, all five had ranked the same officer, currently a battalion commander in South Korea, at the top of their lists. None of them knew Lieutenant Colonel Colin L. Powell personally, but his résumé overflowed
with achievement and his service record was virtually flawless.

The five agreed that Powell would have a slot, but they were divided
over which college this star candidate should attend. Three of them, all
alumni of the Army War College at Carlisle Barracks in Pennsylvania,
adamantly insisted it was the place for him. But Julius Becton, newly promoted to major general and presiding over the meeting, had other plans.
His own alma mater, the National War College in Washington, had more
to offer an officer so clearly on his way to the top. The NWC was the military's Harvard, Yale and Princeton rolled into one. When the others dug

in their heels, he threatened to sabotage their other leading candidates, assigning them "ones" on his own priority list and thus lowering their overall scores.

As the debate continued, Becton tossed the race card onto the table, arguing that Powell had earned the best possible opportunity and that rewarding such a promising minority officer was good for the Army at a time when it was trying to demonstrate its commitment to integration in the highest ranks. "Back in those days, you could have very heated discussions" about the relatively new concept of affirmative action, he later recalled. "You can't do that anymore." Becton eventually prevailed, and Powell was assigned to enter the National War College in September 1975.

Powell would long remember his year in Korea as the most satisfying in his military career. It was there, after the disappointments of Vietnam, that he found at least a glimmer of the idealized Army of his boyhood dreams, in which hard-charging, seat-of-the-pants officers molded men from the soft clay of youth. For the first time since his company command at Fort Devens, he had hands-on control of troops. He was their father figure, their disciplinarian and cheerleader, their confessor and source of all wisdom and truth.

Not that anyone at headquarters in Washington was paying much attention to anything happening in Korea. The armed forces were wallowing in a deep trough of self-doubt and finger-pointing as the agony of Vietnam ground slowly to an end. The Army was bloated with resentful, substandard troops and still fighting an uphill battle against drug abuse and racial conflict. To the distracted brass, the 50,000 U.S. soldiers stationed in South Korea were leftovers from a nearly forgotten war and a drain on their diminishing resources.

Twenty years after the armistice with the North, much of South Korea remained a rubble-strewn, treeless wasteland. The economic miracle that would eventually turn the country around had begun to take root in Seoul and other urban centers, but the countryside was still bleak and impoverished. Facilities at Camp Casey, the Army's sprawling 2nd Division headquarters midway between Seoul and the demilitarized zone to the north, were appalling: filthy, two-decade-old "temporary" war housing, poorly heated buildings and vehicles with no fuel. Racial tensions were high, and drug problems were even worse than they had been in Vietnam. Something as innocuous as a barkeep's failure to equalize the number of Motown and country music records in a jukebox could lead to a brawl; eventually the Korean bars outside the Camp Casey gates were segregated into black and white bastions, and neither side was welcome on the other's turf.

Near the top of Powell's growing list of maxims was his belief that "there are no problems, only challenges," and Korea offered a wealth of them. His year at Camp Casey was like a long-running episode of the popular American television series *M*A*S*H,* an acerbic comedy based at a fictional Korean War Army field hospital where privation and nonsensical edicts from faraway bureaucrats were overcome with a soldier's ingenuity, improvisation and wit. Diesel-powered heaters, left cold in the frigid Korean winter for want of a small part that was never resupplied, turned toasty after Powell, rummaging through the supply depot, discovered a forgotten cache of suitable widgets buried under dusty boxes of World War I–era gas mask canisters. When the trucks that were to transport Powell's battalion back to base after a nighttime field maneuver ran out of gas, he led his half-frozen, exhausted men on a triumphant twelve-mile jog back, earning them an award. Camp Casey was filled with characters, many of them worthy of their own television series: strutting, self-appointed black leaders who thought with their fists; the Army chaplain who pursued his flock onto the dance floors of off-base fleshpots; the semicrazed division commander who wore an Old West six-gun in a tooled holster and was known to all as "Gunfighter."

Short on spit and polish and willing to break the rules to get his way, Major General Henry E. Emerson was exasperating and inspirational in equal measure, a man of Pattonesque gruffness who was paradoxically ahead of his time in experimenting with the "humanist" methods of personnel management that would soon be in vogue throughout the Army. "Gunfighter" set up classes so that unlettered soldiers could earn their high school diplomas, organized all-night rock concerts for young men he worried were missing out on formative stateside experiences, and forced participation in no-holds-barred contact sports as substitute combat for bored and testosterone-pumped troops. Emerson decreed an end to racial violence—"There ain't gonna be no goddamn racism. I want it all gone by eight in the morning!"—and showed no mercy to repeat offenders. He encouraged the troops to be nice to one another by ordering them to attend weekly screenings of *Brian's Song,* a 1971 cinematic tearjerker about the friendship between a black professional football player and his terminally ill white teammate.

"I can easily put that man's occasional excesses into perspective," Powell later wrote. "In the end, results are what matter. While I served under

General Emerson, AWOLs in the division dropped by over 50 percent. Reenlistments jumped by nearly 200 percent. And while impetuous youths might occasionally punch each other out, racially related brawling practically disappeared." Officers like Emerson, he believed, were slowly picking up the pieces of the broken Army and gluing them back together into something they could all be proud of again.

By now Powell had friends in high places and experience in working the Army personnel system. He knew he was probably headed to one of the senior service schools but would have an interim year to kill immediately after returning from Korea. Barely four months into his tour, he wrote to Joe Laitin, the curmudgeonly OMB press secretary who had befriended him and served as a guide through the federal labyrinth during his White House fellowship, asking for behind-the-scenes help in arranging a next assignment back in Washington. Laitin was close to Defense Secretary James Schlesinger and wrote back with an assurance that Powell's file would be placed on Schlesinger's desk. He suggested that Powell make a "casual" stop by the Pentagon's senior civilian suites during an April 1974 visit home, since "it takes six months for anything to move in that place even when God orders it be done." When Powell returned to Washington that September, a temporary slot in the Pentagon's manpower planning office was awaiting him.

Powell was not, in Harlan Ullman's view, a great student. But to the War College instructor, who prided himself on being a good judge of both ability and character, the lieutenant colonel was a fascinating mixture of down-to-earth accessibility and an aloofness that Ullman defined as "inner dignity." He was "extremely smart, but he did his best to try and conceal it. He wasn't being stupid, but he wasn't arrogant. He could grabass the guys," but a certain separateness was "in his genes." Even in the class of 141 officers and diplomats who were by definition part of the nation's elite, Powell stood out.

Ullman was a rare bird in the military, a Renaissance man who hobnobbed with the great and powerful, largely by virtue of his wife's pedigree as the daughter of an English lord. Barely in his thirties, he was a decorated Vietnam veteran with a Ph.D. in international affairs and the youngest instructor at the college. Intrigued by Powell, he invited Colin and Alma to dinner at his Georgetown home, and the two couples became fast friends.

It was Ullman who intervened to keep Powell's advancement on track when a crisis arose during his year at the War College. Powell, who had received yet another early promotion, this time to full colonel, had gotten word of his next assignment as a brigade commander with the 101st Airborne at Fort Campbell in Kentucky. It was the next step up the Army's ladder to the top, but the commander of the 101st, Major General John Wickham, ran into a personnel problem and insisted that Powell take up the position months before his college course was completed. Ullman agreed to cover for him, listing Powell as present long after he left.

At the end of the course, Powell's faculty adviser rated him "above average" on leadership and potential and a "front runner ... [who] continued to perform well especially if sufficiently challenged," but lowered his marks to "average" on performance and recommended that he not be selected as a distinguished graduate or considered for further accelerated promotion. Ullman felt it would be "useful to be singled out as one of the best people," however, and successfully interceded to have Powell named as one of twenty-eight distinguished War College graduates in the class of 1976.

The Powells were eligible for on-base housing in Kentucky, and Alma anticipated that Colin's newly elevated rank would entitle them to something expansive. The three-bedroom bungalow that awaited them was a disappointment. After glumly examining the flimsy construction and linoleum floors, Alma concluded it looked like low-income civilian housing.

The children were fascinated with their first real taste of life on a military base, but the adjustment was difficult. A significant number of their classmates in the on-base school were black, most of them the children of enlisted men or noncommissioned officers. The Powell children were not entirely oblivious to racism—one of Annemarie's most vivid early-childhood memories was of Alma stoically cleaning up the raw eggs that a few unreconstructed white boys in their Woodbridge neighborhood had thrown at their house. But the problem at their new school was not being black; it was not being black *enough*. Their light skin led to a general assumption that they were the products of a mixed marriage. Raised in an all-white suburb by a schoolmaster's daughter and a son of British Jamaica, they were set apart by their manner and accent and taunted for "acting white."

Michael told Linda that he just ignored it when black kids made fun of him. It was what the Powell children had been taught by word and example. Their parents "never talked about race much unless something had happened and there was something to explain," Annemarie recalled.

"They used the phrase all the time: 'My race is somebody else's problem. It's not my problem.'" It was the same formulation Colin had repeated to himself since he had first left home for the Army, and his children would have many opportunities to remember it in the future.

Fort Campbell was a small, self-contained city, and commanding a brigade of more than two thousand of its citizens and their families entailed management challenges far beyond the supervision of several hundred unaccompanied men in Korea. Major General Wickham insisted that officers participate in civic affairs and nudged Colin to become president of the post school board. On his own initiative, Colin took up the cause of expanding the post's small Episcopal congregation. He wrote personal letters to potential parishioners, enlisted Michael and Linda as acolytes, found a piano and procured a processional cross and other accoutrements of High Mass.

Alma had her own responsibilities, organizing school fund-raisers and hospital volunteers and providing a sounding board for women with troubled marriages, difficult children or money problems. The role of mother hen to a community of wives was not what she had trained or studied for. But she came to see the necessity and wisdom of promoting bonds among women whose husbands could be shipped away tomorrow with no assurance of when or if they would be coming back. Besides, it was important to Colin's career. The commanding general thought the right kind of wife was a crucial component of any officer's chances for advancement.

Wickham was a straitlaced West Point man whose career was in some ways a template for Powell's: early advancement, Vietnam, graduate school, the National War College and a series of senior staff positions that had cut into his command experience. His last assignment before Fort Campbell had been as a military assistant to Schlesinger and Schlesinger's successor, Donald Rumsfeld, who had taken over as defense secretary in November 1975. When Rumsfeld gave Wickham the choice of a third star in Washington or a division command, the general hadn't hesitated to opt for the latter.

Powell had worked for an eclectic series of military and civilian bosses over the years—Gettys, DePuy, Malek, Emerson—and had internalized a way of accommodating them that he called "pay[ing] the king his shilling." Rather than confronting his superiors or resisting what he considered nonsensical orders, he prided himself on anticipating what they wanted, needed and would appreciate and providing it with supreme competence and efficiency. He knew that some people would see it as ass kissing, but he viewed it as loyalty. Once the king was paid, he was off your back and you had the operating room and flexibility to push your own initiatives and do things your own way. "I detected a common thread running through the careers of officers who ran aground even though they were clearly able—a stubbornness about coughing up that shilling," he later wrote. "They fought what they found foolish or irrelevant, and consequently did not survive to do what they considered vital."

In temperament and respect for Army rules, Powell's new commander was the polar opposite of "Gunfighter" Emerson. Wickham was a stickler for training, so when Powell was left behind while the division's other two brigades were sent to Germany for an exercise, he spent weeks beating his thirty-nine-year-old body into shape to pass the demanding workout required for an Air Assault badge and then ordered the rest of his brigade to do the same. Responding to spoken and implied Wickham directives, he cracked down hard on AWOL and reenlistment rates, delinquent supply store accounts and drunken driving by off-duty troops. At one point, he ordered the officers' club bar to limit individuals' intake, but the backlash convinced him he had gone too far and he reversed the order.

Wickham's stern style didn't fit all of Powell's management goals. Powell wanted to be liked as well as respected and to build his men into a team bound together by more than submission. Taking a page from Emerson, he promoted brigade sports and visibly shared the competitive enthusiasms of his troops. He made a point of strolling unaccompanied through the streets of his three battalions each afternoon, "deliberately letting myself be ambushed" by enlisted men, noncoms and junior officers who wanted a private minute with him outside the usual chain of command.

Nineteen seventy-six was a presidential election year, and Powell was pleased when the Georgia governor who had impressed him during his White House Fellows' visit to Atlanta won the Democratic nomination. It seemed prescient on his part, since he and Alma, who had been with him on the trip, had remarked to each other at the time that Carter would make a good president. But Powell had no way of knowing when he voted a third time for a Democratic president that the Carter administration would lay the groundwork for a new career direction.

Carter had welcomed the civil rights movement and consolidated its gains in Georgia; he arrived at the presidency determined that his administration would include a representative number of minorities. When his new national security adviser, a prickly Polish immigrant and foreign policy intellectual named Zbigniew Brzezinski, began hiring for the White House National Security Council, Carter told him, "You've got to have blacks on your NSC staff." Brzezinski later recalled that he had "looked around and it wasn't all that easy to find very many in the foreign affairs field." Thinking the military would be a good place to start, he called Carter's new defense secretary, Harold Brown, and asked for a list of qualified black officers.

When the call came from Washington, Powell was less than a year into what he hoped would be a two-year tour at Fort Campbell and more than a little reluctant to give up his command and uproot his newly settled family. But Wickham advised him that it would be unwise to rebuff Brzezinski's summons for an interview. On a frigid February morning a month after Carter's inauguration, Powell found himself on the corner of Seventeenth Street and Pennsylvania Avenue in the nation's capital, staring unhappily at the gray walls and mansard roof of the mammoth Old Executive Office Building. Once home to the Departments of State, War and the Navy, the OEOB now provided executive staff offices for the White House next door. Inside, it was designed to awe, with wide, dimly lit hallways whose floors were polished to a dull gleam, and massive stone staircases climbing into the gloom of its upper levels. As he followed an escort to Brzezinski's third-floor office, the clomp of Powell's Air Assault jump boots echoed through the halls like gunshots. He had deliberately worn them to the meeting, hoping to communicate his reluctance to be there.

Brzezinski was all sharp edges, with narrow eyes and an angular, Slavic face split by a thin, longish nose. His Polish-accented voice cut like a knife and he talked fast, using minimal gestures. He had already studied Powell's résumé and discussed him with the Army and he got quickly to the point. "Colonel, you're going to be detailed to the NSC staff. You'll be working for the President."

"Yes, sir," Powell replied.

"Now, I want you to know this is really a position of serious responsibility and you'll have to work six days a week, sixteen hours a day."

"Yes, sir."

"Terrific.... It's a full-time commitment, so I'm glad you want to be with us. Isn't that right, Colonel?"

"No, sir."

Powell explained that brigade command was important to his career and he wanted to stay with his men. Besides, he knew nothing about the job of senior staffer in the NSC's defense cluster. Brzezinski reminded him that he could have him assigned to the NSC whether Powell liked it or not. Then he paused and smiled thinly. He was looking for people who wanted to be there and to work for Carter, he said, and he would look elsewhere for now.

But Brzezinski wouldn't forget Powell. Of all the NSC interviews he had conducted, the Army colonel was the only person he had offered a job who had turned it down.

The next call came in May, a repeat summons to the NSC for another interview and a new job offer. While in Washington, Powell was also ordered to the Pentagon to discuss a separate position needing to be filled. John Kester, Defense Secretary Brown's White House liaison and political point man, had pulled Powell's name off a list the services had compiled of potential military aides to top Defense Department civilians. A thirty-eight-year-old lawyer with a reputation for playing bureaucratic hard-ball, Kester was looking for an assistant, and the self-assured colonel seemed like just what he needed: an officer with connections and credibility who could circulate at all levels of the Pentagon, keep his ears open and report back to the secretary's third-floor suite. Powell also seemed tough enough to carry messages in the other direction, making sure that staff aides to the military chiefs were fully on board with civilian policy.

Wickham advised Powell that the Army brass wanted him to take the Pentagon job; just as Kester wanted his own eyes and ears inside the military, the Army wanted its own people close to the secretary's inner sanctum. Powell had also been advised that he would not be getting the job he coveted as Wickham's chief of staff at the 101st. He called Kester to say he would accept on one condition: that his desk be located just outside his boss's door. His experience working for Fred Malek in the Nixon administration had taught him the importance of access. Kester's power derived from his position as Brown's gatekeeper, with control over every person and piece of paper that entered and left the secretary's office. Powell would serve Kester in the same capacity.

Kester was impressed that Powell already had an idea of how Washington operated. "I got a sense he was very acute politically," he later recalled. "I was in an intensely political job, and I wanted someone who could understand the role of politics and yet would not get dirty himself.... A lot of my job was fending off the White House, the crazy ideas that would come in from the politicians there. After I became comfortable with [Powell's] judgment, I'd sometimes let him talk to the people in the White House."

There was nothing wrong with political power, Kester felt, but he found in Powell a kindred spirit who agreed that intramural power struggles were like sex: best kept out of view, especially when the children were watching.

The White House fellowship and his seat outside Malek's office at OMB had been Powell's elementary education in high-stakes Washington, but his move to the secretary's suite at the Department of Defense was a leap into postgraduate studies. During his seventeen months with Kester, he alternately admired and was appalled by the way the game was played. On the positive side, Kester was meticulous about recognizing achievement and skilled at calming Secretary Brown's sometimes explosive dislike of political wheeling and dealing. A physicist more comfortable with paper than people, Brown preferred reading heavy defense tomes and scribbling notes at his desk to face-to-face confrontation with the members of Congress who controlled his budget.

But Kester could also be mean and petty in his usually successful efforts to extend his grasp, ostensibly on Brown's behalf, beyond the outer edges of his reach. His goal could be as large as wresting control over senior military promotions from the service chiefs or as small as delaying the return of a telephone call or sitting on routine paperwork as a means of asserting psychological dominance. Powell often applauded Kester's ends but was put off by his means. He made a mental addition to his list of good management habits: don't play games with calls, letters and other paperwork; respond as quickly as possible, since the next time you might be on the other end of the telephone line waiting for an answer.

Sitting in a back seat at Harold Brown's morning senior staff meetings was far more educational than any class at the National War College for learning the interplay between the military and civilian politics. Kester and other senior aides tried to convince Brown of the need to massage congressional egos, at one point suggesting that the secretary host a series of informal dinner-and-a-movie evenings for selected lawmakers and their spouses. As the junior member of the team, Powell was charged with arranging the sessions: choosing a venue, hiring the caterer and selecting a movie.

As the first dinner approached, Brown's wife strongly suggested they impress their guests with that season's popular new disaster movie, *The Swarm*, in which killer bees invaded Texas and wiped out much of the state before being decimated by an all-out military offensive. Powell was accustomed to leaving nothing to chance, particularly where the boss was concerned, and he went to a local theater to preview the film. An early scene of a picnicking couple and their children being stung to a painful death was enough to convince him to make a different choice. Powell selected *House Calls*, a romantic comedy starring Glenda Jackson and Walter Matthau, and though Mrs. Brown turned to glare at him several times during the evening, her husband and his guests were well pleased.

Clifford Alexander, Carter's secretary of the Army and the first black to hold the job, was four years older than Powell and a fellow New Yorker who had pushed against racial barriers from a different direction. A graduate of Harvard University and Yale Law School, Alexander had held senior positions in the Kennedy and Johnson administrations, and in 1967, Johnson had named him chairman of the Equal Employment Opportunity Commission established by the 1964 Civil Rights Act. It was there that he had honed his understanding of the more subtle forms of racial discrimination that followed federally mandated desegregation.

When Alexander arrived at the Pentagon, blacks made up a quarter of the Army's total enlisted personnel and had substantially higher reenlistment rates, yet they remained heavily concentrated in the lower ranks and the military's own data indicated that they were promoted more slowly than whites. Early in his tenure, Alexander rejected a list of proposed general officers on which no black colonels had been deemed worthy of promotion. He sent the selection board back to try again. "My method was simple," he later recalled. "I just told everyone that I would not sign the goddamn list unless it was fair."

Years later, it would become conventional wisdom that Alexander's affirmative action had greased the wheels of Powell's promotion to brigadier general. Powell found the assumption irritating, just as he always disliked being labeled the best black officer or the first black anything. It was true that what had arguably been a disadvantage when he had entered the Army in the 1950s had become a professional asset, and he knew that whether he liked it or not, he was a poster boy—a nonthreatening, nonmilitant black whose presence in the front office allowed whites to hide their own prejudices. But the Army had not cut him any slack. It had given him opportunities to show that he was just as good as anyone else of any color and better than most. Being black might have been the reason his file ended up on Brzezinski's desk on a particular day in early 1977, but it was the contents of the file that had earned him the job offer.

Despite the later assumptions, there was no indication that Alexander's instructions to the promotion board had influenced Powell's career. His name was not on the new list Alexander had ordered up—he already knew that the Army had refused to consider him for promotion to brigadier general in 1977 because it had been barely a year since he had made colonel. He was already far ahead of the others in his "year group" of 1958 and had no need to be singled out for affirmative action. His record was spotless. He had consistently been promoted ahead of schedule, and every one of his military and civilian bosses since he made lieutenant colonel—including Secretary Brown—had urged in writing and in the strongest terms that he be made a general as soon as possible.

Powell's name appeared on the Army's promotion list at the end of 1978, and a general's star was pinned on his shoulder at a ceremony held in the defense secretary's formal dining room the following summer. Arie stood at his side, along with his sister, Marilyn, Alma and the children, a crowd of Jamaican relatives, and friends from his previous postings. The only sad note was that Luther Powell, who had died early that year after a long struggle with cancer, was not there to see his son become the youngest brigadier general in the Army.

When they returned to Washington after sixteen months at Fort Campbell, Colin and Alma could finally afford property closer to the capital. They settled in the Virginia suburb of Burke, a planned community of handsome new homes with neighborhood swimming pools and old-growth trees. Colin immediately went to work while Alma got the three children into school and once again began laying down the roots she knew were important to their sense of stability. "Alma Powell can settle a house faster than anybody I know," Marilyn once marveled. "She can be there for forty-eight hours and have every picture up on the wall."

Colin's career defined his family's universe, but Alma was the center of the children's world. She was the one who created "the feeling that we had a safe and fun and loving place no matter where we moved," Linda later recalled. "She was the one who was there when we came home, she was the one who was fixing up the rooms and making sure we got the right school. She was the one who belonged to us." As he moved up in the military-political world, their father belonged to them less and less. His job in the Carter Defense Department marked the beginning of the second half of a career that would ultimately take Powell to the very top of the military while moving him ever farther away from soldiering. He would spend all but three of the next sixteen years until he retired from the Army in Washington.

For Alma and the children, the Washington years would impose a tension and emotional separation that were in some ways even worse than the physical distance they had endured during his Vietnam and Korea tours. He left the house early each day and returned late, usually bringing work home with him. His children saw him as larger than life, and he was regularly invoked as the keeper of the family's values. But while his paternal aura and high expectations permeated the household, his children's interactions with him became less the familiar flow of daily life and more like rare, treasured snapshots. Michael and Linda never tired of rewatching the family movie where they ran into their father's arms when he came home from his second tour in Vietnam.

The Powell family was not given to small talk; there were few "How was your day?" conversations around the dinner table. Colin did not offer confidences and didn't seek them from Alma or the children. He took his paternal obligations seriously and gave the children regular hugs and kisses, but he retreated into shy formality when it came to more challenging intimacies. As the children reached their sixteenth birthdays, he gave each a long, handwritten letter.

"It was sort of Rudyard Kipling–like," Michael recalled. "The tone was that over the coming years you are going to be exposed to evils from drinking to drugs, from sexual relations to this and that and in the end you're going to be an adult.... Just remember that our philosophy is that we show you right from wrong and the rest is up to you. You don't do things according to our wishes. *You* make the decision of whether it's right or wrong in accord with the ways that we taught you. And he concluded by saying, 'Never forget, there is nothing too bad that you can't come and get our help.'

"The funny thing is that he would follow the letter up in action, but he would never ask you about [it]. You would get the letter sort of anonymously, and he would rarely even ask whether you read it. I always sensed that there was an uncomfortableness on his part to even talk about it."

About a year after his birthday letter, Michael got a second helping of fatherly advice, this time by way of a book, called *Boys and Sex,* wrapped inside a brown paper bag and tossed casually onto the sofa as Colin made his way through the den one Saturday. "If you have any questions, just ask me," he said over his shoulder as he exited hastily to the garage, got into his car and drove away. Despite their oblique delivery, these epistles seemed to have the intended effect, and the Powell children rarely caused their parents any heartache. "Just watching him struggle to get the message across made you admire him so much and made you care about him so much and not want to hurt him so much that you just wouldn't," Michael reflected.

At work, Powell was intuitive and a clear and concise communicator. In his public life he was loquacious, charming and funny, known for an exquisite sense of what was appropriate and a talent for putting others at ease. At home, however, he was subdued and often distracted, especially as his career became more demanding. When the children's friends or dates came to call, he would offer a brief "Hi" if they crossed his path and then ignore them. Before Michael married his college sweetheart, Colin had barely had a conversation with her. Other than an occasional dinner with old friends, he and Alma rarely went out unless it was work-related. On weekends, if he wasn't on the telephone or in his den with work brought home, he liked to putter around in the garage. When he had time for relaxation in the evening, he would park himself in front of the television with a bowl of ice cream, limiting his conversation to "What do you want to watch?" He was a television addict—British comedies, concerts and most of all old movies, preferably musicals. After he had become an international celebrity, profiled everywhere from *The New York Times* to *People* magazine, Linda concluded that her father had "a work personality and a home personality."

In July 1979, Carter reshuffled his Cabinet following the eruption of a long-feared energy crisis that brought severe gas shortages and skyrocketing prices and sent his job approval rating plummeting. Powell's boss, Deputy Defense Secretary Charles Duncan, was named Secretary of Energy, and Powell reluctantly agreed to go along as his assistant to a department that was in crisis mode, with workdays stretching to sixteen hours and beyond. Powell hated the job, although he was delighted when the move brought his first mention in the national media, a blurb in *Newsweek* magazine's "Periscope" column that identified him as the "black brigadier general who was Duncan's top assistant at the Department of Defense" and one of "Harold Brown's whiz kids."

But the additional hours away from home brought Alma to the breaking point. They had never had serious arguments; both tended to respond to marital storms by retreating into their separate corners and waiting for the skies to clear. But now she began to fall into frequent blue moods and even to lash out, accusing her husband of neglecting her and their children. There was a history of depression in Alma's family, and she had sought help in the past for up-and-down periods she believed were exacerbated by the stresses of a growing family and the disruptions of military life. But this was different. Colin came home one night to find her collapsed in inconsolable tears.

They went together the next day to Walter Reed Army Medical Center in Washington. Prescribed medication, Alma saw little improvement for the first few weeks until the treatment kicked in and, as Linda put it, "she came back to being Mom." But Colin remained concerned and went to Duncan after two months on the job to say he wanted out. He returned to his old position at the Pentagon, becoming military assistant to the new deputy defense secretary, Graham Claytor.

The Carter administration hit a new low point in November 1979, when Iranian militants stormed the U.S. Embassy in Tehran, seizing control of the building and taking sixty-six Americans hostage. By the spring of 1980, with fifty-two hostages remaining in the embassy, the administration had developed a top secret rescue plan. The mission was launched during the early evening of April 24, a date chosen in expectation of full moonlight. By the next morning in Washington, however, it was clear that the operation had been an unmitigated disaster. Not only had it failed to achieve its goal; it had resulted in the deaths of eight American servicemen and the loss of seven of the eight helicopters deployed and a C-130 transport aircraft.

Planning for the mission had been so tightly held that even Powell, sitting outside the deputy secretary's office and attending Brown's morning meetings, knew nothing about it until Carter appeared on television the morning after the debacle. A later investigation determined that the operation, which included disparate Marine, Navy and Army components, had been undercut by the decision to develop an ad hoc plan rather than use existing special operations formulas that the military had worked on for years. The overweening secrecy meant that there had been no prior review of the operation other than by those who had drawn it up, the report found. "Rigid compartmentalization" had hampered training and readiness and left no clear chain of command.

When the helicopters ran into heavy dust storms on the way to a secret refueling base inside Iran, dubbed "Desert One," the crews had no contingency plan for breakdowns and time delays. The mission required at least six helicopters for success, and three of the eight deployed were quickly out of commission. Carter, monitoring events from Washington, ordered the operation aborted, and in the confusion of multiple takeoffs from the secret base, a helicopter and a C-130 collided and burst into flames. The other helicopters were left behind as crews scrambled to climb into the remaining C-130 and get out of Iran.

As Powell found out more about the incident, it underscored the lessons he had already learned about the use of force and taught him new

ones that he would remember when it was his turn to plan combat operations at the highest levels. If the mission required six helicopters, far more
than eight should have been dispatched to ensure success. The combination of pilots and support staff from different service branches who had
never trained together, using equipment that was not their own, was just
as fatal an error in the Iranian desert as it had been in Vietnam, where
cobbled-together companies and battalions had lacked the ability to
operate as cohesive units.

Reflecting on the failure, Powell concluded that "You have to plan
thoroughly, train as a team, match the military punch to the political
objective, go in with everything you need—and then some—and not
count on wishful thinking." The roots of the disastrous plan and its poor
execution, he believed, were also found in the failure to rigorously apply
a decision-making formula of the kind that was drilled into every military officer from the first day he put on his uniform: Mission, Enemy,
Terrain, Troops, Time. Following these clear steps would generate a
well-conceived plan for any situation—military or civilian, professional
or personal—but trying to bypass them or take shortcuts courted catastrophe. Each component had to be broken down and analyzed exhaus-
tively. What is the objective, and how will you achieve it? Who is the
adversary, and what do you know about him? What is the nature of the
battlefield? What resources are necessary and available? Who is in charge?
How long do you expect/want the operation to continue? The "decision
loop," as the military called it, mitigated the distorting effects of personality and politics.

The mounting crises on Carter's watch—double-digit inflation and the
energy crisis, the hostages and the failure of the Desert One mission, the
1979 invasion and occupation of Afghanistan by the Soviet Union—
ultimately led to his defeat in the 1980 presidential election. Powell later
assessed some aspects of Carter's record on national security as "not half
bad." Work had begun during the administration on many of the sophisticated weapons systems that the United States would use effectively during the 1991 war against Iraq. But on the whole, Carter's performance had
discomfited the military profession, and Powell and others worried about
a "hollow Army" left decimated by excessive cuts in the wake of Vietnam.
Powell was among the voting majority who handed the presidency to
Ronald Reagan, the actor and former California governor who promised
Americans that their country's best years were just around the corner.

Caspar Weinberger, a lawyer and former chairman of the California
Republican Party, had served as then-Governor Reagan's director of

finance, where he righted a disastrous budget, earned the nickname "Cap the Knife," and propelled himself into the Nixon administration as OMB director. One of a lengthy list of aspirants to be Reagan's secretary of state, he lost out to Nixon protégé Alexander Haig and ended up at the Pentagon, his second choice.

As a White House Fellow at OMB, Powell had had little contact with Weinberger. But when the newly nominated defense secretary scheduled a private evening visit to the Pentagon shortly before Reagan's inauguration, Defense bureaucrats—anxious to please their new boss with a presumably familiar face—dispatched Powell to escort him from his temporary quarters at Washington's Hay-Adams Hotel, just across Lafayette Park from the White House. The Pentagon limousine carried them across the Potomac and down into the building's basement, where Powell showed Weinberger the secretary's private elevator and took him to the third-floor suite for a brief tour before returning him to the hotel. Powell doubted Weinberger's courteous insistence that he remembered the young officer who had served as a temporary aide in the budget office more than eight years earlier, but he worried that any association would lessen his chances of getting out of Washington. He was in his fourth year of Pentagon gatekeeping and was desperate to return to the field.

Reagan's supporters in the military were torn between hope that the new president would keep his campaign promises to reverse the Carter-era defense cuts and fear of Weinberger's reputation as a budget hawk. Congressional conservatives suspected that the new defense secretary was a closet Rockefeller moderate, a worry that intensified when Weinberger tapped Frank Carlucci as his deputy.

A short, wiry man with a bouncy step, Carlucci had been Donald Rumsfeld's wrestling teammate at Princeton University. Several years after Carlucci started his government career as a Foreign Service officer, Rumsfeld had recruited him, along with a young Republican up-and-comer named Dick Cheney, to Nixon's Office of Economic Opportunity. From there, Carlucci had moved to OMB and then to the Department of Health, Education, and Welfare with Weinberger. When Nixon resigned, Carlucci returned to the State Department as the U.S. ambassador to Portugal. He had stayed in government under Carter as deputy director of the Central Intelligence Agency—a betrayal in the eyes of Republican conservatives. But Weinberger had his way, and just after the inauguration Powell found himself with a new Pentagon boss.

Carlucci was pleasantly surprised. He did remember Powell from OMB, although he hadn't followed his career since then. Like Weinberger, Carlucci knew little about defense issues, but he found that Powell "seemed to know everything. He was well liked, and he circulated widely around the building. He talked to people. He had good judgment, common sense and a wonderful personality. You could turn to him and say, 'What the hell's going on in that part of the Pentagon, what's happening in such and such a place?' and he could tell you right off the top of his head." Powell steered Carlucci toward units to visit in the field and helped him decide which demands from the service chiefs he could safely ignore.

Powell's position in the senior Pentagon suite also provided a degree of racial balance to an administration that sorely needed it. He was in high demand—despite Clifford Alexander's efforts, the military was still suffering from a paucity of black faces at the top. Just weeks after the inauguration, Powell was approached to become undersecretary of the Army, a job that would have required him to retire from the service. He turned down the offer and began a steady campaign to persuade Carlucci to send him back into the field. He had found a brigadier general's slot about to open up at Fort Carson, outside Colorado Springs at the eastern foot of the Rocky Mountains.

"He wanted to go," Carlucci later recalled. "He didn't give me a reason, all he said was 'There's an opportunity for me out in Colorado and I'd like to take it.' " As soon as Carlucci could find a replacement, Powell was out the door.

8

He was directly involved in every issue I faced as Secretary of Defense. . . . In every way, Major General Powell's performance was unfailingly superlative. . . . Soldier, scholar, statesman—he does it all.

—Caspar W. Weinberger

Alma thought Fort Carson was the ugliest place on earth. They had seen the Rockies rise above the plains as they drove west across Kansas, but the majestic, snow-covered peaks disappeared behind scraggly Cheyenne Mountain as they approached the city of Colorado Springs. Now that one mountain was all she could see from the window of their flat ranch house atop a treeless hill where no flowers grew. The wind blew constantly, and she could plot the time of day from the thunderstorm that rolled down the mountain's rocky side at three o'clock every afternoon.

There were three houses on the hill: one for the commander of the 4th Infantry Division and one for each of his two assistants. The 4th Infantry was a mechanized division, and most of the post's 140,000 acres were empty, rutted grassland that served as practice ranges for tanks and armored personnel carriers.

Powell's assignment as assistant division commander to Major General John W. Hudachek was supposed to be his last stop before commanding a division of his own. But as he approached the end of his first year there in May 1982, it looked as though Fort Carson might be the last stop of his career. For the first time in more than two decades in the Army, he had ended up on the wrong side of a superior officer, and all his finely honed techniques for "pay[ing] the king his shilling" seemed unable to stop a steady slide in their relationship.

He had been warned to be careful with Hudachek, a cavalry officer and 1954 West Point graduate with a reputation as a hard man to please. Julius Becton had once served with the general and considered him "impossible." Becton, now a lieutenant general and commander of the Army's Training and Doctrine Command (TRADOC) at Fort Monroe, Virginia, had already told the Army chief of staff that Hudachek had "zero people skills" and should never have been given a division command. Richard Lawrence, whom Powell had served under in the Americal in Vietnam and who was now a division commander at Fort Hood in Texas, had told him the same thing.

Chain-smoking and humorless, Hudachek was a notorious screamer. His office assistant, a young captain named Philip Coker who was regularly on the receiving end of his high-decibel blowups, thought the commander disapproved of the more humane post-Vietnam volunteer Army. Far from going out of his way to provide personal support for his subordinates, Hudachek seemed to have problems in any one-on-one relationship. The sole exception was with his wife, the daughter of a highly decorated general, who had the same arm's-length relationship with the Fort Carson spouses that her husband had with the officers.

Powell had started out confident, even cocky, that he could charm this reputed raging bull and excel at the training job he had been assigned, although his initial meeting with Hudachek had been disconcerting. The unsmiling general had shaken his hand, briskly explained the training programs in place and dismissed him. Powell went about his business, learning how to fire a tank gun and dealing with personnel problems, and started jogging every morning to keep in shape. He spent the summer of 1981 at Fort Carson training National Guard troops and even took full command of the post when Hudachek was away at the Army's annual Reforger exercise in West Germany. He relieved the underlying tension the same way he always had, by working in his garage. He had brought home dozens of old-fashioned adding machines from a rummage sale and spent hours dismantling them, salvaging parts from one for another and putting them back together.

Whatever sourness came from above, those beneath Powell were happy to have him there. Lieutenant Colonel Wesley K. Clark, then a high-flying battalion commander, was a Rhodes Scholar who had followed Powell as a White House Fellow. Clark had heard of the new assistant division commander long before he arrived at Fort Carson. "He was eight years ahead of me in the military, a real senior guy. He had a good reputation, and I was really excited." But it was soon clear to Clark and the others that Powell didn't have the support of the commanding general. In one training advisory, Hudachek went so far as to tell the battalion leaders that "you couldn't take advice from [Powell] because he wasn't an armor officer, and he didn't know anything."

When Powell later assessed his year in Colorado, he concluded that he had made several uncharacteristic mistakes. He had felt an obligation to inform Hudachek that division morale, particularly among the officers and their wives, was bad and to point out ways it could be improved. He had proposed changes in the annual inspection system. At one point, he had gingerly suggested that Mrs. Hudachek loosen her grip on spousal activities and allow the other officers' wives more input into the way the commissary, the post schools and other nonmilitary activities on the base were run. More substantively, he had mishandled a dicey personnel situation involving an officer's affair with a sergeant's wife by trying to resolve it himself instead of following the book and turning it over to Army investigators.

Hudachek's own list of complaints about Powell, recounted in a newspaper interview years later, seemed relatively small bore. Powell had ignored instructions to stay in daily communication with him when he was traveling, Hudachek said. During one trip to Washington, he had learned from his wife—not from Powell—that a high-level foreign military officer was visiting Fort Carson. He implied that Powell was borderline insubordinate and said that if the division had ever been summoned to war, he would have recommended that Powell be replaced.

In his first written evaluation of Powell's performance, in May 1982, Hudachek described him as "an aggressive and technically competent BG" who carried out unit training programs effectively. But while he was a reasonable staff officer, Hudachek suggested, Powell was unfit for a more senior command assignment.

Powell read the review as Hudachek sat silently smoking. It was by far the worst report he had ever received, and when he finished reading he looked up at his commander. "You realize the effect this will have?" he asked. Hudachek shrugged, suggesting that it wasn't the end of the world and noting that there would be a second evaluation the following year. Powell left the room, walked down the hall to his own office and sat down, only to get up again and return to stand at Hudachek's desk. Did the general understand that this would probably mean he would never get a division and that it would likely mean the end of his career? Hudachek said he didn't think that would be the case and made clear that the meeting was over.

Powell tried to convince himself that all was not lost, but things only got worse with the arrival of his "senior rater" report in the mail two weeks later. Every officer got at least two annual chances at evaluation, one by his immediate superior and another by the next level of command. Lieutenant General M. C. Ross, deputy commander of the Atlanta-based

Forces Command (FORSCOM), the umbrella organization for U.S.-based active-duty, Reserve and National Guard forces, barely knew Powell and saw no reason to disagree with Hudachek's assessment. Powell was an "excellent" assistant division commander, he wrote, who was "thorough, meticulous and detailed in planning and in supervising training. He deserves fully [*sic*] consideration to be a principal staff officer in a major command headquarters. The rater considers this more Colin's forte than command at this time." Evaluating Powell's potential in the check boxes provided, Ross found him below average.

The Army was under pressure to be more discerning about its promotions, and the officer pyramid narrowed sharply near the top. There was room for only half of the brigadier generals to make it to two stars, and Powell was now officially in the bottom half. He could already hear the gossip at Army staff headquarters in Washington: Powell had been away from the troops for too long and couldn't hack it in the field. After a long afternoon staring at the wall in his office, he went home to spend a sleepless night. He didn't mention anything about the review to Alma. It was not the sort of thing they talked about; she had never even seen one of his efficiency reports. By morning he had decided to start readying his résumé for the civilian job market.

Several weeks after Powell began to mull over the end of his military career, Julius Becton landed at Fort Carson. Becton was in the company of General Richard E. Cavazos, the FORSCOM commander and the Army's highest-ranking Hispanic. The two were old friends; they had been captains together, and in their current jobs they frequently traveled together to posts around the country. Although unaware of Becton's role in steering him to the National War College, Powell had run into him at the Pentagon and elsewhere; both belonged to "The Rocks." After a day of briefings at division headquarters Powell invited the two visiting generals to the house on the hill for some of Alma's home cooking.

Becton and Cavazos had sensed friction between Hudachek and Powell throughout the day and asked about it over dinner. One thing led to another, and finally the whole story came out, ending with Powell averring that he was about to "test the waters" outside the Army. "It blew our minds," Becton recalled. Without even reading the evaluation, he knew that a word such as "excellent"—rather than "superior" or "outstanding"—not only wouldn't push an officer ahead, "they could get you fired." Do us a favor, they advised Powell. "Just sit on it for now and don't do anything."

On their return flight, the two generals agreed they needed to take action. Powell had built a brilliant career thus far, and Becton felt the Army needed men like him, particularly minorities. Without high-level intervention to counter Hudachek's report, Powell would likely go no further. When he got back to his office, Becton put through a call to the Army chief of staff, General Edward C. "Shy" Meyer. It was what those in the rarefied group of three- and four-star generals did for one another— and for the service.

Less than two months after Powell's evaluation meeting with Hudachek, Captain Coker answered the telephone in the general's outer office and patched through a call from the deputy chief of the Army for personnel. After Hudachek hung up a few minutes later, Coker braced himself for the usual explosive shout to "Get in here!" When it didn't come, he walked to the closed door and looked through a peephole to see the general standing silently, his arms crossed, staring out the window. Coker cautiously stepped inside and asked if the general needed anything. "Yeah," Hudachek replied without turning around. "Move me to Korea in a week."

The news, which reached Powell the same day, was astounding. Hudachek was going to South Korea as chief of staff of the Eighth Army. His replacement was Major General Ted Jenes, deputy commander of the Combined Arms Combat Developments Activity (CACDA) at Fort Leavenworth. Powell was to take Jenes's job.

Hudachek was not happy with his new orders, and his wife was even less so. As Coker organized their packing, Powell stopped by the office to ask if the captain would like to come along to Fort Leavenworth as his aide, further infuriating Hudachek. When the division officers and their wives held a party for the Powells in the headquarters building, the commander sat in his office down the hall, refusing to attend.

When the list of new major generals was released in November 1982, barely three months after he left Fort Carson, Powell's name was among those selected to receive a second star during the coming year. At the bottom of a letter of congratulations, Julius Becton scribbled in longhand, "No odds too great to overcome—even Hudachek notwithstanding." Hudachek himself, who was eventually consoled with a promotion to lieutenant general, apparently had no residual bad feelings he wanted to share with a former subordinate who clearly had friends in high places. "Dear Colin," he wrote. "Heartiest congratulations on a well-deserved selection. The Army couldn't have made a better choice."

Their return to Kansas was a welcome respite for the Powells after the difficult year in Colorado. Michael began his second year at the College of

William and Mary in Virginia, having turned down an appointment to
West Point. After a period of resentment at having to leave her third high
school in three years, Linda settled down nicely, and Annemarie seemed
to fit in wherever they went. For Colin, it was a time to unwind and begin
to enjoy the Army again. He recemented his ties with the substantial
community of black officers at the post and began to learn about those
who had come before him.

Deep within the many chapters of Fort Leavenworth history was the
story of the 10th Cavalry Regiment, established there in 1867 as one of
the first four all-Negro units authorized by Congress. Recognition as a
permanent unit did not mean equality, however. Assigned to separate huts
in a marshy lowland, the black troops were ordered not to come within
fifteen feet of whites, and it was not until 1878 that the unit got its first
black officer. But Lieutenant Henry O. Flipper's career as the Army's first
Negro officer came to an abrupt end after only three years, when he
was charged with extortion and, despite his acquittal, dishonorably discharged for conduct unbecoming an officer. In 1976, as West Point prepared to celebrate the one hundredth anniversary of its first black
graduate, the Army finally granted Flipper an honorable discharge and a
review board ruled that he had been negatively singled out because of
his race.

The 10th Cavalry, called "Buffalo Soldiers" by the Plains Indians, who
reportedly compared their hair to the curly pelt of the buffalo, were
eventually joined by the all-Negro 9th Cavalry, organized under General
William Sheridan in New Orleans. Together, they helped push the outer
edge of the American frontier farther west for white settlers. General
John J. Pershing, the namesake of Powell's Pershing Rifles, commanded a
company of the 10th Cavalry in the Indian territories of Montana and
along the Mexican border. For his efforts, Pershing was called "Nigger
Jack" by West Point cadets at the time, an insult that eventually evolved
into "Black Jack," the nickname by which he was known as General of the
Armies of the United States.

Philip Coker was a white member of the modern-day 10th Cavalry; he
had met some of the old, retired black soldiers in Colorado and continued
to research the unit at Fort Leavenworth. Powell learned more about
them from another aging Buffalo Soldiers veteran, the chief barber at a
black-run shop in the town of Leavenworth where he had his hair cut.

Aside from his impromptu lectures on property rights to white classmates during the turbulent 1960s, Powell had rarely felt comfortable talking about race. He had joined "The Rocks" and knew that Julius Becton

and other black officers were among the mentors who had helped shape his career. But he saw no personal profit in racial activism and considered himself largely above, or at least apart from, issues of color.

Yet with the Buffalo Soldiers, Powell began to see himself as part of a continuum, a black soldier who had risen on the backs and shoulders of tens of thousands before him. These were not the discomfiting rabble-rousers who wanted to burn down the country or the criminal trouble-makers at Camp Casey in South Korea but men like Powell himself who had chosen to play by the rules against far greater odds, for far less reward.

He was proud that the Army had come farther and faster toward equal opportunity than most American institutions. In later years, he would become more comfortable using his rank and prestige to speak out in support of affirmative action, always making sure to couple his message to whites with exhortations to blacks on personal responsibility and hard work. For now, it seemed important to recognize the sacrifice and service of men such as Henry Flipper and the Buffalo Soldiers who had started it all at Fort Leavenworth.

Though the post was full of equestrian statues of famous white generals and virtually every building and road was named for someone, the only memorial to the first black units were 9th and 10th Cavalry Avenues, gravel tracks that ran through a field beside the old Buffalo Soldiers cemetery.

With the help of the post's historian, Powell began raising money from around the country for a more fitting memorial, and by the time he left Fort Leavenworth the project was well under way. Ten years later, he would return to Kansas to dedicate the new Buffalo Soldiers Monument. The bronze statue, surrounded by its own park and set atop a waterfall, would depict a black cavalry officer of the nineteenth century mounted on a rearing horse, a rifle in his hand.

The spring of 1983 brought the penultimate act of Powell's rehabilitation in the wake of the Hudachek evaluation. His old commander at Fort Campbell, now-General John Wickham, had been designated by President Reagan and Defense Secretary Weinberger to replace General Meyer as Army chief of staff. As he began his transition, Wickham pulled together a group of colonels and lieutenant colonels for a crash project to recommend priorities and new initiatives for his tenure. He selected Powell to run the team.

After a month of interviews and briefings with officers, soldiers and civilian officials, they concluded that although the Army had recovered from Vietnam, it had yet to develop a marketable peacetime image and was losing out to the Air Force and Navy in procurement. In notes he made to himself during the project, Powell recorded that the predominant view in Congress, which controlled the military budget, was that the 780,000, sixteen-division Army was bulky, plodding and "honest but dumb." And though it had admirably addressed its problems with race, it hadn't developed a strategy to deal with the challenges of a new minority in its ranks: women.

The defense priorities outlined by the group, which called itself "Project 14" after its fourteen members, reflected past lessons of which Powell had personal knowledge—Vietnam and the debacle at Desert One—and was eerily prescient of future threats. In an introduction written by Wesley Clark, who had also been recruited to the team, it warned Wickham of "three particularly adverse outcomes which ought to be guarded against as your highest priorities." The first two were "failure of an Army force to accomplish its mission in a counter-terrorist operation [and] theft or accident involving nuclear or chemical weapons." The final warning was drawn directly from Vietnam. The Army, it said, must avoid the "commitment of significant forces into a combat situation without sufficient capability to dominate our adversaries [or] without the requisite national commitment to finish the operation quickly and successfully."

Belaboring the obvious, the report noted that if the Army could not win wars and accomplish the military missions it was assigned, nothing else would matter. The team reaffirmed the rightness of the new "AirLand Battle" concept, the battlefield integration of forces that had begun to replace the old war-fighting separation of the service branches, which would be perfected during the 1991 Persian Gulf War. It called for expanded Army capabilities in low-intensity conflict and recommended shortening command tours, stretched to thirty months after the debacle of six-month field commands during Vietnam, to two years.

Much of the Project 14 report focused on the Army's image problem and its poor relations with Congress and the media, subjects Powell had studied at the feet of Fred Malek, John Kester and other masters within and outside the Army. It recommended that Wickham approach Capitol Hill and the media with a combination of pragmatism and charm, selective openness and calculated stroking—advice that became the prototype for Powell's own style when his moment at the top arrived.

No Army chief of staff since General George C. Marshall, who later became secretary of both the State and Defense departments, had managed to maintain consistently good relations with Congress, the report noted. "Many started out with good intentions the first year" but became "downright hostile" to lawmakers by the end of their terms. "There are probably good reasons for this fairly uniform change in attitude. Members of Congress are not accustomed to playing by our rules of duty, honor, country. They are sometimes selfish, self-centered, ill-informed and irreverent.... We strongly recommend you mentally prepare yourself to aggressively work with the Congress throughout your tenure.... It won't always be pleasant—but the payoff will be astounding."

The report recommended asking senators and representatives for their advice and praising them for anything they did for the Army. "Promise to stay in touch and do it. (Breakfasts and lunches in your office are a good technique)...they love to be consulted." Wickham should remember their birthdays and anniversaries and "insist that the Congressional oversight committees be fully informed—especially on bad news (it doesn't improve with age).

"Always arrive 20–30 minutes early for Congressional hearings," the report advised. "Use this time to shake hands and chat briefly with every member and staffer. Do some homework on the people involved so you can say something personal and/or positive to each person.... Be willing to occasionally go to the mat with the Congress over a crucial issue...but show flexibility on less important matters.... When disappointments occur in your relations with the Hill (and they will), take the positive approach of 'next time' we will do better. You should be forewarned not to take it personally when a member criticizes the Army."

A similarly proactive strategy was recommended toward the media, including taking reporters along on official trips, meeting regularly with editorial boards and encouraging subordinate commanders to speak to the press.

Wickham had assigned the transition report to Powell as an investment in his future, he later said, to "make sure he got the kind of jobs that would allow his talent to survive.... The value to Colin was the visibility it gave him, as he went around to talk to senior people who knew I had sent him. That gave him credentials and stature with the 'uniforms' of the Army, with those who thought he was a flagpole type"—an officer who spends his time at headquarters rather than paying his dues out with the troops.

The next opportunity Wickham found for Powell, and the final stage in overcoming Hudachek, came fast on the heels of Project 14. Defense Secretary Weinberger's military assistant, an Air Force officer held over from the Carter administration, was leaving, and Wickham recommended Powell for the job. The Army, as always, was eager to have its own man in the key position, and Wickham made it clear that turning down the assignment was not an option.

"Though you might prefer condolences," Wickham telexed him, "congratulations really are warranted for your selection to the key OSD [Office of the Secretary of Defense] billet. You and Alma know what you're getting into, and I admire your sense of service. DOD will be the better for your role there."

The Powells had spent not even a year in Kansas. Wickham arranged for on-post housing at Fort Myers, Virginia, and they pulled up to their new house just as the Fourth of July fireworks were exploding across the river in Washington. Annemarie had been sick on the drive, and Alma spread a pallet on the bare dining room floor for her to lie on until the movers arrived. They all knew that being back at the Pentagon meant that Colin was going to largely disappear from their lives again; even when he was home, he wouldn't really be there with them. The outside of the house was already festooned with wires and special communications gear that had been installed before they even had a chair to sit on. He could never be away from a telephone.

In contrast to Frank Carlucci's laid-back, "Call me Frank" style, Caspar Weinberger was primly formal. Small-statured, perfectly groomed and lawyerly, he was full of quirks that the military men around him found endearing and amusing—his smart salute to the uniformed guards outside the secretary's third-floor suite each time he entered or exited; his ritualistic departure each night, filling his briefcase, closing his drawers, and lining up his chair just so behind his desk; the secret stash of chocolates he munched on throughout the day. On top of his neat desk, he always kept a five-by-seven pad of white, government-issue paper on which he jotted notes to himself throughout the day—everything from reminders to call his wife to the gist of a top secret memorandum or his extemporaneous thoughts about a pending issue. When he got to the end of a pad, he invariably filed it away in the middle right-hand drawer and started a new one.

Weinberger could be stubborn and prickly, but he disliked unpleasantness and face-to-face confrontation. Powell eventually concluded that the secretary's reluctance to be the bearer of bad news and his overwhelming personal loyalty to Ronald Reagan sometimes kept him from giving the president his best advice, especially when it was something he knew Reagan didn't want to hear.

Weinberger idolized Winston Churchill and was an unabashed Anglophile, part of a patina of cultural erudition that Powell found appealing. It wasn't that Powell was embarrassed by his own upbringing and education; his street smarts, common sense and down-to-earth charm had gotten him a long way. But whether it was John Kester's French, Harold Brown's knowledge of the classics or Weinberger's formality, he always felt there was a dimension he lacked.

As he settled in at his desk in the secretary's suite, Powell was pleased to find that one colleague from his brief Pentagon stint at the start of the Reagan administration had prospered in his absence. Richard Armitage had parlayed a job on Weinberger's transition team into a deputy assistantship and had just been promoted to assistant secretary for international security affairs, with responsibility for virtually the entire globe except for the Soviet Union and arms control policy.

Armitage had been warned to "be careful of that Powell," whose reputation as a skillful bureaucratic operator in the Carter Pentagon was a subject of some suspicion within the middle layers of the Reagan team. But the two men had immediately felt a kinship with each other, based most profoundly on their service in Vietnam. Most of the Reaganites either were World War II veterans like Weinberger or had found a way to sit out the country's most recent war. Vietnam veterans tended to feel they knew things other mortals did not, and it had taken only a few conversations to assure Powell and Armitage that they agreed on the basics: the war had been a noble effort in which America's fighting men had been betrayed by the weakness and ambition of the nation's civilian and military leaders.

Although Powell remained determinedly nonpartisan while Armitage was a declared Republican, they shared a disdain for ideology and had a pragmatic, no-nonsense view of the world that put them in the minority among Weinberger's appointees at Defense. After choosing Carlucci as his deputy, the new secretary had placated the far right by filling other key positions with Cold War hard-liners such as Undersecretary for Policy Fred Ikle and Richard Perle, known inside the Pentagon as the "Prince of Darkness," who handled the Soviet and arms control accounts. Powell and Armitage believed in a strong defense but were wary of the use of force and considered themselves foreign policy realists. The more they talked, the more they realized they also shared more liberal views on a range of social issues from affirmative action to abortion that were anathema to the ascendant right-wing orthodoxy. Their only moderately strong disagreement was on the subject of the death penalty; though Armitage was the one with the tough public demeanor, he was completely against it.

Each considered the other a man of high competence and stamina, but they could not have been more physically dissimilar. Still slender as he neared fifty, Powell was physically graceful and radiated calm. Armitage always seemed tightly coiled. Built like a professional weight lifter with a barrel chest, bulging arms and a neck the circumference of a dinner plate, he was almost completely bald. His blue eyes were deep-set and piercing, and his voice was an aggressive growl even when he wasn't swearing like the sailor he once had been.

Raised in Atlanta, Armitage had graduated from the Naval Academy in 1967 and been stationed off the Vietnamese coast on a destroyer when he volunteered as an adviser to the South Vietnamese Navy. After a year of river patrols in the Mekong Delta, he went back for two more tours, and when the Navy wouldn't allow him another he quit the service and returned as a civilian under contract to the Defense Department. He stayed after the bulk of the American troops withdrew in 1973, accompanying Vietnamese Special Forces on ambushes and nighttime raids. Although he always denied it, even many of his friends believed his real job had been undercover work for U.S. intelligence. When North Vietnamese forces entered Saigon in 1975, Armitage helped sail a South Vietnamese naval flotilla full of fleeing sailors and their families to the Philippines, raising American flags on the ships and successfully demanding that Philippine President Ferdinand Marcos let them in.

After a stint as a Pentagon adviser to the shah's government in Iran and a failed business venture in Bangkok, Armitage was steered by Republican friends to Kansas Senator Bob Dole, who took him on as his administrative aide in Washington. In 1979, he left Dole to work on the presidential campaign of George H. W. Bush, and when Bush's bid collapsed, he signed on with the winning Reagan team.

Among the Pentagon's starched uniforms and $300 suits, Armitage appealed to Powell's earthy side, the part that felt most at home in the down-and-dirty brotherhood of field soldiers. "The man cussed like a sailor and spoke sense in simple declarative sentences," Powell explained. "I understood him and he understood me. We had connected immediately." With Armitage on the policy side and Powell in the executive suite, they agreed that close consultation was to both their advantages and established a habit of talking to each other first thing every morning, last thing at night and many times in between.

Once again, Powell found himself in the key position of gatekeeper to power. Weinberger's door was usually closed, with a panel of lights indicating to his staff whether the boss was away (all lights off), in his office alone (white light on), occupied with a meeting (white and red lights on) or in his private bathroom (green light on). Powell's mornings began early, with a perusal of the daily trove of information that ended up on the secretary's desk, including the Early Bird compilation of Pentagon-related print media stories, a folder of cable traffic and intelligence and a digest of television news programs from the night before.

His close relationship with Weinberger and control of access were resented by some; Secretary of the Navy John Lehman, who found Powell opportunistic and overly political, tried to have him fired. More often, senior officers and civilian officials considered Powell a valuable go-between for communication with a secretary whose wishes were sometimes difficult to divine. He was "the guy who could sort of tell you, what did the secretary really say? What does he really mean?" recalled General P. X. Kelley, then commandant of the Marines. "Whether or not Colin had his own interpretation, you don't know. But Colin read Cap Weinberger very, very well."

Powell sat in on nearly all of Weinberger's meetings, whether with the service chiefs, his senior policy staff or members of Congress, and accompanied him on his frequent overseas trips. Powell rarely spoke as he unobtrusively took notes, but his fly-on-the-wall vantage point quickly became a crash course in high-stakes national security policy and high-tension infighting among the administration's most senior officials. As a personal aide, Powell's respectful competence and cool analysis became indispensable to Weinberger. His duties ranged from coat carrier to confidant, and Weinberger would eventually come to consider him "my closest adviser."

Alma was drafted to play a similar role with the secretary's wife. Jane Weinberger accompanied her husband on many of his trips abroad; at the secretary's insistence and despite Powell's concerns about ethics and expense violations, Alma's name began appearing on the Pentagon flight manifests. Jane was in tenuous health, and it quickly became apparent that Alma was to serve as her lady-in-waiting and traveling companion, sitting beside her in the official limousines that carried them to lunches and tourist sites with the wives of whichever officials were on the men's agenda and making their excuses when Jane was tired or unwell. Sometimes it was tedious, but it had its bright moments. "Who else can say they've been where she's been, met who she's met? She used to love to come back and tell us about those trips," Annemarie recalled. When it came time for Powell to move on and Weinberger was interviewing replacement candidates, Jane told Alma that she had only half jokingly insisted that she wanted him to interview their wives, too.

Reagan had campaigned on promises to increase the defense budget, repair the perceived damage done by the Carter administration and restructure America's nuclear weapons arsenal, including development of a space-based missile defense system. His ambitions for foreign policy fell under the broad umbrella of the ongoing Cold War: a pledge to push back Communist inroads in Central America and a renewed effort to find a durable peace in the Middle East that would stem Soviet influence in the region while ensuring Israel's security and a steady flow of oil. But Reagan's diplomatic initiatives often involved the Pentagon in unantici- pated and sometimes unwelcome ways, none more so than the Lebanon crisis that escalated toward a tragic denouement during Powell's forma- tive first year with Weinberger. Lebanon was "a case study of foreign pol- icy calamity," Reagan's biographer Lou Cannon later wrote. More than any other series of decisions, it "demonstrate[d] the naiveté, ignorance and undisciplined internal conflict characteristic of the Reagan presi- dency," teaching Powell military and political lessons that would greatly influence his future decision making.

Like his immediate predecessors, Reagan believed he could help end decades of conflict between Israel and its Arab neighbors. There was some urgency to the task: throughout his first year in office, Israel and Syria—armed, respectively, by Washington and Moscow—had engaged in sporadic shooting matches, both directly and through proxy forces in and around the Lebanese capital of Beirut. In June 1982, Israel invaded Lebanon, sending a massive military force across the border in what it said was retaliation for the attempted assassination of its ambassador in London by the Beirut-based Palestine Liberation Organization. The Israeli Army encircled Beirut, placing the PLO forces, as well as Lebanese civilians, under siege. Amid international calls for peacekeep- ing troops that could bolster the weak Lebanese government and help evacuate the PLO forces, General John W. Vessey, the new chairman of the Joint Chiefs, cautioned Weinberger that it would "be very unwise for the U.S. to find itself in a position where it had to put its forces be- tween the Israelis and the Arabs."

Weinberger agreed, telling Reagan it would be difficult to keep a peace that none of the combatants seemed to want. Weinberger "could not understand why we wanted to get U.S. forces in the middle of that mess," Powell told Lou Cannon in a 1989 interview. "He didn't understand the purpose they were serving." But Reagan's secretary of state, George P. Shultz, and Robert "Bud" McFarlane, the president's deputy national security adviser, maintained that the presence of a small U.S. military force in Beirut could serve the administration's larger foreign policy interests in the region. In July, Reagan ordered a thirty-day deployment of 800 Marines, who were joined by a comparable number of French troops.

Lebanon quickly became a symbolic battleground for an increasingly public war within the Reagan administration. "Shultz and his aides were convinced that Weinberger wanted to be secretary of state," Cannon later wrote, while "Weinberger and his team viewed Shultz as a World War II Marine who spoke out freely on military matters which he knew very little about."

In a speech on the deployment that was largely crafted by Shultz, Reagan declared "a new opportunity for Middle East peace," and the Marines went ashore in Lebanon on August 25. The PLO was evacuated quickly and without incident, and Weinberger persuaded the president to withdraw the U.S. force two weeks early, on September 10.

Four days later, Beirut exploded. In quick succession, the Lebanese president-elect was assassinated, Israeli forces moved into West Beirut and the Christian militiamen they supported entered the Palestinian refugee camps of Sabra and Shatila on the outskirts of the city. Ostensibly looking for terrorists, the militias proceeded to massacre more than eight hundred civilians, including scores of women and children.

"Against this backdrop," Weinberger wrote in his memoirs, "many people urged the President to send in another multinational force." Shultz and McFarlane blamed Weinberger for his eagerness to withdraw the Marines in the first place. In his own memoirs, Shultz accused the defense secretary of setting the bar for a new deployment too high and the military of being "too nervous" to do what was necessary in Lebanon.

Reagan again sided with Shultz, agreeing to send a new Marine contingent more than double the size of the first. As before, the Marines were prohibited from engaging in combat other than in self-defense. Under an agreement signed with the Lebanese government, they were to "provide an interposition force" and a "presence" in the Beirut area. The agreement gave no explanation of which forces the multinational troops would be "interposed" between, the nature of their mission or how they would know when it had been accomplished.

The next year brought a military stalemate and a diplomatic agreement negotiated by Shultz for the withdrawal of Israeli and Syrian-backed forces from Lebanon that quickly fell apart. By the spring of 1983, the situation was becoming increasingly untenable for the Marine "peacekeepers." In April, a car bomb exploded at the U.S. Embassy in Beirut, killing sixty-three people, including the chief CIA analyst of Middle East affairs and seven other agency officials. Israeli troops withdrew to the outskirts of Beirut while Christian and Muslim militias continued battling in and around the city. When Powell took up his duties as Weinberger's assistant that summer, the 1,800 Marines based at Beirut's international airport were coming under regular mortar and small-arms attack and militia fire from the highlands surrounding Beirut. In September, against the wishes of the U.S. commanders on the ground, the White House authorized ships of the U.S. Sixth Fleet standing offshore to shell Muslim positions outside the capital.

Although Shultz, in later testimony before an angry Congress, and Reagan, in his personal diary, described the naval shelling as purely defensive, in effect it turned the United States into a combatant in the Lebanese conflict, implicitly changing U.S. policy from peacekeeping to intervention on the side of the Christians.

Powell had been a light sleeper ever since the Pentagon had installed the bank of special telephones in the Fort Myers house. One extension connected him with the National Military Command Center, and when it rang it usually meant bad news. In the early-morning hours of Sunday, October 23, the Command Center called with an initial report that a huge truck bomb had exploded at the airport barracks in Beirut, killing an unknown number of Marines. Powell's immediate reaction was overwhelming anger at the senseless deaths of the young American boys who had been sitting ducks in the middle of a crazy war they had nothing to do with. As the night wore on and more and more bodies were recovered from the rubble, the telephone rang again and again. By morning the U.S. death toll was 241, more than in any other single day since the World War II battle of Iwo Jima.

The initial domestic reaction to the Beirut attack was overshadowed by the U.S. invasion of the tiny Caribbean nation of Grenada two days later—a bloody coup and perceived danger to American students there had provided an excuse to eliminate Cuban influence on the island. But the distraction quickly dissipated, and Congress began to call for an immediate exit from Lebanon. Although the administration cited America's "vital interests" and insisted that the United States would not "cut and run," it was clear by early February 1984 that Beirut was still a long way from stability, and Reagan ordered the Marines to leave. Weinberger continued to blame Shultz and McFarlane for pushing to send troops into harm's way without a clear objective, while Shultz blamed Weinberger for what he called the Pentagon's reluctance "to contemplate or cooperate with even a limited application of military force to bolster our diplomacy."

When Weinberger channeled his distress into writing a speech outlining a set of rules to govern the commitment of American armed forces overseas, Powell worried that the secretary might be giving potential enemies valuable insight into U.S. decision making and rubbing salt in the administration's wounds. Uncomfortable with public spats, Powell and other close aides gently pressed the impatient secretary to acquiesce to the White House's wishes and at least delay his delivery of the speech until after the presidential election in November. "We talked him out of it all through the '84 campaign so that we wouldn't have another Shultz-Weinberger fight," Powell later said. "It was going to look like an attack."

Weinberger set six prerequisites for armed intervention, a formula that would later come to be ridiculed by some as a simplistic, shorthand list that rejected any deployment short of "overwhelming" military force, and then only when absolute public support was guaranteed. But the argument behind the "Weinberger Doctrine" was far more sophisticated. He warned that force was justified only in response to direct threats to U.S. national interests or those of its allies. Even then, it should be used only as a last resort. But Weinberger did not rule out the use of limited force to attain limited objectives. Along with the possibility of "full-scale military intervention," he anticipated new kinds of conflicts stemming from "terrorist acts to guerrilla action." In an implicit reference to Beirut, he maintained the need for a well-defined objective understood by the American public, Congress and the troops themselves. Once the mission was clear, Weinberger said, the force deployed must be capable of achieving it.

By the time he finally delivered the speech in late November at the National Press Club in Washington, weeks after Reagan's landslide reelection victory over Democrat Walter Mondale and more than a year after the Beirut bombing, public and political attention had moved on. Weinberger's checklist was interpreted by some as an assurance that the United States would not be indiscriminately drawn into combat in Central America and by others as just another round in his ongoing and increasingly rancorous debate with Shultz. The secretary of state had fired his own shot at Weinberger in a speech the previous April, cautioning against what he called a "purely passive strategy" toward a mounting threat from state-supported terrorism—an allusion to Syrian and Iranian meddling in Lebanon. "We cannot opt out of every contest," Shultz warned.

Despite his concerns about Weinberger going public, Powell agreed with his boss. The U.S. military was a lethal weapon: you aimed it at the enemy and fired it with the intent to kill. As he had witnessed firsthand in Vietnam, any uncertainty about the enemy, the goal or the situation on the ground could lead to disaster. Shultz, Powell believed, saw America's armed forces as a "flexible tool of diplomacy" and wondered why "we pay for all this stuff if we can never use it short of World War III." A decade later, when Powell, as chairman of the Joint Chiefs, was resisting an ill-defined U.S. military intervention in the Balkans, an official in the Democratic Clinton administration would ask him the same question. "I thought I would have an aneurysm," he later said of his reaction to a query by then–U.N. Ambassador Madeleine Albright about the use of U.S. troops in Bosnia. "American GIs were not toy soldiers to be moved around on some sort of global game board." By then, major elements of the "Weinberger Doctrine" had become known as the "Powell Doctrine."

Although the military leadership was obliged to give its best advice on the feasibility of any mission, decisions about when and for what purpose to use America's armed forces were up to civilian policy makers and, ultimately, the commander in chief. But in Lebanon, just as in Vietnam, the military's responsibility did not begin or end with following the president's orders. The chain of command ran both ways, obligating officers to obey civilian policy makers while imposing equal responsibility on the upper echelons to protect the lives and interests of the troops below. Weinberger had called for constant reassessment and readjustment of the relationship between the size and composition of deployed forces and their assigned mission. Post-Beirut investigations sharply faulted senior military leaders for their apparent failure to notice and respond to the fact that a small force armed and equipped for peacekeeping had gradually been eased into a quasi-combat situation.

On the Pentagon's map of the world, divided into five large areas of operation, Lebanon was a distant, Mideast appendage to the European Command. Powell thought regional commanders at EUCOM headquarters in West Germany probably had never gone to see what was happening on the ground in Beirut. He promised himself that if he were ever in charge he would stay closely involved in everything American military forces were doing around the world.

By and large, it was a promise he kept when he later became the most hands-on chairman of the Joint Chiefs in history. Air Force General Charles G. Boyd recalled that as a deputy EUCOM commander in the early 1990s, he or his boss, General John M. Shalikashvili, received a direct call from the chairman nearly every day at 7 a.m. Washington time. "Powell wanted to know, 'What's going on in your theater?' He dialed the telephone himself; nobody ever knew out in the front office who he was calling. But he was calling people all over, and they weren't all four-star generals. Some of them were lieutenant colonels that he knew and trusted, and by the time he got his [Pentagon staff] briefing, he already knew what was going on in the world. He had a lot more confidence in that method than he did in the detailed intelligence briefing" delivered to his office each morning. When another decade passed and he became secretary of state, Powell tried to keep his finger on every corner of his global domain in the same manner, beginning at dawn with calls to Europe and following time zones around the world to the Far East before he headed home at the end of the day.

Alma's father had died in 1984, the same year Arie Powell succumbed to cancer. Colin drove his family to New York to see his mother the week before the end, and Alma was struck by how tiny and fragile her mother-in-law seemed in her hospital bed. Arie had little strength left but all of her wits about her, and, true to form, she told them she was worried about the money the hospital was costing and wondered why she couldn't be moved to a hospice. The funeral was held at St. Margaret's, the Powell family church in the Bronx. Colin was unsettled by how radically it had changed. The young new priest had adopted the modern Episcopal service—"unisex, low-key, non-triumphant," Colin thought, and a far cry from the pomp and pageantry of his youth.

Life was moving on. Michael graduated from the College of William and Mary in 1985, and Colin delivered a speech at his ROTC commissioning ceremony. They had never really talked about a career in the military, but Michael followed in his father's footsteps to basic training and parachute school at Fort Benning and later to West Germany as a cavalry officer. Annemarie, the later-in-life child who had her mother's green-eyed sparkle, was still at home.

Linda, two years behind her brother at William and Mary, was a serious student, with Colin's steady gaze under the same skeptical brows. An English major, Linda spent most of her time in the theater department, and by her junior year, she knew she wanted to pursue a career in acting.

But her heart started pounding and her hands grew clammy every time she thought of broaching the subject with her father. Although he rarely raised his voice at home, she had always been intimidated by him as a child.

She was sure he would consider acting a frivolous choice and an unstable lifestyle that didn't fit his serious view of the world and of the responsibilities of adulthood. She still hadn't screwed up her courage to tell him when one day, as he sat on the sofa reading a newspaper, he looked up at her and asked out of the blue, "Have you decided what you want to do when you get out of school?"

Her heart racing, she said "No" without even thinking and walked out of the room. But then she took a deep breath, came back in and said it quickly before she changed her mind: "You know, you asked me and I said I didn't know but really what I think I'd like to do is be an actor."

He lowered his newspaper and to her great amazement said, "Well, I don't really know how you do that. But if that's what you really want to do, you should do it." He mentioned the children of some friends, one of whom was an engineer. "But they don't seem particularly happy. So I think you should do something that's going to make you happy."

Years later, after her father had paid for acting school and she was struggling to earn a living in New York City, he would joke about when she was going to get a "real" job. But when she finally became a successful actress, with enough work to pay her bills and then some, he always went to see her on stage when he could make it, even though she knew most of the shows she was in ranged far outside his tastes. His favorite stage show remained *The Music Man*.

When General Wickham proposed Powell as Weinberger's military assistant, he had made clear to both men that it was a two-year assignment. By the summer of 1985, it was time for Powell to step back onto the more traditional Army ladder if he was to climb to the heights that Wickham and others had predicted for him. Powell was more than ready to leave the Pentagon when the chief of staff called to say he was slated to take over the 8th Infantry, a mechanized division in West Germany. On a subsequent European tour with Weinberger, Powell took a side trip to visit the division commander he would be replacing in just a few months.

But like a bad Army joke—"Not so fast, Private Smith"—Wickham soon arrived at his door with a different scenario. Weinberger had put his foot down and said he could not spare Powell. The Army still found it useful to have him at the secretary's side, Wickham confessed, but the

good news was that he and the secretary had shaken hands on an extension of just one year. In exchange, they had agreed that Powell's departure
would come with a third general's star and command of an entire corps.
Wickham knew that Powell was wary of how it would look inside the
Army; skipping over division command to a higher headquarters could be
a final confirmation of his "flagpole" status. But he thought that Powell, if
anyone, could pull it off.

9

What's amazing about Powell is he's created a comfort
zone among the guardians of the culture.

—Jesse L. Jackson

As if to resanctify his covenant with the service, Powell spent the day
after his July 2, 1986, swearing-in as the commander of the Army's West
Germany–based V Corps on a sentimental journey to Gelnhausen, where
he had begun his career as a green second lieutenant nearly three decades
earlier. In Washington, the nightmare scenarios of the early Cold War
were a receding bad dream. The new Soviet leader, Mikhail Gorbachev,
was promising to take his country in a different direction. But here on the
front lines, Powell's corps of 75,000 soldiers still stared across the Iron
Curtain, watching for signs of Armageddon. He placed a photograph of
his Soviet counterpart, General Colonel Vladislav A. Achalov, on his desk
in Frankfurt to remind him that 80,000 Red Army troops were still staring
back.

Powell promised his corps officers at a welcome meeting that he would
break his back to make sure they had everything they needed to train and
equip their troops. He encouraged discussion and freely expressed views,
he told them, and expected their best advice. But he demanded their
absolute allegiance. "When we are debating an issue, loyalty means giving
me your honest opinion, whether you think I'll like it or not. Disagreement, at this stage, stimulates me. But once a decision has been made, the
debate ends. From that point on, loyalty means executing the decision as
if it were your own."

Life in Frankfurt was the antithesis of the Washington pressure cooker.
His days were calm and ordered, and they ended, for the most part,
promptly at 5 p.m., with time for a quick handball game or a few hours of
work in the garage. Alma was back in the business of mothering the wives
of soldiers, making sure family services were available, hosting teas and
participating in the city's four separate German-American clubs. Linda

was in her last year at William and Mary in Virginia, and Michael was nearby in Europe, leading an armored cavalry platoon in Bavaria. They were down to one child at home—Annemarie had cried all the way across the Atlantic at having to move for the fourth time in five years, this time leaving behind not only her school but a boyfriend and her newly acquired Virginia driver's license.

Powell was an avid newspaper reader; he didn't see how anyone could do an effective job in government without knowing what people on the outside were talking about. But he found it hard to keep up with the week-old copies of *The Washington Post* that arrived at his headquarters by mail, and he missed the initial whiff of scandal that blew across the Reagan administration in early November 1986. It began with the astonishing report that Robert "Bud" McFarlane—who had resigned as Reagan's national security adviser in late 1985—had made a secret visit to Tehran on behalf of the White House six months later. Iran's parliamentary speaker, Akbar Hashemi Rafsanjani, confirmed that McFarlane and four companions had arrived with false Irish passports, bearing gifts that included a cake decorated with a brass key to symbolize the opening of better relations and a Bible autographed by Reagan. McFarland also brought intelligence maps to brief the Iranians on Iraq, with which they were currently at war, and a planeload of military equipment to exchange for Iranian help in securing the release of American hostages held in Lebanon.

The story had deep legal and political implications. Washington had severed relations with Iran in the wake of the U.S. Embassy seizure during Jimmy Carter's presidency. In 1983, the Reagan administration had blamed the theocratic government in Tehran for both the Marine bombing in Beirut and the subsequent kidnapping of a half-dozen American citizens by Lebanese militants. The State Department had designated Iran a terrorist state, Congress had banned American arms sales there, and Reagan had leaned heavily on sometimes reluctant allies to prevent any military assistance whatsoever to the ayatollahs. The administration was publicly neutral in the Iran-Iraq War, but it was widely known that the Americans were covertly aiding Iraq.

Within weeks of the initial revelations in November, a darker and far more damaging story emerged. Beyond cakes and offers of intelligence, the administration had been selling TOW antitank missiles and HAWK antiaircraft missiles to Iran for more than a year—first through Israel and then directly from U.S. weapons stockpiles—in hopes of gaining the release of the Lebanon hostages. Equally astounding, Iran had been charged inflated prices for some of the weapons and the extra funds had been used, in violation of yet another congressional prohibition, to fund a completely separate administration-backed guerrilla war in Central America. Under the supervision of the CIA and Colonel Oliver North, a Marine officer assigned to the National Security Council in the White House, the U.S.-backed Nicaraguan *contras* had used the money to buy weapons from a network of American arms dealers.

The whole operation made a mockery of Reagan's oft-stated insistence that the United States would never negotiate with terrorists. After initially denying that any arms had been sold to Iran, the president acknowledged the sales but continued to deny key aspects of the matter, including any trade for hostages. By the beginning of December 1986, two separate investigations were under way, one in Congress and another by a presidential commission Reagan had been forced to appoint. An independent counsel was about to be named to investigate possible crimes by public officials.

Media reports indicated that knowledge of the Iran initiative had been closely held among a few senior administration officials. Among them were Weinberger and Shultz—both of whom quickly let it be known that they had opposed the arms shipments to Iran and had not been informed about the money diverted to the *contras*—and a handful of their senior aides, including Powell and Armitage. As more details emerged, Oliver North was fired from the NSC and Admiral John Poindexter, McFarlane's successor and North's supervisor as Reagan's national security adviser, was forced to resign. On December 2, Reagan announced that Frank Carlucci, who had left government for the private sector in 1983, had agreed to return to Washington to take Poindexter's place. The next day, Carlucci called Powell in Frankfurt.

Colin told Alma that night that he had turned down Carlucci's offer to become deputy national security adviser. He had waited three years for this command, and Carlucci knew that dragging him away after just a few months could extinguish any remaining hope of bringing his Army career to a prestigious retirement. Although he didn't mention it to Alma, Powell had also told Carlucci that he had been "up to my ears" in the TOW missile shipments to Iran while in Weinberger's office. There was a real possibility, he warned only half jokingly, that he would be indicted along with other senior Reagan officials once the whole messy business was unraveled. He urged Carlucci to check with the White House lawyers and the FBI. They would tell him that this was a bad idea.

Carlucci had no other candidates. There wasn't time for a formal selection process; the White House was in chaos, and he felt as if he were "surrounded by alligators." He wasn't that close to Powell, but they had worked together at OMB and briefly at the Pentagon, and from what he remembered, Powell "knew how to run things. He had a track record I was comfortable with [and] I trusted him. He had experience, he understood the bureaucracy and he was knowledgeable on the foreign policy issues." On short notice, he couldn't think of anyone else with the same qualifications.

Carlucci called the FBI, and on December 5, after two agents interviewed Powell for an hour by telephone, the Bureau formally advised the White House that he was "not considered a subject of the investigation." Weinberger, at Carlucci's urging, called White House Counsel Peter Wallison and assured him that Powell had had "only minimal involvement on Iran" and had just been following the president's orders.

Carlucci enlisted Powell's friends and former colleagues to help convince him that the situation was urgent. Grant Green, a retired Army general and friend who had left the Pentagon with Carlucci and returned to Washington with him, counseled Powell to accept the offer, as did Kenneth Adelman, the head of Reagan's Arms Control and Disarmament Agency and a White House confidant. Weinberger and General Wickham called with the same message. But after Carlucci told Julius Becton of his plan, Becton called Powell to warn him that accepting the job could ruin his Army career for good. And Armitage, who had his own Iran-*contra* problems, thought that Powell should stay as far away from Washington as possible.

When Carlucci called back, he caught Powell at a formal corps event at the Frankfurt officers' club. Every head in the ballroom turned to watch as an aide whispered in his ear and he walked outside toward the dark parking lot, climbed into his official car and picked up the telephone. Again, he asked Carlucci to back off. "Frank, don't do this to me just to get somebody to be your deputy. You've got to assure me that from your perspective the situation is so bad that you think I've got to give up something I've worked a long time for. Do you really understand the career choice you're putting to me?"

"I've been in the [Defense] Department," Carlucci countered. "I know what I'm asking you to do, and I'm telling you it's important."

Powell finally agreed. But before it was made public, he told Carlucci, he needed the cover of a direct presidential request "for my own peace of mind, for my fraternity. The Army has to see it that way. They just can't see it as I'm going off to a bureaucratic job. If you say it's that important, then I've got to hear it from my commander in chief."

Ronald Reagan called as the Powells were finishing dinner in the kitchen on December 12. Reading from a script prepared by Adelman, Reagan said what was required. "General Powell, I know you have only just gotten there. I know how much it means to you and how you've been looking forward to it, but we really do need you back here and I hope you will come." As Reagan spoke, Powell took careful notes, right down to the "God bless you" at the end.

Powell was spared the embarrassment of public testimony during the televised congressional hearings on Iran-*contra* that mesmerized the country in the summer of 1987. But lawyers for the joint House and Senate investigation had interrogated him behind closed doors in April and again in June on the arms transfers to Iran; in July, he had two more sessions with the FBI. It was clear from the beginning, however, that the investigators' sights were set higher than Weinberger's former military assistant.

The genesis of the Iran-*contra* scheme was a June 1985 top secret memo to Weinberger and Shultz from McFarlane—then still at the White House—warning that the Soviet Union was poised to take advantage of instability in Iran. The United States should "encourage Western allies and friends" to outbid Moscow in providing aid and trade advantages, including the "provision of selected military equipment as determined on a case-by-case basis." There was no mention in the memo of the hostages who were being held by Iranian-backed groups in Lebanon, although investigators later determined that concern about the American captives had been a key selling point in gaining Reagan's approval of the arms sales.

McFarlane's memo arrived first on Powell's desk; he sent it in to Weinberger, who passed it on to Armitage with a handwritten notation that the idea of establishing a new relationship with Iran was "absurd." In a formal reply a month later, Weinberger wrote that "under no circumstances . . . should we now ease our restriction on arms sales to Iran." Not only would it undermine American credibility in the world, "it would adversely affect our newly emerging relationship with Iraq." Shultz sent McFarlane a similar response.

Weinberger and Powell later testified that they had had no knowledge that parts of the plan had actually been implemented the same year or that Reagan had approved using Israel as a cutout for weapons shipments. They both acknowledged that they had seen repeated intelligence references in the fall of 1985 to meetings among Iranians, Israelis and

Americans—Powell had ordered the National Security Agency, on Wein-berger's behalf, to make sure all relevant intercepts were copied to his office. But they testified that they had assumed it was nothing but talk. When the White House inquired in November about Defense Depart-ment stockpiles of HAWK missiles and spare parts, Powell told investiga-tors, "I took it as a hypothetical question."

On January 17, 1986, Reagan had signed a secret presidential "finding of necessity" that eliminated Israel's role as the intermediary and author-ized direct U.S. shipments to Iran. Weinberger had disapproved and, based on research Powell provided him, noted that the law required all Defense Department weapons transfers to be reported to Congress. Instead, Powell had found a way to keep the Pentagon one step removed from the scheme by arranging for 4,000 TOW missiles to be transferred first to the CIA, which could then pass them on to Iran. It wasn't until the White House subsequently increased the order to the strange number of 4,508, Powell testified, that "things clicked" and he realized "that a trans-fer had [already] taken place and this is the replenishment of some kind." The additional 508 were to pay back the Israelis for TOWs they had already sent to Iran in 1985.

"In my judgment and to the best of my recollection," Powell told con-gressional investigators in a June 19, 1987, deposition, all he had known before Reagan's January "finding" was that there had been "a conceptual discussion of the initiative to transfer weapons to Iran, and it was heatedly debated within the administration, and no decision was made to transfer any weapons."

Knowing at the time about the 1985 Israeli shipments and replenish-ment agreement was not illegal, but lying to Congress about such knowl-edge was. Powell's answers were carefully constructed and peppered with "best of my recollection" caveats. He knew he couldn't swear that nothing had ever crossed his desk indicating that U.S.-approved Israeli shipments had actually taken place. But as long as he didn't tax his memory, he felt he could still skirt the outer edges of the truth. The investigators could not prove otherwise, and in any event, they didn't press very hard.

Powell's primary interest throughout the investigation was to protect Weinberger, and only once did he feel close to the edge of a precipice. When Arthur Liman, the Senate committee counsel, asked how fre-quently Weinberger had met with Poindexter, Powell replied that it was every week or two.

"You did not take notes generally of these meetings, did you?" Liman asked.

"I would occasionally take notes, sometimes not," Powell said. "But I did not keep permanent sets of notes. Just use[d] them as memory aids and then got rid of them."

"Maybe I should know this, but did the Secretary keep a diary?"

"The Secretary, to my knowledge, did not keep a diary. Whatever notes he kept, I don't know how he uses them or what he does with them. He does not have a diary of this ilk, no."

"Did he dictate memos...?"

"No, the Secretary did not dictate his daily activities, to the best of my knowledge. I've never seen it. He didn't do it and I was with him every day. Whatever notes he took in the course of a day, I don't know what he did with them."

Powell waited tensely for a follow-up, certain that the next question would lead to a discussion of Weinberger's scribbles on the ever-present notepad that disappeared into his desk drawer each night. But the line of inquiry ended abruptly as Liman's counterpart from the House committee jumped in with an unrelated question about Poindexter.

Powell was never mentioned as a suspect or a target of the investigation. But Iran-*contra* would hang over his head almost until he retired from the Army more than six years later and would always be a favorite subject of his critics. In November 1991, Independent Counsel Lawrence E. Walsh was writing his final report—after thirteen indictments and eleven convictions, including of McFarlane, North and Poindexter—when he learned of Weinberger's previously undisclosed notepads. Weinberger had taken the notes from the Pentagon when he left office in 1987 and deposited them with his personal papers in the Library of Congress, where they had been discovered by one of Walsh's investigators. They revealed, Walsh wrote, "that contrary to his sworn testimony, Weinberger knew in advance that U.S. arms were to be shipped to Iran through Israel in November 1985 without Congressional notification, in an effort to obtain the release of hostages, and Israel expected U.S. replenishment."

Walsh reopened his investigation of Weinberger and called Powell for an interview in February 1992. Given some of the notes to look at, Powell agreed that they were a "personal diary," but said he that while he had often seen Weinberger writing on the pads, he had never read them. He had considered them Weinberger's personal property, he said, and had not known their purpose or what the secretary had ultimately done with them.

In March, Weinberger was notified that he was the target of a federal grand jury investigating whether he had lied about what he had known in

1985. Asked by Weinberger's defense team to provide an affidavit, Powell insisted that the substance of the notes "do not suggest to me that Secretary Weinberger knew, at the time that they were prepared, that Israel had sent missiles to Iran. I do not believe that I knew in the fall of 1985 that Israel had sent missiles to Iran. While I believe we may have heard about discussions or proposals or suggestions involving such activities, to the best of my recollection we did not know that any such activities had actually been carried out until long after."

The day after he signed the affidavit, Powell appeared before the Weinberger grand jury; based at least in part on Powell's testimony, according to Walsh, the former defense secretary was indicted on June 16, 1992. Powell himself was not yet off the hook. Years earlier, he had told Congress and the FBI that he knew everything that went on in Weinberger's office, and he swore in the affidavit that he "saw virtually all the papers that went in and out of [Weinberger's] office, and consulted with him on a daily basis."

Although he thought he had been saved in his 1987 testimony by Liman's failure to follow up on questions about the existence of a Weinberger diary, he knew that his sparring with the lawyer might now be seen as dissembling. If Walsh believed there was enough evidence to indict Weinberger for lying, why not Powell? He was called to a final interview by the independent counsel in November 1992 but heard nothing further.

On Christmas Eve 1992, less than two weeks before Weinberger's trial was scheduled to begin, the former defense secretary was granted a full pardon by departing President George H. W. Bush. Powell had to wait until Walsh's final report was issued in August 1993 to learn that he was in the clear. Walsh wrote that Powell had been "privy to detailed information" regarding the 1985 shipments to Israel. While he "generally was a cooperative witness," Powell's 1987 congressional testimony "was at least misleading" and "hardly constituted full disclosure." But the counsel concluded that it would be difficult to prove that Powell had intentionally lied or colluded with Weinberger to conceal the notes. "Thus, while Powell's prior inconsistent statements could have been used to impeach his credibility, they did not warrant prosecution."

Powell thought that Walsh's conclusions were "dead wrong." He was furious at the report's overall implication that the prosecutor could have nailed him but had decided against it. "I was not to be judged on whether or not I actually made false statements," he later wrote. "Walsh simply implied that I did and dropped the matter, leaving the unfair and unfounded conclusion."

But however angry he felt at the time, Powell was virtually the only official involved who had actually benefited from the scandal—with a new job in the Reagan White House. "If it hadn't been for Iran-*contra*," he later acknowledged, "I'd still be an obscure general somewhere. Retired, never heard of."

He thought that Weinberger had been treated unfairly. Despite the secretary's consistent opposition to the arms-for-hostages scheme, Weinberger had ended up the most senior official indicted by Walsh, an undeserved badge of shame after a long and distinguished career in public service. But while Weinberger later wrote that he had considered resigning in protest over the Iranian arms plot, Powell didn't believe it. Whatever affection and respect he had for his former boss, he thought that Weinberger had been hobbled by his reluctance to speak uncomfortable truths to Reagan. It hadn't been enough to complain about the Iran scheme to the likes of McFarlane and Poindexter and then hope it would go away. Real loyalty to a president, Powell concluded, demanded telling him face-to-face when he was making a mistake, something Weinberger could never bring himself to do.

In its wake, Iran-*contra* reinforced Powell's belief, born in Vietnam and confirmed with Desert One, that presidential policy decisions made without a full and honest airing of options and potential pitfalls among a range of senior advisers usually resulted in disaster. In addition, he concluded, operatives such as Oliver North, the self-appointed "elite" who tried to play outside the rules, were poison to any administration.

Different presidents had held widely different views about the organization and role, and even the size, of the National Security Council and its staff. The NSC had been redefined repeatedly in the years since its creation, under the National Security Act of 1947, as a vehicle to coordinate the president's foreign and defense policies. Made up of the president, vice president and secretaries of state and defense, it had begun with a small White House staff and an executive secretary. Various presidents had added chairs to the NSC table, including the CIA director, the chairman of the Joint Chiefs of Staff and other Cabinet officers, depending on the issue. The role of the executive secretary gradually expanded into the job of presidential national security adviser, with a staff that in some administrations numbered more than a hundred officials. The adviser's influence over foreign policy at times eclipsed that of the secretary of state—most memorably in the case of President Nixon's national security adviser, Henry Kissinger. Rivalry between Zbigniew Brzezinski and President Carter's secretary of state, Cyrus Vance, had contributed to Vance's resignation.

Reagan had pledged during his 1980 presidential campaign to downgrade the national security adviser post and restore foreign policy primacy to the Department of State. By the time McFarlane and then Poindexter—numbers three and four of Reagan's six national security advisers—took over the job, friction among Cabinet secretaries and lack of coordination were again the rule. Their penchant for secrecy and Reagan's own inattention to detail had led to Iran-*contra*.

When Powell arrived as deputy national security adviser on January 2, 1987, the White House was in a state of near meltdown. The Republicans had lost control of the Senate and the Democrats had increased their majority in the House in the 1986 midterm elections even before the Iran-*contra* story broke. The heady days of "Reaganomics" and massive defense budgets were long over, and sunny "Morning in America" had become a downpour of bad news. Carlucci and Powell were operating without a net—they had no instructions from the president beyond fixing what was clearly broken.

Powell's two civilian suits had been packed away for years, and the scent of mothballs quickly filled his new office. Compared to his spacious quarters in Frankfurt it was a claustrophobic cubbyhole, wedged between Carlucci's corner suite and the formal West Wing entrance where two Marine guards always stood at attention. His single window looked out over the White House driveway, where a permanent gaggle of television reporters broadcasted live from the White House lawn. The first person to drop by and welcome him on his first morning was the vice president, George H. W. Bush, who bubbled with bonhomie and informed him that they shared a bathroom.

Powell's arrival coincided with Reagan's return from an extended holiday in California, and the president almost immediately entered a Washington hospital for prostate-related surgery. Powell had rarely been in Reagan's presence, and he scarcely saw the president during his first few weeks on the job. When he accompanied Carlucci to their initial Oval Office briefing, two things about Reagan struck him immediately. The first was the high gloss and absence of wear on the president's shoes, as if he had just taken them out of the box for the occasion. It was something that perhaps only a military officer would notice. No matter where or at what time of day, Reagan invariably looked as if he had just stepped away from a formal photo session. His inevitable white shirt was always stiffly pressed and unwrinkled, and he was rarely without a jacket. The second thing Powell noticed was Reagan's remarkable ability to make you feel like the center of the universe as he smiled and shook your hand.

But it was painfully obvious that Reagan was less than engaged as a chief executive. As they sat with him before the Oval Office fireplace and Carlucci began outlining world events and upcoming decisions, it wasn't at all clear that the words were registering. While the president maintained an attentive expression, he offered no responses and asked few questions. Powell quickly learned that this was typical of Reagan. "We would lay out the contrasting views of various Cabinet officers and Congress and wait for the President to peel them back to get at underlying motives. It did not happen," he later wrote. "Most unnerving, when Carlucci presented options, the President would say little until Frank gave his recommendation. And then the President would merely acknowledge that he had heard him, without saying yes, no, or maybe."

"It was scary," Powell told Reagan's biographer, Lou Cannon. "You couldn't go in there and tell him, 'Mr. President, I've just decided the sun will rise in the West tomorrow morning'...but within a zone of reasonableness, he was quite content to give it to you."

After their maiden briefing, Carlucci and Powell walked back toward their offices in consternation. "You know, Colin, this office has been abused in the past," Carlucci said. "You and I have to figure out how the president would want things done, if this is the kind of response we're going to get." Neither McFarlane nor Poindexter had kept records of their conversations with the president. Although they insisted that Reagan had specifically approved the Israeli arms shipments to Iran, the president was equally insistent that he didn't remember having done so. Powell was going to have to accompany the national security adviser to every presidential briefing and take complete notes, Carlucci said. The last thing they wanted was to "get into a kind of Ollie North situation."

Within weeks, they let go nearly half of the bloated NSC staff, eliminated the political-military affairs department that North had headed, and dismantled a secure communications room he had established in the Old Executive Office Building. The only complaint, Carlucci later recalled, came from Bush, who summoned him to warn that "the president is getting nervous" about the deep staff cuts. Carlucci sent a note to the president saying "something to the effect of: This needs to be done. Don't worry, it will come out all right." Reagan never replied.

In an environment where secrecy and closed doors had long prevailed, the new team was a strong, fresh breeze. Ending the NSC's bunker mentality and long working hours, Carlucci announced that he would leave the office when the sun went down—he sometimes slipped out even earlier for a game of tennis—and that, barring emergencies, he would not come in on weekends. The job of restoring order to the national security decision-making process and regaining public trust played to all of Powell's strengths. In Carlucci's view and his own, he was the world's best staff officer—his upbeat and inclusive style and sense of humor, combined with his military bearing and crisp efficiency, radiated competence and confidence.

No one in the Reagan White House had asked Powell about his foreign policy views or whether he was a registered Republican. He had voted for Reagan, not because he knew much about him but because he was disappointed in Jimmy Carter. He still adhered to his split-ticket military philosophy and remained wary of strong ideology of any sort. But he didn't think this assignment was about politics or policy; it was about applying discipline and common sense to the way the White House worked, making the trains run on time and ensuring that all aboard operated off the same schedule.

Carlucci took over most of the office's public functions and, after some prodding from Powell, began to wade through an unattended pile of pending arms control matters. Powell began a review of all covert operations. After shutting down everything the NSC was operating, he assembled a working group and subjected each remaining covert program to four tests, beginning with "Is it legal?" They looked at what each was supposed to achieve, whether it was working and whether it was something the American people would approve of if they knew about it. Once they had eliminated about 15 percent of the programs, Powell and Carlucci sat Reagan down and explained what they had done. They asked the president to certify his approval in writing.

With his abiding belief in chains of command, Powell replaced the structure that had evolved under Poindexter—in which everyone had reported directly to him and he had kept his own thoughts to himself—with a military-style pyramid and separate divisions in charge of geographic regions and issue areas. For the new culture of openness to prevail and the national security adviser to be reestablished as an honest broker among Cabinet departments, lines of communication had to be repaired. Weinberger and Shultz still barely spoke to each other, and neither trusted the national security adviser. In response, Carlucci proposed and Powell set up a Policy Review Group (PRG) of Cabinet deputies to hash out agreement on issues of the day and forward its recommendations for discussion by their seniors at decision meetings chaired by the president.

Powell ran the deputies sessions with a strict formula straight out of his Army training. First, the length of the meeting was set in advance—usually one hour—and it began and ended precisely on time. The PRG convened once or twice a week at a long conference table in the Roosevelt Room, a windowless White House chamber decorated with a massive equestrian portrait of Theodore Roosevelt in his Rough Riders uniform. After he began with a description of the meeting's purpose, Powell called on everyone around the table—"State, what have you got to say? Defense? CIA?"—to briefly outline their positions. Only he was permitted to interrupt, and he was careful to do so only when a presentation veered too far afield or went over the allotted time. Powell would then summarize their positions and open the floor to discussion, followed by another summary, questions and a statement of the message he would carry to the president. "Then he'd wrap it up with the 'to-do's. Here's what you have to do, and you. Take it back to your principals.' And we all would," recalled Richard Armitage, who often represented the Pentagon.

The introduction of military-drill precision to the meetings became something of a joke among the deputies and other officials, but no one complained. After years of obfuscation and intrigue, Armitage thought, "it was like the clouds opening up and the sun coming out."

On February 26, 1987, the presidential commission headed by former senator John Tower issued its Iran-*contra* report, focusing on the operation of the NSC and its staff. In tactful language, it described Reagan's "personal management style" as so disengaged that he either couldn't control his subordinates or was completely unaware of what they were doing in his name.

The new NSC had already implemented many of the report's recommendations, and the following week Powell wrote a list of "talking points" for administration officials to use in explaining to the media how the White House had changed. Almost half the NSC team had been replaced, it said, and "a clear vertical organization and strict lines of authority have been imposed on the NSC staff. There will be no freelancing. The office of political-military affairs has been abolished."

A new position of NSC legal adviser had been created "with the clout to assure full accountability." All existing covert operations had been subjected to a "sweeping review," and a new directive prohibited NSC staff from participating in such operations.

"The President has reaffirmed his strong commitment to making the Congressional oversight process work, and work well," Powell wrote. "Procedures for disclosure and consultation about intelligence matters will be followed." The process of interagency coordination had been "fully restored."

Reagan liked to tell stories he thought demonstrated his lack of racial bias: about his youthful experience as an athlete and radio sportscaster, when he had favored integration in major-league baseball; about the time he had invited two black college football players, traveling to an away game, to stay at his parents' Illinois home after the segregated local hotel had turned them away; about his friendship with black entertainers, especially Sammy Davis, Jr. But his political history—opposition to the 1965 Voting Rights Act, refusal to criticize the segregationist Alabama Governor George Wallace during the worst of the Birmingham firestorm—and his administration's domestic policies said otherwise. Reagan spoke disparagingly of "welfare queens" and opposed making Martin Luther King's birthday a national holiday. His administration fought to reverse a long-standing IRS ruling against tax-exempt status for segregated private schools, and his attorney general, Edwin Meese III, led an effort to end court-sanctioned affirmative action programs for minorities. Few black Americans supported his presidency.

Powell had no doubt that Reagan respected and liked him. The president's apparent blindness to the ongoing African-American struggle was distressing, but Powell decided that Reagan was simply oblivious to a problem he had rarely been exposed to. Powell suspected that Reagan liked the idea of having a black man in the front office, just as he'd liked having the black ballplayers stay at his parents' home. But it was clear that the president's comfort level with having a senior black official in the White House was less an affirmation of racial enlightenment than an erasure of color. Carlucci recalled that Reagan only once commented on Powell's color, saying, "You know, you don't even think of Colin as black."

On the rare occasions that the general subject of race came up, Powell told Lou Cannon, he tried to let Reagan know "that things ain't as great as you think they are, and there are still problems out there to be dealt with. And he always would look pained and interested and anguished" and launch into one of his stock stories about a positive interaction he had once had with a black person. It made Powell far more uncomfortable than it appeared to make Reagan, Powell recalled. He didn't want to become known as the "house black."

Powell had no illusions about the distaste of the administration's conservative constituencies for the Johnson-era victories of civil rights over the so-called rights of southern states. But he thought Reagan could accomplish a lot in the black community if he would simply acknowledge reality from time to time.

One such opportunity arose in May 1987, when Reagan's schedule included a rare appearance before a black audience: a commencement ceremony at Alabama's Tuskegee University and the dedication of a new science center there named for the late Air Force General Daniel "Chappie" James, one of only three blacks to have attained four-star status. Powell usually vetted and provided input for Reagan's speeches on national security and foreign policy issues, but this was a domestic address to which he could make a direct contribution. The paragraphs he offered to the White House speechwriters were, he thought, a strong statement of Reagan's empathy and an acknowledgment that "racism still exists; there is a long way to go." His submission was first rejected and then fought over for days before finally being boiled down to one paragraph of what Powell considered "happy talk."

In the speech, Reagan congratulated the civil rights movement and acknowledged that "the political and legal battle is obviously not over." But he offered no response to criticism of his own policies and called on blacks to stop "dwelling almost exclusively on the negative." All of America, he said, should start paying more attention to "stories of black successes and triumphs" in science, technology and other professions beyond "the attention focused on black athletes and entertainers." The speech was well received by Tuskegee faculty and students, but Powell thought the power had been drained from it.

The president's deputy national security adviser did not have a high profile outside the White House, and Powell remained virtually unknown beyond the Army and the black intelligentsia that kept track of his achievements. He rarely appeared in the media. "I'm glad you were able to catch the MacNeil/Lehrer show because you won't see me on television talk shows too often if I can help it," he wrote in a letter to Gene Norman, his childhood friend from the Bronx. But he made regular exceptions for African-American publications and organizations, feeling a responsibility to make himself available as an example of what hard work and taking advantage of opportunities could accomplish—and thinking it might do the administration's image some good. When a long-standing commitment to address a local black chapter of the American Legion Auxiliary on Veterans Day in November 1987 conflicted with the visit of a senior Soviet team preparing for an upcoming Washington summit with Gorbachev, Powell stiffed the Russians and fought his way through a freak fifteen-inch fall snowstorm to reach the venue at a motel near Howard University. His audience consisted of nine elderly war widows.

He had reached a level where government officials had staffs to answer letters and calls from outsiders, but he still tried to respond personally to everyone who wrote or telephoned. "My thoughts on leadership are rather simple," he handwrote to an ROTC cadet from Iowa who asked for help on a school paper. "Never forget the mission, take care of and love your soldiers, loyalty up and down, self-improvement, take risks, total integrity, don't take yourself too seriously, have fun, and learn from failures." When the White House press office asked why he had returned a telephone call from a columnist it had advised him to ignore, he shot back a memo: "I called him because I return calls."

Powell was leery but flattered when *The New York Times* asked for a profile interview in October 1987. The resulting article, headlined "Case of the Reluctant General," convinced him that he had mastered yet another part of the Washington game. "By all accounts General Powell, a tall, husky man with a quick laugh and even-handed manner, has won the respect of top bureaucratic operatives who often wield sharp knives," it said. He was depicted as modest in attitude but brave in battle and called a "key player" in rebuilding the NSC staff. Army scuttlebutt, the article concluded, was that Powell would eventually be a prime candidate for chief of staff.

Any hope of a quick return to uniform, however, had been put off six months into the White House job when Powell's son, Michael, was seriously injured in an accident while on duty in West Germany. Crushed under a jeep, Michael suffered severe injuries and would need multiple surgeries and months of hospitalization followed by extensive rehabilitation if he was ever to walk again. His military career was over. Colin and Alma had flown to Nuremberg the night of the accident in the hold of a military transport plane; once Michael could be moved, they brought him back to Walter Reed Army Medical Center, a ten-minute drive from the White House, where they could be with him daily.

As Powell's star rose, Weinberger was reaching the end of the road as defense secretary. He was one of only two original Reagan Cabinet members still in office (the other was Samuel Pierce, at Housing and Urban Development, whose department would soon be under investigation by an independent counsel for its own scandal), and much of his time was now spent in a losing battle with Congress over the defense budget. Weinberger's continuing suspicion of the Soviet Union, his hard line on arms control agreements and his unstinting support for the most expansive implementation of Reagan's missile defense initiative were as strong as ever. But the tide had been running in the opposite direction, toward détente and arms control compromise, ever since Gorbachev took over in Moscow. In addition, Jane Weinberger's health had continued to deteriorate, and she needed more and more of her husband's time.

In early November 1987, the White House announced that Carlucci would replace Weinberger as defense secretary and Powell would take over as Reagan's sixth national security adviser. On November 5, at a ceremony in the Rose Garden, Reagan shook Powell's hand and it was done.

Like most things in the Reagan White House, plans had been discussed and decisions all but made long before the subject had ever reached the Oval Office. Howard Baker, Reagan's chief of staff, had come to Powell in mid-October to ask if he would accept an offer to move up to the corner office. Two days later, Carlucci told him he was the only candidate for the job and at an unrelated meeting in the White House situation room shortly thereafter handed him a note that said "Done." Reagan "never laid out his expectations, never provided any guidance; in fact, he had not personally offered me the position or congratulated me on getting it," Powell later wrote. "After ten months in the White House, I was not surprised."

On a personal level, he admired Reagan and saw much in him to emulate. Powell had never met anyone more comfortable in his own skin; Reagan was absolutely confident of who he was and never tried to be more or less. He projected none of the affectations of "American royalty" that some presidents were known for. Powell had grown to appreciate what he thought Reagan symbolized for the country. "He may not have commanded every detail of every policy; but he had others to do that. . . . The man had been elected President twice by knowing what the American people wanted, and even rarer, by giving it to them."

But though Reagan was capable of insight, few subjects captured his interest. On those issues where he did engage, he needed close attention from his aides. Powell kept a handwritten list in his desk drawer of foreign policy issues on which the president's fervent but flawed version of reality risked sending his administration in the wrong direction. Reagan had eventually acknowledged that arms had been traded to Iran in exchange for hostages, but he never really believed it. He liked to compare the Iran episode to the infamous Lindbergh kidnapping in 1932, when a retired school principal from the Bronx had become the intermediary between the family of the flying ace Charles Lindbergh and the unknown person who had broken into Lindbergh's house and stolen his infant son for ransom. (The intervention had failed, and the child had been killed.) In Reagan's memory, his advisers had simply been looking for Iranian intermediaries to help free the hostages in Lebanon. Powell was careful to ensure that a long line of aspiring hostage negotiators who still sought an audience with the president were kept out of the White House.

It was clear that bad or manipulative advisers could steer Reagan down dangerous paths. But good ones had the heavy responsibility of distilling the essence of his foreign policy desires from a sometimes uninformed set of beliefs. As he took over as national security adviser, Powell briefly wondered whether he was the best man for the job. He knew Carlucci had chosen him as his deputy because he was a good manager who solved problems and got things done, not because he was a grand foreign policy strategist. No one had to tell him that he wasn't a Kissinger or a Brzezinski who had spent "most of his adult life sitting around concocting a view of the world," Powell told Lou Cannon. Yet here he was, adviser to a president who would accept almost anything he said about the great issues of the day.

Powell confronted his doubts with the same unemotional analysis he applied to most life decisions. He was fifty years old, the mature product of years of experience and the nation's finest training system. He had a quick mind and proven mental and physical endurance, a talent for navigating bureaucracy and a commanding presence. His career was replete with examples of rising to meet whatever challenge presented itself, and his instincts had proven all but unerring. If he followed his training and his gut, he decided, all would be well.

From his experience with Weinberger and as Carlucci's deputy, Powell had definite ideas about how the national security process was supposed to work. The adviser's job was to "get it all out—all the agendas, all the facts, all the opinions, all of the gray and white and black areas," let the departments and agencies argue and defend their positions, try to guide them to consensus and then formulate recommendations for decision that he would take to the president. If consensus could not be reached, Cabinet officers were free to make their own Oval Office pitches, but Powell reserved the right to tell Reagan why he thought they were wrong. If they ended up mad at him, so be it.

Shultz was eager to leave the contentious Weinberger years behind—and to make sure he knew what Powell and Carlucci, the new defense secretary, were up to—and proposed regular meetings among the three of them. Powell suggested they gather every morning at seven for coffee in his office; that way they would all began the day on the same page. "We knew that if the three of us could agree, that was it," Carlucci recalled. "Because nobody else was going to try to bypass us and try to get to the president, and Colin would just keep the president informed."

Powell, Carlucci said, handled the other two deftly. "He's got that laugh, and he'd just turn to me and say 'Come on, Frank, that's full of crap.' Or 'No, George, don't go in that direction.' And he'd bounce us back and forth with good humor."

But the years of bickering between the State and Defense departments, and Iran-*contra*, had left deep scars. Shultz refused to give up his twice-weekly sessions with the president. And whenever Powell had something of substance to discuss with Reagan, he always made sure that someone he trusted—Howard Baker or his successor as chief of staff, Ken Duberstein, or White House Communications Director Tom Griscom—was in the room and that someone was taking notes.

One of Powell's jobs for Weinberger had been to make sure the secretary looked good in the media, or at least to keep him from looking bad. Now he was getting used to being the subject of coverage himself. Among the most satisfying early mentions was a preview of 1988 by *Defense Week* magazine, which noted that Lieutenant General Colin L. Powell was "in" and Colonel Oliver North was "out."

On the rare occasion when a well-informed journalist nailed him, Powell was willing to take his lumps. But he quickly developed a tendency to strike back sharply at what he considered bad reporting or cheap shots. Spending his first New Year's as national security adviser, he accompanied the traveling White House to Reagan's vacation home in California. While the First Couple and close White House aides attended a traditional New Year's Eve party at Walter Annenberg's opulent Palm Springs estate, Powell joined the White House press corps at its equally traditional holiday bash at a nearby rib joint. Reporters presented him with one cake shaped as a key and another with a picture of a Bible— reminders of the ill-fated McFarlane visit to Tehran. After he laughed, posed for pictures and cut himself a piece of cake, the journalists agreed that he had passed their "good guy" test.

A few weeks later, however, a local Washington magazine put a different spin on the evening. Under the headline "Guess Who Didn't Come to Dinner," *The Washingtonian* reported that "one guest [had been] noticeably missing" from the annual Annenberg party, which it called "a good barometer of real power in Washington." The article noted that Powell was black, and, in case anyone missed the point, it was accompanied by a photograph of Reagan's new national security adviser. It was the kind of innuendo Powell detested: insulting friends of his boss and singling out his race in the same paragraph. He shot off a letter to the editor, pointing out that while he hadn't known the Annenbergs personally, they had called the morning after the party to apologize for not realizing he was in town and to invite him to dinner that evening. "*The Washingtonian* article by photo and words left the suggestion that my being black may have had something to do with my not being invited to the New Year's Eve event," he wrote. "You owe Mr. and Mrs. Annenberg an apology for that suggestion."

While other senior officials spoke only rarely to reporters, and then usually under strict guidelines, Powell's strategy was to overwhelm the media with access to him and his point of view. Watching a news broadcast one evening in his office, he took issue with a story about the administration's policy in the Persian Gulf and looked out his window to where the reporter was speaking to a live camera. When she finished, he banged on the window and motioned her inside. "And she came into my office and I said that is not the way it happened," he later recounted in a speech to military officers. "Here is the way it happened. And she went right back out, as soon as the commercial was over, and she put out my version because she believed my version, she trusted me.

"You cannot underestimate the importance of dealing with the press and media in shaping foreign policy," Powell concluded. "I am not talking about spin control; I am not talking about deception. I am just talking about helping the American people understand the major issues that are out there by being accessible to the press, realizing that they have a job to do, not being afraid of them, and not looking down on them, but just working with them."

Of all the loose foreign policy ends remaining when Powell took over as Reagan's national security adviser, what to do about the Nicaraguan *contras* was among the most difficult. Oliver North's clandestine weapons accounts were closed, but the *contras* were still dependent on U.S. aid for survival. The administration's uphill efforts to persuade the Democratic Congress to reverse its ban on military assistance had been made even harder by the Iran-*contra* revelations and the Democratic majority. Powell did not doubt the White House's view that Nicaragua's Sandinista government was a Marxist-led pawn of the Soviet Union and Communist

Cuba. But despite Reagan's warning that Central American Communists were only a "two-day march" from the Texas border, he found it impossible to believe that the Sandinistas were a credible military threat to the United States or that the Russians had any intention of using them for that purpose. The CIA had already told him that the *contra* force would last another year or two at most and that it had no chance of victory over the Sandinista army no matter how much money and weaponry it received. Powell found the *contra* commanders unappealing, inept leaders who spent most of their time in Miami or Honduras. As the war dragged into its eighth year, he knew from internal White House polling that barely 30 percent of the American public thought it was important that the *contras* stay in existence. Most Americans weren't even sure which side their government was supporting in Nicaragua.

Given their inevitable demise, Powell thought the *contras* were useful primarily as leverage to ensure that a negotiated peace would be to the administration's liking. When Nicaragua's Central American neighbors proposed a deal he thought favored the Sandinistas, Powell threatened to cut their U.S. aid. But threats did not come naturally to him. Mediation and the art of the possible were more his style.

Congress had dug in its heels on further funding for the *contra* war. Powell was popular on Capitol Hill, where he had built a reputation during the Weinberger era by following his own rules: never lying outright, flattering members and making them feel included in decision making. Deftly humanizing the *contra* cause, he told them that the Nicaraguans' plight reminded him of his own anguish as he had waited for resupply helicopters in the Vietnamese jungle in 1963. When he eventually brokered a compromise to supply a small amount of military aid along with a larger commitment of humanitarian assistance that would keep Reagan's promise not to abandon the fighters, the deal was rejected not by the Democrats, but by the Republican Right. House Minority Whip Dick Cheney of Wyoming led the opposition, insisting on substantial military aid or nothing. Cheney, Powell concluded, would rather lose on principle than achieve compromise.

Powell found that Reagan capitulated far more easily than his right-wing backers, and he eventually reached a nonlethal aid agreement with a congressional majority. While conservatives grumbled, more mainstream Republicans and the national media hailed the national security adviser for solving the thorny *contra* problem. Powell was "the grand facilitator of foreign policy, not so much an initiator as a compromiser," whose honest-broker approach "has brought much-needed order to the White House national security process," said the *Los Angeles Times.* In one of its first editorial-page mentions of Powell, *The New York Times* called his handling of the Central America situation "wise" and congratulated him for "moving into the long-vacant middle ground in Administration policy."

During three summits with Gorbachev, the reformist Soviet leader, Reagan had forged a new relationship between Washington and Moscow, including the signing of an unprecedented agreement to destroy nuclear weapons. But as Powell and Shultz met with Gorbachev in April 1988 to plan for a historic presidential visit to the Soviet capital that summer, the prospects for a successful fourth summit did not look good. Across a conference table in the Kremlin's ornate Hall of St. Catherine, Gorbachev railed against a red-meat, anti-Communist speech Reagan had recently delivered to Republican conservatives. Despite all they had accomplished, the Russian fumed, the Reagan administration was "not abandoning stereotypes, not abandoning reliance on force, not taking account of political realities and the interests of others." There had been "backward movement," he said, and the Americans were trying to preach to the Soviets.

Gorbachev paused for breath, put away his notes and stared at them before starting to speak again, this time in a different tone. "We've told you we want to cooperate, we want dialogue; we want to find answers together with the United States." He was serious about opening up the Soviet system, he said, perhaps even imposing term limits on Communist Party officials. He wanted to make his country more efficient and modern and improve its economy. He realized there were human rights issues to address. It was all on the way, he said, but the United States should not push for change faster than Soviet society—or the Communist Party—could adjust to it.

Shultz thought Gorbachev's statement was "remarkable...for the Communist boss of the Soviet Union." For Powell it was far more. Gorbachev's apparent earnestness convinced him that the ruling reality of his professional life had ceased to exist. "He was saying, in effect, that he was ending the Cold War. The battle between their ideology and ours was over, and they had lost." Gorbachev looked directly at him, Powell later recalled, "knowing I was a military man, and said with a twinkling eye, 'What are you going to do now that you've lost your best enemy?' " Powell would retell the story for years to come, citing it as a moment of tectonic realignment in the world.

The CIA, many in Congress and others in the Reagan administration—some of them in Powell's own office—didn't buy it. They had repeatedly warned that Reagan risked being duped by a Soviet leader whose cleverness and appeal in the West made him even more dangerous than his predecessors. Even if Gorbachev were for real, they cautioned, the Communist Party monolith would never let him succeed.

Powell thought the intelligence community's reluctance to grasp the hand Gorbachev was extending was typical of its tendency to let long-held beliefs block its view of reality and of its inability to use common sense. Disagreement over the issue within the administration continued through the end of Reagan's presidency and into the next administration. Eight months after the successful May 1988 summit took place, as the Soviets were preparing to withdraw their troops from Afghanistan after a decade of occupation, the CIA warned that the Red Army was planning to use chemical weapons in a final assault on U.S.-backed mujahedeen fighters there. "There is no question that this planning is being conducted out of Moscow, and almost certainly with Gorbachev's knowledge given the very high military command level involved," Fritz W. Ermath, a senior CIA official seconded to the NSC, warned in an urgent message to Powell. Ermath recommended sending an immediate, strongly worded protest.

There had been unconfirmed reports of chemical weapons use in the years immediately following the Soviet Union's 1979 invasion and occupation of Afghanistan, but nothing since then, and now the Red Army was leaving. No matter what the so-called intelligence said, Powell thought the idea that the Soviets were planning a chemical weapons attack was a ludicrous example of the usual CIA hyperventilation. He scribbled a reply to Ermath: "Thanks for the note. We'll watch carefully but notwithstanding intel reports, I find it inconceivable, almost, to believe Sovs would use lethal CW [chemical weapons]... during the last month of the war and the week before a worldwide CW conference.... I would really be stunned at such a development. Gorby ain't that dumb." The feared chemical attack never occurred.

It was not only the CIA that tended to see what it believed rather than the other way around. Powell had experienced it up close as a military commander and now saw it regularly as national security adviser. In Nashville to receive an award on July 3, 1988, he and Alma had just gone to sleep after an evening at the Grand Ole Opry when their hotel room telephone rang. It was John Negroponte, Powell's deputy in Washington, relaying a Navy report that the USS *Vincennes*, escorting Kuwaiti oil tankers around the Iran-Iraq war zone, had just come under attack by an Iranian F-14 jet. The *Vincennes* had shot the plane down. Powell woke

Reagan to inform him but cautioned the president to wait for further information; there was something about the report that didn't smell right. The F-14 was a fighter jet used for air interception and combat, not a ground-attack plane. And why would Iran send one plane to attack a massive, heavily armed combat cruiser? Twenty minutes later, Negroponte called back to say that the downed plane was not a jet fighter but an Iranian commercial Airbus on a regularly scheduled flight with 290 civilians aboard. All were presumed dead.

When Powell returned to Washington the next morning, the Navy and the Pentagon reported that the ship had tracked the Iranian plane from takeoff at Bandar Abbas, a joint military-civilian airport in southern Iran. They claimed it had been flying outside the standard commercial flight path, had not responded to radio demands to identify itself and had been descending straight toward the *Vincennes* when the ship fired an SM-2 antiaircraft missile at it. The press statement Powell approved for release by the White House did not dispute the military version of events but left wide room for doubt. "We deeply regret the loss of life and are in the process of investigating the incident.... The Vincennes had about four minutes from the time it picked up the target until it was declared hostile. This is a severe constraint. Given these facts, the USS Vincennes took proper defensive action."

The early explanation eventually proved false on nearly all counts. Iran Air 655, a twice-weekly flight to Dubai, had been ascending after takeoff and was well within a recognized civilian flight path when it appeared on the ship's radar. The *Vincennes* itself had been far off course, sailing four miles inside Iranian territorial waters and forty miles south of where it was supposed to be. Although the ship had radioed four separate identification queries to the plane, all but one were on a military frequency that the airline pilot—still occupied with communications with his own control tower—could not receive. The ship had fallen victim to what psychologists call "scenario fulfillment"—those aboard had seen what they had expected to see.

As the facts emerged, Powell could imagine what had happened almost as if he had been there. The technology-heavy *Vincennes* was sailing in hostile waters, sporadically shooting at small Iranian speedboats threatening the oil tankers. Amid the noise and confusion, the commander had likely received a message from the air warning control center below deck. "It's some junior [non-commissioned officer] who's never been in combat before, who can hear the shots [at the speedboats] outside but doesn't know what's going on," Powell visualized. "His adrenaline is pumping like you wouldn't believe, and he suddenly says 'Bogey!' He's looking at his radar screen, and he sees something that's not supposed to be there and it's coming at them. And the commander says, 'What's its attitude?' And the kid says, 'Descending toward us,' when it was actually climbing away."

Someone in the control center shouts, " 'It's a possible Astro,' " the code word for an F-14. "The captain lets a few seconds go by, and he says, 'What's its attitude?' 'Sir, still descending, gaining speed. On course toward us.' The captain turns to the fire control officer and says, 'Prepare to launch.' And a few seconds later, he asks, 'What's its attitude?' 'Descending toward us, rapidly increasing speed.'

" 'Fire.'

"He never checked, he never looked, he never second-guessed what this kid was telling him," Powell concluded of the captain. It was, he thought, a perfect object lesson in command failure. When something doesn't make sense, "some leader has to say, 'Wait a minute. Stop.' "

Four minutes was plenty of time to make an informed decision. And when the Pentagon realized that had not been done, it simply denied reality and covered up. Eight years later, although no wrongdoing was acknowledged, the United States agreed to a compensation package of $61.8 million, to be divided among the families of the Iranian dead.

Still suffering from the aftereffects of scandal and internal schisms, the Reagan administration limped through its final year. There was no grand strategy and no major initiatives. Powell's main objective was to avoid crisis and keep foreign policy on an even keel. He meticulously planned every minute of Reagan's summits with Gorbachev—in Washington in December 1987, in Moscow during the summer of 1988 and a casual get-together on Governors Island in New York Harbor in the administration's waning days—providing the president with strict talking points and keeping close by his side to intervene if Reagan meandered near any rhetorical abyss.

By the summer of 1988, Powell's name was being bandied about as a possible vice presidential running mate for George H. W. Bush, the presumed Republican nominee to succeed Reagan. A month before the Republican Party nominating convention, the idea gained steam with a July 10 column in *The Washington Post* by George F. Will, a leading conservative commentator with close ties to the Reagan administration. Powell "is bright as a new nickel," Will wrote, and his soundness on foreign policy would underscore the weakness of the likely Democratic nominee, Massachusetts Governor Michael Dukakis. "Some say the nation's residual racism would make Powell's nomination politically imprudent," Will wrote. "They are underestimating the country and the capacity of boldness by a conservative party to have a constructive effect."

The outside buzz created a hum inside the White House itself. Frank Donatelli, Reagan's political affairs adviser, sent Powell a memo the day after Will's column asking about "Your availability to be Vice President. Would you like us to work on the floor demonstration" at the convention? Powell scribbled a reply in the same lighthearted vein that he hoped Donatelli had intended. "Frank, I plan to stay in my hotel room under the bed reading Army field manuals."

Powell had little involvement with the political side of the White House and no relationship with the Republican Party. He liked Bush well enough—although he judged that the vice president's racial consciousness was no higher than Reagan's. But he saw no advantage in being pushed to the political forefront at this point in his career, especially if he planned to return to active duty. He was scheduled to spend a day at the mid-August convention in New Orleans only because Reagan was touching down to give a speech en route to his California ranch.

The civil rights leader and Democratic presidential hopeful Jesse Jackson was asked regularly about Powell and managed simultaneously to praise him and dismiss him as something of an "Uncle Tom." "One has the impression he is in the administration, but not of it—really a military man who is now on assignment," he said. "He will not attain hero status from the masses of black people because Reagan has been so indifferent, so insensitive, to blacks. But there is an appreciation of the predicament of his job."

Not all African Americans were as caustic as Jackson about Powell's political prospects. "The 51-year-old Powell is far more than an attractive black man," the liberal columnist William Raspberry assessed. "He is a military man and a foreign policy expert who takes seriously the need to stand up to the Soviets. He is smart, conservative, self-effacing and intensely loyal. His résumé and his personal characteristics would make him a reasonable bet [for the Republicans] even if he were white. But it is his blackness that transforms him into a can't-miss proposition."

Whatever Bush thought about the suggestion, however, he never mentioned the vice presidency to Powell. Bush and Reagan crossed paths at the New Orleans airport during the week of the convention—the vice president was arriving to accept the nomination as Reagan was leaving for California after delivering his speech. As the Air Force One engines idled on the tarmac, the two slipped into Reagan's cabin for a private chat. After takeoff, Powell looked up to see Reagan enter the staff compartment with a small smile on his face. Bush, the president announced, had confided to him his choice of Indiana Senator Dan Quayle as his running mate.

The day after the November 8 election, a victorious Bush returned to the White House. After a brief Rose Garden welcoming ceremony, the president-elect, to Powell's pleasant surprise, invited him into his West Wing office. He wanted Powell to stay on in the new administration, Bush said, and offered him his choice of two positions: CIA director or deputy secretary of state. Powell's first thoughts were that both were a step down from his current position and either one would require him to leave the Army. He told Bush he would think about it, and that night, went to visit Army Chief of Staff General Carl E. Vuono. Vuono assured him the Army wanted him back and offered Powell the four-star job of chief of FORSCOM, the Forces Command in charge of all of the Army's U.S.-based troops as well as the Reserves.

"When I got home," Powell wrote in his memoirs, "I did what I usually do when faced with a personal decision: I drew up a balance sheet. I put 'Stay' on the left side and 'Go' on the right side, since staying in the Army or going out were my only intentions. I did not want to go to the State Department as number two. It would be a demotion. And I did not want to be the nation's chief spook at the CIA. That was not me."

There was another alternative: he had been approached to join several corporate boards and hit the lecture circuit at up to $20,000 a speech. The money was tempting; after thirty years in the Army, his take-home pay was little more than $3,000 a month. He still had one child in college; he and Alma had only once in their marriage purchased a new car. "I'm thinking of quitting the Army," he told his cousin Bruce Llewellyn, who in the past had helped him out with financial advice and assistance.

Ten years older than Powell, Llewellyn was a wealthy entrepreneur who relished the role of clan patriarch. "Don't you want to be [Army] chief of staff?" he asked. Powell told him it would be another eighteen months before the chief's job was open.

"Give it a shot" at FORSCOM, Llewellyn advised, "and we'll see what happens. If after eighteen months you haven't got what you wanted, then you've exhausted all of your options and you can take off." Don't worry about the money, he said. "We'll take care of it."

Powell conveyed his decision to Bush. On December 1, a Defense Department news release announced that Reagan would "nominate Lieutenant General Colin L. Powell for reassignment as CINC, U.S. Forces Command, Fort McPherson, Georgia." The job came with a fourth star.

As Bush's inauguration approached, Powell penned a commentary for *The New York Times* detailing "an extraordinary combination of events, at the end of the Reagan Administration, that offer the world more hope for peace and freedom than at any time in decades." Headlined "Why History Will Honor Mr. Reagan," it was as much a bouquet for what Powell felt had been accomplished during his own two years at the White House as it was a tribute to the outgoing president: the end of the Iran-Iraq War, the Soviets on the verge of leaving Afghanistan, the departure of Cuban troops from Angola, independence for Namibia, Vietnam's withdrawal from Cambodia and "people power" victories against dictators in the Philippines and South Korea, not to mention warmer feelings between the United States and the Soviet Union. "Something else is going on," Powell wrote, "not only peace but the advance of freedom and democracy."

As Reagan left office, Powell was widely hailed for having brought discipline and moderation to the White House after the frightening disarray of Iran-*contra*. Some commentators declared that the unprecedented rise of a black man to a position of such power and responsibility was a watershed event in American racial history. Powell's mere presence in the administration was seen as a credit to Reagan, no matter what he had accomplished.

African-American newspapers cited Powell and his record of mainstream achievement as a welcome addition to the list of minority role models, anointing him a leader whose influence should, if it didn't already, rival that of Jesse Jackson. On top of being national security adviser, he was about to become the fourth black four-star general in American history and one of only two currently on active duty.

But Powell would soon learn that standing on a pedestal invites stones from all directions. Some were not as willing as he was to overlook the social policies of the people he worked for. "If African-Americans fail to embrace Powell, it is understandable," editorialized Detroit's *Michigan Chronicle,* a leading black newspaper. "It is because of the company he keeps."

10

Reluctance to use military force is an American tradition. I can trace it back from Washington to Grant to Eisenhower. Since war is ultimately a political act, not a military act, give political tools the opportunity to work first.

—Colin L. Powell

Forces Command was the least glamorous and arguably the least prestigious of the military's commands. Most of the other commanders in chief, known as CINCs, led unified combat forces of the Army, Navy and Air Force around the world. FORSCOM was responsible for U.S.-based Army forces, including the Reserve and National Guard, and charged with defending the homeland and getting troops ready for deployment overseas. Once they left American shores, they were someone else's responsibility.

When he arrived at Fort McPherson, the FORSCOM headquarters in southwest Atlanta, in April 1989, Powell was in a holding pattern, waiting for General Carl Vuono to retire as Army chief of staff. But limbo suited neither his energy level nor his sense of himself as a gung ho commander. He set out to make the most of FORSCOM, traveling to the far outposts of his domain, dropping in on troops and surprising Reserve units that had never seen an active-duty general before. When 2,000 soldiers were deployed to fight summer forest fires in the Northwest, he flew out to watch them. He was a frequent public speaker in and around Atlanta and made special efforts to appear at black colleges, where his advice was to do as he had done: work hard, seize opportunity and overcome.

He spent long hours thinking about the future of the military. Nothing had shaken the conviction he had formed a year earlier, sitting in Gorbachev's Kremlin, that the Cold War was on its last legs. The inevitable collapse of the Soviet Union would have deep implications for an American defense establishment that had spent the past half century focused myopically on the threat from Moscow. Pentagon spending was already down 12 percent from its 1985 peak, and if the military did not get out in front of demands for a further "peace dividend," the Democratic Congress would cut it to ribbons.

Powell was convinced that the military had not even begun to anticipate this fast-approaching reality. The service chiefs were still fighting among themselves for ever-larger pieces of a shrinking pie and clinging to personnel and weapons systems as if they were their own children. Powell agreed with the more forward-thinking planners on the Pentagon's joint staff that the defense budget would ultimately be reduced by 20 to 25 percent, with cuts in all the branches. The challenges were how to configure what was left to best accomplish a new, post–Cold War mission and how to make sure the cuts didn't go any deeper than that.

Two years in the White House had given him confidence in his own ideas and in his ability to play at the top of the league, and he saw no one better positioned to maneuver among the executive branch, Congress and the military to determine the country's future defense needs. He did not intend to absent himself from what was likely to be the most significant restructuring of the military's shape and mission in a generation.

Powell unveiled his thoughts for the first time just one month into his FORSCOM command, at a closed-door symposium for senior officers and defense contractors at the Army War College in Carlisle, Pennsylvania. He had worked hard on the speech, which he titled "The Future Just Ain't What It Used to Be," scribbling in and scratching out phrases up to the last minute. Ranging far outside the traditional military purview, he described a world in which peace had begun "to encircle the globe"; where the Soviet Union was so mired in political and economic difficulties that it was rapidly becoming a "benign bear"; and where America's attention had shifted from overseas threats to domestic concerns.

"The dangers in this world seem to spring more from its enormous debt problems and the poverty and joblessness that these problems generate than from irreconcilable East-West tensions," he assessed, and a preoccupied Congress was in no mood to alter the downward trend in defense spending. The American people "want us to continue to act the part of a world superpower and leader ... they continue to want a strong defense ... [but] we can't act in the Nineties as if we had the same public consensus of the early Eighties."

The reaction to his remarks, from an audience on the Pentagon payroll, was less than overwhelming. Powell's description of the inexorable decline of the Soviet threat was also rejected by the new administration in

Washington. At a March 21 ceremony welcoming him to the Pentagon, the new defense secretary, Dick Cheney, warned that Gorbachev's political reforms and peace initiatives might be only a "temporary aberration." Those who "want to declare the Cold War ended ... perceive a significantly lessened threat and want to believe that we can reduce our level of vigilance accordingly," he said. "But I believe caution is in order." Standing at Cheney's side, President Bush averred that "Now is not the time for America and its allies to make unilateral reductions, to relax our defense efforts."

A reprint of Powell's speech in *Army* magazine brought a torrent of calls and letters, most of them warning that the Soviet bear would return to bite him. One correspondent from the conservative Heritage Foundation noted that the assessment of analysts far more astute than Powell "was that the Soviet Union will emerge in the early 1990s from its ongoing 'reorganization and modernization' much stronger militarily than it is today."

Bush had ordered up a review of the nation's defense strategy shortly after taking office, tasking Cabinet departments, the Joint Chiefs and the intelligence community with determining "how, with limited resources, we can best maintain our strength, preserve our Alliances, and meet our commitments in this changing but still dangerous world." The document, labeled National Security Review (NSR) 12, was drafted in part by Condoleezza Rice, a Soviet expert from Stanford University recruited by Bush's national security adviser, Brent Scowcroft, to the new National Security Council staff—the same Condi Rice whose father had worked for Alma Powell's uncle in Birmingham. Despite "hopeful signs" in Moscow, the document cautioned, "it would be reckless to dismantle our military strength and the policies that have helped make the world less dangerous, and foolish to assume that all dangers have disappeared or that any apparent diminution is irreversible."

Inside the Pentagon, a steering group established to formulate the Defense Department's contribution to the review failed to reach consensus. Planners working under Admiral William Crowe, the chairman of the Joint Chiefs of Staff, urged a shift in focus from the permanent "forward basing" of massive numbers of American troops in Europe and planning to counter Soviet expansion in the Third World to new threats that would emanate from the Third World itself. Cheney's undersecretary for defense policy, Paul D. Wolfowitz, a former academic and diplomat who chaired the group, disagreed. Wolfowitz shared his boss's conviction that Soviet aggression, in either Europe or the Persian Gulf oil fields, would continue to be the main threat facing the United States.

Powell had mixed feelings about President Bush. As vice president, Bush had once dressed him down sharply, jabbing his finger at Powell's chest during a foreign policy disagreement. A blatantly race-baiting television advertisement run by Bush's presidential campaign had made Powell uncomfortable. On the other hand, most of their personal interactions in the White House had been pleasant, and although Bush had made clear after the election that he wanted to replace Powell with his own national security adviser, he had been solicitous of Powell's future.

The new president had a human touch that Powell appreciated. Michael Powell had married while his father was working in the White House, and when he and his wife, Jane, produced a first grandchild in the spring of 1989, Bush sent a personal letter to Colin and Alma welcoming them to "the grandparents club." When Powell responded with a letter to "President and Mrs. Bush," Barbara Bush shot back a handwritten note on White House stationery, reminding him that when they had first met she had demanded he call her by her first name. "If you don't call me Barbara, I'll kill you," she wrote, drawing a smiley face and signing "Love, Barbara."

But "Barbara and Colin" aside, Powell had no reason to credit rumors that Bush was considering him to replace Admiral Crowe as chairman of the Joint Chiefs. As the youngest and most junior of the eligible four-star generals, Powell was far from the obvious choice. Besides, the chairmanship was usually rotated among the services, and it was the Air Force's turn.

Dick Cheney and Frank Carlucci had known each other since the Nixon administration, and after Cheney was sworn in as Bush's defense secretary, it was only natural he would turn to his old friend and immediate predecessor in the job for advice. Carlucci briefed him on the department, then turned the conversation to a related subject. "Dick, the one decision you're going to make as defense secretary that will be uniquely important is choosing a chairman," Carlucci said. "Frankly, there's only one candidate as far as I'm concerned." He was nearly operatic in singing Powell's praises.

Aside from their wrangling over *contra* aid and a brief congressional visit to V Corps, Cheney barely knew Powell. But the next four years were going to be a rocky time for the Defense Department. He wanted a chairman who would help him exert strong control over the service chiefs and energetically support the president's policies. Although they had sometimes disagreed, Cheney felt Powell had served Reagan well during a difficult period in the White House. The general was clearly a devoted military man, but he had shown he knew how to be loyal to his civilian leaders.

Cheney himself was Bush's second choice as defense secretary, after Texas Senator John Tower was forced to withdraw his nomination amid allegations of personal impropriety. A lifelong politician who had begun his career as a congressional aide, Cheney was a protégé of Donald Rumsfeld, who had brought him along when he became Gerald Ford's chief of staff after Nixon's resignation in 1974. When Rumsfeld had become defense secretary, Cheney had succeeded him at the White House. After Ford lost the presidency to Jimmy Carter in 1976, Cheney was sent to Congress from his home state of Wyoming and had risen steadily in the ranks of the Republican leadership. As Powell had witnessed in the *contra* debates, Cheney's reputation as a tough-minded conservative was well deserved.

As far as Powell was concerned, the most salient fact about Cheney was his avoidance of the Vietnam draft with no fewer than five separate student and family deferments; during his confirmation hearing, Cheney told the Senate Armed Services Committee that he had "had other priorities in the Sixties than military service." Powell also knew that after nominating Richard Armitage to be secretary of the Army, Cheney had failed to back him when Armitage came under fire from conservative Republicans and the billionaire political gadfly Ross Perot. Armitage withdrew his name before his confirmation hearing and blamed Cheney for pulling the rug out from under him. But Powell had no intention of letting his personal doubts about Cheney stand in the way of his career.

In the summer of 1989, as Crowe neared the end of his term, Cheney stopped to see Powell at Fort McPherson on his way back to Washington after a visit to the Tampa-based Central Command. Neither man raised the subject of the chairmanship during conversations in Powell's office or over lunch at his residence, but it was clear to both of them that the meeting was a preliminary test. Cheney noted to himself with approval that Powell seemed well versed and absorbed in his current job and didn't appear to be lusting after power in Washington. Anxious to appear cool, Powell thought he had managed to convey the message that he was perfectly happy where he was and would have to be asked to move.

Beyond the fact that Powell and Cheney shared a basic belief in a strong American defense and had both once been rumored as potential running mates for Bush, it would have been hard to find two men with less in common. Whereas Powell shunned party politics and ideology, Cheney's well-entrenched views were just short of what Powell considered the loony fringes of the Republican Party. With his slight paunch, receding hairline and wire-rimmed glasses, the secretary seemed older than his forty-eight years. He had already suffered three heart attacks—the last one just a year earlier, in 1988, followed by quadruple bypass surgery. Said to be interested in little beyond politics and fly fishing, Cheney was famously tight-lipped and disdained small talk. In contrast, Powell moved easily between the personal and the professional, between casual conversation and crisp briefing. After several months of dogged workouts at FORSCOM, he had shed the effects of too many cheeseburgers in the White House mess and was now as well starched as he had ever been.

The main roadblock to Powell's selection as chairman was the president. Bush thought Powell was smart and easy to get along with; his sense of humor had gotten them through a lot of tense times during the Reagan administration. But he worried that jumping the most junior four-star general to the top of the list might not sit well with the military, and he wasn't anxious to pick a fight. Cheney was adamant, but Bush made his own private soundings among senior officers who were personal friends before giving preliminary approval.

Powell was with Alma at a commanders' conference in Baltimore on August 8 when the summons to Washington finally came. Cheney sent a helicopter to bring both of them to the Pentagon, and within an hour they were climbing the stairs to the River Entrance, facing the Potomac on the building's north side. With Alma waiting, the meeting was brief; Cheney said he had chosen Powell for the chairmanship, subject to Bush's final agreement, and asked if he wanted the job. As always, it was important to Powell to be perceived as being sought rather than seeking advancement. "If you and the President want me, I'll take it and do my best," he responded. "But you know I'm happy in Atlanta and not looking to move."

Word of Powell's selection leaked out almost immediately, sending the White House scurrying to assemble an official announcement ceremony. Alma decided to return to Atlanta, so Michael, still convalescing after numerous surgeries following his accident, stood with his father in the hot August sun as Bush told reporters assembled in the Rose Garden that Powell was his choice for chairman. The president's description of him as a "complete soldier" made all the headlines the next day, along with the information that he was not only the most junior of eligible officers and the youngest to ever hold the chairmanship, but also the first ROTC graduate and the first black.

Powell was a careful student of military rules and customs, and he knew that by all rights he should never have been selected. His career had been full of interruptions, and being bumped up into a corps command with no stop at division level was heresy. But his confidence in his capacity to lead the armed forces was as hard-wired into his self-image as his belief that he was a grunt who had never lost contact with the soul of the military.

The Sunday after the announcement, Powell made the cover of *Parade*, the largest-circulation magazine in the country. The cover photo by the famed Vietnam War photographer Eddie Adams showed him in full military regalia, his chest full of ribbons and his Ranger tab just below the four stars on his shoulder. He had removed his heavy, black-framed glasses and stared at the camera with his chin resting on his hand and a slight smile on his lips. The story was a cumulus cloud of puffery written in the usual *Parade* profile style. Headlined "Have a Vision," it recounted the inspirational tale of a black hero who "rose from humble origins to the top of his profession—and still lives by the values he learned from his parents." At the end was a boxed list of thirteen aphorisms, copied by the reporter David Wallechinsky from among the slips of paper stuck under the glass atop Powell's desk. They were, he wrote, the general's "rules to live by":

1. It ain't as bad as you think. It will look better in the morning.

2. Get mad, then get over it.

3. Avoid having your ego so close to your position that when your position falls your ego goes with it.

4. It can be done!

5. Be careful what you choose. You may get it.

6. Don't let adverse facts stand in the way of a good decision.

7. Check small things.

8. Share credit.

9. You can't make someone else's choices. You shouldn't let someone else make yours.

10. Remain calm. Be kind.

11. Have a vision. Be demanding.

12. Don't take counsel of your fears or naysayers.

13. Perpetual optimism is a force multiplier.

Some of the sayings under Powell's desk glass didn't make it onto *Parade*'s list, including Thucydides' famous observation that "Of all manifestations of power, restraint impresses men most." Others had been collected over the course of his Army career. "Avoid conservatism"—the lesson he had learned at Fort Leavenworth about the dangers of excessive caution. "You never know what you can get away with until you try"—gleaned from Fred Malek's crafty bureaucratic infighting. "Use your intellect to inform your instincts, but trust your instincts"—codification of his deep suspicion of "elite" military units and the intelligence community.

Powell took over the chairman's office on the Pentagon's second floor on Sunday, October 1, 1989. Crowe had cleaned the place out, leaving row upon row of empty shelves specially made to accommodate his collection of military hats. Alma quickly ordered colonial furniture to replace Crowe's low, modern couches. The windows abutting the River Entrance terrace were covered with yellow security paint that obscured a splendid view of the parade ground and the Potomac Tidal Basin ringed with Japanese cherry trees. Powell ordered them replaced with one-way, bullet-proof glass. If a passerby happened to see him, he told his aides, he would wave.

He arranged for the Pentagon historian to deliver enough generic military history books to fill the shelves, but pride of place was given to the personal items he carried from job to job: the marble pen holder he had won at Fort Bragg in 1957 for being "Best Cadet, Company D"; a portrait of Martin Luther King, Jr., given to him by the slain civil rights leader's widow; a shotgun that Gorbachev had given him as a summit gift; and a painting of Henry Flipper leading 10th Cavalry troops across the plains.

He had a special stand for his bronze bust of Thomas Jefferson, whose first inaugural address, he thought, described what America was all about: political tolerance, equal justice, majority rule with protection of minority rights, the supremacy of the civil over the military, fiscal prudence, the open dissemination of information.

Next to a stand-up desk near the window, he kept a tape player and a collection of music cassettes. His favorites were Caribbean calypsos sung in a dialect unintelligible to anyone who hadn't grown up around it. Most were off-color double entendres, such as "Come Water Me Garden" or the all-time classic recorded by every calypso singer worth his salt, "The Big Bamboo" ("I asked my woman what shall I do, to keep her honest and keep love true. She said, 'The only thing I want from you is a little piece of the Big Bamboo.' ")

In the early morning hours of October 2, less than twenty-four hours after his chairmanship began, Powell was awakened by a call from the Pentagon. A major in the Panamanian Defense Forces (PDF) was initiating a coup against the dictator Manuel Noriega and wanted U.S. military support. Powell activated the high-level telephone tree, waking Cheney, who called Scowcroft, who called Bush. Powell also called General Max Thurman, the new commander of the 13,000-troop Southern Command, based in the Panama Canal Zone. Thurman was an old friend; he had served in DePuy's office with Powell in the early 1970s and at the Pentagon during Powell's Weinberger years. The two generals decided that there wasn't enough information about the coup organizers or their prospects of success for the Americans to dive in—a conclusion borne out the next morning when the plotters delayed the action. When the major finally made his move a day later, Powell advised Bush to hold back, judging the operation a "half-assed" effort by a less-than-courageous officer who had neither a plan nor many followers. Within hours after it began, the coup collapsed with Noriega still in power.

The most troubling lesson of the episode for Powell was that even if the president had decided to intervene, the American military had no comprehensive, updated plan for Panama. He ordered Thurman to put everything else aside and develop one. But he was also disturbed by what he saw as the haphazard handling of the administration's first foreign policy crisis. Bush had wanted to break with Reagan's image of being spoon-fed information in formal meetings in the Situation Room—the secure, wood-paneled conference and communications center in the White House basement—but he and Scowcroft seemed to have thrown the baby out with the bathwater, dismantling the Policy Review Group for NSC deputies that Powell had set up and replacing it with nothing. Decision meetings often amounted to informal sit-downs in the Oval Office called on short notice. If you were there when something important was discussed, fine; if you weren't, too bad.

The Democratic Congress quickly homed in on the disarray, but though Powell agreed with some of the criticism in the wake of the aborted coup he was taken aback by the shrillness of the attack. Senate leaders, in particular, excoriated the administration for what they saw as bumbling indecisiveness and a lack of backbone to take the indicted drug trafficker and tinpot dictator Noriega by force. Powell and Cheney were hauled before the Senate Armed Services Committee, whose Democratic chairman, Sam Nunn of Georgia, noted correctly that the United States had spent two years encouraging a revolt against Noriega but had no real plan for what to do when it happened.

On the plus side, Powell was impressed with how Cheney had handled himself. Throughout the Panama crisis and the subsequent political fall-out, he hadn't lost his head or his temper; he'd taken the criticism in stride and protected his people from outside attacks. Despite Bush's testy and somewhat flustered appearance before the press ten days after the coup attempt—in which he denounced congressional criticism as a "stupid argument"—Powell thought the president had performed reasonably well. When the national security team sat down in the White House residence on October 15 to review the matter, Powell noted with approval that Bush acknowledged the congressional hits but said he was "satisfied with the action we took" and remained determined to grab Noriega and bring him to U.S. justice when the circumstances were right.

The opportunity presented itself on December 16, when Noriega's thugs shot an off-duty American Marine lieutenant in Panama City and roughed up a naval officer and his wife in separate incidents. By then, military plans were in place for everything ranging from a surgical snatch of Noriega to a full-scale invasion, and while Bush still preferred informal Oval Office meetings, Scowcroft had reestablished a deputies committee for more orderly decision making. On Sunday, December 17, Bush met with his senior advisers and was given a unanimous recommendation that he launch a major military attack with two operational objectives: to dismantle the PDF and restore democratic government in Panama and to bring the indicted Noriega to justice.

As the president slouched in his chair beside the Oval Office fireplace and chewed on his bottom lip, Powell flipped through maps showing when, where and with which American units—an additional 14,000 troops were to be flown in to join the Southern Command for the surprise attack, for a total of 27,000—the operation would proceed. Bush said little while the room buzzed with discussion and questions. What would they do if Noriega escaped capture? How many American casualties were likely? Finally, the president rose from his chair and silenced everyone. "Okay, let's do it," he said. "The hell with it."

Operation Just Cause was launched just after midnight on December 20, 1989. The Panamanian military was conquered with relative ease and a civilian government was quickly installed, although it was well into January before Noriega, who had managed to elude U.S. forces and then sought refuge in the Vatican Embassy, was taken into custody. There were deployment glitches, complaints from the media about access to the fighting—an internal department study later blamed Cheney and his press secretary, Pete Williams, for an "excessive concern for secrecy"—and allegations that imprecise bombing had caused unnecessary civilian casualties. Both the United Nations and the Organization of American States censured the U.S. action. But Powell was elated that the largest U.S. military operation in more than fifteen years, carried out on his watch, had been a "clean" victory with minimal American casualties—23 killed in action and 324 wounded—and a quick withdrawal.

"By nature, I'm very cautious about the use of the armed forces . . . putting lives on the line," he had told a reporter just days before the invasion. "But when it's clear we're going to use them, well, let's use them." After the inauspicious beginning of his chairmanship, when the failed coup attempt raised doubts for some about whether he had the grit and boldness for the job, he felt vindicated. The media seemed to agree. The political general had "taken clear command of the Pentagon," gushed a lengthy *Newsday* profile after the Panama operation. "In a brilliant if violent thrust, Powell had proven his military mettle."

Lawrence Wilkerson's interview for a job as Powell's speechwriter and special assistant at FORSCOM had been brief. After a fifteen-minute discussion of his background—he was an Army lieutenant colonel who had served in Vietnam, a Far East specialist and a military academic—Powell asked two questions: Could he write a speech for delivery at a black Baptist church? I could sure try, Wilkerson responded. He was white, but he hailed from South Carolina and had some knowledge of the black church there. No need, Powell said crisply, he could do that himself. Did he want the job? Not really, Wilkerson acknowledged. He hadn't volunteered, and he was happy in his current posting on the faculty of the Naval War College. Good, Powell said with a smile. He liked candor. Wilkerson was hired.

When he moved with Powell to the Pentagon several months later, Wilkerson expected resistance to the new chairman from the senior military leadership. "If he walked into a room of three- and four-star generals, there would be a few who would say 'Never commanded a division' or

'Had a battalion for only a year in Korea' or 'Typical ticket puncher. Brigade for a short time and corps for an even shorter time,' " Wilkerson later recalled. "I thought it myself for some time. What kind of soldier is this guy?"

But during months of sitting in FORSCOM meetings and traveling to Army posts around the country with Powell, he had settled on an answer. "If you thrust him in the middle of a major conflict, would he do well as a corps commander? Hell, I don't know. Who knows that about anybody? But his leadership skills were so good that it didn't even matter whether or not his knowledge or experience were as deep as they should be."

It was obvious to Powell that the chairman's office would require all the leadership skills he could muster and that he would have to move quickly to assert his authority. He would be aided immeasurably by a law that had gone into effect in 1986, officially titled the "Department of Defense Reorganization Act" but commonly called "Goldwater-Nichols" after its congressional authors. The end product of years of teeth gnashing on Capitol Hill and in the military over Vietnam and the inability of the service branches to get along with one another, Goldwater-Nichols had reorganized the "joint" staff at the Pentagon into a think tank for the chairman—rather than a place for each service to dump dead-end offi-cers—and had given the chairman himself important new powers. Now designated the principal military adviser to the president and the secre-tary of defense, he was no longer merely a conduit for the consensus views of the Army, Navy, Air Force and Marine chiefs that usually resulted in lowest-common-denominator, back-scratching recommenda-tions. The chairman's advice to the civilian leadership would reflect his own views, informed but not dictated by the opinions of the other service chiefs. Powell would be the first chairman to serve a full term with the new powers, and he was determined to take them as far as they would go.

He had read all about management theory during his many years of military study, including Frederick Herzberg on "job enrichment" and Abraham Maslow's "Hierarchy of Needs." Leadership was an amalgam of personality, process and ideas. Rather than gathering with the chiefs in the "tank," their secure conference room where each normally arrived with a retinue of colonels and other aides, Powell installed a small, round mahogany table in his office and told them that on most occasions they would meet with him there, alone, without note takers or a written agenda. Ostensibly designed to intensify their relationships and diminish posturing, the move also served to solidify his authority and home-turf advantage. He eliminated most of the paper that cluttered even the most mundane gatherings. He was no longer a member of their committee; they were all advisers to the defense secretary and the president, but by law, he was the "principal" one.

"He was a completely different guy" from Crowe, recalled Charles Boyd, who observed Powell's chairmanship both in the Pentagon as a top operations officer for the Air Force chief and as deputy chief of the European Command in Stuttgart. "The thing I thought about Powell was that on any issue he could see the political ramifications of it, while to varying degrees the four service chiefs would see some military angle... something that was going to affect their institution." Unlike the chiefs, whose fealty extended only as far as the executive branch, Powell saw Congress as another power center to woo.

From the chiefs' perspective, Powell was not always forthcoming about his political activities. "Colin was a bit—defensive is not quite the word, but he had to assert himself and make sure everybody knew he was the chairman," Boyd recalled. "Crowe's approach [after Goldwater-Nichols] was, we're not going to do much different.... Powell didn't have any notion of that at all. Powell was quite content to go over to the [White House] principals meeting and not ask anybody's opinion before he went, and not necessarily debrief when he came back."

Powell met with his own senior staff each morning at 8:30—he arrived in the conference room at precisely 8:31 and made it clear that anyone who entered after he did was inexcusably late. As in his sessions with the chiefs, he abolished the formal briefing format and went around the room asking each officer to report on what was going on in his area—no agenda, no charts, no papers. In most cases, he already knew the answers. He had ordered what amounted to a personal switchboard installed in his office, a massive console with direct lines around the building and to headquarters around the world, and he made a round of calls first thing every morning.

He was a stickler for efficiency and preparation, Powell told them, but he liked a light touch around the office. They should expect him to tell jokes, ask about their spouses and children, grill the secretaries about their boyfriends and steal candy off their desks. He wasn't interested in many of the trappings traditionally accorded the nation's most senior military officer. When he traveled, he didn't expect royal treatment. He had no special food requirements; he liked cheeseburgers. He wasn't averse to a shot of rum at the end of a hard day on the road, but they shouldn't go scurrying around looking for any particular brand. He told them he didn't need a special room or bed, and then he proved it by having himself booked at the Holiday Inn on visits to NATO headquarters in Brussels. It was partly genuine, partly designed to let them know that he was different, that he was both approachable and demanding and that he was in charge.

William Smullen had been Crowe's communications aide and press spokesman and had agreed to Powell's request that he stay on. But after a few weeks of twiddling his thumbs, Smullen told his wife he thought he'd made a mistake. The new chairman's work style didn't leave much room for assistance, and he seemed supremely confident of his ability to manage his own public image. Powell was routinely ignoring Smullen's suggestions for interviews and speeches, setting up his own appointments and establishing his own relationships with reporters.

It was only after several months of unhappiness that Smullen was finally called into the chairman's office on the eve of the Panama invasion, sworn to secrecy and told to get ready for several days of major activity. To Smullen's surprise, Powell wanted him at his side in the Command Center. Once the attack began, the chairman allowed Smullen to set up interviews and press conferences and even asked his advice on public statements. Powell finally seemed to have realized, Smullen concluded with satisfaction, that being chairman was a bigger and more complicated job than being a corps commander or even a CINC.

To help smooth the way for Smullen and other aides, Powell handed out a list of rules under the heading "How to Survive as My Aide—Or What Not to Do."

—Don't ever hesitate to ask me what to do if uncertain.

—Don't ever sign my name.

—Never use your money on my behalf.

—Avoid "The General Wants" syndrome—unless I really do.

—Provide feedback but be tactful to those who ask—talks between you and me are private and confidential. Alma has nothing to do with the office.

—Never keep anybody waiting on the phone. Call back.

—I like meetings generally uninterrupted. I ask a lot of questions. I like questions and challenges.

—I like to remain enormously accessible. I like to do things
with people.

—I will develop ways of getting to know what's happening.

—Don't accept speaking engagements without my
knowledge.

—Keep track of whom I have seen.

—I tend to get moody, preoccupied. I will snap but that
clears the air.

—Be punctual, don't waste my time.

—I prefer written information rather than oral. Writing tends
to discipline.

—I like to do paperwork—and I do a lot.

—NEVER, NEVER permit illegal or stupid actions.

—No surprises. Bad news doesn't get any better with time.

—If there is a problem brewing, I want to know of it early—
heads up as soon as possible—I don't like to be blindsided.

—Speak precisely—I often fudge for a purpose. Don't over-
interpret what I say.

—Don't rush into decisions—make them timely and correct.

—I like excellent correspondence—no split infinitives.

The confluence of congressional budget pressure and the disintegration
of the Soviet empire in Eastern Europe began to surge by the fall of 1989,
but the Bush administration was still searching for a new defense strategy.
Normally, the executive branch would develop a policy and hand it over
to the military to implement. But the NSR-12 process had achieved little,
and Powell saw a void to fill. His brief did not extend to foreign policy, but
as far as he was concerned the only way to plan for future defense was to
anticipate what the future world would look like and design an armed
force to address it. It was, he later wrote, "analysis by instinct... I was not
going on intelligence estimates, war games, or computer projections. My
thoughts were guided simply by what I had observed at world summits,
by my experience at the NSC, [and] by what I like to think of as informed
intuition."

In early November, barely a month into his chairmanship, he presented an initial outline of his ideas to his strategic planning staff. The Soviet Union, he predicted, would soon become either a federation or a commonwealth, withdraw from Eastern Europe, decrease its military budget by 40 percent and cut its force levels in half. The demise of the Warsaw Pact and reunification of Germany would present new opportunities for expanding NATO and recasting its mission away from Cold War tank battles in Germany and toward regional concerns. In handwritten notes he titled "Strategic Overview—1994," he anticipated a black majority government in South Africa and projected trouble spots around the world: "Korea, Lebanon, the Persian Gulf, Philippines." Under the subheading "Potential U.S. Involvement," he listed two places: Korea and the Persian Gulf. In one of the few areas where history would subsequently prove him wrong, he predicted an early improvement in relations between North and South Korea.

Standing long-existing practice on its head, Powell concluded that the point of departure for defense planning should no longer be a specific threat—the Soviet Union or any other—but a forward-looking assessment of America's role in the world and the overall capabilities needed to preserve it against future threats large and small, seen and unseen. He envisioned forces organized into four "baskets": an Atlantic force, including heavy air and sealift components to protect U.S. interests in Europe, the Middle East and the Persian Gulf; a Pacific force, primarily maritime; a contingency force with rapid-response and special operations capabilities; and a strategic force to maintain America's nuclear capability. He proposed phased reductions in U.S. forces permanently stationed in Europe and South Korea and a cut in overall Army strength from 760,000 troops in eighteen divisions to twelve active-strength divisions totaling 525,000 troops, with similar reductions in the other service branches. Half of the nation's current 1,000 intercontinental ballistic missiles—and, eventually, all of the Army's tactical nuclear force—would be eliminated. Configured in the right way, with the right training and equipment, it was enough to meet any contingency and, if necessary, to fight two simultaneous wars, and hopefully it would be enough to satisfy Congress's budget-cutting lust. Overall, the military and foreign policy components of the plan were the closest he had ever come to true strategic thinking— a long-term vision of America's place in the world of the future.

Cheney gave Powell's ideas a fair hearing, but both the secretary and Wolfowitz, his chief strategist, remained skeptical that the USSR's collapse was as imminent as Powell seemed to believe. Cheney had already projected that the defense budget could not tolerate cuts of more than 10 percent over the next five years. Bush expressed similar concerns but allowed his chairman to continue working on the issue.

After several years in the upper echelons of political power, Powell found it increasingly difficult to "pay the king his shilling." He had to remind himself to give due deference to the secretary of defense, and it sometimes took an explicit reminder from Cheney himself. The secretary chastised him more than once during the first few months of their working relationship for insisting that all military routes to Cheney's office pass through Powell and for straying too far afield from his military writ into foreign policy. Cheney was far and away the most conservative member of Bush's national security team. Observing the interaction between them, Brent Scowcroft noted that Powell tried whenever possible to avoid contradicting or disagreeing with Cheney, but when it was unavoidable Powell's position was always the more moderate one.

Relations between the two men were proper and professional; they were close only in terms of physical proximity. They never socialized with each other outside the Pentagon, and during more than three years of daily contact they rarely had conversations that were not directly related to work. The nearest they came to personal moments were a few shared lunches in Powell's office—where Cheney, under strict orders from his wife to watch his intake of fat, could sneak a forbidden burger—and a celebratory breakfast after staying up all night during the Panama invasion. When Democratic House members first introduced a bill to end a Pentagon ban on homosexuals in the military, Cheney confided to Powell that he might have a problem leading the fight against it since one of his two daughters was a lesbian. But the discussion was more political than personal. Powell told Cheney that his secret was fairly widely known around Washington and assured him that the chiefs would handle the issue for him and the president.

Powell thought he and Cheney understood each other; they both played by big-league rules—if you screwed up, you were on your own. Cheney gave him a long leash to explore the limits of his power vis-à-vis the services and to continue working on the new force structure, but he made clear he would yank it tight if Powell went too far astray. When Powell told a *Washington Post* reporter in May 1990 that he thought the defense budget could be reduced by as much as 25 percent over the next five years—more than double Cheney's projection—the secretary called him onto the carpet to question his support for the president and ask whether he was still "on the team." Even if Cheney wasn't keeping close tabs himself, Powell always felt under the watchful gaze of his boss's civilian aides—Wolfowitz and his deputy, I. Lewis "Scooter" Libby; and Stephen Hadley, who had taken Armitage's former job as assistant secretary for international security.

Powell continued to work on his restructuring plan while doing his best to placate the chiefs, who not only opposed many of the cuts he envisioned but also resented what they saw as his failure to adequately inform or consult with them. Most of his direct negotiations were with Wolfowitz, who was immersed in writing the overall Defense Planning Guide that would incorporate any force restructuring. Neither Cheney nor Bush had signed off on Powell's proposals yet. But he worked Congress on his own, holding private conversations with Sam Nunn, among others, and continuing to talk to civilian and military audiences—and reporters—about the new military configuration he called the "Base Force" as well as a range of foreign policy issues.

Congress's insistence on major defense cuts grew as Gorbachev survived, the Berlin Wall fell and Eastern Europe blossomed with independence. Although Cheney and Wolfowitz insisted on caveats about the possibility of a Soviet resurgence, they eventually agreed on a blueprint for America's future defense configuration that adopted nearly all of Powell's proposals for downsizing and restructuring. At an Oval Office meeting on June 26, 1990, Bush approved the overall direction of the plan and scheduled a presidential speech to unveil it. After eight months of painstaking negotiation and tinkering, it was a major triumph for Powell. But by the time Bush delivered the speech on the afternoon of August 2, at the annual Aspen Institute Symposium in Colorado, America's attention was diverted halfway around the world. Just hours earlier, four divisions of Iraqi troops, led by Saddam Hussein's Republican Guard and hundreds of Soviet-made T-72 tanks, had crossed the border from Iraq into neighboring Kuwait.

The United States had maneuvered for advantage throughout the 1980–88 Iran-Iraq War while publicly maintaining its neutrality. The Bush administration came into office determined to continue Reagan's surreptitious tilt toward Baghdad in the belief that Iran—the arms-for-hostages deviation notwithstanding—remained the bigger threat to the interests of the United States and its regional ally, Israel. A strong Iraq would check any Iranian thoughts of aggression, and although Washington had occasionally expressed concern about Saddam's human rights abuses and use of chemical weapons, Bush was willing to let bygones be bygones. "Normal relations" with Iraq, including opportunities for U.S. businesses to participate in war reconstruction and the provision of non-lethal military aid, "would serve our longer-term interests and promote stability in both the Gulf and the Middle East," Bush decreed in an October 1989 National Security Directive.

Powell, too, thought Hussein was "a good demon" whose draconian presence kept his potentially fractious country intact as a bulwark against Iran. As Reagan's national security adviser in 1988, Powell had recommended that the Iran-Iraq War end with a cease-fire rather than a negotiated peace, commenting that it would be better if "they stare at each other forever . . . and not turn their attention elsewhere." But by the summer of 1990, as a long-standing dispute with Kuwait over territory and oil boiled over, Iraq's belligerent gaze had shifted south.

Powell would later acknowledge that the Pentagon had waited too long to become alarmed when American intelligence warned in mid-July that Saddam was moving troops toward the border. He opened a close line of communication with General Norman H. Schwarzkopf, the burly, outspoken CENTCOM commander whose regional territory included the Persian Gulf, but the administration adopted a policy of watching and waiting. On Thursday, July 27, the Saudi ambassador, Prince Bandar bin Sultan, had visited Powell in his Pentagon office to tell him that the kingdom saw the dispute cooling and had concluded there would be no Iraqi move against Kuwait. That night, Colin and Alma went to the White House to watch a movie with George and Barbara Bush—the president thought Powell would enjoy the just-released *Memphis Belle,* about a World War II bomber crew flying dangerous missions over Europe.

By August 1, as Iraqi tanks lined up on the border, it was clear that Bandar had been wrong. After briefing Cheney on satellite intelligence, Powell suggested that Bush send an urgent message warning Saddam to back off. But before the idea had wended its way through the White House bureaucracy to the president, the tanks began to roll and Kuwait was overtaken.

Although they had discounted the likelihood of an invasion until it was too late, there was no question among the members of Bush's national security team—Scowcroft and his deputy, Bob Gates, Cheney, Powell, Secretary of State James A. Baker, CIA Director William Webster and the president himself—that Iraq's move threatened U.S. interests. OPEC— the Organization of the Petroleum Exporting Countries—was already immersed in a struggle between producing countries sympathetic to the United States, including Saudi Arabia, and radicals, including Iraq, that wanted to limit production, raise prices and squeeze the industrialized world. With its own oil and Kuwait's, Baghdad now controlled 20 percent of the world's known reserves, and the massive Saudi fields were only an hour's tank drive away. "Naked aggression against an unoffending country" was a serious concern and a legal justification for a response, Scowcroft later acknowledged. "But what gave enormous urgency to it was the issue of oil."

An initial White House meeting the morning after the invasion was chaotic, as an intelligence briefing and a report on early diplomatic consultations quickly descended into an anxious discussion of the stock market and oil prices. Asked for military options, Powell and Schwarzkopf explained that they were limited: a few ships in the Persian Gulf that could hit some Iraqi targets immediately and fighter planes that could arrive in the region within a few days, provided the Saudis gave them permission to land. Powell thought that kind of pinprick attack made no sense. It would let off some American steam but do little to improve the situation on the ground and likely make it worse, with the Americans in no position to follow up on initial air strikes. There was a plan on the Pentagon shelf for defending the Saudi oil fields, Schwarzkopf said; it included 200,000 American troops and would require temporary basing rights from the Saudis and several months to implement.

It was the kind of disorderly session that drove Powell crazy—people talking at random and going off on tangents with no clear agenda or path to a decision. They were all looking for military options but had no idea what they wanted to achieve. He tried to steer the conversation, asking whether getting into a war over Kuwait was in America's interest and proposing that they direct their energies toward defending Saudi Arabia. After the meeting broke up without any answers, Scowcroft was even more distressed by the session than Powell, although for a different reason. All this talk about lines in the sand, he told Bush with some consternation later that day, indicated that the president's advisers considered Iraq's aggression in Kuwait acceptable as long as it didn't cross the Saudi border.

Bush and Scowcroft left the meeting and headed to Colorado for the Base Force speech, while Powell rushed to a telephone to call Alma and check on the surgery Michael was undergoing that morning. On 100 percent disability since his accident, Michael was working in the Pentagon as a civilian on East Asia issues. But he was far from finished with the numerous operations that were gradually rebuilding the lower part of his body. By early afternoon, Michael was in recovery and Powell went to Capitol

Hill with Cheney and Wolfowitz to begin selling the Base Force. But all Congress wanted to hear about was Iraq.

When the team convened again the following morning, the tone had changed. Scowcroft began by saying he had detected a note of "acquiescence" in the previous day's meeting, and "my personal judgment is that the stakes in this for the United States are such that to accommodate Iraq [in Kuwait] should not be a policy option." Jumping aboard, Deputy Secretary of State Lawrence Eagleburger, who sat in Baker's chair while the secretary was traveling overseas, worried that Israel could be Saddam Hussein's next target. Cheney pointed out the potential for a major U.S. conflict with Iraq and warned not to underestimate the size of the military force that would be needed.

Needed for what? Powell asked himself. The talk still seemed all over the map. Just moments before, as they were assembling in the Cabinet Room, Bush had told waiting reporters that he was not considering any military intervention at all. Now they seemed to have moved beyond doing nothing and jumped right over defending Saudi Arabia to an American military rescue of Kuwait. He tried again to nudge the conversation toward specific military objectives and long-term U.S. interests. Both the president and Scowcroft shot glances at him; he knew he was starting to annoy them, but he kept on. He felt there were ghosts in the room—certainly Vietnam, where tens of thousands of young Americans had been killed when senior military leaders had allowed themselves to be co-opted by civilians who refused to face reality; but also Beirut, where 241 Marines had died as pawns in a political game. He felt that no one else in attendance could bring his breadth and depth of experience to bear on the issue—a frontline soldier and a commander, adviser to a secretary of defense and a president. This was *his* Vietnam, *his* Lebanon, and he was damned if history would repeat itself on his watch. The only way to avoid it was to put everything on the table and have an honest discussion.

Later that day, Powell was relieved to hear Bush's decision: they would squeeze Saddam with diplomatic and economic pressure and try to force him to withdraw from Kuwait. For now, American troops would be dispatched only to protect Saudi Arabia from further Iraqi advances. The deployment would require the Saudis' agreement, and Prince Bandar was summoned first to the White House and then to the Pentagon to be briefed on plans to send ships, aircraft and 200,000 troops to the kingdom. If they began immediately, the force would be fully in place by the beginning of December. Cheney and Schwarzkopf would go to Saudi Arabia personally to seek agreement from King Fahd.

After Bandar left, Cheney and Powell sat alone. They normally met at 5 p.m. to discuss the day's events, but this time Cheney did nearly all the talking. Powell was the president's military adviser, he said, not his national security adviser. His job was not to force a discussion or press Bush for policy answers; it was to provide a range of military options and then shut up. The way Cheney said it led Powell to believe that his interjections that morning and the day before had been the subject of a discussion outside his presence, probably between Cheney and Scowcroft. With what was likely to be the biggest crisis of his chairmanship barely two days old, he knew he had misstepped. But the more he thought about it, the less repentant he was. "If it caused me to be the skunk at the picnic," he told an interviewer several years later, they could all "take a deep smell."

On Saturday, August 4, the national security team gathered at Camp David, the presidential retreat in the Maryland countryside, to hear Powell and the CENTCOM officers more thoroughly outline a plan to defend Saudi Arabia. Most of the team returned to Washington that evening, leaving Bush to enjoy the rest of the weekend. On Sunday afternoon, Powell was watching the television news at home as Marine One landed on the South Lawn behind the White House. With cameras rolling, the president stepped from the helicopter and walked to a group of waiting reporters to express his determination "to reverse" the Iraqi invasion. "This will not stand, this aggression against Kuwait," Bush vowed.

Bush was already changing the agreed-upon mission from defending Saudi Arabia to liberating Kuwait, Powell thought uneasily. But when he went alone to the White House at 5 p.m. to brief the president on events over the last twenty-four hours, he kept his concerns to himself.

Within a week, the United Nations Security Council voted to impose full economic sanctions on Iraq, stopping oil exports and prohibiting all imports except food and medicine. American troops began arriving in Saudi Arabia for the operation they called Desert Shield. Flying back to Washington after a quick visit with Schwarzkopf in Tampa on August 14, Powell began to sketch out the update he would give the president at the Pentagon the next day. It was both necessary and desirable that Bush quickly activate Reserve forces, he would say. He had long ago concluded that President Johnson's refusal to call up the Reserves during Vietnam had been an act of political cowardice; when the military had reorganized itself after the war, it had made sure that the Reserves would be a necessary component of any large operation.

All elements of the defensive deployment would be through the far end of the pipeline by early December, Powell planned to tell Bush. If the president wanted to change the mission from defense to offense and keep the buildup flowing without pause until there were enough troops to attack the Iraqis in Kuwait, he had to decide by the end of October.

Powell privately made a list of questions beyond his own responsibilities that he thought would have to be answered before that decision was made. Absent a further Iraqi provocation, going into Kuwait after Saddam's forces would be an act of war. Would the Saudis or the United Nations—or even the American people—support it? Was congressional authorization required? If American troops liberated Kuwait, would they leave a deterrent force in place? Would they move beyond Kuwait into Iraq itself to try to unseat Saddam? Was a weakened or fractured Iraq in America's interest?

As August rushed into September, Powell found Bush increasingly agitated over the status quo of the Iraqi occupation, anxious to do something decisive and repeatedly asking why they couldn't just bomb Saddam out of Kuwait from the air. Powell had been present at the birth of the Air-Land Battle concept after Vietnam, and he was absolutely certain that an air campaign alone was not enough. Bombing could soften up an enemy and degrade its command and control systems, but territorial victories were won on the ground. A premature air attack might spark the very thing they were trying to avoid—an Iraqi move into Saudi Arabia—at a time when the still-deploying U.S. ground forces were not yet ready to take on the 150,000 troops and 1,200 tanks their own intelligence told them Saddam could instantly throw at them.

Just as important, the administration had persuaded much of the world to support its sanctions resolution at the United Nations; why would they want to abandon containment when it was just getting started? A massive public diplomacy effort painting Saddam as an illegal aggressor and soliciting military allies to defend Saudi Arabia was under way, even as American intelligence operatives were covertly trying to promote an internal revolt among his own people. Attacking now from the air would undermine all of it.

Powell's concerns posed a dilemma for him. He had risen steadily through the military and four administrations by maintaining a careful balance between deliberate prudence and intrepid competence. He had been the quintessential staff officer who could make things happen for those with more stars on their shoulders or a majority of votes in their pockets. He had already been burned for speaking beyond his chairman's brief, and his instincts advised caution. But he was worried that Bush was working himself up to do something that was neither politically nor militarily wise and that no one else was telling him to think twice before acting.

In early September, Powell spoke privately with Baker, Scowcroft and Cheney, hoping that they would use their influence to help slow Bush down. Wasn't it their joint responsibility to make sure the president had a good understanding of all the options, he asked, including the possibility that containment would succeed? Were they confident that Bush knew what the military was and was not capable of doing at this stage in the deployment? Of the three, only Baker, the diplomat, thought there was a modest chance that sanctions and the threat of force would persuade Saddam to withdraw. Scowcroft said he didn't think Bush was willing to wait around for sanctions to work. Cheney, having put Powell into his box just weeks earlier, allowed him to vent until finally, on September 24, he invited the chairman to come over to the White House that very afternoon and tell the president what he was thinking.

Powell felt ill-prepared as he and Cheney walked into the sun-brightened Oval Office, where Bush was seated behind his desk engaged in conversation with Scowcroft and John Sununu, the White House chief of staff. He would have preferred a chance to collect his thoughts and present them more formally in the Situation Room, but there was no time for that now. General Powell has something he wants to say, Cheney told the president.

Nearly two months into the crisis, Powell began, Bush still had two broad options available for dealing with Iraq. One was to attack sooner rather than later, with or without additional Iraqi provocation. Although an air assault could do considerable damage, it was unlikely to radically alter the situation on the ground by itself. Hussein might respond by killing large numbers of Kuwaitis, harming American civilians still present in both countries or blowing up the oil fields. If attack was what the president wanted, the best guarantee for success was a full-scale air-land-sea assault, but U.S. forces were not yet in optimum position to do it. He laid out air capabilities and the current stage of deployment, explaining that if they tried to push more troops and equipment through the pipeline now, it would bottleneck. The decision deadline for changing the mission from defense to offense, he reminded, was the end of October; if Bush gave the go-ahead then, they would extend the buildup and be set to launch an attack sometime in January.

Option two, assuming no further Iraqi provocation, was continued containment and strangulation. Saddam had not abandoned Kuwait, but neither had he shown any indication that he was preparing to advance into Saudi Arabia. They could cap the deployment at the defensive level in early December and begin regular troop rotations, with plans to gradually replace the Americans with an Arab deterrent force. They could tighten the sanctions until Saddam cried uncle. The advantages of containment were several: minimal risk to precious American lives, maintenance of international support and stability in the oil market. The possibility of a decision down the road to send more troops and attack if Iraq did not capitulate would still be there. The disadvantages, of course, included at least the temporary surrender of Kuwait.

Powell himself wasn't sure whether his main concern was going to war too soon or going at all when it wasn't absolutely necessary. If Bush had asked him which option he favored, he later thought, he would have recommended keeping sanctions in place for as long as possible, until it was certain they would fail. At the very least, he would have said, don't be tempted to attack now; use the time available to you to build political and public support for war and give the military time to get ready. Because if you order us to move prematurely, we can't guarantee success.

He was relieved when Bush didn't ask. He was satisfied that he had done what the chiefs had failed to do in Vietnam and Beirut and that all the cards were on the table. But there was no point in moving so far in one direction that he risked isolation. It was one thing to be the skunk at a picnic; nobody wanted one stinking up the White House.

Powell considered his presentation a seminal moment for the military, for his own stature as a senior adviser and for the course of decision making on Iraq. But it seemed to have little impact on Bush. Two days earlier, the president had written in his diary of his hardened resolve to forcibly eject the Iraqis from Kuwait and wondered "if we need to speed up the timetable." After Powell finished his pitch, Bush thanked him and said it was "good to consider all the angles." However, he added, he didn't think sanctions were going to work.

As the October decision deadline approached, Powell again went to see Baker. The secretary of state and the chairman spoke frequently outside regular channels, and Powell asked him specifically this time not to tell Cheney about their conversation. "Powell and I were pretty much of one mind," Baker later wrote of their October 19 meeting. While both still believed that containment was a viable option, the White House was clearly far along the road in the other direction—Bush's rhetorical comparisons of Iraq to Nazi Germany and Saddam to Hitler were escalating. War seemed a foregone conclusion, and the two men agreed that they needed to begin laying the groundwork for Bush's acceptance of the political and diplomatic roadblocks that would have to be negotiated and the massive size of the military force that offensive action would require. Baker felt strongly that they needed both United Nations and congressional approval, and he made the case to Bush on Sunday, October 21, over a drink in the White House residence. He found Bush "interested" and "generally sympathetic" to the political checklist he laid out but unwilling to commit himself.

As Baker was meeting with Bush, Powell left for Riyadh to check on Schwarzkopf's progress on the offensive plan he would present for a decision the following week. A preliminary scenario presented by CENT-COM officers in early October had been rejected by the White House as inadequate. The meeting had not gone well; the commanders felt their planning process was being rushed, while Bush and the civilian advisers suspected that the military "didn't want to do the job," as Scowcroft put it.

To Powell's intense irritation, Cheney had then circumvented the military process by asking civilian Pentagon planners to produce what he considered more "imaginative" options. But even Powell agreed that the initial plan, however unfairly hurried, was severely lacking. There was a lot at stake; the lives of American soldiers and their chances of success would depend on the resources and strategy they carried into battle. It was Schwarzkopf's plan to author but Powell's responsibility to make sure that the force was matched to the task at hand and then to sell it to the civilian leadership.

Powell had set up a direct communication channel with the Riyadh headquarters, establishing himself as the sole nexus between the commander in the field and the commander in chief in Washington. The arrangement not only satisfied his own desire for control, it allowed him to serve as a buffer for Schwarzkopf, a volatile man whose fuse had shortened during nearly three months in the Saudi desert. They were of the same Vietnam generation; Schwarzkopf had arrived at the Americal Division as a battalion commander just as Powell was leaving in 1969. They shared memories of an unpopular, failed war that had left the Army in shambles, and they had the same concerns about being forced to launch prematurely into Kuwait with a plan that substituted "imagination" for massive numbers of men and weaponry. When Powell arrived in Riyadh, Schwarzkopf told him with a mixture of belligerence and trepidation that his final plan for the offensive would take nearly half a million troops—

"a force almost as big as the one we sent to Vietnam." Powell promised that there would be no halfway effort. The U.S. military would provide what they both believed was necessary to do it right.

As he prepared for the October 30 decision meeting at the White House, Powell went over Schwarzkopf's new plan again and again, committing every detail to memory. He always tried to speak without notes, believing it engendered confidence in what he had to say and forced his audience to pay attention. His staff had prepared charts and maps detailing all the options and variables, including the current disposition of forces and the defensive strategy, future deployments and the offensive plan.

The offensive, if that was the option Bush chose, would start with a three-phase air assault on Iraq, he began. If Hussein refused to yield, a heavy ground attack from the south and west would follow. In the wood-paneled hush of the Situation Room, Powell moved the red dot of his laser pointer over the two-dimensional terrain. The defensive force Bush had approved in August, totaling 250,000 troops, would be fully deployed on schedule by December 1, he said. The war plan would require at least another 200,000, plus six carrier task forces and additional aircraft. If the president gave the order now, the offensive option would be in place by January 15.

Scowcroft was taken aback by the size of the attack force Powell was proposing. The military, he felt, had moved from reluctance to undertake an offensive operation at all to a deliberately inflated plan designed to make the president think twice about the effort. Bush asked again why airpower wasn't enough, and Powell replied that he would be "the happiest soldier in the Army if the Iraqis turned tail when the bombs start falling." But he didn't believe it would happen, and they couldn't take the chance—if they decided to attack, they would have to seize the initiative and impose their will decisively on the enemy. Don't worry about the numbers, he said. Deploying too few troops would risk a prolonged battle, higher casualties and even failure. After a victory, no one would argue that the force had been too big; people would say they had been prudent.

With American lives at stake, Powell still believed nothing would be lost by waiting, as the Iraqis still hadn't moved one way or the other. But he had spoken his mind on sanctions, and there was no point in bringing the subject up again. With little further discussion, Bush ordered the offensive deployments to proceed and dispatched Baker to gather allies and build support for a new U.N. resolution authorizing war. Saddam would have less than three months to get out of Kuwait voluntarily before the full force of the American military came after him.

That night, Powell sat at home in his study and filed a note to himself. Amazingly, he wrote, the White House had gone past containment without pause or serious debate. But he felt he had done what his conscience and duty required; the American people had elected Bush to make such decisions. Powell had his orders.

Baker spent three grueling weeks on the road, visiting twelve capitals on three continents, and on November 29 his shuttle diplomacy paid off: the United Nations authorized the use of "all necessary means" to drive Iraqi forces from Kuwait if they failed to withdraw by January 15 and to "restore international peace and security in the area." Security Council Resolution 678 passed by a vote of 12–2, with China abstaining and Cuba and Yemen voting no.

The Soviet support for the U.S.-sponsored resolution, while grudging, was unprecedented, and it confirmed Powell's assessment of the new relationship between Washington and Moscow. It also reaffirmed his faith in the United Nations. He had never shared the antipathy of conservative Republicans toward the international body; the United Nations was in the admirable business of preventing and ending wars. The endless diplomatic posturing could be tedious, but the organization had shown its value to American foreign policy, most recently by easing the Soviet exit from Afghanistan and helping to bring the Iran-Iraq War to an end. In a speech at the National Defense University the day after the vote, Powell acknowledged that the U.S.-U.N. relationship had been rocky at times in the past but said he was "bullish" about its future. "I am very supportive of the United Nations," he told an audience of military students and faculty. "And I think that as part of moving into this new era, we should align ourselves more and more closely with [its] activities."

Powell was pleased that a premature launch of the offensive had been avoided; Bush had settled down and let the military follow its plan and schedule. As the end of the year approached and the Iraqis continued to dig in, systematically looting and destroying Kuwait in the process, he finally concluded that the president had been right all along about sanctions—they weren't going to work.

The week before Christmas, Powell and Cheney traveled to Saudi Arabia to check on the troop deployments. Dressed in desert camouflage, Powell was the main attraction at a series of rallies for tens of thousands of American soldiers and airmen bivouacked in sprawling tent cities across the eastern Saudi desert. Cheney, in slacks and a suede jacket, paled beside the chairman, who pumped up his team with all the fervor of a football coach on the eve of the championship game. "If we go in, we go in to win, not fool around," Powell shouted. "When we launch it, we will launch it violently. We will launch it in a way that will make it decisive so we can get it over as quickly as possible and there's no question who won."

With Powell as the visible face of America's fighting resolve, public support for the approaching war grew even as Congress fretted about whether Bush was driving the country toward another unnecessary conflict. Whether he was seen stacking sandbags with the troops or patiently expounding at congressional hearings and Pentagon briefings, the chairman was as compelling a figure on television as he was in person. The presence he had developed when lecturing junior officers at Fort Benning and traveling in the corridors of power translated on-screen into a charisma that captured the popular imagination. *People* magazine declared him one of the "25 Most Intriguing People of 1990," along with President Bush, Saddam Hussein, and the cartoon character Bart Simpson.

But one significant segment of society disapproved of going to war. While 80 percent of white Americans told opinion pollsters they supported going to war over Kuwait, half of black Americans opposed it. Blacks now made up nearly a quarter of the Army, twice their proportion of the overall population, and the Vietnam-era charge that minorities were being used as cannon fodder resurfaced. To Powell, it was pure demagoguery; the high level of black enlistment in the now all-volunteer Army simply showed that the military was more welcoming to minorities than the private sector was. "I wish that corporate America, I wish the trade unions around the nation would show the same level of openness and opportunity to minorities that the military has," he told a congressional hearing just weeks before the war began. "The fact that we have a higher percentage [of blacks in the military] than the percentage that exists in the general population doesn't trouble me at all. That's why *I* came in, to get a job—$222.30 a month." And, he added, "I ain't done bad."

But when the sponsors of the annual Martin Luther King, Jr., birthday celebration on January 22 suggested he withdraw his earlier acceptance of an invitation from King's widow to serve as grand marshal of the Atlanta parade, he sent his regrets.

The first weeks of January were spent going over target lists. The British were nervous about plans to strike suspected biological weapons facilities, fearing the release of poison gas into the atmosphere, and Israel was anxious about possible Iraqi retaliation with chemically armed Scud missiles that could reach Tel Aviv. Cheney wanted to hit the massive statues of Saddam scattered throughout downtown Baghdad, but they were taken off the list when Pentagon lawyers judged that their destruction could not be considered a legitimate war aim.

Everyone's nerves were on edge. After a long and rancorous debate, Congress on January 12 narrowly authorized the president to go to war under the terms of the U.N. resolution. "Between [Bush's] impatience and Norm Schwarzkopf's anxieties," Powell later wrote, "I had my own juggling act. Norm displayed the natural apprehensions of a field commander on the edge of war, magnified by his excitable personality.... At the same time, the President was leaning on me: 'When are we going to be ready? When can we go?' Dealing with Norm was like holding a hand grenade with the pin pulled. Dealing with the President was like playing Scheherazade, trying to keep the king calm for a thousand and one nights."

Even Powell occasionally lost his carefully cultivated calm. "Are you watching CNN?" he shouted to Smullen through the intercom one afternoon in early January. "Get in here!" A retired general was on the cable news station, analyzing American deployments and speculating with discomfiting accuracy about the still-secret offensive plan. "I am so sick and tired of everybody who thinks they have the answers about how we're going to fight this war," Powell shouted at his press aide. "I'm particularly mad at *him,*" he pointed at the television, "because he does it a lot." Slamming his hand on his desk with nearly enough force to break the glass, Powell turned to Smullen. "You figure out how to deal with this. I'll recall his ass to active duty if I have to." Such eruptions were infrequent but not unheard of among Powell's closest staff. Smullen had been through it before; he issued a smart "Yes, sir," then left the room and did nothing.

On January 15, Bush authorized Powell to send CENTCOM the order to execute the offensive war plan the next day. Faxed to a machine in Riyadh that only Schwarzkopf and his top aide had access to, it was one carefully worded paragraph that assumed the U.N. deadline for withdrawal from Kuwait would pass without Iraqi action. If the assumption proved incorrect, it said, "you will receive modifying instructions."

Wednesday, January 16, dawned cold and quiet in Washington. "The calm has arrived," Powell wrote in his journal. There was nothing to do but sit around and wait and watch CNN. The network's correspondents were among the few Americans remaining in Baghdad, and they usually had better information than the CIA about what was happening there. He was jolted upright late in the afternoon when an urgent cable landed on his desk. Intelligence monitors in the Persian Gulf had detected the firing of cruise missiles in the region and sent out a worldwide alert. Powell ran to the command center, grabbed his own intelligence officer and started yelling, ordering him to shut down the nation's entire signals intercept system. "They're our missiles!" he shouted. The element of tactical surprise had nearly been lost.

CNN had kept a live camera running in a Baghdad hotel window, focused on the city skyline, ever since the U.N. deadline expired. At 7 p.m. Wednesday—3 a.m. Thursday in Baghdad—the Iraqi night exploded on television screens at the Pentagon with the unleashed force of more than seven hundred U.S. and allied combat aircraft and the impact of dozens of cruise missiles launched from ships in the Persian Gulf. For the next several hours, there was nothing for Powell to do but wait for Riyadh to call. He walked restlessly across the hall to the chairman's mess to fix himself a bowl of cereal and tried to catch some sleep on the couch in his office.

At around 5 a.m. in Washington, Schwarzkopf finally telephoned with a preliminary assessment. The first round of attacks, targeting Iraqi air defenses, command and control installations, communications facilities and suspected chemical and biological weapons sites, had gone well; only two American aircraft were reported lost.

Just as important, from Powell's point of view, was what the American people would see and think about their modern fighting force. When the first pilots returned to their aircraft carriers, he watched an F-16 roll to a stop and pop open its canopy as reporters on deck rushed forward with notebooks and cameras. He held his breath as the young pilot jumped to the ground, hoses dangling from his sweat-soaked uniform, tucked his helmet under his arm and started to walk away from the shouted questions. Then the pilot stopped and turned toward the cameras. "I'll tell you what it was all about, what it was like," he said. "First I want to thank God that I completed my mission successfully and I got back to my base safely." Powell exhaled in relief. You never knew what would come out of an adrenaline-pumped jet jockey's mouth.

There was more: "I want to thank God for the love of a good woman," the pilot said. He walked a few more steps and then turned again. "I want to thank God that I'm an American." And again: "I want to thank God that I'm an American fighter pilot."

Powell wiped away a few tears.

Barely a week later, the atmosphere in Washington began to turn sour. Iraq had been pummeled by a relentless air attack for days, reporters at the Pentagon briefings and congressional opponents of the war accused. Why wasn't it over yet? How long was it going to last? Was something wrong? Iraqi Scud missiles were crashing into Israel and Saudi Arabia, and there were no indications of an Iraqi exit from Kuwait. Powell and Cheney had tried to stay out of the briefing room and leave the play-by-play to their spokesmen, but Powell finally suggested they hold a press conference both to praise the military's accomplishments and to secure public confidence while dampening expectations of an early end to the conflict.

He sent back the first delivery of charts and maps for his presentation with instructions to simplify them using only those elements that would show up well on television. His intended audience went far beyond the reporters; he would be speaking directly to the American people and Congress, the troops in the field, foreign capitals and Saddam Hussein himself. The media were always looking for sound bites, and he practiced several pithy one-liners, trying them out on Smullen and the vice chairman, Admiral David Jeremiah, and sleeping on it overnight before settling on what he knew would be a surefire headline. The next afternoon, he guided reporters through the 12,000 sorties flown, the hundreds of targets demolished and the coming ground war against Iraqi forces in Kuwait. Then it was time for the money quote: "Our strategy to go after this army is very, very simple. First, we're going to cut it off, and then we're going to kill it."

The hourlong session, broadcast live around the globe, had the desired effect. Although some people still groused that the Pentagon was holding back information and demanded to know when the ground attack would begin, the clamor largely subsided. Powell's tour de force of the war theater and his audacious "kill it" line made front pages everywhere, and many American publications commissioned separate stories about the chairman himself. The briefing had "showcased [him] in a new role, that of an articulate and persuasive spokesman for Bush Administration policy," *The New York Times* reported, while the *Los Angeles Times* editorialized that Powell's "clear and succinct briefing at the Pentagon" was "the best thing to come out of the week." He was a "cool, tough-talking military man," wrote *USA Today*, who had "charmed an agitated press corps" with a performance that "accelerated talk that the 32-year military officer is presidential timber." Powell could well be another Eisenhower, the paper said. "The most widely touted scenario has Powell emerging as a populist presidential candidate in 1996—if President Bush hasn't already turned to him to replace Vice President Quayle in 1992."

By late January, the White House was anxious to begin the ground war. Cheney and Powell decided to make another trip to the region in early February—Cheney wanted to speak directly to Saudi officials and to Schwarzkopf and his commanders. Powell and his staff had spent long hours tutoring the secretary over the last several months on everything from the size of divisions to tank mechanics so that he could speak to the troops, television and the president with authority. Cheney told his aides he also wanted to meet privately with a small group of soldiers, sailors, airmen and Marines in the field and hear their views about when the ground campaign should begin. It would be, he said, his "sanity check."

About twenty servicemen, ranging from privates to lieutenant colonels, were flown to Riyadh from ships, air bases and ground installations in the region to meet with Cheney and Powell in a small room at Schwarzkopf's headquarters. Cheney asked them to go around the room and introduce themselves, explain what they had been doing over the last three weeks and comment about the force's state of readiness. To a man, they said they knew that their road home led through Kuwait and they were ready to start the journey.

In Washington, any concerns the president had had about the military's stomach for the task had long since vanished. Powell's briefings on the progress of the war "conveyed a quiet confidence that was contagious," Bush later recalled. "He had always been willing to do what had to be done, but now I thought he was genuinely enthusiastic."

Powell had no doubt that the troops were ready, but he still wanted to make sure that everything was on the table and that Bush was fully aware of what was about to happen. When the national security team gathered in the Situation Room for a final briefing in the early afternoon of February 22, two days before the scheduled launch of the ground campaign, Powell reported that the Iraqi Army had begun to crack. To his own surprise and despite all his warnings that an air war would not suffice, there seemed to be a small possibility that they could achieve their objective without a fight on the ground. He and Schwarzkopf had discussed it, Powell said, and they had agreed that an Iraqi withdrawal, or a negotiated settlement that met U.S. conditions, might be preferable to extending the war. He explained to the president the potential risks of ground combat, including a high cost in lives and the possibility of an Iraqi chemical weapons attack. They would win, but it would be grim and grisly and nothing like the standoff air war. Scowcroft interrupted, saying that the president didn't need to hear all the gory details, but Bush overruled him.

Powell thought they should at least talk about whether an imperfect peace was a better deal than the satisfaction of smashing the Iraqi Army at the potential cost of thousands of casualties. But Bush was in no mood to consider calling off the attack. At this point, Powell concluded after the meeting, the president probably just wanted to beat the crap out of the Iraqis so it would be clear that they had been defeated. Otherwise, how would he justify this entire enterprise to the American people and the world?

The ground campaign that began on February 24, 1991, succeeded far more swiftly than anyone had anticipated. By the end of the second day, Powell and Schwarzkopf agreed that the Iraqis would be decimated within a week. By day four, with more than 70,000 Iraqi prisoners of war in multinational custody and most of Kuwait liberated, Saddam ordered what was left of his army to withdraw. His troops were nearly surrounded, with only one avenue of escape. Fleeing Iraqis clogged the main highway north, where they became easy pickings for American helicopters and jets. On the morning of February 27, Powell called Schwarzkopf to say they should be thinking of a cease-fire. The doves in Washington were beginning to be disturbed by surveillance images of the highway carnage, he said; so far no one outside the government had seen them, but some reports had already made it to the media from returning pilots.

Powell himself was revolted by the slaughter. He had no sympathy for the Iraqis; they had started this war and were getting what they deserved. But a highway turkey shoot was not the image he wanted the American people to have of their brave warriors. He thought it was "ungallant"— killing for the sake of killing that had little to do with the outcome of a war they had already won.

Schwarzkopf said he thought they could wrap it up the next day, punching eastward and completely closing off the Iraqis' escape route.

In the Oval Office that afternoon, Powell set up his maps and described the state of play. He told Bush that he and Schwarzkopf agreed that their objective was all but achieved and they were in the "window of termination." The Iraqis still making their way out of Kuwait were mostly stragglers under no real command structure. The media were already making references to the "Highway of Death." Everyone in the room wondered whether further bombing along the route would be considered "piling on," recalled Richard Haass, Scowcroft's Middle East deputy and the note taker for the meeting. Baker later remembered Powell saying, with considerable emotion, "We're killing literally *thousands* of people."

No one disagreed when Bush asked whether the time had come to end the attack. Powell went into the president's private study and called Schwarzkopf on the secure telephone. It was possible to stop now, Schwarzkopf said, but he wanted to consult with his commanders one more time. In the early evening, the team reconvened in the Oval Office and called Schwarzkopf again. With his agreement, they decided to declare a cease-fire at midnight, Washington time, ending the ground war exactly one hundred hours after it had begun. "There was a general consensus that we had, in fact, achieved our objectives," Cheney later recalled. The Iraqis were out of Kuwait. "We'd done what we said we were going to do."

After Bush announced to the country that night that the war was about to end, he invited the team upstairs for drinks in the White House residence. Scowcroft left to visit his wife, who was hospitalized with a long illness, and Cheney went home. The others stood somewhat awkwardly in the residential parlor, drinks in hands. The victory they had given the president was not V-E Day, Powell knew; the tyrant, although weakened, was still in his palace. But they had accomplished something historic, he told Bush. They had set a clear goal, assembled the resources to achieve it, built popular support and established a new international precedent for dealing with territorial aggression. American casualties, anticipated in the thousands, would eventually be tallied at fewer than 150 combat deaths. And once the goal of pushing the Iraqis out of Kuwait was achieved, they had stopped—just as they had promised.

11

You show me a general in Washington who ain't political,
and I will show you a guy who ain't gonna get promoted
again, and probably should not be a general in the first
place.

—Colin L. Powell

It's a great day to be back home in New York," Powell exulted to the millions of people who had squeezed twenty deep along lower Broadway to welcome home the troops. On a crystalline morning in June 1991, Colin rode with Alma in a white Buick convertible through the skyscraper canyon, past the towers of the World Trade Center and City Hall. He had turned down the offer of a bulky bulletproof vest to wear under his uniform; Cheney, one car ahead, and Schwarzkopf, one behind, had agreed they would sacrifice security to sleekness for the day.

The war had been over for more than three months, but the parades had continued nonstop. The New York City salute—an estimated 4.7 million people under a downpour of six tons of confetti, two hundred miles of ticker tape and a million yellow ribbons—was the extravagant culmination of celebrations stretching from Atlanta and Chicago to Los Angeles and back again to the East Coast.

Schwarzkopf garnered his share of adulation, but Powell was the rising star of the postwar euphoria. A nation eager for new military heroes was fixated on the charismatic black general who had guided it through Desert Storm as the apotheosis of victory, patriotism and global power. He was "a living, breathing recruiting poster with a beer-barrel chest, a blacksmith's arms and the bearing of a centurion," declared a profile in the *Los Angeles Times*. Powell, beamed Republican Senator John McCain—the son and grandson of admirals and a hero in his own right as a Navy fighter pilot and ex–prisoner of war in North Vietnam—was "the greatest military leader this country has produced since World War II."

In April, Powell had thrown out the first pitch at the Yankees' season opener and led scores of reporters and cameras on a celebrity stroll down Kelly Street in the Bronx. At Morris High School, his alma mater, he had extolled the virtues of hard work and a strong family. "I remember the feeling that you can't make it," Powell had told the largely black and Hispanic student body. "But you can."

Republican pundits openly called on Bush to dump Dan Quayle, seen as a drag on the 1992 reelection ticket, and take Powell in his place.

Exhilarated and sometimes overwhelmed, Powell tried to limit his appearances to events that honored the military as a whole and to stay away from those he considered undignified—he found Schwarzkopf's dance with Mickey Mouse at a flag-waving tribute in Tampa particularly appalling. He sometimes worried that official Washington would not look kindly upon his being singled out for such adoration. In a repeat of the last time he had been touted as a running mate on the presidential ticket, the one person whose opinion counted most—George Bush—had not mentioned anything to him about the vice presidency.

But it was hard to resist taking personal credit for the overwhelming victory that had occurred during his chairmanship and on his terms. It was a payoff for the previous two decades, from Vietnam through the painful rebuilding of the Army, and a validation of what journalists were now calling the "Powell Doctrine"—no military commitment without decisive force, a clear objective and popular support. The label smacked of Weinberger's similar checklist, and Powell himself avoided using it. But it was his strategy, and it had worked. "If in the end war becomes necessary, as it clearly did in Operation Desert Storm, you must do it right," he said in a speech to veterans at the Vietnam War Memorial. "You've got to be decisive. You've got to go in massively. You've got to be wise and fight in a way that keeps casualties to a minimum. And you've got to go in to win."

If the military leadership had acted differently in Vietnam, he believed, there would have been fewer names on the memorial's black granite wall. "The parades we are now seeing across America for the men and women of Desert Storm are important national celebrations. If you're a veteran of Vietnam," he said, his voice welling with emotion, "the parades will be for you, too. But you won't be there to redeem yourself. You need no redemption.... You will be there to share in the adulation, to accept some of the applause you were denied and to be recognized for the true and brave patriots that you are.... The Desert Storm parades may also serve to finally, as Lincoln said, bind up the wounds of Vietnam."

Although most Americans rejoiced in the victory, Desert Storm's after-math on the ground left a bad taste in some mouths. The monarch they had restored to his throne in Kuwait was no democrat, and the tyrant in Baghdad was still in power. Iraq was deeply divided along ethnic and sec-tarian lines, and Bush had encouraged the majority Shiites in the south-ern part of the country—hated, feared and long oppressed by Saddam Hussein, a minority Sunni—to rise up against him. But Saddam had lashed out like a wounded beast, killing and uprooting the rebellious Shi-ites by the thousands. Bush, with strong support from Powell but sharp disapproval from other advisers, including Paul Wolfowitz at the Penta-gon, turned his back on them, dismissing the uprising and the vicious repression as an internal Iraqi affair. At the northern end of the country, ethnic Kurds were given similar treatment by Saddam and driven into the treeless mountains near the Turkish border, where the U.S. military even-tually gathered them into refugee camps and began dropping relief sup-plies. The United States, Britain and France, acting under what they asserted was U.N. authority, imposed "no-fly zones" in the skies across northern and southern Iraq, from which the Iraqi Air Force was banned.

Among the administration's harshest critics were conservatives who decried Bush's refusal to march to Baghdad and unseat Saddam. Those who had decided to stop the war once Kuwait was liberated were often called upon in the coming years to defend the decision as militarily, polit-ically and morally justified.

Cheney vigorously rejected any notion of regret and said he had been "comfortable" with the decision. "We could have gone on," he told re-porters nearly fifteen months after the end of the war. U.S. troops could have captured Baghdad, but "I don't know how we would have let go of that tar baby once we had grabbed hold of it.... How many addi-tional American casualties would we have had to suffer? How many additional American lives is Saddam Hussein worth? And the answer I would give is not very damn many."

Bush never wavered in his certainty that they had done the right thing in leaving Iraq to the Iraqis. "To occupy Iraq would instantly shatter our coalition, turning the whole Arab world against us, and make a broken tyrant into a latter-day Arab hero," he wrote in the memoirs he co-authored with Brent Scowcroft in 1998. "It would have taken us way beyond the imprimatur of international law ... assigning young soldiers to a fruitless hunt for a securely entrenched dictator and condemning them to fight in what would be an unwinnable urban guerrilla war. It could only plunge that part of the world into even greater instability and destroy the credibility we were working so hard to reestablish."

Even Wolfowitz, who had argued unsuccessfully in the days immediately following the cease-fire that U.S. forces should reengage to protect the Shiites and establish a "liberated" enclave in southern Iraq, thought the 1991 war's accomplishments were underappreciated, in part because victory had been relatively quick and painless. "It was a war which demanded almost nothing from the American civilian population, not even higher taxes," he later wrote. "Ironically, if more American lives had been lost in defeating the Iraqi army and liberating Kuwait, there would probably be more widespread appreciation" for what the American military had achieved. "Certainly fewer people would suggest that perhaps we should have gone on to Baghdad."

The assumption of civilian policy makers, from Bush on down, was that a Saddam weakened by war would not last long. They believed that the United States had prepared the ground for his internal overthrow—if not by the Shiites, then perhaps by elements of his own disillusioned military.

Powell agreed that such a scenario was possible but was less than sure that it would be a positive outcome. Once Bush had decided to go to war, Powell had focused on keeping the military goal in plain sight and not heading off on what he considered quixotic missions with potentially disastrous consequences. "I kept insisting we have a clear statement of what we were trying to achieve so that we'd know we achieved it and could make a clear decision [when] to stop. If somebody had said the mission was to defeat the Iraqi Army and change the nature of the regime in Iraq, that was a different military mission," including occupation of territory and protection of Iraqi citizens that might require an even larger force than the half million soldiers they had sent. And once you got to Baghdad, how would you get out? How would the war end?

"It was not our intention to totally decimate the entire Iraqi Army, it was not our intention to go to Baghdad," he said in one of a round of television interviews on the first anniversary of the war. "Had we done that, we would have gotten ourselves into the biggest quagmire you can imagine trying to sort out 2,000 years of Mesopotamian history."

If Bush had ordered the Army to fight its way to the Iraqi capital, Powell would have saluted and found a way to do it. But that did not mean he would have thought it was a good idea. Like most of the rest of the administration, he believed that Iran, and to a lesser extent Syria, were the primary regional threats and that Iraq served as a crucial bulwark against them. An extended war risked breaking Iraq into sectarian and ethnic pieces—and then what kind of bulwark would there be?

Powell could be reduced to tears by the warmth of his own extended family or the patriotism of a young pilot, but in affairs of state he was no sentimentalist. "Our practical intention," he later wrote, "was to leave Baghdad enough power to survive as a threat to an Iran that remained bitterly hostile toward the United States." He believed that leaving Saddam in power was, on balance, a good thing. Even if the Iraqis ousted him themselves, his replacement would not likely be any better for American interests and could conceivably be worse. The Iraqi dictator needed to be punished for his Kuwait adventure, but as long as he was kept on a short leash, the best option was to leave him there.

The newly esteemed U.S. armed forces escaped relatively unscathed from the postwar finger-pointing. But Powell himself was singled out just months after the cease-fire by complaints from the other side—those who felt Desert Storm should never have been fought in the first place. In a book published in early May, *Washington Post* reporter Bob Woodward revealed Powell's early concerns about the rush to combat and his efforts to slow Bush down during the buildup. Some members of Congress who had opposed the war were outraged that Powell had failed to share with them his belief, according to Woodward's *The Commanders,* that continued sanctions were a better option than war. Others suggested that Powell had leaked classified information to the author. No sources were named in the book, but it was hard to read its description of White House deliberations without concluding that Woodward had had extensive conversations with the chairman.

Woodward, who had earned fame for unraveling the Watergate conspiracy leading to Richard Nixon's resignation in the early 1970s, had first approached Powell at the beginning of his chairmanship in October 1989, immediately after the aborted Panama coup. Congress was heaping scorn upon the White House and news stories painted the then-new chairman of the Joint Chiefs as "the fair-haired boy who had fallen flat on his face." Anxious to respond, Powell had provided Woodward with a lengthy interview on the Panama situation. The resulting *Post* article, while accurate, was not particularly helpful to Powell's position, and he later compared the experience of seeing his thoughts and actions translated through a reportorial filter to "posing for what you think is going to be a reasonably flattering photo, only to find out that the photographer has chosen to print the shot of you with your mouth hanging open." But when Woodward later returned with an appeal for assistance on a wider book about Pentagon decision making, Powell was interested. Certain he could influence Woodward's analysis, he agreed to help.

The focus of the book eventually narrowed to two case studies: the successful Panama operation in December 1989 and the lead-up to Desert Storm. Powell met twice with Woodward in his office at the Pentagon—three days before Iraq's invasion of Kuwait and again in early January during the air war—and talked to him by telephone from home. Alma, who distrusted reporters in general and Woodward in particular, thought it was a bad idea. William Smullen warned his boss that he shouldn't be talking to a reporter from his home telephone. But, as Smullen had already observed, Powell was used to being his own image maker and thought he did a good job of it. He knew there were risks involved in close dealings with journalists; they were always waiting to pounce on a stupid or indiscreet answer, and the good ones weren't satisfied with a clever turn of phrase. But he thought that, on balance, he gained far more from talking to them than by ignoring them.

Unlike most senior officers and government officials, Powell didn't fear or disdain the media. On the contrary, he believed they had a legitimate role in a healthy democracy and that an administration lied to, ignored or trifled with them at its own peril. The new world of satellite broadcasts and twenty-four-hour news cycles had made them powerful and potentially useful players in foreign and defense policy.

He had seen for himself the immediate and widespread dissemination of information soon after the end of Desert Storm. While traveling in northern Iraq during Operation Provide Comfort, the military's postwar effort to aid displaced Kurds, he had visited the farthest south U.S. Marine checkpoint near Zakhu, where there was a camp housing 300,000 Kurdish refugees. The camp lay beside a principal highway to Baghdad, and only a few hundred yards separated a Marine roadblock from one manned by the Iraqi military. On the day of Powell's visit, a long line of Iraqi civilian automobiles traveling south was waiting for the Marines to let them through and as he walked along the road a voice emerged from a small red car: "Hello, Mr. Powell. I know you from CNN."

"That's really scary," Powell said with a laugh to the astonished Marine officer at his side. When another Iraqi called out to him by name, he walked over to chat. "If you see Mr. Saddam Hussein," Powell said with a grin, "tell him I said hello. Tell him I'm going to kick his ass."

The Commanders had been released with great fanfare, beginning with a front page *Washington Post* excerpt on May 2, 1991, the day before its official publication. Powell had nearly choked on his morning coffee when he saw it. Instead of the portrait he thought he had drawn of a wise administration and its heroic military, the book described a nervous, trigger-happy president who had rebuffed the judicious counsel of his chairman. The *Post* headline alone—"Book Says Powell Favored Containment; Image of Harmony on Gulf Policy Dispelled"—was likely to seriously rattle a White House that promoted a public image of seamless agreement. Powell's first thought was that he had made a mistake so serious it could cost him his career. He was not only depicted in both word and thought as favoring sanctions over war; he was also pictured as at times privately scornful of other top officials, including the president.

Powell's eventual support for Bush's war decision seemed like a mere footnote to the long saga of his angst. Although more than half of the book was devoted to Operation Just Cause in Panama, nearly all of the media frenzy created by *The Commanders* centered on what was always big news in Washington: dissension at the highest ranks of government. In a May 13 cover story, *Newsweek* labeled Powell "The Reluctant Warrior." He was "cool and smooth on the surface," *Newsweek's* account of the Woodward book read, but "the Chairman of the Joint Chiefs of Staff was wary of Bush and his clubby circle of advisers. Powell favored squeezing Iraq with economic sanctions rather than going to war...just like many Democrats on Capitol Hill." The chairman, it said, had spent "hundreds of hours" with Woodward, and "Washington was abuzz last week that the JCS chairman would so blatantly defy Bush's oft-stated insistence on secrecy at the top."

Powell quibbled with parts of the book, but it was a largely accurate recounting of his version of events and he had only himself to blame for the uproar. Woodward had the "disarming voice and manner of a Boy Scout offering to help an old lady across the street," he later recalled, and he had lapped it up. Alma could barely restrain herself from saying she had told him so.

The book caused Powell some painful moments at the Pentagon, where those who hadn't taken kindly to his leadership changes concluded that he had been more interested in his personal reputation than in the war. But the reader he was most concerned about brushed off the controversy as much ado about nothing. On the morning the *Post* article appeared, long before the worried calls from friends and arch looks from colleagues began, Bush was on the telephone to Powell. "Colin, I don't pay attention to all that crap," the president told him. "Don't worry about it. Don't let them get under your skin."

Asked by reporters that afternoon whether he and Powell had disagreed over the war, Bush didn't hesitate. "How could we have disagreed when you see such a superb military operation?" Powell's job was to give the president his best advice and then carry out his decisions, and that's what he had done, Bush declared. "If there's anybody that has the integrity and the honor to tell a president what he feels, it's Colin Powell, and if there's anybody that is disciplined enough and enough of a leader to instill confidence in his troops, it's Colin Powell." He was too busy to read the book himself, Bush said, but the things that had been brought to his attention were simply not true. "Nobody's going to drive a wedge between him and me."

When such assertive support failed to dampen speculation about Powell's standing in the White House, Bush told Cheney that he wanted to hold a public ceremony to announce Powell's reappointment as chairman, months before his current two-year term was due to expire at the end of September.

Cheney said nothing to Powell about the Woodward controversy, leaving him with the feeling that the secretary didn't mind letting him dangle in the wind a bit. When Cheney told him of the reappointment, Powell started to thank him, then realized Cheney had had nothing to do with it. It all had been Bush's idea.

On May 23, 1991, Powell stood at the president's side in the Rose Garden as Bush told reporters, "I am taking this step now to demonstrate my great confidence in his ability and the tremendous respect that I have for him. It's personal and it's professional." Powell's advice throughout operations in Panama, "and of course most important in the Gulf was absolutely remarkable," Bush said. "And the confidence I have in him is reflected in the confidence the men and women of our armed forces have in General Powell and I have seen it first hand and it has not diminished in any way."

Whatever concerns he had about the president, Powell thought, this was what he liked and would always value about him. Bush was a *mensch*.

The Senate was not willing to let Powell off so easily. The week before his reconfirmation hearing, scheduled for September 27, Armed Services Committee Chairman Nunn and the committee's ranking Republican, John Warner of Virginia, sent him a long list of questions about advice he had given Bush in the lead-up to the war. Suggesting that he had shared confidential information with Woodward, they asked whether a Pentagon investigation was under way.

Powell's written response was testy. He was "unaware of any investigations ... or any perceived need for one." He had exchanged no documents with Woodward, and "my conversations were similar to conversations I, and most government officials, regularly hold with correspondents and authors. I did not discuss classified or sensitive information or conduct myself in any inappropriate manner." He had kept Cheney and the service chiefs apprised of his talks with the reporter—they had spoken with Woodward themselves—and "there was nothing secret, conspiratorial or mysterious" about his cooperation.

Although Warner had signed on to the queries, Nunn and his staff were the driving force behind them. Powell had made a point of maintaining good relations with the Democrats' chief defense policy maker over the years, establishing a back-channel line of communication with Nunn that had paid off in smooth congressional cooperation on a range of issues. But the Georgia senator's unyielding opposition to what turned out to be a popular and successful war had threatened Nunn's hopes of winning his party's presidential nomination in 1992. Powell thought that Nunn couldn't care less what he had told Woodward; the senator was simply trying to get the respected chairman of the Joint Chiefs to say he had shared Nunn's conviction that Desert Storm was a bad idea.

Despite the Senate's concerns, however, *The Commanders* had only enhanced Powell's popularity over the summer of 1991. The caution and hesitation it revealed were seen as prudence, and most Americans seemed as reassured by Powell's initial reluctance to go to war as they were by the victory itself. His approval rating in a series of nationwide polls soared above 80 percent—far higher than that of any politician in the country. Pundits called on both political parties to sit up and take notice. "This guy is a master politician," *New York* magazine political reporter Joe Klein wrote, favorably contrasting Powell with Cheney. Powell, Klein wrote, "is a leader, not a staff guy. He runs on instinct more than intellect (though he's no dummy). He's a dynamic presence, not just another suit." Although he had worked most prominently for Republican administrations, Powell was a registered Independent, Klein noted, and the "Democrats would do well to consider this book a calling card, perhaps even a *billet-doux*."

Nunn was not impressed. When the reconfirmation hearing finally began on Friday, September 27—three days before the end of Powell's term—the senator announced that they would have to hold a second session after the weekend since the committee had not finished reviewing Powell's responses to its written questions. Visibly irritated, Powell told the committee he had "no second thoughts ... no conscience problems" about his conversations with Woodward. *The Commanders* was "a combination of fact, of fiction, of accurate quotations and in some cases not so accurate quotations," he said, although he didn't specify which parts he considered fiction. "That's the sum and substance of it, Mr. Chairman, and I really have little more to add."

The session went on to other defense matters and ended with Nunn expressing confidence that they could send Powell's reconfirmation to the Senate floor for approval after a committee vote on Monday. "I certainly hope so, Senator," Powell said curtly. He had been "advised by counsel" that his current term expired at midnight September 30, after which "I can no longer serve as principal military adviser to the President." Warner tried to wind up the tense exchange with a joke, asking Powell, "Does your pay stop?"

Having broken Powell's legendary calm, Nunn went for the jugular, sending yet another long list of questions to the chairman over the weekend. Powell angrily threw the thirty pages on the floor of his office and told his aides he would not answer them. Paul Kelly, his legislative assistant, quietly picked up the scattered papers and, unbeknown to Powell, sent them down to the general staff director to answer. When Kelly showed him the proposed responses on Monday morning, Powell threw them into the trash. "You just don't get it," he told Kelly sharply. "I'm not answering." He typed out a single clipped paragraph telling Nunn and Warner he had nothing more to say and ordered Kelly to deliver it to Capitol Hill.

Nunn and Warner put through a call to Cheney. No senior military officer had ever refused to answer questions from Congress, they warned; if the rest of the committee knew of the chairman's abrupt nonresponse, his reconfirmation might be in jeopardy. Cheney passed the message along to Powell without comment.

The senators were in a foul mood on Monday, not least because Bush had surprised them over the weekend by announcing, without consultation, a major new reduction in nuclear weapons. Powell spent most of the hearing reassuring them that there would still be sufficient armaments to annihilate the Soviet Union several times over if it became necessary. When the first mention of the book finally came, he nearly lost control. The conservative Wyoming Senator Malcolm Wallop suggested that such a benign view of Soviet intentions might be a mistake, noting that "the book *Commanders*" made it clear that the Pentagon had misjudged Saddam Hussein's intention to invade Kuwait and been totally unprepared for it.

Powell interrupted him sharply. "That's absolutely wrong, Senator."

"Well," Wallop continued, "that's what the book—"

"I don't care what the book said, Senator," Powell again interrupted, saying that there had been a plan on the shelf for just that scenario. Wallop dropped the subject, and Powell was spared having to acknowledge that he and his staff had, in fact, been slow to recognize Saddam's intentions.

In the end, it was the committee, not Powell, that blinked. By late afternoon, the senators had worn themselves out; they agreed unanimously to recommend Powell's approval for another term, and the full Senate quickly followed with unanimous consent. As far as Powell was concerned, they had little choice. He knew how popular he was with the American people—and so did the senators.

The Democrats, as Joe Klein had advised, soon began paying attention to Powell. In December 1991, he was visited at the Pentagon by the Marine veteran Ron Dellums, a popular black congressman from Oakland, California. Powell didn't know Dellums well; they had interacted at congressional hearings and occasionally crossed paths at social events. "Man, I've been talking to people . . . senior members of the Democratic Party," Dellums began, his voice slipping into what Powell dismissively thought of as "brother talk." The 1992 presidential primaries were still months away, but Dellums had clearly been sent by the Democrats to feel out Powell's party preference. If he ended up as Bush's running mate, as many Republicans hoped, he would be the Democrats' worst nightmare, Dellums said. If he would consider coming over to the Democrats, it would be a dream come true.

Powell had a ready answer: as a serving military officer he had no political affiliation, and he planned to stay in uniform until he retired. But five months later, he received another Democratic feeler, this time from a more compelling messenger—the powerful Washington lawyer Vernon Jordan. Jordan's close friend, former Arkansas Governor Bill Clinton, was about to become the Democratic Party's presidential nominee.

Powell had first bumped into Jordan, literally, one night in 1987, as they were both trying to make an early escape from the Gridiron Dinner, an exclusive white-tie get-together on Washington's annual calendar of self-important events. Whites usually assumed that all prominent black men knew one another, but Jordan and Powell didn't really become acquainted until they were later invited to dinner by Charles Duncan, Powell's old boss in the Carter administration and a friend of Jordan's. The two clicked immediately, and their friendship quickly advanced to at-home suppers with their wives.

In early 1989, Jordan had made a point of inviting Powell, then commander at FORSCOM, to a fancy party he threw for his mother's eighty-second birthday at the Ritz-Carlton Hotel in his hometown of Atlanta. The Jordan family was intimately familiar with Fort McPherson—Mary Belle Jordan had worked as a cook in the officers' club when it was all white, her postman husband had delivered mail there, and their sons, Vernon and his brother, had earned pocket change collecting errant balls on the whites-only military golf course. In his youth, Vernon had thought of Fort McPherson as a military version of a southern plantation, and he knew it would please his mother to know that a black man now ran the place.

Jordan and Powell recognized in each other the qualities necessary for blacks to achieve high station in the white world, but they had traveled markedly different paths to get there. An imposingly tall, dark-skinned man with soulful eyes and a courtly manner that masked an iron will, Jordan was a son of the segregated South, raised by poorly educated but striving parents. Unlike the horror Powell's Jamaican family had felt over his decision to enter ROTC, Jordan's mother had insisted he join the college military program upon his arrival at DePauw University, a liberal arts college in small-town Indiana where he was the only black freshman. "All the white women I work for are sending their boys to the ROTC," she told him. Vernon unhappily and only briefly complied. After earning his law degree from Howard University in 1960, he enlisted instead on the front lines of the civil rights movement, eventually rising to the top of the National Urban League. In 1980, he was shot in the back by a white supremacist in an Indiana parking lot, a near-fatal attack that required a long recuperation and led to his departure from the movement to join a leading Washington law firm.

Jordan was already a well-known national figure, but he was now attracting new attention as a political power broker through his nearly two-decade-long friendship with Clinton. Although he had not yet discussed it with the candidate, Jordan was sure that Powell's popularity, national security gravitas and color would bring votes to any ticket. Besides, he had a feeling that "Colin [was] a Democrat wrapped in Republican swaddling clothes."

Jordan asked if he would be interested being Clinton's running mate. Powell gave him the same answer he had given Dellums: he would not leave the military to run for office. Moreover, he said, even if he could see his way clear to becoming a registered Democrat—which, at the moment, he couldn't—he would never campaign against the president. Bush had selected him as chairman and had stuck by him when it counted, and running against his own record in the Bush administration was unthinkable.

Jordan knew that Powell was a loyal soldier, he later reflected. "But that didn't mean I should not drop the handkerchief."

Just as it insulated him from racial tensions, Powell's uniform served as camouflage on America's partisan battlefields. He liked his image of political neutrality and fostered it at every opportunity. He had helped formulate and carry out the policies of two Republican presidents at the highest levels—and voted for both of them—but he wasn't shy about revealing that he had also cast ballots for John F. Kennedy, Lyndon Johnson and Jimmy Carter, or that FDR had been the patron saint of his childhood. His deep-seated aversion to party politics was both acquired, at the feet of his early military commanders, and innate. He was a born negotiator, more politic—pragmatic, diplomatic, shrewd—than political.

He felt little emotional or intellectual pull from either party. In his experience, Republicans were more reliable stewards of the military and the country's finances. But on social issues such as abortion and affirmative action—issues where he thought the Republicans were becoming alarmingly extreme—he was far more in tune with the Democrats. He was convinced that Bush didn't agree with the sharp Republican turn to the right, but the president seemed, at least so far, either unwilling or incapable of leading the party back to the center.

Despite Powell's frequent disavowals, Richard Armitage and his other friends in the shrinking Republican center were half convinced he would jump at the opportunity to run as Bush's vice president if it were offered to him. With Bush's reelection chances sinking as fast as Powell's popularity was rising, they told him, the party would be grateful to have him. He wouldn't have to mold himself to platform planks he disagreed with; he could just emphasize the ones he supported: a strong defense and an entrepreneurial economy. He could be the one to turn Bush's fortunes around and lead the GOP back to moderation. There were moments when Powell actually believed them. But beyond his concerns about fitting in with the Republicans, three obstacles stood in his way.

Above all else, he was an active-duty Army officer, determined to reach his goal of retiring with the maximum thirty-five years of service in 1993, and even to think aloud about politics seemed an act of disloyalty to the service and to his commander in chief. Just as important, Alma was dead set against his running. In a rare press interview targeted straight at those urging him on, she had put her foot down unequivocally, telling *Women's*

Wear Daily that electoral office was "not anything either one of us would seek or have any idea about." They had discussed it, but "not with any seriousness at all." Her husband joked about it, she said, while "I simply say 'Listen, I don't want any part of this.' "

The biggest obstacle, however, was Bush's decision to stay with Dan Quayle as his running mate for reelection in 1992.

Powell used Bush's last year in office as a time to enjoy and consolidate his own prestige and that of the military. He won budget battles for the Base Force plan, engineered an expansion of high school and college ROTC programs and oversaw the erection of the Buffalo Soldiers Monument at Fort Leavenworth. He took Alma on her first visit to Jamaica, where he was hailed as a native hero, if once removed; and to Africa, where they visited ports in Senegal and Sierra Leone that had been departure points for millions of black slaves transported to the New World.

As the postwar jubilation dissipated and the economy weakened early in the election year of 1992, Bush's campaign went into a tailspin from which it never recovered. The nation needed something desperately, Powell thought, and the president just couldn't figure out what it was. He knew that Bush was not in top form—the president had acknowledged that the medication he was taking for a newly diagnosed thyroid disorder affected his alertness—and Powell began to wonder if Bush were truly ill. Never a polished speaker, he seemed positively dopey at times on the campaign trail. "Listen to Governor Clinton and the Ozone Man," he shouted at one stop, referring to Senator Al Gore of Tennessee, the self-styled environmentalist Clinton had chosen as his running mate. "This guy [Gore] is so far off in the environmental extreme, we'll be up to our neck in owls and out of work for every American. This guy's crazy. He is way out, far out. Far out, man." Bush's dog, Millie, he said, "knows more about foreign affairs than these two bozos."

Powell had rarely come face-to-face with the reality of racial injustice in America, but he was shocked on April 29, 1992, when a Los Angeles jury acquitted four white police officers charged with brutally beating Rodney King, a black construction worker and ex-convict who had been arrested after a high-speed car chase. The incident fourteen months earlier had been captured on a bystander's video camera and broadcast around the world. Powell and many others had believed that no fair-minded person could deny that the officers had been guilty of using excessive force.

Within hours of the acquittal, largely black neighborhoods in Los

Angeles erupted in the worst race riots since the assassination of Martin Luther King twenty-four years earlier. Protesters marched on police headquarters, fires burned out of control and whites were attacked on the streets. As California Governor Pete Wilson and Los Angeles Mayor Tom Bradley summoned the state National Guard to supplement the local police, Powell advised the military to be ready to intervene if ordered to do so. The chairman was not in the chain of command that would be activated in such an eventuality, but if and when Bush asked, Powell wanted to be able to tell him they were prepared.

As he watched the chaos in Los Angeles on his office television, Powell was sickened at the thought of sending troops to fight fellow citizens, especially African Americans. As much as he deplored the violence, he saw it as the release of pent-up fury after years of continuing inequality. When the riots spilled over into a third day and began to erupt in other cities, Scowcroft called to ask for help on a speech Bush intended to deliver that night. Powell was unsurprised and only marginally offended; he had nothing to do with domestic law enforcement or civil rights policy, but minority perspective was in short supply in the White House. He called the speechwriters' attention to Rodney King's tearful appeal that afternoon for blacks and whites to stop fighting and "get along," something he thought Bush could build on to voice an understanding of the underlying inequality that still plagued the nation. Keep the law-and-order stuff, he advised, but use King's statement to segue into a healing message.

At nine o'clock on the night of Friday, May 1, Powell excused himself from a formal dinner at a downtown Washington hotel and told his staff to find a room where he could watch the president's speech. He was startled to hear Bush announce he had decided to federalize the California National Guard and would send 4,500 Army and Marine troops to help restore order in Los Angeles. He was "instructing General Colin Powell to place all those troops under a central command," the president said—news to Powell.

Bush described the videotaped King beating as "revolting" and pledged a federal investigation. Most of the rest of the speech was tough reassurance that the perpetrators of "the wanton destruction of life and property" in Los Angeles would be brought to justice. He concluded with a call for Americans to "keep working to create a climate of understanding and tolerance" and "lend their hearts, their voices, and their prayers to the healing of hatred." But he never mentioned the underlying cause of black rage or King's appeal to "get along."

Powell was scheduled to deliver a speech of his own the following Monday at Fisk University in Nashville, his wife's alma mater. Most of it was already written, but he tore it apart over the weekend; the largely black audience would expect him to talk about Los Angeles, and it was one of those rare moments when his emotions overcame his caution on the subject of race.

"As I saw those pictures on my television set," he told a hushed commencement audience of parents and students, "my heart hurt.... I didn't want to believe what I was seeing. Violence—by the police or by the mob—is not the answer.... It shouldn't be; we've come too far for this. But it did happen. And we see once again what a long way we still have to go. Because the problem goes beyond Rodney King. The problem goes beyond Los Angeles. It goes beyond the trial of those four officers.

"The problem goes to the despair that still exists in the black community over the inability of black Americans to share fully in the American dream. Too many African-Americans are still trapped in a cycle where poverty, violence, drugs, bad housing, inadequate education, lack of jobs and loss of faith combine to create a sad human condition, a human condition that cannot be allowed to continue if this nation is to hold its rightful place in the world."

Each of them, he told the graduates, had a responsibility to believe in themselves and believe in America. "I want you to fight racism, I want you to rail against it. We have to make sure that it bleeds to death in this country once and for all," he said. But "As you raise your families, remember the worst kind of poverty is not economic poverty, it is the poverty of values. It is the poverty of caring. It is the poverty of love."

The speech gained national news coverage, both for what it said and the color and position of the speaker. "Of the millions of words spoken and written in the aftermath of the Rodney King verdict and the Los Angeles riots," wrote David Broder of *The Washington Post,* one of the nation's top political columnists, "none were more pertinent, pointed and eloquent."

Powell's only regret was that he thought it was the speech George Bush should have delivered.

Bush's rhetoric moved farther to the right as he sought to capitalize on Clinton's inexperience and reputation as a philanderer and draft dodger. Pandering to its core of socially conservative voters, the Republican Party awarded the keynote slot at its August convention in Houston to the right-wing populist Pat Buchanan, who had made a strong showing in the party primaries. In what the media later dubbed the "culture war" speech, Buchanan warned that Clinton would bring "abortion on demand, a litmus test for the Supreme Court, homosexual rights, discrimination against religious schools, [and] women in combat." It was "not the kind of change we can tolerate in a nation that we still call God's country."

In suburban Virginia, Michael Powell called his sister Linda in New York to see if she was watching the convention. They agreed that it looked like "a Nazi youth rally," and Michael "could not imagine his father involved in what the Republican Party had become."

Powell cast his usual absentee New York ballot—for Bush—and spent election night, November 3, at home. Clinton won with 43 percent of the popular vote to Bush's 34.7 percent, with the rest taken by the third-party candidate Ross Perot. After a day or two, Powell called the president with his condolences. "It hurt like hell," Bush told him. Colin and Alma were puzzled when Barbara Bush telephoned that night to invite them and their children and grandchild to Camp David for the weekend; surely the First Family had closer friends with whom to commiserate. When they arrived Friday afternoon to find that they and Bush's brother were the only guests, Powell concluded that the president and his wife probably just wanted to spend time with someone who wasn't part of the political process.

As the early dusk of fall approached, they dressed in heavy coats and took off on the president's version of a "power walk" around the secured perimeter of the forested compound. Bush and Powell walked ahead of the others, and the president chatted amiably and inconsequentially for a time before abruptly switching the subject to his defeat. It was particularly painful, Bush said, that a group of retired senior military officers, including Powell's predecessor, Admiral William Crowe, had come out for Clinton despite the challenger's draft record compared to his own World War II service. "I just never thought they'd elect him," Bush lamented. "Don't understand it."

After dinner that night in the main cabin, they settled in to watch a new British movie, *Enchanted April*, a romantic comedy about four women friends vacationing together in post–World War I Italy. Powell noticed that Bush dozed off several times before it was over.

Two days before the election, Vernon Jordan had tried again. Anticipating victory, Clinton had asked Jordan and Warren Christopher, a California attorney who had served in the Carter State Department, to head his transition team, assembling names and a vetting process for potential senior officials in the new administration. Over dinner at Powell's house, Jordan asked if Powell would consider serving as Clinton's secretary of state or defense. "If I had gotten the green light from Colin, then I would have assaulted Clinton," Jordan later recalled. "But I didn't get the green light."

There was still the question of loyalty to Bush and his policies, and Powell was already thinking ahead to what he would do after his Army retirement. Alma had had little life of her own throughout their now-thirty-year marriage, and he had promised her that this would be his last government job, at least for as much time as it took to translate his experience and celebrity into enough money to secure their financial future. After a lifetime of living on military wages, and sending three children to college, they had minimal savings. They lived in a grand house at Fort Myers, but the only home they owned was the one they had bought years before in Burke and kept as a rental property. Don Regan, President Reagan's onetime chief of staff, had once told Powell that "if you really want to be somebody in this town, you've got to go out and make a buck on your own. The 'fuck you' money. Until then, you're never really free." During his last year in the service, Powell took out an extra-large life insurance policy. He would be fifty-six years old in April, and just in case he didn't make it to the private sector he wanted to be sure Alma would be left with a comfortable lump sum.

Tom Clancy, the best-selling author of novels on military and intelligence themes and a longtime friend, had queried Powell in the midst of the Gulf War about writing his autobiography. "Whether or not you want to do a book about yourself is a very personal decision," Clancy said in a letter. "Speaking for myself, I think you have an interesting story to tell. You are an American success story: son of immigrants makes good." The downside was that "autobiographies are often self-promotion and are invariably seen as such," he said. But the money "is not bad. You could, I think, count on a seven-figure advance." As the new administration headed into office, Powell began consultations with Marvin Josephson, whose literary agency also handled Henry Kissinger. He and Alma started looking at houses in McLean, a pricey Washington suburb near the CIA headquarters in Virginia.

The hundred-mile trip from the Pentagon to Gettysburg, Pennsylvania, took mere minutes by helicopter. But when overcast skies turned into a driving rain on the morning of Thursday, November 19, Powell and William Smullen climbed into the chairman's armored car for a two-hour drive to the Civil War battlefield where Powell had scheduled a speech. When he called back to the Pentagon from Gettysburg at midday, there was a message from Bill Clinton. The president-elect wanted to see him at 3 p.m. at the Hay-Adams Hotel. Powell finished his speech, compressed the rest of his Gettysburg schedule and climbed back into the car.

As his driver sped through the storm down Interstate 270 toward Washington, Powell wrote some notes to himself on the military issues Clinton would likely want to discuss. He was eager to meet the man who had brought the Bush administration crashing to the ground. It was conventional wisdom, at least in the media, that the nation's most prominent soldier was contemptuous of Clinton's evasion of the Vietnam draft. Powell might have felt that way in the 1970s, but not anymore. He wasn't happy that Clinton was the first president since World War II who hadn't served and that he was one of the mostly white guys who had wangled draft deferments. But at least Clinton had spent the war speaking out and demonstrating against it, unlike the right-wing, "let's kick the crap out of them" types he had worked with who were eager for everyone else to fight the battles they championed—Richard Perle and Frank Gaffney from the Reagan Pentagon, Cheney with his five deferments and "other priorities," or Dan Quayle, who had sat out Vietnam in the Indiana National Guard. The Republicans had tried to nail Clinton for doing what many of them had done, Powell thought, but at least Clinton wasn't a hypocrite.

When they pulled under the sheltering portico of the Hay-Adams, Powell left Smullen in the car, checked in with Clinton's newly expanded Secret Service detail and took the elevator up to the opulent penthouse suite. George Stephanopoulos, Clinton's deputy campaign manager, told him that the president-elect was running late.

Clinton had arrived in Washington the day before to meet with Bush and congressional leaders. To the delight of the national media and his image handlers, he had spent the afternoon strolling along Georgia Avenue, a major north-south artery that traversed some of the poorest and most crime-riddled neighborhoods in the District of Columbia. In accounts Powell had read in the morning papers with a mixture of admiration and eye rolling, Clinton had hugged and high-fived everyone from vendors to the homeless, all the while scarfing scallops from a neighborhood Chinese carryout. He had greeted a fellow alumnus from Washington's Georgetown University with a bit of "brother talk," shouting "Yo, my man!" That night, he had dined with Democratic potentates at Vernon Jordan's house.

The next morning, the president-elect had jogged around the National

Mall in shorts and a T-shirt. He had stopped for a cup of decaf at a local McDonald's, where, among other things, he had told patrons that he admired Colin Powell. By the time he reached a midday news conference, word had leaked of his plans to meet with Powell that afternoon, and a questioner asked whether he would offer the chairman a Cabinet post. Nothing of the sort had been discussed, Clinton replied. "I've never even met him. I think he's a very eminent American who's capable of doing nearly any job in this country, including the one that I've just been elected to, but I've had no conversations with him about anything like that."

Powell's national stature made him both attractive and dangerous to Clinton. Keeping the general as a senior member of his team would help vaccinate the new president against Republican charges that he was weak on defense and would help curtail any thoughts Powell himself might have of running against Clinton in the future. But having him in the new administration would be risky, especially if Powell should disagree with Clinton on a major issue. Clinton had discussed the possibility of Powell as a running mate early in the campaign with Dick Morris, his political adviser, but had been convinced Powell wouldn't do it. Despite his public disclaimers, Clinton had also sanctioned Jordan's most recent approach to Powell about a possible Cabinet position but had decided to drop the idea when Jordan told him of Powell's demurral. Months later, Clinton told Stephanopoulos he was convinced that Powell would have taken the job of secretary of state if he had pressed him at the Hay-Adams meeting.

When Clinton eventually walked into the penthouse living room, Powell's first impression was that the youthful president-elect was "bigger and more vital-looking than his TV image. He seemed relaxed and unawed by what he had just accomplished." Clinton offered Powell a seat, sat down and presided over coffee, cookies and cigars. He scored an immediate first point by saying he had wanted to meet Powell ever since he had seen a tape of the chairman's speech at Morris High School a few months after the Persian Gulf War and proceeding to mention several specific passages.

As the conversation continued, Powell offered an indirect reassurance that, despite Clinton's antiwar past, the new president would have the military's full support. He was the commander in chief, Powell later recalled telling Clinton. The military didn't care who or where he had been. He was not just the president or the head of state to them. He was the commander of the armed forces of the United States. It was important that Clinton understood that they would follow where he led, and it was important that he hear it from Powell.

Clinton asked about Bosnia, one of the new countries that had emerged from the recently dismembered Yugoslavia, where Serbian militiamen loyal to Belgrade were systematically killing Muslims. Bush had taken Powell's strong advice against direct military intervention. Wasn't there some way, Clinton wondered in an echo of Bush on Iraq, that they could influence the situation with airpower without committing troops on the ground? Here we go again, Powell thought. "Not likely," he replied, but he said he would have his staff look into it. They talked about war-ravaged Somalia, where American troops were participating in U.N. food deliveries to a starving population, and Haiti, which was collapsing from within and offered another potential venue for U.S. military intervention. Clinton asked about the Middle East, and Powell advised appointing a high-level emissary rather than letting the secretary of state get bogged down with endless shuttle diplomacy. Powell brought up Clinton's campaign pledge to end the ban on homosexuals' serving in the armed forces and suggested he take it slowly, saying "This is a big, big problem for [the military], and it ain't going to be easy."

The only downside of the meeting, as far as Powell was concerned, was Clinton's indication that he would nominate Wisconsin Representative Les Aspin to be his defense secretary. Aspin had been Powell's bête noire as head of the House Armed Services Committee, denouncing the Base Force cuts as insufficient and calling for a bigger, faster "peace dividend." That provided an opening for Powell to deliver to Clinton a short speech he had prepared in his head. His two-year term as chairman wasn't up until September, he said, but his "fingerprints" were all over a dozen years of Republican defense policy and he would go earlier if that was what Clinton wanted. If he stayed, he would serve the new commander in chief loyally. "Anytime I find that I cannot, in good conscience, fully support your administration's policies because of my past positions, I will let you know. And I'll retire quietly, without making a fuss."

The last thing Clinton wanted was for the nation's most popular African American and four-star general to resign. He later described the meeting as a success. "Despite our differences, General Powell made it clear that he would serve as best he could, including giving me his honest advice, which is exactly what I wanted."

Powell was in high spirits when he returned to the car after more than an hour. Clinton, he told Smullen, was enormously curious and had asked great questions. He was young, animated, and sharp as a tack; he knew every issue about every country they had discussed. His focus was on the economy, and he seemed very pragmatic. When Richard Armitage received Powell's report on the meeting, his Republican heart sank. "I'm sorry," Powell said with a laugh. "I like this guy."

If the initial encounter between Clinton and Powell was high tea, Stephanopoulos later recalled, the first formal meeting between the new president and the Joint Chiefs of Staff was high noon. Sitting on opposite sides of the long oak table in the Roosevelt Room just five days after the January 20 inauguration, they had a brief, pleasant discussion of current defense matters before the conversation turned to what the chiefs wanted to talk about: gays in the military.

Gay and lesbian groups had supported Clinton's campaign with time and money, and he had promised them he would end what he saw as a historically unfair ban. Everyone knew that thousands of closeted gays were already serving honorably in the armed forces while being forced to live a lie. Under existing policy, those whose sexual orientation was revealed were made to resign; over the past decade, the military had kicked out 17,000 homosexuals.

The media had been hammering the issue since long before the election, looking for a clash between the liberal draft dodger and the conservative, uptight armed forces. Powell had addressed the issue publicly just ten days before the new president was sworn into office. If Clinton followed through on his promise, he said in a speech at the U.S. Naval Academy in Annapolis, Maryland, "We must conform to that policy. The debate will be over." Those who couldn't square such a policy with their personal moral beliefs, he said, would "have to resign."

Powell had kept his own opposition to lifting the ban as far away as possible from morality. It was a question of good discipline and order—two things the military depended on to function. The presence of open homosexuals would be a source of endless friction and potential violence in the restrictive military world where soldiers lived and fought in such close proximity.

Proponents of lifting the ban had compared discrimination against gays to that against blacks and called attention to the seeming irony of Powell's position. "Your reasoning would have kept you out of the mess hall a few decades ago," Colorado Congresswoman Pat Schroeder, a liberal Democrat, wrote Powell in the days after the debate was first joined. He rejected the comparison and wrote in a prickly response that he "need[ed] no reminders concerning the history of African-Americans in the defense of their nation.... Skin color is a benign, non-behavioral characteristic. Sexual orientation is perhaps the most profound of human behavioral characteristics. Comparison of the two is a convenient but invalid argument."

Beyond Schroeder and her liberal ilk, Powell knew that most of Congress, including Nunn and many other leading Democrats, was on his side and would quickly enact legislation to overrule Clinton if he tried to reverse the ban by executive order. But the strongest opposition was within the military itself. The four service chiefs had demanded the meeting with Clinton during the first week of his presidency.

As he stated his case to the chiefs, Clinton's voice was strained and scratchy from too much talking and too many late nights. They listened respectfully but "weren't there to be persuaded," Stephanopoulos concluded from his seat against the wall behind the president. "They had the congressional troops they needed to fortify their position. Their message was clear: Keeping this promise will cost you the military. Fight us, and you'll lose—and it won't be pretty."

Knowing that the chiefs would give Clinton an earful, Powell had suggested blandly that the president hear from them individually. Carl Mundy, the Marine commandant, "was most vehement," Stephanopoulos recalled. But Powell, speaking last, "was the most effective. He leaned his thick forearms into the table, his clasped hands pointing straight at the president, and laid down a marker: The armed forces under Clinton's command were in 'exquisite' shape, he said. We shouldn't do anything to put that at risk. We'd never had full civil rights in the military, and it would be impossible to maintain morale if gay and straight soldiers were integrated."

Clinton agreed to delay any action for six months while he considered the views of senior officers. Harry Truman, he knew, had allowed the military years to overcome its resistance to desegregation. But the longer the emotion-laden issue dragged on, the more likely it was to drown out the economic initiatives he hoped to push early in his term. "I was more than willing to hear them out," Clinton later said of the chiefs, "but I didn't want the issue to get any more publicity than it was already receiving, not because I was trying to hide my position, but because I didn't want the public to think I was paying more attention to it than to the economy. That's exactly what the congressional Republicans wanted the American people to think."

As the meeting drew to an inconclusive close, Powell proposed an alternative that fell far short of the total lifting of the ban that Clinton had pledged during his campaign. Powell called it "Stop asking and stop pursuing." While a presidential commission studied the issue and the chiefs conferred, he suggested, the ban for those already outed—voluntarily or otherwise—would stay in place. But recruits would no longer be asked about sexual orientation and commanders would stop investigating suspected gays.

Clinton was noncommittal. He thanked the chiefs graciously and told them not to worry about being tough with him. If these were easy issues, he said, "somebody would have solved them long before us." Powell was pleased and optimistic that he had shown the president a possible way out of the dilemma while giving up virtually no military ground.

When the inconclusive results of the meeting were made public, issue partisans and the media pounced. Some articles congratulated Powell for upholding American morality and military honor, while others said he was thinking of resigning in disgust over Clinton's proposal. On the other side of the spectrum, he was slammed as a homophobe who had forgotten his roots. One newspaper columnist concluded sadly that Powell had passed up a chance to inspire the country to overcome its prejudices and had "consigned himself forever to the footnotes of history, to the fine print that mentions the lives of men who could have been great but refused to be."

Still others questioned Powell's loyalty to the president and suggested "that a clash is in the making on the matter of civilian control of the military." *Time* called him "The Rebellious Soldier" and suggested he wouldn't finish his tour, and a front-page, above-the-fold story in *The New York Times* confirmed it on February 10: "Joint Chiefs' Head Is Said to Request Early Retirement." The story mentioned Powell's unhappiness with Clinton's proposed cuts in the defense budget and his disagreement with the gay issue and said that Defense Secretary Les Aspin was "considering" whether to accept his resignation.

Less than a month into the Clinton administration, Powell was miserable, hailed by conservatives as an ideological compatriot, trashed by liberals as a right-wing race traitor and accused simultaneously of insubordination and bureaucratic cowardice.

Smullen's home telephone starting ringing off the hook as soon as the *Times* article hit the wires the night before its publication. Reporters wanted confirmation that Powell was quitting; Smullen denied it with little effect. When he arrived at the office at 6:30 the next morning, Smullen was met on the front steps of the Pentagon by a CBS crew wanting an interview with the general. Powell was just leaving home when Smullen called to warn of what awaited him. He rushed in from Fort Myers and headed straight for the steps to tell CBS he had no intention of resigning over the gay issue. Smullen took off to the ground-floor booths where most television correspondents did their broadcasts and arranged additional live interviews. At 11 a.m., Powell rode across the river to the CNN bureau near the Capitol. "I have no intention of leaving early for the purpose of expressing any disgruntlement… with the policies of the new administration," he told the news anchor Bernard Shaw. "I'm not down in the Pentagon writing any… resignations or break-my-sword letters."

It was true that Powell had considered early resignation, although not—at least initially—because of the gay issue. He had told Aspin at their first luncheon meeting in the new secretary's office that he might ask to leave during the slow summer months before his term expired at the end of September. It would give his successor a chance to handle the next year's budget planning, he had said, and give him a chance to get a head start on private-sector life. His thirty-five years would officially be up in June, and he would need an extension to complete his term as chairman. He had told Cheney the same thing just before the election, in the event that Bush won.

But it was also true that since the inauguration he had become frustrated and depressed that the dispute over gays in the military was overtaking every other issue. As far as Powell was concerned, it was a policy disagreement, not a moral conundrum—and certainly not a resignation issue per se. He had told Clinton what he and the chiefs believed, but thought he had made it clear that he would do what the commander in chief ordered. He had never been attacked by liberals before, particularly as a bigot; it bothered him far more than he had anticipated, and he spent more than a few moments thinking that maybe he *should* resign. There was no point in staying around if this was going to go on for the next seven months. But the *Times* article had forced his hand, and now that he had publicly declared he was staying, resignation under virtually any circumstances was off the table.

If things didn't look much better the morning after the published rumors of his resignation, Powell regained his footing shortly thereafter. The president himself was part of the solution. Whether out of genuine respect for Powell's views or, more likely, because he couldn't afford for the general to leave in a huff, Clinton enveloped him in a close embrace, consulting him regularly on issues military and otherwise. He called him on the telephone, held Powell back after group meetings for private consultations and invited him over for informal White House chats. Powell spent more quality time alone with the president during his eight months with Clinton than he had during his years with Reagan or Bush. Drawn to the persuasive abilities they recognized in each other even as they were unspoken rivals, Clinton and Powell were like magnets that could both attract and repel.

Once he regained his equilibrium, Powell fended off critics of them both with his usual panache. However much he disagreed with Clinton on gays in the military, he would not tolerate what he saw as disrespect for the president. When an Air Force general publicly called Clinton a "gay-loving, pot-smoking, draft-dodging womanizer," it was Powell, despite Clinton's willingness to overlook the remark, who insisted the man be fired. He accompanied Clinton to the annual Memorial Day speech at the Vietnam Memorial, cooling an angry crowd of veterans with more talk of binding national wounds and a pointed introduction of "the Commander-in-Chief of the armed forces of the United States, President Bill Clinton."

At the same time, Powell worked to maintain his own reputation. When hundreds of graduating seniors turned their backs and released a thousand pink balloons saying "Lift the Ban" as he sat on a dais waiting to deliver the 1993 commencement address at Harvard, Powell applauded their right to protest. He rose to shake the hand of the graduate student who preceded his speech with a denunciation of military bigotry and was drowned in applause. Kenneth Reeves, the black, homosexual mayor of Cambridge who had introduced himself to Powell by saying he disagreed with the chairman on most things, was impressed. "The secret to Colin Powell, I found, is that he is disarmingly charming."

In mid-July, Clinton announced that the temporary policy on gays in the military, now called "don't ask, don't tell," would remain permanently in place along with the existing ban. Billed as a compromise, it was a presidential surrender.

Powell found Clinton smart and appealing, but he couldn't say the same for most of the new defense and foreign policy team. Everything about the professorial Aspin irritated him, from the secretary's rambling thought process and ill-chosen words to his untidy eating habits. Secretary of State Warren Christopher, who rarely spoke in White House meetings, was unnervingly passive. National Security Adviser Tony Lake seemed content to oversee meetings that rambled on for hours and veered far off topic. George Stephanopoulos was one of the few Clinton aides whom Powell felt he could relate to—Stephanopoulos was a sharp urbanite with New York–style street savvy whose questions, Powell thought, often cut through the hours of verbiage.

To Powell's amazement, Clinton's aides seemed to think nothing of interrupting and arguing with the president. Their first NSC meeting after the inauguration set the pattern. "In my days with Reagan and Bush, you walk in, everybody knew where you were supposed to sit and you sat there," he later recalled. "And there was an agenda and you followed the agenda. At this meeting, Clinton was late—that told me something at the beginning. We all went into the Sit Room. Everybody grabbed whatever chair was there. And when Clinton came in—the President—there was no chair. We'd already taken the chairs around the table. We were now at the coffeehouse. And so we had to kind of make room for the President of the United States and the Vice President of the United States. And it didn't bother anyone—I'm going oh-oh-oh—but everybody just sat around and started chatting. [If] you had come in from Mars and didn't know who was who, you would have joined that conversation [not knowing] who the President was."

Powell was clearly a breed apart. Madeleine Albright, Clinton's ambassador to the United Nations, was both impressed and intimidated by the mere sight of the ramrod-straight general. "Part of the problem was that we were all new and Powell seemed like the grown-up. And this may sound crazy ... but somebody walks in with a uniform and has a chest full of medals and is the hero of the Western world ... there is a certain something about a winning military commander, and if you're a civilian woman, it's even worse."

But despite her admiration, Albright often found Powell exasperating, particularly on the subject of the worsening situation in Bosnia. His view that limited air strikes would accomplish little in getting the Serbs to behave had not changed. If they took out a few artillery positions from the air, he argued, the Serbs would just hide their weapons under the trees or move them somewhere else, and then what would the Americans do? "As soon as they tell me it is limited," Powell had told a reporter when Bush was still in office, "it means they do not care whether you achieve a result or not. As soon as they tell me 'surgical,' I head for the bunker." Clinton had promised during the campaign to be more aggressive than Bush, but neither he nor any U.S. allies had expressed an appetite for sending in troops to topple governments or occupy ground.

Powell saw no more vital American interest in the age-old sectarian battles in the Balkans than he had seen in Lebanon and no point in committing any military forces "until we had a clear political objective." What Albright heard was a refusal to undertake any action, no matter how compelling the reason, short of all-out war. "He replied consistent with his commitment to the doctrine of overwhelming force," she recalled, "saying it would take tens of thousands of troops, cost billions of dollars, probably result in numerous casualties, and require a long and open-ended commitment of U.S. forces. Time and again he led us up the hill of possibilities and dropped us off on the other side with the practical equivalent of 'No can do.'" It was at one of these sessions that she rendered Powell temporarily speechless by asking what was the point of having an army if you couldn't use it.

Albright was not the only one who buckled under Powell's dominance. Despite his early inclination to "do something" in Bosnia, Clinton was reluctant to reject the advice of the general who gave his administration whatever small amount of military credibility it had. Powell simply overwhelmed them all, the diplomat Richard Holbrooke later observed. "He regarded the new team as children. And the new team in turn regarded him with awe."

When Powell retired at the end of September, they were still arguing about Bosnia. Two years later, after the United States and its allies conducted limited air strikes with limited effect, he felt his arguments had been borne out. "I believe in the bully's way of going to war," he told the author Henry Louis Gates, Jr. "I'm on the street corner, I got my gun, I got my blade, I'm'a kick your ass." It was one of his gamier maxims—"a little too...ethnic, and a little too Bronx," he told Gates—and he usually avoided using it in public.

After six tumultuous months in office, Clinton and his senior advisers were exhausted, and top officials scattered in August 1993 for much-needed vacations. Powell had passed up a visit to Long Island, where his cousin Bruce Llewellyn and other wealthy new friends had summer homes, to monitor the escalating conflict in Somalia, another leftover from the Bush administration.

The country on the Horn of Africa was a hellhole without a government, its people starving from drought and upheaval as competing clan leaders vied violently to preside over its disintegration. Bush had sent thousands of U.S. troops there as part of a United Nations–led force to organize and protect humanitarian food distribution; Clinton had already begun planning their withdrawal. But hopes of an early exit were abandoned on June 5, 1993, when twenty-four Pakistani soldiers in the U.N. force were killed by gunmen loyal to the Somali clan leader Mohamed Farrah Aidid. The furious U.N. Security Council, with strong U.S. backing, immediately mandated a military hunt for those responsible, effectively changing the multinational mission from peacekeeping to participation in Somalia's civil war.

U.N. commanders on the ground, led by retired U.S. Admiral Jonathan

Howe—the officer who had replaced Powell as Carlucci's military assistant early in the Reagan administration—announced a $25,000 reward for Aidid's capture and pressed Washington for more firepower. Powell opposed expanding the mission and recommended that Aspin reject an appeal by Howe and Major General Thomas Montgomery, the commander of the U.S. contingent, to send a unit of Special Forces troops to go after Aidid. But after a visit to Mogadishu in July, Albright added her voice to Howe's conviction that nailing the warlord was essential. She carried his request for "tanks, antipersonnel carriers, attack helicopters, and a U.S. Special Forces unit" back to Washington.

In Powell's view, using combat troops to distribute food was bad enough, but Somalia was turning into a repeat of Bosnia, Lebanon and even Iraq: a messy, age-old internal conflict in which America had no strategic interest. His reluctance to expand the force—shared by Marine General Joseph Hoar, head of CENTCOM, the U.S. military headquarters responsible for Somalia—was also colored by his long-standing distrust of the CIA and elite military units that were hunting for Aidid. Intelligence agents were good at collecting information, but in Powell's experience they had an abysmal record of figuring out what it meant. They had no common sense. The warrens of Mogadishu were crawling with spies who swore they could pinpoint Aidid's location. Hoar put the chance of success at one in four, but Powell thought it was closer to one in a thousand. He had always had an ominous feeling about Special Forces; there was bad blood running through their veins that addicted them to ad hoc operations. He considered them self-important cowboys who threw tried-and-true military doctrine to the wind, opening the door to catastrophic failure.

But after several more firefights with Aidid's forces and the deaths of four American soldiers whose jeep ran over a land mine, Powell yielded to requests from the field. He roused Aspin from a fishing vacation in Wisconsin to recommend they send a 400-troop contingent of Rangers and Delta Force soldiers. Clinton, vacationing on Martha's Vineyard, signed off on the order on August 22, and the elite task force arrived in Mogadishu four days later, accompanied by a new surge in CIA operatives.

It was, both Powell and Albright later concluded, a mistake. "Despite increased military pressure Aidid continued to elude capture," Albright wrote in her memoirs. "By mid-September, congressional support for our policy was declining. We had fallen into the trap of personalizing the fight with Aidid, then failing to nab him. U.S. forces had suffered casualties in several incidents and pressure was building to get out."

On September 22, at Washington's urging, the U.N. Security Council passed another resolution, this time stressing a political and economic, rather than military, solution to the Somalia problem. But on the ground, the hunt for Aidid continued and the Pentagon received a new request from Howe and Montgomery. Passed along with approval by Hoar in a September 23 memorandum titled "Protection of Forces in Somalia," it asked again for tanks and Bradley fighting vehicles. Again, Powell was opposed; the American people had agreed to participate in U.N. food aid and nation building, and now they were being sucked into the quicksand of an actual fighting war. He kept asking for justification for such heavy weaponry; ultimately, Aspin, with Powell's recommendation and under pressure from Congress to begin withdrawing U.S. forces, rejected the request.

But at a Saturday-morning White House meeting on September 25, Powell changed his advice. For years, he had preached respect for the commanders on the ground; the commanders in Somalia were emphatically insisting they needed armor to protect American lives. He had concluded that it shouldn't be up to those sitting in air-conditioned conference rooms in Washington to tell them they were wrong. Aspin, Christopher and Lake, however, were in no mood to up the military ante in Somalia. They instead recommended a broad U.S. policy shift toward the political solution outlined in the most recent U.N. resolution. Clinton agreed, but again, no new orders were sent to the troops on the ground. Two days later, after an additional appeal from Powell, Aspin again turned down the armor request.

On October 3, three days after Powell retired from the military and left office, Army Rangers and Delta Force troops trying to nab Aidid lieutenants were trapped in downtown Mogadishu and killed in a furious firefight. Eighteen were killed, and in a horrifying spectacle broadcast around the world, Somali crowds dragged two American corpses through the streets in celebration. Powell thought it was a toss-up whether a few armored vehicles would have helped rescue the Rangers, but a Senate Armed Services Committee investigation of the incident later blamed him, along with Aspin, for leaving the troops with insufficient protection.

The Somalia debacle eventually led, in large part, to Aspin's resignation, but there was plenty of blame to go around. Clinton's team, still smarting from accusations of defense weakness that had begun with the draft-dodging charge and escalated during the gay ban controversy, hid behind Powell as the source of all military decisions. Clinton blamed Powell directly, first for recommending deployment of the Special Forces and then for leaving the White House holding the Somalia bag alone. "If I had to do it again I might do what we did then, but I'd do it in a different way," Clinton told an interviewer in 2000. Powell had come to him after the loss of the Pakistani and American peacekeepers, Clinton said, and told him, "You ought to do this, and then he retired. He left the next week. And I'm not blaming him—I'm just saying he was gone."

Clinton's version of the timing of events, later repeated in his autobiography, compressed into a matter of days the nearly six weeks between his approval of the Special Forces deployment and Powell's retirement. But he made a valid point: he had depended on Powell to keep him out of trouble overseas, and they had traveled together into disaster.

Powell wished he had stuck to his initial instincts on Somalia. He had had nothing to do with the daylight raid that had led to the American deaths, but there was no denying he had advised Clinton that sending the Special Forces was the right thing to do. It made little difference now that he had tried, in his last official conversation with the president, to tell Clinton they had both made a mistake.

On Thursday, September 30—the day of his retirement and three days before the Somalia fiasco—Powell had planned to spend the morning collecting his thoughts for the farewell speech he would give at a ceremony that afternoon, saying good-bye to his staff and organizing a huge contingent of Powell relatives in town for the retirement festivities. At 8 a.m., the White House called to say the president wanted to see him.

It was a bright, early-fall day, and Clinton, just back from his morning jog, suggested they sit outside on the Truman Balcony, looking southward toward the monuments to Presidents Washington, Jefferson and Lincoln. After a moment of awkward humor—"You take the rocker, Mr. President, you need it more than I do"—Clinton said he had no agenda beyond thanking Powell for his service and sharing some quiet time together. They spoke of Powell's plans to hit the lecture circuit and write his autobiography and then rambled through politics. In response to a question from Clinton, Powell intimated that he thought Aspin should be replaced; the defense secretary, he said, enjoyed the confidence of neither Congress nor the military.

Eventually, the conversation turned to Somalia. As Powell later recalled it, he told Clinton the same thing he had been telling Aspin: that the United States could not make a country out of the place; it could not substitute its brand of democracy for centuries of tribalism. "We've got to find a way to get out, and soon." As he said it, Powell heard echoes in his own voice of Weinberger's advice to Shultz a decade earlier: "George, we've got to get out of Beirut."

12

I have not been able to find a perfect fit in either of the two existing parties.

—Colin L. Powell

For more than thirty-five years, Powell had built his life inside the framework provided by the Army. Far more than just a paycheck and a place to go, the Army had molded his thought process and given him a set of values and a yardstick with which to measure his success. It had taught him how to stand and how to speak and told him where to live and what to wear. He had followed its guidelines with equal rigor in the mountains of Vietnam, the halls of the Pentagon and the White House.

On his last day in uniform—September 30, 1993—he was nearly overcome with emotion. The White House and the Pentagon pulled out all the stops for his retirement ceremony at Fort Myers, attended by the Clintons, the Bushes and most of their Cabinets, along with scores of Powell relatives and family friends. It was a military tradition that officers who had served with the honoree attended such festivities; in Powell's case the number of those who had known or worked closely with him, from the Pershing Rifles to the Pentagon, swelled into the hundreds.

Clinton praised him eloquently for "feeling in his heart the awesome responsibility for the lives and livelihood, for the present and future of every man and woman who wore the uniform of the United States of America." The president presented him with the Medal of Freedom—his second—and several carefully selected personal gifts—a tie Powell had once admired, a set of "his" and "her" watches from the now-defunct East Germany, an old Volvo fixer-upper that Clinton arranged to have hauled onto the parade grounds and a first edition of *Pilgrim's Progress*. Powell noted approvingly that Clinton had arrived before the ceremony began and didn't leave until the last Air Force flyover two and a half hours later.

Powell's own speech was stirring and, at the end, tearful. The Army was "my home…my life…my profession…my love for all these many years," he said. But his true debt was to America itself. "I love this country with all my heart and with all my soul. It is a love without limit. I have a bottomless faith in the goodness of this land and in the goodness of its people. I am proud to be an American. I am so proud to have been a soldier."

The next morning, after a raucous celebration at the new Powell family home in McLean, a six-bedroom, million-dollar mansion on a quiet cul-de-sac, there was no early alarm and no chauffeured car waiting to take him to the Pentagon.

Alma was hoping his retirement would begin a new phase in their relationship. Their marriage was solid and the children were well launched, but family rhythms had always been defined more by his absence than by his presence. He had rarely shared details from the professional life that had consumed nearly all of his time and energy; he joked that Alma's inevitable response to a promotion or honor was "That's nice, dear." They were comfortable together, but when he was home, if he wasn't talking on the telephone or secluded in his study, he was in the garage or parked in front of the television. She was looking forward to a chance to putter around the house together. They would go walking hand in hand or—finally—just sit around and talk.

But "the general," as everyone outside his family continued to address him, had other plans.

Tom Clancy had been right about the publishing industry's interest in Powell—Random House had eagerly snapped up his autobiography for a reported $6 million. He hired the veteran nonfiction author Joseph Persico to help write the book, and on the Monday after his retirement they sat down in Powell's basement office and he began to dictate the story of his life into a tape recorder. Persico, a white-haired Navy veteran from upstate New York, had learned politics as a speechwriter for New York Governor Nelson A. Rockefeller and had written biographies of Rockefeller and Edward R. Murrow along with several histories of World War II and its aftermath. He was the perfect fit for Powell—witty and no-nonsense, with a vast knowledge of modern American and military history and an easy writing voice that was a good match for Powell's own accessible style.

Powell was a gifted storyteller. A notorious packrat and meticulous note taker throughout his career, he had the documentation to back up his near-photographic memory. From October 1993 through the spring of

1995, with only occasional nudging from Persico, he spun tales of his childhood, his life in the Army and drama at the highest levels of national policy. It was a genuine American parable that almost wrote itself. With the transcribed tapes, Persico fashioned chapters that he sent to Powell, who revised them and sent them back to be added to the growing manuscript.

The two men rarely disagreed on what should go into the book and what should be left out, but Persico objected strenuously when Powell insisted that they devote several chapters to his chairmanship, the Base Force and the Gulf War. Powell thought the more amusing anecdotes of his service life might overpower his years in the White House and the Pentagon, and he didn't want to be dismissed as a lightweight. The book needed to be a little more "Shultz-ish," he told Persico. George Shultz, the former secretary of state, had published his 1,100-page memoirs in 1993.

Persico countered that Shultz's book had sunk like a rock, as had Caspar Weinberger's, which had been published in 1990 at half the length. People wanted to know about Colin Powell's life, he argued, not about missile defense and the Helsinki Final Act Conference. President Eisenhower's charming personal memoir had been a great success, and Reagan's *Where's the Rest of Me?* had topped the charts. Emulating Shultz and Weinberger "is to set as your standard the Edsel, not the Volvo.... You can't possibly put this boring, dull crap in this great book of mine."

"It's not your book!" Powell shouted.

They finally took the fight to their Random House editor, Harry Evans, who told Persico to give up. "Joe, the guy was a general," Evans ruled. They had to hit the high notes of his career.

Powell sometimes balked when things said in the privacy of his basement seemed too stark on the printed page. He made sure that most of the four-letter words that peppered his casual speech were excised, and he bowed to Alma's concern that any mention of her depression would be a violation of her privacy. He worried about how to describe Bush's poor performance during the 1992 campaign and his own concern that the president was losing it. "The President calling someone a bozo?" he fretted before the book was released. "You can't do that. But the only way I could see writing it—because I'm not a medical expert—was to pose it as a rhetorical question." It ended up as a vague musing: "I have often wondered if George Bush was well during the campaign."

Writing about Dick Cheney was also problematic. Cheney had exercised his right to put Powell in his place when he felt it necessary. Not only had the former defense secretary dressed him down over his reluctance to forge ahead with military plans against Iraq, he had summarily fired—against Powell's recommendation—Air Force Chief of Staff Mike Dugan for giving a careless media interview before the war. Powell's backers thought the move had been directed at the chairman as much as at Dugan. Friends of the former defense secretary thought he still had a chip on his shoulder concerning Powell—the general was too fixated with what Congress and the media thought, and he had gotten more than his fair share of credit for the Gulf War victory.

For his part, Powell thought that whatever personal relationship they had enjoyed had been set adrift at the end of Bush's term. On their last full day in office together, he had walked up to Cheney's Pentagon suite only to find it already packed up. The secretary had left without so much as a thank-you or a good-bye. Powell knew it was just Cheney being Cheney, but an early draft of the manuscript reflected his irritation.

When Richard Armitage read the draft, he could understand Powell's feeling. "I mean, here's Cheney, who took off after working cheek by jowl [with Powell] for four years, through the Base Force, through a war and everything else? Panama? Just walked away without saying a word?" But Armitage thought the draft went too far and advised Powell to soften the language.

Powell relented. He and Cheney thought alike about many things, he wrote in the final version, and "I had developed not only professional respect but genuine affection for this quiet man.... I was disappointed, even hurt, but not surprised [at Cheney's silent departure]. The lone cowboy had gone off into the sunset without even a last 'So long.' "

At least once a week, Powell headed out on the lecture circuit to the Midwest or the West Coast, telling his war stories and giving motivational talks to conventions and corporate boards. The effort required was minimal; he had spent decades polishing his speaking skills in front of much tougher audiences of troops and world leaders. Many of his former Bush administration colleagues traveled the same circuit—he ran into Cheney in San Diego in early 1994 when they were both booked at the Hardware Industry convention—but few could match the size of Powell's crowds, the warmth of his applause or the high fees he regularly commanded.

Alma eventually gave up her hope of spending more time together and accepted an offer to start her own lecture tour. She talked mostly about Colin, recounting the trials of house-training a newly retired husband. He kept inviting people over for lunch and failing to tell her until the last minute, she would say. She would race to the grocery store to find something befitting the stature of his guest and then spend her day cooking, serving and cleaning up. She finally put her foot down and told him he was on his own. "And the next time I left the house," she began the punch line, "he went...for carryout. I came home and they were sitting in the kitchen with food all over. Whoever was with him said, 'He's not much of a cook.' " For the first time in their marriage, she was earning her own income. The speeches built her confidence, and she started to branch out into public service activities.

On September 15, 1994, nearly a year after his retirement, Powell received a surprise call from former President Jimmy Carter. Carter had remained actively involved in world issues since leaving the White House in 1980, sometimes to the annoyance of the administration in power. Clinton had already had his share of Carter interventions. On a trip to North Korea in early 1994 that Clinton had only grudgingly approved, the ex-president had brokered a deal with "Supreme Leader" Kim Il Sung that Washington learned about only when Carter announced it on CNN. When that summer brought another influx of Cuban refugees sailing across the Straits of Florida to the United States, Carter took it upon himself to open negotiations with the Cuban dictator Fidel Castro and ignored the White House's demands to stop.

Now Carter was convinced he could negotiate a peaceful resolution to a growing crisis in Haiti, where turmoil under the military dictatorship that three years earlier had ousted the elected president, Jean-Bertrand Aristide, threatened to send even more Caribbean refugees toward American shores. The United Nations had demanded that the ruling military junta step down, and Clinton planned to send U.S. armed forces to invade the island and restore Aristide to power.

Carter had already recruited fellow Georgia Democrat Sam Nunn to travel with him to Port-au-Prince, the Haitian capital, and Nunn suggested they add Powell to their team. The retired general would provide the mission with a semblance of nonpartisanship, and he could talk to the junta leaders soldier-to-soldier. They thought it was equally important to their efforts that Powell was a black son of the Caribbean. Powell initially begged off, pleading a pressing book deadline and pointing out that Clinton had not approved the trip. But Clinton, boxed in by Carter's increasingly public efforts and anxious to appear willing to exhaust all nonviolent alternatives, signed off at the last minute. He called Powell personally to ask him to go.

The delegation was scheduled to depart on the morning of Saturday, September 17. Clinton instructed them to spend no more than twenty-four hours in Haiti, and to leave the island no later than noon on Sunday. The U.S. military landing would take place no matter what they achieved, he told them, and their negotiating brief extended only to whether U.S. troops would arrive to coordinate a peaceful transfer of power or would storm the island with guns blazing. What Clinton did not tell any of the three envoys was that the countdown to invasion had already begun. The first American paratroopers were due to take off from Fort Bragg at 5 p.m. Sunday; they would drop into Haiti at midnight to prepare the ground for a full-scale naval assault early Monday morning. Navy Special Forces had already infiltrated the island; they were given standby orders to forcibly extricate the negotiating delegation from the Haitian capital if they tarried.

The negotiators landed in Port-au-Prince aboard a military transport just after noon Saturday and were taken to the Haitian military command headquarters across from the city's massive, whitewashed Presidential Palace. The building's second-floor conference room was lined with the portraits of the heroes of the slave revolts that led to Haiti's declaration of independence in 1804. The world's first free black republic and the second independent country in the Western Hemisphere—after the United States—Haiti's rich history had been squandered since then by a series of dictatorships. In 1990, Aristide had become the country's first democratically elected president, only to be overthrown by the military after seven months in office. The international community had demanded that the two generals who led the coup—Raoul Cédras, now head of the ruling junta, and army chief Philippe Biamby—step down.

Tension was as high as the temperature in the muggy, airless room as the meeting with the junta began, and Powell kept his eye on an M16 rifle with a fully loaded banana clip leaning against the wall in easy reach of the Haitians. Carter began by explaining that he, Nunn and Powell all had reservations about a military invasion but they and all Americans would support President Clinton if it came to that. U.S. troops were going to land regardless of the junta's decision; the question was whether they would use force or land peacefully.

The Haitian officers seemed to have eyes and ears for Powell alone, recalled Robert Pastor, a Carter aide who was taking notes of the session. Powell had been watching them with equal intensity, and as Carter turned the floor over to him, he decided that before threatening them he would try to provide them with a way out.

"Perhaps more than any member of our delegation, as a soldier like all of you, as someone who spent 35 years of my life in the military, I think I understand what is in your heart and head at this time," he began. But their shared duty was not to their institutions, he said, it was "to the people. An historic decision has been placed before you: you have been asked to step down at the request of the international community.... I tried to put myself in your position. A very large force is assembled; it will act. I know the commander; I trained the leaders. I know their plan. It will be a massive operation with assault troops. I do not want to see that force launched against your forces and the people of Haiti. There will be a terrible loss of life.

"The alternative that President Carter put before you is to work together to see if it could be a force of friendship to help make a peaceful transition so that the Haitian Armed Forces could be preserved as a key institution working with the Multinational Force." Yielding, he told them, was not only the right course of action but the "honorable" thing to do. "That is my best advice, as a soldier, a friend and someone deeply committed to the welfare of the Haitian people."

Powell glanced occasionally at the M16 as he spoke, calculating whether he could reach it before Biamby. He paused and then started describing what would happen if the junta did not cooperate. The American force would include many U.S. ships and "assault forces with every ability to attack and defend themselves with helicopter gunships and artillery. It will approach the size of U.S. forces during the Panama invasion, but with greater robustness.... If it anticipates resistance, it will come in very heavy." As he spoke, Powell moved his hands to illustrate swooping aircraft and massive troop movements. It reminded Pastor of the mesmerizing briefings Powell had given on television during the Gulf War.

Cédras stared at him. "All that coming?"

"Yes."

But Haiti, Cédras observed, was only a small country. "We used to be the weakest military force in the hemisphere and we're now about to become the biggest military force in the hemisphere when that arrives." He wanted to explain the island's history to his visitors, he said. He began with slavery, French colonialists and the 1804 revolution, finally coming to Aristide more than an hour later. The deposed president, he insisted, was a terrible man and as much a dictator as any of his predecessors. "If he were to return, the entire country would go up in flames."

The envoys listened politely. Carter tried to shift the discussion back toward the logistics of the junta's capitulation, but made little progress.

During a break in the talks, the Americans headed to their rooms at the Villa Creole, a small, bougainvillea-wrapped hotel in the fragrant hills high above the squalor of Port-au-Prince. To try to move the process forward, they drafted an agreement for the junta's resignation and a peaceful American landing and took it back to the command center. Again, there was little movement. Over dinner at the hotel, a Haitian businessman assured them that Cédras's wife, Yannick, was the real power behind the junta. They arranged a meeting with her for the next morning.

The Cédras home was a relatively modest house in a better part of Port-au-Prince. Yannick Cédras and her husband met them at the door with two of their three young children and escorted them back to the kitchen/dining room. After they sat down, she sent the children away and with no preamble said, "Last night, we brought our children into bed with us and I made them pledge that we were all going to die together, to commit suicide, at the moment the invasion occurs." They would all rather perish as martyrs with American bullets in their chests, she said, than as traitors with Haitian bullets in their backs.

For a moment, no one spoke. "It took our breath away," Pastor recalled. "She was serious as shit. I almost felt like crying."

The envoys had been told that Mrs. Cédras—the daughter, granddaughter and wife of Haitian generals—was an admirer of Powell, and they had already decided he would carry the ball for them that morning. Powell said his own wife would understand her loyalty. "But I tell you there is no honor in throwing away lives when the outcome is already determined. You and your husband should accept the inevitable and spare Haiti further suffering." Mrs. Cédras was noncommittal, and her husband never said a word. While they were at the house, Powell was called out of the room several times to take calls from an increasingly agitated Clinton. What were they doing? Did they realize they only had three hours before they had to leave Haiti?

They drove back to the military command center, and as they entered the conference room, the Pentagon general traveling with them pulled Powell aside. "We're in the window," he whispered.

Powell raised his eyebrows in surprise. "In the window? What window?" He had talked with Carter and Nunn about the timing of the invasion, and they were convinced it would be at least another day or two.

"Planes will be taking off in a few hours, and they're coming here," the general informed him. As they sat down to resume their negotiations, Powell quietly relayed the information to Nunn.

Their noon deadline came and went, and Clinton's communications grew increasingly frequent and peremptory. The negotiators had installed a secure telephone in a room down the hall, and they excused themselves every thirty minutes or so to take another call from Washington. As Clinton argued with the envoys, his aides were gathered in the Oval Office, warning the president that Carter and the other two had gone native. Unbeknown to the three Americans in Haiti, the Special Forces extrication team was waiting for Clinton's go-ahead to land a helicopter outside the command center and grab them, shooting any Haitian who got in their way. Carter tried to calm Clinton. "Mr. President, we're there," he insisted. "We've got the agreement, got the essence. We want to finish."

The Haitian generals had finally agreed in principle to stand down but were haggling over the date and conditions of their exit from power. Washington wanted them out of Haiti, but Carter argued that forced exile was a violation of international law. Powell thought it was pointless to quibble about the details when the basic agreement had been struck. "Mr. President, we've got the major thing we want," he told Clinton. "They have accepted the agreement. It would be terrible if we were to fail at this point, to pull out and to have American troops killed when they can come in peacefully." He sounded more certain of the junta's agreement than he actually was.

Biamby left the room in the early afternoon, only to burst back in at around 4 p.m. accompanied by wild-eyed armed guards and shouting that Haitian intelligence—later determined to have been spotters camped with binoculars outside Fort Bragg—had just informed him that paratroopers were boarding a plane. "You lied to us!" he screamed. "You have betrayed us! I'm taking General Cédras to a secure location so we can prepare our defenses."

Carter's face turned red, and his voice rose above the shouts. "You cannot leave! If you leave these negotiations now, your children will die. Haitians will die. You can't assume that responsibility." Powell was astounded. He didn't think the former president had it in him.

Cédras suggested they submit the proposed agreement to Émile Jonaissant, the eighty-year-old judge installed by the junta as a puppet president. The Presidential Palace was only a short distance away, but no one wanted to push through the increasingly agitated crowd surrounding the headquarters and chanting "Death to Aristide." Powell became separated from Carter and Nunn and ended up with Cédras, Biamby and their rifles, squeezed in the back of a Haitian military vehicle whose floor was covered with loose bullets and grenades.

Inside Jonaissant's office, the old man calmly signed the document with no changes, brushing off the resignation threats of his attendant Cabinet ministers. Powell raced off to update Clinton, picking up an open-line telephone on the desk of the first vacant office he came to. "Mr. President, they have now given us free rein. No American soldier will die.... We don't have to get into the fine details right now. We got what you wanted."

Clinton insisted they obtain a personal pledge from Cédras—who had remained silent since they had arrived in the palace—that there would be no resistance to the landing. What about it? Powell asked the general. Cédras said he would give his word, but only if Jonaissant told him to.

Powell turned to Jonaissant. "Will you instruct him to enforce the agreement?" Yes, the president replied. "Well, do it," Powell said sternly.

Jonaissant looked at Cédras and said, "I want you to enforce the agreement." Powell again turned to the general. "You've just been instructed. Are you going to enforce it?" As the others held their breath, the exchange went back and forth several more times until Cédras said he would not disobey his president's order.

It was done. They raced to the airport, climbed aboard the transport and called Washington from the air. The paratroopers had already taken off from Fort Bragg; Clinton ordered the planes to make a U-turn and return home. Pastor was left behind to finish up the details, and at 10 a.m. on Monday, September 19, the first American helicopters landed at the Port-au-Prince airport. As the troops piled off, guns at the ready, Pastor ran across the tarmac, waving his arms and shouting "Don't shoot!" He grabbed the commander, Lieutenant General Hugh Shelton, by the hand. There were no Haitians in sight.

Aristide returned to Haiti in triumph on October 15. The Americans suffered no casualties from hostile fire during the six months they were deployed on the island before being replaced by a U.N. peacekeeping force. Powell was praised as the key element in avoiding war, although some criticized him for having let Cédras and the others off the hook too easily. Powell didn't care. As far as he was concerned, Haiti was no place for a young American soldier to die.

Although White House aides spun the story as a victory for presidential resolve and willingness to use military force, they privately thought Clinton had been embarrassingly trumped by his own negotiators in a battle of wills that could have gone disastrously awry. The returning envoys were hailed as heroes, and Richard Armitage, whose political sensitivities were far more acute than Powell's, warned his friend that it was dangerous to upstage a sitting president or even a former one. Armitage had watched the team's press conference with Clinton, he told Powell. It wasn't that the general had talked too much or said the wrong thing, but he had somehow managed to steal the limelight. "You know, you've got to stop that, man, because you just dominate it." The president might not notice, but those around him certainly would.

Nearly everything Powell had touched throughout his long career had turned to gold, even if others involved were sometimes left looking less than heroic. He had survived Vietnam and flourished. When Iran-*contra* had tarnished a generation in government, he had emerged with his reputation enhanced and credit for restoring order to the Reagan administration. His professional crises, from General Hudachek to *The Commanders,* had faded quickly, and his ability to thrive as a black man among conservative white Republicans had done far more for his own image of personal rectitude and reasonableness than it had for their claims of equal opportunity. A few weeks after his retirement, when a nationwide survey asked respondents to rate leadership figures on a scale of 0 to 100, with 100 indicating "a very warm feeling," Powell came in first at 71. Cheney, with a residual Gulf War glow, was second at 57. Clinton and the Republican presidential hopeful Jack Kemp tied for third place with scores of 55.

Powell had no idea whether his sense of duty or his talents extended to elective office. He had hopscotched the nation from post to post, but outside the walls of the military his own country was still a relative mystery to him. His approach to issues of national import was guided not by an overarching political philosophy but by a list of maxims, his own experiences, common sense and the U.S. Army Leadership Field Manual. He held strong convictions about the use of military power in specific circumstances but had given little thought to the appropriate diplomatic role of the United States in the post–Cold War world. On the domestic front, Powell thought the government should stay out of people's private lives while being stingy with Americans' money even as it provided for the disadvantaged. But he had no ready solutions for the difficult problems of health care, education or poverty.

According to opinion polls, Americans were split on whether they considered Powell a Republican, a Democrat or affiliated with no party at all. Yet every time he appeared in public he was now asked whether he would run for president. He quickly developed a line to avoid the question and get a laugh, responding, "Of what?"

"Don't you feel you have a mission?" pressed one of six hundred telecommunications experts he addressed at a conference in Florida shortly after his retirement. He deflected the question with a grin and a line from the movie *The Blues Brothers:* "We are on a mission from God." Aboard a plane back to Washington the same day, a white man with a southern accent and a business suit spotted him and burst out, "I sure am proud to be sitting in front of the next president. We gotta get rid of Slick Willie and them boys." Powell felt like hiding in the bathroom for the rest of the flight.

As they finished up a taping session early one afternoon five months into the book project, Persico remarked that even he was being deluged with calls of support for a Powell presidency. It was looking inevitable, he said.

"Nothing is inevitable," Powell replied with a laugh. There were other things he could do in public life short of running for president.

"None even remotely comparable," Persico replied. The only thing he had to decide was when to declare and for which party.

Powell turned serious. He had real concerns about the Republicans, he said, and would be interested only if he thought he could help pull the party back from what seemed to be a headlong plunge to the right. As for the Democrats, he could imagine the advice Bill Clinton would give him: "Look, Colin, you can wait until 2000 and go with either party. You could go up in the Democratic primaries against Gore or Hillary. But how would you feel about leaving the speaking tour, trying to get your book finished, establishing an organization, going into the Republican Party primaries and running against a sitting president, one who might be doing well. That's what you face if you go in '96."

As usual, Powell parsed the situation into a "decision loop." "Enemy situation: Bill Clinton, Jack Kemp, Dick Cheney. Friendly situation: I'm in good health, I've retired, the nation thinks about me in a certain way.... I don't know anything about health care, but I know a hell of a lot about national security. Terrain and weather: I'm aging rapidly, I'm not sure that I really want to go through the kind of twenty-four-hour days required for a long period of time."

The mission was to prepare himself and develop a campaign plan to run for president, and to win in 1996. Potential support included Armitage as campaign manager and Kenneth Duberstein and Tom Griscom from the Reagan administration for fund-raising and communications, respectively. "Logistics: Going to need a lot of money. Command and control: Retain complete control over the campaign."

Early polls indicated that Powell was the only potential candidate likely to unseat Clinton in a head-to-head contest. But even if that were true when the votes were actually cast—the presidential election was still more than two years away—he wasn't sure that replacing Clinton was the right thing for the country. They didn't always see eye to eye, but Clinton was a decent president who had America's best interests at heart. If Powell wanted to be a Democrat, maybe he should take up the president's offer to join his Cabinet—there was still talk about replacing Warren Christopher as secretary of state—and run as his Democratic successor in 2000.

With little to no encouragement, "Powell for President" committees were being formed and support and money were being pledged around the country. His fax machine was clogged with advice and appeals to run, and he was getting telephone calls from everyone he had ever known or who thought they knew him. So far, he had ignored them. He didn't have any answers at this point, he told Persico. Anyway, Alma didn't want to hear anything about it.

Proposals poured in for other races, in other places. Republicans in Powell's home state of New York were sure he could unseat Democratic Governor Mario Cuomo. If that didn't appeal to him, he could run for the Senate in his adopted state of Virginia against the incumbent Democrat, Chuck Robb. He turned them all down, but Harry Evans, his Random House editor, was eager for him to stay in the public eye and not to close the door to the presidency before his autobiography was published.

Evans wanted to make sure the Powell persona remained luminous enough to sell as many books as possible, but Powell had never welcomed advice on how to maintain his image. A letter he drafted to Evans in the summer of 1995 reflected both his political uncertainty and a shrewd assessment of his own market value: "Notwithstanding my limited exposure, my profile is as high as it was when I retired. I am enclosing a NEWSWEEK piece where I came in second to Billy Graham and a NY OBSERVER piece which is typical of articles appearing about me around the country on a weekly basis.... I am generating this interest by remaining the 'mystery man' to a great extent. What is he? Will he or won't he? I do not think it is wise for me to tamper with this image. I am also sure we can keep it going for some time."

He would attend an upcoming book fair in Frankfurt, Germany, as Random House had requested, Powell wrote, but it would cheapen his currency if he used his contacts and celebrity, as the publisher also had suggested, to set up meetings with European leaders for the sole purpose of creating headlines. He saw no reason for foreign press interviews. "It strips away my cover and will make no news in Europe unless I [talk about] Bosnia, Clinton, politics, etc." He would make brief remarks at the Frankfurt event, but "If anyone hangs a banner from the autobahn, I ain't coming."

The November 1994 midterm elections dealt the Democrats a devastating blow, with the loss of eight seats in the Senate and fifty-four in the House of Representatives. It was the biggest turnover since 1946 and enough to give the Republicans control of both chambers. The defeat reawakened Clinton's interest in bringing Powell into his Cabinet, with the same mixed motives as in 1992. The addition of the respected black general would strengthen his administration's anemic foreign and defense policies even as it added racial heft. Although Les Aspin had been replaced by his deputy, William Perry, shortly after the Mogadishu disaster, the uninspiring Warren Christopher remained secretary of state. Clinton's attention to Powell was also an insurance policy: co-opting the general now would keep him out of the presidential competition in 1996.

On a Sunday morning six weeks after the midterm election, Clinton called Vernon Jordan at home. He was thinking of making a change at State, the president said, and wanted Jordan to feel out Powell again. Jordan, who was recovering from stomach surgery, dragged himself out of bed and to the White House, where he placed a call to Powell from the Oval Office.

"Don't go to church," he said, "because I'm coming to have church with you."

Again, Powell's answer was no. He was committed to his book, he told Jordan that afternoon, and the spring 1995 deadline for the manuscript was fast approaching. Jordan didn't need to be told that Powell disapproved of the style and some of the substance of the administration's foreign policy. Equally unspoken was the recognition by both men that joining the administration now would preempt Powell's decision on whether to run for president himself.

Jordan reported back that Powell was not interested but didn't want to have to tell the president no to his face. Clinton was undeterred and called Powell at home that night to ask him to stop by the White House in the morning. Powell spent much of the rest of the night thinking about it, and the next day, in more polite terms, he gave the president the same answer he had given Jordan. At least one part of his political future had been decided—he wasn't going to be a Democrat.

The Republicans had their own Powell dilemma. More popular than any of the half-dozen likely contenders for the party's nomination, he posed a particular danger to Bob Dole, the seventy-year-old Republican leader in the Senate, who by early 1995 had emerged as the front-runner. Powell knew Dole, although they were far from close. When he had been Reagan's national security adviser, Dole would sometimes summon him to Capitol Hill to knock some sense into recalcitrant conservatives—the "hard rocks" in the party, Dole called them—who were balking at some Reagan initiative they considered insufficiently hawkish toward the Soviet Union.

Dole's advisers were pushing him to resolve the problem by persuading Powell to run as his vice president. One of Dole's close political friends, former New Hampshire Senator Warren Rudman, had broached the subject with Powell as early as the spring of 1994. What if Dole agreed from the outset to serve only one four-year term, Rudman had asked, leaving Powell a clear shot at the presidency in 2000 and 2004? Although Powell had changed the subject without responding, Rudman told Dole he hadn't said no. Since then, Dole partisans had raised the issue regularly with Powell.

Powell didn't want to be asked. He had no interest in being anybody's number two, and whatever appeal his popularity might add to the Republican ticket, he doubted that Dole could unseat Clinton.

Harry Evans needn't have worried about keeping his nascent author in the headlines. In speeches around the country throughout 1994 and 1995, Powell revealed just enough of his evolving views on domestic issues to maintain interest in his possible candidacy. "The American people are going to have to come forward with a consensus that we are all prepared as a family to suffer a little more, either by accepting less from the federal government, doing with less in the way of entitlements, [or] paying more taxes if that's what it takes to put this nation on a solid economic footing," he told a crowd of 2,600 in Cleveland in late 1994.

When he was asked directly if he would run for president after a February 1995 appearance at Trinity University in San Antonio, his reply was Delphic: "There is no real passion in me to run for office. But I don't want to rule it out." Now that he was retired from the Army and traveling around the country, he said, "I expect I will develop a political philosophy. Time will tell whether I find that my personal philosophy fits one or the other of the two major parties or whether I just remain independent. I think it important for me to have something I believe in rather than have my beliefs fit a party just for the purpose of saying I belong to it."

Divining Powell's partisan leanings became a favorite political parlor game. He praised elements of both Republican and Democratic initiatives and claimed friends across the board. He criticized Clinton's foreign policy as "zigging and zagging—waffling, some might call it" and in the next breath charged that the "Contract with America," the conservative blueprint being touted by the new Republican congressional majority, risked undermining the Constitution. He spoke eloquently of his own upbringing and "the need to re-create the American family," but he shocked conservatives by allowing that "it doesn't even have to be a two-gender family."

On the lecture circuit, he was a combination of larger-than-life hero and regular guy. Now dressed in hand-tailored suits, he was physically vigorous and exuded energy and authority. He provoked gales of appreciative laughter with stories about his early Army life and his current self-portrait of an aging retiree whose wife refused to fix his lunch. "One of the saddest figures in all Christendom is the Chairman of the Joint Chiefs of Staff, once removed, driving around with a baseball cap pulled over his eyes, making his strategic choice as to whether it's going to be McDonald's or Taco Bell." He took them inside the Oval Office and the Kremlin and to military camps in the Kuwaiti desert, tugged at their patriotic heartstrings and then made them laugh all over again. Putting on a New York Jewish accent, he described the scene at a White House treaty signing between Israeli Prime Minister Yitzhak Rabin and Palestinian leader Yasser Arafat. "Arafat...is so taken with the moment that he starts to pull me toward him and hug me and give me a two-cheek kiss. But I can only stand so much new world order..."

Aside from the visibility and income the lecture circuit provided, Powell was also learning more about the country and using his celebrity platform to draw attention to an issue about which he had become increasingly passionate: children and minorities in need. At nearly every stop on his speaking tours, he took time out to make quiet visits to local schools and Boys and Girls Clubs, sometimes speaking to an audience of only a few dozen children. At the District of Columbia's Lorton Prison, he spent three hours trying to persuade three hundred mostly African-American inmates, many of whom confessed that they had thought of him as an "Uncle Tom," to persevere in the face of poverty and racism and to love and care for their often estranged children. When he finished speaking, they crowded around him for autographs.

Beyond his words, Powell's mere existence seemed to make Americans proud of the country that had produced him, and of themselves as its citizens. He talked openly about race to whites in ways that were both nonthreatening and inspirational. "How did I deal with racism? I beat it," he said in San Antonio. "I said ... 'I'm going to destroy your stereotype. I'm proud to be black. You carry this burden of racism, because I'm not going to.'"

Powell was not the only member of his family who had made it in white America. There were judges, executives and diplomats among the Powell and McKoy descendants. His cousin Bruce Llewellyn, a leveraged buyout expert who owned the Coca-Cola bottling company in Philadelphia and had served in the Carter administration, was one of the richest men in the country. But Llewellyn had a more jaundiced view of the state of racial equality in the United States and thought Colin let whites off the hook too easily. "He gives a great speech," Llewellyn once said of his cousin. "He gets all them white people coming up off the chairs, clapping and feeling good about themselves. He talks about America, the great land of opportunity, and how a poor West Indian kid with Jamaican parents and living in the south Bronx can work his way to be the chairman of the Joint Chiefs of Staff.... They all love this shit. They all love the idea that, 'Gee, we weren't prejudiced. A good man came, and we gave him his shot.' White people love to believe they're fair."

Black voters were less enamored of Powell. Although nationwide polls indicated that he would win a two-way race, 75 percent of African Americans said they would vote for Clinton. Virtually every black leader of consequence was a Democrat, and their views of Powell were diverse. He was the most viable potential black candidate who had ever come along, and many felt that since he was sound enough on most of the issues they cared about they could overlook those areas in which their views diverged. "Not only would I support him; I'd work my ass off for him," declared the author and academic Roger Wilkins. Representative Kweisi Mfume, a Maryland Democrat and former chairman of the Congressional Black Caucus, called Powell "the best that we can be.... I told him that whenever he decided, please count me among the persons he would call first." Marian Wright Edelman, the head of the liberal Children's Defense Fund, said that after hearing Powell speak, "I had to force myself to remember that we disagree on certain military policies. He certainly has a central core of integrity."

But other African Americans saw Powell as a newcomer or even a no-show in the fight for equality who had made his bed with the opposition. Jesse Jackson, so far the only black man to have actually run a presidential campaign and still mulling a 1996 bid, resented what he considered Powell's free ride in the largely white-owned media. "He's a phantom candidate," Jackson snapped to the author Henry Louis Gates, Jr., in the summer of 1995. "We can all have positive assumptions [about Powell], but we still don't know. We do know that very right-wing white people can trust him. They can trust him to drop bombs. We know that Reagan could trust him. Historically, there's been this search—whites always want to create the black of their choice as our leader. So for the white people this nice, clean-cut black military guy becomes something really worth selling and promoting. But have we ever seen him on a picket line? Is he for unions? Or for civil rights? Or for *anything?*"

With his uniform, his light skin and his island heritage, Powell didn't even seem *black* to most whites, observed the longtime Democratic politician and civil rights activist Julian Bond, an admirer. "You put Colin Powell and any other Mr. Black Man up there, and it becomes just that—it's Colin Powell and Mr. Black Man. Probably because of his Caribbean background, he has a kind of diction that isn't black American. He's verbally not black." Some black analysts predicted that his pleasing demeanor wouldn't survive a campaign. "Once the ugly attacks and assaults really begin, Colin Powell will be forced, to some degree, to come out swinging," the Harvard philosopher and social critic Cornel West told Gates. "Then they'll say 'Oh my god, he *is* a black man. Look at him. He's full of rage. He's been that all the time.' "

But so far, at least, there was little evidence of rage in Powell's speeches around the country. Instead, he gently chided the nation for losing sight of its better self. "We should sacrifice for one another, care about one another, never be satisfied when anybody in this group is suffering and we can do something about it," he told a National Sporting Goods Association convention in Chicago in August 1995. "That's what we've been missing. That's what's causing this angst in our public consciousness, the sense that we've lost the ability to care and sacrifice for each other.... We've lost the sense of shame, we've lost the sense of outrage. The solution isn't some new program, more government, it's not just screaming at the television, it's not screaming at our politicians or watching them scream at each other."

He avoided offering specific solutions to most domestic problems—sometimes out of political calculation, sometimes out of genuine indecision—leaving individual Americans to assume that because they liked and respected Colin Powell, he must think like them. The country was wallowing in a post–Cold War malaise and suffering an economic slump. Clinton seemed indecisive and ineffective, and the Republicans had grown increasingly harsh and obstructionist. Powell stood shining in the breach, the nation's number one "heroic figure" to self-described conservatives and liberals alike. No politician matched the breadth of his support across race, gender, income group or party. He was, as *Time* magazine noted in an admiring cover story, "something of an empty ideological vessel into which voters pour their own beliefs."

The national swoon was sometimes too much even for Powell. The *Time* cover story, he told a friend, was "a major barf." On rare occasions, the media itself seemed embarrassed by its exorbitant admiration. "Even by the standards of modern media excess," reported *The Washington Post*—which had made its own contributions to Powell-mania—"there has never been anything quite like the way the press is embracing, extolling and flat-out promoting this retired general who has never sought public office."

Among the bouquets showering Powell in the spring and summer of 1995, the occasional weed sprouted. Most, but not all, grew from ideological roots. Powell was a confirmed multilateralist and a proponent of the "new world order" in which American sovereignty would be handed over to a "global government," warned the right-wing *New American* magazine. He had been "packaged under a false label and marketed by the same snake-oil hucksters who have sold us deadly political poison many times before." Moreover, he had "sacrificed every principle that he was sworn to uphold" on the altar of personal ambition.

In an article that echoed charges they had made in a book about the Gulf War, two *New York Times* journalists wrote that "a careful look at [Powell's] performance shows someone who's less a modern MacArthur than a master bureaucrat, skillful in dealing with the press and adept at escaping blame for questionable decisions, risk-averse to the point of timidity." He had tried to avoid the very Gulf War that had made him a national hero, they pointed out. Once the war began, they charged, he had argued successfully to end it too soon, ensuring that America would be mired in a low-level struggle to contain Baghdad for years to come.

Others combed his career for character flaws. *The New Republic* contended that "Powell often disagreed with the Army or the government, or with the direction of the country. But he rarely spoke out. Rather, he made a point of keeping his head down and doing his job." If he hadn't brushed off Tom Glen's letter on military abuses in Vietnam, the article suggested, the horror of My Lai might have been uncovered sooner (although Glen himself later said he had praised Powell in 1995 television interviews that were never broadcast). If he had publicly revealed his distaste for the Iranian arms scheme and refused to facilitate the shipments, the *New Republic* reporter Charles Lane suggested, perhaps the Iran-*contra* scandal could have been avoided.

The presidential drumbeat also breathed new life into earlier allegations that Powell had usurped civilian authority during his chairmanship. In a lengthy treatise that provoked a torrent of debate among defense policy experts, the military historian Richard H. Kohn charged that Powell had crossed the military-civilian line with his 1989 pronouncements on the pending demise of the Soviet Union and incipient world trouble spots. In the Powell Pentagon, Kohn argued, defense planning and the Base Force had been conceived without consulting the service chiefs and in circumvention of "the established programming/budgeting procedures in place in the Defense Department since the early 1960s. He developed his plans without any guidance from the President or the Secretary of Defense, and he sold the plan to the White House and Congress, in spite of Secretary of Defense Dick Cheney's initial disagreement with its assumptions about the Soviet threat and opposition from other Pentagon civilians."

Powell had maneuvered to force President Clinton to compromise on the issue of gays in the military by effectively announcing to the world that "the President could be rolled," Kohn wrote. Democrats were afraid to challenge him, he concluded, because "they saw no profit and much danger in criticizing the first African-American Chairman of the Joint Chiefs" whose reluctance to use military force overseas matched their own.

In early May 1995, Powell took advantage of a scheduled speech in Bermuda for a brief vacation with Alma. They stayed at the home of John Swan, the elected premier of the self-governing British colony, whom Powell had befriended when he was in the Reagan White House. As they sat around the swimming pool on a balmy spring afternoon, Powell talked about the pressure he was under to make a run for the presidency. Swan was enthusiastic, pushing hard to persuade him to seize a once-in-a-lifetime opportunity. Alma, who had remained silent through most of the conversation, suddenly burst out, "I don't want any part of it. Somebody will try to kill him."

Powell was amazed at both the opinion and the emotion in her voice. He hadn't expected her to be enthusiastic about the White House, but it was heresy for an Army wife to express such concerns in terms of personal safety—what did she think he'd been doing all those years in Vietnam and Korea?

Alma had been biting her tongue for months while her husband wrote his book, delivered his speeches and basked in the nation's adoration. Whenever anyone asked what she thought about the presidency, she said they hadn't really discussed it. The truth was that they hadn't—but that didn't mean she hadn't thought long and hard about it. "You think everybody loves Colin Powell," she told friends and relatives. "Well, everybody does not love Colin Powell."

He lived on a pedestal and was applauded whenever he walked out the door. She was the one who gingerly took the mail from the postman every afternoon and thumbed through the hate messages scattered among the fan letters. She was the one who peered nervously out the window as strangers drove slowly and ominously around the cul-de-sac outside their house, staring and pointing at their unfenced yard. Those who loved Colin could be nearly as frightening as those who did not—one glassy-eyed, disheveled man had appeared at their front door to say he had driven straight through from Florida to tell her husband he had to run for president.

She thought he was naive to ignore the impact a major African-American candidate would have. She had grown up in the South and knew firsthand the racial hatred that he had never really experienced.

The only member of the Powell family who thought his candidacy was a good idea was their son, Michael—"the little politico," Colin laughingly called him—who had a new law degree and a job in the Justice Department. Colin's sister, Marilyn, feared that no matter how many whites showed up at his speeches to cheer and say they would vote for him, there were a lot of Americans who would never accept a black president. She was proud of what he'd done for his country but thought it was enough. Bruce Llewellyn put the fear more bluntly: "I could just see some guy sitting there saying, 'Over my dead body this guy is going to be President of the United States.' " Except the dead body would be Colin's.

Annemarie thought her father was "too good to be put into that political environment where you have to make choices that are going to be compromises to get elected . . . to please a certain group of people." Linda feared an end to their privacy and the opening of all their lives to public consumption.

The choices and compromises had already begun. As they worked on the final draft of the book, Persico was disturbed to see that Powell had excised two sentences from the last chapter outlining his political philosophy. He was "a fiscal conservative with a social conscience," the passage began, and neither of the two major parties fit him comfortably. But Powell had removed the rest of the passage, which read, "I am troubled by the political passion of those on the extreme right who seem to claim divine wisdom on political as well as spiritual matters. God provides us with guidance and inspiration, not a legislative agenda." When Persico protested, Powell responded that it might not be worth what it could cost in book sales and future employment. Get a grip, Persico argued; it was one of the most powerful messages in the chapter, and it was what he believed. Powell agreed to reinsert the sentences.

Until it was published, the book was an extension of the cover his uniform had provided for decades, a blind to hide behind while politics swirled around him: "Don't bother me, I'm writing. When I'm finished, all will be revealed." Random House had scheduled its release for mid-September 1995 and planned a major promotional campaign, including a coast-to-coast tour with stops in two dozen cities and visits to Paris and London. Bookstores were competing for personal appearances, and many agreed to purchase at least the required two thousand copies of the book to qualify. *Time* magazine was set to run excerpts, and the major television networks were vying for the first postrelease interviews.

At 8 a.m. on Saturday, September 16, Peggy Cifrino's telephone startled her out of a sound sleep. Cifrino, along with William Smullen, had left her Pentagon job to work for Powell in his retirement. She was scheduled to meet him at 11:30 that day at the Crown Books outlet near his home in McLean for the inaugural book signing. But the store manager was on the telephone begging her to come right away. He had arrived that morning to find scores of people who had camped overnight in the parking lot and a line that ran around the next block. Television trucks were already setting up for live broadcasts, and reporters wanted to come inside the store.

News of the mob scene only reinforced Alma's decision to stay home. She had found the book a revelation—she was familiar with the events in his life over the years, "but it was the first time I knew what he thought about it." But she had never shared his enthusiasm for crowds.

Powell fought his way into the building amid cheers and flashing cameras. As he sat behind a table and began signing the 600-page volumes, Smullen kept track of the numbers, and by the time they finished hours later, Powell had penned his name in more than 3,000 books. Over the next four weeks, it was the same wherever he went. Smullen calculated that it took slightly less than seven seconds for Powell to be handed an open book, smile, scrawl his name across the title page and hand it back.

Powell's arrival was a major news event in each new city. Book reviews in smaller venues were inevitably raves, but even the more prestigious, big-city newspapers and magazines were almost universally charmed by the easy telling of his life story, titled *My American Journey*. It hit the top of *The New York Times*' best-seller list by the end of its first week. Foreign-language versions were released as quickly as the book could be translated, although not always the entire text and not always with the approval of Random House. Saudi Arabia left out some of the Gulf War parts, and Cuban President Fidel Castro wrote Powell to say that his government had done its own Spanish translation and had "printed only a few copies for some of our top officials." He sent Powell a copy, saying there would be "no charge" for the translation if the publisher wanted to print a Spanish edition for distribution elsewhere.

Random House was overjoyed and kept the presses rolling far beyond the initial printing of a million copies. Like every nervous first-time author—particularly one who has laid out his own life history—Powell was relieved, gratified and, not incidentally, pleased at the lucrative sales. But what overwhelmed him was the outpouring of interest, care and even love from the massive crowds he encountered in city after city. As he climbed into the backseat of the car with Smullen after each event, he would shake his head and say, "Do you believe this?"

At every stop, the crowds begged and pleaded with him to run for president. "At first I think he was stunned by it," Smullen recalled. "Then a little bit scared, in the sense of not wanting to declare a political preference. People would say, 'I don't care what you are, General. I'm a lifelong Democrat and even if you're a Republican you can count on me and all the people in my family.' He listened to it time and time again. I suppose you go from surprised to scared to pretty soon being struck by how good it sounds."

By the time the tour was over, with 60,001 books personally signed and sales well on the way to more than a million, his decision was all but made.

13

This guy would make a great president.
—George W. Bush

By the end of the book tour, it was clear to Powell that the American public saw him as far more than a celebrity in uniform. There was serious national interest in a Powell presidency, and he was seriously interested in going for it. He felt no real allegiance to either of the major political parties and at first assumed he would run as an Independent. But when he began during the summer of 1995 to look at the numbers—money, organization and electoral votes—it seemed unlikely that a third-party ticket could succeed. He might change the face of American politics for the future, but the "Powell Doctrine" applied to political as well as military warfare: there was no point in launching an attack unless you intended to win.

Powell knew the Democrats would be happy to have him on their side in some capacity, but not as their presidential candidate, not this time. He had no interest in being Clinton's second in command—Clinton would continue with Gore, in any case—and no chance of wresting the nomination from a sitting president.

That left the GOP. Considering the rightward drift of the party, he calculated he was at best "55 percent Republican." It was the party of order and responsibility, and in his experience it took stewardship of the nation's defenses more seriously. His economic views were moderate Republican orthodoxy: tax increases were bad, but budget deficits were worse. Powell believed in a modified trickle-down theory in which helping the rich to prosper would eventually benefit the poor. "Once these kids come out of school, there has got to be a capitalistic entrepreneurial system that is just burning up the place to create jobs for these kids. And therefore you've got to get the tax burden off business," he told an interviewer. He agreed with the Republicans that the social programs devouring much of the nation's riches—welfare, Medicare, Medicaid—needed reform, although not at the expense of the most vulnerable.

But the remaining 45 percent of his political makeup was considerably to the left of the Republican vanguard. Powell considered himself "a liberal sort of guy" when it came to not interfering in the personal lives of others, and he differed sharply with the Republican platform on the issue of abortion. Children should be taught how to avoid pregnancy, he felt, but if a pregnant woman did not wish to give birth, "if she chooses to abort, that's her choice. So that's pro-choice."

He believed in affirmative action as an opportunity leveler but thought predetermined quotas were insulting. He had no problem with private firearm ownership—he had been given a number of guns over the years, although they were packed away gathering dust—but he supported registration programs and waiting periods before purchase. He considered himself a religious man, but he thought that prayer and other forms of religious expression belonged at home or in God's house and not in schools or the government. He believed that the family was the source of most of the goodness in the world and bore primary responsibility for instilling moral values and a sense of community in children. But the government's role was to help families prosper, not to define what constituted a couple.

Powell was convinced that most Americans rejected extremes on both sides of the political spectrum and wanted to travel the same pragmatic middle road as he did. His political comfort zone resided with the people he knew best, Republicans like Carlucci and Armitage who had shared Reagan's defense and economic goals but had limited enthusiasm for much of the social agenda that had now become the party's battle cry. He felt little in common with the zealous authors of the "Contract with America" who were now running the Congress. The more he thought about it, the more he believed his candidacy could be the beginning of a Republican realignment, the first step in leading the party's majority back to its rightful place in the center. It was a personal challenge almost as great as the presidency itself.

"The Christian Coalition is out there with their contract, and the Contract with America was certainly anchored on the right side of the Republican political spectrum," he concluded. "But there are a lot of other Republicans out there, I have found as I've traveled around the country, who are a little bit more to the left of that point on the spectrum, and I think they will be heard from in due course."

Moving the party to the center might also break the Democrats' hammerlock on blacks' votes. The 25 percent of African-American voters who told pollsters they would choose Powell over Clinton was nearly double Ronald Reagan's 1980 percentage and two and a half times Bush's 1988 share.

The racial component of a potential presidential run was complicated for Powell. He had no more desire to be a poster boy for black achievement in politics than in the Army. But even at his elevated status, there were still times when a perceived racial slight stuck in his throat. It was rarely intentional; it usually involved well-meaning whites trying to find a connection with him on first meeting by saying they had known some other famous black person, often a military figure such as Chappie James or Rock Cartwright. What he wanted to say in response, but never did, was "Why do you think I give a damn? Did you know George Patton? Curtis LeMay? Why do you feel it necessary to tell me you knew Chappie James?"

As a younger man, he had been offended by the black street demonstrators and rabble-rousers who threatened to tear down their own neighborhoods along with the white establishment. Now in comfortable middle age, he had come to see them as a necessary part of the evolution that had widened the cracks in American racism over the past thirty years. The Black Power types, Martin Luther King, Jr., Thurgood Marshall, Chappie James and the Buffalo Soldiers had all contributed in different ways to the same goal. His own role, he thought, had been to demonstrate that African Americans didn't belong in some national subcategory where they competed among themselves for "best black." He knew that neither whites nor blacks saw him as the preeminent leader of the nation's African Americans—Jesse Jackson and even the Nation of Islam's Louis Farrakhan were judged to be more influential. Powell had succeeded by competing with whites on their own terms.

The winds of the slave trade had deposited his ancestors on a small tropical island rather than in the larger colony to the north, and the result was that he was more Caribbean American than African American. His beliefs were rooted far more deeply in the British Jamaica of his parents than in the Harlem of his birth. His own explanation for his success as a black man recalled the distinctions West Indian immigrants of his parents' generation had drawn between themselves and American blacks. "To some extent I have transcended race in general America," he told *Ebony* magazine in 1995. "But I know why. I speak well. I don't look that black. I don't have some of the stereotypical patterns with which white people have defined us." He insisted he was proud of his color and made sure "everybody knows I am as black today as I was yesterday." But it was a difficult line to walk—defining himself as simultaneously different from and the same as most other people of color—especially for a man thinking of a political career. He wanted blacks to fight against racism, but not by sealing themselves off from the majority culture. "We can't walk away from the rest of America and go off into our own little world.... Our language is English—the Queen's English. Don't give me any silliness about Black English or African roots. We don't live there; we live here. We've got to make our life and our future in this broader American society and we cannot separate ourselves."

Most of the companies where he spoke on the lecture circuit had minority outreach programs and vice presidents for "diversity," but he thought those were just ways for whites to feel better about themselves by creating a special place for blacks. It was like "Black History Month." Why did black Americans have to have a special month? Weren't they Americans all year long? Some African Americans lauded the redrawn congressional boundaries in southern states that had created black majority districts and resulted in the election of more black members to the House of Representatives. Powell considered them a form of "ethnic cleansing" that left more districts with lily-white constituencies that "no longer have to worry about black folks. They got rid of them all." Racial redistricting, he felt, was "disastrous for Americans, and more particularly disastrous for black people. If white folks don't have to deal with you because you have gone off somewhere, they are pleased not to have to deal with you. And they should be made to deal with us because we are Americans."

But for many blacks, particularly those at the bottom of the economic ladder, the salient fact about Powell remained that he had held high positions in Republican administrations. The Democrats, and Clinton in particular, seemed far more in touch with their lives and needs, a reality that would be unavoidably emphasized in a presidential campaign.

To Vernon Jordan, a friend of both Clinton and Powell, it was ironic that Powell's racial credibility was questioned by black leaders such as Jackson who had spent their lives fighting for equal opportunity. "There is nobody around here passing out assignments. We all seek our own assignment, and we choose different roles. That's what the civil rights movement was all about. Going across the Edmund Pettis Bridge was not to suggest that we all ought to come out the same on the other side. And we did not. There are those who say Vernon Jordan and Colin Powell ought to be doing thus and so. Well, Colin Powell and Vernon Jordan have to do what they think they can do with what they have."

Both men could recite from memory lines from *Purlie Victorious,* Ossie Davis's satire of life in the Jim Crow South that was first produced on stage in the early 1960s. The butt of the play's jokes, a comically addled white landowner, is run rings around by amused blacks who allow him to believe he still owns their lives. "Some of the best pretending in the world" is done by blacks in front of whites, says the protagonist, Purlie Victorious Judson. As the curtain falls, he sardonically invites his fellow African Americans to "do what you can for the white folks."

As Powell saw it, he had spent his life "doing what he could" to help whites get over prejudices some of them didn't even know they had. In the process, he felt, he, too, had widened the cracks for those who followed him.

By the last week of October 1995, the den in Powell's McLean house and a small office suite he had rented in Alexandria, Virginia, had become political war rooms. The telephones rang constantly, and the fax machine buzzed with advice from consultants and unsolicited exhortations from at least three national "draft Powell" committees. The activist core of the Powell bandwagon was composed of Rockefeller Republicans who saw the right wing leading their party astray and considered Powell their new Eisenhower. But there were also ideologues among his supporters whose pragmatic determination to unseat Clinton trumped their concerns about Powell's social liberalism. In the middle of it all, Powell held court, listening and questioning assessments of available money and his prospects in the Republican primaries.

Regardless of where he stood in opinion polls, he lagged far behind the current contenders for the nomination in both organization and fundraising. Kansas Senator Bob Dole, Texas Senator Phil Gramm, the maverick magazine publisher Steve Forbes and Pat Buchanan had emerged as contenders and had been campaigning energetically all year. Powell would need at least $60 million to mount a credible race. He had no real campaign structure beyond the business leaders who called to pledge future money, the self-appointed draft committees and a lot of regular people who said they would vote for him. The Iowa caucuses were just around the corner in February, with primaries in New Hampshire and a rash of southern states not far behind. But Powell's backers consulted one another and concluded that a run for the nomination was viable, provided he moved quickly.

It seemed that the whole world, or at least the entire political machinery of the United States, was waiting for him to decide. Internal GOP polls indicated that Dole would likely beat Powell in the primaries but that only Powell could unseat Clinton in the general election. He would do so by laying claim to a good number of votes from Democrats and Independents along with moderate Republicans, whose positions on many issues were anathema to core party constituencies. As far as the ideological and religious Right were concerned, he might be able to put their party in the White House, but a Powell administration would be tantamount to a coalition government. His victory as a Republican would only delay the fundamental national shift to the right that they envisioned.

Powell's message was one of strength and healing, and he told his speech audiences that "We have to start thinking like a family again." But the battle being waged within the Republican family was not going to be settled by compromise and reconciliation. It was a theological war over the role of government in society, a "fight to the death," in the words of the conservative William F. Buckley, Jr., the revered founder of *National Review* magazine. Those who saw Powell as the new Eisenhower should recall that Eisenhower's battle in 1952 had not been with Adlai Stevenson, the liberal Democratic nominee, Buckley wrote. "The differences between Stevenson and Eisenhower were mostly matters of emphasis.... The real fight in 1952 was between Eisenhower and [Republican] Senator Robert Taft," who fought, and lost, the nomination on a promise to end Franklin Roosevelt's New Deal. The Right had grown in power since then, Buckley noted, and Powell's supporters would soon learn that he wasn't the man to preside over the coming internecine combat.

Republican National Committee Chairman Haley Barbour made a pilgrimage to Powell's office at the end of October but emerged no wiser about the general's intentions. House Speaker Newt Gingrich was sent by Ken Duberstein to talk to Powell about running. Although Gingrich later maintained that he thought Powell's candidacy would be good for the country and the party, his motives at the time were mixed. His own supporters came from the ideological Right, and he still hadn't closed the door on running himself.

"Everybody who was hard right was worried about Powell," Gingrich later recalled. "If you were right-to-life, a conservative Republican, Powell represents the other wing.... I was dubious he could get the nomination." Single-issue primary voters—largely abortion opponents—would be against him, and the question was whether Powell could draw enough moderates into the primaries to overcome their determination. Gingrich told him he thought it would be nearly impossible to accomplish such a feat "from a standing start in November."

That was Gingrich's counsel as a professional politician. On a personal level, he told Powell, "If it isn't a calling so large you have to do it, it is going to be so brutalizing and so exhausting, you're going to be so battered, you shouldn't do it."

Newsweek magazine had already revealed that Alma was on medication for depression. Oliver North, now the host of a radio program popular among conservatives, told his audience that "This guy is not a Republican" and demanded answers on "his real role in the so-called Iran-*contra* affair, his real role in the cover-up of the My Lai massacre in Vietnam, his role in what was done to prevent Desert Storm."

The right's full broadside landed on November 2, when a handful of prominent conservative activists held a press conference to attack Powell's military record, vilify him on social issues and warn that his candidacy would tear the Republican Party apart and hand victory to Clinton. Paul Weyrich, the founder of the right-wing Moral Majority, accused Powell of foot-dragging on the Gulf War and giving only lukewarm support for Reagan's "Star Wars" missile defense project. Powell's popularity was "the last gasp of the Washington establishment," Weyrich said.

Frank Gaffney, who had served with Powell in the Weinberger Pentagon and said he considered him a friend, nonetheless described Powell as "a risk-averse and politically hypersensitive military officer." Grover Norquist, the president of Americans for Tax Reform, accused Powell of being a closet "tax-and-spend" Democrat who had failed to sign the "no new taxes" pledge Norquist had set before declared Republican contenders.

The handful of conservatives who were defending Powell—among them, William Kristol, Quayle's former White House chief of staff and now publisher of the magazine *The Weekly Standard;* former Reagan education secretary William J. Bennett; and even Richard Perle, the anti-Soviet "prince of darkness" from the Reagan Pentagon—had "taken leave of their senses" in the name of racial correctness, said Morton Blackwell of the Leadership Institute, a self-described "training center" for future conservative politicians. "If General Powell were a white general holding his views they would not consider for a minute supporting his nomination," Morton assured reporters at the press conference. Carol Long, director of the National Right to Life Political Action Committee, said that if Powell sought the Republican nomination, "our top priority during the primaries will be his defeat."

The ugliness of the session offended even some conservatives who had strong doubts about Powell. Powell himself was taken aback, particularly by the criticism of his military record, although he told anyone who asked that it was all part of the American way and people were free to say whatever they wanted. In any case, it was clear that those speaking against him were shouting into the wind. His poll numbers remained high, and the mainstream media treated him like a national hero.

The media's softball treatment of Powell was particularly frustrating to Clinton, who saw himself under constant siege by a belligerent and hypercritical press. When George Stephanopoulos tried to calm the president during one angry tirade in the Oval Office, insisting that journalists would go after Powell once he actually became a candidate, Clinton exploded. "You're wrong! You're wrong! You're wrong!" he shouted, pointing a finger in Stephanopoulos's face. "They'll give him a ride, even though he wouldn't do half the things I've done as president. They're just going to give him a free ride."

Clinton was convinced he would lose if Powell was the Republican nominee. "He'll take away blacks, he'll separate himself from the congressional Republicans, he'll run a great campaign, and he'll beat me bad," the president told his chief political adviser, Dick Morris. Their internal polls confirmed it. But the same polls, Morris assured him, said that Powell would never make it through the conservative-dominated Republican primaries.

Away from the adoring crowds of his book tour, Powell's euphoria drifted into uncertainty and indecision. In the span of just a few weeks, he went from feeling certain that he should run to doubting his decision to convincing himself that it was wrong for him and his family—only to be tempted again.

In late October, with help from Joe Persico, he drafted a speech announcing his candidacy for the Republican nomination. His plan was to deliver it just before Thanksgiving at his alma mater, City College of New York.

He had decided to run, he would tell them, because he knew the American people wanted change. They wanted a government that was both smaller and more responsive to their needs, and leadership that shared their values. His Republican Party would build a prosperous and inclusive society at home even as it restored America's prestige abroad. As a political moderate, he would eschew rigid ideology and mudslinging. As a soldier, he would say, he had learned both to listen and to lead.

But even as he thought about the campaign, Powell drafted a second speech, this one explaining why he would "not be a candidate for president or for any other elective office in 1996."

By the end of October, Powell was changing his mind daily, sometimes hourly. For a man who prided himself on decisiveness and self-knowledge, it was agonizing. He felt like a windshield wiper, his world reduced to a rhythmic "no, yes, no, yes, no." He would go to bed at night thinking "no" but would "wake up every morning and say, 'Have I made the right decision?' And then I'd call somebody, or I'd see somebody else...and I'd be all atwitter again." He had always had to watch himself in times of crisis to avoid overeating and ballooning. Now he was losing both weight and sleep.

"I saw him go from a healthy, happy guy to a very tired, uncertain person," William Smullen recalled. "Uncertainty is just not his middle name. He's always confident of what the next decision, the next step in life is going to be."

Beyond most of his immediate family, many of Powell's friends were also opposed to the idea of him running, or at least wary of it. Harlan Ullman, his long-ago professor at the National War College, offered a detailed analysis. "I think your absolute strengths are as a leader, problem facilitator and solver, and motivator...your principal contributions have been ones of character and accomplishment; you are a superb role model...an honest broker and facilitator of the first order.... You are also tough to bullshit, another virtue," Ullman wrote in a lengthy letter.

"I would say that your political weaknesses are experiential.... In some ways it was 'too easy' in that [military] environment...and I'm not sure that you have been challenged as much as you would be in a race for the roses. I would have thought that given this background and your strength of character, the banalities and 'corrupting' or demeaning practices of politics would turn you off, particularly fund raising and some deal making, aspects of political life in which Clinton excels and Dole is quite comfortable.

"You have always worked 'for someone,' providing you a degree of political cover; that may not work so well when there is no such cover.... Finally, you are honest, direct and nicely irreverent—traits I admire but ones that may get you into political trouble."

A major question, Ullman wrote, was whether Powell could translate his vision for an America of strength and fairness into a strategy for leading the country as opposed to merely a platform for winning the election. He recalled the last scene in a favorite movie, *The Candidate,* in which a pure-hearted liberal activist played by Robert Redford is persuaded to run for the Senate. He sells his soul to the Democratic Party machine and at the end, after winning against all odds, asks, "What do we do now?"

"I do not think that the 'man' alone will qualify as the 'message' if it is the presidency you seek," Ullman warned.

Duberstein encouraged him to run, while Armitage remained opposed. On "yes" days, when Powell told them to start forming an exploratory campaign committee and making calls to prospective donors, Armitage would burst out, "Don't do it! Don't do it!" He tried to convince Duberstein privately that Powell was close to cracking. "He can deal with it," Duberstein responded.

Armitage was not so sure. He was not only a political adviser, he had been Powell's closest friend for more than two decades. They knew all of each other's jokes and war stories; they finished each other's sentences. But Armitage, who had once worked for Dole on Capitol Hill, considered himself more knowledgeable about the dark underbelly of both the Republican Party and electoral politics in general. He knew that Powell was "a tough person and a very disciplined person. But he's not a mean person.... To run for the presidency, you have to have a bit of a mean streak in you." Armitage was afraid his friend would get hurt.

Alma's concerns weighed more heavily on Powell. For thirty-three years, she had supported his career decisions, and she and Colin both knew she would acquiesce if he insisted it was the right thing to do. But she hoped he would not.

Her depression had been under control with medication for more than fifteen years, but Colin still vividly remembered the helplessness he had felt the day he found her collapsed in tears. She wanted nothing to do with the exposure and pressure of a national campaign or a life in the White House, and he told himself it would be a lot to ask of her. Alma was no shrinking violet; sometimes she even liked the limelight, and she knew how to handle herself in it, he reasoned. "But she can ration it, she can gauge how much she wants to do and doesn't want to do. For all those years in the military, it was my life to which she was attached. For the first time she had her own life.... She was no longer harnessed to me, and she did not want to be harnessed like that again. And we were not kids anymore."

But however important the views of his family and friends, the answer had to come from him alone, and he began to worry about his inability to make a clear and final choice. The familiar "decision loop" didn't seem to work anymore; he would get halfway through and then start again in the other direction. It wasn't *being* president that concerned him—he was confident he could inspire and lead and thought he was developing the foundation of a political philosophy, although he worried that he was still underinformed on many domestic issues. But he hated the whole idea of politics and campaigning—the demeaning scramble for money, the closed-door deals and trading of favors—almost as much as he hated the possibility of losing.

It came down to two fundamental questions, he concluded. The first was whether he had a duty to run. He felt overwhelmed by the public clamor for his candidacy and the compressed time frame for a decision, "pushed by events and pressure and pulled by a sense of obligation. A lot of people were saying 'You're the first black who's ever been in a position like this. How could you not do it?' " But his whole life was anchored in the belief that skin color had nothing to do with a man's abilities or with what he stood for. People simply wanted a hero, a man on a white horse, and they had chosen him before they had even heard what he wanted to do for the country. At least initially, he would be running on the basis of his popularity—or, worse, his celebrity—rather than his political agenda. "People would turn out for Charles Manson, too," he once observed cynically after a day of adulation on the book tour.

The second question was how much he wanted it. Ironically, some of the best advice he had received came from Dan Quayle, a man Powell had held in low esteem as vice president. They had talked a few times during the fall of 1995, and then one night at home he heard Quayle being interviewed on television about the presidency. He couldn't remember the exact words, but the gist of it stuck with him. You simply have got to want it from the depth of your stomach or your soul, he remembered Quayle saying. And if you don't feel that, then no matter what anyone tells you, whatever else you think, you shouldn't do it. You can't do it.

The one thing Powell was sure of was that his soul, his stomach and every other part of his being were telling him no.

On Friday, November 3, he told Alma definitively that he would not run. Over the weekend, he and Persico worked on the draft of the speech Persico called "Option 2: No Go," faxing copies between McLean and Persico's home in Albany, New York. The "Go" speech had been fairly easy to compose, but they were having trouble with this one. Persico thought that the basic reason for declining, which he shorthanded as "I just don't want to do it. It's not me. It's too much for my family," had the virtue of being true but was too narrow. They were looking for a more positive message about the country. Powell had rejected Persico's proposal of an "Option 2a: Crack in the Door," in which he would simply say he hadn't decided yet. But he was not going to shut the door completely on some future campaign, perhaps in 2000.

On Saturday, a shiver went through the Powell family with the news that Israeli Prime Minister Yitzhak Rabin, another soldier turned politician, had been shot dead by a radical Jew who had simply walked up to him at a peace rally and pulled out a gun. Standing in the kitchen of their southern California home when they heard the news from Tel Aviv, Colin's sister, Marilyn, and her husband looked at each other and shook their heads. It was exactly what they feared for Colin.

At home on Monday evening, Powell told Armitage and Duberstein of his decision. Smullen booked the ballroom of the Ramada Inn near Powell's Alexandria office for Wednesday at 3 p.m. Scores of reporters had bivouacked for weeks in front of Powell's house, waiting for him to declare himself. To keep the lid on until the formal announcement, Powell decided to travel to Philadelphia on Tuesday for a scheduled speech to the American Society of Travel Agents convention.

He stopped first at the University of Pennsylvania, shutting the door on his media tail for a private talk to a group of students whom he assured he hadn't yet made up his mind about whether to run. At the convention center, he delivered his standard praise of American greatness and his call for family responsibility. Three thousand travel agents leapt to their feet, applauding deliriously and cheering him on to the presidency, and suddenly the windshield wiper took one last swipe.

He left the hall and called Alma. Maybe he had made the wrong decision, he told her. Maybe he shouldn't make the announcement so quickly. When Powell retold the story years later, he laughed and slapped his hand down on the desk in front of him, indicating what Alma had done with the telephone. Within minutes she had called Armitage with venom in her voice and a demand that he "do something." "She just bit into me," Armitage later recalled. "And I said 'Alma, wait a minute. What happened? I'm on your side on this.'" He couldn't understand what was going on with Powell; they had talked that morning and there had been no change of heart. Armitage tried to reach him to argue the case against running once again, but by the time he got through, Powell had already come down to earth. "I'm fine," he said. "I'm back. I'm back."

Smullen started calling reporters at 8 a.m. Wednesday, telling them Powell would hold a press conference that afternoon. Just before 3 p.m., he took Colin and Alma, Michael and his wife, Jane, Linda and Annemarie through an underground parking garage and in a back door to the hotel. The only place to wait unseen was in the kitchen adjacent to the ballroom, and they lined up amid plates of salmon being readied for dinner. Powell looked awful, Smullen thought—in addition to the weight loss and lack of sleep, he had gotten a haircut that morning and hadn't had time for a shampoo. His normally slicked-down hair looked as though he'd stuck his finger in an electric socket. But Alma was beaming. "You're a happy woman, aren't you?" Smullen asked her. "Yes, I am," she replied.

The ballroom was packed. As the family filed in, Alma ignored the chair set out for her and walked to stand at Colin's side by the podium. He had shortened his speech and written the main points on note cards.

He was honored and grateful for the faith and confidence so many Americans had shown in him, he said, and he had spent long hours consulting with friends and advisers and "talking with my wife and children, the most important people in my life," about the sacrifices and changes that came with a presidential campaign. "Ultimately, however, I had to look deep into my own soul, standing aside from the expectations and enthusiasms of others," and he had failed to find the same passion and commitment for a political quest that he had felt every day of his life as a soldier.

Electoral politics was "a calling that I do not yet hear. And for me to pretend otherwise would not be honest to myself, it would not be honest to the American people.... And therefore I cannot go forward. I will not be a candidate for president or any other elective office in 1996."

He said he would continue to speak out on major issues and would try to find ways "to help heal the racial divides that still exist within our society." He would do so "as a member of the Republican Party and [would] try to assist the party in broadening its appeal. I believe I can help the party of Lincoln move once again close to the spirit of Lincoln."

There was a flood of questions. Was it true he didn't have the stomach for the "down and dirty" of American politics, that he was used to having his own way and was retreating from a fight? Powell answered that he understood how dirty it could be and that anyone who sought the office should be prepared to run the gauntlet. The conservative attacks had "rolled off my back," he insisted. In a pleasurable jab toward Frank Gaffney and the others, he said he couldn't get too excited "when somebody who never served in the military jumps up and attacks me for my thirty-five years of service."

He told them he agreed with Republicans' calls for reforming welfare and other social programs but worried about the "harshness" of abandoning those who truly needed a safety net. He said he had no interest in the vice presidency for 1996 and deflected questions about a possible presidential run in 2000. For now, he said, he was going to "work as a Republican in the months ahead, trying to broaden the appeal of the party."

Powell's Republican declaration was almost as big a surprise as his announcement that he would not run. His sister, Marilyn, like Alma a registered Independent, thought of the picture of FDR that had hung in their childhood living room and imagined their parents "spinning in the ground, like whirling dervishes." In New York, Bruce Llewellyn wondered if his cousin had lost his mind.

"I don't know that I felt I had to," Powell later reflected on the decision to declare a party allegiance. "I felt I should leave something out there as to what I believed in and what I might do with respect to political life or commenting on things, and I just didn't want to hide any longer saying 'I'm on the book tour and I'm thinking about it' or 'I'm a soldier.' I had no reason not to declare an affiliation.... I felt kind of an obligation...to come out of the closet." He wasn't closing the door on the presidency forever, and he had done the math that argued against an Independent candidacy. If he wanted to leave himself an opening for the future, when there was time to build a campaign from the ground up, it had to be as a Republican.

Armitage had tried to talk him out of it, arguing that the party was rushing in a direction neither of them wanted to go and it was doubtful they could stop it. "You've got the freedom to stay out," he said. "I'm already identified as a Republican. For me to leave, I'm not a big shot, it's a different statement. You can just stay out. Don't declare." But Powell told him he was convinced his political future lay in "bringing the party back."

Giddy with relief and exhaustion after the announcement, the Powells headed home to McLean on the tree-lined George Washington Parkway. Once inside the house, nobody talked about the presidency or the Republicans; it was as if they had all been out at a party and had come home happy. To Annemarie, the lifting of their yearlong family burden was "like being cured of cancer."

At the White House, George Stephanopoulos walked into the Oval Office to give Clinton the news. "It's because of his sense of duty," Clinton responded. "McClellan was the only sitting general to run against his commander in chief. Ike could have run against Truman, but he waited." The president returned to his paperwork, then glanced up at Stephanopoulos over the top of his reading glasses. "Too bad for Al," he said with a grin. The vice president would be a candidate to succeed Clinton in 2000. If Powell chose to run then, he would be Gore's problem.

That afternoon, Vernon Jordan had boarded an airplane in Dallas, heading home to Washington after a J. C. Penney board meeting. During the flight, the clearly disappointed pilot came on the loudspeaker to tell the passengers, "Colin Powell just announced he is not going to run for president." After they landed, Jordan went home to get his car and drove to Powell's house, arriving at about 7 p.m. The television trucks and reporters had packed up and left, and the street was empty.

He rang the bell, and Powell answered the door. They embraced and walked to the kitchen, where the family was sitting around the table eating just-delivered pizza and drinking Cokes. Jordan was impressed. "I decided that was the measure of the man," he later said. "Four hours earlier, he had the world in his hand. The media were all there. Now, there were no friends, no booze, just them. He was relaxed. . . . He was at peace. As my grandkids would say, he was cool."

Many conservatives doubted the authenticity of Powell's official conversion to Republicanism but saw his declaration, along with his decision not to run for president, as a positive outcome. His noncandidacy meant the core constituencies on the far right had nothing to fight about, even as Powell's party membership would bring the party moderate votes and maybe even some blacks. And he could still draw a bigger crowd and more media coverage than just about anyone in the country aside from Clinton. As the electoral season moved into full swing during the spring and summer of 1996, Powell was flooded with requests for campaign appearances from Republican congressional candidates.

With rare exceptions, he turned them down. He considered his image and physical presence to be valuable commodities, and he husbanded them carefully. In any case, he never felt comfortable with what he dismissed as "the whole campaign thing." The fact that many of the appeals came from candidates Powell knew disagreed with him on a range of issues was reason enough to say no. Senator Strom Thurmond, the one-time Dixiecrat presidential candidate, wrote that "It would be an honor if you would visit South Carolina to assist my re-election efforts. You are highly respected in our state and your appearance would be a tremendous asset to my campaign." Powell responded that he was "booked pretty solidly for the next several months."

Gingrich asked Powell to serve as guest of honor at his principal fund-raiser in the fall. "To no surprise, the National Democratic Party has recruited a multimillionaire philanthropist to challenge me," Gingrich wrote. "This is an attempt to hinder the national campaign effort by attacking me at home. Your presence in my district would excite our base of supporters and energize the local media." Powell declined. "While I am proud to be a Republican," he responded, "my plans and schedule for the foreseeable future will not permit me to participate in fundraising or campaign activities."

Democrats who feared he would show up in their states wrote to remind him that many of his positions were similar to their own. "As you know, any appearance by you on behalf... of the Republican Party would no doubt include your tacit support for my Republican opponent," wrote Max Cleland, a Vietnam veteran running for a U.S. Senate seat in Georgia. Cleland had heard that Powell was planning to campaign for Dole in Atlanta. "I would hope you would not do that," he wrote. "I believe this nation needs more people in the Senate like you and me, people in the 'sensible center.' "

Dole, who by the end of March 1996 had locked up the Republican nomination, was harder to turn down. Rather than approach Powell directly, he asked Armitage to serve as a go-between to solicit Powell for his campaign. Powell knew he couldn't very well call himself a Republican and refuse to stump for the party's presidential candidate, and he agreed to make a few appearances. "I felt an obligation to help," he said later. "But I did not want to spend my time running around to campaign rallies. I think I did two, just to show that I wasn't against [Dole]."

Despite Powell's public expressions of disinterest in the vice presidency, there was still talk of a Dole-Powell "dream ticket" that would send Clinton down to defeat. Dole thought it might be possible to convince the general, but for months he danced around him without asking for his hand. The closest he ever came was a meeting carefully choreographed by Duberstein two months before the 1996 Republican National Convention.

Powell had been invited to a June 9 fund-raiser for Virginia Senator John Warner and was led to believe that Dole, who would also be attending, would pop the question there. He sent the invitation back to his assistant Peggy Cifrino with a scribbled note saying he would be en route to California that day. For good measure he added instructions to Cifrino to "verify if Sen. Warner is pro-life or pro-choice." Organizers of the event quickly came back saying they would reschedule for another day at his convenience, and Cifrino messaged him that "Warner's campaign office says he is pro-life. However, we called his congressional office anonymously, saying we were Virginia voters and wanted to know his position. His legislative aide would not commit to either label."

Told that the fund-raiser had been moved to June 8 to accommodate him, Powell grudgingly agreed to make an appearance. "Make sure they understand that I am only an attendee," he told Cifrino. "I am not a sponsor, a host or an honoree. I am not to be listed or advertised on the invitation."

As arranged, Dole and Powell left the main party and stepped into another room alone. As Powell remembered it, he took the initiative in the conversation, making it clear he did not want to be asked about the vice presidency and saving Dole the embarrassment of being turned down. Dole was a heroic World War II veteran and a nice guy. But Powell found him less than inspiring as a candidate, and Dole's increasingly right-wing domestic rhetoric made him uneasy. Even if he had changed his mind about elective office and the vice presidency, he would have had to think long and hard about running with Dole.

The Republican National Committee did not know quite what to do with Powell. His disdain for retail politics and his insistence on holding the party and its candidates at arm's length were irritants. Powell showed up where and when he wanted, seemed largely uninterested in hewing to the party "message" (at least on social issues) and did not ask for permission or approval to speak to the media or anyone else.

He agreed to address the August 12 nominating convention in San Diego, and as the event drew near, RNC Chairman Barbour pleaded with him to arrange any and all media appearances through the party's Office of Media Support Activities. In a letter to Powell also signed by Dole campaign chairman Scott Reed and convention manager Paul Manafort, Barbour reminded him that "all senior Republicans have cooperated fully with this system by referring all television, radio and print media scheduling requests to the Media Support operation, and by not making commitments to do any broadcast, cable or satellite interviews." The system allowed the party to "best coordinate and project its daily messages to the media." Powell did not reply.

Negotiations over the San Diego address were tortured. "If they wanted me at the convention, which they did, and they wanted me to deliver a message to the American people about the Republican Party," the message was going to be about "a party that was not yet fully there in my own view with respect to certain issues," Powell later recalled. "So if they got me, they had to expect me to talk about those things that were on my mind and in my heart."

A recalcitrant Powell was far better than no Powell at all. After the negative fallout from the "culture war" convention in 1992, the Republicans were eager to parade Powell as the star example of their welcoming philosophy. "General Powell's presentation is all about the 'soft' themes we want to promote—inclusion, leadership, opportunity, responsibility, change, vision of the future," read an internal convention planning document. "He should be our Walter Cronkite (the most trusted man in America). To him we leave the chore of summing up all the positive things we have said about Americans."

The convention choreography called for Powell to deliver the opening night keynote address. He would follow Nancy Reagan's sentimental speech about her husband, who was now suffering from Alzheimer's disease. At the end of her remarks, she would introduce a video montage of the Reagan presidency, after which the lights would come up to reveal Powell standing at the podium. "During appropriate portions of General Powell's speech," read the RNC planning document, "moving or still visuals can be programmed onto the screens behind the podium in support of his text. The last visuals to freeze behind him are President Reagan on one screen and Senator Dole on the other. General Powell's final remark is that the time is now for a strong, honest, true American hero who says what he means and means what he says to lead us forward to the new millennium (as Dole's image takes over both screens)." Powell scrawled "NO!" across his copy of the document.

In a form letter sent to all speakers, Barbour wrote that the committee anticipated "working closely with you on the nature of your remarks in order to ensure each presentation enhances the objectives of the convention." Convention planners would retain "initial drafting responsibility, advance speech review [and] final editorial control." Powell was assigned the veteran Reagan speechwriter Aram Bakshian to draft his remarks.

One of several prominent Republicans who declined to address the convention under Barbour's conditions, Powell told them he would write his own speech and edit it himself. Bakshian was permitted to do a little shaping, and senior officials—including Dole—could look at it when he was finished, he said, but he would allow no substantive changes.

He arrived in San Diego late in the evening on Sunday, August 11, flying with Smullen aboard a private corporate jet arranged by the RNC. He made sure that the plane would take him back home first thing Tuesday morning after his Monday-night appearance, long before Dole was scheduled to arrive at the convention. Except for a late-night party for Nancy Reagan, he turned down all requests to mingle with Republican luminaries and fat cats. He set up his own media interviews, scheduling tapings late Monday night after his speech to be shown on the morning network news shows.

Most convention delegates were eager to bask in Powell's celebrity, although some were less than happy about what they assumed he would say. Ward Connolly, a prominent black Republican much applauded by the right wing for his sponsorship of a California referendum outlawing affirmative action in the state's university system, had threatened to walk out of the convention hall if Powell mentioned the subject during his speech. As Powell stood in the wings waiting to take the stage, he made sure he knew where Connolly was seated—down in front, just to the right of the podium.

"I come before you this evening as a retired soldier, a fellow citizen who has lived the American Dream to the fullest," Powell began. "As someone who believes in that dream and wants that dream to become reality for every American."

He said the right things about Dole—"a man of strength, maturity and integrity"—and touched many of the usual Republican buttons: "family values," "pro-growth" economic policies and lower taxes. He never mentioned defense or foreign policy; the climax of the speech was about what Powell thought the Republican Party should be: compassionate, inclusive, fair-minded and standing for "equal rights . . . for all."

"I became a Republican because I want to help fill the big tent that our party has raised to attract all Americans," he said. "You all know that I believe in a woman's right to choose abortion. And I strongly support affirmative action." He heard scattered boos and paused for a moment before moving to the next line: "And I was invited here by my party to share my views with you because we are a big enough party and big enough people to disagree on individual issues and still work together for our common goal: restoring the American dream." By the time he finished the sentence the hall was on its feet, clapping and chanting "Co-lin, Co-lin, Co-lin." Powell glanced down with a slight smile at the immobile Connolly and thought to himself, "Go ahead and walk out. I dare you."

He knew the applause didn't mean that the majority of the delegates agreed with him any more than Connolly did. "I was applauded wildly . . . [because the] last thing [the convention organizers] wanted was to have Santa Claus booed."

He put more of an edge on his message when he made the rounds of the network television booths later that night. "I can talk to a group of Fortune 500 folks," he told ABC News, "and I look around the room and it's a wonderful group and guess what? They're all white. They're all men. Then I can go into an inner-city school that doesn't have books, that doesn't have proper paint on the walls, that are falling apart, and they're all black. The color of your skin still does count in this country as a means of being left behind, and so I think affirmative action still has a role to play."

His views on affirmative action and abortion "represent the views of many, many millions of Republicans who are out there," he asserted in an interview recorded for NBC's *Today* show the next morning.

It was those perceived millions, and not the overwhelmingly conservative delegates, that Powell hoped were listening to his first major political speech. If the party was going to be pulled away from the clutches of the Right, he thought, the silent majority needed to know that someone on the inside agreed with them and would stand up and speak out. For one night in San Diego, at least, he was a politician.

Whether Powell misjudged the views of the Republican "millions" or simply lost interest, his push for party realignment lapsed as quickly as it had begun. For the next several years, after Clinton was comfortably reelected to a second term, Powell's involvement in the GOP and politics in general was minimal. He remained the party's most popular figure and continued to draw substantial Democratic support—repeated national polls judged him the most trusted person in America and he regularly ranked among the most admired people worldwide, keeping company with Pope John Paul II and Mahatma Gandhi. In an epilogue to the paperback edition of his book, he wrote that he knew he had disappointed many people by deciding not to run, and "I couldn't escape the feeling, in some ways, that I was disappointing myself." But he had had no real second thoughts. He could not imagine going through weeks of indecision and uncertainty again, and in late 1997—as Republican hopefuls were already organizing for the 2000 presidential race—he firmly shut the door on a Powell candidacy.

For the next several years, he retold his life story in paid speeches, made nonpartisan appeals for personal responsibility and public fairness and, for the most part, stayed away from the hot-button social issues. On the few occasions when he spoke out, it was usually to reject the prevailing Republican dogma. He supported Clinton's call for arms control treaties and joined other military leaders in backing a comprehensive ban on nuclear tests that was killed by the Republican Senate. He sharpened his digs at racial prejudice—Americans opposed to special preferences didn't seem to mind it when it came to things like college admission bonuses for student athletes or tax benefits for the wealthy, he sarcastically told one interviewer. "We're not against preferences. We're just against any preference that is related to the color of a person's skin." When a Democratic senator wrote asking for his views on a proposed constitutional amendment to protect the American flag—a perennial conservative favorite—he wrote back to say that if he were a member of Congress he would vote against it. "Destroying a piece of cloth... [does] no damage to our system of freedom which tolerates such desecration."

Seeking other outlets for his prodigious energy and leadership skills, he immersed himself in volunteer work with disadvantaged and at-risk youth. He joined the boards of directors of the Boys and Girls Clubs, the United Negro College Fund, the Children's Health Fund and the predominantly black Howard University. In April 1997, he agreed to serve as the chairman of a three-day summit on American volunteerism hosted by Clinton and former president Bush. In its wake, he founded his own nonprofit organization, called America's Promise, to solicit funds and social activism from corporations and direct them toward worthy programs for children.

Powell undertook a crusade to rescue the country's endangered youth with all the zeal he had once devoted to training young soldiers. He persuaded major corporate sponsors to establish internships and jobs programs for disadvantaged teenagers and personally visited scores of schools and Boys and Girls Clubs across the country to make sure the targeted youths took advantage of them. On the lecture circuit, he added pro bono stops to speak to students, opening himself to questions on every subject ranging from the size of his shoes (12EE) to what it was like to work in the White House or to be shot at in war. His message to them never varied: stay in school, obey your parents, work hard, seize opportunity and don't make excuses. He guilt-tripped his publisher, Random House, into supplying books to schools and persuaded America Online, whose corporate board he joined in 1998, to provide free computer training at after-school centers. Using his media savvy and celebrity as bait, he crisscrossed the country recruiting state and local governments to pledge more resources to youth and community service organizations.

One such recruitment drive for America's Promise took him to San Antonio in the fall of 1997, where he joined Texas Governor George W. Bush at a rally to kick off a statewide effort to boost volunteerism. "We've heard the call," Bush told a gathering of 1,000 students and dignitaries at the city's municipal auditorium. "Our answer is this: General Powell, Texas is reporting for duty."

At a postrally press conference, the two men joked about early news reports that the governor—the eldest of former president Bush's four sons—was considering his own run for the White House in 2000. "We look forward to great things from this man in the future," Powell told a crowd of cheering Texans. When he demurred in response to the inevitable question about his own future, Bush pointed at him and said with a grin, "This guy would make a great president."

Powell pointed back and returned the compliment. "As would this guy."

14

Dear General . . . I am greatly encouraged by your appointment.

—George F. Kennan

Every summer, George and Barbara Bush gathered friends and family to cruise the Greek islands aboard a borrowed yacht. Powell had remained close to the former president, and in July 1998 he and Alma found themselves sailing the Aegean Sea along with Bush children, grandchildren and cousins, including the twin, teenaged daughters of their son George. His wife, Laura, a former librarian, was quiet compared to the other members of the boisterous clan. But the Powells found her a pleasant traveling companion.

Laura's husband had opted out of the two-week vacation. Back in Austin that month, he had scheduled a meeting at the governor's mansion with a group of defense and foreign policy experts assembled to help him consider a run for the presidency in 2000. Convened by George Shultz, the invitees included Dick Cheney and Cheney's former Pentagon aide, Paul Wolfowitz. Schultz had also invited Condoleezza Rice, the Soviet expert from the first Bush administration's National Security Council. An avid sports fan, Rice had first met the governor in 1995, when they had bonded in admiration of the rows of signed baseballs—mementos from Bush's days as managing general partner of the Texas Rangers—that filled the polished wooden bookshelves of his statehouse office.

Now provost at Stanford University, Rice was coolly efficient and had a way of explaining complicated issues that put the untutored and little-traveled Bush at ease. A month after the meeting in Austin, she was invited to the Bush family compound in Kennebunkport, Maine, for further talks with the governor. After several days of outdoor recreation and conversations about current events, she agreed to take on an official role as his principal campaign foreign policy adviser.

By fall, Rice was joined by Wolfowitz, who had done similar service for Bob Dole four years earlier. They quickly expanded the team to include others from previous Republican administrations: Richard Perle and Dov Zakheim from the Reagan Defense Department; Robert Zoellick from the Bush State Department; Stephen Hadley, Wolfowitz's aide under Cheney; and Robert Blackwill, who had worked with Rice on the Bush NSC. They called themselves "the Vulcans," after the fifty-six-foot statue of the Roman god of fire that looked down from a hill above downtown Birmingham, the southern steel town where Rice had grown up.

The eighth member of the team, suggested by Shultz, was Richard Armitage, who had spent the Clinton years running his own international consulting firm and, like the others, was eager to return to government. Armitage initially hesitated joining; he was holding out for Arizona Senator John McCain to declare himself a candidate for the Republican nomination. The Bush team had made clear that his allegiance had to be all or nothing, Armitage told McCain, and there would be no changing horses if McCain entered the race. But at the time, the senator was not ready to make a decision.

Although Armitage kept Powell, his closest friend, apprised of the Vulcans' meetings, neither Bush nor Rice sought the general's advice or made any attempt to bring the nation's most popular Republican and best-known defense expert onto the team. Powell was happy to keep his distance. He knew "Sonny," as he referred to the younger George Bush, only in passing. The president's son had been around the White House during the Bush administration; Powell had met him at occasional social gatherings and at the 1997 America's Promise event in Austin.

Powell's initial impression was that candidate Bush was "still getting his sea legs." His early speeches were faltering, and he was clearly over his head in most foreign policy and defense discussions. But Powell considered himself part of the extended Bush family, with the personal loyalty that kinship entailed. "It wasn't as if I was a stranger, or that anybody had to worry or could imagine that I would not be for Sonny when the time came," he later reflected. But Bush was a long way from capturing the nomination, and Powell saw no reason to commit himself.

Most of the Vulcans had worked with Powell in the past and some had mixed feelings about him. He and Wolfowitz had collaborated on defense planning at the Cheney Pentagon, although they had clashed over aid to the Shiites in southern Iraq at the end of the Gulf War. Perle and Powell had sharp ideological differences, but Perle had written a glowing review of *My American Journey* and predicted approvingly that Powell would win the presidency if he ran in 1996. Zakheim had defended Powell against allegations that he had overstepped his authority as chairman of the Joint Chiefs. Blackwill was a senior arms control negotiator in the Reagan administration—Powell had turned him down for a job on the NSC staff—and had served in the Bush White House.

Rice and Powell connected on several levels. Alma knew the Rice family from Birmingham, and her sister had once dated Condi's uncle. In the first Bush administration, Powell and Rice were among the few minorities. Although he was far above her in seniority and she was nearly young enough to be his daughter—it was difficult for him to think of her as a senior strategist—he respected her intelligence and had always been kind to and solicitous of her. After he retired from the military and she moved to California, they had kept in occasional touch; she was active in the Boys and Girls Club in Palo Alto when he served as national chairman of the organization. On visits to Washington, she occasionally stopped by for dinner with Colin and Alma.

The Vulcans' reluctance to seek Powell's counsel was part ideological—his service in the Clinton administration and outspoken multilateralism made him suspect to some—and part generational. Most of the Vulcans were in their forties or early fifties and considered themselves worker bees, meeting regularly and holding thrice-weekly conference calls as they brought Bush up to speed on international affairs and equipped him with foreign and defense policies. But they all recognized the status the sixty-three-year-old general would lend to their efforts; once they were prepared to unveil their candidate to the nation and the world, they could bring Powell down from Mount Olympus to publicly bless him.

Yet however distant he was from the campaign's foreign policy deliberations, as the author James Mann noted in his 2004 history of the Vulcans, Powell was "central to its politics." There were regular leaks to the media that he was a behind-the-scenes member of Bush's brain trust. Campaign operatives eager to dispel the notion that their candidate had a weak grasp of foreign and defense affairs hinted that Powell would travel with Bush on international fact-finding trips and gave assurances that he would be Bush's top choice for secretary of state. But no one in the campaign ever approached Powell about such a trip, and there was no substantive discussion of a Cabinet position.

In fact, there was no contact at all between Powell and Bush as the primary race heated up in late 1999 and early 2000. Not only did the Vulcans feel they did not need his input, Bush's political managers were wary of

Powell's celebrity and of his interest in McCain, who had finally declared his candidacy and emerged as the main competition for the Republican nomination. McCain told reporters outright that he would invite Powell to be his secretary of state.

Powell hedged his bets by sending a $1,000 check to each campaign and insisting publicly that he had no preference. "I think that the Republican Party has two leading candidates who are very, very strong," he told CNN interviewer Larry King in December 1999. "I could support either one of them and in due course will make a judgment." Although McCain was far more conservative than Powell, he was also a maverick in the Republican ranks who was hard to pigeonhole. And despite Powell's willingness to excuse Clinton's draft dodging, he still tended to divide the Vietnam generation into those who had answered their country's call to military service and those who had ducked it. McCain was a decorated veteran who spent five and a half years as a prisoner of war in North Vietnam, while Bush had joined the Texas Air National Guard and never left home.

But while Powell made no public statements about his availability for either candidate, he was more than ready to move back into government service and deeply interested in the job of secretary of state.

Since his retirement from the Army, he had hobnobbed with dozens of company presidents and CEOs, all of them multimillionaires or even billionaires, and had closely studied their lifestyles. He and Alma had long since started buying new cars regularly; they talked about traveling the world and buying a vacation home. America's Promise was well established, and it was getting harder for Colin to work himself up for yet another paid speech on leadership and motivation. Alma, who could usually sense his moods even if he didn't immediately share his thoughts, told him it was time to start something new. Returning to government would mean more years of sixteen-hour days, and the income cut would be substantial. But they were already wealthy beyond their wildest dreams. His income from speaking engagements alone, delivered at the rate of eight to ten a month with fees sometimes reaching $100,000, would exceed $6 million in 2000.

Powell felt he still had years of service in him and that he knew as much as or more than anyone in the country about diplomacy and the use of force. He had been involved in foreign affairs for much of his working life and had a firm vision of how to make and keep friends and influence others while preserving and increasing national strength. There was an admirable precedent for a military officer becoming secretary of state: General George C. Marshall, who had led the reconstruction of post–World War II Europe in the Truman administration, was a revered figure to Powell. The job was the perfect fit; it would utilize all of his strengths yet required no political pandering. It was only later that the distance he intentionally put between his policy interests and Bush's political interests would return to haunt him.

Bush sealed up the Republican nomination in early spring 2000, vanquishing McCain in the "Super Tuesday" round of state primaries with the help of a nasty smear campaign impugning the war hero's character. As Bush and Vice President Gore joined in battle during a season of relative peace in the world, they focused mostly on domestic issues: taxes, the environment, education and health care. Foreign policy had not been a major presidential campaign issue since Vietnam.

To the limited extent that Bush felt it necessary to lay out his worldview, he spoke of a strong yet prudent America that would defend its values but not impose them on others. He promised to surround himself with leaders such as Powell for advice and support. "No question that a man of Colin Powell's stature would send a strong signal to America that I know how to attract the best minds in America," Bush said a week after the Super Tuesday vote.

On April 26, 2000, Bush traveled to Washington with several purposes in mind. To demonstrate his conversance with world affairs and foreign leaders, he planned to meet with visiting Russian Foreign Minister Igor Ivanov, who was in town to prepare for a June summit in Moscow between Clinton and Russian President Vladimir Putin. To soften the harsh tone of his primary campaign and reach out to Democrats, he scheduled a conversation on Social Security with Nebraska Senator Bob Kerrey. He would headline a major Republican fund-raising dinner. But another meeting did not appear on his public schedule: a private breakfast in his Washington hotel room with Powell. It was the first time they had seen each other since Powell's visit to Austin two and a half years earlier.

Afterward, Bush sent Powell a brief handwritten note thanking him for his time and "for the candid discussion and your willingness to help my campaign." He signed it "With respect." Powell's response, three days later, was breezy and noncommittal: "Dear George, I enjoyed our breakfast. You and Laura look great. Stay well, Colin."

In an indication that he already enjoyed the standing among foreign leaders that Bush was seeking, Powell had also met with Ivanov during the Russian's visit. Moscow was concerned about Bush's plans to expand Reagan's original "Star Wars" missile defense plan far beyond the pared-down development program Clinton had authorized. To Putin's dismay, Bush had indicated that he considered the 1972 Anti-Ballistic Missile (ABM) Treaty with Moscow—which prohibited deployment of such defensive systems—an obsolete impediment to U.S. national security. Ivanov wanted Powell's thoughts on the matter and, like most others outside the campaign, believed the general had an inside track with Bush.

The campaign was finally ready to publicly showcase Powell as a supporter on May 23, at a Washington press conference to unveil the candidate's views on nuclear weapons and strategic defense. The event was timed to preempt an upcoming speech by Gore and to put Bush out in front on defense issues before the upcoming Clinton-Putin summit. McCain was out of the picture, and Powell was happy to oblige.

In preparation, the Vulcans sent Powell two working papers drafted by Rice and Hadley. They argued that Clinton (and presumably Gore) was "locked in a Cold War mentality" and failed to recognize that America's offensive nuclear force could and should be significantly reduced, even unilaterally, from levels already agreed upon by Washington and Moscow. A Russian nuclear attack was no longer the primary threat to American security, and resources should be shifted toward a comprehensive defensive system—shared with the Russians if they wanted it—to deflect ballistic missiles. The system would protect against the real danger now facing the nation and the world: possible nuclear attack by "retrograde" states either seeking or already possessing nuclear weapons and the missiles with which to deliver them.

"The President cannot wait until that horrifying day when North Korea or Iraq launches—or threatens to launch—a nuclear attack against the U.S. or its key allies," Rice wrote. The ABM treaty, by preventing development and deployment of a defensive shield, "makes it impossible to do what we must do to defend ourselves."

For Powell, the most appealing part of Bush's plan was the outreach to the Russians as potential allies and the pledge of additional offensive weapons reductions, something he had been invested in since his Reagan days and had continued to push as chairman of the Joint Chiefs. He was agnostic about eliminating the ABM Treaty and lacked the missionary zeal with which some Republicans pursued missile defense. But he could live with both objectives. As Bush outlined his plans to reporters at the National Press Club in Washington, Powell stood behind him in silent support along with other Republican defense and foreign policy heavyweights—Shultz, Henry Kissinger, Brent Scowcroft and Donald Rumsfeld. Although not a Vulcan, Rumsfeld was in charge of a smaller campaign group that was studying how to fully implement Reagan's missile defense vision.

As intended, the media took special note of Powell's presence, and he and Bush deflected several questions about his role in a future Bush administration. Asked about the extent of his support for Bush's "foreign policy vision," Powell replied, "I support the governor. I look forward to the governor's election as President of the United States."

Two days after the news conference, on May 25, Powell visited Bush in Austin, ostensibly for another America's Promise session. As reporters sweltered outside on the statehouse lawn waiting for them to emerge, the two men sat down together in Bush's office. There was no discussion of missile defense, foreign policy or Cabinet choices, and Powell's most enduring memory of the conversation was Bush's determination to become president. "He essentially said, 'I'm going to run for all it's worth,'" Powell later recalled. "'Don't let there be any doubt in your mind, I am going to win.'"

Earlier the same day, Bush had hosted South African President Thabo Mbeki; the campaign planned to use photographs of them strolling together on the lawn to illustrate the governor's foreign policy acumen. With Powell in the same spot an hour later, the Associated Press's account of the day noted that Bush had garnered "an added visual political payoff by rubbing shoulders with two prominent black leaders." For the Powell shot, props were positioned on the lawn: several little red wagons (the America's Promise symbol) and a group of elementary school children, all white except for two Hispanics brought to stand at the front. The idea, Bush's adviser Karen Hughes explained, was "to showcase...Governor Bush's inclusive message." There was nothing out of the ordinary about it; Gore's campaign arranged the same racially balanced backdrops for his speeches.

After they spoke to reporters about children and volunteerism, Powell was asked about the vice presidency and issued his stock rejection: "I am not a candidate.... I'm not seeking it, and the governor knows that." Even if Powell were interested, any chance of being chosen as Bush's running mate had been effectively eliminated when Bush had asked Dick Cheney that spring to head his vice presidential search committee. Although Cheney and Powell had worked closely together at the Pentagon and learned to live with their differences, they had ended their association after the last Republican administration at arm's length and had grown no closer during the intervening years. The distance between them owed as much to personality as it did to ideology. Powell was put off by Cheney's dour certitude; Cheney thought that anyone as smooth and popular as Powell was inherently untrustworthy.

Powell went on to answer a question the reporters hadn't asked: other than the vice presidency, he said, "one has to listen when a president asks you to consider a job. I'm not looking for a job right now, but obviously I will do what I can to assist the governor with advice and friendship. And in due course, we can talk about whether or not there might be a role for me in his administration." If Bush wasn't going to bring up the subject of secretary of state in private, Powell figured he might as well say his piece in public.

Bush chuckled and said it was "a little premature to be discussing different slots. But obviously if I were to win, he would be a man that I would like to talk to about how to make sure the world was peaceful and the country was prosperous."

A week before the July 31, 2000, Republican nominating convention in Philadelphia, the question of the vice presidency was finally mooted when Bush selected Cheney himself as his running mate. As he had been four years earlier, Powell was scheduled as the keynote speaker on the convention's opening Monday night. The party was still struggling to promote an inclusive, "big-tent" image, and Powell was still its most prominent black member. He drafted a variation of his America's Promise speech on providing the nation's children with the values and tools they needed to develop into competent and caring adults. That was fine with the convention planners; it meshed nicely with Bush's campaign theme of "compassionate conservatism."

A twist on traditional conservatism, the "compassionate" version rejected both the Right's "benign neglect" of the poor and the Left's search for the "root causes" of social problems. It explicitly recognized the government's responsibility to meet the needs of disadvantaged Americans by promising to assist them in developing self-reliance and values that would enable them to help themselves. As Bush explained it, much of the government's burden, as well as federal resources, should be shifted from traditional welfare programs to state and local governments, churches, and community organizations—what he called "armies of compassion"—which were better suited to the task. More traditional conservatives were skeptical; it was "hot air at best and, at worse, a slur on past Republican accomplishments," including efforts to get the federal government and its pocketbook out of the social welfare business altogether, according to one scholar. Many Democrats considered "compassionate conservatism" a hypocritical, meaningless phrase designed to soften the appearance of hard Republican edges and blur the boundary between church and state.

As Bush moved closer to the nomination, Powell tasked Lawrence Wilkerson, his former Pentagon aide, now on his private staff, with examining how effectively compassionate conservatism had worked in Bush's "No Child Left Behind" education program in Texas, where he had cut state funds to underperforming schools. The assignment signaled to Wilkerson that Powell had finally started "to get really serious about the prospect of being a principal Cabinet officer for a Republican administration."

Powell approved of what he learned about Bush's governorship. "To me," he told cheering delegates at the convention, compassionate conservatism was "just caring about people."

Just as in 1996, Powell's address made little reference to foreign or defense policy. Instead, after lauding American strength and goodness, he warned that the nation's children were inadequately educated and cared for. Bush's Texas agenda, he said, had responded to the "deepest needs" of minorities. He congratulated the governor for attending that year's annual NAACP meeting, where Bush had outlined "his plans for housing and health and education programs to help all Americans." Bush had "spoke[n] the truth to the [NAACP] delegates when he said that the party of Lincoln has not always carried the mantle of Lincoln," Powell said. "I know that with all his heart, Governor Bush welcomes the challenge. He wants the Republican Party to wear that mantle again."

Minority concerns had to be addressed "not just during an election year campaign…it must be every day, and it must be for real," Powell said. "The party must listen to and speak with all leaders of the black community, regardless of political affiliation or philosophy." Republicans "must understand the cynicism" created among blacks when "some in our party miss no opportunity to roundly and loudly condemn affirmative action that helped a few thousand black kids get an education, but you don't hear a whimper when it's affirmative action for lobbyists who load our tax code with preferences for special interests." To reclaim Lincoln's mantle, he said, they had to prove to minorities every day that the Republicans offered them a real choice. "If we give them that choice, it will be good for our party. But above all, it will be good for America."

Although his address included as much reproach of the Republicans as it did approval, Powell's appearance was an enormous boost for the party's image. The convention's opening night had been carefully staged to portray a commitment to education and diversity, and he was preceded on stage by Laura Bush and a gospel choir. But the truth was that the Republican platform had gone downhill since 1996 in terms of the domestic issues Powell cared about. The diversity on stage did not extend into the convention hall, where there were only a handful of nonwhite delegates, with nearly a dozen state delegations containing no minorities at all.

The evening's program, the conservative commentator David Frum noted critically, was "like that scene in *Singin' in the Rain* where the sound track and the video don't quite mesh.... You look at the platform. This is a staunch, firm conservative party.... The images that they're projecting, however, are not just soft but also rejecting traditional Republican [tenets]." The intent was to speak to two different audiences, Frum said, and "the hope is...that each will hear different portions. The question will be what happens if the same audience hears both."

Despite his enthusiasm four years earlier for expanding the political center, Powell's distaste for party politics had left him with few avenues of influence over the conservative activists who set domestic Republican priorities. His America's Promise appeals had been determinedly nonpartisan. But at least he had told the convention what it still needed to hear, he thought. To Powell's ears, "compassionate conservatism" sounded like the beginning of a solution to the tangle of mixed party messages. He agreed with Bush that minorities and the poor shared responsibility with the government for their own betterment. He believed in bootstraps—as long as everyone had equal access to boots.

Once again, Powell made the rounds of television interviews late Monday night after his speech and left for home early the next morning, turning down pleas from party officials to appear at donor and delegate parties. Bush was still campaigning around the country and wouldn't arrive in Philadelphia until just before he accepted the nomination on Thursday. Pressed by reporters during a stop in West Virginia to reconcile Powell's call for affirmative action with the party's explicit rejection of it, Bush said he hadn't read Powell's speech ahead of time but that it was "an important message" that reinforced his own dedication to minority recruitment.

The Bush team was pleased with Powell's contribution. "Your speech to the Republican National Convention was absolutely out of the park," Rumsfeld wrote to him from Chicago. "It could not have been better. Congratulations, and thanks."

Powell made a handful of appearances with Bush during the final months before the election, always no more than an hour or two by plane from

Washington so that he could quickly return home or complete his own lecture schedule. Just as he had with Dole in 1996, Powell drove the Bush campaign to distraction with demands to know who the audience would be and who else was scheduled to appear on stage. To the candidate's gimlet-eyed handlers, Powell's presence was a mixed blessing—he could be counted on to draw big crowds, although he refused to be scripted and the audience tended to cheer louder for him than for Bush. But they couldn't ignore the value he added to the campaign, and even when he wasn't around, Powell was a constant virtual presence at Bush's side, offered as proof of the candidate's competence. Asked in New Hampshire in mid-October to "tell us the names of people you would surround yourself with" as president, Bush offered Powell at the top of his list.

"If you're George Bush, and the biggest weakness you have is foreign policy, and you can have Cheney on one flank and Powell on the other, it virtually eliminated the competence issue," Newt Gingrich later recalled of the campaign. "And in Powell's case, he is an African American, chairman of the Joint Chiefs, best-selling writer, most trusted man in America. Lots of good things."

Beyond Bush's commitment to missile defense, the outlines of his foreign policy and defense plans remained fuzzy. In his one major campaign speech on the subject, in November 1999, he had spoken of "the modesty of true strength. The humility of real greatness." Only one of his three debates with Gore, at Wake Forest University in North Carolina less than a month before the election, focused on foreign policy. Powell sat prominently next to Laura Bush in the front row of the audience and nodded approvingly as Bush spoke of reaching out to allies and disparaged the "nation-building" deployments of the Clinton era. "Our military is meant to fight and win war," Bush said. "That's what it's meant to do. And when it gets overextended, morale drops." He would be "judicious as to how to use the military. It needs to be in our vital interest, the mission needs to be clear, and the exit strategy obvious."

America under a Bush administration would use its power to expand freedom and protect its alliances, he pledged, and other nations would respond with respect rather than envy. "It really depends upon how our nation conducts itself in foreign policy. If we're an arrogant nation, they'll resent us. If we're a humble nation, but strong, they'll welcome us."

After the debate, Powell and Armitage went to the "spin room," where spokesmen for each campaign tried to convince journalists that their standard-bearer had prevailed. They had been nervous about the debate— "scared to death" was how Armitage put it—and were relieved at Bush's relatively polished performance and the absence of any major gaffes. But

Armitage noted with concern that reporters "ripped the door down" trying to get to Powell as soon as they spotted him. From his Vulcan vantage point, Armitage had concluded that there were some people inside the campaign—Karl Rove, Bush's chief political adviser, in particular—who had strong misgivings about Powell.

The November 7 presidential election was one of the closest in American history, and the final tally was a long time coming. For more than a month after the vote, contested ballots were recounted in Florida and brought before the courts. On November 30, as the balance seemed to be tipping in Bush's favor, Powell traveled with Cheney and their wives to Bush's 1,600-acre ranch outside the dusty, east-central Texas crossroads town of Crawford for a public display of togetherness and confidence. Before lunch, the three couples walked outside to talk to waiting reporters. Bush said Powell was there to talk about "national security matters and foreign policy matters" and coyly insisted that there had been no Cabinet discussions. Powell, tieless and wearing a casual leather jacket, said that no one had asked him yet to be secretary of state.

In the end, there was no vetting of Powell by Cheney or any other campaign officials and no deep policy examinations. Having profitably embraced and been embraced by the general in the last weeks of the campaign, there was no reason for Bush to balk now. Powell later recalled that he and the governor had done most of their talking about the job in the backseat of cars between events on the four days they had campaigned together that fall, but he couldn't recall an explicit invitation from Bush to serve in his Cabinet. Once the U.S. Supreme Court declared the Florida recount officially over in early December, Powell later said, "It just sort of happened as it was assumed to happen."

On December 16, three days after Gore conceded defeat, Powell again flew to Texas, this time to be unveiled as Bush's first Cabinet nominee. Powell and Cheney stood on either side of the president-elect as he read from prepared remarks to reporters gathered in a Crawford public school auditorium. Pledging to "conduct our foreign policy in the spirit of national unity and bipartisanship," Bush said, "our next Secretary of State believes, as I do, that we must work closely with our allies and friends in times of calm so that we will be able to work together in times of crisis. He believes, as I do, that our nation is best when we project our strength and our purpose with humility." Turning to Powell, Bush invoked Harry Truman's tribute to George Marshall. "He is a tower of strength and common sense. When you find somebody like that, you have to hang on to them. I have found such a man."

As Powell moved to the microphone, Bush blinked back tears. It was an emotional moment, he later explained, "because I so admire Colin Powell—I love his story."

After thanking Bush and recognizing Cheney—"we have been through many adventures together, and many more adventures await us in the future"—Powell launched into an expansive foreign policy tour de force. Speaking without a text, in far more detail than Bush had provided during or since the campaign, he drew a blueprint of engagement and strong, expanding alliances that would be "the center of our foreign policy activity." The administration would work closely with China and Russia, discussing areas of disagreement "in rational ways." Nations that pursued weapons of mass destruction would not "frighten" us, he said. "We will meet them. We will match them. We will contend with them." He spoke of the revolution in information technology, previewed an expansion of global trade and promised to rebuild the State Department after years of poor management and budget cuts.

The new administration, Powell said in response to questions, would "remain very much engaged" in the Middle East. "I expect it to be a major priority of mine and of the Department," reflecting America's ongoing commitment to Israel's security as well the fulfillment of "the aspirations of the Palestinians." Noting that Saddam Hussein had not yet complied with international demands to account for and dismantle Iraq's illicit weapons programs, Powell said that "my judgment is that the sanctions in some form must be kept in place until they do so." He spoke at length about American military deployments in Bosnia and Kosovo and promised to "spend time discussing" missile defense with U.S. allies before any steps were taken.

Armitage watched the performance on television, and Powell called him afterward to ask how he had come across. His speech had been impressive, Armitage said, but Powell's easy articulateness, compared to Bush's apparent lack of sophistication, had actually been a little discomfiting to see. He repeated what he had told Powell after witnessing his appearance with Clinton following the Haiti negotiation in 1994. "It's about domination," he said. "Be careful in appearances with the president." Powell, pumped up and pleased with himself, brushed off his friend's caution.

But the contrast between Bush and his designated secretary of state was widely noticed. "Powell seemed to dominate the President-elect who had just nominated him, both physically and in the confidence he projected," *The Washington Post* reported. According to the *Boston Herald*, "Some political observers wonder if Powell, with worldwide stature and deep foreign policy experience, may eclipse his boss. During a brief press conference following the announcement, all of the questions were directed at Powell while Bush stood by silently, cracking a joke at one point."

The New York Times foreign affairs columnist Tom Friedman worried half seriously that Powell might wield too much power over Bush. "I sure hope Colin Powell is always right in his advice to Mr. Bush," Friedman wrote after the Crawford announcement, "because he so towered over the President-elect... that it was impossible to imagine Mr. Bush ever challenging or overruling Mr. Powell on any issue. Mr. Powell is three things Mr. Bush is not—a war hero, worldly wise, and beloved by African-Americans. That combination gives him a great deal of leverage. It means he can never be fired. It means Mr. Bush can never allow him to resign in protest over anything."

William Smullen, Powell's aide in retirement, knew that Powell had given extensive thought to his remarks. He had intended to stake out his territory and take advantage of the opportunity to declare himself. "At the time, he probably figured he had nothing to lose," Smullen later reflected. "If they don't like it, screw them. That's fine for the moment, but it can come back to haunt you."

Before joining the Bush team, most of the Vulcans had written and spoken publicly about foreign policy issues ranging from Iraq and the Middle East to Russia, China, North Korea and the United Nations. Some of them were on record with a far more muscular posture than Powell's promise of tempered strength and pragmatism, envisioning a new era of "American exceptionalism" to replace the multilateralism of Bush's father and Clinton.

But those issues had rarely been debated inside the team during the campaign, and certainly not with a relative outsider such as Powell. Bush, who was far more interested in domestic issues, saw no reason for concern about possible conflicts among his top advisers. "I don't think we had big worldview kinds of discussions at any point that I can remember," a senior Bush administration official who was closely involved with the campaign later recalled. "The main things were that the president, then governor, had a strong view that America was sort of central to world peace and security, [and would] exercise strong leadership, and we had a few relationships that had to be built very strongly. I don't think there was any question that Colin Powell was the kind of person that you were going to want doing this."

Powell's stature—his "ability to fill up a room," in the official's words—was just as important as his judgment and experience. "He's politically very savvy with people. If you're secretary of state, you have to be able to walk in to [French President] Jacques Chirac or [British Prime Minister] Tony Blair and operate, not as an equal, but to represent the United States in that strong way. And he brought all of that."

Armitage, who was fairly cynical about campaigns in general and this one in particular, thought that Powell's foreign policy expertise ranked far below his political popularity and "ability to fill up a room" on the list of things the Bush team wanted from the general.

Rice, the closest Vulcan to Powell next to Armitage, was slated to become Bush's national security adviser. She had stayed out of the often acrimonious ideological and policy debates among the Republican elite during the 1990s, including the divisions over Powell's potential presidential candidacy. As far as she was concerned, it was all part of the usual—and usually pointless—Washington maelstrom. She dismissed what she knew were unresolved differences over the inconclusive end to the Gulf War and what to do about Iraq in the future. As long as everyone was on board with the basic Bush goals, she thought, a clash of ideas over how to achieve them would be a good thing.

Gingrich, who had left Congress after the 1998 election but remained a powerful figure with close ties to the more hard-line side of the incoming team, wasn't worried about Powell. "I thought, and I think Bush thought, that [Bush] would go from education to Social Security.... I think he really thought that essentially he'd be a domestic president. And have a really bright national security adviser and a world-respected secretary of state and a vice president who knew virtually everybody on the planet. And that those three would really do foreign policy. Rumsfeld would do defense transformation."

Bush's choice of Donald Rumsfeld for defense secretary, the same position he had held in the Ford administration a quarter century earlier, allayed conservatives' concerns that Powell would dominate both foreign and defense policy. In the web of intrigue already being spun around and within the nascent administration, it was held that Cheney's memories of Powell's charisma and influence as chairman had impelled him to press for a strong Pentagon counterweight to the new secretary of state. Rumsfeld had been Cheney's mentor when the new vice president–elect had first entered government in the 1970s. Cheney knew him to be a tough customer who could more than hold his own against Powell.

Some reports chalked up the selection of Rumsfeld as an early defeat for Powell, a spin that Powell and Armitage assumed was coming from inside the White House transition team itself. They had both favored Pennsylvania Governor Tom Ridge, a Republican moderate, for the job of defense secretary. When Ridge was rejected, reportedly at the urging of Cheney, they decided they could live with the next prospect in line, conservative Indiana Senator Dan Coats. But Bush and Cheney, who interviewed Coats together in Bush's suite at the Madison Hotel in downtown Washington, thought the senator lacked the necessary heft to both reform the Pentagon and balance Powell's power. Rumsfeld had been under consideration to head the CIA when Cheney proposed him for defense secretary.

It had been assumed throughout the campaign, certainly by Armitage himself, that as the leading Vulcan on defense issues he would be given the powerful policy-making job of deputy defense secretary. But within days of Rumsfeld's appointment, word began to spread that neither Cheney nor Rumsfeld wanted him. A Pentagon gossip column in *The Washington Times,* a frequent outlet for conservative thought, reported concerns that "centrists" in the new administration, including Powell, planned to use Armitage to " 'neutralize' defense conservatives and their standard-bearer, Mr. Rumsfeld."

Despite Rumsfeld's gracious note to Powell after his convention speech, Powell had no real relationship with the Defense nominee. The youngest man ever to hold the job when he was first appointed in 1975, Rumsfeld was now nearly the oldest, second only to George Marshall, who had taken over the Pentagon for a year during the Korean War at the end of his career. Despite there being only five years between them, Rumsfeld seemed like a different generation to Powell, who recalled that he had been only a colonel the last time Rumsfeld headed the Pentagon— a lifetime ago in military terms. He telephoned Rumsfeld after the nomination to congratulate him and to plug Armitage for his number two, although he assumed that Rumsfeld had already "done his homework" and knew that Armitage was Powell's close friend. "And I'm sure people had said to him, 'Hey, wait a minute, if you've got Armitage over here, you've got Powell over here. You've got a mole.' "

When Armitage was finally summoned by Rumsfeld to an interview two weeks before the January 20 inauguration, the meeting was short and sour. Several years later, after Powell had been alternately amused and infuriated by the countless ideological battles subsequently waged inside the Bush administration, he still thought the story was funny. "So Don, in typically charming fashion, says to Rich, 'Well, you know, there's only a fifty percent probability that you'll get this job,'" he recounted. "And Rich, being Rich, says, 'No, Mr. Secretary, on that basis, there's a zero percent probability I'm going to get this job.' And they talk for a few minutes and Rich leaves."

Flapping his arms and laughing, Powell acknowledged that Armitage was a Vulcan. "But he didn't have wings like the rest of them," he said.

As he moved to select a deputy secretary of state, Powell faced the prospect of a mole inside his own department. Paul Wolfowitz was one of several disappointed defense secretary hopefuls who had indicated an interest in the State Department job. In addition to serving as a top aide to Cheney at the Pentagon, Wolfowitz had worked with Rumsfeld (as well as Armitage) as a Dole adviser during the 1996 campaign and had served on Rumsfeld's committee studying missile defense. But while Powell considered Wolfowitz a friend and intellectual powerhouse, he knew they were not "ideologically in gear." More significantly, from Powell's point of view, Wolfowitz had a reputation as a careless and distracted manager, unsuited to the kind of reorganization and team building needed at the State Department. Powell proposed the job of U.N. ambassador as a better fit for Wolfowitz's considerable talents. But Wolfowitz turned down the offer and was quickly chosen for the job Armitage had wanted as Rumsfeld's number two.

Armitage was far from enthusiastic when Powell asked *him* to take the deputy position at State. If he couldn't be at Defense, he said, he would just as soon continue his private consulting business. But Powell said he needed him, and Armitage acquiesced.

For conservatives who saw Powell as a threat, there was comfort in having him and Armitage confined to the same department, effectively diminishing their power to one vote in the anticipated policy battles to come. Wolfowitz, as Armitage's opposite number at Defense, would check his influence, just as Rumsfeld would be more than a match for Powell.

Powell remained unconcerned by the widespread reports of internecine plotting already swirling around him; he had been through the same kind of bureaucratic skirmishing in other administrations and had a good win-loss record. As far as he was concerned, the only view that really counted in any administration was the president's. Powell's attention was focused on Bush, and he was confident that he and the president-elect were on the same foreign policy wavelength.

"Remember what he was saying?" Powell later recalled. "Compassionate conservatism. He was talking about partnerships and reaching out. There may have been some in the group that had very strong views about some issues. But the Bush I knew and had gotten to know, the son of a father who believed all these things, the conversations I had all dealt with partnership, the U.N., et cetera. Obviously there were some challenges out there, with Iran, Iraq and North Korea and some others." But they would deal with them.

For all Powell's confidence, he still had not had a substantive conversation with Bush about foreign policy and what he wanted from his secretary of state. The moment finally came on December 28, when the president-elect invited him to a one-on-one dinner. Powell was eager for the opportunity; his largely favorable impression of Clinton had been formed over a similar session, when they had sat down alone for more than an hour just after the 1992 election. The circumstances were different—Clinton hadn't chosen Powell, who had already been in place as chairman of the Joint Chiefs—but the wide-ranging exchange of views about the world and the nation had given them a chance to size each other up.

After a long conversation with Bush over steaks in a back room at Morton's, a downtown Washington restaurant favored by political movers and shakers, Powell felt he had all the answers he needed. "I was sure I was working for a guy, would be working for a guy, who would understand who I am and what I believed."

The day after his return from Crawford, Powell had paid a visit to Madeleine Albright, Clinton's secretary of state for the last four years. The government was always on the alert for possible terrorist attacks—less than three months earlier, the guided missile destroyer USS *Cole* had been blown apart during a refueling stop at the port of Aden, Yemen, killing seventeen American sailors—but he found the amount of security surrounding Albright's home in Georgetown to be almost comically excessive. There were armed agents around the property and an escape vehicle with its engine running positioned outside the front door.

Even before his nomination, Powell had been inundated with outside studies and reports from blue-ribbon panels and commissions describing the State Department as dysfunctional and physically dilapidated. Some critics obviously had partisan axes to grind, but there was ample objective evidence of problems, many of which had predated Albright but worsened under her leadership. Successive budget cuts had reduced foreign affairs funding from $5.05 billion in 1994 to $3.64 billion in 2000. The reports referred to "woefully inadequate" information technology that had not been updated for years and a physical presence overseas that was "near a state of crisis." Recruitment was stagnant, and only about half of those who had left through retirements and resignations in recent years had been replaced. Congress had fought with Albright at every opportunity and pummeled her with depressing regularity, most recently after reports that secret documents and a computer had disappeared from the State Department building.

Albright's home fortress mirrored the bunker mentality rumored to afflict the State Department's seventh floor, where the secretary and her top aides had their offices. Her personal detail from the Diplomatic Security Service, the department's own protective force, conducted security sweeps of other offices inside the building when she deigned to visit. A draconian, buildingwide crackdown after the computer disappearance had further demoralized employees who already felt cut off from their closeted boss. Powell had received a torrent of letters from insulted former U.S. ambassadors and Foreign Service officers who were now barred from entering the department without an escort.

He had some sympathy for the pressure Albright was under, but when he visited he found her cynical and bitter. "You'll be very welcome" at the department, she told him in a diatribe that Powell thought said more about her own management style than it did about her employees. "Everybody will love you initially, because you're nice and everybody loves you. And the Foreign Service will think you're going to be great for them. But you watch, in six months they'll hate you. And in six months, you'll hate them."

As Powell recalled the conversation, Albright said she had "tried everything" to reach out. "I used to go to the cafeteria, I did this, I did that. But it didn't work, and it's just the way they are."

The more dire the warnings he heard about the department, the more enthusiastic Powell became about the challenge ahead. He took as much pride in his leadership and team-building skills as he did in his policy expertise, maybe even more. Management was an art, and he considered himself a master. The 45,000 State Department employees in the United States and abroad—including 4,500 Foreign Service officers—would be his new infantry division.

On a Sunday evening just after Christmas, Marc Grossman, a career officer serving as Foreign Service director general, was driving his young daughter and her friends around suburban Virginia to look at holiday lights when his cell phone rang. General Powell wanted to talk to him, the operations center announced, and Grossman turned around to shush the girls as his soon-to-be boss came on the line. Powell got straight to the point. He was moving into the transition suite of offices on the State Department's first floor the next day, and he wanted Grossman to be the first appointment on his schedule. The director general handled all personnel issues for the Foreign Service, and Powell wanted to demonstrate that the department's troops would be his first priority. Would it be all right if he visited Grossman's sixth-floor office in the morning?

Grossman was momentarily speechless. Powell's presence upstairs would incite a riot; people would line the hallway trying to get a glimpse of him. And it was a violation of protocol for the incoming secretary of state to be walking the upper levels before the outgoing one had even left. "I'll come to you," he finally blurted out.

When he walked into the transition suite the next day, Grossman had a presentation ready to deliver to Powell. "I told him we needed more people...that I'd done the numbers and the most important thing I needed from him if he really wanted to make an impact was to hire." He gave Powell an initial goal: an internal review by the department's Bureau of Human Resources put the total staffing deficit at 1,158. "Then I tried to give him a picture of where everybody was, and we talked about jobs and who might fill jobs."

Powell's return pitch, Grossman recalled, was that the department was a great place for them all to work and he was going to make it even better. "He clearly wanted me to carry that message out. He wanted me to go out and say, 'I met Colin Powell and this is what Colin Powell was going to be about.'"

The long ballot recount had shrunk the usual two and a half months between the election and inauguration of a new president to just a few weeks. Democrats in the Republican-led Congress had no quarrels with Bush's initial Cabinet choices, and confirmation hearings were scheduled to take place even before Bush was sworn in. With the media reports of his Crawford performance in mind as he prepared for his January 17 session before the Senate Foreign Relations Committee, Powell asked Wilkerson to research everything Bush had said about any foreign policy subject that was likely to be even remotely controversial.

The hearing was a virtual lovefest between Powell and the senators, even those who disagreed with Bush's insistence on pushing forward with missile defense and decreasing the U.S. presence in Bosnia. Powell gave the requisite support for both policies but said soothingly that the administration would consult with its allies before making any precipitate moves. As he addressed other issues, Powell felt that Bush's broad policy outlines during the campaign gave him room to maneuver. "We are attached by a thousand cords to the world at large, to its teeming cities, to its remotest regions, to its oldest civilizations, to its newest cries for freedom," he said in an eloquent case for multilateralism. The United States, he said, had interests everywhere in the world and would not withdraw "into a fortress of protectionism or [an] island of isolationism."

The new administration would be bold but wise in its overseas commitments, he said. Focusing on great-power relationships, he spoke of China as "a giant trying to find its way in the world." It was not a strategic partner, "but neither is China our inevitable and implacable foe. China is our competitor, a potential regional rival, but also a trading partner willing to cooperate in areas where our strategic interests overlap." Ties with Russia would be constructive, he said, but Moscow needed to "get on with reform." The administration would not hesitate to criticize either country when it came to respect for the rule of law and human rights.

In response to questions, he called for talks with North Korea, continued U.S. involvement in Middle East peace negotiations and greater attention to Africa and the spread of HIV/AIDS. "With powerful economies such as South Africa's and, eventually, Nigeria's and other transforming African states, we begin to change the lives of Africa's poorest people, who are so desperately in need, and we need to help them. It is our obligation."

Powell warned that the State Department needed more resources for everything from personnel to a new communications system and increased security, and he said that he would be back to Capitol Hill with specific requests. He promised to "keep the number of political ambassadors in check" and to favor career Foreign Service officers for senior appointments.

Asked about Iraq, Powell called for enhanced sanctions in cooperation with U.S. allies and the United Nations. "As long as we are able to control the major source of money going into Iraq, we can keep them in the rather broken condition they are in now. Mr. Saddam Hussein can put a hat on his head and shoot a rifle in the air at an Army Day parade, but it is fundamentally a broken, weak country.... His only tool, the only thing he can scare us with are those weapons of mass destruction, and we have to hold him to account" with sanctions and the reinsertion of U.N. weapons inspectors.

When it was over, Committee Chairman Jesse Helms, an archconservative Republican from North Carolina, said, "I'm aware of no opposition to Colin Powell from anybody" and asked for a motion to approve him. The vote, both in the committee and later on the Senate floor, was unanimous.

The secretary of state's private seventh-floor office, with just enough room for a desk and chair and a pair of couches snuggled around a coffee table, was a cubbyhole compared to the far more expansive quarters of the chairman of the Joint Chiefs and most other Cabinet officials. Off a quiet, red-carpeted hallway, the path to the womblike inner sanctum wound past an anteroom and through a high-ceilinged, funereal parlor furnished with eighteenth-century American heirlooms. When Smullen first visited the suite on the day after the Saturday inauguration, he found it cold and unwelcoming. Following the usual procedure for a change in administration, the desktops and drawers had been emptied and the walls stripped of the paintings Albright had selected from the department's art collection. Smullen asked if something could be done to make the place look a little warmer. When he was told that historical portraits could quickly be made available, he looked at a list and chose two that he thought would be especially meaningful to Powell: Thomas Jefferson, the nation's first secretary of state, and George Marshall. He asked that they be hung inside the parlor entrance, across from the door to Powell's office and visible from his desk.

When Colin left home on Monday, January 22, 2001, Alma reminded him that he wasn't in the Army anymore. "Don't treat them like an infantry battalion," she warned. But that was precisely how he planned to address his new troops. He liked to start every new command with a bang, a gimmick that would shake them up and distinguish him from his predecessors. At the Reagan NSC it had been the crisp, military-style meetings and the elimination of the secretive operations office established by Oliver North. At the Bush Pentagon, it had been as simple as changing the office furniture and making the chiefs meet him alone without their usual coteries of aides. For the State Department, where oppressive security had come to symbolize pervasive mistrust and the seventh floor's separation from the rank and file, he decided to throw open the doors and mingle with the masses.

He temporarily turned down the secretary's staff car and driver, told his assigned Diplomatic Security agents that he'd find his own way to work and drove his Chrysler PT Cruiser from McLean across the Potomac River and into Washington. He stopped on the way to pick up Grant Green, the retired Army general he had recruited to help him start putting the department in order. Green had been a senior manager in the Weinberger Defense Department and executive secretary at the Reagan NSC during Powell's tenure. Along with Smullen, who would serve as his chief of staff, Powell was also bringing along Peggy Cifrino as Smullen's deputy and Wilkerson, who would have a place on his policy-planning staff.

The morning rush-hour traffic on the George Washington Parkway was backed up, and they arrived late at 8:15, pulling into the circular drive of the recently renamed Harry S. Truman Department of State Building, an unlovely pile of granite covering two city blocks. Hundreds of department employees, hoping to get a look at their new celebrity chief, were waiting in the main lobby and broke into cheers and a full minute's worth of applause as he walked through the glass doors. He shook some hands and climbed halfway up a set of stairs to a mezzanine overlooking the crowd.

"I am not coming in just to be the foreign policy adviser to the President, although that is what the principal title is," he told them. "I'm not just coming in to serve the foreign policy needs of the American people. I'm coming in as the leader and the manager of this department." He was impressed at the quality of the people there, he said, and made clear that the walls dividing the executive offices from the rest of the building would be lowered. "You will ... find that I like to hear things directly. I am going to be asking so many of you to come up and tell me directly what you think.... You are the experts. You know what is going on. You know your accounts better than I know your accounts, and I want to hear from you as directly as I can with a minimum number of layers in between." It was straight from his Army leadership playbook—the "officer in the field" is always right, at least until proven otherwise.

That morning and at a buildingwide "town hall meeting" three days later, Powell peppered his remarks with military jargon and delighted his new soldiers by apologizing in advance for any occasional lapses "back into my original language, which is Infantry." Translators would be provided, he said to rounds of laughter. He talked of "frontline troops" and reminded potential slackers that "I am still a general." He would not bring in a lot of political appointees and special envoys, he told them, because they were already "a great group of company commanders, battalion commanders, sergeants, privates, all working together." He had high standards, and "if you perform well, we are going to get along fine. If you don't, you are going to give me push-ups."

Marc Grossman was dazzled by Powell's technique. "This guy, he's used to standing up in front of ten thousand uniformed military people and it's 'Hooo-ahhhh, let's go. I'm your guy. Follow me.' And people here loved it."

One on one, Powell was equally compelling. "I've never really met anyone else who handles himself that way," marveled a regional assistant secretary. "Maybe they're taught in the military to make eye contact and not forget your name." The official recalled that after six months of near-daily contact with the secretary of state in the senior Bush administration, James Baker still couldn't remember his name.

In early discussions with the heads of regional and issue bureaus, Powell's orders were an about-face from the locked-down Albright days, when all outside contacts required approval up the chain of command and most of the staff had been reluctant to risk an independent opinion. They were now not only allowed but encouraged to raise questions and to maintain their own contacts outside the building.

"Our instructions were to talk to Capitol Hill as often and as clearly and as honestly as we possibly could," recalled another assistant secretary. "It made a huge difference. What it told everybody was, 'We trust you. You're a professional.' " Richard Boucher, the career Foreign Service officer who headed the Bureau of Public Affairs, was told to spread the word that no prior clearance was required to return calls from reporters. The only rules, he recalled, were: "No surprises . . . just tell us what's going on. And no recriminations. . . . If somebody was out there testifying or making a speech or even talking to a reporter on the record, you had to really screw up to get a phone call saying, 'Why did you do it that way?' "

Powell quickly made good on his promise to consult directly with experts in the building. Edward Walker, the assistant secretary for Near East Affairs (NEA), was "sitting at my desk and all of a sudden this light on the phone comes on. I'd never seen it lit before and I yelled out, 'What the heck is this?' And everybody comes in and I pick it up and get this 'Hi, Ned. Could you come up here for a minute?' He called me himself. He just pushed the speed dial that said NEA. So suddenly we had to label this button on my phone that nobody had known what it was." They were told not to let anyone else answer the secretary's direct line to their offices; if he called and no one picked up after five or six rings, Powell said, he'd call back later. He had become a dedicated computer geek in recent years and handed out his home e-mail address liberally, telling aides he checked his computer regularly in the evening and on weekends. Assistant secretaries found that he often responded to messages within minutes.

When he was helping Bush prepare for the president's first trip out of the country—a daylong visit to Mexico in mid-February—Powell asked the Mexico desk officer, the lowest rung on the regional chain, to accompany him to the White House for a briefing. It was a privilege heretofore reserved for only the most senior officials, and word spread quickly through the State Department's labyrinthine corridors. Powell started wandering around the building himself, dropping by offices on random visits. Whenever possible, he took the regular elevator up to the seventh floor rather than the private one reserved for the secretary. He personally escorted visiting foreign dignitaries down to the lobby and out to their cars, often stopping to talk to reporters or chat with whoever was standing around. Once when he spotted a group of interns waiting to be escorted upstairs for a tour of the elegant eighth-floor diplomatic reception rooms, he walked over, introduced himself, and took them on the tour himself.

But Powell's laid-back style extended only to the limits of his military decorum and his expectations of high performance. Early on, when the president asked a junior department official in Powell's company a question and the reply was "Yeah," others in the room swore they could see the hair on the back of the secretary's neck stand up straight. Tardiness to the daily 8:30 a.m. senior staff meeting was not tolerated, nor was showing up unprepared. "Top up my database," he would say to the assembled under-secretaries and assistant secretaries. He usually had a long list of questions, many of them from early-morning telephone calls and e-mails with his network of personal contacts in high places around the globe, the five newspapers he read at home each morning while riding his exercise bike and his constant perusal of the Internet. "He'd ask, 'Why did so and so say this? What happened here? Why are we doing this?' " recalled a regular morning attendee. "You had to know the answer right away, and if you didn't know the answer don't try to fake it. Just say, 'Sir, I'm behind. I'm sorry. I'll find out.' And you better have an answer by the time you got back to your office."

Just as he had with Reagan's broken National Security Council, Powell lifted their spirits and energized their minds. He knew a lot of it was gimmickry, but he thought gimmicks were often useful to set a tone and build a strong team. It didn't have much to do with the new president's foreign policy, but it built a foundation of personal loyalty to Powell's own leadership that for most in the department would prove unshakable over the next four years.

"Here was a guy who understood institutions, who was going to rely on the institution and support it. It was just what we'd been waiting a decade to hear," recalled a senior career officer. "We were like the Army at Valley Forge when George Washington showed up."

15

I've had tough days. I've had great days. . . . There are days where things don't go so well and a position you might have been pushing isn't successful. . . . That just comes with the business. And if that's going to put you into a blue funk, then you're in the wrong business. . . . I've been shot at for real, as opposed to the way I get shot at now.

—Colin L. Powell

Kofi Annan anxiously awaited the February 14 arrival of the new U.S. secretary of state at U.N. headquarters in New York. Powell's decision to make the United Nations his first out-of-town destination after the presidential inauguration was a good sign, Annan thought.

In his many years at the United Nations, the last four as secretary-general, Annan had seen the organization become a political football in Washington, applauded one day and condemned the next. What the new American president thought about the institution was a relative mystery. In one of his few comments about the United Nations during the campaign, Bush had dismissed its deliberations as "an opportunity for people to vent." He didn't seem very interested in the world beyond U.S. shores. His experiences outside North America had been limited: a few brief stops in Europe; a visit to Beijing in 1975, when his father had been ambassador to China; an official trip to Gambia when the senior Bush was president; and a tour of the Middle East with fellow state governors in 1998. Annan knew that the Republican Party and Bush's own advisers were divided between those who were suspicious of international organizations in general and the United Nations in particular and those who thought they were an important part of U.S. foreign policy.

Annan assumed that Powell fell into the latter category, but this meeting would set the initial tone for the United Nations' relations with the new administration. The two men weren't strangers; their paths had crossed several times when Powell was chairman of the Joint Chiefs of Staff and Annan, an international civil servant from Ghana, served as head of U.N. peacekeeping operations, including multinational forces in Somalia and the Balkans.

The secretary-general's suite on the thirty-eighth floor of the U.N. Secretariat, beside the East River in Manhattan, was opulent and serene compared to the dark, worn offices in the building below. Plush gray carpeting muffled the approach along a wide corridor. Escorts wearing formal dress and speaking in hushed voices guided visitors to the reception and conference rooms, furnished with earth-tone leather chairs selected by Annan's Swedish wife. It was an atmosphere that engendered formality and diplomatic distance, but when Powell walked in he greeted Annan as an old friend.

They talked in general terms about the ongoing Israeli-Palestinian conflict and agreed on the importance of continued American and U.N. involvement. Powell said the administration would work to revamp U.N. sanctions against Iraq. They discussed peacekeeping and programs in Africa, and Powell gently lobbied for an American appointment to a vacant senior position in the office of the U.N. High Commissioner for Refugees. Annan and his aides were relieved and encouraged. There was none of the bullying, peremptory tone that some American representatives adopted and that they had feared would mark the new administration. Powell was relaxed and well versed on the issues, as they had expected. But more importantly, this was a secretary of state who seemed confidently prepared to do business with the United Nations on a practical and nonideological basis.

At a joint press appearance after their meeting, Annan was beaming. "I am extremely happy that the Secretary of State's first visit outside the U.S. is to the U.N.," he said.

Later that day, Powell traveled to the U.S. Mission to the United Nations, located just across the street, for a separate meeting with ambassadors from the "P5," the five permanent members of the U.N. Security Council: Britain, France, China and Russia, along with the United States. The Security Council was the United Nations' international policy and enforcement body, composed of the P5 and a rotating membership of ten other nations selected by region. Resolutions adopted by the General Assembly, where all of the nearly two hundred member nations took part, had only whatever moral authority they could muster. But Council decisions carried the force of international law.

Like Annan, the P5 representatives got the message that Powell intended to convey: he was "reaching out" to the international community. His visit meant that the new administration took the United Nations seriously. But here, Powell also had specific business to conduct. "The meeting was devoted to Iraq and only Iraq," recalled one P5 ambassador.

They knew as well as Powell did that the U.N. sanctions that had restricted Iraqi trade since the Gulf War a decade earlier were falling apart. Repeated Security Council demands that Saddam Hussein stop abusing his own people, relinquish all weapons of mass destruction—including biological and chemical weapons and a possible nuclear weapons program—and open his doors to U.N. inspectors had become an international joke. Saddam had barred all weapons inspections since the end of 1998. Meanwhile, the Iraqi dictator was getting rich from profits and kickbacks from illegally sold oil. He was using the proceeds to buy more weaponry and build himself more extravagant palaces while blaming the international sanctions for the fact that Iraqis didn't have enough food to eat. Well-publicized pictures of starving Iraqi children had become a propaganda nightmare for the P5. Some nations were already trading with Iraq on the sly, and there was mounting pressure to abandon the restrictions altogether.

The Bush administration wanted to solve the sanctions problem, Powell told them, and was preparing a new policy that would increase the pressure against Saddam while forcing him to feed his own people. The United States would seek cooperation from the United Nations through dialogue and negotiation.

The Arab world and Iran had been the subjects of Powell's first State Department briefing after he took office. He had invited Condoleezza Rice, who was concerned about the region, as a useful demonstration of how the NSC and the department would work closely together in the new administration. Edward Walker, the regional assistant secretary, had begun by telling them that the United States was engaged in secret discussions with the Libyan government of Muammar Qaddafi. Libya was under U.S. and U.N. sanctions because of its terrorist ties, and Qaddafi was looking for ways to get the restrictions lifted. He had started to cooperate with the Central Intelligence Agency on terrorism issues.

The so-called peace process between Israel and the Palestinians was in tatters, Walker continued. A Palestinian uprising, or *intifada*, had broken out in the West Bank the previous August, prompting Israel's military occupation of the territory. Last-minute attempts by Clinton to broker a deal that would stop the escalating violence had failed. The Israeli government had since fallen, and the smart money was on the conservative Likud Party to win the upcoming elections, making the hard-line Ariel Sharon the prime minister. Hopes for progress were slim, and the department placed much of the blame squarely on the back of the Palestinian leader Yasser Arafat, who was unwilling or unable to control extremists' attacks against Israeli civilians. Powell remarked that Clinton had telephoned him on Inauguration Day to warn that Arafat could not be trusted and advise him to travel to the region as soon as possible to make his own assessments.

Walker briefed Powell and Rice on former secretary Madeleine Albright's efforts to open a dialogue with Iran's unyielding Islamic government. He devoted considerable time to Iraq, advising them that current U.S. policy could not be sustained much longer. For the past decade, that policy had consisted of three separate branches, each rooted in the inconclusive end to the Gulf War. First, there was the as-yet-unsuccessful effort by U.S. and allied intelligence agencies to promote Saddam's overthrow by Iraqis themselves. Congress's impatience with his continued existence had led to the adoption in 1998 of the Iraq Liberation Act, which authorized funds for active Iraqi opposition forces, most of them in exile, and set "regime change" as an official U.S. goal. The act, and a more muscular policy toward Iraq in general, had been strongly backed by conservative Republicans—including many now holding high positions in the new administration—who charged that Clinton had withheld appropriated aid to the exiles and been too timid in using American military power. During the campaign, Bush had promised to implement the act in full, but he had given few clues to exactly what he had in mind.

The second policy branch was military containment, with a U.S. troop deterrent based in other Persian Gulf states and U.S. and British air patrols over the "no-fly zones" they had established over two thirds of Iraqi territory. Saddam was prohibited from flying his own aircraft in the zones, but Iraqi antiaircraft weapons on the ground fired regularly at the patrols, particularly in the southern part of the country.

Finally, there were the U.N. sanctions, another instrument of containment and the policy branch that the State Department was most directly responsible for. With a number of countries flouting the rules restricting trade with Iraq, and a losing public relations battle, the sanctions were on the verge of collapse. The Russians and the French—both P5 members—were among those wanting to end them altogether, and even the British weren't convinced that the sanctions should continue. The State Department had already started fashioning a temporary fix, Walker reported. If the rules could be narrowed to focus only on Iraqi oil exports and imports of weapons and their components, it would be harder for other countries to cheat the system and for Saddam to blame the United Nations for starving his people.

"I believe the big [foreign policy] issues are going to be China and Russia," Bush had said early in his presidential campaign. "There will be moments when situations, incidents will flare up. It's important for the President to think globally. But in the long run, security in the world is going to be how do we deal with China and how do we deal with Russia." When the new president sat down with his national security team for the first time on January 30, however, the Middle East was the only item on the agenda.

Powell noted favorably that the president arrived in the Situation Room exactly on schedule at 3:35 p.m. and took his seat at the head of the table. There was none of the annoying formlessness of the Clinton National Security Council. Each participant—the vice president, the secretaries of state, defense and the Treasury, the chairman of the Joint Chiefs of Staff and the head of the CIA—had an appointed place. Rice sat across from Bush; Dick Cheney was at the president's right hand; and Powell was at his left. Donald Rumsfeld sat to Powell's left, with General Hugh Shelton, the chairman of the Joint Chiefs, beside him. Treasury Secretary Paul O'Neill and CIA Director George Tenet were seated beyond Cheney.

When the NSC members met without the president—as they usually did—they were called the national security "principals committee," and Cheney had pushed Bush to break precedent and appoint him chair of those sessions rather than the national security adviser. In most administrations the vice president himself was not even a regular attendee, but Cheney had already signaled that he expected to play a major role in the formulation of foreign and defense policy, assembling his own team of advisers that would rival the NSC staff in influence, if not in numbers. He lost his initial battle to control the principals' agenda, however, when Bush announced at the January 30 session that "Condi Rice will run these meetings" when the president was not there. "I'll be seeing all of you regularly, but I want you to debate things out here and then Condi will report to me."

None of the Cabinet deputies had yet been confirmed by the Senate, so the "second" chairs along the walls were occupied by those on the lower rungs of the departments. The exception was I. Lewis "Scooter" Libby, Cheney's former Pentagon aide, who needed no confirmation as the vice president's new chief of staff. Powell was accompanied by Edward Walker.

As the senior Cabinet official, Powell was asked to speak first and told them that the expanding spiral of violence between Israel and the Palestinians was the region's most urgent crisis. Bush expressed strong support for Israel but said he wanted to make his own appraisal of both Sharon and Arafat before committing himself to involvement. His reluctance was no surprise. Even if there had been a clear path to progress, Bush was loath to automatically adopt any initiative left over from a predecessor whose foreign policy he had harshly criticized during the campaign. Powell agreed that Clinton had overextended himself in his last-minute attempt to broker a Palestinian-Israeli deal and had left the situation in "a real mess." But a hands-off approach was untenable, he said. The United States had unique influence over both sides, and moderate Arab leaders and America's allies in Europe expected it to be used to help stop the violence and seek a solution. Cheney and Rumsfeld disagreed, advising the president that any involvement in the intractable dispute beyond aid and rhetorical support for Israel was a waste of his political capital.

The discussion moved on, and it quickly became apparent that powerful voices around the table were far more interested in Iraq than in the bogged-down Mideast peace process. "We have a regime change policy that isn't really regime change," Rice told them. The administration needed a strategy that would actually put pressure on Saddam. Powell agreed that the sanctions were full of holes. But they could be salvaged at least temporarily, he said, by shifting "from a list of what is allowed to a list of what is prohibited"—specifically, weapons and their components. Manipulated by Saddam, the sanctions were "not endearing us to the Iraqi people, whose support we're hoping to elicit—if I understand our position correctly—to help with overthrowing this regime." As he explained the new proposals Walker and his staff had developed, however, it was clear to Powell that "nobody liked the sanctions, except me and, grudgingly, the President."

"Why are we even bothering with sanctions?" Rumsfeld asked. Saddam was just using them as a smoke screen behind which he was reconstituting the weapons programs that had been dismantled by U.N. inspectors after the Gulf War. Although Rumsfeld and his deputy-nominee, Paul Wolfowitz, had for years been part of the conservative phalanx pushing for aggressive action to oust Saddam, he said he didn't give a damn about sanctions or even regime change, "but I do care about weapons of mass destruction." He went on to describe Iraq's increasingly bold defiance of the no-fly zones, including attacks against American and British jets targeted from command-and-control sites located inside Saddam's "home territory" between the northern and southern zones. Current rules of engagement limited U.S. ability to retaliate. The United States hadn't lost any pilots yet, General Shelton added, but it was only a matter of time before one would be shot down and killed or captured.

Powell thought the no-fly program was of limited value; it risked the lives of American pilots and had cost a fortune in manpower and equipment to maintain over the years—nearly $1.5 billion in the last year alone. However flawed and in need of revision the sanctions were, at least they accomplished something. Even if Saddam were pilfering a few billion dollars in illegal profits each year, the United Nations was controlling many, many billions more of his oil revenue. Without sanctions, Saddam would have an unrestricted supply of components to develop both weapons of mass destruction and the missiles to deliver them far beyond his own borders. The truth was that if they didn't have sanctions, they didn't have much of a policy at all.

When Tenet's turn came, he unrolled several table-size surveillance photographs showing command and antiaircraft formations on the edge of Baghdad and structures he identified as possible chemical weapons factories. They all got up out of their chairs to look at the clusters of buildings in the desert, but it was hard for the untrained eye to reach any firm conclusions about their purpose. On-the-ground American intelligence inside Iraq was poor to nonexistent, Tenet acknowledged, and there was no progress to report on the efforts to foment Saddam's overthrow.

The principals were instructed to come back with more detailed plans to address the problems that had been outlined. All three branches of the policy would remain for now, they agreed, with adjustments. Powell would work on upgrading the sanctions regime while Tenet put together a more robust intelligence program and new covert action plans. Rumsfeld would look at refinements for the no-fly patrols and reexamine overall military options for dealing with Iraq. As he left with Powell, Walker thought the meeting had been very businesslike, belying early reports of tension among the principals and rumors that Bush was less than capable of handling a sophisticated foreign policy discussion. The president had asked good questions and seemed genuinely interested in listening to the answers.

They gathered again on February 5 to report on their homework assignments. Powell detailed the status of planning for what were now called "smart sanctions"—a name he disliked but one that had managed to stick. A decision had already been made by the White House to fund exile opposition groups for new anti-Saddam activity inside Iraq. On the military front, Rumsfeld outlined and the president subsequently approved a new set of "response options" against attempted Iraqi attacks on American and British aircraft. Pilots were to be given leeway to target radar, antiaircraft and command-and-control centers beyond the no-fly zone lines. The military response would escalate if a pilot was shot down or if Saddam's forces launched a direct attack against the northern Iraqi Kurds or the southern Shiites whom the no-fly policy was designed to protect.

Although there was no direct discussion of an imminent threat from Iraq or an offensive U.S. military strategy, it was clear to several of those present that the new palette of policy options heralded a significant change from the Clinton era. The United States would no longer feel constrained about using its military on the ground in Iraq.

On February 16, Powell accompanied President Bush on the president's first foreign trip—a day with the newly elected Mexican president, Vicente Fox, at Fox's private ranch in the central Mexican state of Guanajuato. As the two delegations faced each other across a conference table and began to discuss immigration issues, White House Spokesman Ari Fleischer slipped into the room to motion Condoleezza Rice away from the table. "Why are we bombing Baghdad?" he whispered.

"What? We're not bombing Baghdad," she whispered back.

"Well, CNN says we're bombing Baghdad."

Rice excused herself to find a television and quickly sent someone back to retrieve Powell. Karen Hughes, Bush's top communications adviser, was called out next, and "pretty soon it's just the President sitting there with the Mexicans," one administration official present later recalled.

Using the unpublicized new "response options" Bush had recently approved, American and British aircraft had hit some twenty military communications targets far inside Iraq, including on the outskirts of the capital. The strikes "had set off the air raid system in Baghdad and all hell was breaking loose. It was much closer to Baghdad than any of us had realized," the official said. The Iraqis were already parading injured civilians in front of CNN cameras. Rice returned to the conference room and asked if they could take a short break.

The White House team viewed the attack as a potential disaster, not necessarily because of what had happened in Iraq but because it inevitably would overshadow the plan that had been carefully laid out for Bush's day. He had criticized Clinton for ignoring Latin America and had placed improved hemispheric relations high on his own agenda. "This is our great trip to Mexico," the official recalled. "We've decided to go to Mexico first and show our great solidarity with our neighbor." When Bush and Fox appeared at a joint news conference later that day, White House aides feared most of the questions would now be about Iraq.

Rice, Powell and Hughes quickly briefed Bush on the situation, stressing the importance of not expressing any surprise to reporters. They suggested that Bush emphasize that the strikes were a "routine" operation that he had known about in advance.

When the questions came, Bush responded according to the hastily composed script. "The commanders on the ground, rightly, make the decision as to how to enforce the no-fly zone," he said. "I want to assure those who don't understand U.S. policy that this is a routine mission. Some of the missions require the Commander-in-Chief to be informed. This was such a mission.... We will continue to enforce the no-fly zones.... It is a part of a strategy, and until that strategy is changed, if it is changed at all, we will continue to enforce the no-fly zone. But, anyway, the decision is made on the ground."

For good measure, Rice used the word "routine" or "routinely" four times in her own comments to reporters. Fleischer said it five times while briefing the media but stumbled in trying to explain why such attacks fell within the no-fly engagement rules. "The President made two points and was crystal clear on both of them," he responded obscurely. "The President's actions and his words are supported by all but the most partisan Americans." It was the first time—but would be far from the last—that the administration responded to doubts about its foreign policy by challenging the motives of the doubters.

Despite Bush's assurance that the bombing was all "part of a strategy," the national security team realized that it had only narrowly escaped looking both incoherent and uninformed. To the White House's relief, news reports described the attacks as an indication of well-planned administration resolve on Iraq and the incident was quickly overtaken by other events.

Among the many expressions of congratulation and advice Powell had received in the weeks following his nomination, one had special resonance. George F. Kennan, at age ninety-seven the oldest living veteran of the Foreign Service and an American foreign policy legend, introduced himself in a lengthy personal letter as the founder and first director of the department's policy planning staff. His initial assignment from then-secretary George Marshall had been to develop the Marshall Plan for post–World War II reconstruction of Western Europe, Kennan explained. "I say all of this only that you should know that I am not entirely without experience in the service of a military man serving as Secretary of State."

He would not presume to advise Powell on foreign policy, Kennan wrote. But he wanted to offer some observations on the position of secretary, an office that "has in recent decades, in my view, been seriously misused and distorted." The secretary's job was twofold: to serve as the president's "most intimate and authoritative adviser on all aspects of American foreign policy" and to lead the department and the Foreign Service. Neither job could be adequately performed when the secretary traveled extensively outside Washington, as had been the practice of most of Powell's recent predecessors.

"I see such travels to have a number of undesirable features," he wrote. "The absence of the Secretary of State for prolonged periods deprived the President, so long as it endured, of what should have been the latter's widest, most qualified, and most responsible source of advice on foreign policy problems." Kennan also disapproved of the recent proliferation of "special envoys" to undertake missions that he believed were far better left to professional diplomats. If ambassadors in America's embassies weren't capable of doing the nation's most important business abroad, they shouldn't be there in the first place, he wrote, adding that the title of "ambassador" had long been abused.

It would be some time before Powell fully appreciated Kennan's warning about trips away from the president's side, and his absences from Washington would have consequences that not even Kennan could have anticipated. But Kennan's remarks on leadership of the department and the value of the career Foreign Service already rang true.

As he had promised his State Department troops, Powell got rid of most of the existing "special envoys" and tried to resist the pressure exerted by all new presidents to make appointments on the basis of partisan or ideological purity or as payback for campaign support, rather than diplomatic expertise. He had gone personally to the White House to ask that Clinton-appointed ambassadors with children still in school abroad be allowed to stay in place until the end of the school year. Beyond a coterie of senior aides he brought with him from previous jobs— Armitage as deputy secretary; Grant Green as undersecretary for management; and William H. Taft IV as legal adviser, similar to the job Taft had held as the Defense Department legal counsel under Weinberger— nearly all of his appointments were career diplomats and civil servants. He selected Richard Haass, the NSC Near East director in the first Bush White House, as head of the policy planning office.

For the important post of U.N. ambassador, Powell persuaded John D. Negroponte, a former Foreign Service officer who had been his deputy national security adviser in the Reagan administration, to give up a lucrative job in the private sector. Tall and patrician, Negroponte had been born in London and educated in the Ivy League, and he admired Powell's old-school rectitude. The two men shared a high threshold for the use of force and a deep respect for the United Nations as a flawed but vital institution that served American interests.

But Powell was experienced enough in government to know that there were favors to repay after every election and that Bush had the right to impose. A few weeks after the Supreme Court confirmed Bush's victory, Cheney had called with a recommendation to "take a good look at John Bolton" for a senior job. Bolton, a Republican lawyer with experience at the Justice and State departments, had been part of Bush's legal team during the Florida ballot recount, Cheney explained. "You could help yourself a lot if Bolton was in the Department," he said without further elaboration.

Bolton had spent the Clinton years at the American Enterprise Institute, a Washington think tank that was the out-of-power home to many conservative Republicans. Powell did his own research on Bolton and found him on the far right of the party's foreign policy views, with a reputation as a bureaucratic brawler. In addition to Cheney, North Carolina Senator Jesse Helms, the conservative chairman of the Foreign Relations Committee, was one of Bolton's biggest fans. Bolton, Helms said when Powell called for a reference, was "a man with whom I would want to stand at Armageddon."

When they met for an interview, Bolton handed Powell two articles he had written for *The National Interest* that he said illustrated his views. One outlined Bolton's objections to the new International Criminal Court, the permanent tribunal for prosecuting war crimes that Bush had already made clear he would not support. Bolton, who had written extensively on the general ineffectiveness of international organizations, thought the court would impinge on American sovereignty. Powell did not disagree; like most military men, he rejected any ICC jurisdiction over American soldiers assigned abroad lest they be subjected to politically motivated prosecution. The second article was an admiring treatise on Edmund Burke, the eighteenth-century Anglo-Irish author and politician whom many considered to be the father of modern conservatism.

Powell set the articles aside and explained that he had already chosen Marc Grossman for the job Bolton wanted, undersecretary for political affairs. He offered, and Bolton declined, a position as department counselor, a nonspecific senior adviser slot used by previous secretaries for special assignments. They finally settled on another of the department's five undersecretary positions: arms control and international security. The focus of the job was nonproliferation, and its first major task would be following through on Bush's determination to get rid of the ABM Treaty blocking the proposed National Missile Defense program, or NMD, as it was now widely known.

Bolton became the most senior of Powell's White House–promoted aides, and as time went on many in the State Department came to consider him a spy in their midst who reported directly back to Cheney. Powell thought of Bolton as an interesting challenge, more a rambunctious and aggressive terrier than an infiltrator. "The book I had gotten on John was that John will push the edge constantly, and he will get you in trouble on a regular basis," Powell later recalled. If he was not kept on a tight leash, Bolton would "break china all over the world." But his energy and aggression, if properly monitored, could be useful. Powell had dealt with men like Bolton before; he was sure it was just a question of pointing him in the right direction. But he was already sensitive to suggestions that he was under Cheney's thumb, and when the first news reports suggested that Bolton had been forced on him, he told his spokesman, Richard Boucher, to make sure reporters at the State Department "understand that I don't have anybody working for me that I didn't want."

The potent résumés and reputations of Cheney, Powell and Rumsfeld— along with Bush's perceived lack of sophistication and Rice's comparative youth and inexperience—had sparked strong interest, both within and outside the government, in who would exercise the most influence over the administration's foreign and defense policies. Once the team was in place, every comment and action was seen through the prism of a perceived battle for power and influence over the president.

Powell's first trip to the Middle East, in late February 2001, "signaled that after eight years in the wilderness during the Clinton administration the State Department was back on the map," *The New York Times* reported approvingly. During his four-day swing to assess Arafat and the newly elected Israeli prime minister, Ariel Sharon, and to introduce "smart sanctions" to skeptical Arab governments, Powell had "left an impression of a Secretary of State imbued with authority and confidence," the *Times* concluded.

But others saw the trip as a worrisome early sign of an ascendant Powell "multilateralism." *The Weekly Standard* chronicled "the damage done" and accused Powell of kowtowing to Arafat. "Smart sanctions" were a continuation of Clintonian weakness and "a sign of retreat" from needed confrontation with Iraq. Powell's meetings with Arab despots such as Syrian President Bashar Assad, a *Washington Post* columnist said critically, were more public relations than policy and constituted an "unfortunate reversal" of the toughness demonstrated by the February 16 air attacks on Iraqi military installations.

The divergent media assessments reflected differing views within the administration itself. Some analysts defined the schism as between those who had been most closely associated with Ronald Reagan's "visionary" policies and those who adhered to the elder President Bush's multilateral pragmatism. But Powell had served in both administrations, Cheney in the "pragmatic" Bush camp and Rumsfeld in neither.

David Rothkopf, whose 2005 book *Running the World* examined the modern history of the National Security Council, attributed the "core tension" within the administration of George W. Bush to a clash between "traditionalists" and "transformationalists." Traditionalists such as Powell saw foreign policy "as a way to manage our relations within a diverse global community, moving in the direction of our ideas, but recognizing the limitations on us and the need to balance the optimal with the practically possible," Rothkopf wrote. Transformationalists "decry such views as moral relativism or as implying a willingness to subjugate our national interests to the wishes of the larger community of nations; in any event, their view is that we need to make the world more like us."

Other labels were applied to the often overlapping subsets of "transformationalists" on the Bush team: "neoconservatives," whose definition of national interest extended beyond geographic security and material concerns to the spread of democratic ideology, and "exceptionalists," who believed that America's power and "rightness" gave it both the authority and the responsibility to set the rules for the rest of the world.

Powell was all for the spread of democracy but thought the best way to achieve it was through example rather than coercion or exhortation. His views on the use of force were well known; far from shying away from the "multilateralist" and "traditionalist" labels, he embraced them. The dif-

ference between him and the "transformationalists," he thought, was one
of experience and training. As a soldier, he had been taught to consider
alternatives and maintain flexibility. Cheney, Rumsfeld and their minions
were politicians and think-tankers—ideologues, idealists and intellectu-
als who had spent the wilderness years of the Clinton presidency formulating strategies that had yet to be tested in the real world.

Attempting to remake the world was "just not his intellectual style,"
said a foreign policy veteran of several Republican administrations who
respected Powell but found him lacking in strategic vision. "This is a guy
who came into the job with instincts and a kind of practical, reasonable
approach to American foreign policy. A sense of 'We'll see what's there,
we'll deal with the problems.' Or, as he would say, 'the challenges.' "

As far as Powell was concerned, the outside criticism was all part of
the Washington game and was irrelevant to the way he did his job. He
took his cues from the president, and Bush had given no indication he
was unhappy with his secretary of state. As for the vice president, Powell
thought he had learned how to handle Cheney years before. Rumsfeld
was still something of a mystery but was unlikely to cross Powell's foreign
policy tracks too often. Overall, Powell thought his working relationships
with the rest of the team were good. Rice and her NSC, despite all the
high-powered alpha men around the principals' table, seemed to be settling in well and doing their job. Events over the next several months,
however, would make these early assessments seem naive.

Under a 1994 accord with Communist North Korea called the "Agreed
Framework," the Clinton administration had promised eventual U.S.
diplomatic recognition and material benefits in exchange for North
Korea's freezing and ultimately dismantling its nuclear weapons program.
Progress toward normalization of relations—and discussions over North
Korea's development of long-range missiles capable of delivering nuclear
warheads—had stalled during the final months of 2000. Clinton had sent
Albright to Pyongyang, the North Korean capital, in October. In a frantic
round of last-minute negotiations before leaving office, he had tried
unsuccessfully to schedule his own meeting with Kim Jong Il, the North
Korean dictator.

Clinton officials had visited Powell at his home one evening during the
presidential transition to brief him on the status of the North Korea initiative, and Clinton himself had filled in President-elect Bush during a
meeting at the White House. But six weeks after the inauguration, on the
eve of a March 7 Washington visit by Kim Dae Jung, the president of

democratic South Korea, the Bush principals had not yet held an exten-sive policy discussion on the subject.

At the top of the South Korean agenda was Kim Dae Jung's "sunshine policy" of using economic and social incentives to nudge the North toward national reconciliation. Clinton had been wholly supportive, and the South Koreans were anxious to gain similar backing from Bush, along with a promise to continue U.S. talks with Pyongyang. But the govern-ment in Seoul had been taken aback when Bush seemed rigid and awk-wardly ill-prepared during a telephone conversation between the two presidents in February. Charles "Jack" Pritchard, a Clinton holdover who handled Korean issues on the NSC staff, sat in on the call and was sum-moned back to work at the White House that night by Rice, who asked him to put together more background information about Kim and his "sunshine policy." Pritchard wondered why Bush had not wanted the information before, rather than after, the telephone call.

Just days before his Washington visit, Kim irritated the White House by hosting Russian President Vladimir Putin at a summit in Seoul. In what seemed a cavalier slap at one of Bush's highest priorities, they had signed a communiqué stressing the importance of preserving and strengthening the ABM Treaty as the "cornerstone" of global security. "That kind of got everybody's nerves jangling," Powell later recalled. Rice, in a message delivered through her South Korean counterpart in Seoul, made clear that the American president was not pleased.

On March 6, the day before Kim's arrival, a reporter asked Powell about Bush's overall plans for the two Koreas. He replied that the admin-istration supported South Korea's efforts toward rapprochement with the North and would continue to coordinate its own policy toward Pyongyang with Seoul. "We do plan to engage with North Korea to pick up where President Clinton and his administration left off," Powell said. "Some promising elements were left on the table."

The story didn't make the front page, but *The Washington Post*'s inside-the-paper headline the next morning—"Bush to Pick Up Clinton Talks on N. Korean Missiles"—immediately set off alarm bells at the White House. Rice was on the telephone to Powell before his regular 8:30 a.m. department meeting. "We've got a problem," she said. "Have you read your newspaper yet?"

Powell thought his comments had been relatively benign—simple placeholders for a policy that had not yet been hammered out. He was convinced that what had really triggered a White House reaction was his use of "the fatal word: 'Clinton.' " The Bush team's loathing of Clinton went far beyond policy differences, and Powell himself was already tainted in the eyes of some by his service in the Clinton administration. It was the "Satan's finger on Earth" theory of foreign policy, observed one senior State Department official. "Steer clear of anything that 'he'—Clinton—put his mark on. Every new administration is skeptical of its predecessor, but this was something different."

Some in the White House saw Powell's remarks less as an innocent mistake than as a witting attempt to subvert Bush's will, or at the very least as an arrogant disregard for what the president thought. "He knew," one senior Bush aide said firmly of Powell. "We had had a meeting with the president the day before Kim Dae Jung came. Everybody knew where the president stood, that he wanted to take a tough line."

Rice told Powell that the *Post* story needed to be corrected before Bush and Kim faced the media after their talks. Journalists waiting outside the Oval Office that morning were surprised to see the secretary of state slip out of the in-progress meeting and approach them with a statement. The conversation was going well, Powell reported. President Bush had "forcefully made the point that we are undertaking a full review of our relationship with North Korea, coming up with policies that build on the past, coming up with policies unique to the administration, the other things we want to see put on the table. And in due course, when our review is finished, we'll determine at what pace and when we will engage with the North Koreans." If there had been "some suggestion that imminent negotiations are about to begin," he said, "that is not the case."

After the meeting, Bush told reporters that he didn't trust North Korea to honor any nonproliferation agreement. Until there was an ironclad way to verify the North's compliance, he said, there would be no more U.S. discussions with Pyongyang. With the South Korean president standing awkwardly at his side, the rebuff of a U.S. ally was clear. For those who specialized in reading between the lines in Washington, however, the day's most startling development had been the swift and public nature of Powell's trip to the White House woodshed.

At the State Department, anxious officials saw their leader's comeuppance as a bad omen. To Lawrence Wilkerson, it was a power play with Dick Cheney's fingerprints all over it. It reminded him of when Defense Secretary Cheney had abruptly fired a top general who made intemperate remarks just days before the 1991 Persian Gulf War to make the point that Cheney, not Powell or the military, was in charge.

"He's not easily stunned, but he was stunned by that," William Smullen said of the Korea incident. "But the one thing about Powell is that he's a very resilient sort who can say, 'Okay, we had a bad day but we're going to do better. We're going to get this right.' "

Powell quickly moved to reassure his troops, shrugging off the put-down at a staff meeting that afternoon. "That was why people didn't panic," a senior Powell aide later recalled. "He said he had 'made a mistake and got crossed up with the president.' But I can also remember him sitting there and saying, 'Don't worry about this. This will come our way in the end because we're right about it, and we're going to have to talk to the [North] Koreans about their nuclear program.' " North Korea was an undeniable threat, Powell told them, but unless the administration planned to start a war with Pyongyang it would have to resume some sort of dialogue.

Weeks later, when reporters asked Powell if the administration had sent mixed messages on North Korea, he laughed and said, "Yeah, and I delivered both of them. Sometimes you get a little too far forward on your skis, that's all."

Powell's confident optimism quickly overtook any worry he might have had about the Korea incident. Bureaucracy was a series of tactical skirmishes in a long campaign, and a single day's setback counted for little. But just a week later he again found himself "crossed up" with the White House.

The issue this time was the Kyoto Protocol, an international agreement that committed highly industrialized countries to gradual cuts in emissions of the "greenhouse gases" that most scientists blamed for a worrisome rise in the earth's temperature. The American energy industry and many in Congress strongly opposed the accord—named for the Japanese city where it had been negotiated in 1997—as unfair, since large developing countries and potential competitors such as China, India and Brazil were exempt from its provisions. Clinton had not even submitted the protocol for Senate ratification, and Bush had no intention of doing so. Some in the new administration argued that global warming did not even exist, although Bush had agreed during the campaign that climate change was a concern. He had pledged support for domestic emissions reductions, including limits on the carbon dioxide that spewed from the smokestacks of American power plants.

U.S. allies in the European Union and Japan, where there was far more consensus on the seriousness of global warming, strongly supported Kyoto. In early March 2001, as Bush prepared for upcoming international meetings in which the issue was sure to be raised, Christine Todd Whitman, the former New Jersey governor and new head of the Environmental Protection Agency, recommended that the president "continue to recognize that global warming is a real and serious issue." Bush, Whitman wrote in a memo, should "indicate that you are exploring how to reduce U.S. greenhouse gas emissions internally and will continue no matter what else transpires. Mr. President, this is a credibility issue for the U.S. in the international community." She called White House Chief of Staff Andrew Card to schedule an early appointment with the president.

The State Department had only peripheral involvement in energy issues, and Powell assumed that the administration would agree to disagree with its allies on Kyoto as it formulated its own initiatives. The White House had appointed a task force—headed by Cheney—to develop a new energy policy. Powell thought that all they had to say to the Europeans and the Japanese for now was that they were "working on it." But on the morning of March 13, Rice called unexpectedly to say, "We're going to have to do something on Kyoto."

"Right now? Why?" Powell asked.

The president had received a letter from Nebraska Senator Chuck Hagel and three other Republicans who opposed Kyoto and wanted a "clarification" of his policy on domestic emissions reductions, Rice said. The vice president's office had drafted a response, and she was sending it over for Powell to read.

The draft, written for Bush's signature, emphasized the high priority the president placed on national energy production and said he had decided against mandating emissions reductions. It was a reversal of Bush's campaign pledge, but Powell was not interested in the domestic political implications. After reading the letter, he called Rice back to say, "The policy's okay [but] we've got to put something in this letter that says, 'And we're going to work with our friends and allies to see how we can move forward together on emissions.' And then we're going to have to go talk to our friends and allies about this before we do it."

At Rice's urgent request, he quickly sent the White House new language to reassure America's allies. "She called back and said, 'It didn't make it,' " Powell later recalled. "It didn't pass whoever was grading the papers that morning—a combination of the President, Cheney, Condi and who knows who else was in there—and I said, 'Okay, I'm on my way over. We've got other language . . . slow this thing down until I get there.' " Hagel's letter was a week old, and it was unclear to Powell why the White House suddenly felt compelled to rush a response. He left his office immediately for the short drive to Pennsylvania Avenue.

He found the president, Rice and several others in the Oval Office, where they had just finished a meeting and were waiting for Bush's next appointment. "When can we talk about Kyoto?" he asked.

"It's gone," Rice replied.

"What's gone?"

"The letter."

"Gone where?"

Rice told him that the vice president had just left to hand-deliver the letter to Capitol Hill. The meeting Bush had just completed before Powell's arrival that morning had been with Whitman, who had left the Oval Office in a daze after being told the president would not accept her recommendations. She had passed Cheney, dressed in his overcoat and putting the response to Hagel in his pocket, on her way out.

Powell was astounded. "They all got together...and said to hell with everybody else and they just signed it with no reference to our allies, no reference to 'Let's work with them and find a way forward on carbon emissions' or whatever," he later recalled. "Cheney was anxious to get it up there, so he just walked it up.

"And when the president looked at me and said, 'Well, we wanted to get it up to the Hill to Hagel right away,' I said, 'Well, you're going to see the consequences of it.' And we all kind of smiled. And the next day we started seeing the consequences of it and didn't get rid of it for another year. Because people said, 'What the hell is this all about?' "

News of the letter, followed by a statement from Rice to E.U. ambassadors that Kyoto was "dead," drove the first of what would be many wedges between the Bush administration and traditional U.S. allies in Europe. At the time, the White House was puzzled by the uproar. Bush had opposed Kyoto during the campaign, they told themselves, so what was the problem? Some administration officials eventually recognized that the matter at least could have been handled with more finesse. However bad the Americans considered the accord, Kyoto "was kind of like this crystalline superstructure [the Europeans] had set up, a symbol" for commitment to improving the environment, a senior Bush aide later acknowledged. "And we walked by and knocked it off the table. It was even worse than that...we knocked it off the table and said, 'Oh, did we hit something?' "

Powell took the sequence of events as a warning about the nature of the Bush administration's decision-making process. There was nothing like the formal options papers he had prepared for Reagan after consultations with the Cabinet; the less formal but decisive discussions among senior advisers in front of the Oval Office fireplace under Bush's father; or even the endlessly tedious NSC debates with Clinton. In this administration, presidential decisions seemed to come out of the ether.

More than a year later, when Powell mentioned to *The New York Times* that the Kyoto announcement "was not handled as well as it should have been," the wrath of the White House again descended on him. "I blurted out the truth," he later recalled. "They were all mad at me that day, too." By then, however, his skin had grown thicker. "What are they going to do?" he asked his aides. "Send me to Vietnam?"

The administration's first full-fledged foreign policy crisis arrived in April, and with it came an opportunity for Powell finally to show what diplomacy and tactical maneuvering could accomplish. A Chinese F-8 fighter jet and a U.S. Navy EP-3 reconnaissance aircraft had collided sixty-two miles off the Chinese coast, sending the smaller Chinese plane and its pilot crashing into the South China Sea. The American pilots issued a "Mayday" call and steered their wounded aircraft toward the nearest landing strip, on the Chinese island of Hainan. As the plane shuddered to a stop, the rest of the twenty-four-member crew was busily destroying documents and sensitive interception equipment.

Beijing immediately charged that the American plane, on what it called an illegal spy mission, had intentionally struck the fighter. U.S. officials said that the Chinese pilot had been harassing the slow-moving intelligence plane when his own aircraft strayed too close, hit the Americans and lost control. There was no denial that the EP-3 was spying—it made regular tours up and down the coast collecting electronic transmissions, often with Chinese jets buzzing around it like angry bees. But while China claimed that its territory extended two hundred miles into the sea, the rest of the world recognized only twelve miles and the plane had been flying in international airspace.

After two days, as Bush publicly demanded the return of the crew and plane and China insisted on U.S. acceptance of blame, an official apology and the end of all surveillance flights, the incident escalated into a confrontation reminiscent of the dark days of the Cold War. The administration was under pressure from congressional hawks, media pundits and China hard-liners within its own ranks to retaliate. Sanctions on Chinese exports, cancellation of Bush's scheduled visit to Beijing that fall and opposition to China's bid to host the 2008 Olympics were all under consideration.

At the State Department, "We were trying to figure out where the president's head was at," Armitage recalled. The Chinese ambassador was summoned to the seventh floor, where Armitage suggested he warn his government "to be cool, don't do anything stupid here, we'll figure it out." The United States was sorry for the loss of the pilot, he said, but China should realize that his actions could have left a whole plane full of American military personnel dead.

Despite Bush's initial harsh rhetoric, the White House was concerned that a long-term standoff—with American captives in the middle—would provoke uncomfortable memories. "We were balancing not saying anything that made us look weak and not defending American interests" against "Let's not have a hostage crisis," recalled one senior official. "We sent a message to the Chinese very early on: 'Don't parade our people. Don't do anything to humiliate our people, or you will really have trouble.' " With no progress made by the third day, Bush authorized Powell to begin negotiating a solution.

Staying up most of the night on the telephone with Chinese officials and the U.S. ambassador to Beijing, retired Navy Admiral Joseph Prueher, Powell began to explore what it would take to loosen Beijing's grip on the crew members. He applied the same tactics he had used with Haiti's generals in 1994: determine your own red lines, and within those parameters try to give the other side what it needs. An early missive to Vice Premier Qian Qichen expressed regret for the presumed loss of a Chinese life. "I want to take this opportunity to let you know that President Bush is very concerned about your missing pilot," Powell wrote. "His thoughts and prayers are with the pilot's family and loved ones, as are mine and all Americans." When the Chinese went too far in their demands—insisting on acknowledgment that the original flight path of the American plane had violated their airspace—Powell instructed Prueher to tell them he would not even take the idea to the president.

A week after the April 1 collision, agreement was reached on the text of an official letter addressed to the Chinese foreign minister and signed by Prueher. The United States expressed "sincere regret over your missing pilot and aircraft" and asked that the Chinese people and the pilot's family be told "that we are very sorry for their loss." Regret over entering Chinese airspace was limited to the landing on Chinese soil.

The letter confirmed that the two sides would meet to "discuss the incident," including "possible recommendations whereby such collisions could be avoided in the future, development of a plan for prompt return of the EP-3 aircraft, and other related issues." The English-language version of the letter deliberately avoided the word "apology," whereas the

Chinese version used a character suggesting "deep expression of apology or regret." It was a linguistic subterfuge that satisfied both sides, and the crew was released.

Most public accounts of the controversy and its settlement portrayed Bush as having shown both flexibility and firmness, moving confidently to protect American citizens while wisely averting a major conflict. There was some grumbling from the right—the lesson of a "humiliating" U.S. apology in response to Chinese extortion would not be lost on Saddam Hussein, wrote *Weekly Standard* editor William Kristol. But Powell and Armitage dismissed it as the usual carping by people who would never be pleased with them. "We could have done anything, we could have gone to war, [and] they'd have been mad, too," Armitage said.

The Office of the Secretary of Defense (OSD), which had largely stayed out of the negotiations, reasserted itself once the crew was released, pushing aside Prueher—who was denigrated as a Clinton appointee—to insist that the EP-3 belonged to the Pentagon and the latter would handle its recovery from the Chinese. Rice, who was pleased at the outcome of the crisis, ribbed Rumsfeld: "Well, Don, Colin said, 'Sorry.' Maybe you ought to find a way to say, 'Pretty please.'" Months later, after Beijing rejected the Pentagon's insistence that Americans be allowed to repair the plane and fly it home, the Chinese dismantled it and sent it to the United States in boxes.

For those keeping score at the State Department, the Pentagon's failure underscored the diplomatic victory. The gloom of March quickly lifted, and "we were feeling pretty lusty and bold," as Armitage put it. But as Washington began to wilt in the first humid waves of the summer of 2001, it became clear to Powell and his aides that it was the China experience—not Korea or Kyoto—that was an aberration in the way the Bush administration wanted to do business.

Europe reacted with amazement, closely followed by overt hostility, to its first glimpses of Bush's foreign policy. Headlines on the continent were scathing: "North Korea: Bush Irritates the Asians"; "Climate Agreement: The United States Abandons the Kyoto Protocol"; "World Court: No Support from United States"; "Iraq: Bombing Instead of Diplomacy." In Britain, Bush was dubbed the "Toxic Texan," and the French newspaper *Libération* put a cartoon of the American president on its front page, with black smoke pouring from his smokestack head. In Germany's *Süddeutsche Zeitung*, he was "Bully Bush," and even *The Economist*, which had endorsed Bush's presidential candidacy, lamented that Europe had been looking forward to "the smack of firm leadership... [but] so far it seems all smack and little leadership."

The perceived insults to traditional U.S. allies continued unabated: Rumsfeld said he intended a unilateral withdrawal of American troops from NATO peacekeeping operations in Bosnia; Bush announced with no allied consultation that the United States was ready to move "beyond" the ABM Treaty to deploy missile defenses; and the administration declared its opposition to internationally drafted enforcement mechanisms for a biological weapons treaty and to a ban on nuclear testing. To much of the world, Bush's foreign policy appeared far from "humble."

In the months following the China incident, Powell had a series of what he considered respectable successes: a trip through Africa, where he emphasized the administration's commitment to help conquer the AIDS virus that was tearing the continent apart, and a fence-mending tour of Asia. The results of a White House review of North Korea policy were finally released in early June, making new demands of Pyongyang but at least opening the door to renewed talks. Powell argued successfully against the precipitate withdrawal of U.S. troops from Bosnia and for extended discussions with Russia before a peremptory pullout from the ABM Treaty.

But even the most noncontroversial issues seemed to provoke intense debate and endless "policy reviews," and by early summer the cumulative weight of the constant skirmishes began to weigh on him.

A growing antipathy between Powell and the State Department, on one side, and Cheney, Rumsfeld and their senior staffs, on the other, extended far beyond specific policy disagreements. It was institutional, ideological and even personal. The ever-loyal Armitage thought simple jealousy had a lot to do with it. Powell's enormous stature with the American people and the media seemed to engender an impulse to cut him down to size, no matter what the issue. He and Cheney had both emerged from the Gulf War as national heroes. But whereas Powell had risen in popularity and been practically offered the White House on a silver platter, Cheney had largely disappeared from public view and his own bid for the 1996 Republican nomination barely got off the ground.

Rumsfeld also had made a run for the Republican presidential nomination, in 1988. But his campaign had collapsed in a bitter early loss to Bush's father, whom he regarded as a lightweight more interested in public relations than in substantive policy. He had the same opinion of Powell, and additionally thought of him as a specter of the plodding, old-fashioned, troop-heavy military of the past. Rumsfeld intended to transform the armed forces by making them smaller, swifter and equipped with sophisticated technology and missile defense.

Powell had hated civilian second-guessing when he was in charge of the armed forces, and he was now determined to stay out of military matters. But he privately thought that "transformation" was nonsense. He had been through countless "transformations" in his Army career; the military was constantly changing and adjusting to meet new priorities and threats and would continue to do so with or without Rumsfeld.

Beyond any personal animus among the principals and their departments, diplomacy was "traditionalist" by definition. Richard Perle, the former Weinberger aide who had become a neoconservative guru and now served as an outside adviser to Rumsfeld, considered the State Department "bereft of ideas" and out of place in an administration with a new vision for the exercise of American power. Unrelenting in its efforts to "reconcile the irreconcilable, to negotiate the unnegotiable, and to appease the unappeasable," Perle wrote in a book published midway through Bush's first term, the State Department—like the Democrats— continued to wallow in "business as usual, beginning by placating offending allies and returning to the exaggerated multilateral conceit of the Clinton administration."

Powell's first-day pep talk and his pledge to listen to the views of the diplomatic "officers in the field" may have pleased the Foreign Service, but they confirmed to administration conservatives that he fully subscribed to the propitiating worldview of his State Department underlings. One powerful conservative official found an anecdote in Powell's 1995 autobiography that he thought perfectly illustrated the secretary of state's unfortunate attitude. Powell had written of his admiration for General Henry Emerson, the "Gunfighter" under whose command he had served in South Korea, and of Emerson's insistence on putting the welfare of his troops above all else. At Emerson's retirement ceremony, Powell wrote, the Gunfighter had instructed him to order the assembled officers to turn and salute a parade ground full of enlisted men. To Powell, the symbolic gesture had "said everything that had to be said about armies and about who, in the end, most deserves to be saluted." At the State Department, the official concluded, Powell was clearly more interested in what the troops below him thought than in what the president wanted.

Washington was accustomed to conflict between the State and Defense departments, and Powell himself had had a front-row seat at the infamous Shultz-Weinberger disputes under Reagan. In the administration of

George H. W. Bush—now known as "Bush 41" to distinguish him from his son, the nation's forty-third president—Powell had skillfully maneuvered between Secretary of State James Baker and Defense Secretary Cheney. He had established his own relationship with the president and become the most powerful chairman in the history of the Joint Chiefs of Staff. But past experience was turning out to be a poor guide to the new reality, and Powell was slow to grasp the extent of his—and the State Department's—isolation within Bush's national security team.

He saw Bush frequently, though never alone. He found the president better spoken and more thoughtful in private than his public posturing as a rough-hewn, plain-spoken Texan would indicate, although Bush had an irritating tendency to interrupt everyone from his Cabinet officers to visiting heads of state. But while Bush publicly praised Powell's abilities and stature, their relationship remained stiff and formal.

Powell's interactions with Rumsfeld, with whom he spoke nearly every morning in an early conference call with Rice, were largely cordial. But gruffness was clearly the defense secretary's managerial stock-in-trade, and Powell heard stories from former military colleagues about Rumsfeld's peremptory treatment of his own civilian and military staff. In principals' meetings, Rumsfeld tended to speak in rhetorical circles and avoid committing himself to a position. But he bombarded the White House with a constant flow of memos, brief and with direct language that seemed to appeal to the president's no-frills style.

Cheney's taciturn personality seemed to Powell not to have changed at all since the days of Bush 41. The vice president was now simply in a more powerful position to impose his conservative views than he had been as defense secretary.

The principals' sessions stuck to precise agendas but usually avoided real debate or conclusions. One State Department official who attended a number of early meetings found Rice "incredibly quick and focused" in the chair and finely attuned to the powerful egos of the men over whose deliberations she presided. "She can read the vice president's twitches," the official remarked. When a confrontation threatened, "she would defuse it... or kind of intuit where something was heading and shape it. She was a master at it—always running the meeting but making it clear she was not butting heads with any of the real powers—Cheney, Rumsfeld and Powell."

In the Shultz-Weinberger years, conflicts at the top had often been smoothed over by good working relationships between the department staffs, where the nuts and bolts of policy coordination took place. But as the Bush administration reached the midpoint of its first year, divisions below the principals' level seemed, if anything, even deeper than those at the top. Meetings of the national security "Deputies Committee," where policy options were supposed to be ironed out for consideration by the principals, were often inconclusive. With Rice's deputy, Stephen Hadley, in the chair, Paul Wolfowitz or Policy Undersecretary Douglas Feith attended from the Pentagon. "Scooter" Libby or his deputy, John Hannah, sat in the vice president's chair. Libby, Hadley and Wolfowitz had all worked together under Cheney at the Defense Department and were of like mind on most issues.

Armitage or Grossman usually attended from State, and they found the sessions to be exercises in frustration. It seemed to them that no matter what the subject was, the positions taken around the table were always the same: the diplomats would talk about partnerships and alliances and the others would call for "bold" action. The meetings began without direction and ended without agreement. The State Department representatives always had the feeling that "the real business was being done somewhere else," one official later recalled. "Someplace where we weren't invited." As the chasms deepened, Armitage began to think the deputies' meetings were "just another way to get in the gerbil cage" and spin around on a wheel that went nowhere.

When his aides vented their frustration to Powell, he told them to keep their powder dry. He was playing for the long term, he would say; his way was not to seek confrontation but to prevail by working quietly and persistently over time. Powell thought Bush was being pulled in conflicting directions by different people on his team and differing instincts within himself—his Yale-Harvard education versus his Texas background. The president was throwing red meat to the conservatives on issues such as North Korea and the Middle East, but Powell was confident that circumstances and experience would eventually provide the perspective Bush needed.

It wasn't until late in the summer of 2001 that Powell's equanimity began to falter. A spate of media stories portrayed the secretary of state as "facing a steeper learning curve than he anticipated" and "on a short leash...nothing more than a silent symbol or a messenger boy." With Powell at the diplomatic helm, one critic wrote, "it is hard to think of another administration that has done so little to explain what it wants to do in foreign policy." Bush's political adviser Karl Rove was said to feel privately that Powell was not living up to his advance billing and had not managed to forge a comfortable relationship with the president.

The assumption on the State Department's seventh floor was that the anonymous shots had been fired from inside the administration. Powell "wasn't thinking about quitting, he was thinking about 'How am I going to manage this? How am I going to handle it [and] make sure my stuff gets out first?' " Richard Boucher recalled.

His protective senior staff decided the secretary was being outspun. They had their own spies in the Pentagon and the White House and regularly received clandestine copies of e-mails circulating in the enemy camps. The missives pointed out where Powell had deviated from conservative orthodoxy and provided talking points for the media about his waning influence. Powell's aides launched a counteroffensive, arranging on-the-record interviews with columnists and reporters they thought might be more sympathetic to his views. Department media briefings began to emphasize that the secretary was meeting regularly with the president. When *Time* magazine planned a cover story on him, Powell and senior department officials opened their offices for interviews.

But when the *Time* article appeared the first weekend in September, its headline, "Odd Man Out," was the first clue that their strategy had backfired. Considering that he was the brightest star in the Bush administration's firmament, the magazine asked, why was the light he shined on policy so dim? "I've been struck by how not struck I am by him," said one of a number of unnamed officials quoted in the piece. Powell was described as "marginalized" and "chum in the water" for conservative sharks, and was said to be leaving "shallow footprints." His achievements—continued U.S. troop participation in the Balkans, bringing the aircrew back from China, the administration's eventual acquiescence to talks with North Korea—had sprung not from Powell's own initiatives but from "cleaning up messes" left by rambunctious conservatives. Powell had yet to put a "distinctive mark" on U.S. foreign policy.

Smullen and Boucher, who had both pushed Powell to do the *Time* interview, took the brunt of his wrath over what all of them saw as a calculated attack by official sources the magazine had sought outside the State Department. Smullen knew that in addition to whatever immediate pain the article caused Powell, a label like "odd man out" had a way of sticking. It was certainly not helpful to the international relationships the secretary was trying to cultivate. Reflecting on the article several years later, Smullen saw it less as a realistic depiction of Powell's first eight months in office than as a fairly accurate prognostication of the future that none of them at the time, least of all Powell, seriously anticipated.

Powell found some consolation in the fact that *Time* had eviscerated

Rumsfeld a few weeks earlier for alienating both Congress and the uniformed services with his abrupt style. The article noted that the defense secretary had failed to win requested increases to the defense budget. The administration was widely perceived as flailing on both defense and foreign policy, and Powell knew that the betting in some smart Washington circles was that Rumsfeld would be the first Bush Cabinet member to go. But Rumsfeld hadn't made the *Time* cover, and the gist of the story about the defense secretary was that he was ineffective outside the administration, not isolated within it.

Powell felt he had taken a serious hit and he was sure that once again the shots had been fired from behind the administration's own lines. Lawrence Wilkerson, who had been at Powell's side since before his chairmanship, saw the effects on him. "He had had so many years of success—and I include in that going all over America making speeches where audiences of fifty thousand and upwards would fawn over his every word—that he had come to believe not that he was invulnerable, but that with his persuasiveness, charisma and celebrity, he could just about persuade anybody to do anything. And I think it came as a shock to him as he began to realize that it wasn't going to work out that way."

"The fact of the matter is that was a really bad time," Powell later acknowledged. He marked it as the moment when he first realized that the cards he had brought to the table—experience, persuasiveness and ability—were not necessarily the winning hand he was accustomed to. There were "strong ideological differences" over a range of issues, and it appeared that ideology would trump most other imperatives inside the Bush administration. Powell still had cards to play, but the deck was undeniably stacked against him.

It was not the kind of realization that a commander shared with his troops. At their first morning staff meeting following the *Time* cover story, senior State Department officials waited nervously to see what the secretary would say. Powell made no reference to the article during the session but turned back as he started to leave, as if with an afterthought.

"You know, I've been around this town for a very long time and I know that sometimes you're up and sometimes you're down," he told them. "Sometimes they do it to you and sometimes you do it to them. But you always get a chance to do it to them. So I'm fine. The president knows the work that you do and that I do. He appreciates the work that we all do, and we're going to keep on doing it."

16

We're Americans. We don't walk around terrified.

—Colin L. Powell

Powell was a reluctant traveler and not much of a partygoer, but on Monday, September 10, 2001, he felt relaxed at an evening fiesta in a brightly lit Spanish colonial courtyard in the Peruvian capital of Lima. It was the beginning of a two-day trip—a meeting in Lima of the thirty-four foreign ministers of the Organization of American States, followed by a stop in Colombia—and he was relieved to be away from Washington's fixation with his standing inside the administration. There had been continued fallout at home from the *Time* story, but just before he had left things had finally started looking up for diplomacy. The Israelis and Palestinians had agreed to high-level talks, and the White House principals, at a session the previous Friday, had discussed a possible Bush-Arafat meeting at the annual U.N. General Assembly session later in September.

Early Tuesday morning, Powell was due to hold a bilateral breakfast meeting with the OAS host, the newly elected Peruvian president, Alejandro Toledo. U.S.-educated, with a doctorate in economics from Stanford, the half-Indian Toledo was Peru's first-ever chief executive from among his country's long-oppressed indigenous majority. He had campaigned on promises of jobs and economic growth and planned to ask for Powell's help in delivering. At 7:45 a.m. at the government palace on Lima's ornate central square, they sat down with their respective aides at a round table set with fruit and coffee in a room adjacent to Toledo's office.

Speaking in fluent English, Toledo was reaching the end of a long appeal for U.S. tariff relief on Peruvian cotton exports when Powell's executive assistant, Craig Kelly, entered the room and handed the secretary a note. An airplane had crashed into one of the two 110-story World Trade Center towers in New York City. It was 8:10 a.m. in Peru, one hour earlier than in Washington, and the incident had happened just twenty-five minutes before. "Oh, my God," Powell said as he looked up at Toledo, who was sitting directly across from him with a sun-filled window at his back. There had apparently been a terrible accident, he explained, relaying the contents of the note. They discussed the misfortune for a moment and resumed the meeting.

The note said nothing about the size of the aircraft or the damage done; the assumption around the table was that a private plane had gone tragically astray. Powell thought it was curious that Kelly had interrupted him; the meeting was almost over, and every day he was handed dozens of similar "watch notes" about something happening somewhere in the world, usually things he couldn't immediately do anything about.

Within minutes, Kelly returned with a second note. Another plane had hit the other World Trade Center tower; both planes had been large commercial jets, and both towers were on fire. It was immediately clear to everyone in the room that a terrorist attack had taken place. Roberto Dañino, Toledo's prime minister, didn't hesitate to ask what was on all of their minds: "Who's behind it?"

"Osama bin Laden," Powell said immediately, before cautioning that they should wait for confirmation. The Saudi-born bin Laden and his international terrorist network, al-Qaeda, had been held responsible for numerous attacks over the past decade, including truck bombings of the American embassies in Kenya and Tanzania in 1998 that had left hundreds of people dead. But the initial assumptions that "one of theirs" had been responsible for the last major terrorist attack on U.S. soil—the 1995 bombing of a federal office building in Oklahoma City—had turned out to be wrong, Powell recalled; that had been "one of ours."

To the astonishment of Toledo and Dañino, Powell then returned to the subject of Peru's economy. They had reached only number nine of the twelve items on the Peruvian agenda, and he insisted they continue until the scheduled end of the meeting at 8:30. Dañino thought Powell's emotional control was remarkable. "Obviously, inside he must have been devastated. But he just went back to talking." When the Americans finally left the room, the Peruvians rushed to Toledo's office, turned on the television and sat transfixed before the scenes of chaos and confusion in New York. They were still sitting there half an hour later when the first tower fell to the ground.

Kelly and Richard Boucher rushed to keep up as Powell hurried along the palace corridor and down a stairway. Without stopping, he spoke over his shoulder to Kelly. "Get the plane ready. We've got to go home." Did he still want to go to the OAS, where the meeting was scheduled to begin at 9:30? Kelly asked. It would take ninety minutes to fuel and prepare the secretary of state's specially outfitted Boeing 757 for takeoff. Agreeing he would first go to the meeting, Powell climbed into a waiting limousine as the rest of his entourage scrambled into a line of white vans. Powell called Armitage from the road, just in time to learn that a third plane had crashed into the Pentagon, but he spoke to no one else in the administration. Bush had been visiting an elementary school in Florida when the news of the attack reached him, and the Secret Service had whisked him away on Air Force One. He was en route to a secure Air Force base in Louisiana. Cheney was in the bunker beneath the White House. Powell had no instructions.

The OAS ministers had gathered on the other side of the city at Lima's modern Hotel Oro Verde for a morning of speeches. They were scheduled to vote that afternoon on something called the Democratic Charter, a statement of joint principles for the hemisphere that had taken years to negotiate. When Powell arrived, it was clear that the opening of the session had been delayed as word of the attacks spread.

The half dozen members of the official U.S. delegation went to an upstairs holding room in the hotel, where the television was tuned to broadcasts from New York. The first tower had already fallen, and they stared in shock at the video replay. Before they could begin to absorb it, live pictures showed the second tower collapsing. No one said a word.

Informed that the ministers had suspended their schedule to vote on a resolution of solidarity with the United States, Powell entered the chamber and took his seat. The Latin Americans, eager to express their outrage and extend their condolences, began delivering long-winded speeches. Time was ticking away, but Powell had had extensive practice in staying calm during moments of crisis. There was no point in shouting or reaching for the telephone; the plane was not yet ready, and there was nothing else he could do in the meantime. He tried to concentrate on what he was going to say.

Finally, the assembly turned to him. He had no notes, but the words flowed without effort. He thanked his Peruvian hosts and expressed his deep appreciation to the ministers. "A terrible, terrible tragedy has befallen my nation," he began. "But it has befallen all of the nations of this region, all of the nations of the world, and befallen all those who believe in democracy.

"Once again we see terrorism, we see terrorists, people who don't believe in democracy.... They can destroy buildings, they can kill people, and we will be saddened by this tragedy; but they will never be allowed to kill the spirit of democracy. They cannot destroy our society. They cannot destroy our belief in the democratic way. You can be sure that America will deal with this tragedy in a way that brings those responsible to justice. You can be sure that as terrible a day as this is for us, we will get through it because we are a strong nation, a nation that believes in itself. You can be sure that the American spirit will prevail over this tragedy."

It was important, Powell told them, that he stay there long enough to cast the U.S. vote in favor of the Democratic Charter. "Terrorism...is everyone's problem and there are countries represented here who have been fighting terrorism for years and have seen horrible things happen. It is something we must all unite behind. And we unite behind it as democratic nations committed to individual liberties, committed to the rights of people to live in peace and freedom in a way in which they and not terrorists select their leaders or define how they will be governed.... I ask, Mr. Chairman, if it would be at all possible for the [charter] resolution to be moved forward so that I can be a part of the consensus."

As their convoy raced to the airport after the unanimous vote, Boucher was struck by the instinctive rightness of what Powell had said and done. "He knew from the start that what we needed were friends. We didn't know who did it, we didn't know why. But we needed democratic friends—that was the only way, whatever this was, that we were going to beat it."

In suburban Virginia, Alma was about to leave home for a hair appointment. The television was on in the kitchen as she stood talking on the telephone, and she looked up just as the second plane hit. They had round-the-clock security when Colin was there, but with him out of the country there was no one to tell her to stay put. She drove the short distance to the salon but left minutes later after someone came tearing through the door to say that a plane had crashed into the Pentagon. Back home, Michael called and then quickly came to her while his wife, Jane, went to pick up their two boys from school.

In upper Manhattan, Annemarie also had the television on as she sat in her apartment over a bowl of cereal. Her sister, Linda, had briefly stopped by on her way to a morning tennis match, and they had seen the images of the first plane's impact. After the second crash, Annemarie decided to take the subway to her job at a midtown television studio. Far from the mushrooming chaos at the southern end of the island, the New Yorkers sat stoically on their morning commute. But as word spread of what some of them had just seen or heard on the news, a low-grade panic set in, and they poured off the train at the next stop. Annemarie's cell phone was ringing as she climbed the station stairs toward what was still a brilliant, blue-sky morning. Linda told her that a third plane had just crashed into the Pentagon and she couldn't get through to their mother or brother.

Annemarie began walking back uptown, eventually reaching Linda's apartment. It was there that the State Department's Diplomatic Security agents found them, packed them into separate cars and sped away. They were taken to the Waldorf-Astoria Hotel, where the State Department maintained an apartment for its U.N. ambassador, and instructed not to leave. For the rest of the day and into a sleepless night, they sought comfort from Alma over the telephone and stared at the television images of the horrific events outside.

The city of Washington was in a panic. Traffic gridlocked as office buildings hurriedly emptied and frantic parents rushed to collect their children from school and make their way home. At the White House, things were only slightly more orderly. Richard Clarke sat in the Secure Video Conferencing Center across from the Situation Room facing a bank of monitors on the wall, each filled with the face of a senior government official waiting to give information or receive instructions. As head of the Counterterrorism Security Group, Clarke was the NSC's top terrorism official, and Condoleezza Rice had just turned coordination of the government's immediate response to the attacks over to him.

Clarke instructed the Federal Aviation Administration to clear the skies of all commercial aircraft—a fourth airliner, piloted like the others by hijackers who had commandeered the controls, had just crashed into a field in western Pennsylvania. Countless passenger jets were still in the air, and no one knew if any others were under the control of terrorists. Clarke ordered the dispatch of combat fighters over major cities, and Cheney, after being whisked by the Secret Service to the Presidential Emergency Operations Center bunker under the East Wing and consulting Bush by telephone, authorized the shoot-down of any threatening aircraft. With the security situation in the capital still uncertain, Air Force One stopped only briefly in Louisiana before taking the president to the underground Strategic Command Center at Offutt Air Force Base in Nebraska.

Clarke was being bombarded with sketchy information. CNN reported that a car bomb had exploded at the State Department, and he shouted at

Armitage's big, bald head on one of the monitors. "Rich, has your building just been bombed?"

"Does it fucking look like I've been bombed, Dick?" Armitage got out of his chair and disappeared from the screen, saying that he would check for himself. There had been no bomb.

Aboard the secretary of state's plane, teeth-grinding anxiety was barely concealed under a surreal surface calm. Communication with Washington during the seven-hour flight from Lima was all but impossible; the commercial satellites used by the on-board telephones were jammed with traffic. Powell had a couple of brief, unsatisfactory conversations with Armitage from the cockpit radio and one with Rice. Cynthia Church, a press aide on board whose Navy officer husband worked in the destroyed portion of the Pentagon, was desperate for information; the secretary tried to comfort her and used part of his brief time with Armitage to make sure the man was safe.

At the back of the aircraft, Powell briefed the dozen or so reporters who had accompanied him on the trip. His information was spotty; he told them that the State Department had not been bombed but reported erroneously that a fifth plane had also crashed near Camp David. Bush had spoken to the nation from a secure facility, he said; Cheney was in Washington, and emergency national security systems were operating. He had no word of casualty numbers in New York or at the Pentagon, he said, and "I don't know the answers to any of the questions you might pose to me with respect to responsibility or what triggered it. I just don't know."

Powell spent most of the flight alone in his cabin at the front of the plane, writing questions to himself and some initial answers on a legal pad. What did he have to do? What was the State Department's role? Who did he have to call? Who did he have to reach out to? There were U.S. embassies and personnel around the world to protect and Main State, as the department's Washington headquarters was known, to mobilize and lead.

If bin Laden was behind the attacks, that meant going after him in Afghanistan, where he was being sheltered by the Taliban, the ultraconservative Islamic movement that had fought its way into control over most of that country after the Soviet withdrawal in 1989. Clinton had bombed al-Qaeda's terrorist training camps in Afghanistan after the 1998 embassy attacks in Africa but had failed to eliminate bin Laden. This time, it might take a full-fledged ground war, and although Powell no longer had a formal defense role, he couldn't help but consider what it would mean for the military. He had experience putting an invasion force together—if that was what Bush decided to do—and knew how long it took and what was involved beyond assembling troops. However the president chose to respond, they would have to seek cooperation from neighboring countries and basing rights for troops and aircraft. Just as in the Persian Gulf War, they would need a coalition of allies to provide moral, monetary and perhaps military assistance.

When they were halfway to Washington, Boucher walked into the cabin. He had been making his own list of things they had to do, he told Powell—official statements and press conferences and speeches. Powell stared up at his spokesman. "You've got to understand," he said. "This changes everything. Absolutely everything."

The sun was low in the west when they flew up the Potomac and swung around in a U-turn over Washington to descend toward Andrews Air Force Base, southeast of the city. Officials and reporters alike pressed against the windows on one side of the aircraft for a clear view of the national monuments, the White House and the smoke still rising into the sky above the Pentagon.

Powell's first official briefing on terrorism had taken place on December 20, 2000, even before he was sworn in as secretary of state. He had asked Clarke and his team—all still working under President Clinton at the time—to give him a full rundown on bin Laden. Intelligence had indicated that al-Qaeda was planning direct attacks against the United States and likely had sleeper cells already in place inside the country. After the inauguration, Cheney and Rice had received the same briefing.

The Republicans had harshly criticized Clinton for failing to move effectively against al-Qaeda, and Clarke proposed immediate action. Among other things, he suggested shipping arms to the loose association of anti-Taliban Afghan tribal armies known as the Northern Alliance and arming the unmanned Predator aircraft that flew surveillance missions over al-Qaeda training camps. But during the administration's first few months, other foreign policy matters—the ABM Treaty and the Russians, China and the Middle East—had seemed more pressing. Although Rice had agreed to hold Clarke over from the previous administration, the plan he had proposed still carried the Clinton aura and was deemed in need of a full review. The matter had been deferred to the deputies committee.

Following several delays as the deputies were confirmed by the Senate, the terrorism plan had finally appeared on their agenda on April 30. In four meetings during the spring and summer of 2001, Clarke had pushed for early action on al-Qaeda and Afghanistan, but the deputies were deeply divided. Armitage, representing the State Department, supported the expansion of CIA support to the Northern Alliance, although he noted that several of the anti-Taliban warlords were considered unreliable thugs, drug traffickers and human rights abusers.

Wolfowitz, in the Pentagon's chair, disputed Clarke's assessment of the al-Qaeda threat, suggesting that the more immediate terrorist danger to the United States came from Iraq. He pushed hard, but without success, for an initiative he had been advocating for years: the establishment of a U.S.-protected, opposition-run "liberated" enclave around the southern Iraqi city of Basra, where anti-Saddam members of the Iraqi military could surrender and switch sides. Powell and Armitage would chuckle every time Wolfowitz made the case; it reminded them of a similar U.S. gambit during the Vietnam War called *Chieu Hoi*, or "Open Arms." Powell thought the idea that Iraqis would say to themselves, " 'Ah, the Americans have taken fourteen acres of southern Basra. Let's go turn ourselves in!' " was ludicrous. Even the White House was unimpressed. "The idea was never taken seriously at higher levels," recalled a senior Bush aide.

As the deputies' discussions continued, Clarke grew increasingly testy with Wolfowitz's fixation on Baghdad. There was no evidence of a direct threat against the United States emanating from Iraq, he argued, and no known Iraqi association with al-Qaeda. Deputy CIA Director John McLaughlin agreed and noted that the terrorist groups headquartered in Iraq, such as the one led by the Palestinian Abu Nidal, had been largely out of commission for nearly a decade. Rice's deputy, Stephen Hadley, whose youthful, buttoned-down appearance reflected his distaste for uncontrolled debate, proposed a compromise: they would focus first on formulating a general policy toward Afghanistan and the related issue of Pakistan; later, they would turn their attention to examining Iraqi-sponsored terrorism.

There were some actions Powell could take without waiting for the results of a full policy review. Helping the Northern Alliance and other groups in Uzbekistan and other Afghan border states and taking military action against al-Qaeda camps, should the president authorize it, would require agreements with other countries in the region. He sent emissaries to Uzbekistan, Kazakhstan and other former Soviet satellite nations north of Afghanistan to request stepped-up support for the anti-Taliban opposition. He also reactivated a moribund U.S.-Russia working group on Afghanistan and turned its management over to Armitage.

Pakistan, which borders land-locked Afghanistan on the south and east, was one of only three nations in the world to maintain diplomatic ties with the Taliban regime (the others were Saudi Arabia and the United Arab Emirates). Washington's relations with the government in Islamabad, the Pakistani capital, were strained; once among the leading recipients of American aid, Pakistan had been under U.S. sanctions, along with India, since the neighboring rivals had both tested nuclear weapons in 1998. Additional constraints had been imposed on Pakistan following the 1999 military coup that had brought to power its current ruler, General Pervez Musharraf. Using vague promises of rapprochement with Washington and assistance in resolving Pakistan's long-standing difficulties with India, Powell had begun pressing Islamabad to convince the Taliban to eject al-Qaeda from Afghanistan. A letter sent to Musharraf over Bush's signature early in 2001 had made the same demand.

But despite these efforts, concerns about bin Laden and al-Qaeda were as far down on Powell's immediate priority list as they were for the rest of the administration's national security team.

The summer of 2001 had brought an escalating flow of CIA warnings to the White House that al-Qaeda was planning "something spectacular." But the counterterrorism initiative, wending its way slowly from the deputies to the principals, had received little attention. Bush was focused on his campaign pledges of tax cuts and education reform. The president spent most of August vacationing at his Texas ranch, and it wasn't until September 4—one week before the attacks in New York and Washington—that a principals meeting was scheduled on the issue. With little discussion, they agreed to what the deputies had recommended. The president would issue a directive along the lines of Clarke's original proposal, ordering increased pressure on the Taliban to eject al-Qaeda and allocating more money for the CIA to arm the Northern Alliance. Rice told Bush that it would take at least three years to deliver results. On Tuesday, September 11, the document was still awaiting the president's signature.

Powell's plane landed at Andrews at dusk, just after the president had arrived aboard Air Force One. Bush's performance throughout the chaotic day, in brief sound bites from various landing spots, had been disappointing; he had appeared disoriented and uncertain. As a Marine helicopter whisked him from Andrews back to the White House, his speechwriters were busy working on a more formal statement, scheduled for delivery from the Oval Office at 8:30 p.m., to reassure the traumatized nation.

Young Luther Powell with his cousin, Nessa Llewellyn, after both had arrived in the United States in the early 1920s.

Luther Theophilus Powell, always known as a natty dresser, in his twenties.

Colin Luther Powell, age seven.

The boys from the Kelly Street neighborhood in the early 1950s. Colin Powell is second from right.

Young Colin and his prized bicycle in the Bronx.

A high school camping trip to New Jersey was as far as Colin had traveled from the Bronx.

The Powell family: Luther, Marilyn, Arie and Colin, at Marilyn's college graduation in Buffalo in the mid-1950s.

In a group ROTC portrait of the Pershing Rifles at City College of New York in 1957, twenty-year-old Colin Powell is second from the right in the front row. On his right is his friend and role model, Ronnie Brooks.

Colin and Alma Powell on their wedding day, August 25, 1962.

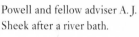

Powell and fellow adviser A. J. Sheek after a river bath.

Army of Vietnam Battalion Commander Captain Vo Cong Hieu and his American adviser, Captain Colin Powell with Vietnamese children in the A Shau Valley, Vietnam, 1963.

A family gathering in 1970, during Powell's student days at George Washington University. Second row, left to right, Powell's brother-in-law Norman Berns and Marilyn Berns, Luther and Arie Powell, Alma and Colin. Front row, left to right, Colin and Alma's children Linda, Michael and baby Annemarie with Marilyn's daughters Leslie and Lisa.

Powell, bottom right, received the Soldier's Medal, the Army's highest award for non-combat heroism, after pulling survivors from a November 1968 helicopter crash in the South Vietnamese jungle despite his own broken ankle.

Major Powell on his second Vietnam tour, Duc Pho, 1968.

Lieutenant Colonel Powell at Camp Casey, South Korea, 1973.

Colonel Powell with troops on a training exercise at Fort Campbell, Kentucky, 1976.

Battalion commander Colonel Powell greets visiting Defense Secretary Donald Rumsfeld during a 1976 visit to Fort Campbell.

In the White House Rose Garden on November 5, 1987, President Reagan announced Powell's appointment as national security adviser, replacing Frank Carlucci, right. Carlucci replaced Caspar Weinberger left, as Secretary of Defense.

The Powell family in the late 1980s, outside the Oval Office. Left to right, Annemarie, Michael, Linda, Coli and Alma.

National Security Adviser Powell briefs President Reagan and White House Chief of Staff Howard Baker. Powell's deputy, John Negroponte, is in the background.

Much of the White House staff traveled with Reagan on his frequent vacations at his California ranch.

President Bush appoints General Powell chairman of the Joint Chiefs of Staff, August 10, 1989. Left to right, Bush, Defense Secretary Dick Cheney, Powell, retiring chairman Admiral William Crowe.

Powell briefs President Bush and senior officials on Operation Desert Storm war plans, 1990. Left to right, CIA Director Robert Gates, Powell, National Security Adviser Brent Scowcroft, White House Chief of Staff John Sununu, Bush, Vice President Quayle, White House Spokesman Marlin Fitzwater.

President Bush speaks by telephone with British Prime Minister John Major, while Powell consults with General Norman Schwarzkopf for a status report on the war on February 27, 1991. Left to right, Powell, Sununu, Gates, Bush and Scowcroft.

Cheney and Powell greet airmen at a U.S. base in Saudi Arabia, February 10, 1991, four weeks after the launch of the Operation Desert Storm air campaign.

Waving to well-wishers gathered along Michigan Avenue in Chicago in May, 1991. Powell was the star attraction in parades across the country to welcome home Operation Desert Storm troops.

Much to the dismay of Richard Armitage and his other Republican friends, Powell decided in this first meeting with President-elect Clinton that he liked the new Democratic chief executive.

Powell calls on reporters while Alma stands at his side on November 8, 1995, as he announces he will not run for president.

Erecting a big tent for the Republicans at their presidential nominating convention.

Picnicking at the chairman's residence at Fort Myer; Powell and his first grandchild, Michael's son Jeffrey.

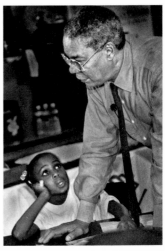

The Bushes, the Clintons, and most of both of their Cabinets showed up for Powell's retirement ceremony on September 30, 1993. Vice President Gore is over Powell's left shoulder.

Visiting children at a Washington, D.C. Boys and Girls Club, part of Powell's youth crusade while out of government

President Bush meets with his national security advisers at Camp David on September 15, 2001. Left to right, President Bush, Powell, Defense Secretary Donald Rumsfeld and Deputy Defense Secretary Paul Wolfowitz.

White House Chief of Staff Andrew Card, National Security Adviser Condoleezza Rice and Powell chat in the Oval Office as Bush has his picture taken.

Bush, Powell, Rice and Rumsfeld sit through a long afternoon at a NATO summit in Prague on November 2 2002.

At a news conference after a meeting between U.N. Secretary General Kofi Annan and representatives of the fi permanent members of the U.N. Security Council, September 12, 2003. Left to right, British Foreign Secretary Ja Straw, French Foreign Minister Dominique de Villepin, Russian Foreign Minister Igor Ivanov, Annan and Powe

Secretary of State Powell presents "the facts" about Iraqi President Saddam Hussein to the U.N. Security Council on February 5, 2003, as CIA Director George Tenet, left, and U.S. Ambassador to the United Nations John Negroponte listen.

Vice President Cheney makes a point to Powell as they wait for a ceremony to begin on the White House South Lawn, May 19, 2003.

resident Bush and his secretary
state share a light-hearted
oment in this undated White
ouse photo.

Anxious to show unity after reports of discontent during the summer of 2003, Bush hosts Powell and Deputy Secretary of State Richard Armitage at his ranch in Crawford, Texas.

With Alma at his side, Powell says good-bye to State Department employees on January 19, 2005.

Launching a public relations offensive on Iraq, President Bush invites former secretaries defense and state to the White House on January 5, 2006. Left to right, Cheney, Bush, Ric Powell and Madeleine Albright.

Powell rode into Washington in an armed convoy, speeding to the State Department along city streets now nearly empty except for police and military vehicles. After a brief consultation with his senior staff, he arrived at the White House as Bush was finishing his televised remarks. Terrorists had attacked "our way of life, our very freedom," the president had said. Although he made no specific charge of responsibility, Bush warned that "We will make no distinction between the terrorists who committed these acts and those who harbor them." He reemphasized the point when he sat down in the Situation Room at 9:30 p.m. with his "War Cabinet," as the national security principals would henceforth be known.

Rumsfeld, who had spent part of the morning helping evacuate the wounded from the Pentagon, had brought his own list of steps that needed to be taken. He urged retaliation—the Pentagon had identified forty-two major bombing targets in Afghanistan—but warned that it could take up to two months to put together a full-fledged military operation. With the new reality barely twelve hours old, the principals were all but certain of bin Laden's responsibility but sure about little else. How would they mount a military offensive in a remote land of deserts and mountains seven thousand air miles away? What about other countries where al-Qaeda had established a presence? What should be the other elements of a comprehensive antiterrorism policy? How should they deal with Pakistan? With few answers, they adjourned until the next day.

Colin had been unable to make contact with Alma on the flight back from Peru. He assumed that she and the children and grandchildren were fine—they were a military family that knew how to respond to crises, and the Diplomatic Security Service would ensure their safety. When he finally arrived home near midnight, he and Alma spoke only briefly before going to bed. As he always did when his problems were professional rather than personal and he needed to face the next day with a clear head, he fell quickly into a deep sleep.

For Alma, the Pentagon attack would revive a role from which she thought she had long since retired. A few days after September 11, Kathleene Card, the wife of Bush's chief of staff, called to express a concern shared by many administration spouses. Their husbands were gone during the day and into the night; emergency plans were for staff only and no one had told them what to do in the event of another attack. Alma helped organize the women—and at least one husband whose wife worked in the White House—into a support group, and they met regularly for months at a local church. "That's what I could do," she later recalled. As a military commander's wife, "I had had a lot of practice. One of them said, 'But if they evacuate our husbands, will someone come and get us?' I said, 'No, dear, nobody will come and get you. You're on your own.' " They set up a telephone tree and talked about how they could protect their children.

Powell was far from alone in concluding within hours of the September 11 attacks that they had "changed everything." As the nation looked to Bush for reassurance and leadership, demanding retribution and protection, the president quickly recognized that history would judge him by how—and how effectively—he responded. With full backing from Congress and the American people and the support of much of the world, he declared the nation at war with international terrorism; the coming battle, he said, would be "a monumental struggle of good versus evil."

In the days following the attacks, Bush met with congressional leaders and traveled to New York to visit "Ground Zero," the stories-high pile of smoking rubble that had once been the World Trade Center towers, where rescue workers were still searching for survivors. When he gathered his full Cabinet for the first time on Friday, September 14, he choked up as they stood and applauded him. It was an emotional week for everyone; like all Americans, administration officials were deeply worried about their families and their wounded nation. Concerned that Bush would lose his composure when he spoke at a memorial service at Washington National Cathedral later that day, Powell waited until everyone sat down and then passed the president a note. When he had to give an emotional speech, Powell wrote, he tried to avoid words like "Mom" and "Pop" that caused him to well up. Bush read it and smiled, telling his Cabinet that the secretary of state had just advised him: "Don't break down." The room erupted in tension-relieving laughter.

The War Cabinet—Cheney, Powell and Rumsfeld, along with Rice, Tenet, Treasury Secretary O'Neill, Joint Chiefs Chairman Shelton, FBI Director Robert Mueller, and Attorney General John Ashcroft—met each morning and afternoon. While Tenet's CIA quickly unveiled its plan to send covert units into Afghanistan to help the Northern Alliance, the Pentagon struggled to formulate military options. Rumsfeld returned to the issue Wolfowitz had raised with the deputies months before: Shouldn't they broaden their response to include Iraq? Cheney suggested that larger states known to support terrorism were easier targets than Afghanistan. After one meeting, Bush took Clarke aside and asked him to gather any information he could find on the question of a possible Iraqi link to the New York and Pentagon attacks.

It seemed clear to Powell that some of his colleagues were trying to use the events of September 11 to promote their own policy obsessions and settle old scores. In 1991, there had been no dissent when Bush 41 opted to end the Gulf War with Saddam Hussein still in power. But it had become part of conservative lore that Powell had been the driving force behind the decision. The neoconservatives in particular, he thought, had made entire careers out of demanding that the "mistake" of 1991 be corrected.

Powell had no sympathy for Saddam and wasn't opposed in principle to moving against him at some point. But not now. In his confirmation hearing, he had described Iraq as "fundamentally a broken, weak country" that could be brought to its knees—or at least contained—by sanctions. Its military force was a mere shadow of what it had been in 1991, and the United States was keeping a close eye on what Baghdad was doing. It would be bad policy and pure folly even to consider striking Iraq now. The American people wanted to know who had assaulted New York City and Washington, leaving thousands dead, and what the administration was going to do about it. There was no indication that Iraq—or Iran, North Korea, Syria, Cuba or any of the other countries at the top of the conservative hit list—was responsible. The guilty party was Osama bin Laden, and the administration knew where he lived.

When Powell was not in White House meetings, he spent much of his time fielding a flood of condolence calls and offers of assistance from his foreign minister counterparts around the world. The U.N. Security Council passed a resolution of condemnation, and NATO, for the first time in its history, invoked the mutual-defense provisions of its charter. Powell found that setting up a coalition against al-Qaeda was like "snapping Legos together"—the whole world shared America's pain and outrage. The one potential problem was Pakistan and its relationship with the Taliban. Once Bush sorted through the internal debates over whom to target and settled on Afghanistan, as Powell was certain he would, they would need Pakistan in the U.S. camp.

Powell and Armitage decided that they had neither the time nor the inclination to beat around the bush with Pakistani President Musharraf. He had to be told in no uncertain terms that it was time to choose sides. Sitting in Powell's office two days after the attacks, they sketched out a list of nonnegotiable demands and handed it to a visiting Pakistani intelligence official, telling him they wanted an answer the next day. Pakistan was to end all logistical support for al-Qaeda and close its borders to the terrorists; give the United States blanket access to its airspace, ports and borders and share all intelligence and immigration information; condemn the September 11 attacks and "curb all domestic expressions of support for terrorism"; and ban its citizens from crossing the border to Afghanistan to join the Taliban. Once there was firm evidence of bin Laden's responsibility for the attacks, Pakistan must join the United States in demanding that the Taliban hand over the terrorists. If the Afghans refused, Pakistan must sever all relations and end all support for the Taliban and assist the United States in every way in the destruction of al-Qaeda. Taken as a whole, it would be a tall order for a military dictator whose population included numerous Islamic militants and whose own military intelligence service had helped put the Taliban into power in the first place.

As he sent the message to Musharraf, Powell felt a rush of satisfaction. "We didn't show that list to anybody," he later recalled, reflecting his frustration with the short White House leash that tethered him on most issues. "We didn't coordinate it with anybody, we didn't share it. We just did it. The next morning, I told the president we'd done it and we were going to follow up." After the Cabinet meeting on Friday the fourteenth, he called Islamabad for an answer. "As one general to another," he told Musharraf, "we need someone on our flank fighting with us. Speaking candidly, the American people would not understand if Pakistan was not in this fight with the United States." As soon as the conversation was over, Powell put through a call to Bush to tell him that the Pakistani leader would comply in full with their demands.

Bush ordered the War Cabinet to Camp David over the weekend of September 15 to discuss a final plan of action. Rumsfeld brought Wolfowitz, and Tenet was accompanied by McLaughlin and CIA counterterrorism chief J. Cofer Black. Armitage was absent; he had been sent to Moscow to engage the Russians in what he called a "no-shit conversation" about the shared threat of terrorism. Several Cabinet secretaries—Powell, Rumsfeld, O'Neill and Ashcroft—brought their wives.

Each of the officials was assigned one of the eleven cabins scattered throughout the wooded, 125-acre compound. When they gathered on Saturday morning at 9:30 in Laurel Lodge, the largest of the stone-and-wood structures, Bush had already been up for hours walking his two dogs, jogging and calling the presidents of Spain and Mexico. Before the meeting began, a small pool of reporters was ushered into the wood-paneled conference room to photograph the assembled officials, most of whom were wearing zippered jackets over their casual khakis or blue jeans to ward off the early-fall chill. The principals had arranged themselves in their White House seating pattern around the massive conference table: Cheney to Bush's right, Powell to his left and Rumsfeld beyond Powell.

Bush had already made several decisions. The war against the terrorists and those who harbored them would have to be fought on many fronts—intelligence, financial and diplomatic as well as military. The United States would hit them with all available resources, but "in a smart way." He already had the right goals and the right rhetoric, Bush thought. What he needed now were action specifics: What, exactly, were they going to do?

Once the media had left, Bush offered his customary prayer and an introductory statement before motioning for the secretary of state to speak. Powell reported on his conversation with Musharraf and the status of international support. O'Neill followed, saying that the stock market would reopen Monday and updating their progress in tracing the paths of the hijackers before they had boarded airplanes in Boston, Washington and Newark on the morning of September 11. They already had a good idea of the identities of the nineteen terrorists divided among the planes: all appeared to have been Arabs, and U.S. intelligence had tentatively confirmed that at least fifteen of them were Saudi Arabian nationals. They would find out a lot more, O'Neill said, as they continued tracking the financial transactions the terrorists had made during the varying lengths of time they had been living in the United States. The money trail should lead not only to the direct perpetrators but up the chain to whoever was behind them.

Tenet handed out thick packets of information, titled "Going to War," that outlined what the CIA knew about worldwide terrorist groups and how they could be destroyed in Afghanistan and beyond. Phase one would target al-Qaeda's operating base in Afghanistan, with CIA paramilitary teams deployed with the Northern Alliance, U.S. military Special Forces inserted on the ground and efforts to enlist anti-Taliban (though also anti–Northern Alliance) tribes in the southern part of the country. The packet included a proposed presidential order giving the CIA virtual carte blanche to go after terrorists worldwide with all necessary means.

The direct military strike options against al-Qaeda, outlined by General Shelton, were not encouraging: they could hit the al-Qaeda camps and even some Taliban targets with sea- and air-launched cruise missiles and manned bombers. No one was very enthusiastic; the air attacks were the kind of "pinpricks" Clinton had launched in 1998, and they could tell from satellite photos that most of the camps they knew about were already empty. They could combine air assaults with some ground troop insertions, but any substantial deployment would take weeks if not months and would require the cooperation of neighboring countries.

When the discussion moved to the wider world of terrorism beyond Afghanistan, Wolfowitz returned to the question of Iraq. The enemy in Afghanistan was elusive, he said, while Iraq was rich in targets. Its corrupt regime was brittle and ripe for toppling. There was a 10 to 50 percent chance that Saddam had been involved in the September 11 attacks in any case, he asserted; they would have to go after him sooner or later.

When Powell remarked that the international coalition that was quickly coming together against al-Qaeda would likely fall apart if the military targets went beyond Afghanistan, the president shrugged and said he didn't care if they had to go it alone.

After breaking for lunch, they reconvened, and Bush asked them to go around the table and offer recommendations based on what they'd heard in the morning session. Once again, Powell spoke first. They should begin to implement the campaign Tenet had outlined, he said, and issue a warning to the Taliban—supported by pressure from Saudi Arabia and Pakistan—with a deadline for ejecting al-Qaeda. If, as they all expected, the Afghans did not comply, they would launch a sustained air campaign against known al-Qaeda sites. Public support and allied backing would be important, and they should be prepared to effectively present the evidence against bin Laden. As far as targeting other state sponsors of terrorism, Powell said to Bush, they could wait until "a time of your choosing." It was a phrase the president had used in his National Cathedral speech the day before.

Powell thought that Wolfowitz was blowing smoke about the ease of attacking Iraq. CENTCOM, the military's regional command with responsibility for the broad swath of countries between the Horn of Africa and Central and South Asia, would already have its hands full in Afghanistan. To Powell's relief, neither Rumsfeld nor Cheney seemed to support an early move against Saddam Hussein, and a consensus was reached to adopt Tenet's plan. Bush thanked them for their input and said he would let them know of his decision.

Powell, Rumsfeld and their wives returned to Washington that night while the Ashcrofts and O'Neills stayed at Camp David and joined the Bushes for what the president called "comfort food": fried chicken, mashed potatoes and corn bread. After dinner, they relaxed with jigsaw puzzles and songs around the piano. While Ashcroft played and Rice sang along, Paul O'Neill sat by himself in a corner reading through the hefty pile of documents Tenet had distributed earlier in the day. Replete with plots to "neutralize" terrorist enemies around the globe, the broad action plan Tenet offered had no provision for civilian or congressional oversight. O'Neill, who had spent a quarter century as a corporate executive and found Bush's management style disturbingly disjointed, later recalled hoping that the president would actually read the material carefully before he relinquished so much decision-making responsibility to an agency no one had elected.

When they reconvened at the White House on Monday morning, Bush said they would move forward immediately with Tenet's plan. The Pentagon would prepare a second stage of action along the lines of the broadest military option outlined by Shelton: cruise missiles, bombers and troops in Afghanistan. Other tasks were assigned: Ashcroft would complete a new legislative package for Congress to authorize expanded legal authority for the FBI to track terrorists in the United States; O'Neill would work on finding and seizing terrorists' assets; Powell would continue to organize international support—paying special attention to Pakistan—and draw up an ultimatum for the Taliban.

Barely a week after the towers had fallen, American arms were flowing to the Northern Alliance while CIA and Special Forces personnel were operating on the ground in Afghanistan. At home, new security laws were enacted to catch terrorists already inside the country and to keep others from entering. An army of analysts and accountants followed money trails through the dozens of countries believed to harbor al-Qaeda operatives and terrorist fellow travelers.

As expected, the Taliban refused to eject al-Qaeda, and on October 7, American cruise missiles and aircraft began to punish Afghanistan. By the end of the year, with additional U.S. and allied troop deployments, the bulk of the enemy's forces had been killed or captured or had escaped into the rugged mountains along the Afghanistan-Pakistan border. The United Nations organized a conference of non-Taliban Afghan tribal leaders, and on December 22 Hamid Karzai, an India-educated, ethnic Pashtun from southern Afghanistan, was installed in Kabul as president.

For Powell, the tragic events of September 11 had turned the page on the most unhappy period he had ever experienced in government service. With a new unity of purpose and urgent challenges facing them, the principals finally began working as a team and most of the internal sniping ceased. Powell was no longer the "odd man out," and his crisis management and leadership skills, along with his international standing among potential allies in the fight against al-Qaeda, were in high demand. The attacks, he confidently told *The New York Times,* had "hit the reset button" on American foreign policy.

Inside the State Department, there was an invigorating new sense of direction. "Most Americans were vulnerable and shocked to the core" after September 11, Richard Boucher recalled. "But we had the feeling that we could deal with this. We can do something about this. Powell had that feeling.... There was an enormous diplomatic aspect to it—lining up coalition partners, signing democracy charters, getting NATO, the OAS, Pakistan, Central Asia on board. It was all going to have to be taken care of, and he was going to do it. It defined his job the way nothing before had defined it."

For the first time since the spy plane crisis with China, there were clear foreign policy problems for Powell to address—beginning with Pakistan—and no internal roadblocks to prevent him from solving them. Although he wasn't naturally given to thinking in terms of grand global strategies, he also saw a larger opportunity in the war on terrorism. The situation obviously called for a multinational response; the United States shouldn't want to fight alone and didn't have to. Terrorism was a common threat against which the nations of the world could rally, one that could supersede their competing self-interests. It was a chance to revitalize and expand, under American leadership, the international relationships and interdependence that had lost much of their reason for being with the end of the Cold War and the fall of the Soviet Union.

With Iraq as a notable exception, virtually every country in the world had condemned the September 11 attacks, and most were contributing in some way to one or more aspects of the response. It remained to be seen whether the fledgling cooperation from nations such as Iran and Syria— which themselves harbored terrorist groups—would amount to much. But Powell felt it was worth exploring.

There was one front on which the new internal and international equations following September 11 seemed to have little effect. Throughout the summer before the attacks, Powell had continued to press regularly for White House attention to the escalating violence between the Palestinians and Israelis. European allies and friendly Arab governments were increasingly uneasy over what they saw as Bush's lack of interest in the peace process. The Saudi Arabian leader, Crown Prince Abdullah, whose country provided both oil and military basing facilities to the United

States, had sent a personal letter to the president in August voicing his discontent with U.S. policy. Palestinian suicide bombers had killed scores of Israeli civilians, and Ariel Sharon, the new Israeli prime minister, had responded with tanks, troops and targeted assassinations of Palestinian militant leaders. Bush seemed to have abandoned all pretense of balance to cheer on Sharon while making no effort to stop the carnage. That was his prerogative, Abdullah noted, but the president had to realize that such actions made it difficult for Saudi Arabia to maintain a public friendship with the United States.

Cheney, Rumsfeld and their senior aides continued to urge Bush to think small in terms of any Mideast initiative, although Powell privately questioned why the defense secretary was being allowed a decisive say on what was essentially a diplomatic issue. The Pentagon was emerging as a major voice on foreign policy, often in opposition to what the State Department advocated. Powell felt that his own senior staff was a good mix of nonpartisan professionals and political appointees, while Rumsfeld's group of senior civilians, most of whom had close ties to the vice president, was a "pure litmus test" on a whole range of issues. In Powell's estimation, you had to be "a very strong neoconservative to get on the [Pentagon] team, and they all brought in the theories and things they had been working on for years with the presumption that the State Department is the enemy." Although their obsessions tended toward foreign policy—Israel, Iraq, China and missile defense—rather than social issues such as abortion and affirmative action, Powell considered them "the soul mates of the guys who had the press conference in [19]95, asking me not to become a Republican."

On the Middle East, he had to admit that Cheney and Rumsfeld were right to believe that the chances of Bush's succeeding where so many of his predecessors had failed were slim. Sharon and Arafat were intransigent old men and implacable foes who were unlikely ever to agree about anything. Bush had not been dealt any aces in his Mideast hand. But the United States had a major historical role to play in the region whether the vice president and the defense secretary liked it or not. It simply wasn't possible, Powell thought, for the president of the United States to say, " 'No, it's too hard. I don't want to waste energy on it.' "

Powell had made a second trip to the region in June 2001, not because he had high hopes of progress—he considered every visit to the Middle East "like a root canal...awful"—but because he thought it had to be done. On his return, he had convinced first Rice and then Bush that even if there were no ready solutions to the conflict, at the very least the administration should signal its concern about and commitment to trying to find one. With their approval, Powell's staff had gone to work on a major policy speech for him to give on the subject.

After September 11, however, the speech was put on indefinite hold. The possibility of a Bush-Arafat meeting, discussed just days before the al-Qaeda attacks, was now out of the question. The United States had labeled Arafat a terrorist in the past, and now Bush had declared all terrorists equal.

In his new "with us or against us" view of the world, Powell thought Bush tended to see the Israeli-Palestinian situation in black-and-white terms—"Sharon good, Arafat bad." Powell felt the need to constantly remind the president of the stakes involved for U.S. security and international alliances. Cheney and Rumsfeld, neither of whom seemed to have a visceral feeling about the issue beyond the domestic political price of involvement, now argued that Bush might appear irresolute in the war on terrorism if he didn't stand firm against the Palestinians. For many top Defense Department ideologues—Wolfowitz, Undersecretary for Planning Douglas Feith and Feith's deputy, William J. Luti, along with Richard Perle—the conflict fell squarely within the parameters of the worldwide antiterrorist crusade Bush had launched. Any pressure on Israel to negotiate with Arafat amounted to appeasement of terrorists and a betrayal of a leading U.S. ally. In their view, whatever sustenance Palestinian militants drew from dictatorships such as Syria, Iran and Iraq made it all the more important to go after those regimes. Once they were replaced with democratic governments, the Mideast swamp would dry up.

Powell referred to Rumsfeld's team as the "JINSA crowd." JINSA, the Jewish Institute for National Security Affairs, was a Washington-based organization that equated U.S. national security with strong backing for Israel's defense needs. Feith, a Washington lawyer who had actively opposed Mideast peace talks for most of his career, had served on its board, as had Perle and Cheney.

To Mideast experts at the State Department—including William Burns, who had replaced Edward Walker as assistant secretary for Near East Affairs, and his two principal deputies, Ryan Crocker and David Satterfield—those views reflected an upside-down and dangerous reading of the situation. Justifiably or not, the plight of the Palestinians was a rallying cry throughout the Muslim world. Until the conflict with the Israelis was resolved, they believed, it would remain a valuable recruitment tool for Islamic terrorists, and the United States—as Israel's prime economic, military and diplomatic backer—would be a target. It was far from al-Qaeda's only reason for attacking America, but it was one the administration ought to pay more attention to.

"There were a lot of caricatures of the arguments people were making during that period," recalled a State Department official involved in the debates. "The reality we kept trying to stress was that you can't not make a serious effort on this issue, if only because it matters to everyone else in the region. Making a serious effort at least allows you to get a hearing on other issues." Powell needed little convincing from his staff. Israel had as much right as the United States to defend itself against terrorism, but the vast majority of Palestinians weren't terrorists and had legitimate griev-ances against Israel that were recognized by the United Nations and important U.S. allies. Continued progress against al-Qaeda would depend in significant measure on help from governments in the Arab world, prin-cipally Saudi Arabia, Jordan and Egypt. Part of the price for that cooperation—as well as for their acceptance of Washington's urging to democratize their own governments—was stepped-up American involve-ment in the Mideast peace process.

After September 11, Burns and State Department Mideast adviser Aaron Miller had continued working on Powell's postponed speech. They proposed breaking no new policy ground; America was still pledged to a strong and secure Israel and support for a negotiated settlement of land issues with the Palestinians. The administration still backed the so-called Mitchell Plan, a series of confidence-building steps between the two sides proposed in April 2001 by George Mitchell, a former U.S. senator who Clinton had dispatched to the region. It still advocated the Tenet Plan, a dormant security agreement brokered by the CIA director. But the process was stalemated, the violence was ongoing and Powell believed it was time to up the American ante, at least rhetorically.

At Powell's urging, Bush had agreed to include a statement on the peace process in his address to the annual opening of the U.N. General Assembly on November 10. The meeting brought all the states in the unwieldy new international antiterrorism coalition together under the same roof for the first time—the vast assembly hall was filled with close U.S. friends and new allies of convenience—along with the mistrustful and the openly hostile. After noting that any one of them could be the next terrorist target, Bush warned that there would be "a price to be paid" by those nations who were on the wrong side of history. Full of bombast and resolve, his address ignored the diplomatic conventions most heads of state followed even when they had a dose of bad medicine to administer; there were none of the customary pro forma promises to address world underdevelopment and poverty. Despite his frequent pauses, the General Assembly largely ignored Bush's applause lines.

The one-paragraph reference to "a just peace in the Middle East" that had been inserted near the end of the speech seemed out of place. "We are working toward a day when two states, Israel and Palestine, live peacefully together within secure and recognized borders," Bush said, and the United States would do "all in our power to bring both parties back into negotiations." But it was the first time any American president had explicitly referred to a Palestinian state, and the Arabs were pleased. Segueing back to his larger theme, the president cautioned that "peace will only come when all have sworn off, forever, incitement, violence and terror."

Powell's own Mideast speech was finally scheduled for delivery at the University of Louisville on November 19, but internal disputes continued up until the last minute. The controversy, a senior White House official later insisted, was primarily over the timing of the speech and "whether it might be misread, in terms of [a lack of] support of Israel's right to defend itself." In anticipation, Powell later recalled, the Israelis "start[ed] bitching...and they've got marvelous channels to bitch in. They come to New York, and New York comes to Washington, and Washington comes to me. This was causing a great deal of nervousness in the White House." It was clear that "if I had walked in to the President and said, 'You know, Mr. President, on second thought, I don't think I should give this speech,' he would not have said, 'Oh, no, you've got to.' He might even have breathed a sigh of relief."

It wasn't the kind of thing that Bush would bring up directly with Powell, however. As usual, the message was transmitted through an anxious Condoleezza Rice, who told him that the president "just wonders whether you really need to give this speech." Powell replied via the same channel. "I know the Israelis don't like it," he told Rice. "I'm sure there's stuff in here the Palestinians don't like. That's the awful part of this portfolio." But the administration had to be "on the record comprehensively, and not just with one paragraph."

The United States and Israel, Powell told the Louisville audience, were "bound forever together by common democratic values and traditions. This will never change." But despite the fading hope for peace in the region, the Bush administration had "a vision of a region where Israelis and Arabs can live together in peace, security and dignity." In a concise statement of his own views, he said that solutions would "come about only through hard work, common sense, basic fairness and readiness to compromise. They will not be created by teaching hate and division, nor will they be born amidst violence and war."

Both sides would have to face "fundamental truths," Powell said. Palestinians would have to accept that "Israelis must be able to live their lives free from terror as well as war.... There must be real results, not just words and declarations.... Whatever the sources of Palestinian frustration and anger...however legitimate their claims, they cannot be heard, let alone be addressed, through violence." But Israel would have to realize that the "humiliation and lack of respect" it was inflicting on the Palestinians was "just another path to confrontation." Israel's settlement activity on Palestinian land must stop, along with its military occupation of Gaza and the West Bank.

He announced that he was sending Burns and a new "senior adviser," retired Marine Corps General Anthony Zinni, to the region to work on implementing the Mitchell and Tenet Plans and helping to arrange a lasting cease-fire. The Bush administration, he vowed, "will stay engaged.... The Middle East has always needed active American engagement for there to be progress, and we will provide it."

Although the Israelis thought it went too far and the Arabs thought it did not go far enough, the speech at least accomplished its purpose of conveying the administration's interest. Powell saw it as an internal triumph—proof that his patient persuasion could influence the president—and as a public signal at home and abroad that he was in charge of the nation's foreign policy.

After such a lengthy and contentious buildup, he was as nervous as a Broadway actor awaiting opening-night reviews as he flew back to Washington. He arrived in time for a late-afternoon Cabinet meeting and was relieved when Bush slapped him on the back and congratulated him. Asked by reporters what personal influence he would use to get the peace process moving, Bush pledged his involvement. "Our objective is to convince both parties to make a conscious decision to come to the peace table," he said. "And when they do so, we're more than willing to help."

Not only was the president "very complimentary," Powell later recalled, in short order he was claiming the Mideast initiative as his own. "If Cheney had had his way," Powell noted with satisfaction to a senior aide, "that speech never would have been given."

Anthony Zinni had been lured out of retirement by Burns and Armitage, two of his closest friends in government. Until Powell publicly announced his new appointment as a "senior adviser," he had never even spoken to the secretary of state about the job. Zinni's background was similar to Powell's—the son of an Italian immigrant father, he had grown up in working-class Philadelphia and served two Vietnam tours on his way to high command. But they knew each other only in passing, primarily from when Zinni had served as deputy commander of the Kurdish aid effort in northern Iraq during Powell's chairmanship of the Joint Chiefs. Several years after Powell left the Army, Zinni was named head of CENTCOM, where he was responsible, among other things, for running the no-fly zone patrols over Iraq. His familiarity with the Arab world and its leaders and his outspoken insistence on the need for U.S. engagement in the peace process had not endeared him to the current Pentagon leadership.

Two days after Powell's speech, Zinni traveled to Washington from his home in Williamsburg, Virginia, for briefings at the State Department. Told on arrival to meet the secretary in the basement parking garage, he found Powell waiting for him, reading the newspaper in the backseat of his official car. It was only when Zinni climbed in that he learned they were headed to the White House.

Bush, Cheney and Rice had gathered in the Oval Office. After an introduction by Powell and some small talk, the president looked at Zinni and asked, "What's your mission?" Zinni was surprised; it was the administration's initiative, not his, and he still hadn't received any instructions. He improvised something about "bringing the parties together." Trying to think of more to say, he noted that Israeli Prime Minister Sharon was due to visit Washington in the coming week. "Fine," Bush said. "Good." End of meeting. Neither Cheney nor Rice had uttered a word. Zinni had the impression that Powell had prevailed upon the president to shake his hand and wish him well, but there was no sense that Bush had bought into his mission. As they got up to leave, Zinni later recalled, the president said something to the effect of, "Well, Colin, this is your baby...you convinced me, now it's your show."

As 2001 drew to a close, Powell felt that the trials of the administration's first year were behind him. The war in Afghanistan was largely won, and his Mideast initiative had been launched. In early December, he found himself heading to Moscow on an important task for the president—the first time he had been there since accompanying Ronald Reagan to the 1988 summit with Mikhail Gorbachev.

Considering Russia's significance to the United States, it was surprising that the secretary of state had not visited sooner. Both Rice and Rumsfeld had been there over the summer for talks about weapons reductions and the ABM Treaty, a fact not lost on those who kept track of Powell's relative standing within the administration. Early suspicions that Powell was soft on the Russians and less than enthusiastic about Bush's plans to scrap the treaty had not subsided.

The truth was that he felt little passion for either the treaty or the missile defense system it was inhibiting. But he saw no point in gratuitously offending Moscow by peremptorily withdrawing from the accord, at least until the United States was ready to begin testing and deploying the system. In the meantime, Powell had convinced Bush and Rice that they were better off trying to negotiate amendments to the treaty—or at least giving the Russians time to get used to the idea of scrapping it altogether. Bilateral talks had been ongoing for months at various levels, including the Rumsfeld and Rice trips. Bush had met with Putin on four occasions, and Powell had held more than a dozen sessions with Foreign Minister Igor Ivanov in Washington and other international venues. A joint negotiating committee was meeting regularly, with John Bolton leading the U.S. team. But the Russians remained adamantly opposed to amending or ending the treaty, and the question of how long they should be placated had become a contentious one among the principals.

When Powell argued at one particularly testy NSC meeting in mid-fall that they should make a last push with Moscow, he felt it necessary to insist explicitly that he was not opposed to the NMD program. "We're going to go forward with missile defense," he assured them. It was important to do so "without fracturing a relationship or causing more trouble than we need to cause, but one way or the other we're going forward... and if it takes getting out of the ABM Treaty there's no resistance from me." Using an analogy they had all heard from him several times before, he reminded his colleagues that even the American colonists had formally stated their case—with the Declaration of Independence—when they broke with the British crown. But as NMD development deadlines approached, Powell had acknowledged that time was running out.

He was assigned the task of personally notifying Putin that they had reached the end of negotiations and that Bush was about to officially announce the United States' withdrawal from the treaty. When he left Washington on December 3, the main purpose of his trip was disguised with interim stops in Turkey and Central Asia for consultations on the Afghanistan campaign. He flew to Moscow from Kazakhstan on the evening of December 9 and headed to the Kremlin the following morning with Alexander Vershbow, the U.S. ambassador to Russia. Far from the opulent Hall of Saint Catherine where Gorbachev had once told Powell and George Shultz that the Soviet Union was on its last legs, Putin and Ivanov received them in a small but tastefully furnished office. There were a desk and a table, and four armchairs that had been set apart in a circle.

Bush had remarked after his first meeting with Putin that summer that he had looked into the Russian president's eyes and gotten "a sense of his soul." To Powell, Putin's emotionless, ice-blue stare said more about his years with the Soviet spy agency, the KGB, than it did about his "soul." Already briefed by Ivanov on what he was about to hear, Putin maintained a stony silence while Powell spoke. "Mr. President, President Bush wanted me to come to see you personally to talk about this," Powell began. Despite extraordinary effort and goodwill on both sides, he said, their differences over the ABM Treaty were irreconcilable. The United States had no desire to threaten the Russian Federation or to harm their bilateral relationship or Russian interests. Putin, he said, was no doubt aware of the urgency the Bush administration attached to the NMD program as other countries, including Iran, were developing long-range missiles capable of reaching American shores. Because of this concern, which Russia itself should share, President Bush had decided he had no choice but to abrogate the treaty in the name of "supreme national interest."

As Ivanov and Vershbow took hurried notes, Putin stared blankly at Powell. He finally replied, "Well, I think you're making a big mistake. Tell the President I disagree." He began a lengthy and spirited defense of the treaty he said had preserved world peace for the past three decades. As for missile defense, he said, "You don't even know if it will work."

Putin paused, and Powell steeled himself for more. But in much the same way as Gorbachev had railed against the United States and then abruptly switched gears to calmly outline his plans for major Soviet reforms, the Russian leader suddenly smiled. "Now we don't have to talk about that anymore," he said dismissively. What was done was done, he said, and they should start working together on a new strategic framework.

Faced with his inability to alter the American plans, Putin had decided to accept them, place his cooperation in the bank as a credit to be used in the future and move on. It was a tactic Powell would see the Russian leader adopt many more times over the next three years, and it convinced him that his initial assessment of the ABM situation had been the right one: be firm but give them some time; reassure them that you're not out to get them; and eventually they'll come around.

Bush had begun his presidency pledging to move aggressively on missile defense and to put a stake through the heart of the treaty. Divergent camps had labeled it as either a bold move befitting the world's sole super-power or arrogant unilateralism that would offend traditional and potential allies. Yet on December 13, when the president publicly announced that the United States would withdraw from the treaty, it provoked little more than a collective domestic and international shrug. Five months later, despite the Pentagon's objections, Bush acquiesced to the Russians' demands for a new accord affirming the strong U.S.-Russian relationship and acknowledging plans to further reduce existing weapons stockpiles. In May 2002, the United States and the Russian Federation signed a two-page Treaty of Moscow.

Powell considered it a triumph both for Bush and for himself. The president had stuck to his principles but allowed everyone ample opportunity to vent. More important, he had given his secretary of state time to soften the blow and arrange a graceful exit. Powell had proven to his own satisfaction that diplomacy was alive and well in the Bush administration—and that he had some trump cards of his own to play.

17

Ultimately, a Secretary of State can succeed only if he or she is close to the President and is treated by him as the center of the policy process.

—Henry A. Kissinger

President Bush completed his first year in office with the highest public approval rating ever recorded for a president: more than 80 percent of the nation thought he was doing a good job. Stunned and fearful in the immediate aftermath of the September 11 attacks, Americans had been reassured by his resolute, forceful response to al-Qaeda and the Taliban in Afghanistan. His declaration of a global war on terrorism had reawakened their confidence and fighting spirit. He told them he had a plan to keep them safe, and they were more than willing to give him the room and the resources needed to implement it.

Powell was heartened by the new level of comity among the administration principals and confident of his good standing with the president. His successful efforts to broaden the antiterror coalition and bring Pakistan on board were widely applauded, and there had been only minimal internal resistance to close cooperation on the issue with the United Nations. The Mideast initiative was underway and the ABM Treaty had been smoothly disposed of. He had also made significant progress on his pledge to revitalize the State Department itself, doubling the number of applicants taking the Foreign Service exam, cutting in half the amount of time from exam to service entry and increasing the number of minority diplomats. His plan to put an Internet connection on every diplomat's desktop was well under way.

On January 15, 2002, Powell embarked on a weeklong trip to Japan and South Asia. The timing was dictated not only by the need to drum up more international contributions to pay for post-Taliban reconstruction and to visit the new U.S. Embassy in Kabul, but also to address an escalating border crisis between nuclear-armed neighbors India and Pakistan. Open warfare between the two risked atomic conflagration even as it distracted Pakistan from assisting the United States' efforts to track down al-Qaeda fighters still on the run, including Osama bin Laden himself. It was a particularly satisfying trip for Powell. He defused the India-Pakistan conflict, at least temporarily, and there was minimal interference in his diplomacy from the White House and the Pentagon. Unlike the fervor they felt for some other parts of the world, no one in the administration had strong ideological feelings about the balance of power between India and Pakistan. As long as he kept the others abreast of what he was doing, they didn't seem to care.

But as he shuttled between New Delhi and Islamabad, Powell received a disturbing call from William Taft, his State Department legal adviser and friend of three decades, that indicated that the new collegiality around the principals table was less than it appeared. In Powell's absence, Taft told him, Bush had made a crucial decision regarding al-Qaeda and Taliban captives from Afghanistan. Approving a Justice Department opinion backed by the vice president, the defense secretary and the White House legal counsel, the president had ordered that neither group would be granted prisoner-of-war status and that the United States would not be bound by the Geneva Conventions in its treatment of them.

It was a move reminiscent of the Kyoto incident, when the State Department's objections had been overridden in hurried secrecy without Powell's input. He put through his own call to the White House. "You'd better hold on," he warned Rice angrily. "I think we're making some mistakes here."

The White House had begun addressing the question of what to do with prisoners captured in the war on terrorism within weeks of the September 11 attacks. As a first order of business, a small working group led by White House Counsel Alberto Gonzales and including legal counsels to Cheney and Rumsfeld, as well as officials from the Justice Department, determined in early November that the captives should be barred from federal courts and granted no constitutional guarantees. Instead, the group recommended, the military should be given the power to imprison and interrogate them indefinitely and to convene special tribunals to prosecute them.

On Saturday, November 10, at a small White House meeting on the subject chaired by Cheney, a directive was approved for Bush's signature. It authorized the military to detain anyone the president or his representative determined had "engaged in, aided or abetted, or conspired to commit" terrorism. Although "full and fair" judgment was pledged, detainees had no promise of a presumption of innocence or a public trial. The State Department and the NSC staff had not participated in the discussions, and neither Powell nor Rice was aware of the decision until the president—after a lunchtime discussion with Cheney—signed and released the order on November 13.

Taft told Powell that they had no basis on which to object to the plan, although the "more normal" course would have been to bring the captives before courts-martial under the provisions of the Uniform Code of Military Justice. But there was legal precedent for the special commissions, and it was certainly within the president's power to establish them, Taft concluded.

The next question was where the detainees would be imprisoned and interrogated before prosecution. A growing number of captives were already being temporarily held at various facilities in Afghanistan controlled by U.S. forces. A new interagency group met in Washington during November and December to consider options for more permanent placement. Although the State Department participated, it was not a leading player in the discussions, which eventually settled on establishing a prison at the U.S. Navy facility at Guantánamo Bay.

Located at the southeastern tip of Cuba, the Guantánamo base's forty-five square miles of land and water were first leased to the United States in 1903, shortly after U.S. forces defeated Spain's Caribbean fleet. Under a 1934 treaty signed by Washington and Havana, the lease could be broken only by "mutual consent"; although the Cuban dictator Fidel Castro had long ago declared the accord invalid, the United States still claimed occupancy. Guantánamo's initial attraction for detaining and interrogating terror captives was its easy defensibility—the entire facility was bordered by water and a fenced and mined no-man's-land.

Its other advantage was its physical and legal distance from the United States. During the 1990s, Guantánamo had been used to house tens of thousands of Haitian and Cuban "boat people" apprehended by the Coast Guard on their way to U.S. shores. The facility had prevented the refugees—nearly all of whom were eventually denied U.S. admission—from attaining the right of appeal they would have had on American soil. Now, the administration concluded, Guantánamo could serve the same purpose of keeping enemy prisoners away from U.S. courts.

Still to be decided was whether federal or international law had any jurisdiction over how the captives were treated during their detainment and interrogation. The military was particularly concerned about the Geneva Conventions, the international treaties promulgated after World War II to govern wartime treatment of captured enemy soldiers and civilians. The conventions had been incorporated into domestic U.S. law with the 1996 War Crimes Act, making American officials liable at home for violating their provisions abroad. In early January 2002, the Pentagon queried the Justice Department for an opinion on whether the conventions or the War Crimes Act applied to treatment of al-Qaeda or Taliban fighters.

A forty-two-page draft memorandum circulated on January 9, 2002, by Deputy Assistant Attorney General John Yoo concluded that neither group was entitled to prisoner-of-war status or any protection at all under Geneva. Al-Qaeda, Yoo wrote, was a stateless entity with no rights under international law. The Taliban was similarly deemed to be without protection since Afghanistan, although a Geneva signatory, was a "failed state" whose treaty rights Bush could "suspend" at will and "restore" if and when a more suitable government was in place. Since the Geneva Conventions did not apply, Yoo reasoned, neither did the War Crimes Act. The same analysis held true for customary international law, the uncodified agreements governing behavior among states. In any case, Yoo concluded, the president's constitutionally mandated responsibility to protect the United States during wartime trumped any international obligations. The administration could do whatever it wanted with the detainees.

By the time Yoo circulated his draft, international criticism of the handling of prisoners by U.S. forces had already erupted in response to published photographs of the initial group of captives, hooded and in chains, arriving at Guantánamo in early January. Asked by reporters about the treatment, Rumsfeld suggested at a January 11 Pentagon news briefing that they would be "handled not as prisoners of war, because they're not, but as unlawful combatants [who] do not have any rights under the Geneva Convention." He made no distinction between al-Qaeda and the Taliban but said that the military planned, "for the most part, [to] treat them in a manner that is reasonably consistent with the Geneva Conventions, to the extent they are appropriate."

Rumsfeld's statement came as the State Department was formulating a reply to Yoo's draft opinion. In Taft's view, Yoo had completely misread international law. "Both the most important factual assumptions on which your draft is based and its legal analysis are seriously flawed," Taft wrote in a cover letter accompanying his own thirty-seven-page analysis. The concept of a "failed state" had no legal basis, he noted, and the Geneva Conventions contained no provision for one signatory to unilaterally suspend the rights of another.

He could not advise "either the President or the Secretary of State that the obligations of the United States under the Geneva Conventions have lapsed with regard to Afghanistan or that the United States is not bound to carry out its obligations under the Conventions as a matter of international law," Taft wrote. Though al-Qaeda members might not qualify as prisoners of war, the conventions contained other provisions that could affect their treatment. As for Taliban captives, they had a legitimate claim to POW status, and Geneva called for any doubts to be resolved on the basis of a case-by-case determination for each individual prisoner. "In previous conflicts, the United States has dealt with tens of thousands of detainees without repudiating its obligations," he concluded. "I have no doubt we can do so here."

Although he mentioned the disagreement to Powell, Taft did not describe the legal arguments in detail. Despite Rumsfeld's public comments on the treatment of prisoners, the president had not yet made a determination. The debate was still only among lawyers, Taft felt, and was far from ready to rise to the level of the principals, let alone the president.

Yoo replied to Taft's memo on January 14. The State Department's comments were "valuable," he wrote, but mistaken, particularly on POW status for the Taliban. The Justice Department was working on its opinion, he said, and would send Taft a copy of its next draft.

Lawyers at Justice, Defense and the White House already considered the State Department a weak link in the national security chain. Not only were its legal interpretations as narrow as possible, it also seemed unappreciative of the fact that winning this unconventional war on terrorism would require unconventional means. "In general, the State Department was the outlier on a lot of these issues ... advocating a more lenient or less muscular, less aggressive approach," recalled Bradford Berenson, an associate counsel in the White House legal office.

On January 18, with Powell in Asia, Taft was informed that the president had approved the Justice Department interpretation, determining that neither al-Qaeda nor Taliban detainees were covered by the Geneva Conventions and that neither group was eligible for POW status. Although the White House made no formal announcement, Rumsfeld issued written instructions to the military the next day. There would be no POW designation, he wrote. Treatment would be "consistent with the principles" of Geneva "to the extent appropriate and consistent with military necessity."

Taft was astounded. They were in the middle of an unresolved inter-agency debate—every memo he had seen had been stamped "DRAFT"—and there had been no formal opinion from the attorney general. It was no accident, he thought, that it had all transpired while the secretary of state was out of the country.

Powell told Rice he wanted to talk to the president in person. He usually preferred to work within the bureaucratic structure, resisting any impulse to march into the Oval Office with a personal complaint. Even if he had had a closer, more informal relationship with Bush, "his feeling was that you don't go in there demanding things, you don't go in hot and bothered," recalled one of Powell's senior aides. "Instead, you play the game with the cards you are dealt.... He's not the kind of guy who goes in there and forces himself on the president the way others would." Powell felt strongly that principals' meetings were the proper forum in which to debate such disagreements.

But once again the president's decision on a matter of international importance seemed to have materialized out of thin air; there had been no high-level meeting or debate over prisoner treatment, and Bush had apparently ruled without a full consideration of the issue. Treaties and relations with other countries were the State Department's responsibility, yet there had been no discussion of the Geneva Conventions in Powell's presence. As he wrapped up his South Asia trip, Taft sent him the relevant documents and brought him up to speed over the telephone.

In an Oval Office meeting shortly after he returned to Washington on January 21, Powell urged the president to rethink the issue. American soldiers depended on Geneva for their own safety, he said, and a unilateral disregard of the conventions would put them at risk in this and future conflicts. "I said I wanted everybody covered, whether Taliban, al-Qaeda or whatever," he later recalled, "and I think the case was there for that." He understood the urgent need for intelligence about future terrorist acts, he said, but contrary to what Bush might have been told, Geneva did not prevent interrogation of detainees. Interrogators could ask any questions they wanted; they just couldn't try to get answers by treating prisoners in an inhumane or degrading way.

Bush was notoriously unwilling to reconsider any decision he had already made. He didn't like being second-guessed, and he made his annoyance clear to Powell. But he agreed to convene an NSC meeting on the issue the following Monday, January 28.

Powell's satisfaction at winning reconsideration was short-lived. He awoke Saturday morning to find the news of his dissent on the front page of *The Washington Times* in the form of a leaked four-page memo sent to Bush the day before by Gonzales, the president's legal counsel. The document, later said to have been drafted by Cheney's counsel David Addington, dismissed Powell's case for a reversal of the decision as "unpersuasive." The attorney general had "delegated" his authority to interpret the law to Yoo, and Justice's view was definitive. "Nevertheless," the memo added, "you should be aware that the Legal Adviser to the Secretary of State has expressed a different view." By implication, Bush had not been previously informed of the State Department's lengthy disagreement with the opinion from Justice.

Bush had already defined the war on terrorism as "a new kind of war," the Gonzales memo reiterated, and "this new paradigm renders obsolete Geneva's strict limitations on questioning of enemy prisoners and renders quaint some of its provisions." Since the president had ordered that U.S. personnel "provide humane treatment to enemy detainees," even as he determined they had no status under Geneva, the United States would retain "the credibility to insist on like treatment for our soldiers."

Powell was beside himself with rage, less at the substance of the memo than "at the way the process was being pushed. It was not being put in *The Washington Times* in order to have a balanced view of the issues," he later said. "It was in *The Washington Times* in order to try to screw me." Whoever had leaked it, he said, wanted to "blow me out of the water" before high-level debate was formally joined.

Powell's suspicions regarding the source of the leak centered on the offices of Cheney and Rumsfeld. Both had tried to squeeze Powell out of the decision-making process in the past. No one at the White House appeared eager to find out, but Bush himself was clearly anxious not to push his popular secretary of state too far. Before the day was out, he telephoned Powell with a soothing acknowledgment of the secretary's irritation and a renewed promise that the Geneva issue would be fully discussed at the Monday meeting.

Powell prepared his own memo for the meeting, outlining the liabilities of publicly dismissing Geneva, and sent it to both Gonzales and Rice. Not only was it legally indefensible, he wrote, "it will reverse over a century of U.S. policy and practice ... and undermine the protections of the law of war for our troops, both in this specific conflict and in general." Since U.S. forces had already been ordered to treat prisoners according to Geneva "principles," why refuse to invoke the conventions in the first place? Recognizing the treaty would provide "the strongest legal foundation for what we actually intend to do ... [Geneva] presents a positive international posture, preserves U.S. credibility and moral authority by taking the high ground, and puts us in a better position to demand and receive international support."

The "case-by-case review" that Geneva required for Taliban captives might well conclude that some were entitled to POW status, Powell wrote. "This would not, however, affect their treatment as a practical matter." He asked that the president be given "a much clearer understanding of the options available to him and their consequences."

At the Monday meeting, General Richard B. Myers, who had replaced General Shelton as the chairman of the Joint Chiefs of Staff, indicated that military lawyers had persuaded him that wholesale rejection of Geneva posed risks for U.S. troops. Rumsfeld did not dispute Myers's concerns but felt it was enough for the president to say that treatment of prisoners would be "consistent" with the conventions. The meeting ended inconclusively; over the next several days, more memos were circulated with little change in positions.

On February 7, Bush signed an executive order adopting the "new paradigm" language for the war on terrorism. Based on Yoo's Justice Department analysis, the order said, the president had determined that "none of the provisions of Geneva" applied to al-Qaeda. Although the Constitution gave him the authority to suspend the conventions with regard to the Taliban fighters, Bush maintained, he had chosen not to do so "at this time." The order stipulated that Taliban captives were legally entitled to Geneva protections but added a caveat that made the decision meaningless. Rather than the case-by-case prisoner-of-war determinations the conventions mandated for individuals whose status was disputed, the order made a blanket determination in advance that all captured Taliban were "unlawful combatants" who did not qualify as POWs. "Of course," it concluded, "our values as a Nation, values that we share with many nations in the world, call for us to treat detainees humanely, even those who are not legally entitled to such treatment." Reaffirming the instructions Rumsfeld had transmitted to military commanders nearly three weeks earlier, Bush said that detainees would be afforded humane treatment "consistent with the principles of Geneva."

The decision was widely portrayed in the media as a partial victory for Powell, at least as far as Geneva coverage for the Taliban was concerned. But his own view was that it was a pointless distinction; in practice, there was to be no difference in the treatment afforded al-Qaeda and Taliban prisoners. "I didn't agree with it," Powell later recalled. "The president knows I didn't agree with it. But it got him out of the problem he had. And it's been causing us problems, I think, ever since."

Shortly after the order was issued, lawyers representing Justice,

Defense and the White House began a series of closely held discussions and exchanges of memos on methods of prisoner interrogation
and interpretation of a different treaty—the international Convention
Against Torture and Other Cruel, Inhuman or Degrading Treatment or
Punishment—that would continue for the next two years. This time, the
documents were not circulated to Powell or to Taft, and the State Department was not invited to the meetings.

It had been decades since Powell had puzzled over a mechanics manual
and taken apart his first automobile engine. With little time now to spend
in the detached garage outside his home in McLean, he missed the calming effect of hands-on problem solving that required patience and adher-
ence to basic principles. But he had adopted a similar approach to foreign
policy. Although quick, aggressive action was sometimes required, he felt
that most differences between nations were best resolved with persever-
ance and a step-by-step approach to fixing what was broken.

In the fall of 2001, Powell had persuaded the White House to adopt a
policy of patient activism in the Middle East. But less than two months
after his Louisville speech, the initiative he had launched was foundering
and Anthony Zinni had returned to Washington with the future of his
mission uncertain. Despite a promising beginning, Zinni's negotiations
had been put on hold when Israel interdicted a freighter sailing through
the Red Sea from Iran with fifty tons of illicit weapons destined for Yasser
Arafat's Palestinian Authority. With Arafat's bad faith confirmed, the
Israelis responded by sharply increasing their military presence in all of
the West Bank's population centers and placing the Palestinian leader
under virtual house arrest in his government compound in the city of
Ramallah.

At a White House meeting four weeks into the new year, the principals
examined the administration's options. Was it worth sending Zinni back
to the region to resume negotiations with both sides? Or, as Cheney and
Ariel Sharon advocated, should they declare Arafat an irredeemable terrorist and sever all ties with him once and for all? Powell was as disgusted
as anyone with the Palestinian suicide bombings that regularly slaugh-
tered Israeli civilians and with Arafat's empty promises to do something
about the militant groups responsible for them. But Israel was far from
blameless in the endless spiral of violence, and Powell hadn't changed his
view—reinforced by a steady stream of calls and visits from Arab and
European foreign ministers—that the United States could not afford to
disengage from the Palestinians' chosen leader or from the peace process

itself. He was pushing Arafat hard, Powell insisted. They should give the situation a little more time.

Jordan's King Abdullah made the same argument to Bush during a visit on February 1, conveying that he was also speaking for his colleagues in Egypt and Saudi Arabia. They had no desire to defend Arafat, Abdullah said, but getting rid of him would create an extremely dangerous political vacuum. Meanwhile, the Palestinian people were suffering under Israel's increasingly harsh occupation and the virtual shutdown of civilian life in the West Bank. There had to be specific American demands made of Sharon as well as Arafat, Abdullah argued. The White House needed to finish what it had begun with Bush's U.N. speech in November. Although the Jordanian king was assured that no decision had been made on severing ties with Arafat, Bush told him there would be no U.S. pressure on Israel to withdraw its forces from the West Bank or to ease up on Palestinian civilians until the terrorist violence stopped.

It was left to Powell, after his own meeting with Abdullah, to remind the world of Bush's professed goal of Palestinian statehood. With the king at his side, he told reporters, "We will not give up hope and we will continue to work ... with both sides in as balanced a way as we can to get back to a process that will lead to a cease-fire and the negotiations that we must have ... to arrive at a peaceful solution to this crisis."

The first week in March was the bloodiest yet in the eighteen-month-old *intifada*. With Ramallah still under siege, Israel bombarded Palestinian government and security buildings and invaded two West Bank refugee camps, charging that the camps were sheltering militants. A failed Israeli attempt to assassinate a leader of Hamas, one of the main Palestinian groups responsible for the suicide bombings, had left two women and their four children dead.

As Bush rejected new appeals from Egypt and Saudi Arabia to intervene, Powell publicly voiced his own concerns. "Prime Minister Sharon has to take a hard look at his policies to see whether they will work," he said during a congressional budget hearing in early March. "If you declare war against the Palestinians thinking that you can solve the problem by seeing how many Palestinians can be killed, I don't think that leads us anywhere." Although he was similarly harsh in his criticism of Arafat, his balanced blame of both sides was a marked departure from the usual White House rhetoric.

As international pressure escalated along with the violence, Bush finally acknowledged that he had to take action. But the White House had an additional reason for changing course: it was about to launch its first outreach effort, in the form of a rare overseas trip by Vice President Cheney, to enlist Arab support for regime change in Iraq.

Iraq had been only temporarily removed from the administration's front burner after September 11. Throughout the fall of 2001, as the principals focused their attention on the war in Afghanistan and al-Qaeda, their deputies continued to skirmish over how and when to move against Saddam Hussein. From the Pentagon, Paul Wolfowitz and Douglas Feith pushed for more assistance to Iraqi exile groups, accusing the State Department of undercutting the anti-Saddam opposition by restricting funds to the Iraqi National Congress, a London-based group headed by Ahmed Chalabi. A Western businessman who had left Iraq as a child, Chalabi was a favorite of Richard Perle and had direct access to the vice president's office. State was suspicious of Chalabi and his associates and questioned how they had spent the money they had already received under the Iraq Liberation Act. The department had been moving to strengthen its own ties with a different center of anti-Saddam power: the Kurds in northern Iraq.

Leaders of the two main Kurdish groups were in close contact with Powell's office, and when the State Department's Near East Bureau suggested in November 2001 that an emissary be sent to meet with them in person, Armitage saw an opportunity to one-up the Pentagon. While the Defense Department was wasting its time with the "Bayswater set," he told aides, referring to the upscale London neighborhood where many of the INC leaders lived, State would be on the ground dealing with "real" people in Iraq. In December, William Burns' deputy, Ryan Crocker, was dispatched to meet with the Kurdish leaders.

Although Armitage kept him apprised of the deputies' increasingly unproductive and fractious sessions, Powell was determined to stay above the fray. As the president's principal foreign policy adviser and the senior member of the Cabinet, he felt that any issue important enough for his direct involvement should be discussed with the principals or with Bush himself rather than underlings in the offices of Cheney and Rumsfeld. He was reluctant to overtly weigh in on military decision making, but his personal Pentagon grapevine was well tended. Powell was rarely in the dark on what was happening on the other side of the Potomac. Many of his senior aides—including Armitage, Green, Smullen, Wilkerson and Assistant Secretary for Legislative Affairs Paul Kelly—were retired military officers with Pentagon contacts of their own.

Once victory in Afghanistan was ensured, Bush had privately instructed

Rumsfeld in late November 2001 to dust off the military's Iraq invasion plans, which had been on the shelf with minimal updates since the 1991 Gulf War. Rumsfeld had delegated the assignment to General Tommy Franks, the CENTCOM commander, with express orders from the president that it be tightly held, Bush later explained, lest, "it would look like . . . I was anxious to go to war."

The subject was not formally brought before the National Security Council until December 28, when Franks traveled to Bush's Crawford ranch to update the vacationing president on his progress. The others sat in via videoconference—Powell, Rice, White House Chief of Staff Andrew Card and George Tenet from the White House Situation Room, Cheney from his vacation home in Wyoming and Rumsfeld from his own ranch house in Taos, New Mexico.

They did not discuss the rationale or advisability of an attack. The case that had been made from the beginning of the administration and reemphasized since September 11, was still on the table: Iraq was a state sponsor of terrorism with an evil regime that brutalized its own people. The president had warned that those who "harbor" terrorists were as guilty and liable for punishment as the terrorists themselves. Saddam Hussein had used chemical weapons in the past, both in his own country and against Iran during the 1980s. Since being driven out of Kuwait in 1991, he had thumbed his nose at a long list of U.N. resolutions. In 1998, he had barred U.N. inspectors looking for the weapons of mass destruction that even the Clinton administration had been convinced were there.

Cheney, in particular, had continued to voice concern over Iraq in his frequent private conversations with Bush, warning that Baghdad could turn its deadly weapons over to al-Qaeda. "The Vice President, after 9/11, clearly saw Saddam Hussein as a threat to peace and was unwavering in his view that Saddam was a real danger," Bush later recalled.

Rumsfeld saw the possibility of attacking Iraq—a far more ambitious prospect than the relatively small-bore war in Afghanistan—as an opportunity to quicken the pace of his proposed defense "transformation." He had told Franks that he wanted the existing Iraq invasion plan replaced with an entirely new concept that would use some of tactics that had worked well in Afghanistan: heavy reliance on sophisticated, well-targeted precision weaponry and Special Forces that would lessen the need for large numbers of combat ground troops. Although Franks hadn't discussed the ultimate goal of the mission with Rumsfeld, he assumed that the objectives were "to remove the regime of Saddam Hussein" and leave behind a unified Iraq with no weapons of mass destruction.

Bush ended the December 28 Crawford session by telling the entire group to "remain optimistic that diplomacy and international pressure will succeed in disarming the regime." His request for invasion plans was precautionary, he said, in case other means failed. "We cannot allow weapons of mass destruction to fall into the hands of terrorists," he told them, repeating Cheney's concerns. "*I* will not allow that to happen." When he and Franks met with reporters after the meeting, Bush said only that they had discussed operations in Afghanistan. He did not mention Iraq, and none of the reporters asked about it.

Planning continued through the winter, as Rumsfeld repeatedly pressed Franks to come up with new "iterations" requiring ever-lower force levels. Powell felt the exercise was prudent but assessed that they were still far from a presidential decision on Iraq or even a workable war plan. U.S. military forces—particularly the Reserves—had been stretched thin by domestic security demands after September 11 and by the Afghanistan campaign. Stocks of sophisticated weaponry were depleted, and the CIA was still struggling to expand its intelligence network inside Iraq. Although the Pentagon estimated that it would be ready to invade by the fall of 2002, it seemed more likely that Bush's decision would be as long as a year away.

Powell buttressed his personal knowledge of the military's deployment constraints with his confidence in Bush's pledge to use diplomacy and international pressure before resorting to force. He was certain there was still plenty of time to get Iraq right; despite Cheney's alarmist claims, he saw no convincing evidence connecting Iraq to al-Qaeda or the September 11 attacks. He was convinced that the best way to prevent proliferation of Iraqi weapons was to get the inspectors back into the country.

But if Bush ultimately did decide an attack was warranted, they would need allies. International resistance to such an endeavor—outright rejection, in some cases—would take time and patience to soften. The whole idea seemed far in the distant and unlikely future. "Iraq isn't going anywhere," he told an interviewer a week after September 11. "It's in a fairly weakened state. It's doing some things we don't like. We'll continue to contain it." He had seen nothing since then to change his mind.

Despite the administration's attempts at secrecy, word of the Pentagon's Iraq war planning quickly reached the media. Far from denying his willingness to consider the use of force, Bush publicly rattled his saber, using his State of the Union Address on January 29, 2002, to warn of an "axis of evil" made up of Iraq, Iran and North Korea. Each of the three, Bush said, was "arming to threaten the peace of our world" with weapons of mass destruction and sponsorship of terrorists. "I will not wait on events, while dangers gather," he said. "I will not stand by, as peril draws closer and closer."

Powell had little taste for such rhetoric. It reminded him of Ronald Reagan's "evil empire," a phrase much beloved by neoconservatives but one he considered unnecessarily provocative and relatively meaningless in the context of the pragmatism he knew had marked U.S.-Soviet relations in the final years of Reagan's presidency. But he saw little reason to press for any rhetorical moderation on Iraq. The public threats, he thought, were not without value. Congress and the American people, as well as potential allies, would begin to wake up and weigh in on the issue before the White House could carry it too far. And there was always the possibility that Saddam Hussein would be sufficiently rattled to agree to new U.N. weapons inspections.

In his public statements, Powell became as belligerent as the next Cabinet official. "The President is examining a full range of options of how to deal with Iraq," he told Congress the week after Bush's "axis" speech. Regime change was "something the United States might have to do alone. How to do it? I would not like to go into any of the details of the options that are being looked at, but it is the most serious assessment of options that one might imagine." But he took care to soften the message with diplomatic reassurances. "It doesn't mean that an invasion is imminent," Powell told the *Financial Times* just days after his congressional testimony. Sanctions and support for the Iraqi opposition were still firm pillars of administration policy, he said, and "if there is ever a point where we believe it's necessary to do something else, we'll do it. But one shouldn't think that there is some plan on the President's desk now waiting for him to sign off on. There is not."

Immediately after the State of the Union speech, Cheney's office announced he would make a twelve-nation swing through the Middle East in mid-March to consult on antiterrorism issues. Having served as defense secretary during the 1991 Gulf War and later as president of Halliburton, which did a lot of business in Arab countries, the vice president "knows the region well and has many long-standing relationships with people in these countries," a Cheney aide told reporters.

White House officials made clear that the underlying purpose of the trip was to solicit Arab support for regime change in Baghdad. Among the scheduled stops were at least nine nations deemed potentially willing to assist in the effort—Egypt, Oman, the United Arab Emirates, Saudi Arabia, Bahrain, Qatar, Jordan, Israel and Turkey. Although none of them would publicly declare their support for an invasion, General Franks told Cheney in a top secret briefing he and Rumsfeld had prepared, most of them would be happy to see Saddam gone.

But as the trip approached, Arab governments evinced far less interest in talking about Iraq than about the conflagration in the West Bank and the Bush administration's minimal efforts to stop Israeli aggression. As Powell and the State Department had warned repeatedly, the plight of the Palestinians came first in the Arab world, if only because regional governments saw it as a useful distraction from domestic political pressures for reform. After keeping the erupting Middle East at arm's length since the suspension of Zinni's mission, Bush decided it was time to send him back to the region.

In a hastily arranged Rose Garden news conference on March 7—three days before Cheney's scheduled departure—the president announced Zinni's return and publicly recast the purpose of the vice president's trip away from the war on terrorism and toward what he said was an ongoing effort to bring "peace and stability" to Israelis and Palestinians.

Standing at the president's side with Cheney, Powell said little. It was enough that the White House had finally gotten the message. Whatever Cheney planned to tell the Arabs about Iraq, he thought to himself with some satisfaction, the vice president was about to get an earful on the importance of the Mideast peace process.

At first, Cheney's Mideast marathon seemed to spark some forward movement. As Zinni negotiated between the Israelis and Palestinians on the ground, Arab leaders meeting in Beirut approved a proposal by Saudi Crown Prince Abdullah to exchange Arab recognition of and peace with Israel for Israel's withdrawal from the West Bank territories it had seized in the 1967 "Six-Day War." The Arab initiative was vague and incomplete, but at least it signaled that the leaders were working toward a solution. On the morning of March 27, Rice gave an upbeat report to Bush and the just-returned vice president in the Oval Office. As he left to give a speech in South Carolina, the president was optimistic about the issue for the first time in months.

That evening, however, all optimism was shattered when a suicide bomber detonated a massive explosion at a restaurant in the Israeli coastal city of Netanya. Thirty people, most of them gathered for a Passover Seder, were killed, and more than a hundred others were injured. Israel responded in a fury with massive new troop movements into West Bank cities, starting with increased fortifications surrounding Arafat's Ramallah headquarters. Tanks rolled into Bethlehem, the home of numerous Christian holy sites, and trapped two hundred Palestinian fighters and dozens of Franciscan monks inside the Church of the Nativity. But while Bush initially voiced support for what he called "Israeli self-defense," it quickly became apparent that the world—and the Arab world in particular—was expecting more from the American president.

On April 1, Bush convened an NSC meeting to consider two proposals for action. One was a presidential speech that would demonstrate his concern and outline a way forward. The other was an emergency visit to the region by the secretary of state.

Rumsfeld was against the idea of a trip. They shouldn't waste Powell's stature on something that was hopeless, he argued, and this situation clearly was. Powell's antennae immediately perked up at the uncharacteristic display of what he tartly characterized to himself as "Don's Christian compassion," and he quickly concluded that it was just another backdoor attempt to talk Bush out of engagement. But "the president knew he had to do something because they were just killing him on this," Powell later recalled. "And he said, 'No, I want Colin to go.' "

When the meeting ended, Powell walked with Bush back toward the Oval Office. In the West Wing hallway between Rice's door and that of the vice president, Bush turned and looked at him. "I really need you to do this for me," the president said. "I know how hard it's going to be. It's going to be very bad. But you've got enough standing...you'll get burned, but you can handle it. There'll be enough of you left when it's over."

Bush wanted the problem to go away but had no clear sense of how to make it happen. Rice felt bad for Powell, she later told him, but they didn't have any better ideas. The situation was falling apart, and an all-out war could erupt. At the very least, she thought, Powell would be "a calming presence" in the region and would "show that America cared."

The administration's unwillingness to set any more specific goals for the trip gave Powell pause, but he had been impressed by Bush's admission of need and willingness to plunge ahead. "Don didn't want to touch it," he recalled. "Dick didn't want to touch it. Nobody wanted to touch it, and Condi doesn't have sympathy for this account. But the president stuck with it."

Powell thought that Bush had a bad habit of driving headlong down blind alleys or going along for the ride when policy was being driven by Cheney, often with Rumsfeld in the jump seat. But at least the president was usually willing to apply the brakes before crashing into a wall, and he seemed to understand that his secretary of state was there to steer him back toward a reasonable course. As Powell and others anxious about Bush's sense of direction saw it, that was what had happened in a series of first-year crises—the initial hard lines on China and on troop withdrawal from Bosnia, the refusal to talk to North Korea and the move toward peremptory withdrawal from the ABM Treaty. In each case, Powell saw himself as having brought the president back from the brink of disaster. Sometimes he failed, as he had with the Geneva Conventions dispute. But he felt he was succeeding, in fits and starts, with the Mideast peace process.

Serving as a brake on rash presidential actions and misguided policies was not the forward-looking role Powell had envisioned for himself as the nation's chief diplomat. But as time went on he had begun to see it as an honorable and indispensable service to Bush and to the nation. If he sometimes ended his days in frustration, he still generally awoke each morning with a sense of purpose and new possibilities. It was in his nature to see most glasses as half full and not to dwell on setbacks.

Bush returned to the Rose Garden on April 4, 2002, to reaffirm that "the outlines of a just settlement are clear.... Two states, Israel and Palestine, living side by side, in peace and security." Yasser Arafat had promised to control terror attacks but had failed. "I call on the Palestinian people, the Palestinian Authority and our friends in the Arab world to join us in delivering a clear message to the terrorists: blowing yourself up does not help the Palestinian cause. To the contrary, suicide bombing missions could well blow up the best and only hope for a Palestinian state." Israel, he said, "faces hard choices of its own." There must be a stop to Israeli "incursions into Palestinian-controlled areas," a freeze in the expansion of Jewish settlements and an end to the "daily humiliation" endured by peaceful Palestinians living under Israeli occupation.

"I expect results," the president averred.

Turning to his secretary of state beside him, Bush announced that Powell was on his way to the region "to seek broad international support for the vision I've outlined today." The secretary would work to implement "an immediate and meaningful cease-fire; an end to terror and violence and incitement; withdrawal of Israeli troops from Palestinian cities, including Ramallah; [and] implementation of the already agreed-upon Mitchell and Tenet plans, which will lead to a peaceful settlement." After Powell briefed journalists in the White House press room following the speech, Bush spokesman Ari Fleischer decreed that the secretary of state could not be quoted by name. The president had spoken, Fleischer said, and statements by anyone else would detract from his message.

There was little meat on the bones of Bush's "vision." In a series of high-level meetings before his departure, Powell found himself repeatedly fending off attempts to tie his hands. Israel had prohibited entry into Arafat's besieged compound, and the White House was not eager to legitimize the Palestinian leader by demanding that Sharon allow a personal visit from Bush's representative. Powell argued that it was impossible for him to meet with Sharon but not with Arafat. Reports from Ramallah described a desperate situation there, with no electricity or fresh water. Powell needed to check on Arafat's physical condition even as he delivered him a stern message. Besides, he reasoned, appearing to let the Israelis tell the United States what to do was hardly a useful message to send the Arabs. The day after Bush's Rose Garden statement, however, Fleischer told reporters that Powell had "no plans to meet" with Arafat since the secretary would be seeing only "leaders in the region who continue to work for peace."

Powell planned a first stop in Madrid for multilateral talks with Javier Solana, the European Union foreign policy chief; U.N. Secretary-General Kofi Annan; and Russian Foreign Minister Igor Ivanov. All were critics of the Bush administration's performance in the Middle East, and Powell hoped to persuade them to join forces in a common strategy for peace. It was an idea that had already occurred to Annan, who had developed a close relationship with Powell. Both men knew that one of the reasons it had been so hard for the allies to work together was that the Israelis and Palestinians played them off against one another. If the United States, the United Nations, the European Union and the Russians could unite, Sharon and Arafat would have nowhere else to turn. Powell additionally hoped that the backing of other players would provide ballast for his arguments inside the administration.

One proposal discussed by the newly formed Madrid "Quartet" was a conference of Mideast leaders under its auspices. The idea was to hold a meeting along the lines of the one cosponsored by the United States and Russia during the presidency of Bush's father, which had led to nearly a decade of relative peace. But the younger President Bush, who had traveled to Texas for a meeting with British Prime Minister Tony Blair at his Crawford ranch as Powell left for the Mideast, told a television interviewer that he saw little point in holding a "summit."

"I was going to try to see if I could get some discussion ... going," Powell later recalled. "I thought it would be useful to hold out the promise of some kind of conference." But "as my plane was taking off, there were people back here shooting it down. 'No conference. Shouldn't talk to Arafat. Shouldn't do this, shouldn't do that.'

"I was on my own. I kept making up stuff, and every time I made stuff up and sent it back for clearance, I'd get a lot of rudder checks about 'Don't do that.' " Before embarking, he had tried to lower expectations by saying publicly that he did not anticipate coming back with a peace agreement. "I may not even have a cease-fire in hand," he warned.

Zinni thought Powell's trip was a bad idea. The Israelis were almost as stunned and angered by the Passover bombing as Americans had been by the September 11 attacks. Sharon, with widespread support from the Israeli public, had ignored Bush's call to withdraw his troops from the West Bank. Arafat was full of promises but had taken no visible steps to deal with Hamas and Islamic Jihad, the two organizations responsible for most of the suicide attacks. It was becoming increasingly clear that neither leader was capable of constructing a lasting peace—Arafat would never take the first steps to get the process under way, and Sharon would never make the territorial concessions necessary to complete it. But innocent people on both sides were suffering and dying, and the situations in Ramallah and Bethlehem had become untenable. By the time Powell finally arrived in Israel on April 12, Zinni had changed his mind. "I think [Powell] felt, we all felt, that this was a last chance."

Powell made it clear to Sharon that he expected unfettered access to Arafat, and on April 14 he traveled to Ramallah in an armed convoy. Most of the buildings in the Palestinian compound had been reduced to rubble, and the bare ground was littered with the skeletons of burned vehicles. Israeli tanks and troops had blocked access to the only structure left standing, where Arafat was holed up with dozens of aides and—Israel claimed—a collection of wanted terrorists who had taken refuge in the basement. Powell, Zinni and William Burns walked five hundred yards across a no-man's-land under the gaze of heavily armed, black-garbed Israeli SWAT teams and snipers from both sides. Powell had insisted that they travel without bulletproof vests; they were diplomats, he said, not combatants.

Inside the compound, the smell of unwashed bodies and garbage was overpowering. Zinni thought all the Palestinians looked as though they were on their last legs—until they reached an ebullient Arafat, who pumped their hands and cheerfully exclaimed, "I am under siege!"

During five days of diplomacy that included side trips to Syria and Lebanon, Powell met twice with Arafat. He had always found the Palestinian leader politically untrustworthy and personally unsavory. Arafat promised everything but produced nothing. Invariably dressed in olive drab fatigues, with his trademark stubble and a traditional *kaffiyeh* on his head, he would always try to sidle up to Powell as a "fellow general." On Powell's second visit, the day before he was scheduled to return to Washington, he led Arafat away from his aides and into a side room.

"There is no one left in Washington who will talk to you," he told the Palestinian leader soberly. "You have got to change." If Arafat didn't give him anything to work with, he warned prophetically, it was likely to be the last time they would ever see each other.

The White House's interest in allowing Powell to take risks or spend Bush's political capital on the Mideast conflict had been minimal at the start of his trip. By the end, it was nonexistent. Armitage, manning the ship of State at home, relayed comments passed along to him by journalists: unnamed "senior administration sources" were telling them that the secretary was overcommitting the president, showing too much deference to the wrong people and accomplishing little on his trip. Powell's meetings with Arafat and a side visit to Syria, which openly aided the Hezbollah militia in Lebanon and Palestinian militant groups, were seen by conservatives as confirmation that he had fallen under the sway of suspected Arab sympathizers in the State Department.

Powell was scrupulous about informing the White House, usually through Rice, about what he was doing whenever he traveled overseas. Some of his internal critics saw the national security adviser herself as overly chummy with the secretary of state. No one knew "the number of times [Powell] had informal conversations with Condi," a conservative senior official later assessed. "The times when he said, 'Okay, Condi, I think I'm going to do this...' and she'd say, 'Okay, go ahead and do it.' And then Rumsfeld and Cheney would wake up and say, 'What? Where did this come from?' It happened over and over again."

In many of his conversations with Rice, however, Powell was on the receiving end of expressions of concern. He assumed that her admonitions, sometimes approaching actual dressings-down, reflected "the views of somebody in the White House" that were not necessarily her own. The Mideast trip was "ten of the most miserable days imaginable," he later recalled, and not only because of the intransigence of Sharon and Arafat. Rice was on the telephone constantly, both directly and through Armitage, worrying that Powell was going too far and telling him to hold back.

On the night of April 16, as he prepared to leave Israel for home the next day, the calls came nonstop. He had little to show for the mission; despite Bush's demands, Israeli officials had withdrawn only a small number of troops from the West Bank and were continuing their sieges of Ramallah and Bethlehem. Although Arafat had publicly criticized the terrorist attacks under pressure from Powell, suicide bombings continued. When a bomb exploded during Powell's visit, he raced to the site and issued his own condemnation. Despite the White House's disapproval, he had spoken publicly of a possible "regional or international conference" that would include both Israeli and Palestinian officials, and he planned to make the same point in his departure statement the next day.

"The White House went crazy when they heard what I was going to say," Powell recalled. "They said, 'Why don't you just leave?'"

"I've been here for ten days," Powell said he replied. "I'm the secretary of state. I'm representing the president. He sent me over here. I can't just say, 'It's been nice,' sign the guest book and leave." He could practically hear the growling and gnashing of teeth over the telephone.

He worked through the night and into the early hours of the morning, struggling to craft a statement that would be acceptable both to the White House and to his own sense of what needed to be said, giving both sides of the conflict a message that was simultaneously stern and hopeful. To the aides traveling with the secretary, it was a painful exercise to witness.

Powell was his own best speechwriter, and the result was a masterful but vague commitment to keep on trying. He would discuss the idea of a regional conference with Bush as soon as he arrived in Washington, he said. Zinni and Burns would stay behind to continue working, and "I plan to return to the region and move ahead on all aspects of our comprehensive approach."

The day after his return to Washington, Powell met with Bush in the Oval Office. Reporters were ushered briefly into the room as the two sat before the fireplace, and one asked the president whether he supported an "international peace conference." Bush ignored the question and reiterated his determination to fight terror around the world. Ariel Sharon, he said in response to another question, was a "man of peace."

Less than three weeks after Bush had warned that he "expected results" in the Middle East, there were none to show. Sharon's troops were still in place despite Bush's demand for withdrawal "without delay," and the Palestinian violence continued unabated. Suddenly, the president who had appeared so forceful and confident in the months after September 11 seemed overwhelmed and unable to find his footing on this and a range of other foreign policy issues.

Afghanistan, once seen as a rousing success, was becoming an irritant.

Osama bin Laden and most of his top lieutenants remained at large, and the multinational coalition was arguing over how to move forward with a lasting security system for the country. Bush's promised reconstruction of the Afghan infrastructure and economy had yet to get off the ground. At the same time, trade agreements promised to a number of countries had failed to materialize. Bush's initiative on immigration, like nearly everything else outside the war on terrorism, had stalled. While Powell was out of the country in April, the White House had embarrassed itself by tacitly supporting a coup against Venezuelan President Hugo Chávez that had ultimately failed. Brent Scowcroft, Bush 41's national security adviser and a highly respected foreign policy analyst in Washington, observed that the administration seemed "in real danger of being overextended."

Bush was wedged between the Arabs' demands for a firm plan and a timetable for progress toward Palestinian statehood—along with nudges from Powell and the Europeans not to drop the ball—and insistence by his political supporters at home on wholehearted support for Israel. *The Weekly Standard* accused the administration of deviating from the moral absolutism of the war on terrorism with "ham-handed" efforts to "appease" the Arabs at Israel's expense. Karl Rove, Bush's political adviser, warned the president that Powell's visits with the highly unpopular Arafat had already caused slippage in the public's view of Republican officials.

The effort to juggle Mideast policy nearly collapsed on April 25, when Saudi Crown Prince Abdullah arrived for a visit with Bush at his Crawford ranch. The meeting—with Cheney, Rice and Powell in attendance—had been scheduled weeks earlier as part of Bush's then-newfound activism. But Abdullah, tacitly exerting the leverage of Saudi Arabia's massive oil reserves and its geographic importance to a potential Iraq invasion, made clear from the outset that he was disappointed in Bush's lack of Mideast follow-through. He brought a book of photographs and presented the president with a videotape of scenes of Palestinians' distress and outraged reaction on Arab streets.

Over lunch, Abdullah listened while Bush spoke vaguely about the difficulties of making progress and Cheney began to shift the subject toward Iraq. The crown prince said that he appreciated the conversation but had come for answers. "I can't go back empty-handed," he complained. What, exactly, was Bush going to do about the crisis and, most immediately, about Arafat's ongoing encirclement in Ramallah?

As Bush again began to temporize about the difficulties, Abdullah waved his hand dismissively and said he had heard enough. Calling to his aides to prepare his private jet, he gathered his flowing robes around him and announced that the meeting was over. It was a ploy the Saudis had planned among themselves in advance, and Abdullah's translator, as scripted, quickly interjected that perhaps the discussants should take a break. They all rose from the table and retreated to separate corners.

"It was an ugly scene," Powell later recalled. He walked outside and accosted Prince Bandar, the Saudi ambassador, shouting, "What the hell did you do? How did you let it get to this?" Bandar shouted back, and Bush came out to investigate the commotion. Eventually, Powell joined Abdullah and his foreign minister, Saud al-Faisal, back inside. "Whatever disappointment you're carrying around, you can't walk out," he told the Saudi leader, with Bandar interpreting into Arabic. "You can't go. You can't do it to us . . . to yourselves . . . to the Palestinians. This would be an absolute disaster." They sat and talked for nearly half an hour, joined by Rice.

Having made their point, the Saudis returned to the table. "The next thing you know, they were all hugging and kissing each other, and the president goes into the room and the crown prince says, 'I love you like a son,' " Powell recalled.

The administration had its own problems with the Saudis. The country was ruled by a self-appointed monarchy that remained in power by appeasing Islamic fundamentalists. They had been less than fully cooperative in the investigation of the Saudi nationals who had hijacked the September 11 flights. Abdullah's defense of the Palestinians was a disingenuous distraction from his government's own problems. But he had successfully called Bush's bluff. Although administration officials professed no recollection of the line, one Saudi present at the meeting later insisted that the president had turned to Rice during the final round of hugs and kisses and told her to "call Sharon and tell him my ass is on the line."

The weeks and months that followed Powell's Mideast trip were a blur of diplomatic and political activity. Sharon and Arab leaders leapfrogged one another with visits to Washington, and the competing sides of Bush's national security team vied to turn the president in one direction or the other. Powell and the State Department's Near East Bureau had some successes, convincing Bush to personally press Sharon to end the Ramallah and Bethlehem sieges and to push for a timeline of steps by both sides. The Palestinians were less than helpful; a suicide bomb exploded in May while Sharon was sitting in the Oval Office with Bush. Cheney, Rumsfeld and their deputies continued to advocate giving the Israelis wide latitude to expand their military operations, a view seen as more consistent with both the war on terrorism and domestic political priorities.

When Bush finally emerged on June 24 to fill in the blank spaces of his Mideast "vision," the speech he gave was clearly the product of unresolved internal disagreement. It began with a demand that the Palestinians replace Arafat with new elected leaders "not compromised by terror." He still anticipated the creation of a Palestinian state, Bush said, but the United States would not support its establishment "until its leaders engage in a sustained fight against the terrorists and dismantle their infrastructure." In the second half of his speech, he reiterated his months-old demand that Israel withdraw its troops from the Palestinian territories and called for an Israeli commitment, once the Palestinians had resolved their leadership problems, to negotiate a secure and fair border.

"With intensive effort by all," he said, a "final-status agreement" between the two sides could be achieved "within three years from now. And I and my country will actively lead toward that goal." Powell spent the afternoon telephoning reporters to make sure they wrote about more than the explosive first half of Bush's remarks. There was real substance in the speech for the Palestinian side, too, he insisted.

However actively Bush may have intended to lead, he fell far short of his stated objective. Over the rest of his first term in office, there would be many other U.S. pronouncements on the Mideast peace process and demands for progress. A painstakingly composed "road map" for settling security and political issues was eventually formulated by the "Quartet" Powell had established in Madrid. Arafat was ultimately replaced by other leaders, although he remained the power behind the Palestinian throne until his death in late 2004.

The eight months between November 2001 and June 2002 had been a high point of U.S. efforts to find a solution to the conflict. But by the end of Powell's tenure as secretary of state, Israel and the Palestinians would be no closer to permanent peace than they had been at the start.

For Powell, it became an exercise in futility. Occasional glimmers of hope were repeatedly snuffed out in equal measure by the intransigence of the parties on the ground and the deadlock within the administration. The White House's early desire to hold the peace process at arm's length had been briefly overcome after September 11 by concerns that the unresolved conflict would interfere with the war on terrorism. But by the time of Bush's June 2002 speech, plans for an invasion of Iraq were well under way, drowning out any argument about the importance of making real progress on the peace process before invading an Arab country.

Instead, Bush came to subscribe to the belief long espoused by neocon-servatives that Baghdad was a first and necessary stop on the road to peace in Jerusalem. In a combination of ideological conviction and economic realpolitik, they posited that the replacement of one Arab dictatorship with a democracy would break the region's autocratic tradition and serve as a transforming example for the rest. Several countries were candidates for regime change: Syria, Libya, even Iran, an Islamic state bordering Arab lands. But Iraq, with its unquestionably brutal dictator and history of regional aggression, its well-educated population and its massive oil reserves, was seen as the perfect place to start.

As Richard Perle explained, "If a tyrant like Saddam Hussein can be brought down, others are going to begin to think ... [and] begin to act, to bring down the tyrants who are afflicting them [all] in pretty much the same way." Nervous regional despots would then "accelerate whatever efforts they might make anyway to reform themselves internally and to open their political process." The result would be a fundamental change in the Arab-Israeli dynamic.

The neoconservative thesis reinforced Bush's own post–September 11 belief that his administration had a singular "calling," as the president often described it, to rid the world of terrorists and replace dictators with democrats, by force if necessary. "I think the JINSA crowd had a lot to say about it," Powell later reflected on the White House's attitude toward the peace process. Bush "saw Sharon fighting terrorism, he saw bombs going off in Israel. That affected him deeply. Israel was a democracy! Freedom! And he saw all of these Arab states that were not democracies."

18

Nothing else holds the special excitement of a rumored resignation. The problem was that a line of thought had grown up in Washington that if you don't like what's going on, then you should pull out.

—George P. Shultz

I understand that every couple of weeks, whenever somebody makes a determination that something didn't go my way—whether it did or not—there's an obligation to write something that suggests I'm ready to go off the cliff." Powell was visibly annoyed as he stood in the aisle of the secretary of state's official aircraft and lectured reporters embarking with him on a ten-day, eight-country trip to Asia. The immediate cause of his irritation was a front-page article in the previous day's *New York Times* headlined "Embattled, Scrutinized, Powell Soldiers On." It was one of many on the same theme published during the last week of July 2002 as the latest round of speculation about his future got under way.

Why was it, Powell asked, that when *he* won a round at the White House there was no speculation about who *else* might resign in protest?

"I serve the president," he repeated in what had become a well-worn response to questions about his standing within the administration, "and I can assure you he's pleased."

But as the plane crossed the Atlantic into the night sky, what the reporters really wanted to know was whether Powell himself was pleased. His life in the Bush administration had to be dispiriting. How could he *not* be unhappy with the president's June decision to suspend the Mideast peace process until the Palestinians got rid of Yasser Arafat? And just a few days ago, Bush had cut off U.S. funds for an international family planning program that Powell had personally praised, after antiabortion groups had objected to it.

"Do I wish everybody always agreed with me?" he asked. "Yes. But I don't find this all so rare and unusual." He had spent nearly twenty years working at the highest levels of government, and there were always internal disagreements, he reminded the journalists. "I can hold my own."

It was a rare display of defensive pique from a man who refused to publicly acknowledge the existence of the Washington parlor game of "who's up, who's down." He liked to look forward, not back, Powell often said. "Colin Powell's Rules," the list of maxims that were still handed out by his office upon request, were mostly cheery and optimistic. But he had other, unprinted rules that served him equally well. At the top of that list was "Never let them see you sweat."

Powell's outburst shortly after departure was the last visible drop of perspiration for the remainder of the Asia trip. By the time he reached his first stop the next morning, in India, he appeared to have left his irritation half a world behind. Rushing from private meetings to press conferences over the next ten days, he juggled the ongoing dispute between India and Pakistan and discussed terror, trade and military aid during brief touchdowns in Thailand, Malaysia, Singapore, Indonesia and the Philippines.

Alma had come along for the ride but kept her own itinerary. On the plane between stops, she stayed in the forward cabin as Colin made frequent forays, in his stocking feet and wrapped in a sweater or a windbreaker, into the separate staff and press compartments. Whether huddling in the aisle with aides or chatting and swapping off-color jokes with whoever happened to be awake as the plane hurtled through the sky, he was in unfailing good humor. The tour of Asia was a rare chance to conduct real diplomacy, free from the constant gaze of critics and backstabbers back in Washington.

His official meetings went well, and the press was favorable. In most of the Asian capitals, Powell's motorcade swept through streets lined with smiling people eager for a glimpse of the celebrity diplomat. At U.S. Embassy staff receptions held in his honor, he stood patiently for snapshots, his arm around the shoulders of an endless procession of secretaries, gardeners and security guards.

The high point of the trip was a two-day stop at the annual meeting of Southeast Asian foreign ministers in Brunei, the Delaware-sized sultanate on the northern edge of the Indonesian island of Borneo. In addition to nailing down a tough new regional security agreement, Powell held a groundbreaking meeting with his counterpart from North Korea. It had been more than a year since the administration had finished reviewing its North Korea policy and announced—as Powell had proposed in the spring of 2001 before being contradicted by the White

House—that it was willing to open bilateral talks. But the policy had stalled as first Pyongyang, then Washington, balked at setting up an initial meeting. Knowing that Foreign Minister Paek Nam Sun was going to be in Brunei, Powell decided to arrange a symbolic informal chat over coffee.

The meeting had not been vetted by the principals, and administration hard-liners were caught off guard by an initiative they assumed had been cooked up by Powell alone. He had, in fact, discussed the idea with Rice, but it had been closely held to give the White House plausible deniability in case it blew up in Powell's face. The president had to deal with conflicting constituencies at home, and the secretary of state considered it part of his job to serve as Bush's "wind dummy" to check the prevailing breeze. "I'm *supposed* to go out and do these things, and if I get picked off first base, I get picked off first base," he said. It was a time-honored maneuver that Powell sometimes used with his own staff when he didn't want to get too far out in front on an issue. In this case it succeeded—for a brief period, at least—in jump-starting the dialogue with North Korea. It may have left some in Washington "grinding their molars," he said, but there had been no criticism from the president.

The annual Asia conference traditionally ended with a dinner and skits in which the foreign ministers entertained one another by good-naturedly making fools of themselves. At her final appearance in 2000, Madeleine Albright had donned a bowler hat and sung "Thanks for the Memories." Powell, in 2001, had invited ridicule with an off-key version of "El Paso"—the Marty Robbins song he had sung to South Vietnamese soldiers in the A Shau Valley forty years earlier. A tape had immediately been leaked to CNN and broadcast around the world.

This year, extensive preparation had gone into his performance, whose central joke involved videotaped appeals from Bush, Armitage, Alma and a throng of poster-waving ersatz demonstrators arranged outside the State Department—all insisting that Powell save the nation from humiliation by not performing. But Powell, the story line went, had insisted. When the video ended, the lights went up to reveal Powell on stage with a microphone in his hand and a chorus of his senior staff snapping their fingers and shuffling behind him as he warbled "Some Enchanted Evening" in a passable baritone.

He went straight from the dinner to his departing aircraft, still laughing and so pleased with himself that he decided to stage a reprise for the aides and journalists who had not been invited to the dinner. As the plane rose over the South China Sea toward his next stop, a video player and microphone were hooked up and the secretary of state danced and sang in the aisle between the bulkhead and the bathrooms.

His portrayal as a disgruntled passenger on a never-ending roller-coaster ride within the Bush administration was a distraction made all the more irritating because the media, in Powell's view, frequently muddied the facts. It was true that Bush's June 24 speech on the Israeli-Palestinian conflict had been the subject of long and difficult negotiations between the State Department and the rest of the national security team. But Powell thought he had come out even, with equal emphasis given to getting rid of Arafat, restraining the Israelis and promoting Palestinian statehood.

The flap over the United States' contributions to the U.N. Population Fund, he thought, was a nonstory. He chose his battles carefully and had decided long before to avoid emphasizing his disagreements with Bush and the Republican Party over social issues. When he once let an opinion slip—telling a global audience on the MTV youth music channel that anyone who was sexually active should use condoms to protect against HIV infection—many of the president's most ardent conservative backers had accused him of encouraging unmarried sex and demanded he be fired or at least made to apologize. Instead, the White House simply pretended he hadn't said it. When the administration went on one of its rampages against family planning aid, he had learned, it was easier to quietly redirect the targeted foreign assistance to another equally worthy overseas cause.

But Powell's insistence that he won more battles than he lost was not the way many in Washington and the rest of the world saw it. However self-assured the secretary of state was, the "odd man out" portrayals that had diminished in the wake of September 11 had now resurfaced. Visiting foreign officials and ambassadors made sure that their official conversations with the Bush administration extended beyond the State Department. "It was not a happy circumstance," recalled a senior U.N. official. "In previous administrations you might have had three centers of power—the White House, State and the Pentagon. Now you had a fourth—the vice president's office. It is a very complex terrain for foreigners to deal with when they come in for a quick visit of a day or two. They want to see the secretary of state and Condi Rice, if possible. But it became clear after a while that State didn't speak for the administration." Whenever his own envoys returned from lower-level meetings to report Washington's agreement on a particular issue, the U.N. official said, the first question he asked became "Was somebody from the White House there, or was it only State?"

Many of the top foreign officials Powell dealt with believed that his worldview was closer to their own than to what they encountered elsewhere in the administration. They pored over his comments and analyzed his demeanor for confirmation. He never spoke in overt opposition to administration policies on the Middle East, acknowledged one foreign minister who met with Powell frequently on the subject, "but he's said many things that are clearly understood to mean that." Yet as the views of European nations and other allies began to diverge ever more sharply from those of Washington, Powell's artful defense of the White House's policies began to make them wonder if he had been assigned the role of "good cop" and sent to soothe their concerns while those with real power disregarded them.

Some of Powell's closest overseas counterparts told themselves and one another that they would resign in protest rather than tolerate what they assumed Powell put up with. Searching for an explanation, they speculated that his military background made him unwilling to question orders or that any black man who reached the top in America must have done so by toeing the line.

"I'm sure, when he declared he was a Republican in 1995, he did not expect this brand of Republicans to come to the White House," one foreign minister mused. "But still, as secretary of state, I think he allowed other departments to interfere in the process in a way they shouldn't have. Of course, the president has allowed them to do so. He should have gone to the president and said, 'Look, I'm the secretary of state, not these guys. If you don't want me, I'll get out. But as long as I'm secretary of state, this is how things should be.'

"Maybe he did," the minister concluded with a contemplative shrug.

Armitage fretted that Powell's arm's-length relationship with Bush was exacting a heavy toll on both the administration's policies and his friend's reputation. "He never had a bad relationship with the president," Armitage later explained. But "I felt sometimes that the president himself viewed Powell almost the way he viewed his father, as an elder . . . it wasn't a question of [Bush] not liking him; it was 'He's kind of my father's generation,'" even though Powell was closer in age to the younger Bush. Cheney advanced his views through daily access to the president, and Armitage was sure that Rumsfeld had regular private meetings at the White House. The defense secretary's pithy, one-page memos regularly made their way to the president's desk. Lengthy State Department analyses, their authors feared, ended up in the Oval Office trash can.

For his own part, Powell remained confident that the real Bush was the one he had seen and heard during their first extensive foreign policy discussion, at their one-on-one dinner the December after the election. On the rare occasions when they spoke privately, there was evidence that Bush listened to, and even acted on, the secretary of state's advice. "The President has good instincts...an instinctual grasp" of issues, Powell often told his skeptical aides. But he usually followed that assessment by noting that Bush "has got these rough edges—his cowboy, Texan rough edges—and when he gets them exposed, there are other people who know how to use them" to their advantage.

At Armitage's urging during the summer of 2002, Powell began to request regular meetings with the president outside the NSC structure—twenty or thirty minutes a week with just Rice present. One of these sessions was scheduled to take place on August 5, the day after Powell's return from Asia, to talk about Iraq. He knew that no decision on an invasion had been made, he told Rice, but he was concerned that the president wasn't getting all the information he needed on the options before him.

Although the administration publicly described its work on Iraq as contingency planning that was far from the point of decision, let alone implementation, activity had expanded rapidly on all fronts during the first half of 2002. General Franks continued refining his invasion plan, urged by Rumsfeld to make it smaller and quicker and with the shortest possible launch time once the president gave the order to attack. In one version presented to Bush on July 19, Franks said he had been steadily moving forces into Kuwait and now had two brigades on the ground. Within three weeks, he said, two more brigades could be in place, and, along with a Marine unit already stationed nearby, the ground force would approach 50,000, enough for a running start across the Iraqi border. Another two divisions could arrive within an additional two to three weeks, for a total of more than 100,000 troops to march to Baghdad from the south.

Powell later recalled that he was "always uneasy about the low numbers." "They were making up for mass with technology and speed and cleverness and special operations, [assuming that] what they did in Afghanistan they can repeat in Iraq." Yet the two countries, and situations, were vastly different—one rural and backward, the other highly organized with a sophisticated, albeit degraded, army.

Goldwater-Nichols, the 1986 defense reorganization act, had streamlined the chain of command from the president through the defense secretary and directly to the unified commanders. But it also made the chairman of the Joint Chiefs of Staff the president's principal military adviser. General Richard Myers, the current chairman, did not seem to be a major factor in the administration's Iraq planning, and Powell worried that the service chiefs had been cut out of the process altogether. Even Cheney, as defense secretary, had given then-Chairman Powell a far freer rein than Rumsfeld appeared to give Myers. What Myers might have done with additional authority was an open question; as an Army man, Powell questioned the Air Force general's knowledge of the requirements of a ground war. He had a great deal of respect for Franks and assumed the CENTCOM commander knew what he was doing, but Franks and Rumsfeld seemed to be the only ones at the Pentagon with any real input to the president.

The lead-up to the 1991 Gulf War had been a starkly different process: different personalities and a different style of analysis, presentation and decision making. Powell was not at all sure that the current state of affairs was serving the president, or the nation, well. In "his" war, Powell had been the main military conduit to both the secretary of defense and the president, and General Norman Schwarzkopf at CENTCOM had spent the five months of military buildup in the Persian Gulf region with his troops. It was Powell who had conducted the briefings in Washington and answered the president's questions. He considered it a major part of his job at the time to restrain Bush 41's eagerness to take action until all options were considered, a broad international coalition was assembled, the forces were readied and an exit strategy was assured.

Franks made several trips to visit the new U.S. headquarters established in Qatar, along the Persian Gulf, and he checked in regularly with Arab leaders in the region. But for the most part, he seemed to Powell to be at Rumsfeld's constant beck and call, running up to Washington every few days from CENTCOM headquarters in Tampa to brief the defense secretary or the White House on each new wrinkle in the war plan. If Schwarzkopf had been given that kind of access to the White House during the 1991 war run-up, "he and I probably would have killed each other," Powell later reflected wryly. "We know each other well, but we are remarkably different guys and we had a good understanding about it. It was my job to convey to the president and to the secretary what Norm thought we should do. Getting to what Norm thought we ought to do took a lot of work between me and Norm, because I didn't always agree with him. And I used my staff, and the Joint Chiefs, in a different way than [General] Myers." Powell knew from the military grapevine that the service chiefs—particularly Army General Eric Shinseki—were concerned about the direction of the war planning and felt shunted aside by Rumsfeld.

Powell assumed that Rumsfeld's reported disdain for the uniformed military hierarchy at the Pentagon had a lot to do with him. Cheney, Rumsfeld and their top aides, he knew, considered him "the anti-Christ"—the general who had accumulated too much power as chairman and used it to argue against the 1991 Gulf War. It was widely believed in Washington that Rumsfeld owed his selection as defense secretary in large part to Cheney's desire to limit Powell's influence at the Pentagon.

Powell considered the stories about his role in the Bush 41 administration to be revisionist history. "Where I really got my authority and influence [as chairman] was from my relationship with Dick Cheney," he contended. "If Dick Cheney didn't want me to use what Goldwater-Nichols gave me, he would have—" Powell drew his finger across his throat in an "off with his head" gesture. "He was quick to tell me when I was off the farm."

As the administration's war planning progressed in 2002, Powell was constrained as much by his own respect for the chain of command as by Cheney and Rumsfeld's desire to keep him out of it. "I'm the secretary of state, not the defense secretary or the chairman of the Joint Chiefs or the national security adviser," he would admonish his aides when they expressed concern over Iraq. Among the principals, he emphasized the importance of getting "the right number of troops," but he did not press the issue or offer his own estimate of what that number might be. Whatever Powell thought of Rumsfeld and his acolytes, he was reluctant to second-guess Franks. "Tommy Franks is no rookie," he said. Franks had studied the same military doctrines as he had, and "Tommy was the one coming forward with the numbers as a result of his analysis."

In the years following the 1991 war, some had criticized the half-million troops Powell had deployed against Iraq as excessive. He thought the carping was typical of those who knew next to nothing about warfare; if he had to do it again, he wouldn't change a thing. The proof was in the low number of casualties: 148 American combat deaths and 467 wounded. Of 116,000 coalition sorties flown, they had lost 75 aircraft, none of them in air-to-air combat. But it was clear that they wouldn't need as many troops this time. The Iraqi Army had been reduced by at least 60 percent since Powell's war, and sanctions had blocked the import of parts for tanks and planes for years. He was concerned that Franks was taking the number for the invasion force too low, Powell later acknowledged, but "I did not die on my sword over it."

In mid-January 2002, just four months after the September 11 attacks, a little-noticed article in *The Washington Times* reported that the Pentagon had launched its own secret effort to develop a case for attacking Iraq and overthrowing Saddam Hussein as part of the war on terrorism. The so-called mainstream media—led by *The New York Times, The Washington Post* and the major television networks—had little use for *The Washington Times,* a conservative daily funded by the eccentric self-proclaimed "messiah," South Korean Reverend Sun Myung Moon. The State Department paid far more attention to the mainstream papers.

Established under Paul Wolfowitz by Douglas Feith, the Pentagon effort was overseen by Feith's deputy, William J. Luti. Luti, a retired naval officer and former aide to ex–House Speaker Newt Gingrich, had come to the Pentagon from Cheney's office. Chief among the new office's multiple tasks was a closer examination of all intelligence information to find links between Iraq and al-Qaeda and evidence of Saddam Hussein's weapons of mass destruction that other analysts might have overlooked or underappreciated. The office, which maintained close contact with "Scooter" Libby and his deputy, John Hannah, on the vice president's staff, also managed the Pentagon's relationship with its favored candidate to replace Hussein, the exiled leader Ahmed Chalabi, a leading supplier of anti-Saddam intelligence.

Intelligence analysis was normally the province of the CIA, and the State Department was nominally in charge of the administration's relationship with Chalabi and his Iraqi National Congress. But at the White House and the Pentagon, both the CIA and the State Department were considered insufficiently aggressive on the subject of Iraq and unnecessarily hostile toward the INC.

Even without a central role in planning for the war, however, the State Department found the Iraq momentum hard to ignore. Ryan Crocker, the NEA deputy who had been sent to Afghanistan to help organize a post-Taliban political structure, believed that the difficulties he had encountered there would pale beside the challenges of a post-Saddam Iraq. Iraq was a far larger, more sophisticated country with a prominent place in the Arab world, with deep ethnic and religious differences that had been suppressed for decades by the dictatorship the administration was now planning to remove. Saddam's ouster would leave a major power vacuum in the country and in the region. Though few in the department thought that invading Iraq was a good idea, they decided someone should start preparing for its aftermath.

In April, the Near East Bureau launched a project it called the "Future of Iraq," enlisting two hundred Iraqi academics, business leaders and experts in everything from education and oil policy to governance and national security to draw up a blueprint for reconstructing and running their country after Saddam was gone. The idea had originated months earlier with Edward Walker, the former assistant secretary who had left government in mid-2001 to take over a Washington think tank on Mideast issues, as a vehicle for drawing together Iraqi military and political exiles, particularly among Hussein's minority Sunni sect.

When the State Department had invited Walker to lead the project, the Pentagon and some lawmakers had objected on the grounds that he was considered hostile to Chalabi and the INC. The NEA took over the management of the initiative itself, inviting the participation of the INC and five other groups identified as eligible for U.S. aid under the Iraq Liberation Act.

Headquartered in a small, first-floor office near the State Department cafeteria, the program was physically and psychologically far removed from Powell, who had larger problems on his mind during the spring and summer of 2002 and was happy to delegate the task to those with the expertise to deal with it. Although he shared the concern of his Mideast experts about a possible postwar disaster in Iraq, he paid little attention to their efforts. That "absence of buy-in" from the secretary, said one official who worked on the Future of Iraq project, would later undermine its influence.

Throughout the summer and fall of 2002, the Pentagon's secret intelligence analysis office and the State Department's Future of Iraq project toiled separately, one eagerly compiling evidence to justify taking Iraq apart and the other seeking ways to put it back together again. The officials involved rarely spoke to one another, and each group had little, if any, knowledge of or interest in the other. The only obvious overlap between them was the participation of Ahmed Chalabi.

The deputies committee had started regular meetings to discuss Iraq in the spring of 2002. Once again, however, Armitage and Grossman found the sessions more frustrating than elucidating. The best that could be said of them, Armitage joked, was that they "always started on time," although "OSD [Office of the Secretary of Defense] would be a little late. We'd have the meeting. There would be a summary of conclusions eventually sent out, which might or might not reflect what actually happened at the meeting. People would be given assignments, which the State Department would eventually complete and others would do if the wind suited them, if they felt like it.... Marc and I used to joke that the worst words in the English language were 'Remanded to the Deputies.' "

Libby nearly always attended for Cheney, as did Wolfowitz or Feith from the Pentagon. Since there had been no official policy decision on invading Iraq, the meetings had an air of unreality about them. The deputies considered and again rejected Wolfowitz's idea of an independent "enclave" in southern Iraq, they recycled discussions on whether Saddam Hussein could be overthrown by exiles or his own military and they spoke about regime change through U.S. military force. "We knew what we were talking *about,* but we didn't know what we were talking *for,*" recalled one State Department participant. "We didn't know whether secretly a decision had been made."

By early June, the official said, State Department staffers below the deputy level were coming back from their own interagency meetings on Iraq with "a funny feeling. They would say, 'Our counterparts at the Pentagon and the vice president's office are too cocky. It's like they know something we don't.' "

When Richard Haass, the head of State's Office of Policy Planning, asked Rice point-blank after a meeting during the first week in July whether the White House was "really sure that we wanted to put Iraq front and center at this point, given the war on terrorism and other issues.... She said, essentially, that that decision's been made, don't waste your breath."

Haass reported the conversation to Powell, but he had the feeling the secretary thought he was exaggerating its significance. Powell, Haass thought, underestimated the determination of those who wanted to go to war and who intended to do so sooner rather than later.

Powell was playing his own hand cautiously. They probably *did* need to do something about Iraq, especially if there was a danger that Saddam would hand over weapons of mass destruction to al-Qaeda. But his belief that they did not need to rush toward the use of force against Baghdad had not changed. There was much to be done before they reached that point.

"My recollection of Secretary Powell's view and my own," Armitage later said, was that the administration should take its time to "get this right.... Get your domestic [situation] right, get Afghanistan solidified, give us time to take on the diplomatic" effort that would be a crucial component of a war decision.

But like it or not, Iraq was beating at Powell's door. European and Arab allies, agitated by the administration's increasingly bellicose rhetoric, were demanding clarification and consultation. The once-secret military planning was now regularly on the front pages of newspapers across the country, with accounts of tens of thousands of troops and hundreds of warplanes being readied for action. At the West Point commencement in June, Bush outlined a new preemptive military strategy for the United States. Deterrence and containment had worked during the Cold War, he said, but "new threats also require new thinking.... Containment is not possible when unbalanced dictators with weapons of mass destruction can deliver those weapons on missiles or secretly provide them to terrorist allies." He never mentioned the word "Iraq," but no one doubted the intended target of "preemptive action when necessary to defend our liberty and to defend our lives."

Cheney made frequent public references to Iraq's weapons of mass destruction, expressing certain knowledge that Hussein was "working on nuclear" weapons. In a series of media interviews, Richard Perle warned that there was "no time to lose."

Domestic anxiety over the apparent speed of the race toward Baghdad was also rising. The Senate, temporarily under Democratic leadership after the defection of one of its Republican members, scheduled hearings to learn more about the administration's intentions, and even some prominent Republicans began to ask questions. One of them, Nebraska Senator Chuck Hagel, the outspoken opponent of the Kyoto Protocol, was also a Vietnam veteran and member of the Armed Services Committee. In an August 4 television interview Hagel said that Bush was wise to plan for contingencies on Iraq. "But the real question here is what's the urgency of the threat?... What comes after Saddam Hussein? Would we do this in a unilateral way with no allies? What would we hope to gain? What would be the reactions—economic, political, diplomatic reactions—to whatever action we would take?

"If we would move in a preemptive way against Iraq, that would change a doctrine that this country has had as long as we have existed.... I'm not saying that isn't the right doctrine, but think this through a little bit." Hagel noted that it was the thirty-eighth anniversary of the Gulf of Tonkin Resolution, in which Congress had given President Johnson open-ended authority to wage war in Vietnam. "We didn't ask any of these questions before we got into Vietnam. That's why this process is so important now."

Brent Scowcroft, a leading proponent of the last war against Iraq, was also a guest on the same Sunday-morning news program. The Palestinian-Israel conflict and the global war on terror were far higher national security priorities than Iraq, Scowcroft cautioned, and both would be jeopardized by an invasion. "The president has announced that terrorism is our number one focus. Now, Saddam's a problem, but he's not a problem because of terrorism." The primary link between al-Qaeda and Saddam, he said, was that they shared "an intense dislike of the United States."

Invading Iraq to overthrow Saddam, Scowcroft warned, would result in "an explosion in the Middle East" that "could turn the whole region into a cauldron and thus destroy the war on terrorism." If the administration was worried about Iraq's weapons of mass destruction, he advised, it should "get to the U.N. to insist on an inspection regime that is no notice, any time, anywhere, and so on. The administration says Saddam would never agree to it. But if he doesn't agree to it, that gives you the *casus belli* that we don't really have right now."

On the same day that Scowcroft and Hagel were voicing their concerns, Powell was on the last leg of his Asia trip, heading home from his final diplomatic stop in Manila. When his plane set down at dawn for refueling at Hickam Air Force Base in Hawaii, beside the placid waters of Pearl Harbor, he stayed aboard while the others climbed out to stretch their legs and watch the Sunday sunrise. Powell's requested meeting with Bush on Iraq was scheduled for the next day, and he was working on notes to himself to make sure his every concern would be aired.

On Monday, August 5, Powell headed to the White House at 4:30 p.m. for a war-planning update from Tommy Franks. Afterward, he joined Rice and Bush upstairs in the residence for a conversation that extended into dinner. It was his longest uninterrupted talk with the president since before the inauguration. Working through his notes, Powell mentioned all the potential consequences that Bush would have to consider before making a decision to invade Iraq, from the destabilization in the Middle East and abrupt fluctuations in the price and supply of oil a war would cause to the attention and energy that it would sap from the larger war on terrorism and every other foreign policy priority. War would dominate the rest of Bush's term, Powell warned, as well as his reelection effort.

If the president decided to go ahead, they would need allies for money, troops and postwar assistance. Having other nations participate, Powell said, was not just the politically correct, multilateral thing to do, it could help determine the success of the mission. Franks had already outlined the foreign bases to which he wanted access, including permission to march an entire division through Turkey into Iraq from the north. At the moment, however, most of the world opposed an invasion.

If they ousted Saddam Hussein and took over Iraq, what would they do with it? "When you hit this thing," Powell later recalled telling the president, "it's like a crystal glass... it's going to shatter. There will be no government. There will be civil disorder.... I said to him, 'You break it, you own it. You're going to own it. You're not going to have a government... not a civil society. You'll have twenty-five million Iraqis standing around looking at each other.' "

When Bush asked what he would recommend, Powell replied unequivocally, "Take it to the U.N."

Powell's approach to Bush was much the same as the one he had used with the president's father at a similar stage of planning for the 1991 war against Iraq. As chairman of the Joint Chiefs, he had gone to then-President Bush not to advise him on whether to send Americans into combat but to make sure the president would make an informed decision. "My responsibility that day," Powell later wrote of his visit to the White House on September 24, 1990, "was to lay out all the options for the nation's civilian leadership. However, in our democracy it is the presidents, not the generals, who make decisions about going to war." By spelling it all out, "I had done my duty." Powell's goal this time was the same: to slow down the decision-making process by pointing out likely complications. The United Nations could provide an alternative to war, but it could also be a crucial ally in both combat and postwar reconstruction. Bush couldn't have the latter unless he was prepared to first explore the former.

Rice thought the session went well. Powell's appeal on "the upside of making an aggressive approach at the U.N. and the downside of not doing that," she later judged, had made sense.

"He sure did, he did say that," Bush acknowledged long after the Iraq invasion in response to a journalist's question about the substance of his August 5 session with Powell. "And my reaction to that is, is that my job is to secure America. And that I also believe that freedom is something that people long for."

Pressed for more specific information, Bush explained that Powell's job was to be "tactical. My job is to be strategic. Basically what [Powell] was saying was, was that if in fact Saddam is toppled by [the U.S.] military, we better have a strong understanding about what it's going to take to rebuild Iraq." He knew the secretary of state felt strongly that the United Nations was the way to go, he said, but others in his administration, including the vice president, "had seen how feckless the United Nations had been on this issue and were uncertain as to whether or not the United Nations would be able" to force Saddam from power.

Throughout Bush's first term, no other exchange would better illustrate the wide gulf between Powell's view of the world and the responsibilities of governance and those of Bush, his vice president and the rest of his national security team. They defined leadership as grand strategy and "vision." Tactical concerns were a distraction, and those who raised them were timid, disloyal or simply wrong.

Powell was a tactician by nature and experience and was wary of self-described visionaries. Spreading "freedom" around the world was not much of a game plan, no matter how much firepower you had. Achieving a vision—whether it was democracy in Iraq or an Arab-Israeli peace—required an assessment of the terrain between you and your objective, a realistic plan for how to traverse it and the flexibility to maneuver around unforeseen obstacles. No strategy survived contact with the enemy intact; that was one of the first things every combat officer learned.

British Prime Minister Tony Blair had been pressing Bush for months with the case Powell was now making. A centrist who had pulled his Labour Party from the ideological left to the middle and led it to electoral victory in 1997, Blair had been a friend and political soul mate of Bill Clinton's. On the eve of Bush's inauguration, Clinton had advised Blair not to underestimate the new American president and to "get as close to George Bush as you have been to me." Blair's own advisers had worried about the likelihood of forging a friendship between the driven, intellectual Briton and the conservative Texas cowboy. Their first attempt, a get-acquainted visit by Blair to Camp David in February 2001, was a carefully scripted weekend that ignited little real warmth.

Bush and Blair had subsequently crossed paths several times during the spring and summer of 2001, but it was not until September 11 that their relationship finally jelled. It was immediately clear to Blair that the terrorist attacks would radically alter America's relationship with the rest of the world and that it was important for Britain, as the United States' closest ally, to demonstrate strong support. Nine days later, Blair occupied a prominent seat in the House Visitors' Gallery next to Laura Bush as the president told a shaken U.S. Congress that the country was at war.

Blair had a solid record of concern about Iraqi weapons of mass destruction. He had spoken regularly about the subject since his earliest days as prime minister, calling Saddam Hussein an "evil dictator" and a "threat to world peace." In a seminal foreign policy address in Chicago in 1999, Blair had outlined what he called the "doctrine of international community," a justification, in certain circumstances, for direct intervention in the internal affairs of other nations. But while Bush spoke of the

United States' right to engage in unilateral "preemptive" war against perceived adversaries, Blair's doctrine was internationalist and humanist,
stemming from the failure of Western governments to intervene to prevent genocide in the Balkans and Rwanda during the 1990s.

Blair had a deep personal belief in the United Nations, reinforced by
domestic political necessity—the international organization was held in
high esteem in his country. Unlike the Bush administration, Britain saw
no basis in international law for one state's imposition of "regime change"
on another and no convincing evidence of a connection between al-
Qaeda and Saddam Hussein. Bush's insistence that Iraq posed an urgent
threat that could be addressed only by Saddam's removal would be difficult and perhaps impossible to sell to the British people and the rest of the
world.

Yet Blair considered it crucial that the Americans not be left to wage a
crusade on their own. He saw his task as persuading Bush to package the
Iraqi threat in language the United Nations would accept. The Security
Council had long demanded that Iraq relinquish its weapons of mass
destruction, and Saddam had made a fool of it by first impeding and then
barring weapons inspectors operating under a U.N. mandate. If Bush was
determined to invade Iraq, he would have to make the case on the basis of
disarmament.

Like Powell, Blair had urged Bush to direct America's immediate
response to September 11 toward al-Qaeda and Afghanistan and to set
aside Iraq for the time being. "He was very concerned that this shouldn't
be a trigger for a huge split between Muslims and the rest of the world" or
be allowed to undercut the Mideast peace process, a senior Blair adviser
later recalled. On Bush's behalf—although not at his request—Blair had
spent much of the fall of 2001 after the al-Qaeda attacks traveling frenet-
ically through the Middle East and to Russia and the rest of Europe trying to solidify support for the war on terror and reassure worried
governments that the Americans would not go off the deep end.

By the spring of 2002, it was clear to Blair that the administration's Iraq
war planning was well under way. In its search for justification, Blair's own
advisers cautioned, the White House seemed to be shaping its intelligence analysis—particularly on the question of Iraq's ties to al-Qaeda—
to conform to its unilateral intentions. Directing the administration
toward a more measured, disarmament-based approach, they agreed, was
as important to Britain as standing shoulder to shoulder with the United
States in its time of need.

In April 2002, immediately after announcing that he was sending Powell to the erupting Middle East, Bush had invited Blair to spend a weekend at his ranch in Crawford. Over the course of the visit, Blair pushed for a continuation of U.S. engagement in the Mideast peace process while nudging Bush toward seeking broader support and an international mandate for action against Iraq. "The U.K. would support military action to bring about regime change," Blair agreed, "provided that certain conditions were met," according to a secret British government record of the meeting. The conditions were that "efforts had been made to construct a coalition/shape public opinion; the Israel-Palestine Crisis was quiescent; and the options for action to eliminate Iraq's WMD through U.N. weapons inspectors had been exhausted."

At a news conference immediately after the meeting, however, Bush offered no such caveats when he told reporters that he had "explained to the prime minister that the policy of my government is the removal of Saddam, and that all options are open."

Blair, standing beside him, stiffened visibly. "The president is right to draw attention to the threat of weapons of mass destruction. That threat is real," he said. "How we deal with it, that's a matter we discuss."

The Crawford meeting marked the beginning of what would be a steady refrain in Blair's conversations with Bush. At every opportunity, the prime minister's message was, "You could do this on your own. You have the military strength to go into Iraq and do it," recalled Christopher Meyer, Britain's ambassador to the United States. "But our advice to you is, even a great superpower like the United States needs to do this with partners and allies. And the best way of trying to get a good coalition together is to exhaust the processes which the U.N. offers."

The British government's political instincts were aligned with the views of the State Department, and Powell had developed a close relationship with Blair's foreign secretary, Jack Straw. Over the past several months they had spoken by telephone almost daily, and it was clear to both of them that the Iraq train was barreling down the tracks with few brakes applied. On July 23, Straw was one of several advisers who told Blair that "military action was now seen as inevitable" by Washington and there was "no patience with the U.N. route ... [and] little discussion ... on the aftermath."

Blair had started sending Bush short notes and lengthier analyses of shared concerns, establishing a correspondence reminiscent—at least in one direction—of the letters exchanged between Winston Churchill and Franklin Roosevelt during World War II. In July, he wrote to Bush again, laying out the case for taking the Iraq question to the United Nations. By the time Powell had his August 5 talk with the president, the ground had been well prepared.

On August 6, Bush departed Washington for a monthlong summer hiatus in Crawford. Powell felt he had made a convincing case for going to the United Nations and repeated it to Cheney, Rumsfeld and the rest of the principals at a meeting chaired by Rice a week later.

Rice was supportive of the idea, and the discussion turned to whether Bush should talk about Iraq in a speech he was already scheduled to deliver to the annual opening of the U.N. General Assembly on September 12. Cheney objected, warning that the United Nations was nothing more than an international debating society where they would become hopelessly bogged down.

After a long discussion, however, the vice president changed his approach. Bush *should* talk about Iraq in his U.N. speech, he said, and should use the occasion to remind the United Nations that Saddam Hussein was already in violation of a long list of Security Council demands. These weren't American resolutions, Bush should tell them; they were U.N. resolutions. Who could complain if the United States was preparing to carry out the already expressed will of the international community?

When the principals met with Bush on August 16 via videoconference, the president agreed that his speech should focus on Iraq. Later that afternoon, Rice flew to Texas for further discussions. The more Bush thought about it, the more he liked the idea of putting the onus on the United Nations itself to follow through on its demands of Saddam Hussein.

Victory in hand, Powell left for a brief vacation in the Hamptons on Long Island. George Kennan had been right about spending too much time out of town. He did not want to leave Washington, he told his staff, unless it was absolutely necessary, since "when he was out of town bad things happened." But the city was in the August doldrums, and he felt confident that the Iraq train had been slowed. He and Alma had been invited to stay at the summer home of a friend, Ronald Lauder of the Estée Lauder cosmetics empire; Jack Straw was going to fly over from London, and the two would have a chance to consult face-to-face.

One sunny afternoon, Powell took Straw and his wife for a drive along the narrow lanes lined with multimillion-dollar houses and stopped at the nearby home of his cousin Bruce Llewellyn, a dyed-in-the-wool Democrat. The cousins enjoyed good-natured political sparring, and Powell's favorite jab was to ask Llewellyn about the night he had spent in the Lincoln Bedroom during the Clinton administration, a widely distributed perk that later became associated with allegations of "selling" the White House for political gain. Standing in his driveway in gardening shorts and a T-shirt, Llewellyn took his own shot, ribbing Powell and Straw on the rampant war talk in the media. "Am I crazy," he wondered innocently, "or do I remember one of you guys said something about peace in our time?"

"That's it," Powell stopped him with a laugh as he started the car. "That's enough."

In the August heat, the simmering Iraq debate boiled over. Scowcroft, joined by former Secretary of State James Baker, amplified his public warnings against precipitate, unilateral action. Separate op-ed newspaper articles by the two prominent members of the Bush 41 administration were interpreted by the media as reflecting concerns shared by the president's father. Members of Congress, particularly in the Democratic Senate, raised insistent questions about Bush's war plans. The leaders of Germany, France and Russia publicly announced that they would not support an invasion, and Kofi Annan, the U.N. secretary-general, said a preemptive attack would be "unwise."

Anthony Zinni, whose Mideast assignment had again fizzled, spoke out in a Florida speech on August 23 that drew wide notice. "Attacking Iraq now will cause a lot of problems," Zinni said—and he knew a lot of prominent generals, including Powell, who saw things the same way. But "in fairness to President Bush, because I work for him . . . [he] has invited the debate and he allows anyone who has a view to speak to the debate. I mean, within his own administration you hear different views."

On August 26, Cheney struck back during a speech to the Veterans of Foreign Wars convention in Nashville. Zinni, an invited VFW guest, joined him on the dais, and the two men, who hadn't seen each other since Cheney's Mideast trip in March, shook hands and chatted. The vice president began, as expected, with remarks about the valor and value of veterans. But halfway through, as he discussed the war on terror, he switched abruptly to the subject of Iraq.

"The case of Saddam Hussein," Cheney said, "a sworn enemy of our country, requires a candid appraisal of the facts." As the elderly veterans looked confused, Zinni sat up straight in his chair. "This guy is going to make the case for war right here," he thought in amazement. "Right here in front of these guys in wheelchairs."

"There is no doubt that Saddam Hussein now has weapons of mass destruction," Cheney continued. "There is no doubt that he is amassing them to use against our friends, against our allies and against us." The situation was urgent, he said, and "time is not on our side.... The risks of inaction are far greater than the risk of action." As for seeking new weapons inspections through the United Nations, "a return of inspectors would provide no assurance whatsoever of [Hussein's] compliance with U.N. resolutions."

No one had warned Powell that the speech was coming. It was by far the most frightening and assertive statement about Iraq's weapons and intentions that anyone in the administration had made to date. It took both the nature and the immediacy of the Iraqi threat to a new level, beyond existing intelligence estimates, and clearly represented a preemptive attempt to pull the rug out from under the resumption of U.N. inspections before they even got started.

When a BBC interviewer asked Powell three days later whether he and Cheney were on the same page regarding Iraq, Powell offered his standard refutation of serious tension inside the administration. "The President always encourages us to debate," he said. "I think one of the strengths of the President's national security team is that we all have known each other for many, many years in very different capacities. I used to have Condi Rice's job. I used to work for Dick Cheney when he was Secretary of Defense and I was Chairman of the Joint Chiefs of Staff. So we all know each other well and we can have full, open debate without pulling our punches."

Then, without mentioning the substance of Cheney's charges, Powell proceeded to contradict him. "We know that [Iraq] had weapons of mass destruction 12 years ago. And we know that in the four years since the inspectors were removed that they have been continuing to pursue that kind of technology, both with respect to chemical and biological weapons. Now, how much more they have done since 1998, what their inventories might be like now, this is what is not known and this is one of the reasons it would be useful to let the inspectors go in.

"The President is examining all of our options—political, diplomatic, military," Powell continued. "He has said to all of our friends and allies around the world he will consult closely with them, and that of course includes consulting with the United Nations."

Zinni, who quickly emerged as a prominent critic of the administration's Iraq policy and eventually of the war itself, later recalled worrying that Powell, whom he greatly admired, would be "pissed at me" for speaking out. He asked Armitage, with whom he had a much closer personal relationship, to find out if Powell wanted him to pipe down. No, Zinni recalled Armitage telling him, Powell was far from mad. "You're fine," Armitage assured him. "It's great."

·   ·   ·

As the White House speechwriter Michael Gerson began working on Bush's U.N. speech, the administration's separate camps each provided input. The United States already had international legal authority to launch an attack based on Iraq's "material breach" of a decade's worth of Security Council resolutions, the Pentagon argued. The president should simply inform the United Nations that he would act when he chose to do so. The State Department countered that none of the existing resolutions authorized the use of force as punishment for noncompliance and no Security Council member would buy that line of reasoning. What they needed was a new resolution demanding that Saddam allow weapons inspectors to finish the job that had been suspended in 1998 and outlining specific consequences if he failed to comply.

Bush returned to Washington from Crawford on Sunday, September 1. The next day, Powell went to the White House to seek the president's assurance, in the wake of Cheney's remarks, that their first-stage goal was to get U.N. inspectors back into Iraq. Bush agreed, although he was skeptical that inspections would accomplish much. At a meeting with congressional leaders on September 4, the president announced that in addition to going to the United Nations, he would ask Congress for authorization to do what was "necessary to deal with the threat" from Iraq. The administration had already decided internally that it needed no congressional approval, but strong legislative backing would help pressure the United Nations.

On September 6, the principals met at Camp David to try to reach consensus on the U.N. speech. Their conversations were normally businesslike, with a heavy blanket of civility muffling any disagreements, but on this Friday evening Cheney and Powell began to go after each other. No voices were raised, but it was clear to both that a battle had been joined. The skirmish ended inconclusively, but Powell knew he was about to get reinforcements for the next round in the person of Tony Blair, due to arrive at Camp David the following day.

The British were well aware of Cheney's views. There was no office comparable to the vice presidency in their parliamentary system, but it was obvious that he held considerable influence over Bush. When Blair's Marine helicopter set down at the presidential compound on the morning of September 7, he, too, was unsure of what Bush planned to say to the United Nations.

"What we didn't know," recalled a British official who accompanied the prime minister, "was if [Bush] was going to say, 'I'm fed up, I've had enough of this organization and I'm not going to waste any more time. We've passed all these pointless resolutions' or ... 'You better shape up, we'll give you a chance.' And our argument was, let's give them a chance. Let's see what we can do.... We know you find it frustrating and bureaucratic and slow and ponderous, but give it a shot."

If he were ever to support military action against Iraq, Blair first needed Bush's commitment to seek a new Security Council resolution on weapons inspections. To show the world—and British voters—that they had done everything they could to avoid war, they had to say to Saddam, "This is it. You're in Last Chance Saloon, mate."

The vice president sat in on the discussion. He said little, and Blair assumed that Bush wanted him present as the leading opponent of the United Nations. Foreign visitors often found Cheney's silence disconcerting; his immobility and hooded eyes contrasted starkly with Bush's frequent fidgeting and habit of interrupting his guests. Blair made his pitch, but Bush offered no promises.

Bush later referred to the September session with Blair as "the *cojones* meeting," using a Spanish vulgarism for "testicles" to indicate that he had asked for and received the prime minister's backing for war. The British, however, remembered it as the moment when they had conditioned their support for an invasion on Bush's commitment to first pursuing the diplomatic track.

As Bush's speech went through multiple drafts, the call for a U.N. resolution demanding new inspections was inserted and removed several times. Powell insisted to the other principals that the president couldn't stand up and demand that the United Nations take action without saying what he wanted it to do. The speech would need a punch line. In a meeting on September 10, as he prepared to leave for New York, Powell clashed with Cheney again. What if Bush asked for a new resolution and the Security Council refused? Cheney asked. Rumsfeld waffled as usual, and again they adjourned with no consensus recommendation for the president.

With no word from Bush by the evening before the speech, Powell appealed to Rice and she made one final round of the principals by telephone. "Look, there really is a decision to be made," she told them. If they had a final view they wanted to express to the president, now was the time. Later that night, she assured Powell that the resolution language would be included.

On the morning of September 12, heads of state and foreign ministers representing nearly two hundred nations filed into the massive General

Assembly chamber at U.N. headquarters in New York. As the delegations found their seats, alphabetized by country name along curved, rising rows in the amphitheater-like room, there was a shared sense of wary anticipation.

Kofi Annan, who feared that Bush was about to shatter the precarious balance of interests that had kept the international institution alive for more than half a century, had launched a preemptive strike the night before. Due to speak immediately before Bush, he had guaranteed the morning headlines by releasing the text of his remarks early, including a warning that invading Iraq without U.N. support would be a grave mistake and a violation of international law. "No country," Annan said, "should reject cooperation as a simple matter of political convenience." Powell moved to calm the secretary-general, taking him aside as the session was about to open to urge him to "wait and listen" to Bush's speech. "You will not be displeased."

Bush appeared dwarfed in the huge chair at the front of the chamber where speakers waited to be introduced. For once he was still, with his feet flat on the floor and his hands folded in his lap. He stepped up to the lectern amid respectful but unenthusiastic applause. Powell, sitting with Rice among the delegates behind the small, white-on-brown placard reading "United States," followed along in the written text as Bush called for an end to Saddam Hussein's "decade of defiance."

"All the world now faces a test," Bush said, "and the United Nations a difficult and defining moment. Are Security Council resolutions to be honored and enforced, or cast aside without consequence? Will the United Nations serve the purpose of its founding, or will it be irrelevant?" As he neared the punch line, Powell realized with alarm that the call for a new resolution did not appear in the prepared text. But he breathed a sigh of relief as Bush, rectifying what the White House later insisted had been an inadvertent mistake, improvised the words that were not on his TelePrompTer. "We will work with the U.N. Security Council for the necessary resolutions," he pledged, to make one more attempt to secure Iraqi disarmament without resorting to force.

Rice told reporters that afternoon that Powell would immediately begin negotiations with members of the Security Council on a new resolution. The process would be brief, she said. "It's not as if the U.N. doesn't know what Saddam Hussein needs to do."

Powell made the rounds of television interviews and placed personal calls to selected print journalists. The resolution could be negotiated in a matter of days, he predicted. "We know [Saddam] continues to pursue weapons of mass destruction. People can argue at what rate and how many he has," he said, but the new inspections would brook neither deceit nor delay. Asked whether he would seek one resolution that would include both a set of demands and the consequences Baghdad would face for not meeting them, Powell said he didn't want to tip his "negotiating hand." Some Council members, led by France, were already insisting that there be separate resolutions, one with inspection demands and, if it later became necessary, another to authorize punishment. "If everything could be wrapped up in one," Powell demurred, "that would be neat."

Later in the afternoon, Powell hosted the Security Council ambassadors at the Waldorf-Astoria. All were pleased that an imminent, unilateral attack appeared to have been avoided, but few were happy that invasion remained on the table. The other permanent members, with the exception of Britain, resented being asked to bend to America's will. Although France and Russia had little doubt that Iraq maintained an active weapons program, they disagreed with Bush's assessment of the urgency of the threat it posed. Many of the others, from Africa, Latin America and Asia, had histories of being under the thumb of colonialists and didn't like the idea of big-power military occupation under any circumstances.

Even if a decision to invade were eventually made, Powell assured them, any resulting military occupation would be brief. Throughout its history, he said, the United States had never claimed territory captured by conquest. French Ambassador Jean-David Levitte raised his eyebrows and passed a note to Adolfo Aguilar Zinser, his colleague from Mexico. Powell's historical analysis, he wrote, apparently didn't apply to California and the rest of the southwest territory seized during the Mexican-American War. Aguilar Zinser smiled appreciatively.

Having won the interim battle, Powell quickly moved to protect his right flank by establishing his bona fides inside the administration as a believer in the Iraqi threat and a firm supporter—should diplomacy and international pressure fail—of the use of force. Almost overnight, his carefully couched public assessments of the state of Saddam's weapons programs were transformed into certainty. "We do know that he has stocks of biological weapons, chemical weapons," he said in an October interview. Later that month, he added that the U.S. government had sure knowledge that Saddam was "trying to acquire nuclear weapons" and that only the threat of military force would capture his attention. "One thing you can be sure of: He isn't going to disarm, he is not going to let the inspectors in, unless he is fearful of a conflict that would remove him from power.... If peace can be maintained while disarming Saddam Hussein and disarming the Iraqi regime, fine. But if it takes conflict, we must keep the prospect of conflict there or else he will not cooperate."

A tough posture by the secretary of state, he felt, would keep Washington hard-liners at bay and would also help convince the skittish Security Council to take the matter seriously. Council members had to realize that Bush was fully prepared to leave them behind. If they wouldn't deal with the Iraq problem, he warned in a radio interview, "then the United States, with other likeminded nations, may have to deal with it. We would prefer not to go that route, but the danger is so great, with respect to Saddam Hussein having weapons of mass destruction, and perhaps even terrorists getting hold of such weapons, that it is time for the international community to act, and if it doesn't act, the President is prepared to act with likeminded nations."

Powell's statements conformed to the talking points now being issued on a daily basis by the White House Iraq Group, established in August to coordinate an administration-wide public posture for each stage of the confrontation with the United Nations, Congress and ultimately Baghdad. Its efforts had been evident when newly alarming assessments of the advanced state of Iraq's nuclear weapons program had emerged in the days leading up to Bush's U.N. speech. A September 8 front-page story in *The New York Times,* attributed to "administration sources," revealed that Iraq had purchased "thousands of specially designed aluminum tubes, which American officials believe were intended as components of centrifuges to enrich uranium." No one knew when Iraq would have a nuclear weapon, the story said, but "the first sign of a 'smoking gun,' [officials] argue, may be a mushroom cloud."

Asked about the story that morning in a television interview, Cheney readily affirmed that the aluminum tubes, intercepted during shipment to Iraq, were designed to produce "what you have to have to build a bomb." Rice told a reporter that the tubes were "only really suited for nuclear weapons programs" and that Saddam was "actively pursuing a nuclear weapon." They might not be able to ascertain the exact moment when Iraq had passed the point of no return, she said, echoing the *Times* story, "but we don't want the smoking gun to be a mushroom cloud."

Powell's own newly aggressive language caused consternation among those who had long assumed that his emphasis on diplomacy meant he was a secret soldier in the antiwar camp. In one of the more caustic criticisms, Harry Belafonte, the Harlem-born and Jamaica-raised calypso singer and political activist, compared Powell to a plantation slave trying to please his master. "In the days of slavery, there were those slaves who lived on the plantation and [there] were those slaves that lived in the house," Belafonte said in a radio interview that quickly spread across the country and around the world. "You got the privilege of living in the house if you served the master.... Colin Powell was permitted to come into the house of the master. When Colin Powell dares to suggest something other than what the master wants to hear, he will be turned back out to pasture."

Powell, who always resented any effort to tie his color to the way he did his job and for whom foreign policy and race relations occupied separate universes, was livid. "If Harry had wanted to attack my politics, that was fine," he said in response to Belafonte's comments. "If he wanted to attack a particular position I hold, that was fine. But to use a slave reference I think is unfortunate and is a throwback to another time and another place that I wish Harry had thought twice about using."

Powell and the State Department began drafting a Security Council resolution demanding Saddam Hussein's complete cooperation with inspections to verify and destroy his illegal weapons programs. The demand would elicit one of two responses they thought, either of which would keep the United States on the higher moral plane. Either Saddam would refuse and the world would join together to overthrow him by force of arms and build a new Iraq, or he would acquiesce, be rendered toothless, and war would be avoided.

Rumsfeld's office thought the idea that two hundred inspectors running around a country the size of Texas were going to uncover Hussein's covert weapons stocks and development programs was a fantasy. Powell was kidding himself if he thought the United Nations would accomplish anything, but at least the Security Council negotiations would keep him busy and out of the way. Wolfowitz took the lead in preparing the Pentagon's own version of a draft resolution, with draconian demands the Council was almost certain to reject. That would clear the way for a U.S. declaration that the United Nations was "irrelevant." If the harsh resolution should somehow pass, Saddam would either fail to comply or the inspections would uncover the weapons. Either way, the United States would then be justified in forcibly removing him.

The drafters of the Pentagon resolution were infuriated just days after Bush's U.N. speech when Iraq presented the United Nations with a letter saying that the inspectors were welcome back into the country. Irritation with the ploy was further inflamed by the knowledge that Kofi Annan himself had helped the Iraqis fashion the communication to address U.S. concerns. A second red flag for the hard-liners came with an initial estimate by UNMOVIC, the United Nations Monitoring, Verification and Inspection Commission, that once a resolution was approved it would be weeks or perhaps months before it was ready to begin work in Iraq. It could then be as long as a year before the team made a preliminary assessment of Iraq's weapons programs. That time frame would leave the growing U.S. force in the Persian Gulf in limbo far beyond the optimal invasion date, now tentatively set for somewhere between January and March 2003.

In Washington, an interagency group was formed to hammer out the various approaches to the resolution. The group reached early agreement on so-called "red lines" for inclusion: Iraq must be declared already in "material breach" of previous U.N. resolutions. There would be harsh new inspection guidelines. Most important, the resolution had to promise "serious consequences" for Iraqi defiance—diplomatic code words for war.

Wolfowitz's draft ordered the inclusion of U.S. officials and military forces as members of the inspection teams on the ground. The Americans could demand that UNMOVIC initiate an inspection of any site they chose. Iraqi nuclear scientists, who Cheney claimed were already working under Saddam's orders to restart a weapons program dismantled in the 1990s, were to be taken outside the country for interrogation. The final "action" paragraph gave advance approval for the use of "all necessary means" to punish Baghdad for noncompliance—an automatic trigger of "serious consequences."

To Powell's irritation, the Pentagon had once again claimed a full voice in what was clearly a diplomatic task. Cheney's aides also attended all meetings on the resolution, adding an additional heavy thumb on the hard-line side of the balance scale.

On most issues, Cheney's staff was far more threatening to the State Department than Rumsfeld's was. Powell saw the vice president's office as "a very powerful constituency that you had to deal with. They took positions on issues, they pushed language changes.... And they pushed them not only through the [normal] mechanism, but the vice president of course was with the president for a good part of every day."

Cheney's attendance at every principals' meeting made this administration unlike any other Powell had ever served in. The vice president participated in the discussions just as he had fifteen years earlier, when he had served as defense secretary. The difference now was that Cheney had far more power and Rumsfeld sat in the Pentagon chair. Together, they formed a majority bloc on any issue. General Myers was in the seat Powell had occupied as chairman of the Joint Chiefs. But while Chairman Powell had sometimes aligned himself with the State Department behind the scenes, Myers was firmly in Rumsfeld's pocket and had no independent voice on major issues.

Disagreements among the national security principals were nothing new in Washington. But those earlier battles had frequently revolved around policy disputes and had little ideological tint. In the Bush administration, the ideological disputes extended and often intensified all the way down the pecking order. The lineup of Powell versus Cheney and Rumsfeld was duplicated among their deputies and undersecretaries: Armitage did battle with Wolfowitz and Libby, while Grossman butted heads with Feith and Hannah or another member of Cheney's second string. Early suspicions that Cheney's acolyte John Bolton was a mole in the State Department seemed to be borne out as officials from the vice president's office and the Pentagon arrived at meetings with advance knowledge of State's positions. Minutes circulated after interagency meetings sometimes included new positions that had not been stated in the discussions or summaries that bore little resemblance to the overall balance of a debate.

Since assistant secretaries of state frequently found themselves unable to resolve arguments with their counterparts at Defense and in the White House, Powell spent a significant amount of his time dealing with lower-level conflicts that had forced their way up the department chain of command. "There was a time when every day between three and four o'clock I had to get fed all the fights everyone below me was having with the Pentagon," one assistant secretary of state recalled. "Fights over instructions to an embassy, negotiations over base rights, or some ridiculously aggressive cable OSD wanted to send out." After moving several links up the chain without resolution, the matter would be brought before Powell to intervene with Rumsfeld. "He would call Rumsfeld and then call me back and say, 'Okay, Don says he never gave any such instruction and it's okay for the cable to go.'

"So I'd call back my counterpart and say, 'My boss talked to your boss,' and then he'd talk to Rumsfeld and call me back and say, 'Well, Rumsfeld didn't really understand the issue, so hold the cable.' I'd call Powell again and say, 'Guess what? It didn't work. You're going to have to call Rumsfeld again.' And he would say, 'Dammit.' And then he'd call me back again and say it was okay.

"Once when it happened a third time, Powell told me, 'Just sign the goddamn cable out in my name.' "

Often the problems stemmed from differences in management style. Rumsfeld's senior aides appeared to have little decision-making authority, a problem compounded by the fact that the defense secretary did not encourage questioning or requests for clarification from those beneath him.

The exasperation between departments went both ways. Many senior Pentagon officials, in particular, considered the State Department a rogue agency insufficiently committed to the president's policies and overly solicitous of foreign sensitivities. Depending on what they thought of Powell, they saw him as either agreeing with State's rebellious views or refusing to discipline those who got out of line.

In previous administrations, resolving such internecine squabbling had been the job of the National Security Council staff and the president's national security adviser. Confronted by repeated turf battles, Powell found himself harkening back to his own management of the interagency process in the Reagan White House—a combination of military discipline and running interference for Cabinet secretaries. But most members of Rice's staff seemed unable or unwilling to lock swords with Rumsfeld or Cheney or their underlings. Rice herself was a source of frequent exasperation to Powell. With the vice president as a major policy player, her position was doubtlessly more complicated than his own had been in the job. But at times Rice seemed willfully blind to the damage being done by these intramural disputes. More dangerously, in Powell's view, she tended to echo back to the president what she thought he wanted to hear rather than what he needed to know.

With no direction from the top, both sides of the dispute over the U.N. resolution claimed the president's backing. Wolfowitz insisted that Bush had agreed that the harshest demands were "nonnegotiable," while the State Department was equally certain it had presidential approval to negotiate anything and everything beyond the "red lines." Eventually, Powell made a tactical retreat and Wolfowitz's draft was circulated in New York.

Britain, an intended cosponsor, refused to align itself with a draft resolution it considered "totally unsellable" to the rest of the Security Council. France, Russia and China declared it dead on arrival, saying they would agree to nothing with an "automatic trigger" that would allow any one nation to determine Iraqi noncompliance and carry out a punishment in their names. Powell was not totally displeased. At least the other Council members had seen what he was up against; perhaps it would motivate them to agree to a resolution with more teeth than the initial inclinations of several members had called for. A frightened United Nations, he felt, was not necessarily a bad thing at this stage.

By mid-October the Council was deadlocked, and Powell once again turned to the British for reinforcement. He was consulting with Jack Straw several times a day, even as David Manning, Blair's foreign policy adviser, conferred with Rice. The Manning-Rice connection was a direct line to Bush that avoided the Cheney-Rumsfeld roadblock; eventually Rice was persuaded to accept "the art of the possible," as one senior British official put it.

On October 23, a substantially revised draft resolution, cleared with Bush himself, was circulated at the Security Council. Although most of the harsh inspection language remained—along with a new provision inserted by Cheney that gave Saddam thirty days upon passage to submit a full declaration of all of his chemical, biological and nuclear weapons programs to the Council—"all necessary means" and the automatic trigger were gone. Over the next few weeks, Powell negotiated with the French over vague language to put in its place, agreeing that if Iraq failed at any point to comply, the Council would immediately convene to "consider the situation." A final paragraph reminded Iraq that it had been "repeatedly warned . . . that it will face serious consequences as a result of its continued violations of its obligations." The resolution did not say what those consequences would be.

On October 30, Hans Blix, the Swedish head of UNMOVIC, traveled to Washington with Mohamed ElBaradei, the Egyptian director general of the International Atomic Energy Agency, which would conduct the nuclear part of the inspections. Powell, who had invited them to meet with the president and vice president, believed the White House would be impressed by their sober-mindedness. Blix was as "reliable as a Volvo," he thought—high praise from a man who had taken apart and put back together a number of the Swedish cars.

Their first session was with Cheney, who for once did most of the talking. The security interests of the United States were the prism through which he viewed the world, he told the two. If the Iraqi inspections did not produce results the United States was "ready to discredit inspections in favor of [forcible] disarmament." Blix made a pitch for U.S. intelligence sharing to help them find Saddam's weapons, but he left with the impression that Cheney was more interested in putting them on notice than he was in exchanging information.

Blix and ElBaradei walked to the Oval Office, where they found Bush a stark contrast to the peremptory vice president. The president was friendly and respectful, Blix noted, and he seemed almost "boyish" as he told them to disregard reports that he was a "wild, gung ho Texan" bent on war. He would not wait long for results, Bush said, but as long as inspections were progressing he would give them his full support. Rice, who sat in on the meeting, thought that bringing the two to Washington had been a smart move by Powell.

Rumsfeld's office made one final effort to derail the resolution, recommending in writing to the president just days before the Security Council voted on it that he abandon the effort as an unnecessary restriction on the United States' power. But Bush declined, and Powell breathed a sigh of relief.

Powell barely slept during the first week of November, and negotiations over final words and commas, in telephone calls across oceans and time zones, occupied nearly all of his waking hours. After a lifetime in the military and government, his family was used to his frequent absences and preoccupations. But the end stage of the U.N. resolution happened to coincide with family demands that could not be ignored. Annemarie, his youngest child, was getting married. Relatives were coming from around the country and from Jamaica and beyond, and his presence, in body and spirit, was required over three days of activities—the rehearsal dinner, the wedding itself and a celebratory nuptial brunch.

Powell, as always, had shared little of what was going on at work with his family, and Annemarie had paid no attention to the drama at the United Nations. All she knew was that her soon-to-be in-laws were coming and an absent or distracted father of the bride would not make for a good first impression. She worried about his celebrity around dozens of new relatives—it would be a lot like the constant stream of admiring or just plain curious strangers who sidled up to him at the mall or the hardware store. Sometimes he didn't handle it well, particularly when he had a lot on his mind.

On November 2, the day of the wedding, Alma had to stand at the top of the basement stairs and call down that if he didn't come up from his office and get dressed soon he would miss giving his daughter away. Still on his cell phone as he and Annemarie rode together to the ceremony, he snapped it closed just before escorting her up the aisle. The next day, he fell asleep in a chair at the brunch. But overall, his daughter assessed, "he turned it on like a champ."

On the other end of Powell's telephone that week, in rapidly revolving succession, were Straw, French Foreign Minister Dominique de Villepin, and their counterparts in Russia, China and the rest of the Security Council nations. If Powell wasn't talking to one of them, he was in deep discussion with John Negroponte, his firm ally in the negotiations as U.S. ambassador to the United Nations.

Far from the administration's initial assurances that a new resolution could be written and approved within days, the tortured negotiations had lasted seven weeks. Security Council Resolution 1441 was finally tabled for a vote on the morning of November 8, 2002. As Negroponte walked across First Avenue from the U.S. Mission to the United Nations just after 9 a.m., his cell phone rang with a call from the ambassador of Syria, the last holdout among the Council's fifteen members. Powell and Blair had been pressuring and cajoling the government of President Bashar Assad for weeks, but they remained unsure which way Damascus would lean.

Making his way through the U.N. lobby and into the Council chamber, Negroponte smiled to himself as he ended the call and dialed Powell's direct number in Washington. After a brief conversation, Powell hung up and called Rice, who passed along the news to the president just as fifteen hands went up around the Security Council table, signaling unanimous agreement.

Within the hour, Bush stood in the White House Rose Garden before dozens of reporters, photographers and television cameras to praise the United Nations for rising to the challenge he had placed before it. But with the passage of the resolution, he warned, "the world must not lapse into unproductive debates over whether specific instances of Iraqi non-compliance are serious. Any Iraqi noncompliance is serious because such bad faith will show that Iraq has no intention of disarming.... America will be making only one determination: is Iraq meeting the terms of the Security Council resolution or not? The United States has agreed to discuss any material breach with the Security Council, but without jeopardizing our freedom of action to defend our country."

At the president's side on that crisp early-November morning, Powell basked in a dual victory as Bush turned to thank him for "his leadership, his good work, and his determination." It was hard to say which was sweeter—the Security Council success after seven weeks of intricate, nonstop negotiations or the major intramural triumph. For the moment, however brief it would ultimately turn out to be, there was no question who was "up" in the administration.

19

Experience proves that the man who obstructs a war in which his nation is engaged, no matter whether right or wrong, occupies no enviable place in life or history.

—Ulysses S. Grant

I'm here to serve the President, not to protect my popularity. I'm not a fool, I don't waste my popularity, but when the President said to me . . . "I need you to go to the U.N. and present the case," yes, it's my job. I'm the Secretary of State. Who should I turn to? Who should I ask?

—Colin L. Powell

Iraq's declaration of its weapons programs, delivered to Hans Blix in early December 2002 under the terms of Resolution 1441, left much to be desired. There was little new information in its 12,000 pages, many of which were reprinted documents that had already been given to U.N. inspectors in the 1990s. Even Blix, who thought the first few weeks of inspections had gone relatively well, concluded that Iraq had passed up a chance to explain what had happened to tons of chemical and biological weapons agents and munitions never accounted for. Baghdad claimed that the material had long since been destroyed, but it offered no proof.

The Security Council members all agreed that Iraq probably still had some biological and chemical weapons—or at least the know-how and materials to quickly produce them—and still aspired to build a nuclear bomb. Saddam Hussein had used mustard gas and other chemicals during the Iraq-Iran War and against Iraqi Kurds in the 1980s. U.N. inspections begun after the 1991 Gulf War had destroyed large quantities of WMD stockpiles and delivery systems. An undeclared nuclear weapons program had been discovered and dismantled. But the abrupt end of the disarmament effort in 1998 had left many questions unanswered.

The CIA had concluded in 2000 that "we do not have any direct evidence" that Iraq had reconstituted its WMD programs, "although given its past behavior this type of activity must be regarded as likely." Baghdad "has had the capability to reinitiate" both chemical and biological weapons programs, the agency assessed, but "without an inspection monitoring program . . . it is more difficult to determine if Iraq has done so." It also reported that "low-level theoretical R&D [research and development]" on a nuclear program had "probably continued," although "a sufficient source of fissile material remains Iraq's most significant obstacle to being able to produce a nuclear weapon."

By October 2002, however, possibilities and probabilities had somehow become certainties. A National Intelligence Estimate (NIE), hurriedly compiled in response to demands from a nervous Congress that was being asked to authorize military action, judged that "Iraq has continued its weapons of mass destruction (WMD) programs in defiance of U.N. resolutions and restrictions. Baghdad has chemical and biological weapons as well as missiles with ranges in excess of U.N. restrictions; if left unchecked, it probably will have a nuclear weapon during this decade."

Britain released its own lengthy assessment shortly after Bush's September 2002 speech at the United Nations. Iraq's WMD program was "active, detailed and growing," Prime Minister Blair told Parliament on September 24. Saddam Hussein had "existing and active military plans for the use of chemical and biological weapons, which could be activated within 45 minutes," Blair said, and "he is actively trying to acquire nuclear weapons capability."

Intelligence agencies elsewhere had arrived at similar, if not quite so apocalyptic, conclusions. Where other governments parted ways with the Bush administration, however, was on the imminence of the Iraqi threat and the manner in which to confront it. Even Blair had strong doubts about the key element in Washington's case for urgent action: that Saddam had ties to al-Qaeda and might supply weapons of mass destruction to the terrorist network.

Although Cheney, in particular, made frequent references to a relationship between Iraq and al-Qaeda, the administration acknowledged that it had no proof of an Iraqi connection to the World Trade Center and Pentagon attacks. Yet in a major speech in Cincinnati on October 7—three days before the Senate voted to authorize the president to wage war against Iraq—Bush drew a direct line between Baghdad and international terrorists targeting the United States.

"Many Americans have raised legitimate questions about the nature of the [Iraqi] threat, about the urgency of action—why be concerned now—about the link between Iraq developing weapons of terror and the wider war on terrorism," Bush said. The danger was real, he insisted, and would "only grow worse with time." Iraq not only possessed stocks of WMD but also had ballistic missiles that could carry them to nearby countries. Iraq was also exploring the use of UAVs—unmanned aerial vehicles—that could reach the United States. But "of course, sophisticated delivery systems aren't required for a chemical or biological attack," he warned. "All that might be required are a small container and one terrorist or Iraqi intelligence operative to deliver it. And that is the source of our urgent concern about Saddam Hussein's links to international terrorist groups."

Iraq and al-Qaeda not only shared a common enemy—the United States—they had "high-level contacts that go back a decade.... Iraq could decide on any given day to provide a biological or chemical weapon to a terrorist group or individual terrorists," Bush continued. America "must not ignore the threat gathering against us. Facing clear evidence of peril, we cannot wait for the final proof—the smoking gun—that could come in the form of a mushroom cloud."

A number of U.S. intelligence officials questioned the reliability of reports of al-Qaeda ties to Iraq. Sporadic contacts between the two had been noted over the years, but the intelligence was not firm and its significance was unclear. Saddam was a secularist, unlikely to share the Islamic fundamentalist aims of al-Qaeda. The State Department's own Bureau of Intelligence and Research (INR) and analysts at the Energy Department had raised questions about some of the WMD evidence, particularly the aluminum tubes allegedly imported to develop an Iraqi nuclear weapon. A report that Hussein had sent an emissary to Niger in 1999 to purchase uranium to be processed into fissile material had also been questioned by INR and was dismissed by a former Foreign Service officer, Joseph Wilson, who had been sent to Africa by the CIA to investigate in early 2002. The CIA's concerns about the Niger report had led to its excision from Bush's Cincinnati speech in October. But by December the claim had reappeared, when a State Department "Fact Sheet" composed by John Bolton's nonproliferation bureau charged that the Iraqi WMD declaration, among other things, had "ignore[ed] efforts to procure uranium from Niger."

The day the fact sheet was released, Powell pressed ahead with his own harsh public assessment of Saddam's deception of the world community and tepid cooperation with the inspectors. "The world is still waiting for

Iraq to comply with its obligations," he told reporters. "The world will not wait forever...Iraq can no longer be allowed to threaten its people and its region with weapons of mass destruction."

Many of the administration's most vociferous hawks argued that the CIA had, if anything, underestimated Iraq's WMD. They mistrusted the intelligence community as a hidebound, process-obsessed bureaucracy unable to see beyond what was visible to the naked eye. Powell was similarly suspicious, but for the opposite reason. In his experience, dating back to his days at the Pentagon, intelligence analysts were too willing to infer reality from what they couldn't see. Yet in the Bush administration's internecine battles, the CIA had become an ally of sorts of the secretary of state. Intelligence director George Tenet was one of the few plain speakers in the Kabuki-like discussions among the principals, and Powell saw no reason to question the October NIE.

But the thought that Iraq's weapons stockpiles might be difficult to find, if they even existed, had at least occurred to Powell. Lawrence Wilkerson, who had replaced Smullen as his chief of staff, had met with several former U.N. weapons inspectors now working at the Sandia and Lawrence Livermore National Laboratories, who warned that Saddam's weapons were either completely gone or deeply hidden and might never be found. When Wilkerson relayed their assessments to Powell one day in mid-November, the secretary looked at him with raised eyebrows.

"I wonder," Powell said idly as he turned to walk back through the doors connecting their offices, "what we'll do when we put half a million troops on the ground in Iraq and search it from one end to the other—and find nothing." Wilkerson wrote down the words on his desk calendar so he wouldn't forget them.

While the White House was preoccupied with Iraq, Powell had additional things on his mind over the winter of 2002–03. When Bush announced on January 15 that the administration would oppose an affirmative action case then before the Supreme Court, the secretary issued a rare public dissent, telling a media interviewer that he remained "a strong believer" in programs such as the one under challenge at the University of Michigan. But he tempered his implied criticism of the president's stance with a personal assurance of Bush's deep belief in diversity.

In truth, Bush had put Powell into the same difficult position as had the president's father and Ronald Reagan. All made strong rhetorical commitments to racial justice but failed to match their words with deeds. Bush's relationship with African Americans had gone steadily downhill, and he had declined invitations to speak at the annual NAACP convention since the campaign. Asked at a press conference in July 2002 to respond to critics of his civil rights record, he said sarcastically, "Let's see. There I was, sitting around...the table with foreign leaders, looking at Colin Powell and Condi Rice." His remark was widely criticized by black leaders as blatant tokenism.

Among the foreign policy issues demanding Powell's attention, U.S. intelligence had discovered a secret uranium enrichment program in North Korea that violated the 1994 Agreed Framework and indicated that the country was again working on nuclear weapons. For once, the State Department was left to deal with the issue. "We know that the president wants to keep North Korea out of the way so he can concentrate on Iraq," a senior British official in close consultations with the White House noted in January 2003. "They have remitted the issue to State...so that it does not get in the way" of the plans for Saddam Hussein. Powell continued trying to organize talks with Pyongyang.

The White House kept the Mideast peace process at arm's length and would not allow Powell any closer. The "Quartet" that he had set into motion the previous summer had completed work on the new "road map" of steps leading toward Palestinian statehood. But Bush refused to sign off on its release, arguing that no new demands should be made of Prime Minister Sharon until after the Israeli elections scheduled for late January. Powell, who had assured the other Quartet members, the Palestinians and Arab allies that publication of the document was imminent, was left to explain the delay.

Powell insisted in an interview with *The Washington Post* on January 8, 2003, that the administration had everything under control. "But I have to kind of lean back at the end of the day as I'm working all these problems and say, 'Whew, boy.' We've got Iraq, we've got North Korea and the Middle East is still intractable." Amid the challenges, he pointed out, there had been some notable successes. The expansion of NATO to include seven new members from Eastern Europe had gone off without a hitch at a November summit in Prague. The United States was actively involved in efforts to stop a civil war and genocide in Sudan, and "we have a very strong and growing relationship with China, after everybody thought we had blown it with the [spy plane] incident in April of 2001." India and Pakistan had calmed down, and both governments had strengthened their relationship with Washington. Just that morning, Powell said enthusiastically, he had updated the president on the progress being made on Afghan reconstruction.

To Powell, life was a series of challenges to be dealt with and then balled up like pieces of wastepaper. You threw each one over your shoulder and moved on to the next. Some—such as Iraq—took more time and effort to resolve than others, he said, but "I'm not the least bit disturbed. Being the chief diplomat of the United States means problem solving. I think I can go back and read the memoirs of all my predecessors and they've all gone through periods like this. If we solve every one of the [current] problems...I can assure you there will be a new set."

He laughed as he told a story from his days as a green lieutenant in West Germany. One night, he and some other young officers had sat drinking in the Gelnhausen officers' club while their captain, Tom Miller, lectured them for the umpteenth time on how much they had to learn.

"You guys think you're really hot stuff," Miller had growled after a few too many beers. "You've got all your little troops in bed and you're sitting here patting yourselves on the back about how you solved all the world's problems today. And you're going to go home and lie down with your little wives and sleep well.

"But you know what? While you're sleeping, the world is going to get fucked up all over again and you're going to have to get up in the morning and start at the beginning."

The ever-shrinking size of the invasion force being planned for Iraq was a growing source of concern for Powell. Military war games conducted during the 1990s, many of them under Anthony Zinni's CENTCOM leadership, had recommended a ground force of more than 400,000 combined U.S. and allied troops to conquer, control and pacify the country. Rumsfeld was planning to deploy about half that many.

Although he remained reluctant to press the issue, Powell made a few calls to Tommy Franks as the plan was being adjusted, questioning the force numbers and the length of the supply and communications lines. Franks thought that Powell's military service had earned him the right to an opinion but not a veto. After they had talked, he would report the conversations to Rumsfeld. The defense secretary advised him to be "calm and professional" in his dealings with Powell and to "answer his comments, one by one." Any doubts should be put out on the table for the NSC, Rumsfeld said; "otherwise, we'll look like we're steamrolling." But the size of the force never came up for serious NSC discussion.

Franks's plan called for the bulk of the invasion force to enter Iraq from the south through Kuwait. A second, northern front would be established with at least 40,000 U.S. troops moving into Iraq from Turkey. The State

Department's job was to persuade the Turks to agree to the off-loading of an armored division from ships in the Mediterranean, which would then transport its equipment across hundreds of miles of Turkish territory to Iraqi Kurdistan. Powell thought it would be a stretch. But Franks, strongly supported by General Myers and his vice chairman, General Peter Pace, as well as by Rumsfeld's office, was asking for a virtual carte blanche from the Turkish government.

"There was a lot of confusion about what [the Pentagon] did and didn't want" from the Turks, recalled one senior State Department official who worked closely with the issue. "How many Americans, how much stuff... the plan kept changing, the numbers kept changing.... We drove the Turks crazy." The campaign to win Turkish approval—begun in July 2002, months before the Security Council passed the Iraq resolution—was greatly complicated by several factors. Turkey was in the midst of domestic political uproar, headed toward elections in November. At the same time, it was fighting an uphill battle for European Union membership and struggling with renewed international pressure over its occupation of the Mediterranean island nation of Cyprus.

The Turks ducked and weaved through the summer and fall of 2002, placing conditions on the number and transport of U.S. troops and demanding monetary compensation and other emoluments—they wanted, they said, at least as much money as Pakistan was getting to cooperate with the war on terrorism. Turkish public opinion was overwhelmingly against an invasion, and the country's leaders were nervous about participating in an endeavor that many E.U. members clearly opposed. The Pentagon seemed willing to accede to whatever demands the Turks made, sending Wolfowitz to Ankara several times to speak directly to military leaders.

The State Department worried that Defense was oblivious to the challenges it was posing to Turkey's fragile democracy. In addition to popular disapproval, the Kurdish population spanning the Turkey-Iraq border was historically at odds with the central government in Ankara and strongly objected to any Turkish military involvement in Iraq. Powell's office tried to send Marc Grossman along whenever Wolfowitz headed toward Ankara.

Turkey eventually joined the long list of internal issues dividing the administration. Cheney and Rumsfeld believed that the State Department opposed the war and suspected it was not trying hard enough on the diplomatic front to win Turkish agreement. Powell was later criticized for not having made a personal trip to Ankara. A few days after Turkey's

November 4 election, a senior Cheney aide telephoned the department's Bureau of European and Eurasian Affairs and ordered that a new ultimatum be sent to the Turks with a two-day response deadline. The aide dictated wording that he said had been approved by the vice president himself and was not to be altered or cleared with anyone else at State. The bureau immediately violated the latter instruction and informed the seventh floor, which ordered the message transmitted as dictated, along with instructions to the Turks to bypass the State Department altogether and send their response directly to Cheney's office. If the vice president wanted to conduct his own diplomacy, so be it. Turkey, as State had anticipated, replied that it had no government in place to consider the request, which would have to be submitted to a parliamentary vote.

UNMOVIC inspectors could not say with certainty that Iraq had weapons of mass destruction, Hans Blix reported to the Security Council on January 9, but neither could they say it did not. So far, they had found no "smoking gun." Inspections were continuing, and Baghdad—despite its bogus declaration—seemed to be cooperating on the ground.

Blix privately agreed with one of Rumsfeld's favorite circumlocutions: "The absence of evidence is not the evidence of absence." His gut instinct told him that Iraq still maintained WMD stockpiles and weapons programs and had the documents to prove it. But it was going to take some time to unravel all the layers of Iraqi subterfuge.

Time was something the White House was not willing to provide. In December 2002, when the bulk of the troop deployment was just beginning, the president had rejected Cheney's argument that Iraq's failure to accurately declare its weapons programs was reason enough to call off the inspections and set a firm invasion date. The force was not yet ready. But Franks now estimated that they could make a "rolling start" into Iraq by mid-February, with other troops following as they arrived. After six weeks of inspections, it was clear to Powell that Bush was losing patience.

The NSC met regularly to review the status of both military planning and the diplomatic effort. But the principals had never discussed the pros and cons of the war itself. Powell had no doubts about where the others stood—"Cheney thought we had no option; we should do it right away, should have done it last year." Rumsfeld always waffled when Powell was around, but Powell knew what Rumsfeld's deputies thought and had no reason to think they weren't speaking for their boss. Rice had been telling them individually since just after Christmas that the president "really feels he has to do this," and she gave no indication that she disagreed.

There was never "a moment when we all made our recommendations and [Bush] made a decision," Powell later recalled. As far as he knew, the president had decided "in his own mind, by himself" that an invasion was the only option.

When Bush asked him to stay behind to chat after an Oval Office meeting on January 13, Powell already knew from Rice what the president wanted to tell him. They sat down in the two chairs in front of the fireplace. As Powell remembered the conversation, Bush said, " 'I really think I'm going to have to take this guy out.' And I said, 'Okay, we'll continue to see if we can find a diplomatic way out of this. But you realize what you're getting into? You realize the consequences of this?'

"He said, 'Yes, I do.' "

Powell felt there was no point in repeating what he had been telling the president since August about the importance of allies and the difficulty of trying to put a broken Iraq back together. He assumed that Bush knew what the secretary of state thought and was clearly not asking for his opinion now. If asked, Powell later reflected, "I would have said, 'Let the diplomatic process play out as long as you can.' It wasn't time [for a decision on] the thirteenth of January. It just wasn't. He didn't have Blair yet. He didn't have a coalition yet.... He still had to get the forces in place which were not there yet."

Bush asked if he could count on Powell's support, and Powell answered in the affirmative. "I didn't need his permission," the president later said when asked about the meeting. According to White House logs, the conversation lasted twelve minutes.

When he thought immediately afterward about what Bush had said, Powell divined a difference between "reaching a conclusion and [making] a decision to be implemented." Bush had concluded that war was the only way to resolve the situation, but he had yet to order the invasion. No matter what Franks said about the troops being ready, the deployments were not yet complete and the Turkish question remained unanswered. Powell decided he still had Bush's approval to continue pushing the diplomatic process. By his reckoning, there were at least "another six weeks of this game to play out." Nothing had really changed, he thought. If Saddam capitulated completely, they could still avoid war, and the best chance of achieving that was to convince him that the Security Council was speaking with one voice. Alternatively, if Saddam dug in his heels, it was essential that the United States have as much international support for an invasion as it could muster. Either way, the diplomatic effort had to continue.

"The president had come to a conclusion...but he didn't say in the same breath, 'And don't try to keep me from doing it,' " Powell later explained. "So you keep doing what you're doing and maybe things will break differently or not."

He would continue to play the game while time remained on the clock, but it was clear that Bush would brook no additional delay. Even if Powell had wanted to protest, the moment for real dissent had long past, one disappointed senior State Department official later reflected. The only argument against invasion that might ever have succeeded—that it would undermine the larger war on terrorism—"would had to have been made early on," in the spring and early summer of 2002. It was an argument that Powell had not made. Instead, the secretary had tried to play for time and erect roadblocks to slow the march to war, in hopes that something would stop it. But the administration hard-liners, in their hurry to get to Baghdad, had rolled right over him.

"It's easier to see in hindsight," the official said, "but I think what happened is that we convinced ourselves that you could make these tactical arguments, like the U.N. resolution. But we were guilty of ducking the big issue" of whether or not going to war at all was wise policy.

There had been times in the past, and there would be more in the future, when the White House undercut Powell in the performance of his duty or when the cumulative weight of lost battles and misguided policies became more than many of his friends and colleagues thought he should be willing to bear. But those who would later cite the January 13 meeting with Bush as a moment when he should have considered resigning on principle misunderstood both his undaunted sense of the possible and his view of the Iraq situation.

Powell had long known that Bush was determined to resolve the issue one way or the other. He differed with the president on whether the time for diplomacy and inspections had now run out, but ultimately that was Bush's decision to make.

Powell saw similarities between his own position and that of George Marshall, the first career soldier to become secretary of state and a man of "flawless rectitude and self-command," in the words of one biographer. They had both made their names in the military—Marshall, as Army chief of staff, had brilliantly organized U.S. forces for World War II. Both had spent much of their Army careers in desk jobs rather than in the field of combat. Both were known for their skill in navigating high-level bureaucracy and in handling Congress—President Roosevelt had refused to allow Marshall to command the U.S. invasion of Europe, telling him he was too valuable in Washington and naming General Dwight D. Eisenhower instead. As President Truman's secretary of state, Marshall, like Powell, had lent his prestige and reputation to a chief executive desperately in need of foreign policy gravitas. They were both ardent multilateralists, believers in a strong American defense and largely apolitical—although Marshall, unlike Powell, never felt the need to join a political party or even to vote. Both saw the revitalization of the State Department itself as one of their primary tasks.

One anecdote from Marshall's State Department tenure held particular resonance for Powell. Marshall had objected to Truman's decision to grant early diplomatic recognition to a new State of Israel in 1948—before an Israeli government or recognized boundaries had been established—arguing, among other things, that the United States would be drawn into a war between mobilizing Arab armies and Jewish settlers. In a note to his personal files, Marshall wrote that Truman's insistence was nothing more than a "transparent dodge to win a few votes" from American Jews in a tight reelection year—the same year in which Truman courted black voters with his military desegregation order.

But when Marshall's aides suggested that he should resign on principle over the Israel question, he memorably replied, "No, gentlemen, you don't take a post of this sort and then resign when the man who has the constitutional responsibility to make decisions makes one you don't like."

As Powell paraphrased it, Marshall had said, " 'Nobody made me President. I serve.' " Marshall had "done his job. He had given the President his best advice. He had presented it strongly ... [and] used every, every opportunity he had to press his case, and the ultimate responsibility lay with Harry S. Truman." Powell found the story "a heck of a note of inspiration."

The third Monday in January was set aside each year for a federal holiday commemorating the life of Martin Luther King, Jr. Like many prominent blacks, Powell usually spent the day giving a speech or attending King-related events, and when French Foreign Minister Dominique de Villepin called in early January 2003 to schedule a Security Council meeting for Monday, January 20, he initially begged off. France had just assumed the rotating, monthlong Council presidency, and de Villepin wanted to mark the occasion with a ministerial meeting on global terrorism.

In addition to his King Day plans, Powell was leery of attending a public session that would likely turn into an argument about Iraq. Blix and Mohamed ElBaradei were due to present their next inspections report to the Security Council on January 27. Powell saw little point in adding another opportunity for debate before then. It would only provide anti-U.N. forces in the administration with more evidence that the United Nations—and particularly putative U.S. allies such as France and Germany—could not be trusted.

The White House saw France as an arrogant pretender to world-power status, and Bush was personally furious at Germany, which had just assumed one of the ten nonpermanent Council seats. German Chancellor Gerhard Schröder had promised support on Iraq, but now that his political party was struggling in a reelection campaign, he had turned against Bush to pander to public opinion. Rumsfeld derisively referred to both countries as "old Europe."

Powell had his own differences with the Europeans but had argued to the other principals that they had to be given a respectful hearing. When he reported that "the Europeans are worried about this or that, they're nervous, they don't trust us, the tendency within the administration was to say, 'And they're full of shit,' " recalled a senior official privy to the conversations. "Powell would say, 'They're full of shit, and we've got to deal with them.' He was the only one who would say that."

De Villepin did, in fact, want to talk about Iraq, but not in public. He was convinced that the Americans intended to use the upcoming January 27 Security Council session to declare that inspections had failed and should be ended, when as far as France was concerned the process had only just begun. He agreed with Powell that the issue could blow up in an argument for all the world—including Saddam Hussein—to see. Instead, de Villepin wanted to schedule a noncontroversial public meeting on the general topic of global terrorism as a smoke screen behind which the foreign ministers could consult privately on Iraq. With any luck, they could then avoid a high-profile eruption in the session with Blix a week later. Assured that Iraq would not be raised in the January 20 public session and informed that other foreign ministers had already accepted de Villepin's invitation, Powell grudgingly agreed to attend.

De Villepin called the Security Council to order at 10:30 a.m. on January 20. Its agenda, he said, was the search for ways to "strengthen the mobilization of all against terrorism." Kofi Annan and Jack Straw gave five-minute presentations, and then it was German Foreign Minister Joschka Fischer's turn. After offering a stock assessment of terrorism's "strategic threat to peace," Fischer broke ranks.

"Allow me to comment here on the current situation," he said. "We are greatly concerned that a military strike against the regime in Baghdad would involve considerable and unpredictable risks for the global fight against terrorism." It would have "disastrous consequences," and Germany rejected the very idea.

Fischer's remarks startled Powell, whose thoughts had been wandering during the antiterror boilerplate. He immediately started to rewrite his own comments while Straw picked up the gauntlet to announce that "there has to come a moment when our patience must run out and we are now near that point with Iraq."

Russian Foreign Minister Igor Ivanov parried back, saying that success in the global war on terror would depend on unity and respect for international law. "We must be careful not to take unilateral steps that might threaten the unity of the antiterrorist coalition." Russia, he said, favored "a political settlement of the situation concerning Iraq."

When Powell's turn came, he reminded them that they had all joined together to approve Resolution 1441 and would have to face the logical consequences if Baghdad failed to comply with their demands. "We cannot fail to take action that may be necessary because we are afraid of what others might do. . . . However difficult the road ahead may be with respect to Iraq, we must not shrink from the need to travel that road."

Powell was annoyed at the turn the session had taken but thought that nothing of great significance had transpired. "I didn't see it as a huge catastrophe," he later recalled. When the meeting adjourned, the foreign ministers headed off for lunch with de Villepin at the French ambassador's residence.

De Villepin was late in arriving, and his luncheon guests milled around for forty-five minutes waiting for the meal to begin. Ambassadors and aides had been sent to tables in a separate room, where they could listen to the high-level conversation through microphones that the French had tastefully concealed in the ministers' floral centerpieces. Once the host arrived, all that the ambassadors could hear above the clattering of dishes and cutlery was pleasant banter and conversation. The disagreements in the Council chamber seemed to have been forgotten.

But as Powell left the lunch to return to Washington, his cell phone was ringing. "Did you hear what Dominique did?" Rice asked with evident agitation.

"What?" Powell replied.

The French foreign minister had held a press conference at the United Nations immediately after the Council meeting, which explained his delayed arrival at lunch. De Villepin had told reporters that it was clear that Iraq's WMD program was "frozen" and could be contained while

U.N. disarmament continued. "Nothing justifies cutting off inspections to enter into war and uncertainty."

The crisis in Iraq represented a test for the Security Council, de Villepin continued, and "if war is the only way to resolve this problem, we are going down a dead end." Unilateral military intervention without Council approval "would be perceived as a victory for the law of the strongest, an attack on the rule of law and on international morality." Although he never used the word, he all but pledged that France would veto any resolution to activate the "serious consequences" alluded to in Resolution 1441. "We believe that today nothing justifies envisaging military action," he concluded.

The French position was no surprise to Powell; he and de Villepin had discussed it at a private meeting the night before. French President Jacques Chirac's national security adviser had met with Rice in Washington a week earlier and had come away convinced that the decision to invade had already been made. Though Powell had insisted the door to peace was still open, de Villepin thought his language was identical to what France had heard from Rice and interpreted it to mean that "diplomacy was no longer relevant."

But the French foreign minister's public declaration that "nothing" would justify war was a devastating blow to Powell. It was difficult to decide what to be more furious about, the actions of de Villepin and the Germans or the inevitable reactions to them by his colleagues in the White House. His leverage on Iraq in the administration, never high to begin with, was now severely—perhaps irrevocably—destroyed.

"Essentially, I was still pushing for diplomacy, and [now] the White House could say, 'What are you doing? The French are making it clear that they're going to hose you on this,'" Powell later reflected bitterly. "It certainly reinforced [the White House] case that we weren't going to get a diplomatic solution. Or worse, that the French were trying to take away" any hope that the Security Council would ever authorize the use of force. De Villepin had given aid and comfort to administration hard-liners, who argued that the diplomatic effort had been pointless all along. His remarks had made a unilateral U.S. invasion more, rather than less, likely.

"The die was cast after that," a senior State Department official later recalled. "We gave up on our theory" that a united international front was possible.

Media reports described Powell as having been "ambushed" by the French. His aides made some choice comments of their own about de Villepin to journalists, but Powell was convinced that the White House had played up the incident to the media and "made it more of a story than it was. Frankly, I think the White House is responsible for the 'double-cross' story," he later said. " 'Powell got double-crossed. Poor Powell went up there and we warned him not to and he got skunked by the French.' "

For their part, the French believed that Powell had long since lost whatever battle he was fighting within the administration. De Villepin's comments, they were convinced, had simply given Powell the public jus-tification he needed to switch sides and join the hawks. "The decision to go to war had already been taken," a senior French official later insisted. "Colin Powell, like it or not, had to support the policy or say good-bye to this administration. His choice was clear."

The day after the Security Council session, reporters were ushered into the White House for a few words from the president as he began a meeting with a group of economists. Asked if he was frustrated by the French, Bush replied that Saddam Hussein was playing games with the inspectors and the world, just as he had in the 1990s. "It appears to be the re-run of a bad movie," he said. "It's clear to me now that he is not disarm-ing...and we will lead a coalition of willing nations to disarm him. Make no mistake about that." Asked when he would decide, Bush said flippantly to laughter from his guests, "I will let you know when the moment has come."

The administration was under rising pressure at home and abroad to back up its assertions that the threat Iraq posed was both real and imminent. The Vietnam generation knew that war "cannot be sustained without the informed consent of the American people," Delaware Senator Joseph Biden, the senior Democrat on the Foreign Relations Committee, said in a radio interview. The Republicans, who had recaptured the Senate in November, were more willing to take Bush's word for it but worried that their constituents might not agree. "There is no informed consent at this point," agreed Senator Chuck Hagel on the same radio program. Bush "should be prepared to lay it all out...not just for our allies...but for the people in this country. I think people...are very unsure and unsettled about this."

Washington and London had been consulting since the previous fall on the need to reveal more details of what they called "the case" against Iraq. Tony Blair, who had a far bigger domestic public relations problem than Bush, was particularly concerned that the political timetable was begin-ning to lag behind the growing military deployment. The intelligence agencies and Douglas Feith's operation in the Pentagon were adding new evidence every day, and the White House was wrestling with the trade-off between building the most convincing case for war and waiting too long to unveil it.

Just before Christmas, Tenet and McLaughlin had briefed Bush, Cheney and Rice on specific intelligence they thought could be declassified to back up their conclusions on Iraq's WMD and ties to al-Qaeda. The case was a "slam dunk," Tenet had said. But Bush was unimpressed with their presentation; the evidence lacked dramatic punch and was too complicated for the general public to understand.

On December 28, CIA officials had made another try, this time in front of the NSC. Once again, they were told to return to the drawing board and look more carefully at "new intelligence that had been collected" since the National Intelligence Estimate had been issued in October. In mid-January, after a third CIA effort was found wanting, officials in Cheney's office and the NSC staff began to rework "the case" to turn it into a more compelling narrative.

Called to a meeting in the Situation Room on Saturday, January 25, Armitage was instantly suspicious. The purpose of the session, he later recalled, was for "Libby and 'the boys'—not further defined, but I assumed it was Bill Luti and [John] Hannah, the usual suspects" on the hard-line side—to present their version of the justification for an invasion. Wolfowitz was present, along with Rice's deputy Stephen Hadley, Bush's speechwriter Michael Gerson, White House Communications Director Dan Bartlett and Karl Rove. Karen Hughes, Bush's longtime adviser from Texas, was also there. Powell was traveling abroad that weekend, and Armitage put through a call to him as soon as the session was over.

The meeting had been "bizarre," he told the secretary. "The word 'hyperbole' was flashing in neon lights." In feverish language and with references to intelligence described as "conclusive," the new version of the case had both expanded the substance and increased the urgency of the threat from Iraq.

Powell had left the day before for the World Economic Forum, an annual five-day gathering of international political and business leaders in Davos, Switzerland. Richard Haass, who had drafted the address Powell was to deliver to the forum on Saturday, had arrived there several days earlier and reported to the secretary that the meeting thus far had been marked by relentless antagonism toward the United States. Some of the attendees were waiting to attack Powell; many more were certain that he privately agreed with their disapproval of the administration's Iraq policy.

The reasonableness and pragmatism that infuriated both the hidebound Right and the far Left at home—the "empty ideological vessel" that had allowed the broad center to feel political kinship with Powell as he had contemplated a race for the presidency in 1995—also characterized his image abroad. As secretary of state, he had become "a dress-up doll" to much of the world community, in the words of his spokesman, Richard Boucher. European liberals, in particular, liked to "dress him up in their own clothes—they'd take Colin Powell and say, 'Well, he must be a vegetarian pacifist like me. Because he's an eminently sensible person; I'm an eminently sensible person and I'm a vegetarian pacifist.' "

Powell wanted his speech rewritten to let them know they were wrong, both about him and about the United States. Fresh from de Villepin's betrayal at the Security Council, he was fed up with European pontificating and holier-than-thou claims to the moral high ground. The United States had been carrying the weight for countries like France and Germany for years, he thought, building up their economies after World War II, protecting them first from the Soviet Union and now from an international terrorist threat. In return, they offered nothing but contempt. He had his problems with the White House and others in the administration, but that did not mean he was ready to let his country, his government and himself be insulted.

When Powell entered the auditorium on Saturday, about half the audience stood to welcome him while the rest offered modest applause. "I've been here for just over a day," he began, "long enough to speak and meet with a number of you, long enough to hear directly and from others much of what has been said about the United States over the last two or three days, about whether America can be trusted to use its enormous political, economic, and above all military power wisely and fairly.

"I believe—no, I know with all of my heart—that the United States can." From Afghanistan to Africa and Latin America, he said, the Bush administration was working to build democratic institutions. Relations with Russia and China had never been better. The administration was seeking a diplomatic solution to the North Korea problem, using its influence to bring Pakistan and India back from the brink of war and struggling with the immensely difficult Mideast peace process. Differences with Europe were inevitable, he said, "but difference should not be equated with American unilateralism or American arrogance. Sometimes differences are just that—differences."

They had joined together to give Iraq a final chance to disarm, he said, and Iraq had "failed the test." Repeating some of the most damning allegations the administration had made, Powell asked, "Where are the mobile vans that are nothing more than biological weapons laboratories on wheels? Why is Iraq still trying to procure uranium and the special equipment needed to transform it into material for nuclear weapons? These questions are not academic. They are not trivial. They are questions of life and death, and they must be answered." The longer they waited, he warned, "the more chance there is for this dictator with clear ties to terrorist groups, including al Qaeda, to pass a weapon, share a technology or to use these weapons again." The evidence was there, he insisted, and the United States would reveal it to the world "in the days and weeks ahead."

Those who had expected Powell to validate their concerns about the war were disappointed. Far from apologetic, he was outspoken and at times uncharacteristically emotional. "I don't think I have anything to be ashamed of, or apologize for, with respect to what America has done for the world," he said in response to a question from a former archbishop of Canterbury—the spiritual leader of his own Episcopal Church. Time and again over the last century, he said, "We've put wonderful young men and women at risk, many of whom have lost their lives. We've asked for nothing but enough land to bury them in." The line, which he had used often in the past, almost always brought tears to his eyes.

The response was appreciative, but he won few converts to the Iraq cause. "He's a decent guy, but I don't think he changed any minds," said Gareth Evans, a former Australian foreign minister, who was in the audience. "We don't need much evidence, just enough to know that [Saddam] is lying. But there's not enough yet…if you want international support."

Powell returned from Davos on Sunday night "pretty fired up," Armitage recalled. "He felt he'd really done the nation a service by sitting in front of the snarling masses and giving a good presentation. He got, he felt, a respectful hearing. And he felt that the United States…got some respect. He was buoyed."

On Monday, January 27, Blix told the Security Council that Iraq was cooperating with the process of inspections—including granting unfettered access to all sites—but not the substance. There were "strong indications," for example, that Iraq had produced more anthrax before its weapons stockpiles were destroyed after the 1991 war than it had acknowledged. Yet no evidence was offered to explain what had happened to it. "Iraq appears not to have come to a genuine acceptance—not even today—of the disarmament which was demanded of it and which it needs to carry out to win the confidence of the world and to live in peace," Blix said.

Despite these concerns, he continued, inspections were proceeding and they would achieve verifiable disarmament of Iraq "in a reasonable period of time." For the Bush administration, the report was infuriating. Blix had said straight out that Iraq wasn't cooperating, yet he was asking for more time. ElBaradei's report on nuclear inspections was even worse. The IAEA's work in Iraq was "steadily progressing and should be allowed to run its natural course," he said. Within a few months, they should be able to provide credible assurance that Iraq had no nuclear weapons program.

John Negroponte attended the meeting for the United States while Powell remained in Washington. At the White House, Bush told his secretary of state what Powell already knew from Armitage: that the administration was ready to present its evidence against Saddam in detail. " 'We've really got to make the case, and I want you to make it,' " Powell recalled Bush saying. " 'You have the credibility to do this. Maybe they'll believe you.' "

"The case" against Saddam, Powell was told, had been assembled in three separate parts: weapons of mass destruction, ties to international terrorists and human rights violations. Karen Hughes suggested that the segments be presented to the Security Council on three consecutive days, beginning the following week on Wednesday, February 5. Powell replied that his fellow foreign ministers would not sit still for a three-day lecture and most were unlikely to be convinced no matter what he said. Their target audience was American and international public opinion, he said, and they needed a presentation that was serious, specific and succinct.

Despite the alarms Armitage had sounded, Powell assumed that with a little tweaking he could turn the document provided by the White House into something that would fit his voice and style. But he was taken aback on Tuesday, January 28, when he received the first segment on Iraq's weapons of mass destruction. Its forty-eight single-spaced pages—drafted, he assumed, in the vice president's office by John Hannah under "Scooter" Libby's tutelage—were a ready-to-deliver speech replete with drama, rhetorical devices and a kitchen sinkful of allegations with no sourcing or caveats. Acutely aware that he would be selling his own reputation as much as the specific facts, Powell picked up the telephone to tell Rice he needed more time to get it into shape.

During his State of the Union address to Congress that same night, the president planned to announce that the secretary of state would present the evidence to the Security Council on Wednesday, February 5—just one week away. "Condi, please," Powell implored, "let's just tell the president that we're going to put in the State of the Union that Secretary Powell will be going to the U.N. next week. Don't put a date."

"She said, 'Right, right, of course,'" Powell recalled, "and she runs away to change the speech. Then runs back about five minutes later" to call him and say, "'There's good news and bad news. The good news is we can change the speech.'" The bad news, she said, was that the White House had already told the press, in a preview of the State of the Union address, that Powell's presentation would be made on February 5.

"I could have gotten two more days," Powell later said wistfully. "Whether it would have made any difference or not, I don't know."

At 10 a.m. on Wednesday, January 29, Powell walked through the inner doorway to Wilkerson's office. "Here you go," he said, dropping the White House WMD document onto his chief of staff's desk. Wilkerson and a half dozen others from the State Department—including the speechwriter Lynne Davidson, who had previously worked for Tenet, and Barry Lowenkron, a senior CIA officer before he joined Powell's policy planning staff—planned to set up shop at CIA headquarters across the Potomac in Langley, Virginia, where they would turn the document into what Wilkerson called "a Colin Powell speech." Hannah and William Tobey, the NSC counterproliferation director, would meet them there to answer any questions they had.

"We were going out to the agency and live there until we got the presentation ready," Wilkerson later said. "We didn't know the hugeness of the task, but we knew immediately we were going to have to squirrel ourselves away somewhere, because we had to have graphics" drawn from highly classified intelligence material. The White House had detailed its own graphics team—the best in the government—to work with them.

Wilkerson's first reaction was that the document reminded him of his favorite Ian Rutledge novels. Inspector Rutledge, a creation of the author Charles Todd, was a fictional Scotland Yard detective who confronted murder and psychological mayhem in post–World War I Britain. Even if the document wasn't fiction, it sure read like it.

Wilkerson was an expert in Powell's views and moods. Except for a time immediately following Powell's retirement from the military, he had spent most of the last thirteen years working for him. They weren't bosom buddies, and to some extent their relationship would always be one of four-star general to colonel. Outside the office, they shared a commitment to working with disadvantaged youths—Wilkerson managed Powell's personal sponsorship of a downtrodden middle school in the District of Columbia, and Powell helped out with several of Wilkerson's local community projects. At the State Department, Wilkerson was known for his unyielding loyalty to the secretary and for his attention to detail. If anyone would make sure that all the i's were dotted and the t's crossed in the speech, Powell and Armitage felt, it was Larry.

Wilkerson's task was to make the most convincing, evidence-backed case possible. In recent months, Powell's language on Iraq had become almost as loose as Cheney's. Powell had read the October NIE and daily reports since then but had little more than a cursory knowledge of the intelligence underlying some of the most damning charges. In his Davos speech he had cited allegations that his own State Department analysts questioned, including the attempts to import uranium and nuclear-related aluminum tubes as well as the ties between Saddam and al-Qaeda. But that had been only an indictment; this would have to be a complete, trial-worthy prosecution, designed to convince a skeptical jury that capital punishment, in the form of decapitating the Iraqi regime, was warranted. They had to throw out anything they could not prove and buttress every fact with two or more layers of ironclad sourcing.

In addition to proving the case against Iraq, Wilkerson felt, they would have to protect Powell's integrity against powerful forces within the administration—particularly Cheney—who had long been out to tarnish it. The secretary had laughed when he described how the vice president, after a discussion of Powell's upcoming presentation, had poked him jocularly in the chest and said, "You've got high poll ratings, you can afford to lose a few points." Cheney's idea of Powell's mission, Wilkerson thought, was to "go up there and sell it, and we'll have moved forward a peg or two. Fall on your damn sword and kill yourself, and I'll be happy, too."

By early Wednesday afternoon, seven days before the presentation, Wilkerson and his team were huddled in the CIA director's conference room taking the WMD document apart sentence by sentence. Things were not going well. Hannah had brought a clipboard with a three-inch stack of paper that he thumbed through to cite the generic origin of each allegation—reports from the CIA, the Defense Intelligence Agency, foreign intelligence, the Iraqi National Congress and even newspaper articles. Tenet and McLaughlin—backed up by Robert Walpole, the chief CIA officer for nuclear programs; Lawrence Gershwin, the agency's top adviser on "technical" intelligence; and several other specialists—were constantly dispatching aides out of the room to find the original source material.

In some instances, the "evidence" was, in fact, found in an official intelligence report, but only as unconfirmed information that had not been cited in the report's conclusions. "They had left out all the caveats, all the qualifiers," Wilkerson recalled. In a few instances, they had even changed the meaning of the intelligence. A Senate investigation of the speechwriting process conducted after the invasion would later conclude that the Powell team had had to eliminate "information that the White House had added ... gathered from finished and raw intelligence," some of which had come from only a single source with no corroboration at all.

After wrestling with the document for hours, they had made it through only a few pages. "This is not going to meet your time schedule," Tenet said to Wilkerson. "We've got to move faster than this." Wilkerson readily agreed, relieved that the CIA director had voiced what he himself was thinking. At Tenet's suggestion, they decided to scrap the White House document altogether and start from scratch, using the October NIE as their base.

Late that night, after the senior CIA and White House officials had left for the day, Wilkerson and his colleagues watched a film he had borrowed from the State Department archives of Adlai Stevenson's historic speech to the Security Council at the height of the Cuban Missile Crisis in 1962. The Soviet Union had angrily denied charges that it had deployed nuclear-armed missiles on the island ninety miles off the Florida coast. Stevenson, the U.S. ambassador to the United Nations at the time, had responded with irrefutable proof in the form of twenty-six grainy, poster-sized black-and-white photographs of missile sites shot from a U-2 reconnaissance plane, displayed on easels at the front of the Council chamber for all the world to see. That "Stevenson moment," Wilkerson told them, was the effect they were after.

Libby and Stephen Hadley joined the process the next day, and Powell himself appeared at the table on Thursday afternoon. Cheney had called Powell to say he hoped the secretary would "take a good look at Scooter's stuff," and Boucher recalled Libby himself appealing to Powell to look more carefully at the now-discarded White House document and at a twenty-five-page supplement on Iraq's ties to terrorism. "Powell said, 'I don't want to. I want to use what Larry's been working on.' "

They settled into a routine. The CIA turned over the office suite of the National Intelligence Council—the internal organization that coordinated with other members of the intelligence community to write National Intelligence Estimates—to Wilkerson and the others engaged in the nitty-gritty of composing the speech and providing material to the graphic designers lodged in the agency's basement. At around 5 p.m. each day, the writing and research team would move to Tenet's conference room with senior officials, eventually including Rice and Armitage, to spend hours going over the new text and verifying the sourcing for Powell. Although the crowd sometimes reached as many as twenty or thirty people, no one from the Defense Department appeared. Wilkerson received calls from the offices of both Wolfowitz and Feith, however, and he assumed that Tobey and Hannah were "covering for them."

Powell insisted that any intelligence that had come from Ahmed Chalabi's exile group be eliminated. He was told by the CIA that evidence of Saddam's mobile laboratories for biological weapons—one of the most damning charges—had been corroborated by four separate sources, including an Iraqi chemical engineer, a civil engineer and an Iraqi military defector. It was, Tenet said, "totally reliable information." CIA analysts showed Powell drawings they had made of the truck and rail-mounted labs, based on descriptions that the sources had verified in every detail. Powell thought they looked like cartoons.

They argued over how to interpret intercepted communications about Iraq's weapons—a number of them recorded since the October NIE— between Iraqi military officers. None seemed definitive, and Wilkerson was worried that they might not mean what the analysts said they meant. In one of the exchanges, he later recalled, "Captain Ibrahim" had been told by a superior officer to "take nerve agents out of his CEOI [Communications and Electronics Operating Instructions]. Well, suppose he's being told to take nerve agents out of the instructions because there aren't any nerve agents? There were a number of things like that, where we said there were at least two, opposite interpretations." Despite Wilkerson's concerns, Captain Ibrahim stayed in the speech as evidence of existing WMD.

They examined satellite imagery said to reveal prohibited items. Powell was shown, and rejected, a grainy picture of what analysts said was an unmanned aerial vehicle (UAV) site near Basra. It was impossible to tell where it was or even what it was, he argued. Instead, he approved a U.N. photograph of a generic Iraqi UAV, taken years earlier, to illustrate charges in the speech that Saddam was developing drones that could spray deadly WMD on population centers.

CIA analysts showed the team additional photographs they said conclusively revealed chemical weapons production and storage facilities but then insisted that the pictures were too sensitive to be used in a public presentation. Those they were willing to release often appeared—at least to the uninitiated in the room—to illustrate nothing more than trucks parked beside buildings. The analysts insisted that the pictures showed things like Iraqis "moving a prohibited vehicle out," but who could be sure? Wilkerson wondered. "It could be because [the Iraqis] wanted to hide it. Or maybe a general was telling them to move it out because he was supposed to have gotten rid of it six months ago. We were beginning to get leery of our own presentation."

Boucher, too, thought the photographs were less than definitive. "Don't you have a picture of chemical weapons canisters being moved around?" he asked Tenet at one point. "Something we can point to and say: 'That's a chemical weapon.'" Tenet replied that no country had left prohibited weapons "out on the lawn" since the Cuban Missile Crisis. "They know we're looking at them. So we have to go with other things that tell us what they're doing." In each photograph, Tenet said, analysts searched for a "signature"—a telltale positioning of buildings or vehicles—to interpret what they were seeing. In any case, he said, they had multiple sources for each conclusion they had drawn.

They spent hours discussing the aluminum tubes Saddam had tried to import. The Energy Department and the State Department's INR continued to disagree with the CIA's assessment that the tubes were clearly designed for nuclear enrichment. McLaughlin, who had brought one of the intercepted tubes to the table and rolled it back and forth as they argued, insisted that the CIA analysis was correct. The agency, Powell later recalled, "pulled in their experts and swore on a stack of Bibles that they'd done every analysis imaginable, and [the tubes] simply were not for rockets, but for [uranium] centrifuges." The tubes stayed in the speech, although with a brief mention of the disagreement among U.S. government agencies as to their purpose.

Bush had referred in his State of the Union address to Iraqi efforts to obtain uranium from Africa—the same information the CIA had successfully argued should be excised from his Cincinnati speech the previous October because of questionable sources. No one suggested that it be included in Powell's presentation.

The twenty-five-page White House document detailing Saddam's ties to terrorism was, if anything, even more problematic than the WMD portion. Powell retreated with Tenet to the director's private office to talk through "what we really know" about the relationship between Iraq and al-Qaeda. The CIA had repeatedly questioned charges by the Pentagon and the vice president that a senior Iraqi intelligence official had met with one of the September 11 hijackers in Prague during the spring of 2001, and even the Czech government had said it wasn't true. But Powell was shown the transcript of an interrogation of a captured bin Laden aide who swore that al-Qaeda operatives had received biological and chemical weapons training from Iraq. The Prague reference was cut, and an extensive passage on the weapons training was inserted. They agreed that Powell would refer to the overall relationship as an "association." It was an area where Powell's aides later concluded he had compromised his—and their—better judgment.

Tempers began to fray as they moved into the weekend. Tenet and McLaughlin became irritated with Hadley, who kept pressing to reinsert language and information from the original White House draft. Powell exploded at McLaughlin, who supplied tortured, five-minute answers to one-sentence questions. Increasingly, the secretary looked to Tenet for final reassurance. "George would give the kind of answers the secretary liked," Wilkerson recalled. "Whether you liked that 'slam-dunk' language or not, George, to his credit, would say, 'Absolutely, Mr. Secretary, I stand by that.' " Individual intelligence items were described as having "A" or "A+" reliability.

Powell later recalled that most of their time was spent "trimming the garbage" of the White House's overwrought verbiage and uncorroborated specifics from the speech. Once that was done, Wilkerson concluded long afterward, "what we were all involved in—groupthink isn't the right word—it was a process of putting the data to points in the speech rather than challenging the data itself."

Another senior administration official who sympathized with Powell's effort saw it as a perfect example of the secretary's determination to make the best possible hand out of the cards he had been dealt. "Powell began the process with a [document], a lot of which came out of the vice president's office, which was a piece of crap. And he really worked on it. He brought together this whole team of people, and he pared it back and pared it back and probably got rid of 90 percent of the bullshit in it. When you're in government, that's not a bad couple of days' work.

"He knew he had a lot riding on it," the official continued. "This is not a careless man. He was not going to throw away his credibility or his reputation.... Did he do everything he should have done, in retrospect? No ... but that's what government is all about. This is not an open-ended, academic inquiry. This is a politically constrained universe you're working in."

As he constructed his hand, Powell saw no reason to suspect that the cards were marked or to question the game itself.

On Monday, February 3, Powell joined Rice and McLaughlin at a lunch Rumsfeld hosted in his office, where they briefed a small group of influential former officials whose views were likely to be sought by the media after the presentation. The group included former defense secretaries Frank Carlucci and Robert McNamara; former secretaries of state Henry Kissinger and Madeleine Albright; William H. Webster, a former CIA director; and former national security advisers William P. Clark from the Reagan administration and Zbigniew Brzezinski from the Carter administration. Brzezinski, who had publicly questioned the urgency of the Iraqi threat, came away impressed by their unanimous certainty. "They didn't go into any of the evidence, but they very specifically made it clear that this is not assertion, this is not hypothesis, this was actual knowledge."

Brzezinski was not opposed in principle to using force against Saddam Hussein—as long as military action was undertaken in the right way and for the right reasons, based on "compelling" evidence, which he had not yet seen. "But your doubts, honestly, tend to shrink when three people whom you respect, whom you trust, whom you have known for years, tell you they *know*." His own experience in government had taught him "what it means when they say they know … there is certain data that leads to the conclusion that this is a fact. It's not something which is just loose talk.

"I felt, at that particular moment, maybe reassured is the wrong word," Brzezinski later recalled. "I felt more inclined to say to myself, 'Well, if they *know*, it must be so.' "

Colin did not ask Alma to accompany him to the United Nations; normally she had no interest in brief domestic turnarounds. But this time, she invited herself. She could tell that her husband was drained. "I knew he needed me," she said. "He needed to know I was there."

When he arrived in New York on Monday afternoon, Powell was as nervous as Wilkerson had ever seen him. Wilkerson himself was anxious; they had done a prodigious amount of work, he thought, but they had done it far too fast for the monumental importance of the event. After they rehearsed for a while, Wilkerson and Barry Lowenkron continued to tinker while Powell left for an hourlong meeting on North Korea with the Chinese foreign minister.

Tenet, McLaughlin and their staffs had also come to New York, and the entire group convened at the U.S. Mission on Tuesday. Powell was worried that the language in the speech was still too methodical and technical to win over an audience. His best performances were modeled on what he had learned as a young instructor at Fort Benning and under General DePuy at the Pentagon: use a map or some slides, a rough outline or a few key phrases, and then speak naturally. He always knew his material cold, but it was technique that clinched a sale. This time there was little room for technique. Each sentence had been carefully crafted and debated ad nauseam, and he was going to have to read directly from the text.

On Tuesday night they had a final, full-dress rehearsal. The cafeteria on the top floor of the U.S. Mission had been reconfigured into a mock-up of the Security Council chamber, with screens and speakers for the audiovisuals. Powell used a stopwatch to check his timing, clicking it off every time someone interrupted with a question or comment. The speech was seventy-five minutes long.

When he finished, the tension of the last several days seemed to dissipate like the air escaping a balloon, leaving him calm and tired. He felt he had done everything he could do. Departing for his room at the Waldorf, where he hoped to get a good night's sleep, he reminded Tenet that "you're going to be there with me tomorrow." He expected the CIA director to sit in full view of the television cameras, just behind him at the Security Council table. Tenet replied, only half jokingly, that he was the one who would have to face the intelligence committees in Congress if there were any mistakes. He was at least as invested in the presentation as the secretary, he said.

Powell told Boucher and Craig Kelly, his executive assistant, to make sure that Tenet was waiting in the side room they would pass through on their way into the Security Council chamber the next morning. Later he changed his mind and called Tenet from his room to tell him he would swing by the CIA director's hotel and pick him up on the way to the United Nations, just to make sure.

Wilkerson and Lowenkron were awake for much of the night. Amid a flurry of last-minute telephone calls, Tenet's staff expressed concern that too much had been taken out of the terrorism section of the speech. At one point in the wee hours, Wilkerson got a government courier to carry the final text, locked in a briefcase handcuffed to his wrist, to the CIA director's hotel. He heard no more complaints.

The next morning, they finished setting up the equipment in the Security Council chamber at 8:45 a.m., less than two hours before Powell was due to speak.

When Adolfo Aguilar Zinser walked into the Security Council on Wednesday morning, the first things he noticed were the video screens and computers that had been installed for Powell's multimedia presentation. It was a sure sign, Mexico's U.N. ambassador thought with some disdain, that "this show wasn't for us. It was for an international audience, for the U.S. media."

Outside, New York City police officers directed limousine convoys through the high iron gates and onto the circular U.N. driveway, where they deposited arriving foreign ministers and dignitaries. Television satellite trucks were lined up wheel to wheel along First Avenue, and reporters stood shivering in the icy February wind as they shouted into handheld microphones.

The speech was being broadcast live around the world, but a long line of spectators, hoping to watch history being made firsthand, snaked through a white security tent. Every seat in the visitors' gallery was filled when Powell entered the chamber just before 10:30 a.m., smiling and stopping to shake hands as he made his way across the floor. By the time he took his chair at the horseshoe-shaped Council table at the center of the room, with Tenet seated behind his right shoulder and Negroponte behind his left, his features were composed in a mask of gravity.

With war hanging in the balance and the power and prestige of the United States on full display, it was a moment of high drama that owed as much to the player as to the play. A nationwide poll released just that morning had found that "when it comes to U.S. policy toward Iraq," Americans trusted Powell more than Bush by a margin of 63 to 24 percent. His reputation as the "reluctant warrior" and as the administration's leading dove—arguably its only one—would lend incalculable credibility to the case he was about to make.

"I cannot tell you everything that we know," he began after a brief introduction. "But what I can share with you, when combined with what all of us have learned over the years, is deeply troubling." The facts and Iraq's behavior "demonstrate that Saddam Hussein and his regime have made no effort—no effort—to disarm as required by the international community." He moved quickly into his first demonstration, an audiotape of two Iraqi officers he said were discussing the concealment of a "modified vehicle" on November 26, 2002, the day before inspections began. As the scratchy Arabic words echoed through the chamber, an English translation appeared on the video screen.

"My colleagues," Powell said, "every statement I make today is backed up by sources, solid sources. These are not assertions. What we are giving you are facts and conclusions based on solid intelligence."

For an hour and fifteen minutes, he condemned what he called Saddam Hussein's efforts to conceal and to lie about his weapons programs. He played more tapes, showed satellite photographs and displayed artists' renderings of the mobile biological weapons labs he said had been described in detail by eyewitnesses. He showed a picture of an aluminum tube he said had been intercepted in an Iraq-bound shipment and of the wooden crate it had been packed in. He held up a small vial of white powder—fake poison that had been carried to New York in Boucher's pocket. "Less than a teaspoon of dry anthrax... about this amount... shut down the United States Senate in the fall of 2001" when it arrived in an anonymous envelope, he said. Although there had been little suggestion of Iraqi involvement at the time, Powell implied a connection, saying that Iraq had never accounted for 25,000 liters of anthrax that U.N. inspectors in the 1990s estimated it had retained. It was enough, he said, for "tens upon tens of thousands of teaspoons."

He spoke of the "sinister nexus between Iraq and the al Qaeda network, a nexus that combines classic terrorist organizations and modern methods of murder." Saddam was currently harboring a "deadly terrorist network headed by Abu Musab al Zarqawi, an associate and collaborator of Osama bin Laden and his al Qaeda lieutenants." In far more detail than any administration official had offered publicly to date, he described Iraqi training of al-Qaeda operatives in chemical and biological weapons production, attributing the information to a "senior terrorist operative" now in U.S. custody.

"Some believe, some claim, these contacts do not amount to much," he said. "They say Saddam Hussein's secular tyranny and al Qaeda's religious tyranny do not mix. I am not comforted by this thought."

The foreign ministers and other officials around the table were silent. Iraqi Ambassador Mohamed Al-Douri furiously scribbled notes. Kofi Annan sat pensively, making steeples of his long fingers. Joschka Fischer twiddled with his pen, drummed his fingers and cleaned his glasses. Dominique de Villepin leaned forward and stared at Powell intently while Jack Straw nodded his head in agreement.

"We know that Saddam Hussein is determined to keep his weapons of mass destruction, is determined to make more," Powell said in closing. "Given Saddam Hussein's history of aggression, given what we know of his grandiose plans, given what we know of his terrorist associations and given his determination to exact revenge on those who oppose him, should we take the risk that he will not some day use these weapons at a time and a place and in a manner of his choosing, at a time when the world is in a much weaker position to respond?

"The United States will not and cannot run that risk for the American people." The Security Council, in Resolution 1441, had given Iraq one last chance, he said. "Iraq is not, so far, taking that one last chance. We must not shrink from whatever is ahead of us. We must not fail in our duty and our responsibility to the citizens of the countries that are represented by this body."

The other ministers followed his presentation with statements of their own, most of which seemed to have been prepared before Powell spoke. None appeared to have changed his or her views in light of Powell's revelations.

Chinese Foreign Minister Tang Jiaxuan said he hoped that any country that possessed evidence would turn it over to the inspectors and called for the "utmost effort" to work toward a political solution. Igor Ivanov agreed and said that Powell's information had provided more, not less, impetus to continue inspections. De Villepin noted that there were still "grey areas" in Iraq's cooperation with inspectors, a good reason to increase the number of U.N. personnel on the ground.

Much of the world seemed similarly underwhelmed. British reaction was divided, with conservative commentators agreeing that Powell had proven the case for war, while liberal ones, along with the majority of the population, remained doubtful. Among Iraq's neighbors, *The Jordan Times* said that "these new elements did not amount to convincing evidence of Iraqi noncompliance, or that Iraq presents any real or imminent danger to any party." But an editorial in Israel's conservative *Jerusalem Post* exulted, "Scratch everything we've said about Secretary of State Colin Powell. We love him."

Saddam Hussein told Tony Benn, a visiting British member of Parliament, "[t]here is only one truth.... As I have said on many occasions before ... Iraq has no weapons of mass destruction whatsoever."

But if world opinion largely rejected Powell's argument as a justification for war, his speech was an overwhelming success at home. U.S. public opinion shifted literally overnight to support for dealing forcefully with Iraq. A *Newsweek* poll taken just after the speech found that half of all Americans surveyed were now ready to go to war, compared to only a third the previous month. Three out of four Americans who told *Los Angeles Times* pollsters that they had watched, listened to or heard about Powell's presentation said that the United States had proved its case against Iraq.

A *Washington Post* editorial called the evidence "irrefutable" and said that Powell's case made it "hard to imagine how anyone could doubt that Iraq possesses weapons of mass destruction." Even the war-wary *New York Times* said that Powell had made "the most powerful case to date that Saddam Hussein stands in defiance of Security Council resolutions and has no intention of revealing or surrendering whatever unconventional weapons he may have." Mary McGrory, the grande dame of liberal polit-ical columnists and one of the harshest critics of the administration's hawkish stance, said she had been persuaded. "I'm not ready for war yet," McGrory wrote. "But Colin Powell has convinced me that it might be the only way to stop a fiend, and that if we do go, there is a reason."

Republican politicians were euphoric, and many previously skeptical Democrats said they had been convinced. Senate Minority Leader Tom Daschle of South Dakota called the speech "a powerful, methodical and compelling presentation," and California Democratic Senator Dianne Feinstein, who had expressed strong doubts about the allegations made in Bush's State of the Union address, now conceded that "I no longer think inspections are going to work." "If Saddam Hussein does not disarm," said Massachusetts Senator John F. Kerry, now a Democratic presidential con-tender, "he will have chosen to make regime change the ultimate weapons enforcement mechanism."

Powell received high praise when he appeared before the Senate For-eign Relations Committee the day after the speech to testify on the State Department budget. "I'd like to move the nomination of Secretary of State Powell for President of the United States," Democrat Joseph Biden gushed.

It fell to a Republican to bring the love fest back to earth. "Easy there," said Richard Lugar of Indiana, the committee chairman, admonishing Biden with a smile.

Although a majority of congressional Democrats closed ranks behind the president, some still spoke out against the push toward war. Senator Edward Kennedy of Massachusetts conceded that Powell had made a "strong case" but said the administration had not yet demonstrated that "war is the only recourse." Former Vermont Governor Howard Dean agreed, saying he had heard little from Powell "that leads me to believe that there is an imminent threat warranting unilateral military action by the United States against Iraq."

Those closest to Powell were glad it was all over but were worried about both him and the nation. Alma had a sense of foreboding; her husband, she thought, was being used by the White House. Colin's daughter Linda listened to the speech on the car radio as she drove from New York to Vermont. She had heard her father speak in public countless times but found this performance unsettling. His voice was strained, she thought, as if he were trying to inject passion into the dry words through the sheer force of his will.

Wilkerson, who had left the United Nations immediately after the speech and returned to his hotel room to fall into a deep sleep, awoke depressed. He would later come to think of that week, and its dramatic culmination, as "the lowest moment of my life." Back in Washington, he ordered special plaques with Powell's signature made up for the State Department aides who had worked so hard to make the presentation happen. When they were handed out, Powell asked Wilkerson why he hadn't ordered one for himself. Wilkerson replied that he didn't want one.

20

I wish some things had been done differently. I wish Don
Rumsfeld and Colin Powell had forced the Defense and
State Departments to work more closely together.
—General Tommy Franks

Iraq diplomacy was on life support, still breathing only because Tony
Blair refused to pull the plug. British public opinion and the Parliament
were demanding a new Security Council resolution with explicit U.N.
approval for war. Blair needed to demonstrate that he had gone the extra
mile to obtain it. There was still a chance, he insisted to the Bush administration, that France and most of the fifteen Council members could be
brought on board.

Like Powell, Blair knew by January 2003 that President Bush had made
his decision and that war was a virtual certainty. Blair had no intention of
withdrawing his support; it was the timing of the invasion that was now in
play. General Tommy Franks had said that U.S. forces could be ready to
invade by mid-February, but Blair did not share Bush's sense of urgency.
If delay would win them additional Security Council backing, he felt, it
was well worth it.

On Friday, January 31, as Powell was crafting his U.N. presentation,
Blair had flown across the Atlantic for emergency consultations with the
president. His plans to travel by helicopter from Andrews Air Force Base
to Camp David, where Bush intended to spend the weekend, were dashed
by a threatening snowstorm, and the British delegation drove into the
capital in a convoy of SUVs under a low gray sky. Arriving at the White
House just before lunch, Blair found the president in a restless mood.

As far as Bush was concerned, the United States had all the authority it
needed for the use of force. Not only had Saddam Hussein failed to comply with twelve years of previous U.N. resolutions, he had fallen short of
the full and complete compliance with inspections demanded by 1441,

the resolution negotiated by Powell in November. But Blair's own legal team had indicated—and would later formally advise him—that any claim to a U.N. mandate for war without a new resolution might not hold up under an international legal challenge.

Although Blair was under no illusion that he had any veto power over Bush's plans, he was not without leverage. The 44,000 troops he had pledged were not an indispensable part of the Pentagon's invasion plan, but they were Bush's only real basis—along with 2,000 Australians and a few hundred Poles—for claiming that a robust international coalition would accompany U.S. forces into Iraq. Conservative Presidents Silvio Berlusconi of Italy and José María Aznar of Spain had both voiced support without promising troops; they had the same problem as Blair—widespread domestic opposition to attacking Iraq without a clear U.N. mandate.

After several hours of discussion with the prime minister, Bush grudgingly agreed to go back to the Security Council for a new resolution. At a joint news conference late in the afternoon, he glared testily at Blair and cut off questions from British reporters. He would welcome Council action as long as it came "quickly," Bush said. But he made it clear that it was Blair, and not he, who thought a new resolution was needed. "This is a matter of weeks, not months. Any attempt to drag the process on for months will be resisted by the United States. And as I understand the Prime Minister—I'm loath to put words in his mouth—but he's also said weeks, not months."

After a light supper at the White House, Blair drove back to Andrews through falling snow in the early-winter darkness. He had spent six hours on the ground, the same amount of time as it would take him to fly back home.

Hans Blix had not been impressed by Powell's February 5 presentation of the case against Iraq. His UNMOVIC inspectors had already visited some of the sites shown in Powell's satellite photographs—they had examined records, interviewed personnel and found nothing—and the other sites were on their list for future inspections. The intercepted communications were intriguing but did not necessarily mean what Powell said they meant. On the question of a nuclear weapons program, the IAEA disagreed with the CIA's analysis of the aluminum tubes Powell had cited. Both Blix and Mohamed ElBaradei found it curious that Powell had made no reference to Iraq's efforts to purchase uranium from Africa, a key allegation in Bush's State of the Union speech just a week before.

Blix outlined his reservations in his next update to the Security Council on the morning of Friday, February 14. Iraq's compliance was still not perfect, he said, but the inspectors were making real progress. Powell, sitting opposite the Swedish diplomat at the Council table, responded sharply that Iraq was still "playing tricks" on the UNMOVIC team. But despite their public sparring, the two men had a cordial relationship; Blix felt that Powell, unlike Cheney and others in the Bush administration, had always treated him with courtesy and respect and didn't seem hell bent on war. After their public showdown, the two men met for a private lunch in the Security Council Delegates Lounge and Powell listened closely to Blix's ideas about how they could wrap up the inspections and reach conclusions about Iraqi WMD relatively quickly.

At Powell's suggestion, Blix telephoned him at home the following Sunday with more details. He had checked with ElBaradei, Blix said, and they were agreed that remaining weapons questions could be answered by April 15 provided Saddam cooperated. Powell, who knew that the White House was looking for approval of the war rather than a way to avoid it, told Blix that April would be too late.

The prospects for passage of a new resolution were dim. The administration could count on only itself and Britain among the five permanent Council members and only Spain and Bulgaria among the current ten nonpermanent members. The other three P5 members—Russia, China and France—thought that inspections were making progress and should continue, as did Germany and Syria. The remaining six—Mexico, Chile, Pakistan, Cameroon, Guinea and Angola—were undecided or reluctant to take a position that was sure to offend one of the two powerful sides of the debate. Powell's job, at least until Bush determined he had had enough, was to seek the necessary nine-vote majority and persuade the P5 opponents to abstain rather than veto a war measure.

Through the rest of February and into March, Washington and Paris vied for votes; Dominique de Villepin flew to the undecided countries while Bush made personal calls to Moscow, Beijing and other capitals. At times, the jostling for a majority seemed almost comical. When de Villepin traveled to Africa but was unable to see the president of Guinea, who had fallen ill and left the capital for his home village, the State Department tallied a vote for the U.S. side. But word was soon received that a local witch doctor attending the president had advised him against war with Iraq. Walter Kansteiner, the assistant secretary of state for Africa, immediately arranged to hire a second witch doctor, who was dispatched to the village to change the president's mind.

Powell met with visiting foreign ministers and spent hours on the telephone, but he made no personal forays abroad. Critics compared him unfavorably to James Baker, the Bush 41 secretary of state who had circled the globe garnering international support for Operation Desert Storm in 1991. But beyond his reluctance to leave Washington at such a crucial time, by early March Powell had finally come to see the diplomatic effort as pointless. After French President Jacques Chirac publicly declared in mid-February that he would have "no choice" but to oppose a war resolution, Powell's determination to continue negotiations until the last possible moment seemed moot. He now saw the French, Russians and Germans as direct enablers of Saddam's intransigence and, indirectly, of Bush's war plans. And Baker's diplomacy, unlike Powell's, at least had enjoyed the backing of his own president. A final window for the invasion date had already been set for mid- to late March, and Powell knew the White House viewed the United Nations as little more than a sideshow to be endured and then cast aside when the main event commenced.

In the Delegates Lounge and in private meetings among Security Council ambassadors, the American secretary of state was the subject of endless speculation and no small amount of disappointment. For two years—at least until the February 5 speech—it had been an article of faith for many of their governments that Powell respected their views and was always willing to negotiate, even if his power was limited. Now he seemed to have yielded completely to administration hawks who had no interest in anything less than full authority from the world to do what they wanted, when they wanted. When some Council holdouts indicated that they would support a last-ditch British proposal to set benchmarks for Saddam's strict compliance with inspections, the White House declined to sponsor the measure. Ambassadors joked darkly among themselves that the only benchmark the United States would accept as proof that Saddam had disposed of his weapons was if he agreed to swallow them all on live television.

On Monday, March 17, with no more votes guaranteed than the four they had counted at the start, the United States and Britain declared Security Council negotiations over. Powell spent the morning relaying the news to foreign minister colleagues before announcing to reporters at the State Department that "the moment of truth is arriving." The next day, Blair won parliamentary endorsement for Britain's participation in the use of force, despite massive defections in his own Labour Party, thanks to support from opposition Conservatives. At 6 a.m. Washington time on Thursday, March 20, after an overnight bombardment of Baghdad, the first U.S. ground contingents crossed the Kuwait border into Iraq.

The American force totaled 241,000, including both combat and support units in the Persian Gulf region as well as the 4th Infantry Division, moored hundreds of miles from Iraq. It was less than half the number Powell had sent to expel Iraq from Kuwait in 1991. The new Parliament in Ankara had ultimately rejected the United States' request to cross Turkish territory, and General Franks had opted to leave the division aboard its ships in the Mediterranean. If he had been in charge, Powell thought, he would have quickly moved the division to support the main invasion force in the south, which he considered disturbingly thin. But as he kept reminding his staff, he was not in charge. He had raised the issue with Franks, who had politely rejected his advice.

The White House claimed that forty-four countries were part of a "coalition of the willing" in support of military action, but most had promised little more than permission to put their names on the list. Twelve years earlier, Operation Desert Storm had been conducted under a full U.N. mandate with a broad coalition of troops—along with tanks, ships and aircraft—from throughout Europe and the Arab world. Most of that war's $61 billion cost had been borne by countries other than the United States.

In a series of public opinion surveys, Americans had consistently indicated a reluctance to "go it alone," and Bush recognized the political advantages of at least the appearance of multilateralism. But Rumsfeld remained publicly dismissive of the need for allies. On the eve of the invasion, he had made it clear that even British assistance was superfluous, telling a Pentagon press conference that Britain's role was "unclear" and the invasion plan could easily proceed without Blair's troops. The defense secretary's offhand remark, made as Blair was insisting to his own Parliament that Britain's support was crucial to the effort, sent London reeling and demanding an explanation. The Pentagon quickly issued a "clarification"; Rumsfeld said he had "no doubt" of Britain's "full support" for the effort to disarm Saddam.

If not for the administration's rush to war, Richard Armitage later observed, "I think we could have gotten a bigger coalition going in. Clearly, I felt time was on our side. The fact of the matter is that the Department of Defense was not interested in coalition warfare. They were not."

Morale sagged at the State Department, where many had been convinced that even if Powell could not head off the invasion he would at least prevail in delaying it until there was time to build a genuine international coalition. "I think Powell believed for a long time ... that the president was just throwing red meat to the Cheney-Rumsfeld universe and in the end would side with him," mused a senior department official.

"And in fact, the opposite happened, which was that *we* were the ones that were getting the little bits, the kibble, and that in the end the decision went with them.... [Powell] convinced all of us to believe that this would come out our way in the end. And it didn't."

Nearly two months before the war, Bush had signed a directive giving the Defense Department authority over all postcombat operations in Iraq. Powell had not objected; the military would be best positioned during the first few weeks after victory not only to maintain security but to ensure that the immediate needs of Iraqis were met and civil authority was established. In anticipation of a massive displacement of civilians expected to flee from the fighting in fear of biological and chemical weapons, nongovernmental organizations and the U.S. Agency for International Development were poised to follow advancing troops with food, shelter and water. Powell assumed that the United Nations would quickly be brought in to help organize an interim Iraqi government and eventual democratic elections, as it had in Afghanistan.

Just a week into the military operation, Tony Blair flew to Washington again for a meeting with Bush to "work out the details" of securing U.N. endorsement for a post-Saddam government. Like Powell, Blair was eager to move beyond the Security Council arguments and "to get America and Europe working again together as partners and not as rivals." When the two leaders next met, however, in Belfast in early April, Bush made it clear that the United States would remain in charge of all aspects of Iraq's reconstruction for the foreseeable future. The United Nations would have a "vital" role to play, he said, although no U.S. official would venture an opinion on what that meant.

General Franks's light, lean "transformational" plan projected U.S. victory within two months. As a firm believer in established military guidelines, Powell was well aware that both the Army Field Manual and Joint Staff doctrine warned of the need to quickly exploit combat success with a well-organized transition to peace. Franks himself was concerned about the need to deploy civilian experts to manage the postwar process and install an Iraqi administration, and he worried that the military had neither the resources nor a comprehensive set of policy options to establish a civil authority.

Yet Franks's plan optimistically called for U.S. troop withdrawals to begin by summer. Numerous studies both within and outside the military had raised concerns about the potential for postwar difficulties and the need to keep significant numbers of troops in Iraq during the crucial stabilization period. One study, by way of comparison, noted that the United States and its allies had put twenty-five times more money and fifty times more troops into Kosovo, the Serbian province they had occupied in 1999, than they had into Afghanistan, and the difference showed in terms of Kosovo's economic and political development under U.N. administration. Eighteen months after the military victory in Afghanistan, the government in Kabul controlled virtually nothing beyond the outskirts of the capital, and reconstruction was sluggish at best.

In mid-December, months before the war began, Powell had tasked NEA Assistant Secretary William Burns with preparing "a memo on everything that could go wrong" after a military victory. Burns and his deputy, Ryan Crocker, worked into the night to produce a dozen single-spaced pages that they titled "The Perfect Storm."

The memo explained Iraq's complicated ethnic and religious divisions and the tight lid Saddam Hussein's dictatorship and his Sunni-dominated Ba'ath Party had kept on them for decades. Released from his brutal control, Iraqi factions—especially the majority Shiites and the Kurds—might try to settle accounts and would vie, perhaps violently, for dominance over the minority Sunnis or even for territorial separation. The Sunnis themselves would not give up political power easily. Powerful exile figures from all factions would flood Baghdad to compete with and perhaps overwhelm emerging local leaders, while other countries in the region, including Iran, Saudi Arabia and Syria, would try to exert influence on their newly liberated neighbor. A whole new political framework would have to be established, along with a private economy to replace Saddam's centralized system that supplied at least 60 percent of the Iraqi population with everything from jobs to rationed food and fuel. After years of sanctions and corruption, Iraq's infrastructure was in tatters.

The earlier conclusions of the State Department's Future of Iraq project—compiled into thirteen volumes that were handed over to Rumsfeld at the end of 2002—included the possibility of widespread looting and lawlessness and emphasized the need to quickly repair Iraq's infrastructure. In studies conducted during the winter of 2002–03, both the Army War College and the Marine Corps Warfighting Laboratory had warned that the initial months following victory would be difficult yet crucial to the ultimate success of the mission. "The possibility of the

United States winning the war and losing the peace in Iraq," the Army report warned, "is real and serious."

In a harsh December 2002 document titled "Planning for a Self-Inflicted Wound," Anthony H. Cordesman, a widely recognized civilian expert in military strategy and the Middle East, warned that the Pentagon's postwar planning was "uncoordinated and faltering" and based on ignorance about Iraq and the region. "Far too many 'experts,'" Cordesman wrote, "have (a) never been in Iraq to the point of having practical knowledge of the country, and (b) have concentrated on the threat so long that they have little intelligence data on the workings of its government, civil society and economy." A joint study by the Council on Foreign Relations and the James A. Baker III Institute for Public Policy at Rice University warned of possible anarchy and the need for the U.S. military to quickly turn to humanitarian efforts and law enforcement.

In early February, Powell's assistant secretaries for law enforcement, human rights and refugee issues put their own concerns into writing. In a memorandum pointing out potential "serious planning gaps for post-conflict public security," they noted that CENTCOM's focus on "its primary military objectives and its reluctance to take on 'policing' roles" could lead to problems. "We are willing to provide technical assistance and help CENTCOM" develop postwar plans to avoid humanitarian and human rights problems, the three wrote to their immediate superior, Undersecretary of State for Democracy and Global Affairs Paula Dobriansky. "We think it is crucial that Department Principals continue to be strong advocates for these issues in Iraq Principal meetings and we will prepare talking points accordingly." Powell himself, they indicated, would have to press the case.

Less than a month before the invasion, Army Chief of Staff General Eric Shinseki had told a Senate hearing that a U.S. force "on the order of several hundred thousand soldiers" would be required to occupy Iraq after the initial combat victory. "We're talking about post-hostilities control over a piece of geography that's fairly significant, with the kinds of ethnic tensions that could lead to other problems," Shinseki cautioned. "And so it takes a significant ground-force presence to maintain a safe and secure environment, to ensure that people are fed, that water is distributed, all the normal responsibilities that go along with administering a situation like this."

Two days after Shinseki's February 25 testimony, however, Paul Wolfowitz called his estimate of several hundred thousand troops "wildly off the mark." There was no historical reason to believe that free Iraqis would fight against one another or the United States, Wolfowitz told Congress. "I am reasonably certain that they will greet us as liberators, and that will help us to keep [troop] requirements down."

Moreover, Wolfowitz said, the Pentagon anticipated that many countries that were objecting to the use of force would be eager to help once Saddam was gone. "There is simply no reason to assume that the United States will or should supply" the bulk of military forces needed for postwar stabilization, he said. "I would expect that even countries like France will have a strong interest in assisting Iraq's reconstruction."

The peaceful, democratic Iraq the administration expected, one enthusiastic White House official privately assured a reporter, would bring "big-time vindication" for the administration's policy of preemptive use of force.

On May 1, President Bush stood on the deck of the aircraft carrier USS *Abraham Lincoln,* thirty miles off the coast of San Diego, and declared that "major combat operations in Iraq have ended." The ship, en route to California from Hawaii, had delayed its arrival in port to sail in wide circles offshore and provide a suitable venue for the presidential announcement. While the rest of the White House party made the ten-minute trip from San Diego to the ship by helicopter, Bush flew in with a flourish aboard a Navy jet and emerged decked out in a pilot's flight suit. The dazzling television image of the victorious commander in chief, speaking to 5,000 blue-shirted sailors assembled in brilliant sunshine under a banner reading "Mission Accomplished," was everything White House image makers had hoped for.

The war, as confident hawks had predicted, had been a "cakewalk." The Iraqi Army put up little resistance to the U.S. military juggernaut marching toward Baghdad, and after several days of battles with Saddam's elite Republican Guard forces on the outskirts of the capital, American troops reached the city center on April 9, just three weeks after they crossed the Kuwaiti border. Scattered fighting continued around the country— Saddam Hussein himself managed to escape and was in hiding—but Iraq was effectively under U.S. control. American casualties had been relatively light, with 139 dead and 542 wounded. Although ground troops went into battle with special suits to protect them from Iraqi biological and chemical attacks, no weapons of mass destruction had been deployed.

Far from tempering internal administration disputes, victory in Iraq only exacerbated them. The Pentagon's civilian leadership—with energetic support from the vice president's office—restricted participation by Powell's Mideast experts in the Office of Reconstruction and Humanitarian Assistance (ORHA), set up by Defense Undersecretary Douglas Feith in February to manage civilian administration in postwar Iraq. When Jay Garner, the retired lieutenant general picked to head ORHA, invited Thomas Warrick, the director of the Future of Iraq project at State, to join his team, Rumsfeld told Garner that orders from "a high level" had vetoed Warrick's participation.

Powell and Armitage assumed that meant Cheney, since the only higher authority was the president. Bush, Armitage grumbled, wouldn't even know the names of State's senior Mideast team. When the department subsequently sent Garner a list of available regional experts, Rumsfeld turned them all down, provoking an angry letter from Powell requesting that the defense secretary "clarify" the Pentagon's understanding that nonmilitary tasks in Iraq—including the distribution of humanitarian aid and the reestablishment of Iraqi ministries—were to be handled by civilians under Pentagon authority. Eventually, a handful of current and former State Department officials—excluding Warrick—was permitted to join ORHA.

Garner found that the "intense rivalry" between the two departments had prevented any real prewar coordination on a blueprint for establishing a functioning infrastructure and civil administration in Iraq. Interagency sessions had focused on possible catastrophes such as oil well fires and the potential need to feed and shelter civilians displaced during the fighting. The Pentagon was in charge, and it had not invited the State Department to participate in finalizing its political plans for Iraq, assuming it had actually made such plans. "What we wondered was whether Feith and Company were providing all of this in a way we didn't see," recalled one State Department official who attended many of the interagency meetings. "There was this gaping void out there. Since we all assumed early on that we weren't going to be able to...deliver a ready-made government that could assert sovereignty, we would have to do something. What was it we were going to do? We didn't have a clue."

The role of exiles in the new Iraq was a source of endless dispute. One of the few actual shouting matches in the normally decorous principals' meetings had erupted in the White House Situation Room just before the invasion, when Powell defended State's refusal to turn more U.S. government money over to Ahmed Chalabi until the INC complied with congressional demands to account for the funds it had already received. It was, Powell later recalled, "a thoroughly vivid moment."

Defense Department civilians tended to keep their dealings with the expatriates away from the State Department. In March, when the media reported that the Pentagon had begun recruiting exile technocrats to take over Iraqi ministries, Rumsfeld's aides insisted to their State counterparts that they were not involved in any such program. Channel surfing at home one night in early April, Marc Grossman, the number three official at State, was amazed to see Wolfowitz on the screen explaining to a reporter how he had begun six weeks earlier to gather Iraqi Americans for precisely that purpose. The camera panned through a warren of Pentagon-leased offices in Crystal City, on the Virginia side of the Potomac outside Washington, where what the reporter called "an elite group of exiles" sat working at computers. The doors of the offices were posted with crude signs reading "Ministry of Justice," "Ministry of Oil," and so on.

Wolfowitz's view was that "we ought to go in and establish an Iraqi provisional government the day we got there," he later elaborated. As U.S. forces swept quickly through southern Iraq in late March on their way to Baghdad, Rumsfeld sent memos to the White House proposing the immediate installation of an exile-led administration in already liberated territory. Within days, Chalabi and his 600-man militia had been flown aboard U.S. military aircraft from an outpost in Kurdish territory to the conquered city of Nasiriyah, 225 miles southeast of Baghdad on the Euphrates River.

Powell's reaction was "How stupid could you be?" Who would believe that America's only interest in Iraq was the promotion of democracy if it would not even allow Iraqis to choose their own government? For once, Bush and Cheney agreed, and they vetoed the plan.

With White House approval, Powell seized the opening and dispatched the NEA's Ryan Crocker and Zalmay Khalilzad, an Afghan-born NSC official designated as a presidential envoy, to southern Iraq to begin a series of regional meetings with indigenous civilian leaders. The idea, Powell said, was to "bring forth representatives of the different groups in those regions to see who wants to be part of the new government of Iraq." Garner, who agreed with the initiative, announced that he expected that "the nucleus of a temporary Iraq government," to be called the Iraqi Interim Authority, would be in place in a month or two.

The idea barely got off the ground. Powerful Shiite clerics, suspicious of American motives and making their own political calculations, refused to attend the regional meetings. Kofi Annan, despite a personal appeal from Powell, declined to send a representative until the U.N. role in postwar Iraq was clarified. Chalabi, established in Nasiriyah with his militia, told reporters he wasn't interested. He expected, he said, to be in Baghdad in short order to set up a national government.

Meanwhile, after several days of euphoria following the arrival of U.S. troops in Baghdad, the Iraqi capital erupted in a frenzy of crime and looting. American soldiers, without orders, manpower or a plan to intervene, stood by while government facilities were stripped of everything from furniture and fine art to plumbing and electrical wiring. When the ORHA team finally arrived on April 21, it found that seventeen of nearly two dozen government ministries had been completely destroyed. The Iraqi civil servants Garner had expected to call upon to restart the country—as well as the local police and military forces needed to restore order—had vanished. The telephone system no longer existed, and members of Garner's team found themselves walking the chaotic streets of the city forlornly asking passersby if they knew anyone who worked for the government.

The White House and the Pentagon, fending off rising criticism of inadequate postwar planning, described the destruction as both natural exuberance and understandable revenge for years of mistreatment under Saddam. Ongoing violence was blamed on Saddam loyalists, and delays in providing electricity, water and medical care were attributed to the decrepit state in which the dictator had left the nation's infrastructure. Wolfowitz, who had assured Congress in February that there was no reason to expect extensive postwar violence in Iraq or an extended need for U.S. troops, now told concerned legislators that the critics of prewar planning had been misinformed and that the upheaval was no surprise. "Assertions that we are already failing," he told the Senate Foreign Relations Committee in May, "reflect both an incomplete understanding of the situation as it existed in Iraq before the war and an unreasonable expectation of where we should be now."

But internally, the administration was shaken by the unanticipated chaos and anxious to temper expectations about the pace and early success of the reconstruction effort. When Crocker and Khalilzad returned to Washington in early May to brief the White House on progress toward establishing an Iraqi government, Rice told them that the initiative was being abandoned. "If everything had been nice and calm, with no rioting and no destruction, with good order and security, you might have been able" to hold meetings around the country leading to the formation of an Iraqi government, explained one official involved in the effort. "But that was impossible to even think of by May."

By late April, Wolfowitz and "Scooter" Libby had already telephoned the retired diplomat and counterterrorism expert L. Paul "Jerry" Bremer to ask if he was interested in "the job of running the occupation of Iraq." Efforts to quickly put together an Iraqi Interim Authority drawn from leaders inside the country were being abandoned, and ORHA was to be subsumed into a new Coalition Provisional Authority (CPA), they told him. The new plan, a variation on one proposed by Feith months before, left the Iraqis themselves restricted to a twenty-five-person advisory council with virtually no authority for the foreseeable future.

With Iraq spiraling out of control, Powell agreed that it was the best option they had—far better than handing over governing power to the exiles. When Rumsfeld called to tell him of Bremer's selection, Powell and Armitage were relieved. They considered Bremer, who had retired from the Foreign Service in 1989 after twenty-three years, a "Powell guy" and someone they could talk to. "We all knew Jerry," said one senior State Department official. "He was a total pain in the ass, a classic Type A personality, but a guy who gets things done, who wasn't ideological."

In a meeting with Bush before his departure for Baghdad, Bremer insisted that the Arabic-speaking Khalilzad be removed from the Iraq account, telling Bush that he needed "full authority" and there could be only one "Presidential envoy." Crocker, who had long experience in the Arab world, was asked to accompany Bremer as his adviser on Iraqi politics. But it was made clear that he would report to Rumsfeld, through Bremer, and not to Powell.

In its less charitable moments, the State Department's upper echelon took grim satisfaction in the Pentagon's early difficulties in postwar Iraq. Rumsfeld and the Pentagon had gotten the complete control they had wanted, and now they would have to live with it. The diplomats would simply bide their time. Armitage called it the "judo approach": using their adversaries' own weight to drop them to the mat.

In the view of both traditional hawks and neoconservatives, Powell's early assumption that the United Nations would play a leading role in postwar Iraq was evidence that he still had not come to terms with American "exceptionalism" and the national security demands of the post–September 11 world. When it became clear after the end of "major combat operations" that U.S. difficulties in Iraq were only beginning, many conservatives blamed Powell and the State Department for the administration's failure to achieve the early postwar peace they had been convinced would be possible under an exile-led government. State's "hostility" toward Pentagon-favored Iraqi exiles, Richard Perle argued in a

2003 book he coauthored with David Frum, had facilitated the political stalemate and anti-American attacks that followed.

The State Department had "opposed the Iraq war to the end and then, after it lost that fight, battled to minimize the role of the most democratically minded Iraqis in the postwar reconstruction of their country.... As a whole, the department regards the war on terrorism with caution, ambivalence and sometimes open disparagement." The department's sins of "multilateral conceit" extended far beyond Iraq, Perle charged. In the days after the September 11 attacks, U.S. diplomats had sought allies among "moderate" members of the Taliban in Afghanistan and within the murderous Iranian regime. They had later pushed for "full-fledged détente with the dictatorship in Damascus," and it was their fault that Turkey had not been persuaded to allow a northern invasion route.

The launch of the war had opened a floodgate of conservative criticism of the State Department as incompetent and actively disloyal to the president. In a speech at the American Enterprise Institute on April 22, former House Speaker Newt Gingrich threw the first public punch, charging that victory in Iraq had been won in spite of the diplomats. The State Department had engaged in "a deliberate and systematic effort to undermine the President's policies" both before and during the invasion, Gingrich said. "The past seven months have involved six months of diplomatic failure and one month of military success." Department activities since the war "indicate the pattern of diplomatic failure is beginning once again and threatens to undo the effects of military victory."

State's coalition building with Europe and the United Nations on the Israeli-Palestinian conflict and its coddling of Mideast dictatorships—Powell was even planning a "ludicrous" postwar trip to Syria, Gingrich gasped—were "a clear disaster for American diplomacy." Overall, he wrote several months after his speech in an article on the same theme, the State Department had "abdicated values and principles in favor of accommodation and passivity" and was "out of synch with Bush's views and objectives." What it urgently needed was a complete restructuring on the order of Rumsfeld's successful transformation of the Department of Defense.

Gingrich had a history with Powell and had long since concluded that the secretary was uninterested in bringing the department into line. The former Speaker had served on one of the several commissions that studied America's national security structure at the end of the Clinton administration and had sent critical reports to Powell as he took office. When the two men had met to discuss the issue in early 2001, Powell had been cordial but dismissive, telling Gingrich that his goal was not to reform the department but to revitalize it by increasing its budget, recruitment and morale.

Accustomed to more receptive audiences, at least among Republicans, Gingrich later said he considered the meeting "one of the decisive, definitional moments of Powell's tenure. It was very clear that Powell had made the decision that he was going to be the advocate of the State Department" rather than the president. The following two years had only confirmed his view that Powell did not understand the "American uniqueness and exceptionalism" that Bush represented. While the president was transforming the world, Powell "ended up...wandering in with the latest Foreign Service idea, and that just sets up constant friction" between him and the rest of the national security team.

In a visit to Armitage in early 2003, Gingrich said, he had found the deputy secretary "condescendingly hostile" to his efforts to point out the error of the department's ways and offer his assistance. Armitage's "arrogance about the Pentagon, his overt hostility to Rumsfeld and the sort of 'us and them' " mentality made it impossible to "have a serious conversation."

Beyond his pugnacious language, Gingrich had accurately drawn the philosophical dividing line between the Bush administration's dominant, Manichean view of a black-and-white world and the pragmatic realism that left Powell perpetually outside the inner circle. When foreign policy problems were seen as moral challenges, they could have only one correct solution, and the United States had a duty to use its unrivaled power to achieve it. Those who temporized and saw virtue in compromise—even in pursuit of the same goal—were seen by the ruling hawks as imperfectly implementing the president's policies.

"There are people who believe that Powell is part of the problem, although they won't say it publicly," explained one White House official who saw the secretary as a gifted diplomat who had allowed himself to be boxed into a corner. "And there are those who say he may not be part of State but there's a cabal inside State—the permanent bureaucracy that doesn't carry out the president's policy—and Powell needs to beat up on them."

Lawrence Wilkerson, who had spent most of his career in the Pentagon, saw the State Department's isolation as a perennial problem in a long line of administrations, even Democratic ones. But under Bush, a low-intensity turf battle had descended into guerrilla warfare. Powell "tried to be a good leader and he was leading troops that, no matter how much he reversed their morale slide, are distrusted by many others. It's part of the culture of the State Department to be distrusted by the rest of the

bureaucracy, especially the White House." But while it was true that Foreign Service officers tended to see things through the eyes of their foreign
constituencies, Wilkerson said, "I would rather have an ambassador who's
gone native and is telling me the truth about the natives than a neocon
who's going out bashing everybody."

Beneath the philosophical plane, down where the day-to-day skirmishes were being fought, Powell and Armitage plotted their counterattack. On the afternoon of Gingrich's American Enterprise Institute
speech, they huddled on the State Department's seventh floor to plan a
riposte. They would point out indirectly that however much the hawks
had opposed U.N. negotiations over Iraq, Bush himself had approved
them, and the White House had also authorized Powell's upcoming trip
to Syria. And they would suggest that Gingrich had long since passed his
prime as a serious player in Washington. Since Armitage was already
known as outspoken and impolitic—"people see me as half crazy"—and
the message they had in mind was "not appropriate for the secretary of
state," they decided the deputy should wield the dagger.

Armitage called a reporter from *USA Today,* the nationally circulated
newspaper, to say that "the Secretary was astonished that Mr. Gingrich
attacked the President." As for his personal reaction to the speech,
Armitage said, "it's clear that Mr. Gingrich is off his meds and out of ther-
apy." As expected, his words appeared prominently in coverage of the
speech the next day.

A number of moderate Republicans, even some conservatives, spoke
out in Powell's defense. But Gingrich was presumed to be close to powerful people in the administration. He certainly reflected the views both of
Cheney and of Rumsfeld, who had selected him as a member of his
Defense Policy Board, the influential group of outside advisers chaired by
Perle. When the defense secretary was invited by reporters to disagree
with Gingrich's remarks, he declined to respond, saying he hadn't read
the speech.

White House spokesman Ari Fleischer said that Bush considered the
secretary of state "an able, able diplomat." But unlike Bush's father, who
had rushed to embrace Powell when he came under attack as chairman a
dozen years earlier, the president himself made no public comment.

Powell held his own fire in public until a friendly Democrat, Senator
Patrick Leahy of Vermont, provided an opening at an April 30 hearing on
the State Department budget. It was "disturbing," Leahy observed, "that
key officials in the administration seem determined to weaken the State
Department."

Ever since Thomas Jefferson, Powell responded, secretaries of state "have been criticized at one time or another for being like diplomats, for trying to find peaceful solutions, to building friendships around the world, to creating alliances. That's what we do. We do it damn well, and I am not going to apologize to anybody. I'm on the offense for the people who work in my department doing a great job. And if you come after them, come after them with legitimate criticism. We'll respond to that. We're not above criticism. But if you come after us just to come after us, you're in for a fight, and I'm going to fight back."

Despite their commander's spirited comeback, Powell's State Department troops were uneasy. Their opponents in the Pentagon were riding high after the successful Iraq offensive, while their own standard-bearer was still dodging bullets. Two years ago, they had seen him as their savior, the man on the white horse who would restore the department's rightful prominence. Now some believed that he had retreated from too many battles, including Iraq and the Mideast peace process, that were far more important than Gingrich's rantings. Powell had arrived in office with a full account in the bank of public trust, but he had allowed Bush to spend it profligately. By serving as the rational face of an irrational administration, he had become its enabler.

"If he had wanted to, he could have used all of his clout" to steer policy in a different direction, said one disillusioned department official. "Here was the guy who, on paper, had everything he needed to be a great secretary of state."

John Brady Kiesling, one of several midlevel Foreign Service officers who had resigned in protest at the start of the war, wrote to Powell of his "enormous respect for your character and ability. You have preserved more international credibility for us than our policy deserves and salvaged something positive from the excesses of an ideological and self-serving Administration. But your loyalty to the President goes too far."

Many others, however, believed Powell was doing everything possible to tame the administration's excesses and that he was the only thing standing between a sustainable foreign policy and utter national disaster. "The feeling in the building was very, very clear," one assistant secretary recalled. "Pray to God that he doesn't resign, because he is preventing much worse stuff from happening. There is plenty of bad stuff going on, thanks to evil mastermind Cheney and his sidekicks Wolfowitz and Rumsfeld, but if Powell weren't here they would be running rampant in ways that we can't even imagine."

On the record, the upper echelons at State and Defense remained dismissive of reports that they were again feuding. The very idea, Wolfowitz told a reporter, was "sophomoric." "Utter nonsense," Armitage agreed, noting that he spoke "every day" with Wolfowitz, his Defense Department counterpart. "Look, we've been colleagues and friends for 20-odd years. Of course we have our differences, but they are not personal." Powell brushed off public queries by rote—the president had selected his team to give him a wide range of advice, and he relished the healthy battle of ideas within his administration.

But in their separate corners, the two sides continued to heap scorn upon each other's tactics and ideas. Powell was keeping score, with eager complicity from the combative Armitage, and some of his closest friends and colleagues began to worry that he was becoming uncharacteristically mired in the daily drama of administration catfights.

"It was the obsession of every journalist," recalled one U.S. ambassador who spoke with Powell regularly at the time. "I think the secretary may have been a party to that. I used to tell him [when] he'd make some reference to one of these intramural squabbles, I'd say, 'Colin, come on.' . . . He would say, 'Well, that's what it's all about here in Washington.' "

With Saddam Hussein deposed and on the run from U.S. forces, defense hawks warned regimes in Iran, Syria and North Korea to "draw the appropriate lesson," as John Bolton put it in a news conference in April. But preoccupation with the chaotic Iraq occupation had at least temporarily distracted the Pentagon, and the White House seemed disinclined for the moment to rattle any additional sabers.

Powell was incapable of wallowing in pessimism for long. As he had so many times before, he turned his back on yesterday's losses and snapped his gaze forward. The war over the war was finished; there were new opportunities in its wake. Syria and the two other "axis of evil" countries had undoubtedly gotten the message from Iraq, and the administration should seize the moment to offer them improved relationships in exchange for improved conduct. Bush was anxious to prove his prewar contention that democracy in Iraq would ignite a spark throughout the Middle East and agreed that it was time to employ diplomacy to "change the dynamics" of the region.

Unable to stop Powell's new diplomatic initiative, administration hawks succeeded in restricting its scope. The internally negotiated talking points for the secretary's May 3 visit to Damascus contained a list of sticks but no carrots. Long-standing U.S. demands included severing all ties with groups on the State Department's terrorist list, particularly the

Palestinian militants, eliminating all prohibited weapons programs and ending Syria's military and de facto political control of Lebanon. All were worthy and important goals, but Syrian President Bashar Assad was fighting his own internal ideological battles. Unless Washington put something "on the table to induce significant changes in Syrian behavior," there was little room for active diplomacy.

Powell also urged a renewed effort to engage Iran, where the ruling ayatollahs were increasingly being challenged by democratic opposition. After secret, indirect talks were initiated with Washington in the early spring of 2003, Tehran sent a message through the Swiss government during the first week in May. Apparently approved by all factions of the divided Iranian regime, it recognized the need to address U.S. concerns on a range of issues—including nuclear weapons, terrorism and support for a two-state solution to the Palestinian-Israeli conflict. In exchange, Iran wanted an end to U.S. sanctions and "axis of evil" rhetoric, and an eventual reestablishment of diplomatic relations. But as usual, the administration was unable to agree internally on a response. Powell thought the possibility of talks was worth exploring, but the only official U.S. answer was a rebuke to Switzerland, which represented U.S. interests in Iran in the absence of diplomatic ties, for "overstepping" its mandate by transmitting the message.

Damascus and Tehran themselves ultimately undercut any nascent hopes of rapprochement. Although Powell told reporters after the Damascus visit that he thought he had convinced Assad of the wisdom of shutting down the operations of anti-Israel "rejectionist" organizations such as Hamas and Islamic Jihad, the groups remained open for business. Any hope of dialogue with Tehran ended with the May 12 explosion of a powerful car bomb in Riyadh, Saudi Arabia, that killed thirty-four people, including eight Americans. Administration officials charged that the al-Qaeda planners of the attack had operated out of Iran. Powell publicly suggested that the talks might eventually be resumed, but Rumsfeld pressed for a more decisive "regime change" option and insisted that "our policy" was not to deal with Iranian leaders at any level. For the remainder of Powell's term in office, the administration's policy toward Tehran would be dominated by Iran's intransigence vis-à-vis Western demands that it publicly and verifiably abandon its controversial nuclear energy program.

The Israeli-Palestinian conflict briefly offered prospects for a diplomatic Renaissance. Just days before the Iraqi invasion, in response to pleas from Tony Blair, Bush had ended months of delay by announcing the

United States' acceptance of the Mideast "road map" of steps toward peace, provided Yasser Arafat followed through with his pledge to establish a new post of Palestinian prime minister. At their Belfast summit on April 8, the president had also reassured Blair that he was prepared to step up his personal involvement in the peace process. When the two leaders emerged for a news conference, Powell watched approvingly from the sidelines as Bush publicly repeated his dedication to a Palestinian state.

In early June 2003, Powell accompanied Bush on a weeklong trip to Europe and the Middle East. At a gathering with five Arab leaders in Sharm el-Sheik, Egypt, Bush offered "my commitment that I will expend the energy and effort necessary to move the [peace] process forward" and warned that Israel "must deal with the settlements" in the West Bank and Gaza Strip. In return, the Arabs declared that they rejected "the culture of extremism and violence in any form or shape."

From Egypt, Bush traveled to Jordan for a meeting hosted by King Abdullah with Israeli Prime Minister Sharon and Mahmoud Abbas, the new Palestinian prime minister. "He was very tough on Sharon" and insisted that Israel be patient and supportive of Abbas, recalled one pleased Arab participant. "He said, 'Look, if I didn't think I could do this, I wouldn't be here. I know I can solve this problem. I'm putting the reputation of the United States on the line.'" To the amazement of the Jordanian and Palestinian delegations, the president quoted Arab leaders to Sharon and insisted that he was prepared to buck domestic political opposition to pressuring Israel. "He said he wasn't worried about the Christian right vote or the Jewish vote" at home.

Bush announced that Rice, working with Powell, would be his personal troubleshooter in negotiating progress on the road map. The move was greeted with relief at the State Department, where memories of the White House's efforts to undercut Powell during his failed April 2002 peace mission remained fresh. "We were not going to have that again," the secretary of state confidently said in a public reference to his widely reported earlier difficulties. He and Rice and their aides, he said, were now working together "like that," he said, linking his two index fingers. "There is no daylight between us."

There was "no question about it," the Arab official recalled. "That period was a high for Powell. He felt that his views prevailed, he felt vindicated." In July, both Sharon and Abbas visited the White House. But in August, before any substantive steps were taken toward implementing the road map, the high spirits and optimism began to unravel with another rash of suicide bombings, followed by Israeli retaliation. Abbas, repeatedly undermined by both Sharon and Arafat, resigned in September.

During the upbeat summer of 2003, Powell also accompanied the president on a five-day trip to Africa, the first ever by a Republican chief executive. It was a chance to focus high-level attention on so-called soft issues about which the secretary cared deeply—development aid and trade for the poorest continent and the AIDS pandemic—and to demonstrate presidential interest in what Powell kept assuring the world was a foreign policy agenda far broader than preemptive war against perceived national security threats.

The long flights aboard Air Force One over the Atlantic and across the African continent also provided Powell with sustained presidential face time away from Cheney and Rumsfeld. In particular, he planned to use the opportunity to explain to Bush the advantages of a more pragmatic and agile approach toward North Korea, a threat arguably more serious than Iraq had ever been. After months of careful positioning, Powell told Wilkerson confidently, he was beginning to "capture" the president on the subject.

As with most other foreign policy issues, Powell was a minority of one among the principals in advocating a long-term diplomatic approach toward North Korea. The lineup, Armitage assessed crisply, was "OSD hard over, although the military was less so. VP's office hard over. Bolton hard over at State and the rest of us wanting to talk to these guys to resolve the issue. Nobody else had equities in it." The planned bilateral talks had never taken place. In October 2002, North Korea had revealed its secret uranium enrichment program—a clear violation of the Clinton-era Agreed Framework. In response, Washington had canceled the fuel oil assistance that constituted its end of the agreement. Pyongyang then ejected U.N. monitors and announced its withdrawal from the Nuclear Non-Proliferation Treaty.

North Korea accused the United States of preparing to invade its territory and demanded direct, bilateral discussions about their differences; Cheney and the Pentagon, which now claimed an equal voice on virtually every foreign policy issue, argued that any conversation with Pyongyang would constitute a reward for bad behavior. Bush himself had what he called a "visceral" loathing for the North Korean leader, Kim Jong Il, and Powell knew the others were "pushing on an open door" in advocating a hard line with the president.

Since being publicly taken to the woodshed on Korea policy in 2001,

Powell had been "careful to bring the boss along slowly and not get too far ahead." In early February 2003, as the administration prepared for war with Iraq, he had launched a trial balloon, sending Armitage to calm Congress's anxiety over the possibility of preemptive "regime change" in North Korea. Powell himself had been otherwise occupied—it was the day before his February 5 Security Council speech—and Armitage had assured the Senate Foreign Relations Committee that "of course" the United States would eventually have "direct" talks with Pyongyang. Within days, Bush shot the idea down, sharply telling inquiring legislators that such discussions were "not my policy."

Later that month, on a lightning trip to Asia that was his only travel outside the country during the two months before the Iraq War, Powell spent a day in Beijing. China, along with other regional powers, was pressing the administration to sit down with Pyongyang. But since Washington now rejected the bilateral, face-to-face talks it had earlier agreed to, while North Korea insisted on them, Powell suggested it might suffice for both to have just one other party in the room—China. Hosting three-way talks was in their interest, he told the Chinese leaders. As Pyongyang's primary diplomatic and economic patron, with a shared border, China did not want an aggressive, nuclear-armed North Korea any more than the United States did. "I said, 'Look . . . you really should want a discussion to take place,'" Powell recalled. "'You really have to be the spark plug in making all this happen.'"

Further work on the initiative, in meetings with the Chinese on the fringes of prewar Security Council deliberations on Iraq, was part of the three-dimensional chess match that Powell thought made foreign policy interesting. Several games were always simultaneously under way, each related to the others. His North Korea diplomacy, Powell knew, was a cause of "great consternation" to the White House, which saw him again acting the renegade dove just as the hawks were spreading their wings on Iraq. "The last thing [Bush] wanted to do . . . because of the political world he lives in" was to appear soft in the face of blatant provocations from Pyongyang.

In Beijing, Powell chose his words carefully, making clear that China would have to hew to the trilateral line in any comments about the talks. "We had to tell the Chinese that the only way I could get this thing going without huge problems back [home] was [for them] to say, 'No, no, there's not going to be any bilateral meeting, this is trilateral.'"

By early April, the Iraq War was under way and Bush was more favorably inclined to consider diplomacy elsewhere. With Rice's encouragement, the president consulted directly with the Chinese leadership, which offered the necessary trilateral assurances. Rumsfeld was adamantly opposed and argued in a series of memos that their goal should be the collapse of the North Korean regime, not dialogue with Kim Jong Il. When he lost that battle, he suggested that Assistant Secretary of State James Kelly be replaced by John Bolton as the head of the U.S. delegation. In the end, Kelly was dispatched to China only after torturous internal negotiations over his instructions for the meeting. Cheney's office and Robert C. Joseph, the hard-line nonproliferation director at the NSC, insisted Kelly be prohibited from talking directly with the North Koreans even on an informal basis. State Department talking points were replaced with a White House version signed by Rice.

The three-way meeting that began in Beijing on April 23 ended a day earlier than scheduled. Kelly outlined the United States' insistence on "verifiable and irreversible" elimination of North Korea's nuclear weapons program. The lead North Korean negotiator retorted that North Korea's nuclear reprocessing program, frozen under the Agreed Framework, had already been restarted and would continue. There was no middle ground.

Over the next two months, intensive diplomatic consultations brought tentative Chinese, South Korean, Japanese and Russian agreement to participate in a new round of talks. North Korea continued to demand an opportunity to negotiate directly with U.S. delegates; China, in particular, pressed Washington to accede to a bilateral dialogue within a six-party framework and to outline potential benefits, from aid to normalization of relations, that could be discussed with Pyongyang in exchange for verifiable disarmament.

When Powell broached the subject on the Africa trip in July, he reminded the president of his own discussions with the Chinese the previous spring. Bush had invited them to play a lead role in the initiative, and the fact that they were now doing so—and actively recommending ways to proceed—was a success for the White House. Allowing an opportunity for American officials to talk briefly to the North Koreans—not, by any means, a "separate" meeting or negotiation, Powell assured him—while providing a blueprint for future peaceful relations would in no way constitute abandonment of U.S. principles. It would "keep the Chinese in," he said, and allow the process to go forward.

Many at the State Department attributed Bush's eventual agreement to the six-party talks, announced as he headed to his Texas ranch in early August, to the fact that much of his national security team—including many in the offices of the vice president and the secretary of defense—were either on vacation or preoccupied with the deteriorating situation in Baghdad.

The prospect of a lengthy stay at his ranch always put the president in good humor. "I got my summer buzz," he said with a laugh to reporters at the White House on Friday, August 1, as he prepared to depart for his annual vacation. "I'm ready to get down there and enjoy the weather." It was an inside joke between Bush—who reveled in the 100-plus-degree temperatures of the Texas summer—and the wilted journalists who were forced to camp out in the makeshift press room at Crawford Middle School.

The presidential idyll had barely gotten under way, however, when it was disturbed the following Monday by a front-page story in *The Washington Post*. Richard Armitage, the paper reported, had recently informed Condoleezza Rice that neither he nor Powell would serve in a second Bush term; if Bush won reelection in 2004, they would be gone the day after the inauguration. The article said that in addition to his unhappiness with the administration, Powell had already promised his wife he would be a one-term secretary. The election was still nearly a year and a half away, the paper noted, but confirmation of the popular secretary of state's intentions could do significant damage to the president's support among Republican moderates and Independent voters.

Powell called it "nonsense . . . just one of those stories that emerge in Washington that reflects nothing more than gossip." In Texas that morning, White House spokesman Scott McClellan avoided the question but declared that both Powell and Armitage were "highly valued members of the President's team and they're doing an outstanding job." Issuing what he called an "update" to Bush's schedule, McClellan announced that the two would arrive in Crawford the following afternoon to dine with the president, spend the night and "continue ongoing discussions on a range of policy priorities."

The White House had "panicked," Armitage later recalled, and quickly planned the Crawford visit as "a big show that we're all together and no one's jumping ship." After their arrival on the evening of August 5, with Alma Powell along for the ride and the photographs, "we drove around the ranch at night, smoked cigars, talked about some ambassadorial appointments and sat down and had cocktails and a lovely dinner." The next morning "we spent about four hours going through the world with the President." No one mentioned the story in the *Post*.

A media scrum quickly assembled after reporters at the school were alerted that the president, his wife and their guests would lunch at the Coffee Station, a small café beside the Crawford railroad crossing. While Alma and Laura Bush chatted in the shade and Armitage hustled out of sight, the president and the secretary of state posed in shirtsleeves under the blistering sun. Bush joked about keeping fit during his vacation, and as the cameras recorded their camaraderie, the two men smiled and obligingly checked their midsections for a telltale paunch.

The question Bush had been waiting for came after a few polite inquiries about the Middle East and the economy. Did the president want Powell in a second Bush administration? "First things first," he responded. He hadn't even been reelected yet. "Listen," he said, gesturing toward the secretary. "This guy has done a fabulous job." The fact that Powell was in Crawford, "talking about issues of importance, should say loud and clear to the American people that he's completely engaged in doing what he needs to do, and that is, serve as a great Secretary of State."

"I serve at the pleasure of the President," Powell demurred as Bush waved, turned away and said with finality, "We're going to get a burger."

The *Post* article had been right in some respects: Armitage and Powell had long since agreed in private that one term with Bush was enough. Armitage had, in fact, requested a meeting with Rice at the White House several weeks earlier. But rather than discussing the future, his message had focused on the past and the present. Venting two years of pent-up frustration and arguing that the president's goals were being damaged, he told her that the National Security Council was "dysfunctional" under her leadership. The NSC was supposed to resolve differences among Cabinet departments, synthesize the advice of senior officials for the president and ensure that they all acted off the same policy script. "You don't resolve things," he criticized.

"And then I went A, B, C, right down" the list, Armitage later recalled. The Pentagon conducted its own foreign policy with no impediment from the national security adviser. Rumsfeld and his deputies regularly dispatched emissaries abroad who undercut the State Department and— in the case of Ahmed Chalabi—had even tried to install their own chosen government in Iraq. The defense secretary's favorite tactic was to come to meetings unprepared and either equivocate or wave off his turn to speak by saying he was not ready. After the meeting, away from reasoned debate, he would provide his input directly to the White House at a time when he could have more influence on a final decision.

When Rumsfeld's senior aides attended meetings without him, they seemed not to have the authority to agree to anything, Armitage said. "We have endless meetings where nothing is resolved. There's no sanction if someone doesn't perform.... I could easily come to a meeting and say, 'Nah...I didn't do what you wanted. So what?'" Since no one in the administration ever got fired, what difference did it make?

Rice thanked him for his input, Armitage recalled, and then said, "I don't want to read about this in the press."

Powell himself had raised similar issues with Rice, although it was not his style to be confrontational with her or to whine. Besides, whatever his irritation at the way the NSC was being run, he thought Rice was only partially to blame. "She tries," he later assessed. "Sometimes she succeeds, sometimes she doesn't. It is not the same kind of system I have operated in before." As President Reagan's national security adviser, he had run a tight ship, with all decision options fully discussed among the principals, then presented and replied to by Reagan in writing.

The defense secretary was definitely a problem, although Powell believed that the main impediment to a more orderly, disciplined process in the Bush administration was not Rumsfeld but Cheney. The vice president's shadow NSC staff had its fingers in every issue, and Cheney himself spent a good part of every day in Bush's presence. The president tended to pay most attention to the last person to whisper in his ear, Powell thought, and that person was usually Cheney. The word Alma used to describe the vice president was "overbearing."

But though Powell had long avoided focusing his concerns on Bush himself, he had to conclude that the president must be satisfied with the way the NSC and the White House were operating. "He didn't check it or stop it or change it in any way. You don't go to the president and say, 'Is this the way you want it?' The president was always in charge. When people say 'You won this one' or 'Cheney won that one,' it's the *president* who decides all this."

Weeks after Armitage's meeting with Rice, an anonymous "Republican former Cabinet secretary" and an unnamed "senior State Department official" were quoted in news articles as describing the NSC as "dysfunctional." Rice called Powell and angrily charged that his deputy had leaked their conversation to reporters. "He called me up and said, 'Jeez, she's really mad,'" Armitage recalled. "And I said, 'I didn't do it.'" But the stories, he told Powell, had only described "what every single policy maker in this town knows." That, Powell replied, had been precisely his response to Rice.

Whatever the next presidential election might bring, Powell expected to complete his current tour of duty. Amid renewed public speculation over his future, he had returned home from Crawford to a stack of messages from concerned family and friends. "I've got eighteen months to go," he told Bruce Llewellyn with a laugh. "I can do this standing on my ear."

As Baghdad baked in the Middle Eastern summer heat, the deteriorating security situation impeded both political and economic reconstruction and Iraq began to slide into a vicious cycle. The administration blamed outside terrorist groups and Saddam-allied "dead-enders" for attacks on infrastructure targets from the electrical grid to water plants. But the absence of promised jobs, services and any form of self-rule left increasing numbers of Iraqi civilians vulnerable to religious and ethnic incitements to rise up against the American occupiers and one another.

When he arrived in May, Bremer had moved rapidly and ruthlessly to bring Iraq under control, informing exiles and "inside" opposition leaders alike that he was empowered by Bush with "all executive, legislative, and judicial functions" and that the transfer of authority to Iraqis had been put off until further notice. With Pentagon approval, CPA decrees banned members of Saddam's Ba'ath Party—virtually the entire former civil government—from official positions and disbanded the Iraqi Army and police force. But the former move left many ministries with no realistic hope of enlisting local management, while the latter left U.S. forces without local security assistance and hundreds of thousands of unemployed men on the chaotic and already dangerous streets. Both actions were later criticized as crucial early mistakes—the result of ineffective or absent prewar planning—in the effort to bring Iraq under control.

It was true, as Bremer later argued, that the Iraqi Army had disappeared before any decrees were issued; senior officers close to Saddam had gone underground and conscripts had abandoned their units, stripped off their uniforms and headed home as U.S. forces advanced. But Powell was convinced that all it would have taken to get them back was to find a few dozen former battalion commanders, give them each $100,000 in cash and tell them to put out the word that payment was available for any of their men who showed up. The Pentagon had missed its chance.

Bremer repeatedly appealed to Rumsfeld for more U.S. troops, or at least a reassessment of the Pentagon's plans to begin withdrawals. There was no reasonable expectation that a new Iraqi force could be assembled, vetted and trained to stem the downward slide within a realistic time frame. The foreign troops that Wolfowitz had assumed would take over postwar stabilization duties had not materialized. Few countries were willing to commit peacekeepers to what was clearly still a war zone, especially without a U.N. mandate and absent U.S. willingness to cede meaningful operational control or provide a timetable for handing Iraq over to an elected government. The United Nations' unhappiness with the state of affairs escalated exponentially when a truck bomb exploded outside the U.N. office in Baghdad on August 19, killing the chief U.N. representative in the country, Sergio Vieira de Mello, and nearly two dozen others.

Over the next several months, a dawning awareness of the depth of the problems in Iraq—and rising complaints from the uniformed military over the way the Pentagon was managing the reconstruction and troop rotations—led the administration to change its mind about dealing with the United Nations. After the usual internal disputes, Powell was authorized to offer an agreement to expedite the process of political reconstruction in exchange for a U.N. mandate for the occupation. But while the concession won international pledges of nonmilitary reconstruction assistance, it failed to draw any significant troop commitments.

Displeased with the Pentagon's mismanagement, the White House inserted a new layer of supervision over CPA operations by establishing an NSC-based Iraq Strategy Group. But in the meantime, a different problem had emerged. David Kay, named after the war by CIA Director Tenet to lead the hunt for Saddam Hussein's stockpiles of biological and chemical weapons, reported to Congress in October that after nearly four months of searching, he had not found any.

Rumsfeld had scoffed publicly at suggestions in the weeks after the invasion that there might not be weapons stockpiles in Iraq. The search was just getting started, he said. "We know where they are." Throughout the spring and summer of 2003, as Kay's team continued to dig dry holes, administration officials dismissed any suggestion that their prewar assessment of the Iraqi threat might have been wrong. Powell, who had staked his personal reputation on his U.N. speech the previous February, was among the most insistent. Over and over again he told questioners, "I stand behind that presentation."

There was occasional cause for optimism. "We found the vans," Powell told reporters on May 30, after the CIA publicly concluded that two truck trailers discovered by U.S. forces in northern Iraq were part of the fleet of mobile biological weapons factories he had described to the Security Council. The "cartoons" he had shown were real, he exulted. "We didn't just make them up one night. Those were eyewitness accounts of people who had worked in the program and knew it was going on, multiple accounts. And when I put them up, showed the four cartoons, people kind of, 'Well, who knows?' Guess what? You should have seen the smile on my face when one day the intelligence community came in and gave me a photo and said, 'Look.' And it was almost identical to the cartoon that I had put up in New York on the 5th of February."

When the State Department's own intelligence bureau, INR, expressed doubts and suggested that the uncovered mobile laboratories were more likely designed to produce hydrogen for artillery practice balloons, Powell sought reassurance from Tenet. "We went out there [to the CIA] and said, 'George, what's your answer to this?'" Powell later recalled. Tenet, he said, responded " 'Nope. We've looked at all the alternative hypotheses, and none of them track the facts.'

"So we kept sailing along, sticking with the story."

With proof of WMD stockpiles still conspicuously missing, however, the media began to publish detailed accounts of a broader pattern of sketchy intelligence, political pressure and deceptive statements in the months leading up to the war. In the first public breach of the White House–constructed wall of secrecy, a recently retired INR analyst, Gregg Thielmann, went public in early June with the bureau's prewar questioning of several elements of the Iraq case. The Bush administration—including Powell—had disregarded its concerns, Thielmann said.

The administration was far from ready to concede that there were no stockpiles, no mobile laboratories and no semblance of what Cheney had called "reconstituted nuclear weapons." Rumsfeld belligerently suggested that Saddam might have destroyed incriminating weaponry as U.S. troops advanced or spirited it into neighboring Syria. Powell headed in a different direction, grasping a lifeline Kay had offered when he told Congress in his interim report on October 2 that the team had discovered "dozens" of what he called "WMD-related program activities" along with evidence of Hussein's "intent...to continue production at some time."

"Although Kay and his team have not yet discovered stocks of the weapons themselves," Powell wrote in an October 7 column in *The Washington Post*, there was ample evidence that Saddam had deceived the United Nations. The team had found "strains of organisms" in the home of one scientist that "could have been used to produce biological agents." There were documents and equipment that "would have been useful for resuming uranium enrichment efforts." Although Kay had acknowledged "a number of explanations" for the mobile laboratories, Powell said, "nothing rules out their potential use" in weapons production.

Even if it were eventually determined that there were no weapons,

Powell said, the "harrowing possibility" that they might have existed—and that they "could" have found their way into the hands of international terrorists—was ample justification for the U.S. action.

Powell had begun to reshuffle the hand he had played at the Security Council eight months earlier into a new formulation of the prewar threat: Saddam had weapons "capability"—evidenced by "dual-use" chemical plants, preserved documents from past production dating back to the 1980s and knowledgeable scientists still living in Iraq. His intent to manufacture weapons for future use was equally clear—he had deployed WMD in the past against domestic enemies and Iran, and he had "associates" among international terrorists who shared his hatred of the United States. "Hussein would have stopped at nothing until something stopped him," Powell wrote in the *Post.* "It's a good thing that we did."

He wrote that he was convinced that the invasion, however flawed in timing and lacking in international support, had been "a good thing." But his new formulation of the justification for war—full of "could"s and "would"s and "might"s—was a pale shadow of his unequivocal assertions to the United Nations that "Saddam Hussein has chemical weapons" and "We know that Iraq has at least seven . . . mobile, biological agent factories."

Even as Powell continued to defend the administration's case for war during the summer of 2003, however, he became aware of problems. Wilkerson later recalled that Powell had walked into his office one day and said, "You're not going to believe what I just got a phone call on." Tenet, he said, had rung to say that one element of the Security Council presentation—intelligence evidence that the Iraqis had armed rocket launchers with biological weapons and hidden them in groves of palm trees as the U.S. invasion force gathered—"might not be accurate."

Over the next few months, Tenet called repeatedly to alert him that John McLaughlin was headed to Capitol Hill to "clarify" elements of the Iraqi evidence for intelligence oversight committees. McLaughlin occasionally placed similar calls to Armitage, who would amble down the hall to the secretary's office to report that "our friends up the river" had passed along word of further doubts.

"They never walked in here and said, 'Hi, Mr. Secretary, we've got some bad news. It all went to hell,'" Powell later recalled wryly of the CIA. It wasn't until the end of the year that he received his first formal notification from the intelligence agency.

It came in a memorandum addressed to Armitage from McLaughlin indicating that information provided by the primary source for the mobile weapons labs, an Iraqi engineer the agency had code-named "Curveball," might not have been reliable. "Then, a couple of days or weeks later," Powell recalled, "either Condi or Hadley told me, 'You know, they were in briefing the president this morning, and Jami [Miscik, the deputy CIA director for intelligence] told the president that two of the four sources are not looking good.'

"And so I said, 'George, two of the four are bad.' " But "the agency was standing behind it, still."

The beleaguered Bush administration received a much-needed boost on December 13, 2003, when U.S. troops pulled a bearded and disheveled Saddam Hussein out of a rough underground hiding place near a farmhouse north of Baghdad. In a news conference two days later, the president warned that "the terrorists in Iraq remain dangerous" and "further sacrifice" by U.S. troops would be required. "Yet it should now be clear to all," he said, that "Iraq is on the path to freedom. And a free Iraq will serve the peace and security of America and the world."

Powell was not listening that morning as the president jubilantly declared 2003 a "year of accomplishment." As Bush spoke to journalists in the Old Executive Office Building, the secretary of state lay in the recovery room at Walter Reed Army Medical Center following surgery for removal of a cancerous prostate. The diagnosis, made during his annual August physical after years of inconclusive tests, had not surprised him. He was a sixty-six-year-old black man, a prime candidate for the disease that disproportionately affected men of his age and race. But confirmation of the cancer had come during the hectic summer debates over Iraq and North Korea, and he had put off the surgery until the end of the year, when things were likely to be relatively quiet.

A week after the operation, still at home and looking gray and weary, he roused himself for a telephone interview with Michael Reagan, the former president's son, now a California radio host. Powell began by urging African-American men to see their doctors for annual prostate screening. "I'll tell you what," Powell said, "I don't fool with my health and I never have, because I don't ever want to miss an opportunity to protect me from something worse. So I have always been faithful about my health, and I recommend that to anybody who cares about living a long and productive life."

As the conversation drifted into foreign policy, he spoke optimistically of the year ahead. There were still problems with Syria and Iran, but both were beginning to "get smart," he said, and it was time for North Korea to do the same. Saddam's capture had made for a "terrific week" in Iraq, although "we still have a lot of work ahead of us. We have to rebuild a society that's never known democracy before. We've got to create jobs. We've got to put in place a satisfactory political system."

Asked what his top priority would be in 2004, however, Powell did not speak about Iraqi democracy or the fight against terrorism but about the scourge of AIDS in Africa and around the world and the need to develop treatments and a cure. "We talk about weapons of mass destruction, we talk about people who are suffering," he said. "But when you look around the world and you look at what is the greatest killer out there that is not only killing people but destroying societies in Africa and in the Caribbean, and increasingly it's going to be the case in parts of Asia and Europe, it's HIV/AIDS."

"I've got to ask you this for a final question," Reagan concluded. "The president gets reelected. Is Colin Powell still going to be our secretary of state?"

Powell wouldn't bite. "You know," he said, "the only answer to that question is that I serve at the pleasure of the president, and I am honored to be a member of his administration."

21

If I had known there were no stockpiles, I never would
have said there were stockpiles.

—Colin L. Powell

Nearly everyone in official Washington called someplace else home.
The capital city traditionally became a ghost town in late December, as
lawmakers headed back to their states for the end-of-the-year holidays
and senior administration officials escaped temporarily to where they
would some day return permanently. The final days of 2003, Bush's third
year in office, found the president at his ranch in Texas. The White House
Web site, normally cluttered with announcements and speech transcripts,
posted videos of the Christmas adventures of Barney, the Bush family
dog, and Cabinet secretaries reading "bedtime stories" in front of a
brightly decorated tree. Agriculture Secretary Ann Veneman chose "Aun-
tie Claus," while Small Business Administrator Hector Baretto read "The
Grinch" in Spanish. Karl Rove, the president's top political adviser,
offered "Santa's New Reindeer."

With the business of state suspended, the executive and legislative
branches gathered their strength for what lay ahead. By the time Washington began to stir in January, the quadrennial presidential election year
would be under way—the first during a time of war since Richard Nixon
promised "peace with honor" in Vietnam. Although the capture of Saddam Hussein just before Christmas had given Bush's job approval rating a
fleeting boost, his reelection hung in the balance amid public concern
that the U.S. "liberation" of Iraq had become a grueling and costly military occupation. Both Iraq and Afghanistan remained "a long, hard slog,"
as Donald Rumsfeld acknowledged within his closed circle of aides. But
Rove had decided the president would campaign on the offensive, warning voters that terrorists still threatened America and that Bush was the
only candidate with the *cojones* to deal with them.

Powell, who had no home outside Washington and disliked vacations, pulled on his khakis and windbreaker and returned part-time to the State Department two weeks after his prostate surgery. The building was quiet, and he sat in his office reading, telephoning and swiveling around in his chair to peck out e-mails on the always humming computer behind his desk. Alma and his staff were concerned that he was overexerting himself; he still seemed wan and tired. But on January 8, as the president tried out his chest-thumping campaign speech on a group of financial backers in Knoxville, Tennessee—"Terrorists declared war on the United States, and war is what they got"—Powell decreed his recovery period officially over and summoned the diplomatic press corps to hear his plans for the New Year.

Far from Bush's aggressive assertions of threats and triumphs, the foreign policy agenda Powell laid out was one of "progress" to build on and "challenges" to meet with the help of America's allies. The administration would continue to expand development assistance and trade opportunities to less fortunate countries, he promised. Advances were being made in Afghanistan, where NATO had agreed to increase its military presence. Negotiations were under way to end Sudan's twenty-year civil war, and there were "interesting developments" in Iran, where "my European Union colleagues from France, Germany and Britain" were jointly pressing for a nonproliferation agreement. Just a year and a half after India and Pakistan had stood on the brink of nuclear war, the two countries had now initialed a plan to work out their difficulties. The six-party talks with North Korea were moving forward, he said, and "we're anxious to have the next round."

The Mideast peace process remained on the "challenge" side of the ledger, as did Iraq, where the number of U.S. deaths was approaching 500. "We regret the loss of life of our brave young men and women," Powell said, but the cause was just and progress was being made. Under a plan announced in November 2003—the product of the administration's despair over the decreasing likelihood of an early exit—a limited transfer of sovereignty was scheduled for June. Although the U.S. military would remain, Bremer's Coalition Provisional Authority would be replaced by an interim Iraqi government that would supervise the writing of a constitution and preparations for elections in January 2005. Iraqi sovereignty would mean a newly prominent role for the State Department, which was preparing to open an embassy and replace the Pentagon as Washington's chief political interlocutor with Baghdad.

"The difficult work is still ahead of putting in place a new government that will be responsive to its people," Powell acknowledged, "but as the President said repeatedly, we are committed to that end, and we will be successful."

Powell was as capable as any of the administration's hawks of using tough, "cut it off and kill it" language. But more often than not, he labored visibly to fit the Bush administration's muscular rhetoric inside his own pragmatic views. "Partnership is the watchword of U.S. strategy in this administration," he had insisted in a published year-end essay identical in tone and substance to his confirmation remarks three years earlier. Those who thought otherwise simply failed "to grasp what American strategy is really all about." Any president who consulted with the United Nations on Iraq, created a "quartet" to guide Israel and the Palestinians to peace and was willing to talk to North Korea, he wrote, was clearly committed to multilateralism.

As the author of each of the multilateral initiatives with which he credited Bush, Powell knew that all of them had been adopted as administration policy only after long, uphill struggles. Each had suffered from mixed signals and missed opportunities as a result of internal disputes, and each remained under siege from within. But Powell's patience was legendary. "Success doesn't always come with a deep pass," he liked to say. "Sometimes it's a ground game... building up, slowly but surely, layer by layer."

Powell's confident march into 2004 was interrupted by a reporter who asked about a piece of unfinished business from the year before. Each day's news now brought fresh indications that the Bush administration had exaggerated the evidence of the Iraqi threat before the invasion, the reporter noted. It was clear that "a lot of probables, a lot of maybes" had been left out of Powell's February 5, 2003, presentation to the United Nations. Given a second chance, would he have "rephrased" his speech?

"No," Powell replied firmly. "I knew exactly the circumstances under which I was presenting that speech... the whole world would be watching, and there would be those who would applaud every word, and there would be those who were going to be skeptical of every word." Whatever doubts were now being raised, he said, the basic conclusions had been solid. "I am confident of what I presented last year. The intelligence community is confident of the material they gave me; I was representing them... they stand behind it."

On Friday, January 23, the CIA announced without explanation that David Kay had been replaced as head of the Iraq Survey Group hunting for weapons of mass destruction. In an interview that afternoon, Kay told reporters that the weapons stockpiles cited as justification for the war did not exist.

As Powell flew the next day to attend a presidential inauguration in the Republic of Georgia, journalists aboard his plane asked him to reconcile his prewar U.N. speech with Kay's conclusions. "You said a year ago that you thought there was between one hundred and five hundred tons of chemical weapons [in Iraq]," said one reporter. "Who's right?"

"I think the answer to the question is I don't know yet," Powell replied. "What is the open question is: how many stocks they had, if any? And if they had any, where did they go? And if they didn't have any, then why wasn't that known beforehand?"

It was the first doubt that any senior administration official had publicly expressed about the central justification for the war. The story made headlines around the world, and Powell was not surprised when Condoleezza Rice called him the next morning in Georgia. He always knew when the White House was going to be upset with him; all he had to do was read the morning papers. "She'd say, 'Oh, we've got a problem, what are we going to do about this? How are we going to fix this?' "

On this issue, he thought, there was little to be done. "The fact of the matter is, you can't ignore the possibility, since the guy we sent there for eight months as *our guy* says there's nothing there," he later recalled telling Rice with exasperation. "So, to say there's *got* to be something there when he, who has been there for *eight months,* says there's nothing there.... You can't do that. You've got to at least accept the possibility." The White House, he advised, should "just be quiet for the weekend."

On Tuesday, January 27, reporters ushered into the Oval Office to watch Bush shake hands with Polish President Andrej Krasniewski asked Bush whether he had any doubts about the prewar intelligence. The Iraq Survey Group would continue its search, he replied vaguely, and it was important to "find out the facts and compare the facts to what was thought." Pressed to respond to Democrats' calls for an independent investigation into the administration's prewar claims, Bush ducked the question. The world, he said dismissively, was "better off without" Saddam Hussein.

Congress demanded to hear Kay for itself, and the next day the former chief weapons inspector told the Senate Armed Services Committee that "it turns out we were all wrong" about Iraq's weapons. His team had combed the country and found no signs of stockpiles, "large or small." Kay said he believed the uncovered mobile laboratories, which the CIA still insisted were for biological weapons production, had more likely been designed to produce hydrogen for balloons. In his judgment, the intercepted aluminum tubes had been configured for conventional use in missiles rather than to produce weapons-grade uranium.

Powell spent the following weekend carefully reading Kay's testimony, highlighting portions with a yellow marker and scribbling notes in the margins. With the first anniversary of his U.N. speech just days away, the Sunday newspapers and television talk shows were filled with comparisons between the charges he had made and Kay's conclusions. At the White House, Bush's political advisers concluded that the president would have to yield to the growing demands for an investigation. But he could shape the work of an independent commission—steering it toward more general questions of intelligence gathering and analysis and away from an examination of how the administration had used the information—and control its timing. Over the weekend, Cheney began calling members of Congress to say that Bush would announce a broad study of intelligence on WMD proliferation, including in Iraq, North Korea and Libya. White House officials let it be known that the commission's work would continue well into 2005, safely beyond the November election.

At a cabinet meeting on Monday, February 2, Rumsfeld began with a status update on the military occupation. Powell then explained how the administration could square the circle of intelligence and threat assessment leading up to the war and "laid out the construct of intent and capability . . . for the Cabinet and the president." Carrying his marked-up copy of Kay's testimony in a blue folder, he left the meeting and headed for a scheduled lunch at *The Washington Post*, where he planned to make the same argument.

He was "absolutely convinced" that the invasion had been the right thing to do, Powell decisively told two dozen *Post* reporters and editors crowded around a conference table in the newspaper's eighth-floor boardroom. "To talk about a threat, you have to look at intent, and then you have to look at capabilities, and the two of them together equal a threat." Regardless of whether Saddam had had weapons stockpiles, he said, the sanctions that had constrained Iraq since the 1991 war had been falling apart, leaving Saddam on the verge of "breaking free" and reconstituting his lethal programs.

Would he still have "recommended the invasion" if George Tenet had told him a year before "that there are no stockpiles?" one reporter asked.

"I don't know, because it was the stockpiles that presented the final little piece that made it more of a real and present danger and threat to the region and to the world," Powell replied. But there was no point discussing hypotheticals, he said, because "the fact of the matter" was that the CIA, as well as intelligence agencies in Britain and elsewhere, had "suggested the stockpiles were there."

But what if he had *known* they weren't there? the reporter pressed.

"The absence of a stockpile changes the political calculus," Powell acknowledged. "It changes the answer you get with the little formula I laid out."

To a White House already reeling from the one-two punch of Kay's conclusions and Powell's comments en route to Georgia, it was another worrisome example of the secretary of state's unwillingness to stay "on message." When his remarks appeared in the *Post* the next morning, "I think the whole White House operation was mad...the NSC, the president—everybody was annoyed," Powell recalled. "White Houses do not respond well to immediate problems in the morning...all the white corpuscles race to the source of the infection, so all the white corpuscles raced to me." After Rice's inevitable telephone call, White House aides quickly began contacting the media to counteract the secretary's remarks. One official, in a reference to the 2001 North Korea dispute, suggested that Powell had once again leaned "a little forward on his skis."

Stopping to chat with reporters outside the State Department the next day as he walked the visiting Kofi Annan to his car, Powell repeated his "capability...intent" formulation. But the "bottom line," he said, was that "the President made the right decision." News reports indicated that Powell's clarification had been "coordinated" with the White House.

Powell had been irritated but not surprised at the internal reaction. Still mulling over the situation a week later in his dimly lit office, he blamed a persistent White House machismo that took aim at "any-thing...that suggests any weakness in the [administration's] position" regardless of common sense. That, and what he saw as a never-ending effort to humble him personally.

"There are people who would like to take me down," he said, jerking his thumb in the direction of the White House some ten blocks away. "It's been the case since I was appointed. By take down, I mean keep him in his place.... And there are those who, whether it was me or anyone else, just love somebody getting in trouble, because it's usually to the detriment of the person getting in trouble and to the advantage of someone else."

The pettiness and wheel spinning—"people getting ready for their 'down' hours and 'up' hours, and all that foolishness"—never ended. What helped him keep his balance was a constant flow of e-mails and calls from a vast network of friends, family and former colleagues outside the capital who assured him that he was the only one making sense amid apparent lunacy. Even if he had had time to think harder about the *Post* reporter's question before answering, he said, he would not have responded differently. "The answer is so right...I don't *know* what I would have recommended if somebody had said, 'There ain't no weapons of mass destruction.' People out in the countryside understand that... people who are living real lives, who read this stuff and say, 'Well, of course. Yeah, of course.' "

The episode reinforced Powell's already deep-seated disdain for politics and its practitioners. Political thought and decision making were often polluted by ideology and the exigencies of the election cycle; soldiers breathed a purer, more rational air. "I was not trained as a politician or a think tank guy or anything else. I was trained to consider all possibilities.

"I mean, if you're attacking and suddenly you get attacked from the flank," he continued, warming to the topic and using his hands to illustrate a military maneuver, "you don't say, 'I'm going to keep attacking straight ahead [and] ignore this new threat coming at my flank.' " He had been asked whether different information would have changed his assessment of the Iraq situation, and "all of my instincts and all of my background and training at that point said the answer to the question is 'I'd have to reconsider.'

"How could you *not* reconsider?" he asked, his voice rising. "If the CIA, after saying for *a year and a half*"—he slapped his desk twice for emphasis—"suddenly says, 'Whoops.' "

He shrugged and brought his hands to rest. "But that's the way it goes."

Powell's annoyance at the White House was coupled with a growing anger at the CIA. Right or wrong, at least Bush had willingly shouldered the ultimate responsibility for the decision to invade Iraq. Powell felt he had done his own duty by privately voicing caution even as he gave the president his full support. But it was increasingly apparent that the intelligence community had been careless with the truth and hence with Powell's most precious commodity—his credibility with the American people.

For a week after Kay's testimony, the CIA had continued publicly to stand by its prewar weapons assessment. But in a hastily arranged speech at Washington's Georgetown University on February 5, George Tenet had finally said, "Whoops." His "provisional bottom line," Tenet said, was that the intelligence community had been "generally on target" in its warnings that Saddam was developing long-range missiles. But the CIA "may have overestimated the progress Saddam was making" on nuclear weapons.

As for biological weapons stockpiles and mobile laboratories—the most specific and damning charges in Powell's U.N. speech—"we are finding discrepancies in some claims made by human sources" to whom the agency "lacked direct access." The CIA, Tenet said, "did not ourselves penetrate the inner sanctum" of Saddam's programs but had "access to émigrés and defectors" along with high-level information from "a trusted foreign partner." The agency was now in the process of "evaluating" questions such as "Did we clearly tell policy makers what we knew, what we didn't know, what was not clear, and identify the gaps in our knowledge?"

Although Powell had been advised in recent months of problems with some of the intelligence sourcing, Tenet's speech was "the first time I heard that the CIA was no longer sticking behind its story" in public, he later recalled. He had been given no advance copy of the CIA director's remarks and listened in his office to Tenet's acknowledgment of "discrepancies" and uncertainties.

Powell stared silently at Lawrence Wilkerson after Tenet finished speaking. "But the question is," Wilkerson said, reaching for a joke, "are you still friends?"

"I don't think so," Powell replied.

Some in the media suggested that Powell should apologize publicly for peddling false information that had pushed the nation toward war. "Is everyone else going to apologize?" he replied angrily within the four walls of his office. "It's not [just] me getting had. I'm not the only one who was using that intelligence...they all stood up in the Senate. The president stood up on this material. Tony Blair stood up on this material.... The whole global intelligence community bears responsibility."

But there was no denying that he had been the most visible and effective salesman of the case that was now unraveling. He already knew that the label would follow him around forever. "I'm the guy who will always be known as the 'Powell Briefing.'...I'm not being defensive, because I did it. But Powell wasn't the only one."

Most members of Congress treated him tenderly when he testified at hearings on the State Department budget during the second week in February. But several Democrats peppered him with questions about the U.N. speech, putting the onus on Bush for taking the country to war on "false premises" and pushing Powell to set aside his "loyalty to the president" in agreement. The secretary threw it back at them, saying he didn't believe that "anyone in America should think that President Bush cooked the books."

Democratic Representative Robert Wexler of Florida remarked dolefully that he had always considered Powell "the credible voice in the administration.... When you reached the conclusion that Iraq represented a clear and present danger to the United States, that meant a lot to me.... But the facts suggest there was a part of the story that was not true."

Clearly at the edge of his vaunted patience, Powell snapped back. "It's not a question of 'Gee, if there are no stockpiles now, why did you tell us there were stockpiles then?' The reason is because we believed there were stockpiles then. We believed there were stockpiles when I said so before the United Nations.... We believed there were stockpiles when Dr. Kay went in. We believed there were stockpiles when our forces went in, and we were surprised that they didn't find them right away. We were surprised Dr. Kay didn't find them. It's not because we knew they weren't there and now we're pulling a bait-and-switch. We believed it at the time. And we believed it not just because we wanted to believe it to start a war. We believed it because the intelligence information available to us said the stockpiles were there."

Media reports and official inquiries—including investigations by the Senate Intelligence Committee and the independent commission Bush appointed in February—would eventually reach conclusions far more damning than the tentative, after-the-fact warning of "problems" that Powell had received from the CIA.

Some of the sources Powell had been assured were fully vetted were, in fact, associated with Ahmed Chalabi's Iraqi National Congress. One of the four sources of the mobile laboratory claim didn't even exist, and the CIA's conclusion that Iraq definitely "had" biological weapons had been based "almost exclusively" on information from one man—an Iraqi defector code-named "Curveball." An asylum seeker being held in Germany, Curveball had never even been interviewed by U.S. intelligence; all of his reports had come secondhand through German intelligence. The only U.S. official ever allowed to meet with him—a military physician assigned to check for signs that he had been exposed to biological weapons—had reported "inconclusive" results and questioned whether he might be an alcoholic. Long before the Iraq War, German officials had warned that Curveball was "out of control" and "crazy" and intimated that he was a fabricator. An examination of his biography suggested that he had not been in a position to see the biological weapons programs he claimed to have witnessed with his own eyes.

Reports of problems with Curveball, it emerged, had been circulating inside the CIA long before Powell had made his allegations public. At the very moment when Powell was preparing his U.N. presentation, at least one CIA official had e-mailed his superior with concern that the secretary of state planned to rely on someone already branded a liar. "This war is going to happen regardless," the senior officer had responded. "The powers that be probably aren't interested in whether Curveball knows what he's talking about." In testimony before the commission, intelligence officials recalled having warned both Tenet and McLaughlin about Curveball, although both men said they had no memory of such discussions. In its report released in March 2005, the independent commission on WMD intelligence concluded that no policy maker—"especially the Secretary"—had been informed of the CIA's doubts.

Richard Boucher, who had sat alongside Powell in Tenet's conference room with Iraq analysts and other senior administration officials as the speech was being written, later found it hard to believe that "somebody in that room didn't know.... Somebody could have said, 'Hey, we don't like this source.' If anybody had said anything like that, it would have been gone. Gone."

Newly revealed information also cast doubt on the allegations of ties between Saddam and al-Qaeda, including the extensive portion of Powell's speech that had been devoted to a description of Iraqi training for al-Qaeda operatives in chemical and biological bomb-making. A Defense Intelligence Agency memo written a year before the Iraq invasion had concluded that the source of the charge—a captured senior al-Qaeda operative—was "intentionally misleading" his interrogators. By February 2004, the operative had recanted his claims and the CIA had withdrawn all intelligence reports based on his interrogation.

If there was one area where Powell had knowingly compromised, Wilkerson said of the many hours they had spent together at the CIA, it was on the question of Iraq–al-Qaeda links. White House officials had been "absolutely adamant" that "Saddam Hussein had...some kind of contact with al-Qaeda or al-Qaeda-like people." Powell, he said, "finally bought that." The secretary had had the last word on everything in the speech, Wilkerson recalled, "but the last word [was] based on his best assessment of what [Tenet] and the others were telling him."

The State Department team that had been with Powell at the CIA eventually concluded that their fundamental mistake had been the failure to "zero-base" the speech. Their starting premise had been that the weapons stockpiles existed, and they saw their task in those frantic few days as culling the best available evidence to prove it. Information that cast doubt on the premise itself was not offered, and they did not ask for it. But the labor-intensive work of removing the more outlandish claims inserted by Cheney's office and paring down the National Intelligence Estimate had clearly not been enough.

While many charged that the administration's flawed assessment of the Iraqi weapons threat had been the product of "groupthink." Powell preferred to call it "inferential thinking. Where you infer something and it goes from an inference to fact, then new inferences, then you go up a chart and the next thing you know ... you see what you're expecting to see even when it isn't there."

Powell and French Foreign Minister Dominique de Villepin had had their differences over Iraq, but they had never stopped talking to each other. By early 2004, relations between Paris and Washington were more or less back on track and the two men were consulting regularly. On February 6, Powell took a needed break from the Iraq revelations and recriminations swirling around Washington to visit the United Nations in New York. Slipping out of a conference on war-torn Liberia, he met de Villepin for a private lunch. Their discussion ranged over the Middle East and the European initiative in Iran and finally reached a subject far from the center of high-level international attention: escalating violence in the Caribbean island nation of Haiti.

Haitian President Jean-Bertrand Aristide—violently overthrown in 1991 and peacefully reinstated in 1994 thanks to the negotiating efforts of Powell, Jimmy Carter and Sam Nunn—was again in trouble. Reelected and inaugurated for another five-year term in 2001, Aristide had gradually lost support at home and abroad as his government fell into economic stagnation and political corruption.

There was plenty of blame to go around for Aristide's failure. The U.S. troops sent to usher him back to the island in 1994 had remained, under U.N. auspices, for nearly two years. But they had left Haiti little better equipped for economic and political development than they had found it. The Bush administration, put off by Aristide's populist rhetoric and suspecting him of drug trafficking, considered him a thug and had long since turned its back on him.

As Aristide supporters and well-armed opposition mobs began to battle in the streets, the White House and leading Republican legislators insisted there was nothing to be done until the Haitians themselves reached a political agreement. But Aristide still had friends in high places in the United States. The Congressional Black Caucus accused the administration of paying lip service to democracy while failing to support

Haiti's popularly elected government. Florida's two senators demanded that Bush take action to prevent an influx of new waves of Haitian immigrants. The likely Democratic presidential candidate, Massachusetts Senator John Kerry, accused Bush of helping to create the unrest by cutting off aid to Haiti. "They hate Aristide," Kerry said of the administration.

Haiti was a complicated issue for Powell. He was reluctant to get into an argument with either the Black Caucus or CARICOM, the association of Caribbean governments trying to negotiate a settlement that would respect Haiti's electoral process. He had expended considerable personal effort in 1994 to preserve Haitian democracy and put Aristide back into office, and he thought it unseemly to be the one to take him out again.

As the violence escalated into its third week, with opposition forces seizing control of the second and third largest Haitian cities, Powell and de Villepin spoke by telephone several times a day. France had little liking for Aristide and traditionally had few qualms about intervening in its former colonies. When a hastily brokered power-sharing plan fell apart, de Villepin suggested to Powell that it was time to give the Haitian president a push out of office.

"The last thing I wanted was Haiti back," Powell later recalled. "I'd gotten rid of it once before. But when it was clear that we were about to have mass murder in the streets of Port-au-Prince...I [had] to do a reverse and get [him] out of there." There was no support for the Haitian president within the Bush administration, and Powell was given an open door to find a solution.

By late February, he and de Villepin had agreed on a plan. To save Powell the discomfort of publicly advocating Aristide's departure, France offered to take the lead. On Thursday, February 26, de Villepin announced that "the [Haitian] regime has reached an impasse and has already shaken off constitutional legality." Aristide's foreign minister, visiting Paris for consultations, was told in more forceful terms that the president should leave.

That same afternoon, as opposition forces closed in on Port-au-Prince, the private American firm that provided Aristide's personal security called the State Department to express concern for his safety. The United States, it was told, would offer Aristide no protection.

On Friday, Powell followed up de Villepin's announcement with a public suggestion that Aristide undertake a "careful examination" of his options. After Bush met with his national security team on Saturday, the White House released a statement describing the crisis as "largely of Mr. Aristide's making," adding that "his own actions have called into question his fitness to continue to govern."

At 10 p.m. Saturday, Powell received a call from the U.S. ambassador in Haiti, who said that Aristide was ready to depart the country. "Then it took all night to get the planes"—eventually a U.S. military aircraft and escort were arranged—"and I had no place to send him," Powell recalled. "Dominique found a place in an hour." By dawn on Sunday, February 29, Aristide was en route to the Central African Republic, another former French possession. It was one of the "virtues of colonialism," Powell later said with unsubtle irony.

Hours after Aristide's departure, Bush announced that U.S. Marines would deploy to the island as the temporary vanguard of an international force. The United Nations voted to send multinational peacekeeping troops; France, Canada and several South American countries volunteered. There were the inevitable pledges that this time around, the world community would do better in Haiti.

Unlike so many issues Powell had dealt with in the Bush administration, this one had been resolved quickly and without undue interference. With just a few telephone calls, the chief diplomats of two First World powers had successfully conspired to alter reality on a small Third World island—a textbook case of pressure successfully applied without sending a single soldier into harm's way. Although the Black Caucus and others were critical of the U.S. intervention, Powell thought a bloodbath had been averted. The cooperation between France and the United States, he noted in an oblique reference to the more unilateral tendencies of the White House and the Pentagon, also demonstrated "the virtues of not cutting off all your friendships."

The one-month Haitian crisis was soon forgotten, and Powell received little credit for adeptly removing it from the administration's already full plate. "Colin Powell is a master of preventive diplomacy," observed one of de Villepin's aides. "But it's very difficult to crow about something that has not happened.... If you solve a crisis when it's hot, you're in the cameras and it's very good for your image. But when you prevent a crisis, nobody cares."

While Haiti provided a brief distraction from the problems of Iraq, North Korea—whose nuclear weapons were undeniably real—remained a far more ominous threat. The first round of six-party talks in August 2003 had ended inconclusively; by the end of the year, the administration was again locked in disagreement over how to proceed.

Pyongyang had sent mixed signals to Washington, defiantly confirming that it possessed a "nuclear deterrent" while declaring its willingness, under certain conditions, to talk about it. Although Bush had assented to the flexible approach Powell had advocated, administration hawks had continued trying to harden the U.S. position. Most of their efforts took place outside of formal discussions, through John Bolton's calls to NSC and Pentagon allies with intelligence from inside the State Department, along with Rumsfeld's memos and Cheney's regular private conversations with the president.

State was responsible for issuing instructions to the chief U.S. negotiator, James Kelly, but Kelly's talking points for the multilateral meetings were regularly revised and stiffened with input from the Pentagon and the vice president's office, and every line required White House approval. Just as the hard-liners made indirect attacks on his position, Powell tried to circumvent them without direct confrontation. Advising Kelly to follow the letter of his instructions but to remain alert for diplomatic opportunities, he drew a distinction between "dialogue" with the North Koreans and direct negotiations. "Make sure there's no table in the area where you meet" the Pyongyang delegation on the fringes of the six-party talks, he told Kelly. "If it's in the corner of the dining room and there are a bunch of chairs around, that's fine. But make sure there's no table. If you're in a corner with these guys and you talk for two hours, fine. But you're not across a table."

At times, the administration's warring camps seemed to expend more energy on plotting against one another than they did on confronting Pyongyang. Bush appeared oblivious to the infighting, and each faction was convinced it had the president's support.

As planning commenced in late 2003 for a second round of six-party talks, North Korea demanded that the United States forswear military action and commence economic assistance in simultaneous exchange for a freeze on its nuclear programs and their eventual dismantlement. The United States countered that North Korea must achieve "complete, verifiable, irreversible dismantlement"—shorthanded as "CVID" in the diplomatic documents—before any benefits accrued.

In early December 2003, China asked that the multilateral partners prepare a "framework" document before talks resumed. A joint U.S.–Japan–South Korea proposal offered "coordinated" steps in which they, along with Russia and China, would provide North Korea with security guarantees once disarmament and inspections had begun. After consulting with Pyongyang, China rejected the informal offer on the grounds that it made no mention of economic assistance. On December 12, a Chinese counterproposal was rejected by Cheney, who objected to the absence of CVID language as the unilateral starting point for discussions.

In the vice president's view, the six-party talks were a venue for the United States to set out its nonnegotiable demands with the support of the other four partners; anything less would be a return to the weak-kneed Clinton policies that had allowed North Korea to expand its nuclear program in the first place. Pyongyang would have to comply or risk facing the consequences.

That a nuclear-armed North Korea was a threat to U.S. national security was not in question. But Powell argued that unless they were prepared to bomb a recalcitrant Pyongyang into submission, their chances of success were better if they at least dangled the possibility of potential benefits in front of North Korea. The other four partners, especially China, were pressing Washington to give a little. Since the Bush administration had invited them to the table in the first place, Powell said, it couldn't just ignore China's views and expect its continued participation.

Kelly began the next six-party round in Beijing on February 25, 2004, with instructions that any resulting joint statement would have to center on CVID. By the second day, North Korea had rejected the U.S. position and demanded that the United States issue a "verifiable, irreversible" commitment to abandon its "hostile policy." When Kelly reported back on the impasse, Powell authorized new instructions, using diplomatic language designed to maintain the United States' position but keep its partners and the North Koreans at the table.

On the evening of February 26, Powell and Armitage were at a black-tie dinner in Washington honoring the businessman and former diplomat John Whitehead and Powell's cousin Bruce Llewellyn. Midway through the meal, they were summoned away for a telephone call from Rice's deputy, Stephen Hadley. The White House, Hadley said, wanted to clarify Kelly's revised instructions before they were sent to Beijing, where it was already the next day. Powell spent a few moments explaining the language he had approved and then handed the telephone over to Armitage. "You take care of it," he said as he returned to dinner.

But the instructions that Kelly eventually received were fashioned not by Powell but by the vice president. Cheney had intervened with Bush that night to replace Powell's language with a tougher line. Based on Cheney's input, the president approved a two-sentence statement noting that the United States had "no intention to invade or attack the DPRK," the Democratic People's Republic of Korea. "The United States further declares that its continued support of the six-party process ... rests on the complete, verifiable, and irreversible dismantlement by the DPRK of all nuclear weapons and all its nuclear programs." Unless Pyongyang agreed, the statement made clear, the process itself was over. There was no further call to Powell before the message was dispatched.

When he realized the next morning what had happened, Powell's fury was only partially abated by the knowledge that the talks in Beijing had moved toward adjournment without a joint statement but with an agreement to meet again. Before Kelly could "figure out what to do" with his new instructions, Powell learned, "the whole thing had gone away."

Scheduled to attend a White House lunch for visiting German Chancellor Gerhard Schröder, Powell decided to arrive early to speak with the president. He later recalled the conversation as terse and one-sided.

"Busy last night, huh?" he asked Bush.

"Didn't they tell you—?"

"No, they didn't," Powell replied curtly. "Fortunately, it didn't go anywhere. Because if Kelly had executed what he was given... if we had shown our friends and insisted on the position that got called out there last night, my judgment, Mr. President, is that we would have blown up the whole six-party framework. It would have been gone."

Months later, as the North Korean talks continued to limp along without resolution, he remained appalled that "we had the two senior political officials in the government sitting there and writing instructions" in the dark of night. He had not confronted Cheney in the wake of the incident. "Why should I?" he snapped. "I talked to my boss. The president knew that they shouldn't have done that."

Reports of poisoned relations between senior members of Bush's team had been the subject of gossip and media analysis for years. But the well of speculation spilled over with the April 2004 publication of a new book by the journalist Bob Woodward.

Plan of Attack examined presidential decision making during the eighteen months leading to the Iraq invasion, from the days immediately following the September 11, 2001, attacks to the first bombs dropped on Baghdad. The White House had assisted Woodward's research; the president himself had sat for a lengthy, on-the-record interview. But other than Bush and Rumsfeld—whose interview transcripts were released by the Pentagon—no sources were identified for the many private, high-level conversations Woodward reconstructed. He wrote that he had spoken "on background" with "more than 75 key people directly involved in the events, including war cabinet members, the White House staff and officials serving at various levels of the State and Defense Departments and the Central Intelligence Agency."

As in 1991, when a previous Woodward volume had described Powell's reservations about the first Persian Gulf war, the secretary of state was once again depicted as privately cautioning the president about the difficulty of invading Iraq. After his August 2002 conversation with Bush, the book indicated, Powell had been left out of the decision loop. He and Cheney were said to be barely on speaking terms; Powell considered the vice president a "powerful, steamrolling force" who was obsessed with proving a direct connection between al-Qaeda and Saddam Hussein, Woodward wrote. Powell himself was described as "semi-despondent."

In the days following *Plan of Attack*'s mid-April release, some people praised Powell for at least trying to slow the march to war while others vilified him for having lacked the courage either to make his views public or to resign in protest. Critics on both sides of the Iraq decision wondered aloud if Powell had given Woodward a version of prewar events designed to enhance his "reluctant warrior" image—now that the reconstruction of Iraq was going badly—and suggested that he was undermining the president's struggling postwar effort.

For Powell, it was a reprise of the fallout from Woodward's *The Commanders* nearly a dozen years earlier. This time around, he told the media, he had only been following the president's orders. "We all talked to Woodward," he insisted. "It was part of our instructions from the White House. . . . It was no secret that all of us were encouraged to talk." As far as his participation in the war decision was concerned, Powell said he had been "included in all of the military planning and preparations . . . we all sat together regularly and discussed the plan, commented on the plan and reviewed the plan." The president had taken Powell's advice to go to the United Nations; once it was clear that the Security Council would not live up to its commitments and responsibilities, his support for Bush's decision "was willing and it was complete."

His relations with Cheney, Powell averred, were "excellent. As Mr. Woodward notes in one point of the book . . . when the Vice President and I are alone, it's 'Colin and Dick.' "

Plan of Attack raced to the top of the nation's best-seller lists, but less than ten days after its release, the nation's attention shifted suddenly to another crisis. Although Powell was relieved to be off the hot seat, shocking new reports from Iraq were cause for far greater despondency than anything going on in Washington.

"Americans did this to an Iraqi prisoner," the CBS *60 Minutes II* broadcast on the evening of Wednesday, April 28, began. On the screen was a photograph of a hooded man draped in a crude shift, standing precariously on a box with his arms outstretched. Wires attached to various parts of his body trailed outside the frame. More pictures appeared of naked men—stacked atop one another, rolled into piles on the floor or standing at tremulous attention. Some had their arms shackled to what were clearly prison bars over their heads; others cowered in terror from snarling dogs. Most of the photographs included one or more American soldiers pointing, posing or laughing.

The souvenir snapshots had been taken by guards on duty at the Abu Ghraib prison outside Baghdad. Once a torture palace under Saddam Hussein, it was now a U.S. military installation where thousands of Iraqis, from common criminals to "high-value" suspected terrorists, were being held. The broadcast and a lengthy story published several days later in *The New Yorker* magazine revealed that the military had already launched a secret investigation of what had gone on there. Completed in February 2004, it had concluded that U.S. military personnel had committed numerous acts of "sadistic, blatant, and wanton criminal abuse" at the prison during 2003.

Powell had been aware for months of reports of problems at Abu Ghraib and knew weeks before the CBS program that reporters were asking questions. But he had not seen the photographs before they showed up on national television. "Nobody was prepared for that CBS show that night," he later recalled. Nauseated and embarrassed for the military and knowing that the revelations would have a severe impact on the United States' image abroad, he nonetheless was not particularly surprised.

Prisoners held by U.S. forces outside the United States in the war on terrorism had been a source of contention between the State Department and the Pentagon ever since hundreds of detainees captured in Afghanistan first had been brought to the U.S. naval facility at Guantánamo, Cuba in January 2002. More than two years after Bush decided the alleged terrorists would be tried in offshore military courts, not a single case had been adjudicated. In the meantime, hundreds more prisoners had arrived, and only three—two Afghans and one Pakistani—had been released.

Friendly governments impatient with the lack of movement had regularly demanded to the State Department that their nationals—including citizens from Britain, Sweden and Australia, among many others who had been detained in Afghanistan—either be charged with crimes or sent home. Powell had written frequent memos to Rumsfeld on the matter, and even Rice had grown increasingly irritated at the Pentagon. The United

States was fully within its rights to hold the captives during wartime, but the absence of any prosecutions was harming the country's relations with its allies and sending a bad public relations message to the Arab world.

"Condi consistently came into the principals meetings and said, 'Don, you've got to do something about these detainees. Don, where's your plan? We want your plan at the next meeting,'" recalled one senior administration official. "Nothing ever happened."

"Our issue with the Defense Department, and the NSC's issue, was why aren't you figuring this out?" said William Taft, the State Department legal adviser. "Go and figure out whether these people really belong [at Guantánamo]. Each one of them.

"The response was very slow," he continued. "They'd say, 'We're working on it. We've got a lot of things on our plate.' And 'They all belong there. These are bad people.' That was what you'd get back."

Beyond the absence of prosecutions, the conditions under which the detainees were being held and interrogated—both in the Guantánamo prison and at U.S. facilities in Afghanistan—were shrouded in secrecy. Dismissed as incapable of understanding the unique demands of the war on terrorism, Powell and the State Department had been excluded from a small circle of officials from the Defense and Justice departments, along with White House Counsel Alberto Gonzales and Cheney's counsel David Addington, who worked in secret throughout 2002 to draw up new guidelines for prisoner interrogation.

By early 2003, international human rights groups that had long questioned the prisoners' indefinite confinement and lack of adjudication had begun to allege that they were being physically abused and to demand information about interrogation practices at Guantánamo. The International Committee of the Red Cross (ICRC), in a confidential report to U.S. military commanders, insisted that the prisoners had legal rights and questioned whether "psychological torture" was taking place. But although ICRC President Jakob Kallenberger visited Powell to express his concerns, he cautioned that his organization preferred to work confidentially inside military channels and did not want its reports made public.

After Vietnam, Powell's generation of officers had rewritten the Army field manuals that were the service's bible. They had been further revised after the Cold War, but Powell still knew them by heart. The manuals laid down strict rules for prisoner treatment and interrogations—and the Uniform Code of Military Justice made torture a crime. But beyond what it was told by the ICRC and other nongovernmental groups, the State

Department knew nothing of the new interrogation rules approved by Rumsfeld and had no confirmation of mistreatment until news stories in March 2003 revealed that two Afghans had been beaten to death while in U.S. custody. Although the military had initially reported that the men had died of natural causes at a U.S. "holding facility" in Bagram, Afghanistan, death certificates given to their families had listed the cause as homicide. The military's own autopsies described multiple internal and external "blunt force injuries." "When we heard about that, we immediately wrote over to the Pentagon, and [Powell] raised it with Rumsfeld," Taft recalled. "We said, 'Wait a minute, you need to look at this.' And they did. But it took a long time."

When Kallenberger paid another visit to Powell in January 2004 to discuss Guantánamo and Afghanistan, he indicated that the ICRC was also preparing a report on the treatment of thousands of prisoners now also being held by U.S. occupation forces in Iraq. Although Powell tried to draw him out, Kallenberger said he was discussing Iraq with "the people in the field" and declined to go into detail. The ICRC report that was handed over to the U.S. command in Baghdad in early February was a horrifying litany of systematic abuse, including brutality and physical or psychological coercion during interrogation, as well as "excessive and disproportionate use of force . . . resulting in death or injury" at Abu Ghraib and elsewhere.

Powell had repeatedly raised the detainee issue at principals' meetings, with little reaction. Cut off from substantive facts inside the administration, he tasked Wilkerson and Taft in early 2004 with putting together a dossier of all classified and public information about prisoner abuse that they could get their hands on, including his own internal memos over the previous two years. They were in the process of compiling it when the Abu Ghraib photos appeared.

The ICRC Iraq report, leaked two weeks later to *The Wall Street Journal*, made it clear that the problem was far deeper than the shameful, after-hours humiliation of prisoners by a handful of unsupervised young guards acting largely for their own amusement. Publication of the report opened a floodgate of leaked documents revealing not only that interrogation methods amounting to torture were in wide use in Iraq, as well as at Guantánamo and facilities in Afghanistan, but that they had been both broadly and specifically authorized by secret legal opinions by the administration. "We read it in the newspaper," Taft recalled.

Powell had not been informed about any of the authorizations because "they didn't trust him," Taft said. "I suspect that went for the whole State

Department. They thought we would leak" the approved interrogation policies to the media. "When you carry that forward, if you've been in government as long as we have...you know that you have to ask the next question. Why will this be a problem if it leaks? Well, because it's not such a swell thing to do, and if it gets out we won't be able to do it.

"They get as far as 'Well, they'll leak it, and clearly that's wrong.' I guess they also knew that what we were going to say was probably not going to be just a bunch of cheerleading, and they didn't want to hear it."

The State Department watched the unfolding prisoner abuse scandal in horror. Although Rumsfeld came under harsh congressional questioning, with some opinion makers suggesting he should be fired, there was no glee over the Pentagon's difficulties. "It was too awful, it degraded all of us," said one senior Foreign Service officer. "It was like being kicked in the stomach and in the head. You have people here like me who have spent twenty years telling other countries not to torture people, that it's bad.... How do I look at our young diplomats and say, 'Go out there and do right by human rights in this world'? It was as depressing and disheartening a time as I've spent in many, many years."

To Powell, the torture scandal was My Lai and Iran-*contra* rolled into one. Many of the soldiers involved had been poorly trained for their assignments and left without supervision. Chains of command and guidelines were blurred, and no one seemed to be in charge. "You've got to understand the nature of military organizations [in order] to control" such behavior, he later reflected. "People take liberty for license, and that gets you in trouble." The secrecy and questionable legal interpretations promulgated in Washington had opened the door to abuse in the field.

Beyond his disgust at the photographs and ongoing concern at the violations of the Geneva Conventions, he worried that the Army itself had been stretched to the breaking point. The Pentagon's civilian leadership seemed unable to grasp the depth of the problems in Iraq; their attitude from the start, Powell felt, had been "War's over. We won. Everything's great." The insurgency had grown and diversified into multiple bands of former Saddam allies and outside terrorists who found ready recruits in the disillusioned Iraqi populace. At the same time, political battles among Iraq's ethnic and religious factions had increasingly turned into armed combat among the militias they controlled. When they weren't directly targeted, the Americans were caught in the middle.

Powell had persistently maintained that efforts to push forward with Iraqi governance and reconstruction were pointless until the security situation was brought firmly under control. The Army rotation system could barely handle the current deployments, and the Reserves had been pushed to the limit—Pentagon proposals that they extend Reserve active-duty tours by two years, he thought, were clearly illegal. Rumsfeld's plans to break down the division-heavy Army into smaller, more agile units was probably a good thing, but the problem, Powell believed, was that the service needed to be bigger overall to meet the demands being placed on it. The institution historically expanded and contracted depending on national defense needs—he and Cheney had authored major contractions at the end of the Cold War—and it could be downsized again when the Iraq conflict was over.

At the State Department, planning for the new U.S. Embassy in Baghdad provided an outlet for frustration and a new focus for combat with the Pentagon. "We are determined to do this better than those guys across the way," one senior official at State said enthusiastically in the spring of 2004. "We're going to run an embassy, and we're going to have people who want to go there and do something right for the United States.... We are not going to leave a mess of our part of this."

But as the scheduled handover to Iraqi sovereignty and the embassy opening approached, negotiations between the two departments over their new division of duties erupted into blistering arguments. The Pentagon was eager to relinquish responsibility for Iraq's political chaos but insisted on retaining control over all reconstruction resources and decisions. "We were fighting over everything—what the chain of command and support mechanisms were going to be, what kind of power the ambassador would have," said one of Powell's negotiators. "They wanted, essentially, to continue the line of authority from the president to the secretary of defense to the embassy."

In mid-May 2004, after a proposed presidential order on the change of authority from Defense to State had gone through numerous drafts without agreement, Powell took the dispute directly to the president and Rice. U.S. ambassadors throughout the world were in charge of aid programs and government-to-government relations at all levels, and embassies reported to the secretary of state, he told them. If the Pentagon insisted on having its way, he saw no point in having an embassy. Rumsfeld could keep Iraq for himself.

Rice had grown nearly as exasperated with the Pentagon as Powell, and on May 11, 2004, Bush signed the State Department's version of the draft. National Security Presidential Directive 36 superseded the prewar order giving total control over Iraq to the Pentagon. It specified that upon termination of the CPA, no later than June 30, "the United States will be represented in Iraq by a Chief of Mission, who on my behalf and under the guidance of the Secretary of State, shall be responsible for the direction, coordination and supervision of all United States Government employees, policies and activities in country, except those under the command of an area military commander."

While the secretary of defense and the CENTCOM commander would retain authority over security and military operations, it directed that "the Secretary of State shall be responsible for the continuous supervision and general direction of all assistance for Iraq."

It was not the end of the argument, however. For the next six weeks, negotiators from Rumsfeld's legal office debated in minute detail the extent to which the military would provide security and logistical support for embassy and other State Department personnel in the war zone. At one point, Pentagon lawyers insisted that the military's extensive facilities for processing casualties would not be made available for shipping diplomats' bodies home from Iraq. One participant described it as "among the ugliest negotiations I've been [involved in] in my career."

A final Memorandum of Understanding governing responsibilities in Iraq, totaling nearly forty pages of fine print, was signed on the eve of the transition to Iraqi sovereignty by Richard Armitage for the State Department and Paul Wolfowitz for the Department of Defense.

Powell was anxious to ensure that the new ambassador was simultaneously on his team and had clout with the White House, but a series of retired senior diplomats and former state governors declined invitations to serve. Finally, John Negroponte, Powell's trusted representative at the United Nations, volunteered for the job. Negroponte arrived in Baghdad on June 28, quickly followed by a new U.S. military commander, General George Casey. As a symbolic affirmation that 138,000 American soldiers and 4,000 embassy employees in Iraq could work cooperatively together no matter what was happening in Washington, they sat down together and wrote two mission statements, each two pages long. Each man signed both documents.

For the first time in decades, a U.S. presidential campaign was focused on foreign policy. The Democratic nominee, John Kerry, had voted with the congressional majority in authorizing military action against Iraq. But he now described it as the "wrong war in the wrong place at the wrong time." Bush continued to depict Iraq as central to the global war on terrorism and assured the nation that America was winning under his leadership.

In October 2004, Charles Duelfer, David Kay's replacement as head of the Iraq Survey Group, submitted a final report on the hunt for Iraq's weapons of mass destruction. In conclusions that contradicted nearly every prewar assessment made by top administration officials, Duelfer told Congress that Saddam Hussein's WMD stockpiles and production capability had been effectively destroyed in Operation Desert Storm and by U.N. inspectors during the 1990s. There was no evidence that Saddam Hussein had made "concerted efforts to restart" a nuclear weapons program. Although the Iraqi dictator had dreamed of reconstituting his arsenal of chemical and biological weapons, there was no indication that he had taken steps to do so.

Echoing Kay's words of eight months earlier, Duelfer concluded that "we were almost all wrong."

Outside the vortex of the campaign, Powell was largely spared a new round of questions about his U.N. claims. He had long since apologized to the extent he was ever going to do so, telling a television interviewer that "the sourcing was inaccurate and wrong and, in some cases, deliberately misleading, and for that I am disappointed and I regret it." Public support for the Iraq War had gone steadily downhill, and a majority of Americans now thought the situation there was getting worse rather than better. Half of the electorate—give or take a percentage point either way, depending on the poll—thought Bush was not doing a good job as president. Powell's reputation had suffered—his own approval ratings had dropped from nearly 90 percent at the beginning of Bush's term to the mid-60s as the November 2 election approached—but he remained far and away the most popular member of Bush's team.

The years of speculation about how long Powell would last were over; it was now clear to all that he had no intention of resigning before the end of the president's four-year mandate. For many, his staying power had been a profound relief. But for those who believed that even a threat of resignation—especially in an election year—would have forced Bush to make significant policy changes, it was a disappointment.

Wilkerson was bitter on Powell's behalf over many things, especially toward Cheney. But as much as he admired and respected the man he had worked under for so many years, he also blamed Powell for failing to take more risks and make more demands of the president. The key disgrace, he felt, had not been Iraq but North Korea, where Bush had agreed to Powell's flexible strategy but repeatedly allowed Cheney to undercut him behind the scenes. If Powell had challenged the White House more forcefully, Wilkerson thought in retrospect, "they would have backed down. . . . I think [Powell] understood that it would have taken a threat to resign. And he wasn't prepared to do that."

Political Washington rehashed moments when Powell might have played his ultimate trump card. Perhaps overestimating their own courage in standing up to the White House, some moderate Republicans insisted privately that they would have lined up behind him if he had only given them a sign.

"It's easy for us to say, why didn't he just go in there and tell the president he's going to resign," reflected one senior State Department official who had thought long and hard about the possibility that Powell would quit. "But this man was a military officer for thirty-five years. When I go to see the president—he's the president, I'm in awe; I understand what the presidency means. But I also understand that I voted for the guy and I'll vote for the next guy. That's the great thing about America. He's not the king, he's a civilian like me. I have consent here.

"But a military officer who's spent decades saying 'whatever the president of the United States tells me to do I will do because that's an order'—that's different."

To retired four-star general and persistent Iraq war critic Anthony Zinni, the answer lay not in Powell's uniform but in his upbringing and his character. "I couldn't do what he does, no way. . . . He has a set of principles and beliefs. He believes in multilateralism, he believes that the world is complicated and that you have to engage it on many levels . . . [and] he keeps on what he thinks is right. He doesn't get sidetracked. I would get so upset when people would attack him—when some of the slimeballs at the Pentagon, starting at the top, would go after him. But where I would in a moment react to it, he stays above it. . . . I just don't have the temperament to be that way; that's why I admire him and respect him."

At the same time, Zinni observed, "Powell is a pretty ambitious guy. I don't think it was in him to stop this by bringing down his president."

Bruce Llewellyn put the same point into sharper perspective: "I don't think he wants to be known as the guy who walked out."

Frank Carlucci, to whom Powell owed much of his career advancement, felt that Powell had been the "right man at the right time" for the Bush administration, although perhaps not for Powell himself. "I'm still close to Dick [Cheney], I think highly of him," Carlucci reflected. But if what he had read and heard about the dynamic inside the administration and its obsession with political manipulation was true, "Colin has been used."

Alma, who considered herself more hardheaded in some ways than her husband, had long since lost her enthusiasm for the Bush White House. Although she still enjoyed the president personally—he had a kind of antic charm and a knack for making her laugh—she deeply resented what she saw as Cheney's arrogant wielding of power. Though her husband might direct his ire over the faulty Iraq intelligence toward the CIA and absolve the White House, she thought Colin had been callously used to promote a war she wished had never happened. "They needed him to do it," Alma said, "because they knew people would believe him." She was furious at the stains they had left on his reputation. But she understood his commitment to try to influence policy from the inside and disagreed with those who thought his departure in protest would have had a major impact. After a brief political thunderstorm and a torrential downpour in the media, it would have been business as usual for the Bush administration. "It wouldn't have changed a thing."

Powell himself had never seriously considered quitting. Among the rules he lived by was one cautioning not to attach one's own ego too tightly to one's position on any issue. Policy debates were the daily grist of government, and the only reason to resign, as he had long ago told the Navy midshipman who had asked about gays in the military, was when a decision "strikes at the heart of your moral beliefs." He believed that the decision-making structure in the White House was deeply flawed and the president had allowed ideologues to lead him in directions that were counterproductive or simply wrong. He had experienced many moments of intense anger and chagrin over the past four years. But he did not believe he had ever been asked to do or support anything immoral.

He had a deep respect for the Office of the President—if not always for its current occupant—and believed that whether George Bush realized it or not, he needed Powell. George Marshall had once said of his relationship with Franklin Roosevelt during World War II, "I never haggled with the president. I swallowed the little things so that I could go to bat on the big ones. I never handled a matter apologetically and I was never contentious." Powell felt that over time he had won enough of the big ones. "I think any good subordinate accommodates himself to the wishes of his superior," he once reflected, although, he quickly added, "Colin Powell isn't George Marshall, and George Bush isn't Franklin Delano Roosevelt."

The Bush administration had clearly manipulated Powell's prestige and reputation, even as it repeatedly undermined him and disregarded his advice. The question was why he had let them. Part of the answer was that he had been winning bureaucratic battles for so many years that he simply refused to acknowledge the extent of the losses he had suffered. Beyond his soldier's sense of duty, he saw even the threat of resignation as an acknowledgment of defeat. He was a proud man, and he would never have let them see him sweat.

As the November 2 election approached, Powell began to vacillate on his decision to leave the administration at the end of Bush's current term. New and potentially more optimistic vistas were opening on a number of foreign policy fronts. Although interim sovereignty had done nothing to calm the violent upheavals in Iraq, the elections scheduled there for January 30 might provide a new incentive for Iraqis to stop tearing their country apart. Yasser Arafat was in a French hospital and reportedly at death's door, creating a possible thaw in the Middle East. Powell had no intention of signing up for another four years, but postponing his departure for several months would provide policy continuity and maybe even an additional measure of personal satisfaction.

Two days after Bush's triumph at the polls, the president gave no hints of his second-term Cabinet lineup as he departed with Rice and Andrew Card for a long weekend at Camp David. Outside conjecture centered on the strength of Powell's commitment to leave versus reports that the president would try to persuade him to stay, at least temporarily. Some speculated that Powell would condition his answer on whether Rumsfeld would be jettisoned. But before the next week was out, it was Powell—not Rumsfeld—who was asked to submit his letter of resignation.

The Senate was expected to confirm Condoleezza Rice as his successor by Inauguration Day, January 20. Until then, Powell would be a lame duck.

Powell was exhausted as his airplane took off from Nairobi on January 9, 2005. It was the end of a six-day trip that had taken him first to Thailand, Sri Lanka and Indonesia to tour coastal areas where a tsunami on the day after Christmas had killed hundreds of thousands of people, then to Kenya to witness the signing of an accord designed to end Sudan's civil war. He was developing a head cold and had been uncharacteristically subdued and even a bit cranky at a hotel dinner with American journalists the night before. Most Bush administration officials treated reporters like the plague, but Powell was usually friendly and sometimes even informative. Most of those who traveled frequently aboard his plane had a lot of respect for him.

It was likely to be his last trip as secretary of state, and Powell's staff had arranged for a cake to be baked in Nairobi and brought aboard with champagne to be enjoyed during the flight. But as staff and reporters gathered around, Powell found the cake wouldn't yield to cutting. He tried to stab it, but the knife pinged off as if the icing were made of concrete. The atmosphere was already filled with jovial melancholy, and it seemed to be a fitting metaphor for his four years with Bush.

Powell had often resisted overseas travel; when a trip was unavoidable, he had conducted his business efficiently and returned to Washington as quickly as possible. Part of the reason was his lack of interest in the tourist stops foreign governments liked to set up for visiting dignitaries. But he was also acutely aware that whatever power he had to influence White House foreign policy was sharply diminished without his physical presence. Since his resignation had been announced on November 15, however, he had undertaken a hectic schedule, with official trips to South America, the Middle East and Europe, in addition to Asia and Africa.

Alma was looking forward to her husband's second retirement, but for now she was glad he was spending so much time on the road. At every venue he was greeted as an old friend, and it was good for him, she thought, to know he would be missed. Back at home a few days before Christmas, he had put on a baseball cap and sunglasses, escaped his security detail and driven himself alone to the ice rink on the National Mall between the Capitol and the White House. Wilkerson was hosting a skating party for the two dozen adolescents who belonged to the Colin Powell Leadership Club at the public middle school Powell sponsored. Being with kids always boosted his spirits, and he mingled for a half hour over lunch at the rinkside kiosk until he was inevitably spotted. After a round of public handshakes and tourists' photographs, he quickly made his way back to his car.

During the busy interregnum between his resignation and his actual departure, Powell was deluged with interview requests and accepted all invitations to talk about foreign policy issues. But he repeatedly turned away questions, asked in a hundred different ways, about conflicts within the administration and his own legacy. He knew the reporters wanted him to "come on [their] television show and whine [my] ass off" as he departed, and he was determined not to take the bait.

By January 19, the day before Bush's second inauguration, Powell's desk had been emptied, his office cleaned out and the portraits of Marshall and Thomas Jefferson removed from the walls. The new occupant could choose her own heroes. At 11 a.m., he went with Alma to the State Department lobby where he had first greeted his new troops four years earlier, this time to say good-bye. Hundreds of people were packed beneath a massive "Thank You" banner hanging from the mezzanine balcony, and he stood smiling as they cheered him.

After basking in a moment of pure elation, he began his farewell speech. He reminded them of their achievements, their sacrifices and the honor of their cause. "We have much to be proud of, but you are the ones who should be proud of what we have done. It has been my privilege to serve you, but you are the foot soldiers of the battalion."

By the end, there were tears in his eyes and in many of theirs. "I am so proud that I have had this chance to serve my nation once again," he concluded. "When I step down from this job I will have had close to 40 years of government service. Thirty-five of those years were in the United States Army," and while his professional "family" had now been expanded to include the Department of State, "I will never not be a soldier."

It was an apt coda to Powell's tenure that he was denied the pleasure of walking out the door to applause and never looking back. The Senate, in a fit of pique over Iraq, refused to confirm Rice as secretary of state for nearly a week after the inauguration, and Powell, having already said his good-byes, remained in office until January 26. He could have stayed home, but it seemed unprofessional to leave his post without a new commander in place. He dutifully headed into work each morning to check the cables from posts abroad and to fix whatever had been broken overnight.

Epilogue

> Leaving is just as natural a thing to me as coming in, and
> there's another unit out there somewhere waiting. I don't
> know what it's called, whether it has a private name or a
> public name. Or maybe I'll just sit around for a while play-
> ing with my grandchildren.
>
> —Colin L. Powell

Within weeks of leaving the State Department, Powell had moved into a spacious, sunlit office in suburban Virginia with a spectacular view of the Capitol and the Washington Monument. His Buffalo Soldiers paintings and the pen set he had earned as "Best Cadet" at ROTC summer camp in 1957 were all in place. The floors below were occupied by America's Promise, the youth assistance organization he had founded in 1997, where Alma remained chairman of the board. No one in the building called him "Mr. Secretary," the title all Cabinet officers carried with them after leav-ing office, or even "Mr. Powell." He had once again become "General."

Despite the familiar career accoutrements, the office seemed uninhab-ited and sterile, and the normally genial general was edgy as he sat down for an interview there in March 2005. He began preemptively with a story about the autobiography he had published nearly a decade earlier, explaining that the most popular part of the best-selling book had been its colorful descriptions of his Bronx childhood and his early years in the Army. He surmised that the latter half, chronicling his rise to power in Washington, probably hadn't interested anyone except his professional colleagues. Since his most recent departure from government, many peo-ple had asked him if he planned to write another autobiographical vol-ume. It didn't seem worth the effort, Powell said with a laugh, because he'd already told all his good stories. "I'm going to grind through [the last] four years? 'First we had the six-way talks...' It becomes another one of those 'Then I had lunch with so-and-so' books."

But the last four years were clearly still on his mind. He had read the articles assessing his tenure as secretary of state and took issue with many of them, particularly the ones that suggested, as he put it, that "Powell must be *so* distraught."

"Why am I distraught?" he asked testily. "We are working on our relationships . . . look at what we've done with Russia, China, NATO, the E.U. Remember, this administration came in saying, 'We've got to get out of Bosnia.' And it was Colin Powell who went there and said, 'We went in together, we come out together.' It took three months before the president could say it, but I staunched that wound until he could heal it. And that's what we've done.

"Afghanistan? I'm the one who got the Pakistanis to go along with it. Without anyone knowing we were doing it, Rich [Armitage] and I did it. And suddenly it's a great achievement. Everybody hated the 'road map'; nobody would ever use the word. And now it's the flavor of the month. . . . Six-party framework [on North Korea]? The E.U. [initiative on Iran]?—I said, 'Let's work with these guys,' and now suddenly we're having meetings to see how we can do more with this process. . . . Liberia. I had to fight my way through that one and finally get the president to put in a few troops. Haiti—we did that without hardly asking anybody else." He had fought for and won the largest increase in U.S. foreign aid since the Marshall Plan—still far from enough, considering the extent of American riches, but a creditable start—had focused the administration's attention and resources on the global HIV/AIDS problem and had restored the workforce and budget of the State Department.

Powell was perhaps unaware that he had placed nearly all of his accomplishments in the context of battles fought within the administration. Many of his victories had been compromised by the very fights it had taken to win them—the administration's policies on the Middle East, Iran and North Korea had ended up more or less where he had hoped they would start in 2001, but much was lost in the interim.

He had not mentioned Iraq, the issue that overshadowed everything else. Much of Powell's legacy as secretary of state, and George W. Bush's as president, would rest on what happened there, and so far there was little basis for history's judgment to be kind. He would always be tagged with the "Powell Briefing" at the United Nations, and some would never forgive him for ultimately supporting the invasion instead of pushing harder to prevent it. Yet he had been the only senior official in the Bush administration who had tried to slow the march to war and the only one to warn of the difficulty of putting a broken Iraq back together again. He had been alone in opposing the White House decisions that had set into motion the chain of events leading to detainee abuses at Guantánamo and Abu Ghraib.

Powell was indeed the "odd man out" in the Bush administration in virtually every meaningful way. He had thought long and hard about the significance of war and its effects; only he, among Bush's top national security officials, knew what combat was actually like—on both the winning and losing sides—and what it meant to send American soldiers to their deaths. Heir to Eisenhower, Rockefeller and the moderate Republican realists who now seemed like anachronisms in their own party, he alone had understood the need for allies and believed that the use of force should truly be a last resort.

"I am who I am," Powell had often replied when State Department aides had urged him to fight more or dirtier. Life had taught him to work hard, obey the rules and not make excuses; to value friends and try to persuade enemies; to respond to prejudice and rigid ideology with reason and patience.

To Powell, loyalty was not merely a matter of obedience, whether to a president or a commanding officer; it was the glue that held institutions together and made them work. His corollary, however, was that those who commanded the loyalty of others were responsible for their well-being. For a general, that meant making sure your troops were properly trained and equipped and deployed in sufficient numbers to ensure decisive victory in combat. For a president, it meant carefully weighing the sometimes disparate needs of the nation, listening to wise counsel and acting to protect both national security and fundamental democratic values. If Powell were to fault Bush, it would be for an absence of balance in the needs he addressed and in the narrow counsel to which he chose to listen.

As time and emotional distance grew between Powell and his tenure as secretary of state, he gradually put the experience into what he felt was its proper context among his life achievements. He had been chairman of the Joint Chiefs of Staff, the architect of Operation Desert Storm and a shaper of the post–Cold War military. As President Reagan's national security adviser, he had helped bring a drowning White House back to shore. He had been a leader of men and had taken up arms to defend his country. He was a credit to his race and to his upbringing. The State Department might have been his longest and most difficult assignment, but at the end of the day it had been just another posting.

The Army, Powell once recalled, had a saying: "When you give up command, turn the flag over to your successor, make sure the station wagon is all packed with suitcases on top and kids inside. Get in and drive off post without looking in the rearview mirror and with the windows up so you can't hear the trash can covers closing on your 'great ideas.' "

Relieved from his latest post, he bought himself a new car—a silver 2005 Corvette—and said that the best thing about not being secretary of state was that "I can drive myself everywhere." He stepped up his participation in the Colin Powell Center for Policy Studies, which he had established in 1997 at City College of New York to promote lives of public service for the children of immigrants. He invested in an Internet firm designed to help consumers control their own health care; joined in an ultimately unsuccessful effort led by Fred Malek, his old boss in the Nixon administration, to purchase a new baseball franchise in Washington; and became a limited partner in a Silicon Valley venture capital firm. His public speaking calendar quickly filled up more than a year in advance, and he tried whenever possible to couple paid venues with volunteer visits to local schools and youth centers. In November 2005, his daughter Annemarie presented him and Alma with their third grandchild—and first granddaughter.

Although Powell sometimes gently skirted the edges of criticizing the Bush administration in public speeches and interviews, he rarely strayed beyond the obvious and never outright attacked the White House. The number of troops sent to Iraq had been "enough troops for war but not for peace, for establishing order," he told one interviewer barely a month after leaving office. "My own preference would have been for more forces after the conflict." The administration had been "too loud, too direct" in trying to convince others to back its Iraq invasion, and Rumsfeld's caustic rhetoric had alienated traditional U.S. allies, he told a German magazine. In an interview with ABC's Barbara Walters in September 2005, he said that Iraq might not "have turned out to be such a mess if we had done some things differently," including sending more troops to manage the occupation and reestablishing the Iraqi military more quickly.

When Bush nominated John Bolton as U.S. ambassador to the United Nations, Powell let it be known that he had privately told senators on the Foreign Relations Committee that he did not think Bolton was the right man for the job. When Senator John McCain proposed legislation to establish the Army Field Manual as the definitive guideline for U.S. troops dealing with treatment of detainees—a measure Cheney personally lobbied against—Powell released a letter supporting the effort. "Our troops need to hear from the Congress," he wrote to McCain. "I also believe the world will note that America is making a clear statement with respect to the expected future behavior of our soldiers. Such a reaction will help deal with the terrible public diplomacy crisis created by Abu Ghraib."

Others close to Powell were far more outspoken about the frustrations of the past four years. After venting his disgust with the administration for months in closed-door academic gatherings, Lawrence Wilkerson finally went public in October 2005. "What I saw for four-plus years was a case that I have never seen in my studies of aberrations, bastardizations, per-turbations, changes to the national security decision-making process," he said in an angry speech to the Washington-based New America Foundation. "What I saw was a cabal between the Vice President of the United States, Richard Cheney, and the Secretary of Defense, Donald Rumsfeld, on critical issues that made decisions that the bureaucracy did not know were being made. And then when the bureaucracy was presented with the decision to carry them out, it was presented in a such a disjointed, incredible way that the bureaucracy often didn't know what it was doing." In response to questions after his speech, Wilkerson acknowledged that the general was "not happy" about his former subordinate speaking out "because . . . he's the world's most loyal soldier."

Powell did not disagree with the substance of Wilkerson's complaints about the administration, although "I wouldn't characterize it the way Larry has, calling it a cabal," he told the British interviewer David Frost. "What Larry is suggesting is that very often maybe Mr. Rumsfeld and Vice President Cheney would take decisions in to the president that the rest of us weren't aware of. That did happen, on a number of occasions." Asked whether he and the defense secretary had argued over postwar planning for Iraq, Powell said only that they had had "some serious dis-cussions, of a not pleasant kind."

After several testy e-mail exchanges, Powell and Wilkerson stopped communicating about anything except their joint work with youth organ-izations. "He can be the most endearing person you'd ever want to meet in your life," Wilkerson later said of his former boss. "The next minute he can be colder than fish." No one, Powell told him, had the right to charac-terize Powell's sense of loyalty.

Several months after Powell left office, as Bush's poll numbers contin-ued to slide, the president called to say that he missed their "talks" and hoped they could get together soon. Powell loyally took the hint and in May 2005 invited Bush and his wife to dinner in McLean—the first time the two couples had ever spent an evening alone together. Although the event had not appeared on the president's public calendar, he arrived with news cameramen in tow, and the two men were photographed smiling together on Powell's front porch. Inside, the talk was pleasant—Bush had already asked Powell to help promote his "No Child Left Behind" education program, which was coming under criticism from states and local school boards. But Powell did not jump at the chance, and the idea eventually faded away.

In the winter, and again in the spring of 2006, Bush called together former secretaries of state and defense reaching back as far as the Kennedy administration for a photo opportunity and a briefing to convince them that the war was going well. They were largely placid events, with only a few sparks of temper and disagreement. Madeleine Albright told Bush that Iraq was "taking up all the energy" of his foreign policy team while nuclear programs in Iran and North Korea spun out of control and the rest of the world suffered from benign neglect. Powell, who attended both sessions and posed unsmiling for group pictures, said little.

Powell had not arrived at high office with plans to remake the world; as he himself often pointed out, he was not a grand strategist. Ideologues and "exceptionalists" visualized the world as they thought it should be and set out on what they saw as the most direct route to creating it. To Powell, change was best sought in increments. He saw the road ahead as a far more complicated series of turns and steps to be navigated cautiously, guided by a set of principles that were tempered by realism and patience.

He would likely have made a good president, bringing honesty, humanity and common sense to government. His election, in either 1996 or 2000, would certainly have changed the course of American political and racial history. Yet when considered as part of the continuum of his life, Powell's refusal to try to reach the top was not surprising. He owed his phenomenal professional success to his ability to work within institutions, not the kind of individualism that the risk of running would have required.

Had he been commander in chief on September 11, 2001, the subsequent three years would have unfolded differently. The retaliatory strike against the Taliban in Afghanistan would have been ferocious, in keeping with the Powell Doctrine. But his deep belief in multinationalism and partnership, along with his inspirational leadership abilities, would doubtless have set America at home and abroad on a far different path.

Powell might have achieved greatness as secretary of state under different circumstances or in a different administration than the one he served—one in which the vice president played a more traditional role and the national security adviser a stronger one. Under Reagan, Bush 41 and Clinton, he had skillfully maintained an array of back-channel allies in Congress and the Cabinet. But in the administration of George W. Bush, there had been no other power center from which he could effectively draw support. The September 11 attacks and the White House's willingness to exploit public fear as a political strategy had effectively eliminated any chance that he would wield primary influence over foreign policy. The balance had tipped decisively toward the neoconservative vision of the world and the use of military force to achieve it. Outnumbered, outmaneuvered and unwilling to change his tactics, Powell was left to push and pull at the margins.

Asked whether a different National Security Council, under more deft and decisive leadership, would have made a difference, Powell shrugged.

"I don't know," he said curtly. "Probably not."

Why not?

"Cheney."

As Bush moved through his second term, there were occasional signs that Cheney's influence was waning and that Condoleezza Rice would use her close relationship with Bush to put a "kinder, gentler face" on U.S. foreign policy. Although criticism of Rumsfeld continued, and a group of retired senior military officers, some of whom had served in Iraq, broke their silence to call publicly for his resignation, the White House vowed he would remain. By the summer of 2006, with war in Iraq still raging and the threat of terrorism still hanging over the nation, the percentage of Americans who approved of the way the president was running the country had dropped into the low 30s.

Powell saw a certain irony in events, but as the months turned into years away from the locus of power he rarely allowed himself to dwell on the past or to spend too much time thinking about where the administration had been or where it was headed. In his own mind, he had rolled up the windows and moved on. He wanted only to be remembered, he said, as "a good public servant. Somebody who truly believed in his country, loved it and served to the best of his ability. And all of the other little chatter that goes on ... is just that—chatter. As long as I'm remembered as somebody who served, that's good enough for me."

ACKNOWLEDGMENTS

I began this book in 2003 in Jamaica, where Colin Powell's parents were born. Eager for a change of pace after nearly two years of nonstop daily reporting on the Bush administration's war on terrorism for *The Washington Post,* I could think of nothing better than spending a week in a tropical paradise under the heading of "research." Oliver Clarke, a friend of many years who runs *The Gleaner,* Kingston's daily newspaper, kindly provided an introduction to one of Powell's cousins. When I called Vernon Meikle, whose mother, Ethlyn, and Powell's mother, Arie, were sisters, he insisted on coming to my hotel to look me over before agreeing to be interviewed.

I learned several things during a two-hour interrogation by Vernon, a retired engineer who is just one year apart from his cousin in age. The first was that Powell's extended family is enormously proud and protective of him. In a clan full of high achievers, he is their brightest star, and they are diligent keepers of his reputation and his heritage. The second thing was that they are extraordinarily generous people. Vernon subsequently became my guide to the homeland of the Powells and the McKoys, escorting me to western Jamaica, where I met many relatives and heard many interesting stories.

Although this book contains little about Jamaica itself, its history and culture informed much of what I wrote, as indeed it informs much of who Colin Powell is. I am grateful not only to those in Jamaica but also to other members of Powell's widespread network of family and friends in Washington and New York and around the country and the world for their openness. I owe particular thanks to Marilyn Berns, Bruce Llewellyn, Julius Becton, Gene Norman and Joseph Schwar.

This is not an authorized biography. But I benefited greatly from Powell's admirable belief that public servants have a responsibility to explain themselves and their official actions, as well as from his conviction that he is his own best press aide. He sat with me for six lengthy, on-the-record interviews, the first five in his State Department office in 2003–04 and the last in 2005 in the Alexandria, Virginia, office he has occupied since leaving government. Because there are many sources of information on his earlier life, his military career and the public events he participated in—including his 1995 autobiography, *My American Journey*—I limited my questions to the period after his retirement from the military and to his tenure as secretary of state. His only condition was that nothing from our discussions appear in print before the publication of this book. I was also fortunate that Powell is fully committed to the world of electronic communications—he answers his e-mails promptly.

Powell granted me unrestricted access to his personal and professional military papers at the National Defense University Library in Washington D.C., where they are collected among those of other former chairmen of the Joint Chiefs of Staff. Susan Lemke, who oversees the library's Special Collections, and especially Scott Gower, who spent many hours assisting me with literally hundreds of boxes of unclassified Powell materials, were infinitely patient and helpful, and I am deeply indebted to them. I am also grateful to Timothy Nenninger, Susan Francis-Haughton and Richard Boylan of the Modern Military Records Unit of the National Archives for sharing their knowledge of the U.S. armed forces over the past half century, and for guiding me through the documentary history of the Vietnam War.

Many of the most helpful U.S. and foreign government sources of information on Powell's tenure as secretary of state spoke to me on background, allowing me to quote them only as generic officials. I regret that I cannot thank them by name. I am especially grateful to those who did speak on the record, inlcuding Richard Armitage, Richard Boucher and William Smullen. Lawrence Wilkerson allowed me to tap his prodigious memory concerning Powell and generously answered questions about matters both profound and mundane. Thanks also to Peggy Cifrino, Powell's assistant for many years; to retired generals William Nash and Charles Boyd, who helped educate me on the culture, history and language of the U.S. military; to Taylor Branch, who knows everything there is to know about book writing; and to Dana Priest and Elizabeth Becker for their friendship and unflagging support.

I owe a deep debt of gratitude to Joseph E. Persico, Powell's collaborator on *My American Journey*, who gave me the benefit of the insight he gleaned from his countless hours of conversations with Colin and Alma Powell.

The Washington Post has been my professional home for most of my career in journalism; it is a wonderful, exciting place to work. I am grateful to *Post* Company Chairman Don Graham, Publisher Bo Jones, Executive Editor Len Downie and Managing Editor Phil Bennett for many things, among them their strong support for and encouragement of this project. Many current and former *Post* colleagues shared their knowledge and insights, including Mike Allen, Rick Atkinson, Dan Balz, Steve Coll, Michael Dobbs, Joe Elbert, Bradley Graham, David Hoffman, David Maraniss, Dana Milbank, Walter Pincus, Tom Ricks and Margot Williams. Lou Cannon not only gave me the benefit of his voluminous knowledge of the Reagan administration and provided transcripts of his own interviews with Powell on the Reagan years; he and his wife, Mary, extended warm hospitality and introductions in California. Glenn Kessler, who expertly covers foreign policy for the *Post,* kept me up to date with both official and unofficial news from the State Department.

I was privileged to have a home away from home at the Carnegie Endowment for International Peace while researching and writing this book. For that and for her counsel and friendship of many years I am profoundly grateful to Carnegie President Jessica Mathews. The entire Carnegie family was warmly welcoming and intellectually stimulating, and I thank all of them—Moises Naim, Joe Cirincione and George Perkovich in particular—for making my time there so rewarding. John Judis, my fellow "Visiting Scholar," was a wise and indispensable sounding board as well as a great guy to grab lunch with.

Liz Dahransoff, my agent, not only took the angst out of the business side of getting a book written and published; she was an insightful reader and invaluable source of encouragement. I am grateful to my editor, Ash Green, who from our first meeting at Knopf in the winter of 2003 provided just the right combination of wisdom and toughness. His assistants, Luba Ostashevsky and Sara Sherbill, were unfailingly helpful and responsive.

I am indebted to Asher Hildebrand not only for his expert assistance as researcher and editor, but for his ability to keep me organized and endure many months of late nights and weekends.

Above all else, thanks to my family. To my mother, Jeanette DeYoung, for always being behind me no matter what. To my husband, Henry Champ, a journalist of great skill and knowledge, without whose love, patience and unqualified support this book never would have been written. And to our children, Katie and Jesse, who were boosters from the start. They keep me sane, make me laugh and bring boundless joy to my life.

NOTES

CHAPTER ONE

3 "I will never not be": Colin L. Powell, "Remarks to State Department Employees," January 19, 2005, State Department transcript.

5 thought he had made clear: Colin L. Powell, author interview. Powell provided
six lengthy, on-the-record interviews between 2003 and 2005 with the author
for purposes of this book. Material from those interviews is subsequently cited
as "Powell interview."

6 the secretary anticipated: State Department officials, author interviews.

6 "begin the process of thinking": President George W. Bush, press conference,
November 4, 2004, White House transcript.

6 Card told Cabinet members: Mike Allen, "Bush Will Not Seek Mass Resignations; President Is Said to Be Pleased with Administration and Eager to Move
Forward," *The Washington Post,* November 6, 2004, p. A8.

6 "The president would like": Powell interview.

7 four terse and bitter sentences: Ron Suskind, *The Price of Loyalty: George W. Bush,
the White House, and the Education of Paul O'Neill* (New York: Simon & Schuster,
2004), pp. 311–315.

7 "Dear Mr. President": Colin L. Powell, letter to George W. Bush, November 12,
2004, Papers of Gen. Colin L. Powell (Ret.), Special Collections, National
Defense University Library, Fort Lesley J. McNair, Washington, D.C. Material
from this collection is subsequently cited as "Powell papers."

7 the White House released: Presidential statements, November 15, 2004, White
House transcripts.

8 "I think you saw": Scott McClellan press briefing, November 15, 2004, White
House transcript.

8 "great honor and privilege": Colin L. Powell, "On-the-Record Briefing,"
November 15, 2004, State Department transcript.

8 "loyalty over leadership": "Good Soldier Powell," unsigned editorial, *The New
York Times,* November 16, 2004, p. 26.

8 "a list of conditions": Mike Allen, "Powell Announces His Resignation; Secretary of State Clashed with Cheney and Rumsfeld; Rice to Succeed Him," *The
Washington Post,* November 16, 2004, p. A1.

9 There had been no list: Powell interview.

9 "There was no way": Lawrence B. Wilkerson, author interview, March 1, 2005.

9 Powell asked his staff: Ibid.

9 Bush seemed puzzled: Powell interview.

10 The war in Iraq: Ibid.

10 "That was really strange": Wilkerson interview.

10 the applause: The account of Powell's appearance at the National War College on September 19, 2005, is drawn from the author's notes of the event.

CHAPTER TWO

13 "What a island": Louise Bennett, "Colonisation in Reverse," *Jamaica Labrish*, 10th ed. (Kingston: Sangster's Book Stores, Ltd., 2003), pp. 179–180.

13 Alice McKoy left her husband: The account of McKoy family life in Jamaica and Alice McKoy's departure from the island is based on author interviews with Alice's grandson Vernon Meikle, July 23, 2003, and her granddaughter Marilyn Berns, November 10, 2003, as well as Colin L. Powell with Joseph E. Persico, *My American Journey* (New York: Random House, 1995), pp. 7–8. Material from that volume is subsequently cited as "*MAJ.*"

13 tens of thousands: Ira De A. Reid, *The Negro Immigrant: His Background, Characteristics and Social Adjustment, 1899–1937* (New York: Columbia University Press, 1939; New York: Arno Press and *The New York Times*, 1969), p. 62. Citations are from the Arno Press edition.

13 Aubrey and Rosena Powell: The description of Top Hill and Luther Powell's upbringing are based on author's visit and interviews with Ernie Bent and Everton Ritchie, July 24, 2003. They are the daughter and grandson, respectively, of Aubrey and Rosena Powell.

14 "He didn't tarry long": Bent interview.

14 He arrived in Philadelphia: Colin L. Powell, "Personal Security Questionnaire," U.S. Army Form DD 398, January 9, 1957, Powell papers.

14 Among the nearly 3.4 million: Reid, *The Negro Immigrant*, p. 235. Appendices to this seminal book on West Indians in the United States in the early twentieth century include immigration tables and statistics from the U.S. Labor Department.

14 he in 1936: "Personal Security Questionnaire," January 9, 1957, Powell papers.

14 They never spoke ill: Berns interview.

15 America was already beginning: For an extensive discussion of immigration debates and restrictions of the period, see Desmond King, *Making Americans: Immigration, Race, and the Origins of the Diverse Democracy* (Cambridge, Mass.: Harvard University Press, 2000).

15 The text in use: Reid, *The Negro Immigrant*, p. 84.

15 98.6 percent: Ibid., pp. 84–85.

15 " 'African (black)' ": "List of Race or Peoples" attachment to "Manifest of Alien Passengers to the United States," SS *Turrialba*, May 2, 1923, www.ellisisland .org (accessed June 10, 2004).

16 Arie arrived at Ellis Island: "Manifest of Alien Passengers to the United States," SS *Turrialba*.

16 Fully a quarter: Nancy Foner, "West Indian Immigration to New York. An Overview," in *Islands in the City: West Indian Immigration to New York*, ed. Nancy Foner (Berkeley: University of California Press, 2001), p. 4.

16 "bananas ripe and green": Claude McKay. "The Tropics in New York," *Selected Poems of Claude McKay* (New York: Harcourt, Brace and Co., 1953), p. 31.

16 Nonwhite women: J. Bruce Llewellyn, author interview, December 2003. Llewellyn, a New York businessman, is the son of Luther Powell's cousin Nessa Lopez Llewellyn.

17 they were considered all but white: Meikle interview.

17 750,000 Africans: Philip D. Curtain, *The Atlantic Slave Trade: A Census* (Madison: University of Wisconsin Press, 1969), pp. 53, 79. Curtain estimates the total slave imports into English North America to have been 399,000.

17 the lingering disadvantages: Elizabeth Thomas-Hope (University of the West Indies at Mona), author interview, July 22, 2003.

17 light skin was aesthetically favored: Milton Vickerman, *Crosscurrents: West Indian Immigrants and Race* (New York: Oxford University Press, 1999), p. 28.

17 They found black Americans' elation: Llewellyn interview; www.nycpolice museum.org/html/faq.html (accessed June 3, 2004).

18 "She was thoroughly British": Shirley Chisholm, *Unbought and Unbossed* (Boston: Houghton Mifflin, 1970), p. 13, quoted in Irma Watkins-Owens, "Early Twentieth-Century Caribbean Women," in *Islands in the City*, p. 31.

18 "displays of emotionalism": W. A. Domingo, "The Tropics in New York," *The Survey Graphic*, Harlem number, March 1925, p. 650, http://etext.lib.Virginia .edu/harlem (accessed June 20, 2004).

18 "West Indians of color": Ibid.

18 Success in America: Llewellyn interview.

18 "Jewmaicans": Malcolm Gladwell, "Black like Them," *The New Yorker*, April 29, 1996. www.gladwell.com/1996/19960429 a black.htm (accessed June 23, 2003).

18 "When a monkey-chaser dies": Reid, *The Negro Immigrant*, pp. 25–26.

18 The British Colonial Society: Watkins-Owens, "Caribbean Women," p. 33.

19 It was Caribbean women: Domingo, "The Tropics in New York," p. 649.

19 "No blacks need apply": Gladwell, "Black like Them."

19 Alice McKoy was part: *MAJ*, p. 8.

19 But what had been advancement: Berns interview.

19 Luther Powell had not lingered: *MAJ*, p. 9.

19 Other family members: Berns interview; Llewellyn interview.

20 In an oft-told family story: Meikle interview.

20 her son still pictured her: *MAJ*, pp. 8–9.

20 she swore the family to secrecy: Berns interview.

20 a nice English name: *MAJ*, p. 13.

20 more than five thousand: Reid, *The Negro Immigrant*, pp. 126–127.

21 Nearly every household: Gene Norman, author interview, August 27, 2003; Berns interview.

22 Colin's friends took to saying his name: *MAJ*, p. 13.

22 Its limits were defined: Norman interview.

22 As far as the Powell children knew: Berns interview.

22 Colin's friend Gene: Norman interview.

22 those kinds of restrictions: Berns interview.

22 Marilyn and Colin: Ibid.

23 a man of some importance: Norman interview.

23 To their own children: Joseph E. Persico, author interview, December 1, 2004. Persico, who collaborated with Powell on his 1995 memoir *My American Journey*, generously discussed with the author material used in preparation for that book.

23 The McKoy daughters: Meikle interview.

23 Luther was the one: Berns interview.
23 "lousy citizens": Meikle interview.
23 gathered around the radio: Berns interview.
23 Powell family politics: Ibid.; *MAJ*, p. 9.
24 Alice's second-born: Meikle interview.
24 By junior high school: Norman interview; *MAJ*, p. 20.
24 The repository: Berns interview.
24 rare youthful misadventures: *MAJ*, p. 18.
24 a remarkable ability: Juanita Norman, author interview, August 27, 2003.
24 Luther and Arie never lectured: Berns interview.
24 their own family pew: *MAJ*, p. 17.
25 When Colin became a teenager: Persico interview.
25 Marilyn was less in awe: Berns interview.
25 Norman's parents said: Ibid.
25 "We've never had a divorce": Ibid.; *MAJ*, p. 24.
25 unthinkable to Luther and Arie: *MAJ*, p. 24.
26 After consulting her sisters: Persico interview.
26 Marilyn worried: Berns interview.
26 Colin took two city buses: *MAJ*, pp. 24–25.
26 "speak straight-forward," Colin L. Powell, civil engineering essay, February 23, 1954, Powell papers.
27 "I went to college": Howard Means, *Colin Powell: Soldier/Statesman—Statesman/Soldier* (New York: Donald I. Fine), p. 76.
27 He lasted through: *MAJ*, p. 25.
27 "my son, the geologist": Meikle, Berns interviews.
27 Marilyn had also been right: Berns interview; *MAJ*, pp. 25–26.
27 Luther and Arie had talked for years: Berns interview.
28 Luther saw a number: Colin and his sister, Marilyn, tell slightly different stories. In Marilyn's version, there was no dream, only the hymn number on the wall, and the payout, $11,000, was delivered in a suitcase. Colin recalled the dream, a $10,000 payout, and delivery in brown paper bags.
28 The Powells bought the house: *MAJ*, p. 30.
28 a hotbed of liberalism: Ibid., p. 26.
29 as he stood at attention: Ibid.
29 he was courted: Ibid., p. 27.
29 "falling domino[es]": President Dwight D. Eisenhower, press conference, April 7, 1954, http://eisenhower.archives.gov/domino.htm (accessed June 7, 2004).
29 The U.S. Supreme Court ruled: *Brown v. Board of Education of Topeka, Kansas* (1954) overturned the "separate but equal" doctrine of *Plessy v. Ferguson* (1896).
29 They partied and chased girls: *MAJ*, p. 28.
30 A leader had to set an example: Ibid., p. 35.
30 Marilyn was relieved: Berns interview.
30 "Relatives Living in a Foreign Country": "Personnel Security Questionnaire," U.S. Government Form DD 398, January 9, 1957, Powell papers.
30 Ronnie Brooks: *MAJ*, pp. 27–28.
30 his first two college summers: Powell papers.
31 his first trip to the American South: *MAJ*, p. 34.
31 a white supply sergeant: Ibid., p. 34.
31 he applied for appointment: "Application for Appointment," U.S. Government Form DA 61, November 8, 1957, Powell papers.

31 they assumed: Berns interview.

31 Brookhart called him: Persico interview; *MAJ*, p. 38.

32 Davis spent four years: Davis became one of only two black line officers in the Army; the other was his father. A squadron commander with the all-black Tuskegee Airmen in World War II, he later became the first black general in the U.S. Air Force.

32 Brookhart had been warning: *MAJ*, p. 38; Persico interview.

32 his Reserve commission: Army protocol required ROTC graduates eligible for Regular Army commissions to wait until West Point had commissioned its graduates. Although *My American Journey* gives June 9, 1958, as the date Powell took the oath of office, documents in his Army files at the National Defense University library indicate that he was sworn into the Reserve on June 10. He was officially commissioned into the Regular Army active duty three weeks later, making June 30, 1958, his "date of rank" for the rest of his military career.

32 Arie had to send: *MAJ*, p. 37; Persico interview.

32 "Do your three years": David Roth, *Sacred Honor: Colin Powell, the Inside Account of His Life and Times* (Grand Rapids, Mich.: Zondervan Publishing House, 1993), pp. 43–44.

32 During the eight weeks: Ibid., p. 46.

32 eighth in his class: "Academic Report," U.S. Government Form DA 1059, October 24, 1958, Powell papers.

33 Colin had been in an airplane: Persico interview.

33 he knew what the rules were: Ibid.

33 "I wanted ... to succeed": *MAJ*, p. 43.

CHAPTER THREE

35 "The way for a young man": Abraham Lincoln to William H. Herndon (Lincoln's law partner), July 10, 1848, *Collected Works of Abraham Lincoln*, vol. 1 (New Brunswick, N.J.: Rutgers University Press, 1955).

35 "In those early years": Colin L. Powell, interview with Armstrong Williams, TV One, July 21, 2004, State Department transcript.

35 the Hessian Corridor: Later in the Cold War, the Hessian Corridor became known as the Fulda Gap, named for the West German town nearest the break in the Vogelsberg Mountains.

36 "give the Reds": Lieutenant General Garrison Davidson, Seventh Army commander, quoted in "This Is the Army," *Time*, October 13, 1961. www.3ad.com/history/cold.war/abrams.htm (accessed June 23, 2004).

36 As his charges shivered: *MAJ*, p. 45.

36 The biggest artillery piece: "Program of the Army's 280 MM Gun, October 15, 1952," Aberdeen Proving Ground Archives, www.geocities.com/CapeCanaveral/8966/Military1.html (accessed June 24, 2004); "M65 Atomic Cannon," www.globalsecurity.org/military/systems/ground/m65.htm (accessed June 22, 2004).

36 a whole class of weapons: *MAJ*, p. 540.

37 Powell's captain described: "Officer Efficiency Report," U.S. Government Form DA 67-4, various dates, Powell papers.

38 "For black GIs": *MAJ*, p. 53.

38 never more than a half-dozen: Isaac B. Smith, author interview, June 26, 2004.

38 a sharecropper's son: Ibid.

38 "We were not about separation": Ibid.

39 As he began to be noticed: Ibid.; Joseph Schwar, author interview, August 13, 2003.

39 Negroes had fought: Charles C. Moskos and John Sibley Butler, *All That We Can Be: Black Leadership and Racial Integration the Army Way* (New York: Twentieth Century Fund, 1966), p. 23.

40 Two hundred thousand black soldiers: Martin Binkin and Mark J. Eitelberg, *Blacks and the Military* (Washington, D.C.: Brookings Institution, 1982), p. 17.

40 "they are not permitted": R. L. Vann, letter to Ernest H. Wilkins (president, Oberlin College), March 4, 1938, "Desegregation of the Armed Forces," Harry S. Truman Library, www.trumanlibrary.org (accessed May 27, 2004).

40 By 1940: Moskos and Butler, *All That We Can Be*, p. 27, quoting Stephen Ambrose, *The Military and American Society* (New York: Free Press, 1972), p. 26.

40 two separate armies: Morris J. MacGregor, Jr., *Integration of the Armed Forces, 1940–1965* (Washington, D.C.: United States Army Center of Military History, 1985), www.army.mil/cmh-pg/books/integration/IAF-fm.htm (accessed June 15, 2004).

40 Negro enlistment increased: Robert P. Patterson (secretary of war) memorandum to the President's Committee on Civil Rights, May 15, 1947, Truman Library.

41 Truman had detected: Bernard C. Nalty, *Strength for the Fight. A History of Black Americans in the Military* (New York: Free Press, 1986), pp. 236–237.

41 The Republicans: David McCullough, *Truman* (New York: Simon & Schuster, 1992), pp. 643–645; Nalty, *Strength for the Fight*, pp. 240–241.

41 Truman had little chance: Nalty, *Strength for the Fight*, p. 241.

41 In November: McCullough, *Truman*, p. 713.

41 The Philadelphia-born Becton: Julius W. Becton, author interview, February 9, 2004.

42 Desperately in need: Nalty, *Strength for the Fight*, p. 259.

42 "Don't let anything happen": Becton interview.

42 Despite the fears: "Integration of Negro and White Troops in the U.S. Army, Europe, 1952–1954," manuscript prepared by Historical Division, Headquarters, United States Army, Europe, 1956, Historical Manuscripts Collection, U.S. Army Center of Military History, www.army.mil/cmh-pg/documents/cold-war/EI-FM.htm (accessed June 28, 2004).

42 He had not seen: Berns interview.

42 he left blank: Colin L. Powell, voter registration card dated October 14, 1960, Powell papers.

43 "Military officers have to be": Persico interview.

43 Luther and Arie had retained: Berns interview.

43 "I did not know anything": *MAJ*, pp. 60–61.

43 "I consider Lt. Powell": "Officer Efficiency Report," August 31, 1962, Powell papers.

43 When his promotion: Berns interview.

43 He was at loose ends: *MAJ*, p. 63.

44 she was furious: Ibid., p. 64.

44 Alma was from: Annemarie Powell, author interview, May 13, 2003; Persico interview.

44 When the appointed evening: Roth, *Sacred Honor*, pp. 49–50; Persico interview.

44 "We took the girls": *MAJ*, p. 64.

44 Alma thought: Roth, *Sacred Honor*, p. 51.

45 The holiday event: Persico interview.

45 When Alma walked: Berns interview.

45 "Beryl planted herself": *MAJ,* p. 66.

46 Her parents never gave parties: Persico interview.

46 Eisenhower was willing: Stanley Karnow, *Vietnam: A History* (New York: Penguin Books, 1984; New York: Viking Press, 1984), p. 235. Citations are from the Penguin edition.

46 more than two dozen: Center of Military History, *Vietnam Studies. U.S. Army Special Forces, 1961–1971,* Publication 90-23, Department of the Army, 1973, www.army.mil/cmh-pg/books/vietnam/90-23.htm (accessed July 5, 2004).

47 "a major blow": Kahin, *Intervention,* p. 133.

47 2,067: Ibid., p. 139.

47 Alma made it clear: Roth, *Sacred Honor,* p. 53.

47 "I'm too old": Sandra McElwaine, "Her American Journey," *Ladies' Home Journal,* May 1996, p. 152.

47 He had never been: This account of the Powells' decision to marry is drawn from Alma Powell interview with *Ladies' Home Journal,* May 1996; *MAJ,* p. 68; and Persico interview.

48 The Powell family: Berns interview.

48 In the end: Ibid.

48 Nothing happened: Ibid.

49 "a cultural one-eighty": *MAJ,* p. 71.

49 Colin's anger rose: The account of the Powell and Schwar families at Fort Bragg is based on author interview with Joseph Schwar, August 13, 2003; and *MAJ,* pp. 73–74.

CHAPTER FOUR

51 "I see these things": Charles Trueman "Buck" Lanham, "Soldier," poem published in *Infantry Journal,* 1936. Lanham retired as an Army major general in 1954 and died in 1978. The verse became a favorite of infantrymen.

51 "the finest thing": *MAJ,* p. 80.

51 number of U.S. military personnel: Among the many official accounts of the early U.S. involvement in Vietnam, this chapter draws from James Lawton Collins, Jr., *The Development and Training of the South Vietnamese Army, 1950–1972* (Washington, D.C.: Department of the Army, 1991), pp. 30–31; "The Advisory Build-up, 1961–1967," *The Pentagon Papers,* www.mtholyoke.edu/acad/intrel/pentagon.htm (accessed June 2004); Jeffrey J. Clark, *Advice and Support: The Final Years, 1965–1973* (Washington, D.C.: United States Army Center of Military History, 1988).

52 "no command jurisdiction": "The Advisory Build-up, 1961–1967," *The Pentagon Papers.*

53 "untraining": Alton J. Sheek, author interview, September 18, 2003.

53 Since they could not: In the early years of the buildup, officers received only rudimentary guidance before being sent into the field with ARVN units. Among the few documentary training records, examples cited here are taken from "Lessons Learned No. 28: Guidelines for Advisors," Military Assistance Command, Vietnam, April 18, 1963, http://carlisle-www.army.mil/usamhi/DL/chron.htm (accessed November 11, 2003); and Martin J. Dockery, *Lost in Translation: Vietnam: A Combat Advisor's Story* (New York: Random House, 2003), Annexes A, B and C.

53 Powell arrived: *MAJ,* pp. 76–80.

54 Field kits: Dockery, *Lost in Translation,* p. 16.

54 "When the battlefield was searched": Major General David Ewing Ott, *Field Artillery, 1954–1973* (Washington, D.C.: Department of the Army, 1975), www .army.mil/cmh-pg/books/Vietnam/FA54-73/fm.htm (accessed August 6, 2004).

54 ARVN soldiers had refused: Neil Sheehan (United Press International), "Vietnamese Ignored U.S. Battle Order," *The Washington Post,* January 7, 1963, p. A1.

55 When white taxpayers complained: Glenn T. Eskew, *But for Birmingham: The Local and National Movements in the Civil Rights Struggle* (Chapel Hill: University of North Carolina Press, 1997), pp. 178–179.

55 Alma's own mother: Roth, *Sacred Honor,* p. 60.

55 Birmingham was ripe: Taylor Branch, *Pillar of Fire: America in the King Years, 1963–65* (New York: Simon & Schuster, 1998; New York: Touchstone, 1999), p. 26. Citations are from the Touchstone edition.

56 when activist volunteers: Roth, *Sacred Honor,* p. 62.

56 The students trampled: Branch, *Pillar of Fire,* p. 77.

56 John Wesley Rice, Jr.: Dale Russakoff, "Lessons of Might and Right. While Others Marched for Civil Rights, Condoleezza Rice's Family Taught Her to Make Her Own Freedom," *The Washington Post,* September 9, 2001, p. W23.

56 He made Alma: The account of Alma Powell's stay in Birmingham in 1963 is drawn from Roth, *Sacred Honor,* chap. 4; Alma Powell interview by Dale Russakoff, summer 2001, courtesy of Dale Russakoff; Persico interview; and *MAJ,* chap. 4.

57 Major George Price: George Price, author interview, February 27, 2004.

57 "The Vietnamese crowded around": *MAJ,* pp. 95–96.

58 The A Shau camp: Ibid., pp. 80–82.

58 Quang Tri Province itself: "National Campaign Plan Briefing," Miscellaneous Documents, 1962 through Secretary of Defense Conference Agenda, 1963, Military Assistance Command, Vietnam (MAAV) Historian background files, Modern Military Records Unit, National Archives at College Park, Md. Material from this unit is subsequently cited as "National Archives."

58 The ambushes usually targeted: Details of advisers' life in the A Shau valley in 1963 are drawn from Sheek interview and *MAJ,* chap. 4.

59 "perform[ing] his duties": "Officer Efficiency Report," September 6, 1963, Powell papers.

59 little sense of accomplishment: *MAJ,* chap. 4.

59 After the first soldier: Ibid., p. 85.

60 in these forests before: Sheek interview.

61 "Colin had an air about him": Ibid.

61 "counterinsurgency at the cutting edge": *MAJ,* p. 87.

61 "deep raids and attacks": MACV to General Earle A. Wheeler (Army chief of staff), memorandum in response to questions, January 21, 1963, National Archives.

62 "There was no front": *MAJ,* p. 89.

62 One day in February: Ibid., pp. 87–88.

62 "We were walking single file": Sheek interview.

62 "For once": *MAJ,* p. 97.

63 "Casualty Message": U.S. Government form DD-173, addressed to Mr. and Mrs. Luther T. Powell, undated, Powell papers.

63 Luther... kept the news from Arie: Berns interview.
63 "vigorous and comprehensive program": "Officer Efficiency Report," September 6, 1963, Powell papers.
63 he just wanted to go home: Persico interview.
64 "first experience of elite people": Ibid.
64 "it is your military obligation": "Lessons Learned No. 28: Guidelines for Advisors," April 18, 1963.
64 Washington was nonetheless convinced: "U.S. Policy 1962–64 (Planned Phased Withdrawal of U.S. Forces)," *The Pentagon Papers.*
64 "any such announcement": John Mecklin (U.S. Embassy public affairs officer), memorandum to William Trueheart (deputy chief of mission), July 8, 1963, included in briefing book prepared for CINCPAC Conference on July 12, 1963, National Archives.
65 "They asked us about": Price interview.
65 The city government: Eskew, *But for Birmingham,* pp. 318–320.
65 An estimated fifteen sticks: "Six Dead After Church Bombing," United Press International, September 16, 1963.
66 To the young Condoleezza: Condoleezza Rice, "Almost like a Train Coming," *Time,* May 29, 2000.
66 The Johnson family: Roth, *Sacred Honor,* p. 64.
66 "has made progress": "U.S. Policy 1962–64 (Planned Phased Withdrawal of U.S. Forces)," *The Pentagon Papers.*
66 Kennedy ordered: "National Security Action Memorandum No. 263," October 11, 1963, Kennedy Library.
66 "actually cloaked a situation": "U.S. Policy 1962–64 (Planned Phased Withdrawal of U.S. Forces)," *The Pentagon Papers.*
67 "all those rear-echelon wimps": Persico interview.
67 Just after 2 p.m.: "Daily Journal, 1 April 63 through 31 December 63," MACV, National Archives.
67 "I had no penetrating political insights": *MAJ,* pp. 102–103.
68 "previous consideration": "MACV Command History 1964," National Archives.

CHAPTER FIVE

69 "In war": Carl von Clausewitz, *On War,* ed./trans. Michael Howard and Peter Paret (Princeton, N.J.: Princeton University Press, 1976, rev. 1984), book 3, chap. 7, p. 193.
69 his first public political act: *MAJ,* p. 113.
70 "For me, the real world began": Ibid., p. 108.
70 Few Army officers: The description of the racial climate at Fort Benning in the mid-1960s, and Powell's views of it, are drawn from Schwar, Becton and Persico interviews and numerous *MAJ* passages.
70 His teachers: Steven Pawlik, author interview, September 8, 2004. Powell was a Fort Benning student of then-Major Pawlik, who later recommended him as an instructor and taught with him.
71 course for new instructors: *MAJ,* pp. 116–117; Persico interview; P. X. Kelley, author interview, September 7, 2004. Kelley, who later became commandant of the Marine Corps, also taught at Fort Benning.
71 "I used to kid him": Pawlik interview.

71   regular American combat units: Kahin, *Intervention,* pp. 306–307.

71   With few exceptions: *MAJ,* p. 120.

71   a different man: Persico interview.

72   The journey: Linda Powell, author interview, May 13, 2004; Annemarie Powell interview.

72   Alma found she liked: Persico interview.

72   In June 1968: *MAJ,* p. 126.

73   He eventually came to see: Persico interview.

73   "Avoid Conservatism": Roth, *Sacred Honor,* p. 147.

73   "We were not eager": *MAJ,* p. 124.

74   "Alternate Strategies": *The Pentagon Papers,* vol. 4, chap. 2.

74   But the war: "Statistical Information About Casualties of the Vietnam Conflict," National Archives, www.archives.gov/research_room/research_topics/vietnam _war_casualty_lists/statis (accessed September 16, 2004).

74   In early July: Persico interviews; *MAJ,* p. 128.

74   Five years earlier: "The U.S. Army in Vietnam," *American Military History* (Washington, D.C.: United States Army Center of Military History), chap. 28, www .army.mil/cmh-pg/books/AMH/AMH-28.htm (accessed September 9, 2004).

75   A half-hour helicopter ride: Ronald A. Tumelson, author interview, September 2004; *MAJ,* pp. 130–134.

75   The majority of Americal casualties: "The U.S. Army in Vietnam," pp. 680–681.

76   "recently healthy": *MAJ,* p. 134.

76   The Americal Division commander: Tumelson interview.

76   the general might want: Ibid.

77   Chu Lai had grown: "Americal Division Operational Report: Lessons Learned for Period 1 Aug. 68–31 Oct. 68," National Archives.

77   There were other dangers: Tumelson interview.

77   "Racial incidents": "Americal Division Operational Report: Lessons Learned for Period 1 Aug. 68–31 Oct. 68."

78   proud to fight: Wallace Terry II, "Bringing the War Home," *Black Scholar,* November 1970, pp. 6–18.

78   The percentage of blacks: Moscos and Butler, *All That We Can Be,* p. 33.

79   "contained dozens of new men": *MAJ,* p. 133.

79   "a macabre statistical competition": Ibid., pp. 146–147.

79   the Americal meticulously reported: "Americal Division Operational Report: Lessons Learned for Period 1 Nov. 68–31 Jan. 69," National Archives.

79   Space was always tight: Tumelson interview; *MAJ,* pp. 137–139.

81   Word that the commanding general's: "11th Inf. BTN Daily Journal," November 16, 1968, National Archives.

81   "What Gettys told me": Tumelson interview.

81   That night, Powell argued: "Duty Officer's Log," Americal Division, November 16, 1968, National Archives.

81   Alma and the children: Persico interview; Berns interview.

82   "With complete disregard": "Award of the Soldier's Medal," General Orders Number 9285, Department of the Army, December 3, 1968, Powell papers.

82   "Far beyond merely dismissing": Tom Glen, letter to General Creighton Abrams, November 27, 1968, National Archives.

83   "information upon which": The Callahan memo and responses are collected in Americal files, National Archives.

84 "a better understanding": "Americal Division Operational Report: Lessons Learned for Period 1 Nov. 68–31 Jan. 69," National Archives.

84 For the soldiers' own celebration: Ibid.

84 "exceptionally outstanding conduct": Major General Charles M. Gettys, letter to the Secretariat for DA Selection Boards, "Recommendation for Promotion," March 3, 1969, Powell papers.

85 Just before lunchtime: "Testimony of Maj. Colin L. Powell, Deputy G-3, Americal Division, taken at Chu Lai, Republic of Vietnam, on 23 May 1969," National Archives. In his 1995 memoir, *My American Journey*, Powell sets this exchange in "mid-March," although initial allegations regarding the My Lai massacre were not made until the end of March 1969 and the first Army investigation in Vietnam did not begin until the following month. There is additional reason to believe that Powell misremembered substantive portions of the interview with Sheehan, perhaps confusing its content with subsequent public reports about the massacre. Although he wrote that the session began with instructions from the interviewer to look through operations log entries for March 1968 and "let me know if you find an unusual number of enemy killed on any day," those instructions are not reflected in the official interview transcript. Similarly, Powell's recollection that he discovered, and reported to the interviewer, a March 16, 1968, entry reporting "a body count of 128 enemy dead on the Batangan Peninsula" does not appear in the transcript. In his recorded and officially transcribed reading from the journal to Sheehan, Powell reported a cumulative total of 21 Viet Cong dead in various encounters with U.S. forces, a figure that comports with initial reports of the day's events that were falsified by participants shortly after the incident in My Lai.

86 Congress demanded: With the exception of Colonel Henderson's report, original documents regarding the My Lai investigations are located in the National Archives.

87 Five weeks after: Oran K. Henderson, "Report of Investigation," Memorandum to Commanding General, Americal Division, April 24, 1968. A copy of the Henderson report was provided to the author by Charles Lane, who published a related story in *The New Republic* on April 17, 1995.

88 The Peers report: "Findings and Recommendations," in "Report of the Department of the Army Review of the Preliminary Investigations of the My Lai Incident," Department of the Army, Washington, D.C., March 14, 1970, www.law.umkc.edu/faculty/projects/ftrials/mylai/findings.html (accessed September 29, 2004).

89 "For the most part": Lieutenant Colonel Colin L. Powell, sworn statement, Department of the Army, August 10, 1971, Powell papers. In hardback editions of *My American Journey*, Powell mistakenly refers to this 1971 statement as testimony given to the Peers Commission on My Lai, which had completed its inquiry the previous year. The reference was deleted in the 1996 Ballantine paperback edition of the book.

90 In response: Means, *Colin Powell. Soldier/Statesman–Statesman/Soldier*, p. 146.

90 "H & I": Persico interview.

91 "lost touch with reality": *MAJ*, pp. 144–145.

91 The absence of unit cohesion: Ibid., p. 144.

91 "witnessed as much bravery": Ibid., p. 148.

CHAPTER SIX

92   "Learn who's who": Colin Powell, notes to self, early 1970s, Powell papers.
92   "This guy": John Saur, author interview, October 13, 2004.
92   Powell's stomach was churning: Persico interview; *MAJ*, p. 152.
93   Saur looked up: Saur interview.
93   As in every course: "Powell, Colin Luther, Permanent Record," George Washington University, Powell papers.
93   "I would be window dressing": Saur interview.
93   coolly impervious: Ibid.
94   It was far from their dream home: Persico interview.
94   Colin resented the $600 gift: Ibid.
94   the drive south: Ibid.
94   Michael and Linda: Ibid.
95   the final version: "Findings and Recommendations," Peers Report.
95   Westmoreland ordered: "Study on Military Professionalism," U.S. Army War College (Carlisle Barracks, Pa.), June 30, 1970, http://ahecwebopac.carlisle.army.mil:4525/F/82YSYT3YD98K461TB351VQFEKQUQMNKCXJ1RRS2U7PED5RE6HP-11560?func=full-set-set&set_number=076352&set_entry=000001&format=999 (accessed October 12, 2004).
95   Ulmer and Malone reported: James Kitfield, *Prodigal Soldiers* (New York: Simon & Schuster, 1995), pp. 107–113.
96   Westmoreland looked around: Ibid.
96   "The worst part of it": Persico interview.
96   Many returning officers: Kitfield, *Prodigal Soldiers,* chaps. 6–7.
97   "I had no ghosts": Richard MacKenzie, "An Officer and a Gentleman," *The Washington Times,* October 8, 1990.
97   "the way our political leaders": *MAJ,* p. 148.
97   the ultimate irony: Persico interview.
97   Two days later: *MAJ,* p. 154.
98   "At a very unpleasant time": David Halberstam, "What We Can Learn from Colin Powell," *Parade,* September 17, 1995, p. 4.
98   A World War II veteran: Lieutenant Colonel Romie L. Brownlee and Lieutenant Colonel William J. Mullen I, "Changing an Army; an Oral History of General William E. DePuy," United States Military History Institute (Carlisle, Pennsylvania), 1986, http://carlisle-www.army.mil/usamhi/Sampler/Changing/ (accessed October 1, 2004).
99   potential "unlimited": "Officer Efficiency Report," August 7, 1972, Powell papers.
99   "I don't shove it in their face": Henry Louis Gates, Jr., *Thirteen Ways of Looking at a Black Man* (New York: Random House, 1987; Vintage Books, 1998), pp. 83–84. Citations are from the Vintage Books edition.
99   walked along a Pentagon corridor: *MAJ,* pp. 161–162.
100 It was only in the South: Moskos and Butler, *All That We Can Be,* pp. 47–48.
100 "The Rocks": Dorian Cartwright, biographical sketch of Roscoe Conklin Cartwright, www.arlingtoncemetery.net/rccartwright.htm (accessed November 3, 2004).
100 "what was expected of them": Becton interview.
101 return the favor: Schwar interview.
101 "On the one hand": Ibid.

101 the fellowship program: Historical materials related to the White House Fellows program were generously provided to the author by former Fellows Commission Executive Director Jacqueline Blumenthal.

102 Schwar thought: Schwar interview.

102 "In particular, I feel": Colin L. Powell, White House Fellow Application, December 14, 1971.

102 "He emphasized": Luis Nogales, author interview, September 3, 2003.

103 Saying he was calling for Fred Malek: Persico interview.

103 the fellows' year: Persico interview; Nogales interview.

104 "The first several days": Nogales interview.

105 Scowcroft... wrote: Brigadier General Brent Scowcroft, letter to Defense Secretary James Schlesinger regarding White House Fellows, September 25, 1973.

105 "tough to resist": Nogales interview.

105 "the error of a greenhorn": *MAJ*, p. 176.

106 "I needed someone": Frederick V. Malek, letter to Howard H. Callaway, August 20, 1973; and Callaway, letter to Malek, September 6, 1973, Powell papers.

106 As far as his family: Berns interview.

106 "Colin Powell to most of these people": Schwar interview.

CHAPTER SEVEN

107 "I got into the Army": Colin L. Powell, Remarks at Brookhaven Boys and Girls Club, Atlanta, Georgia, October 2, 2004, State Department transcript.

107 On a steamy August morning: Becton interview.

108 "Back in those days": Ibid.

109 Korea offered a wealth of them: Persico interview; *MAJ*, chap. 8.

109 Short on spit and polish: Persico interview.

109 "I can easily put": *MAJ*, pp. 179–204.

110 wrote back with an assurance: Joseph Laitin, letter to Colin Powell, January 12, 1974, Powell papers.

110 not... a great student: Harlan Ullman, author interview, November 18, 2004.

110 It was Ullman who intervened: Ibid.

111 "above average": "Permanent Faculty Advisor's End of Year Evaluation of Advisee," May 21, 1976, Powell papers.

111 "useful to be singled out": Ullman interview.

111 After glumly examining: Persico interview.

111 "acting white": Annemarie Powell interview; Linda Powell interview.

111 "never talked about race much": Annemarie Powell interview.

112 The role of mother hen: Persico interview.

112 The commanding general: General John A. Wickham, Jr. (Ret.), author interview, February 16, 2004; "U.S. Army Officer Evaluation Report," April 22, 1977, Powell papers.

112 When Rumsfeld: Wickham interview.

112 "pay[ing] the king his shilling": *MAJ*, p. 220.

112 He knew that some people: Persico interview.

113 "I detected a common thread": *MAJ*, p. 220.

113 Powell's new boss: Ibid., chap. 9.

113 "deliberately letting myself": Ibid., p. 216.

113 "You've got to have blacks": Zbigniew Brzezinski, author interview, November 22, 2004.

114 As he followed an escort: *MAJ*, p. 227.

114 "Colonel, you're going to be detailed": Brzezinski interview.

115 Of all the NSC interviews: Ibid.

115 Kester…had pulled Powell's name: John Kester, quoted in Means, *Colin Powell:* p. 194.

115 the Army wanted its own: *MAJ*, p. 234.

115 on one condition: Persico interview.

115 "I got a sense": Means, *Colin Powell*, pp. 194–195.

115 There was nothing wrong: Ibid.

116 During his seventeen months: Persico interview.

116 Sitting in a back seat: Ibid.

117 blacks made up a quarter: Binkin and Eitelberg, *Blacks and the Military*, pp. 58–61.

117 "My method was simple": Gates, *Thirteen Ways of Looking at a Black Man*, p. 78.

117 His name was not: Persico interview.

118 every one: "Officer Evaluation Reports," July 20, 1974–December 7, 1977, Powell papers.

118 "Alma Powell can settle a house": Berns interview.

118 "the feeling that we had": Linda Powell interview.

119 the family movie: Ibid.

119 As the children reached: Michael Powell, quoted in Roth, *Sacred Honor*, p. 109.

119 About a year after: Ibid.

120 At home: Linda Powell interview; Annemarie Powell interview; Persico interview.

120 "black brigadier general": "Periscope," *Newsweek*, September 3, 1979, p. 15.

121 "she came back to being Mom": Linda Powell interview.

121 A later investigation: "Rescue Mission Report, August 1980," Jimmy Carter Library, http://arcweb.archives.gov/arc/basic_search.jsp (accessed December 23, 2004).

122 "You have to plan thoroughly": *MAJ*, p. 249.

122 The roots of the disastrous plan: Persico interview.

122 record on national security: *MAJ*, pp. 250–251.

123 his second choice: Lou Cannon, *President Reagan: The Role of a Lifetime* (New York: Simon and Schuster, 1991), p. 84.

123 Powell doubted: *MAJ*, p. 253.

124 "seemed to know everything": Frank Carlucci, author interview, November 18, 2004.

124 "He wanted to go": Ibid.

CHAPTER EIGHT

125 "He was directly involved": "Officer Evaluation Report," June 19, 1986, Powell papers.

125 Alma thought: Persico interview.

125 He had been warned: Becton interview; *MAJ*, p. 261.

126 Hudachek seemed: Philip D. Coker, author interview, October 22, 2004; Becton interview.

126 He had brought home: Linda Powell interview.

126 "He was eight years ahead of me": Wesley K. Clark, author interview, February 11, 2005.

127 He had felt an obligation: *MAJ*, pp. 260–261.

127 Hudachek's own list: Woodward, "The Powell Predicament, Part 2" *The Washington Post Magazine*, September 24, 1995, p. W15.

127 "aggressive and technically competent": "Officer Evaluation Report," May 20, 1982, Powell papers.

127 Powell read the review: Persico interview.

128 Powell was an "excellent": "Officer Evaluation Report," June 3, 1982, Powell papers.

128 He could already hear: *MAJ,* p. 271; Persico interview.

128 Becton and Cavazos had sensed: Becton interview.

129 Becton put through a call: Ibid.

129 Captain Coker answered: Coker interview.

129 Powell was to take Jenes's job: *MAJ,* pp. 271–272.

129 Hudachek was not happy: Coker interview; *MAJ,* p. 272.

129 At the bottom of a letter: Julius Becton, letter to Colin Powell, November 19, 1982, Powell papers.

129 "Heartiest congratulations": John Hudachek letter to Colin Powell, November 18, 1982, ibid.

130 the story of the 10th Cavalry: Gail Buckley, *American Patriots: The Story of Blacks in the Military from the Revolution to Desert Storm* (New York: Random House, 2001), chaps. 4–5. Among the many accounts of the history of the Buffalo Soldiers, also see the Army's online history of the 9th and 10th Cavalry Regiments at www.army.mil/cmh-pg (accessed December 30, 2004) and the National Archives at www.archives.gov/exhibit_hall/featured_documents/henry-o-flipper/ (accessed January 3, 2005).

130 first Negro officer: In an unsuccessful petition to Congress in 1898, Flipper wrote that he had "as honorable a record in the Army as any officer in it, in spite of the isolation, lack of social association, ostracism and what not to which I was subjected by the great majority of my brother officers" and had been discharged for "the crime of being a Negro." Favorable action on his case, he wrote, would bring not only "my gratitude and that of my entire race" but "the satisfaction of having righted a great wrong done to a member of a harmless but despised and friendless race." President Bill Clinton issued Flipper a full pardon in 1999.

130 For his efforts: "50 Years on the Road to Equality," National Park Service, www.nps.gov/pwso/honor/pershing.htm (accessed December 30, 2004).

131 Powell began raising money: Coker interview; Persico interview.

132 "honest but dumb": Colin L. Powell, notes taken during the interview phase of Project 14, Powell papers.

132 The defense priorities: Clark interview; "A Transition Report to General John A. Wickham, Jr.," May 27, 1983, Powell papers.

133 "Many started out": "A Transition Report."

133 Wickham had assigned: Wickham interview.

134 "Though you might prefer": General John A. Wickham, telex to Colin Powell, June 2, 1983, Powell papers.

134 they pulled up: Persico interview.

134 Weinberger was primly formal: Ibid.

134 the secretary's reluctance: Ibid.

134–35 It wasn't that Powell was embarrassed: Ibid.

135 "be careful of that Powell": Richard L. Armitage, author interview, April 2, 2004.

136 Raised in Atlanta: James Mann, *Rise of the Vulcans: The History of Bush's War Cabinet* (New York: Viking Penguin, 2004). Various chapters of this work address the

background of Armitage and others who would later serve in the administration of President George W. Bush.

136 "The man cussed like a sailor": *MAJ,* p. 261.

136 Weinberger's door: Persico interview.

137 His close relationship: *MAJ,* p. 298.

137 "the guy who could sort of tell you": P. X. Kelley interview.

137 "my closest adviser": "Officer Evaluation Form," July 29, 1985, Powell papers.

137 "Who else can say": Annemarie Powell interview.

138 Jane told Alma: Persico interview.

138 "a case study": Cannon, *President Reagan,* p. 390.

138 "be very unwise": General John V. Vessey, memo to Weinberger, June 19, 1982, quoted in Cannon, *President Reagan,* p. 398.

138 Weinberger "could not understand": Colin Powell interview with Lou Cannon. Reagan biographer Cannon, who reported on the Reagan presidency for *The Washington Post,* generously provided the author with transcripts of three lengthy, on-the-record interviews he conducted with Powell between 1988 and 1990.

139 "Shultz and his aides": Cannon, *President Reagan,* p. 405.

139 Weinberger persuaded the president: Ibid., p. 407.

139 "Against this backdrop": Caspar Weinberger, *Fighting for Peace: Seven Critical Years in the Pentagon* (New York: Warner Books, 1990), p. 151.

139 Shultz accused: George P. Shultz, *Turmoil and Triumph: My Years as Secretary of State* (New York: Charles Scribner's Sons, 1993), p. 109.

139 "provide an interposition force": John H. Kelly, "Lebanon: 1982–1984," in Jeremy R. Azrael and Emil Payin, *U.S. and Russian Policymaking with Respect to the Use of Force,* Rand Corporation, 1996, www.rand.org/publications/CF/CF129/CF-129.chapter6.html (accessed January 6, 2005).

140 Although Shultz: Ibid.

140 Powell's immediate reaction: Persico interview.

141 Weinberger continued to blame: Kelly, "Lebanon: 1982–1984"; Shultz, *Turmoil and Triumph,* p. 233.

141 "We talked him out of it": Cannon interview with Colin Powell.

141 Weinberger set six prerequisites: Caspar W. Weinberger, "The Uses of Military Power," as prepared for delivery to National Press Club, Washington, D.C., November 28, 1984, www.pbs.org/wgbh/pages/frontline/shows/military/force/weinberger.html (accessed January 12, 2005).

141 Weinberger's checklist: Richard Halloran, "U.S. Will Not Drift into a Latin War, Weinberger Says," *The New York Times,* November 29, 1984, p. A1; George C. Wilson, "Weinberger Bids U.S. Be Cautious; Warning Is Sounded on Use of Military for Unclear Goals," *The Washington Post,* November 29, 1984, p. A1.

142 "purely passive strategy": Don Oberdorfer, "Shultz Defends U.S. Use of Force, Suggests Need for Anti-Terrorist Action," *The Washington Post,* April 4, 1984, p. A1.

142 "flexible tool of diplomacy": Cannon, *President Reagan,* pp. 405–406. Powell went on to tell Cannon that he could see a foreign policy role for the military when it served a sensible purpose, but "Beirut wasn't sensible and it never did service a purpose. It was goofy from the beginning." While serving as Reagan's national security adviser, Powell went further in explaining the connection. "The military should not exist in isolation, as if it bears no relation to political or foreign-

policy needs of the nation. It is a tool of foreign policy," he told reporter Steve Ryan in the September 1988 issue of the *Foreign Service Journal*.

142 "I thought I would have an aneurysm": *MAJ*, p. 576.

142 probably had never gone: Persico interview.

143 "Powell wanted to know": Charles G. Boyd, author interview, January 29, 2004.

143 Colin drove his family: The account of the trip to Arie Powell's funeral is drawn from *MAJ*, p. 301, and Persico interview.

144 she had always been: Marianna Cook, *Fathers and Daughters, in Their Own Words* (San Francisco: Chronicle Books, 1994), p. 28.

144 She was sure he would consider: Linda Powell interview.

144 he had made clear: Wickham interview.

144 Powell was more than ready: *MAJ*, p. 306.

145 Wickham knew that Powell: Wickham interview.

CHAPTER NINE

146 "What's amazing": Jesse Jackson to Gates, *Thirteen Ways of Looking at a Black Man*, p. 88.

146 He placed a photograph: *MAJ*, p. 318.

146 "When we are debating": Ibid., p. 320.

148 "up to my ears": Cannon interview with Powell.

149 "surrounded by alligators": Frank Carlucci, author interview, November 18, 2004.

149 "not considered a subject": Lawrence E. Walsh, "Part VII: Officers of the Department of Defense (U.S. v. Caspar W. Weinberger and Related Investigations)," *Final Report of the Independent Counsel for Iran/Contra Matters*, August 4, 1993, www.fas.org/irp/offdocs/walsh (accessed December 28, 2004). Unless otherwise indicated, chronological references to the Iran-*contra* affair and quotations from testimony and depositions are taken from this report.

149 "only minimal involvement": Ibid.

149 Carlucci enlisted: Carlucci and Persico interviews.

149 "Frank, don't do this": Cannon interview with Powell.

150 Reading from a script: Ibid.; Annemarie Powell, author interview, May 13, 2004.

150 lawyers for the joint: Walsh, *Final Report of the Independent Counsel for Iran/Contra Matters*.

151 he couldn't swear: Persico interview.

151 Powell replied: *Report of the Congressional Committees Investigating the Iran-Contra Affair and Appendices* (Washington: Superintendent of Documents, U.S. GPO, 1988).

152 Powell waited tensely: Persico interview.

152 In November 1991: Walsh, *Final Report of the Independent Counsel for Iran/Contra Matters*. The North and Poindexter convictions were later overturned on grounds that their congressional testimony under immunity had influenced trial witnesses.

153 "do not suggest to me": Ibid.; Sworn affidavit by Colin L. Powell, April 21, 1992, Powell papers.

153 based...on Powell's testimony: In listing the charges against Weinberger, Walsh wrote that his statements "were contradicted by numerous witnesses, including Powell and Armitage."

153 "saw virtually all": Powell affidavit.

153 "dead wrong": *MAJ*, p. 343.

154 "If it hadn't been": Gates, *Thirteen Ways of Looking at a Black Man*, p. 78.

154 Weinberger later wrote: Weinberger, *Fighting for Peace*, p. 383.

154 Powell didn't believe it: Persico interview.

155 two things about Reagan: Ibid.

156 "We would lay out": *MAJ*, pp. 333–334.

156 "It was scary": Cannon interview with Powell.

156 "a kind of Ollie North situation": Carlucci interview.

156 "the president is getting nervous": Ibid.

157 "Is it legal?": *MAJ*, p. 334.

157 In response: Carlucci interview; Persico interview.

158 "State, what have you": Richard L. Armitage, author interview, April 2, 2004.

158 "personal management style": *Report of the President's Special Review Board*, February 26, 1987. The report of the joint congressional investigation, released eight months later, was more direct in concluding that Iran-*contra* had been the result of "secrecy, deception and disdain for the law" within the administration and that Reagan bore "ultimate responsibility" for what had been done. The final report of the independent counsel, in 1993, was still more specific, saying that "the tone in Iran-*contra* was set by President Reagan. He directed that the *contras* be supported, despite a ban on *contra* aid imposed on him by Congress. And he was willing to trade arms to Iran for the release of Americans held hostage in the Middle East, even if doing so was contrary to the nation's stated policy and possibly in violation of the law."

158 Powell wrote a list: "The President Is Already Acting to Reform the NSC System," March 5, 1987, Powell papers.

159 Reagan liked to tell stories: Cannon, *President Reagan*, pp. 520–525; Lou Cannon, "Antidote to Ollie North," *The Washington Post Magazine*, August 7, 1988, p. W16.

159 Carlucci recalled: Carlucci interview.

159 On the rare occasions: Cannon interview with Powell.

160 "racism still exists": Ibid.

160 "the political and legal battle": Gerald M. Boyd, "President Urges Blacks to Attain Skills in Science," *The New York Times*, May 11, 1987, p. 1.

160 "I'm glad you were able": Colin L. Powell, letter to Gene Norman, June 22, 1987, Ronald Reagan Presidential Library, Simi Valley, California.

160 do the administration's image: Powell passed along to White House spokesman Marlin Fitzwater an August 10, 1987, thank-you letter he received after speaking to the Council of 100, an organization of black Republicans. "You'd be amazed at the coverage this got in the black press," he wrote in a memo to Fitzwater. "It suggests to me that maybe we need to do more with this kind of ethnic press"; Reagan Library.

161 Powell stiffed the Russians: Imagene B. Stewart, president, James Reese Europe Unit #5, American Legion Auxiliary, letter to Colin Powell, August 4, 1987, Powell papers; *MAJ*, p. 357.

161 "My thoughts on leadership": Colin L. Powell, letter to Cadet Kevin Richardson, University of Dubuque, February 26, 1987, Powell papers.

161 "I called him because": Powell, memo to Roman Popadiuk, January 12, 1988, ibid.

161 "Case of the Reluctant General": Richard Halloran, "Washington Talk: National Security Council: Case of the Reluctant General," *The New York Times*, October 5, 1987, p. 18.

162 Howard Baker: *MAJ*, p. 349.

162 "He may not have commanded": Ibid., p. 395.

162 He liked to compare: Cannon interview with Powell.

163 "most of his adult life": Ibid.

163 Powell confronted his doubts: Persico interview.

163 "get it all out": Ivo H. Daalder and I. M. "Mac" Destler, "Interview with General Colin L. Powell," November 23, 1999, *The National Security Project*, Brookings Institution, www.brookings.edu/fp/research/projects/nsc/transcripts/19991025.pdf (accessed June 10, 2003).

164 "We knew that if": Carlucci interview.

164 Powell joined the White House press corps: Cannon, "Antidote to Ollie North."

165 He shot off a letter: Colin L. Powell, letter to John Sansing, executive editor, *The Washingtonian*, February 2, 1988, Reagan Library.

165 Watching a news broadcast: Colin L. Powell, address at the National Defense University, December 13, 1989, Powell papers.

166 impossible to believe: Cannon interview with Powell; *MAJ*, p. 339.

166 Cheney ... would rather lose: Persico interview.

166 Reagan capitulated: Cannon interview with Powell.

166 "the grand facilitator": Melissa Healy and James Gerstenzang, "Security Adviser: Gen. Powell—Quest for Compromise," *Los Angeles Times*, June 27, 1988, p. 1.

167 "the long-vacant middle ground": "Keeping Choice Alive on Nicaragua," unsigned editorial, *The New York Times*, September 17, 1988, p. 26.

167 Gorbachev railed: Shultz, *Turmoil and Triumph*, pp. 1098–1100; *MAJ*, p. 375.

168 "There is no question": Internal NSC memorandum, December 30, 1988, Reagan Library.

168 had just gone to sleep: Powell interview.

169 "We deeply regret": "Statement on Gulf Incident," The White House, July 5, 1988, Reagan Library.

169 false on nearly all counts: John Barry and Roger Charles, "Sea of Lies," *Newsweek*, July 13, 1992, p. 29.

169 Powell could imagine: Powell interview.

170 "bright as a new nickel": George F. Will, "Nominate Bork, and Then...," *The Washington Post*, July 10, 1988, p. C7.

171 "Your availability": Frank J. Donatelli, memo to Colin Powell, July 11, 1988, Reagan Library.

171 "One has the impression": Jesse Jackson, quoted in Cannon, "Antidote to Ollie North."

171 "far more than an attractive black man": William Raspberry, "A Dream Ticket for the GOP: How Colin Powell Could Turn It Around," *The Washington Post*, August 10, 1988, p. A19.

171–172 After takeoff: Persico interview.

172 He wanted Powell to stay: *MAJ*, pp. 388–389.

172 "When I got home": Ibid.

172 "I'm thinking of quitting": Llewellyn interview.

173 "an extraordinary combination": Colin L. Powell, "Why History Will Honor Mr. Reagan," *The New York Times*, January 15, 1989, p. E27.

173 "If African-Americans fail": "Congratulations, Colin Powell, but Some Blacks Are Ambivalent," unsigned editorial, *Michigan Chronicle*, December 10, 1988, p. 6A.

CHAPTER TEN

174 "Reluctance to use": Colin L. Powell, remarks to National Press Club, September 23, 1993, Powell papers.

175 the defense budget: Lorna S. Jaffe, "The Development of the Base Force 1989–1992," Joint History Office, Department of Defense, July 1993, www .dtic.mil/doctrine/jel/history/baseforc.pdf (accessed September 23, 2004).

175 Powell unveiled his thoughts: Colin L. Powell, "National Security Challenges in the '90s: The Future Ain't What It Used to Be," address to the Association of the United States Army, Carlisle Barracks, Pennsylvania, May 16, 1989, Powell papers.

176 a "temporary aberration": Leo Rennert, "Defense Chief Takes Hard Line," *Modesto Bee*, March 22, 1989, p. A1; George C. Wilson, "At Ceremony for Cheney, Bush Cautious on Cuts," *The Washington Post*, March 22, 1989, p. A8.

176 a torrent of calls: Wilkerson interview; Bob Woodward, *The Commanders* (New York: Simon & Schuster, 1991), p. 107; *MAJ*, p. 403.

176 "with limited resources": "National Security Review 12," The White House, March 3, 1989, www.fas.org/irp/offdocs/nsr/nsr12.pdf (accessed March 17, 2005); Mann, *Rise of the Vulcans*, pp. 171–172.

176 Inside the Pentagon: Jaffe, "The Development of the Base Force 1989–1992"; Mann, *Rise of the Vulcans*, pp. 172–173.

177 a personal letter: George H. W. Bush, letter to Colin Powell, March 31, 1989, Powell papers.

177 "If you don't call me Barbara": Barbara Bush, letter to Colin Powell, April 11, 1989, ibid.

177 "only one candidate": Carlucci interview.

178 fact about Cheney: Mann, *Rise of the Vulcans*, pp. 175–176.

178 Cheney stopped to see Powell: Woodward, *The Commanders*, p. 109; *MAJ*, p. 406.

179 the most junior four-star: George Bush and Brent Scowcroft, *A World Transformed* (New York: Knopf, 1998; New York: Vintage Books, 1999), pp. 23–24. Citations are from the Vintage Books edition.

179 "If you and the President": *MAJ*, pp. 407–408.

180 "rose from humble origins": David Wallechinsky, "Have a Vision," *Parade*, August 13, 1989.

180 under the glass atop Powell's desk: Persico interview.

181 the personal items he carried: Ibid.

182 he was also disturbed: Ibid. While Powell was troubled by the seemingly ad hoc nature of Oval Office meetings, Bush and Scowcroft make clear in their joint memoir, *A World Transformed*, that they wanted to replace the stilted atmosphere of full-scale National Security Council meetings whenever possible with smaller, less formal decision sessions they felt would encourage frank discussion and avoid leaks.

183 excoriated the administration: Timothy J. McNulty, "Panama Revolt Has Bush, Staff on Defensive," *Chicago Tribune*, October 8, 1989, p. 1.

183 Powell was impressed: Persico interview.

184 "let's do it": *MAJ*, pp. 424–425.

184 "excessive concern for secrecy": Michael R. Gordon, "Cheney Blamed for Press Problems in Panama," *The New York Times*, March 20, 1990, p. A8.

184 "I'm very cautious": Saul Friedman, "Four Star Warrior," *Newsday Magazine*, February 11, 1990, p. 10.

184 "taken clear command": Ibid.

184 Powell asked two questions: Wilkerson interview.

186 "a completely different guy": Boyd interview.

186 "Colin was a bit": Ibid.

186 abolished the formal briefing: *MAJ*, p. 447.

186 He was a stickler: Persico interview.

187 Smullen told his wife: F. William Smullen III, author interview, November 9, 2004.

187 "How to Survive": Undated memo, Powell papers.

188 "analysis by instinct": *MAJ*, p. 436.

189 an initial outline: The discussion of Base Force planning is drawn from three sources: Jaffe, "The Development of the Base Force 1989–1992"; *MAJ*, pp. 436–440; Persico interview.

189 Cheney had already projected: Lawrence J. Korb, "U.S. National Defense Policy in the Post–Cold War World," in *America's Peace Dividend*, ed. Ann Markusen (New York: Council on Foreign Relations, 2001), www.ciaonet.org/book/markusen (accessed March 14, 2005); *MAJ*, p. 440.

190 Scowcroft noted: Bush and Scowcroft, *A World Transformed*, pp. 154–155.

190 defense budget could be reduced: Persico interview; R. Jeffrey Smith, "Powell Says Defense Needs Massive Review," *The Washington Post*, May 7, 1990, p. A1; *MAJ*, p. 255.

191 under the watchful gaze: Powell interview.

192 "Normal relations" with Iraq: "National Security Directive 26," The White House, October 2, 1989, http://bushlibrary.tamu.edu/research/nsd/NSD/NSD%2026/0001.pdf (accessed March 31, 2005).

192 "they stare at each other": Colin L. Powell interview, "Frontline: The Gulf War," PBS, January 9, 1996, www.pbs.org/wgbh/pages/frontline/gulf/ (accessed September 25, 2003).

192 watching and waiting: Powell's views and actions in the lead-up to the Persian Gulf War, unless otherwise noted, are drawn from Persico interview and *MAJ*, pp. 462–480.

193 "Naked aggression": Brent Scowcroft interview, "Frontline: The Gulf War," PBS.

193 even more distressed: Bush and Scowcroft, *A World Transformed*, p. 323.

193 Powell rushed to a telephone: Persico interview; *MAJ*, p. 463.

194 "my personal judgment": Bush and Scowcroft, *A World Transformed*, p. 323.

195 "the skunk at the picnic": Powell interview, "Frontline: The Gulf War," PBS.

195 "This will not stand": George H. W. Bush, remarks to reporters, August 5, 1990, White House transcript.

197 there was a modest chance: James A. Baker III, *The Politics of Diplomacy* (New York: G. P. Putnam's Sons, 1995), p. 301.

197 Bush still had two: Persico interview; *MAJ*, pp. 478–480; Woodward, *The Commanders*, pp. 41–42 (Woodward dates the meeting with Bush in "early October").

198 He was relieved: *MAJ*, p. 480.

198 "speed up the timetable": Bush and Scowcroft, *A World Transformed*, p. 374.

198 "good to consider": *MAJ*, p. 480.

198 Powell again went: Baker, *The Politics of Diplomacy*, pp. 301–303.

199 "didn't want to do the job": Bush and Scowcroft, *A World Transformed*, p. 381.

199 To Powell's intense irritation: Persico interview.

200 "a force almost as big": General H. Norman Schwarzkopf, *It Doesn't Take a Hero* (New York: Bantam Books, 1992; Bantam paperback, 1993), pp. 426. Citations are from the paperback edition.

200 taken aback: Bush and Scowcroft, *A World Transformed*, p. 431.

200 "the happiest soldier": *MAJ*, p. 389.

201 Powell sat at home: Persico interview.

201 "I am very supportive": General Colin L. Powell, Distinguished Lecture Program, National Defense University, November 30, 1990, Powell papers.

202 "If we go in": Barton Gellman, "Gulf Crisis Nearing 'Moment of Truth,' Cheney Tells Troops," *The Washington Post*, December 22, 1990, p. A11; "Powell Joins in Hawkish Pep Talks," *Los Angeles Times*, December 21, 1990, p. 1.

202 "25 Most Intriguing People": "People in the News," Associated Press, December 24, 1990; *MAJ*, p. 500.

202 "I wish that corporate America": Testimony of Colin L. Powell, House Armed Services Committee hearing, February 7, 1991.

202 he sent his regrets: *MAJ*, p. 500. Participants in the parade and a memorial service held at King's Ebenezer Baptist church in Atlanta condemned the then-week-old war against Iraq and called for an immediate cease-fire (Debra Elliott, "National King Holiday Observance Marked by Persian Gulf Conflict," Associated Press, January 22, 1991).

202 The British were nervous: Persico interview.

203 "I had my own juggling act": *MAJ*, p. 498.

203 "Are you watching CNN?": Smullen interview.

203 one carefully worded paragraph: Brigadier General Dick Chilcoate, memo to Colin L. Powell, November 9, 1993, Powell papers. Chilcoate served as Powell's executive assistant at the Pentagon; the eleven-page memo compiles his recollection of several anecdotes from Powell's chairmanship.

203 "The calm has arrived": Persico interview.

204 the firing of cruise missiles: Ibid.

204 what the American people would see: Powell interview, "Frontline: The Gulf War," PBS; *MAJ*, p. 508.

205 The briefing: Michael Wines, "Briefing by Powell: A Data-filled Showcase," *The New York Times*, January 24, 1991, p. A11; "The War According to the Chairman; Briefing Puts into Focus the First Week of the Showdown," unsigned editorial, *Los Angeles Times*, January 24, 1991, p. B6; Lee Michael Katz, "War Could Propel Powell into Politics," *USA Today*, January 24, 1991, p. 2A.

206 "sanity check": Chilcoate memo.

206 "conveyed a quiet confidence": Bush and Scowcroft, *A World Transformed*, p. 469.

206 had begun to crack: Ibid., p. 477; Persico interview.

207 Bush was in no mood: Persico interview.

207 Powell himself was revolted: Ibid; Schwarzkopf, *It Doesn't Take a Hero*, pp. 342–343.

207 "window of termination": Rick Atkinson, *Crusade: The Untold Story of the Persian Gulf War* (New York: Houghton Mifflin Company, 1993), p. 470.

207 "We're killing literally *thousands*": Baker, *The Politics of Diplomacy*, p. 410.

208 "There was a general consensus": Dick Cheney interview, "Frontline: The Gulf War," PBS.

208 he invited the team upstairs: *MAJ*, pp. 523–524; Bush and Scowcroft, *A World Transformed*, pp. 486–487.

CHAPTER ELEVEN

209   "You show me a general": General L. Colin Powell, Distinguished Lecture Program, National Defense University, November 30, 1990, Powell papers.

209   "It's a great day": Robert D. McFadden, "In a Ticker-Tape Blizzard, New York Honors the Troops," *The New York Times,* June 11, 1991, p. A1.

209   "a living, breathing recruiting poster": Rudy Abramson and John Broder, "Four-Star Power; Colin Powell's Career Has Proceeded with the Certainty of a Laser-guided Missile. How Much Higher Will He Go?" *Los Angeles Times Magazine,* April 7, 1991, p. 18.

210   Exhilarated and sometimes overwhelmed: Persico interview.

210   "If in the end": General Colin L. Powell, speech at Vietnam Veterans Memorial, May 27, 1991, Federal News Service transcript.

211   Cheney vigorously rejected: Cheney interview, "Frontline: The Gulf War," PBS.

211   "We could have gone on": Dick Cheney, speech at the National Press Club, May 20, 1992, Federal News Service transcript.

211   "To occupy Iraq": Bush and Scowcroft, *A World Transformed,* p. 464.

212   "It was a war": Paul Wolfowitz, "Victory Came Too Easily," *The National Interest,* Spring 1994, pp. 87–92.

212   "I kept insisting": Persico interview.

212   "It was not our intention": Colin L. Powell interview, *Good Morning America,* ABC, January 15, 1992, Federal News Service transcript.

213   "Our practical intention": *MAJ,* p. 531.

213   leaving Saddam in power: Persico interview.

213   Woodward . . . had first approached Powell: *MAJ,* p. 420.

214   Powell met twice: Smullen interview; Roth, *Sacred Honor,* pp. 212–213.

214   Smullen . . . warned: Smullen interview.

214   "Hello, Mr. Powell": Chilcoate memo.

215   the portrait he thought: Haynes Johnson, "Book Says Powell Favored Containment; Image of Harmony on Gulf Policy Dispelled," *The Washington Post,* May 2, 1991, p. A1; *MAJ,* p. 535; Persico interview.

215   "cool and smooth": Evan Thomas with John Barry, Thomas M. DeFrank and Douglas Waller, "The Reluctant Warrior," *Newsweek,* May 13, 1991, p. 18.

215   "disarming voice and manner": *MAJ,* p. 420.

215   "Colin, I don't pay attention": Persico interview.

216   "How could we have disagreed": President George H. W. Bush, remarks at a photo opportunity with agriculture leaders, May 2, 1991, White House transcript.

216   Cheney said nothing: Persico interview.

216   "I am taking": President George H. W. Bush, remarks in the Rose Garden, May 23, 1991, White House transcript.

216   a long list of questions: Rowan Scarborough, "Nunn Urges Probe of Leaks to Author of Gulf War Book," *The Washington Times,* October 1, 1991, p. A1.

217   Nunn couldn't care less: Persico interview.

217   most Americans seemed: "California: Powell Plaudits, Quayle Qualms," *The Hotline,* June 18, 1991; Gallup Organization, July 31, 1991, Roper Center at University of Connecticut Public Opinion Online.

217   "a master politician": "The Generals: 'Commanders' Stirs Powell Ponderings," *The Hotline,* June 4, 1991.

217   When the reconfirmation hearing: "Hearing on the Renomination of General Colin L. Powell to Be Chairman of the Joint Chiefs of Staff," Senate Armed Services Committee, September 27, 1991, Federal News Service transcript.

218   Powell angrily threw: Paul Kelly, author interview, October 26, 2005.

218   Nunn and Warner put through a call: Persico interview.

218   Powell spent most of the hearing: "Hearing on the Renomination of General Colin L. Powell to Be Chairman of the Joint Chiefs of Staff," Senate Armed Services Committee, September 30, 1991, Federal News Service transcript.

219   they had little choice: Persico interview.

219   In December 1991: Ibid.; *MAJ,* p. 545.

219   Powell had first bumped into Jordan: Vernon Jordan, author interview, February 27, 2004.

220   "All the white women I work for": Vernon Jordan, *Vernon Can Read!* (New York: Public Affairs, 2001), p. 15.

220   "Colin [was] a Democrat": Jordan interview.

221   "But that didn't mean": Ibid.

221   He was convinced: Persico interview.

221   the party would be grateful: Ibid.

222   "not anything": Susan Watters, "Outside the Storm, Veteran Military Wife Alma Powell Maintains Calm on the Homefront," *Chicago Tribune* (reprinted from *Women's Wear Daily*), February 24, 1991, Tempowoman section, p. 8.

222   "Listen to Governor Clinton": Ann Devroy, "Bush, Clinton Begin Finish Line Sprint," *The Washington Post,* October 30, 1992, p. A1.

223   Scowcroft called: Persico interview.

223   "instructing General Colin Powell": President George H. W. Bush, Address to the Nation, May 1, 1992, White House transcript; Persico interview.

224   he tore it apart: Persico interview.

224   "Of the millions of words spoken": David Broder, "The Military Model," *The Washington Post,* May 13, 1992, p. A23.

224   Powell's only regret: Persico interview.

225   "abortion on demand": Pat Buchanan, speech to the 1992 Republican National Convention, August 17, 1992, www.buchanan.org/pa-92-0817-rnc.html (accessed March 15, 2005).

225   "a Nazi youth rally": Roth, *Sacred Honor,* pp. 227–228.

225   "It hurt like hell": *MAJ,* pp. 560–561; Persico interview.

225   Vernon Jordan had tried again: Jordan interview.

226   "if you really": Persico interview.

226   "Whether or not you want": Tom Clancy, letter to Colin Powell, February 10, 1992, Powell papers. In 1999, Clancy married Alexandra Llewellyn, the daughter of Powell's second cousin, Bruce Llewellyn.

226   Powell began consultations: Persico interview.

227   a message from Bill Clinton: Smullen interview.

227   at least Clinton had spent the war: Persico interview.

227   When they pulled under: Ibid.; Smullen interview.

227   Clinton had arrived in Washington: Michele L. Norris and Ruben Castaneda, "On Georgia Avenue, Cheers, Hugs and Carryout," *The Washington Post,* November 19, 1992, p. A1.

227   The next morning: Reuters, "Americans 'Want the Finger-Pointing and Blame-Placing to Stop,' " transcript of Clinton news conference, *The Washington Post,* November 20, 1992, p. A36.

228 Clinton had discussed: Dick Morris, *Behind the Oval Office* (New York: Random House, 1997), p. 156.

228 Clinton told Stephanopoulos: George Stephanopoulos, *All Too Human* (Boston: Little, Brown and Company, 1999), p. 129.

228 "bigger and more vital-looking": *MAJ*, p. 562.

228 the commander in chief: Persico interview.

229 Clinton asked about Bosnia: Ibid.; *MAJ*, p. 562.

229 "Anytime I find": *MAJ*, p. 563.

229 "Despite our differences": Bill Clinton, *My Life* (New York: Knopf, 2004), p. 450.

229 Powell was in high spirits: Smullen interview.

230 "I'm sorry": Persico interview.

230 Gay and lesbian groups: Clinton, *My Life*, p. 483.

230 "We must conform": "Powell Praises Gay Ban, but Says Clinton Is Boss; Conform or Quit, He Warns Officers," *The Atlanta Constitution*, January 12, 1993, p. 1.

230 "Your reasoning": *MAJ*, p. 547.

231 "weren't there to be persuaded": Stephanopoulos, *All Too Human*, p. 123.

231 "was most vehement": Ibid., p. 124.

231 "I was more than willing": Clinton, *My Life*, p. 483.

232 "consigned himself forever": Cynthia Tucker, editorial page editor of *The Atlanta Constitution*, "Colin Powell, of All People, Is Enforcing Bigotry," *The San Francisco Chronicle*, January 29, 1993, p. A23.

232 "a clash is in the making": Jack W. Germond and Jules Witcover, "Clinton and Powell: Who's in Charge?" *The National Journal*, February 6, 1993, p. 361.

232 "The Rebellious Soldier": Richard Lacayo, "The Rebellious Soldier," *Time*, February 15, 1993, p. 32; Eric Schmidt, "Joint Chiefs' Head Is Said to Request Early Retirement," *The New York Times*, February 9, 1993, p. A1.

232 Powell was miserable: Persico interview.

232 Smullen's home telephone: William Smullen memo to Joseph Persico, March 30, 1994, Powell papers.

233 "I have no intention": Paul Quinn-Judge, "Powell Says He Is Weighing Leaving Early; Denies Move Would Be Signal," *The Boston Globe*, February 11, 1993, p. 3.

233 It was true: Persico interview.

234 When an Air Force general: Joe Klein, "Can Colin Powell Save America?" *Newsweek*, October 10, 1994, p. 20.

234 When hundreds of graduating seniors: Gates, *Thirteen Ways of Looking at a Black Man*, pp. 92–93.

234 Powell found Clinton: Persico interview; *MAJ*, pp. 575–577.

235 "In my days with Reagan and Bush": David Rothkopf, *Running the World: The Inside Story of the National Security Council and the Architects of American Power* (New York: Public Affairs, 2005), p. 322.

235 "Part of the problem": Ibid.

235 "As soon as they tell me": Michael R. Gordon, "Powell Delivers a Resounding No on Using Limited Force in Bosnia," *The New York Times*, September 28, 1992, p. A1.

235 "a clear political objective": *MAJ*, p. 576.

235 "He replied consistent": Madeleine Albright, *Madam Secretary* (New York: Miramax Books, 2003), pp. 181–182.

236 "He regarded the new team": John F. Harris, *The Survivor: Bill Clinton in the White House* (New York: Random House, 2005), p. 49.

236 "I believe in the bully's way": Gates, *Thirteen Ways of Looking at a Black Man*, pp. 91–92.
237 Albright added: Albright, *Madam Secretary*, p. 144.
237 using combat troops: Patrick J. Sloyan, "Somalia Mission Control; Clinton Called the Shots in Failed Policy Targeting Aidid," *Newsday*, December 5, 1993, p. 7; Persico interview.
237 "Despite increased military pressure": Albright, *Madam Secretary*, p. 144.
238 He kept asking: John Diamond, "Senate Report Criticizes Powell's Staff on Somalia Raid," Associated Press, October 1, 1995.
238–39 "If I had to do it again": Joe Klein, "Closework," *The New Yorker*, October 1, 2001, p. 44. In his 2004 autobiography, *My Life*, Clinton wrote that he agreed "just a few days before he retired" to Powell's recommendation that Special Forces be sent to undertake a "parallel effort" to track down Aidid. In fact, the United States had strongly supported a U.N. resolution, passed the day after the June 5 deaths of twenty-four Pakistani peacekeepers, that urged apprehension of the perpetrators and called on member states to add additional resources to the U.N. force in Somalia. But Aspin, on Powell's recommendation, initially turned down appeals from both the commander of U.N. forces in Somalia and the commander of the American contingent beneath the U.N. umbrella to send the specialized troops, and did not agree to the request until after four American soldiers were killed on August 8. With approval from Aspin and Powell, Clinton signed the order authorizing the deployment on August 22, and they arrived in Somalia on August 26. Powell retired on September 30. It may be that Clinton confused Powell's recommendation to approve Montgomery's request for armor, made five days before his resignation and twice rejected by Aspin, with the recommendation six weeks earlier to send the Rangers.
239 the president wanted to see him: *MAJ*, pp. 587–588; Persico interview.

CHAPTER TWELVE

240 "I have not": Colin L. Powell, interview with Barbara Walters, *20/20*, September 15, 1995.
240 "feeling in his heart": Bill Clinton, "Remarks at Retirement Ceremony for Gen. Colin L. Powell," September 30, 1993, Federal News Service transcript.
240 The president presented him: Persico interview; Powell interview.
241 "my home … my life": Colin L. Powell, retirement speech, September 30, 1993, Federal News Service transcript.
241 Alma was hoping: Alma Powell, author interview, February 24, 2005.
242 The two men rarely disagreed: Powell interview.
242 "The President calling someone": Gates, *Thirteen Ways of Looking at a Black Man*, p. 80.
242 "I have often wondered": *MAJ*, p. 560.
243 On their last full day: Ibid., p. 568.
243 "I mean, here's Cheney": Armitage interview.
243 "I had developed": *MAJ*, p. 568.
243 Alma eventually gave up: Alma Powell interview.
244 Now Carter was convinced: Robert A. Pastor, author interview, December 2, 2003. Pastor, then the Latin America expert at the Carter Center in Atlanta, participated in the planning, accompanied Carter, Nunn and Powell on the September 17–18, 1994, Haiti trip and was present during all delegation meet-

ings. Unless otherwise indicated, this account is drawn from his detailed notes and recollections.

245 their negotiating brief: *MAJ*, p. 598.

245 The first American paratroopers: House of Representatives Subcommittee on Commerce, Justice, State, Judiciary and Related Agencies, Hearing on Department of State Budget, March 3, 2004, Federal News Service transcripts.

245 Powell kept his eye: *MAJ*, p. 598.

247 "there is no honor": Ibid., p. 600.

248 Powell was astounded: Persico interview.

249 White House aides spun: Harris, *The Survivor*, p. 141.

250 "you've got to stop that": Armitage interview.

250 a nationwide survey: Wirthlin Group survey, November 9, 1994.

250 "Don't you feel": Persico interview.

251 "Nothing is inevitable": Ibid.

251 "decision loop": Ibid.

252 Alma didn't want to hear: Ibid.

252 Proposals poured in: Powell papers.

252 A letter he drafted: Ibid.

253 reawakened Clinton's interest: Stephanopoulos, *All Too Human*; Morris, *Behind the Oval Office*. Both books make several references to Clinton's paranoia regarding Powell.

253 Clinton called Vernon Jordan: Jordan interview.

253 Clinton … called Powell at home: *MAJ*, pp. 602–603.

254 Dole would sometimes: Powell interview.

254 Rudman, had broached the subject: Bob Woodward, *The Choice* (New York: Simon & Schuster, 1996; Touchstone paperback, 2006), p. 43. Citations are from the Touchstone edition.

254 "The American people": Steve Luttner, "Powell Touts Less Government, Talks Taxes," *The Plain Dealer*, November 16, 1994, p. 15A.

254 "no real passion": Robert Shogan, "Powell Carefully Shines His Political Star," *Los Angeles Times*, February 1, 1995, p. 1.

255 "zigging and zagging": John F. Stacks, "The Powell Factor," *Time*, July 10, 1995, cover story; Sam Howe Verhovek, "Powell Deftly Deflecting Questions on Presidency," *The New York Times*, February 1, 1995, p. 12.

255 "One of the saddest figures": Stacks, "The Powell Factor."

255 At … Lorton Prison: Shogan, "Powell Carefully Shines His Political Star."

256 "How did I deal": Ibid.

256 "He gives a great speech": Gates, *Thirteen Ways of Looking at a Black Man*, p. 84.

256 Black voters were less enamored: Richard Benedetto, "Whites, More than Blacks, Back a Powell Candidacy," *USA Today*, October 10, 1995, p. 1A.

256 "Not only would I support him": Gates, *Thirteen Ways of Looking at a Black Man*, pp. 95–97.

256 "I had to force myself": Ibid.

256–57 "He's a phantom candidate": Ibid., p. 75.

257 didn't even seem *black*: Ibid., pp. 82–83.

257 "We should sacrifice": John Walcott, "The Man to Watch," *U.S. News & World Report*, August 21, 1995, cover story.

258 No politician matched: Thomas B. Edsall, "For Powell, Timing Could Be Crucial," *The Washington Post*, April 6, 1995, p. A1.

258 "an empty ideological vessel": Stacks, "The Powell Factor."

258 "a major barf": Woodward, "The Powell Predicament."

258 "modern media excess": Howard Kurtz, "Pressing for Powell: A General Trend; News Media Embrace Would-be Candidate in a Gush of Boosterism," *The Washington Post,* September 13, 1995, p. A1.

258 "new world order": William F. Jasper, "Like Ike," *The New American,* March 20, 1995, p. 21.

258 "a careful look": Michael R. Gordon and Bernard E. Trainor, "Beltway Warrior," *The New York Times Magazine,* August 27, 1995, p. 40.

258 "Powell often disagreed": Charles Lane, "The Legend of Colin Powell," *The New Republic,* April 17, 1995, p. 20.

258 although Glen himself: Thomas B. Glen, Jr., letter to Colin Powell, October 9, 2000, Powell papers. In the letter, Glen apologized for not having contacted Powell sooner. When news stories about his Vietnam letter first appeared in 1995, Glen wrote, he was contacted by both print and television journalists in his hometown of Centerville, Indiana. It was obvious they had been looking for criticism of Powell, he wrote, and were unsatisfied when Glen did not provide it. Instead, he had praised Powell and said Powell's 1968 actions were appropriate to the circumstances. He had been disturbed when none of his comments were published or broadcast, Glen wrote, particularly since he was now a journalist himself—the owner of a weekly newspaper in his small Indiana town. A draftee during Vietnam, Glen wrote that after his wartime service he had enlisted and served in the Regular Army for twenty years, and had then become a reservist. "I have admired your career as a soldier," he concluded the letter to Powell, "particularly as my son served as a Bradley crewman during Desert Storm."

259 crossed the military-civilian line: Richard H. Kohn, "The Crisis in Civil-Military Relations," *The National Interest,* Spring 1994, p. 3.

259 "I don't want any part": Powell interview.

260 "everybody loves Colin Powell": Alma Powell interview.

260 never accept a black president: Berns interview; Llewellyn interview.

260 "too good": Annemarie Powell interview; Linda Powell interview.

260 Persico was disturbed: Persico interview.

261 Cifrino's telephone startled her: Peggy Cifrino, author interview, June 14, 2005.

261 "it was the first time": Alma Powell interview.

262 Fidel Castro wrote Powell: Fidel Castro, letter to Colin L. Powell, November 11, 1995, Powell papers. Writing in tiny script on a piece of notepaper engraved with his name and title, Castro closed by saying "Now that you are a free man, I hope nothing will hinder you from coming one day to Cuba to get acquainted with our country."

262 "Do you believe this?": Smullen interview.

CHAPTER THIRTEEN

263 "This guy would make": Texas Governor George W. Bush, speaking of Colin Powell at a San Antonio news conference inaugurating a statewide volunteerism and community service campaign, September 24, 1997.

263 "55 percent Republican": Powell interview.

263 "Once these kids": Gates, *Thirteen Ways of Looking at a Black Man,* p. 98.

264 "a liberal sort of guy": Ibid.

264 "if she chooses to abort": Colin L. Powell, interview with Barbara Walters, *20/20.*

264 "The Christian Coalition": Colin L. Powell, interview with David Frost, "Talking with David Frost," PBS, September 29, 1995.

265 "Why do you think": Persico interview.

265 neither whites nor blacks: In a nationwide Gallup Poll of blacks and whites in mid-October 1995, 28 percent felt Jackson was "the most important national leader in the black community today." Respondents gave Farrakhan 12 percent and Powell 9 percent.

265 "To some extent": Colin L. Powell, interview with Laura B. Randolph, "Why Almost Everybody Loves Colin Powell," *Ebony,* November 1995, p. 100.

266 "ethnic cleansing": Ibid.

266 "There is nobody": Jordan interview.

268 "fight to the death": William F. Buckley, Jr., "The Role of the State: Powell Not Right Man for Today's Fight to the Death," *The Lakeland Ledger,* November 7, 1995.

268 "Everybody who was hard right": Newt Gingrich, author interview, January 8, 2004.

269 Alma was on medication: Eleanor Clift, "Why the General's Wife Is a Reluctant Warrior," *Newsweek,* November 6, 1995, p. 39.

269 "the last gasp": Paul Taylor and Dan Balz, "Conservatives Fire Away at Powell's Possible Bid," *The Washington Post,* November 3, 1995, p. A18; Ralph Z. Hallow, "GOP Disaster Seen in Powell Run: Conservative Leaders Urge Party to Reject General," *The Washington Times,* November 3, 1995, p. A1.

270 "You're wrong!": Stephanopoulos, *All Too Human,* pp. 389–390.

270 "He'll take away blacks": Morris, *Behind the Oval Office,* p. 155.

270 he drafted a speech: Persico interview.

271 a windshield wiper: Powell interview.

271 "I saw him go": Smullen interview.

271 "I think your absolute strengths": Harlan Ullman, letter to Colin L. Powell, October 24, 1995.

272 "Don't do it!": Armitage interview.

272 "a tough person": Ibid.

272 both knew she would acquiesce: Powell interview; Alma Powell interview.

272 Colin still vividly remembered: Powell interview.

273 "pushed by events": Ibid.

273 "People would turn out": Colin L. Powell, quoted by Francis X. Clines, "Powell Rules Out '96 Race," *The New York Times,* November 9, 1995, p. 1A.

273 some of the best advice: Powell interview.

273 he would not run: Powell interview; Persico interview.

274 He left the hall: Powell interview; Armitage interview.

274 Smullen started calling reporters: Smullen interview.

275 He was honored and grateful: Colin L. Powell, news conference, November 8, 1995, Federal News Service transcript.

276 "spinning in the ground": Berns interview.

276 Bruce Llewellyn wondered: Llewellyn interview.

276 "I don't know": Powell interview.

276 "You've got the freedom": Armitage interview.

276 "like being cured of cancer": Annemarie Powell interview.

276 "It's because of his sense of duty": Stephanopoulos, *All Too Human*, p. 403.

277 Vernon Jordan had boarded: Jordan interview.

277 "the whole campaign thing": Powell interview.

277 "It would be an honor": Senator Strom Thurmond, letter to Colin Powell, August 5, 1996, and Powell reply, Powell papers.

278 "To no surprise": Newt Gingrich, letter to Colin Powell, June 19, 1996, and Powell reply, ibid.

278 "As you know": Max Cleland, letter to Colin Powell, July 15, 1996, ibid.

278 he asked Armitage: Armitage interview.

278 "I felt an obligation": Powell interview.

278 Dole thought it might: Woodward, *The Choice*, p. 347.

278 "verify if Sen. Warner": Colin Powell, memo to Peggy Cifrino, with response, Powell papers.

279 "all senior Republicans": Haley Barbour, Scott Reed and Paul Manafort, letter to Colin Powell, July 22, 1996, ibid.

279 "If they wanted me": Persico interview.

280 "General Powell's presentation": RNC planning document, July 5, 1996, Powell papers.

280 The convention choreography: Ibid.

280 "working closely with you": Haley Barbour letter to Colin Powell, July 29, 1996, Powell papers.

281 Ward Connolly ... had threatened: Powell interview.

281 "I come before you this evening": Colin L. Powell, speech to the 1996 Republican National Convention, August 12, 1996.

281 "I became a Republican": Ibid.

281 Powell glanced down: Powell interview.

281 "I was applauded wildly": Ibid.

282 "I can talk to a group": Colin L. Powell, interview with Charles Gibson, *Good Morning America*, ABC, August 13, 1996.

282 "represent the views": Colin L. Powell, interview with Katie Couric, *Today*, NBC, August 13, 1996.

282 "I couldn't escape the feeling": Colin L. Powell with Joseph E. Persico, *My American Journey* (New York: Random House, 1995; Ballantine, 1996), p. 600. Citation is from the paperback edition.

282 He could not imagine: Powell interview.

283 "We're not against preferences": "Colin Powell on Race," *The Weekly Standard*, December 1, 1997.

283 "Destroying a piece of cloth": Colin L. Powell, letter to Senator Patrick Leahy, May 18, 1999, Powell papers.

283–84 "We've heard the call": Thaddeus Herrick, "Powell Helps Bush Launch Texas-wide Campaign for Volunteers to Help Youths," *The Houston Chronicle*, September 24, 1997, p. A36.

CHAPTER FOURTEEN

285 "Dear General": George Kennan, letter to Colin Powell, January 17, 2001, Powell papers.

285 he and Alma found themselves: Powell interview.

285 Back in Austin: Mann, *Rise of the Vulcans*, p. 249.

286 Armitage initially hesitated: Armitage interview.

286 "still getting his sea legs": Powell interview.

286 Perle and Powell: Richard Perle, "The 'Journey' of a True Hero Who Never Lost His Compass," *The Washington Times,* October 15, 1995, p. B8.

287 Zakheim had defended: Dov S. Zakheim, "Comments on Lawrence J. Korb's 'U.S. National Defense Policy in the Post–Cold War World,' " *America's Peace Dividend,* ed. Ann Markusen, Council on Foreign Relations, www.ciaonet.org/book/markusen/zakheim.html (accessed July 20, 2004).

287 Powell had turned him down: Colin L. Powell, memo to Robert Blackwill, February 11, 1987, Powell papers.

287 The Vulcans' reluctance: The account of the formation and deliberations of the "Vulcans" and of their relationship with Powell is drawn from interviews with several former Vulcans who later became senior Bush administration officials.

287 "central to its politics": Mann, *Rise of the Vulcans,* p. 254.

288 "I think that the Republican Party": Colin L. Powell, interview on *Larry King Live,* CNN, December 21, 1999.

288 Since his retirement: Powell interview.

288 His income from speaking engagements: Steven Mufson, "Speech Fees Help Powell Build Wealth; Cabinet Nominee Worth at Least $27.3 Million," *The Washington Post,* January 17, 2001, p. A1.

289 "No question that a man": Ceci Connolly, "Bush, Gore Clinch Nominations," *The Washington Post,* March 15, 2000, p. A6.

289 several purposes in mind: Michael Kranish, "In Revamped Campaign, Bush Choreographs His D.C. Day. Appearances Aim to Show He Can Deal with Foreign Leaders and Democrats," *The Boston Globe,* April 27, 2000, p. A8.

289 "for the candid discussion": George W. Bush, letter to Colin Powell, April 26, 2000, and Powell reply, April 29, 2000, Powell papers.

289 Powell had also met: Colin L. Powell e-mail to Peggy Cifrino, Powell papers.

290 two working papers: Hadley's outline of a "Potential Nuclear Initiative," dated April 26, 2000, and Rice's speech draft, dated May 2, 2000, were faxed to Powell on May 9, 2000. Powell papers.

291 "I support the governor": George W. Bush, press conference at the National Press Club, May 23, 2000, Federal News Service transcript.

291 "He essentially said": Powell interview.

291 "an added visual political payoff": Glen Johnson, "In Blatant and Subtle Ways, Bush Appeals for Minority Support," Associated Press State and Local Wire, May 26, 2000.

291 "to showcase": Peggy Fikac, "Volunteer Talk Turns Political," *San Antonio Express-News,* May 26, 2000, p. 9A.

291 "I am not a candidate": Ken Herman, "Powell: No. 2 Job? Thanks, but No Thanks," *Austin American-Statesman,* May 26, 2000, p. A11.

292 "hot air at best": Myron Magnet, "What Is Compassionate Conservatism?" *The Wall Street Journal,* February 5, 1999.

293 "to get really serious": Wilkerson interview.

293 "To me": Colin L. Powell, remarks at the Republican National Convention, July 31, 2000, Federal News Service transcript.

294 "like that scene": David Frum, interview on *The NewsHour,* PBS, July 31, 2000.

294 "an important message": Thomas B. Edsall, "Bush Plays Down Split with Powell; Affirmative Action Stances Show Divide," *The Washington Post,* August 2, 2000, p. A20.

294 "Your speech": Donald Rumsfeld, letter to Colin Powell, August 1, 2000, Powell papers.

295 "tell us the names": Dave Boyer, "Bush Speculates About His Cabinet," *The Washington Times,* October 21, 2000, p. A4.

295 "If you're George Bush": Gingrich interview.

295 "the modesty of true strength": George W. Bush, "A Distinctly American Internationalism," speech at the Ronald Reagan Presidential Library, November 19, 1999, Federal News Service transcript.

295 "Our military is meant": George W. Bush, presidential debate, October 11, 2000, Federal News Service transcript.

295 "scared to death": Armitage interview.

296 "national security matters": Mike Allen, "With Eye on Transition, Bush Confers with Powell," *The Washington Post,* December 1, 2000, p. A26.

296 "It just sort of happened": Powell interview.

296 "conduct our foreign policy": George W. Bush, announcement of Colin L. Powell's nomination for secretary of state, December 16, 2000, Federal News Service transcript.

297 "because I so admire": Dana Milbank and Mike Allen, "Powell Is Named Secretary of State," *The Washington Post,* December 17, 2000, p. A1.

297 "we have been through": Announcement of Colin L. Powell's nomination, Federal News Service transcript.

297 "Powell seemed to dominate": Milbank and Allen, "Powell Is Named Secretary of State."

297 "Some political observers wonder": Andrew Miga, "Powell Gets Nod as Secretary of State," *The Boston Herald,* December 17, 2000, p. 1.

298 "I sure hope Colin Powell": Thomas L. Friedman, "The Powell Perplex," *The New York Times,* December 19, 2000, p. A31.

298 "At the time": Smullen interview.

298 Bush ... saw no reason: The account in these paragraphs of thinking inside the Bush campaign is drawn from author interviews with senior Bush administration officials.

299 expertise ranked far below: Armitage interview.

299 As far as she was concerned: Administration official, author interview.

299 "I thought": Gingrich interview.

299 Cheney's memories: Matthew Rees, "The Long Arm of Colin Powell: Will the Next Secretary of State Also Run the Pentagon?" *The Weekly Standard,* December 25, 2000.

300 "centrists" in the new administration: Bill Gertz and Rowan Scarborough, "Inside the Ring," *The Washington Times,* January 5, 2001.

300 seemed like a different generation: Powell interview.

300 " 'Hey, wait a minute' ": Ibid.

301 "ideologically in gear": Ibid.

301 "Remember what he was saying?": Ibid.

302 "I was sure I was": Ibid.

302 Powell had paid a visit: Ibid.

302 Successive budget cuts: "Secretary Colin Powell's State Department: An Independent Assessment," Foreign Affairs Council Task Force Report, March 2003.

303 "You'll be very welcome": Powell interview.

303 On a Sunday evening: Marc Grossman, author interview, February 5, 2004.

304 Grossman was momentarily speechless: Ibid.

304 Powell asked Wilkerson to research: Wilkerson interview.

304 room to maneuver: Ibid.

304 "We are attached": "Confirmation Hearing of General Colin L. Powell to be Secretary of State," Senate Committee on Foreign Relations, January 17, 2001, Federal News Service transcript.

306 the day after: Smullen interview.

307 "I am not coming in": Colin L. Powell, "Secretary Powell Greets State Department Employees, January 22, 2001," and "Town Hall Meeting," January 25, 2001, Federal News Service transcripts.

307 "This guy": Grossman interview.

307 "I've never really met": Former senior State Department official, author interview.

308 "Our instructions were to talk": Former State Department official, author interview.

308 "No surprises": Richard Boucher, author interview, July 7, 2005.

308 "sitting at my desk": Edward S. Walker, Jr., author interview, December 23, 2003.

309 "Top up my database": State Department officials, author interviews.

309 "Here was a guy": State Department official, author interview.

CHAPTER FIFTEEN

310 "I've had tough days": Colin L. Powell, interview with Armstrong Williams, TV One, August 4, 2004, State Department transcript.

310 Kofi Annan anxiously awaited: The description of Powell's February 14 trip to the United Nations is drawn from author interviews with senior U.N. officials.

310 "an opportunity": Mike Allen, "Bush's Gaffes Are Back as Debates Near," *The Washington Post*, October 1, 2000, p. A8.

311 "I am extremely happy": Colin L. Powell and Kofi Annan, press conference, United Nations, February 14, 2001, State Department transcript.

312 The Bush administration wanted: U.N. officials, author interviews.

312 He had invited Condoleezza Rice: Powell interview.

312 had revealed: Walker interview.

314 "I believe the big": George W. Bush, interview with Maureen Dowd, "Freudian Face-Off," *The New York Times*, June 16, 1999, p. A29.

314 "Condi Rice will run these meetings": Suskind, *The Price of Loyalty*, p. 70.

315 As the senior Cabinet official: Discussion of the Bush administration's initial NSC meetings is drawn from interviews with Powell and with several other participants.

315 "We have a regime change policy": Administration official, author interview.

315 "from a list": Suskind, *The Price of Loyalty*, p. 74.

315 "nobody liked the sanctions": Powell interview.

315 "Why are we even bothering?": Walker interview.

316 The United States hadn't lost: Suskind, *The Price of Loyalty*, p. 73.

316 Powell thought the no-fly program: Powell interview.

316 When Tenet's turn came: Suskind, *The Price of Loyalty*, p. 73.

316 All three branches: Administration official, author interview.

316 very businesslike: Walker interview.

317 a new set of "response options": Bob Woodward, *Plan of Attack* (New York: Simon & Schuster, 2004), pp. 10–11.

317   it was clear to several: Walker interview; Suskind, *The Price of Loyalty*, p. 74.

317   "Why are we bombing Baghdad?": The discussion of Iraq bombing during Bush's trip to Mexico is drawn from author interviews with several administration officials present.

318   "The commanders on the ground": President George W. Bush and President Vicente Fox, joint press conference, February 16, 2001, White House transcript.

318   Rice used the word "routine": Mike Allen, "Bush on Stage: Deft or Just Lacking Depth?" *The Washington Post*, February 19, 2001, p. A8.

319   "I say all of this": Kennan, letter to Powell.

320   he admired Powell's: Administration official, author interview.

320   "take a good look": Powell interview.

320   Bolton handed Powell two articles: Administration official, author interview.

321   "The book I had gotten": Powell interview.

321   "understand that I don't have": Boucher interview.

321   "signaled that after eight years": Jane Perlez, "Powell Goes on the Road and Scores Some Points," *The New York Times*, March 2, 2001, p. A6.

322   "the damage done": Robert Kagan and William Kristol, "Clinton's Foreign Policy (cont.)," *The Weekly Standard*, March 12, 2001, p. 11.

322   "unfortunate reversal": Jim Hoagland, "Where PR Won't Cut It," *The Washington Post*, March 1, 2001, p. A19.

322   The divergent media assessments: Among the many analyses of differing currents of foreign policy thought in the George W. Bush administration, see Rothkopf, *Running the World;* Mann, *Rise of the Vulcans;* David Frum and Richard Perle, *An End to Evil* (New York: Random House, 2003); Paul Wolfowitz, "Remembering the Future," *The National Interest*, Spring 2000; Charles Krauthammer, "The Neoconservative Convergence," *Commentary*, July–August 2005; Irving Kristol, "The Neoconservative Persuasion," *The Weekly Standard*, August 25, 2003; Michael Lind, "A Tragedy of Errors," *The Nation*, February 23, 2004; Ivo H. Daalder and James M. Lindsay, *America Unbound: The Bush Revolution in Foreign Policy* (Washington, D.C.: Brookings Institution, 2003).

322   "core tension": Rothkopf, *Running the World*, pp. 396–397.

323   "just not his intellectual style": Former administration official, author interview.

324   Pritchard wondered: Charles Pritchard, author interview, December 13, 2004.

324   "That kind of got": Powell interview.

324   "We do plan to engage": Colin L. Powell, press appearance with Swedish Foreign Minister Anna Lindh, March 6, 2001, State Department transcript.

324   "We've got a problem": Administration official, author interview.

324   "the fatal word": Powell interview.

325   "Satan's finger on Earth": Former administration official, author interview.

325   "He knew": Administration official, author interview.

325   "forcefully made the point": Colin L. Powell remarks on meeting between President Bush and South Korean President Kim Dae Jung, March 7, 2001, Federal News Service transcript.

325   Bush told reporters: Remarks by President Bush and President Kim Dae Jung of South Korea, March 7, 2001, White House transcript.

325   it was a power play: Wilkerson interview.

325   "He's not easily stunned": Smullen interview.

326   "That was why": State Department official, author interview.

326   "Yeah, and I delivered": William Douglas, "Powell Acknowledges Some Miscues," *Newsday*, May 5, 2001, p. A7.

327 "continue to recognize": Suskind, *The Price of Loyalty,* p. 113.

327 "We're going to have to do": The account of Powell's objections to the Kyoto Protocol letter is drawn from author interviews with Powell and other administration officials.

328 She had passed Cheney: Christine Todd Whitman, *It's My Party Too: The Battle for the Heart of the GOP and the Future of America* (New York: Penguin Group, 2005), p. 176.

328 "They all got together": Powell interview.

328 "this crystalline superstructure": Administration official, author interview.

329 "I blurted out the truth": Powell interview.

329 The administration was under pressure: Daalder and Lindsay, *America Unbound,* p. 68.

330 "to be cool": Armitage interview.

330 "We were balancing": Administration official, author interview.

330 An early missive... Powell instructed Prueher: Johanna McGeary, "Safe Landing: A Carefully Engineered Game Plan Helped Bush Bring the U.S. Flight Crew Home," *Time,* April 23, 2001, p. 38.

330 "sincere regret": "U.S. Ambassador's Letter to China's Foreign Minister," *The Washington Post,* April 12, 2001, p. A25.

330 The English-language version: "Resolving Crisis Was a Matter of Interpretation," John Pomfret, *The Washington Post,* April 12, 2001, p. A1.

331 a "humiliating" U.S. apology: Robert Kagan and William Kristol, "We Lost," *The Washington Post,* April 13, 2001, p. A23.

331 "We could have done anything": Armitage interview.

331 "Well, Don, Colin said, 'Sorry' ": Administration official, author interview.

331 "we were feeling pretty lusty": Armitage interview.

331 Europe reacted with amazement: European headlines quoted in Roger Cohen, "America the Roughneck (Through Europe's Eyes)," *The New York Times,* May 7, 2001, p. A10; Bert Roughton, Jr., "On Bush: Europeans Not Hiding Their Dislike of President," *The Atlanta Journal-Constitution,* April 22, 2001, p. 1G.

332 Armitage thought simple jealousy: Armitage interview.

332 he regarded as a lightweight: Bob Woodward, *Bush at War* (New York: Simon & Schuster, 2002), p. 22.

333 he privately thought: Powell interview.

333 "bereft of ideas": David Frum and Richard Perle, *An End to Evil,* pp. 6, 221.

333 One powerful conservative official: Administration official, author interview.

333 "said everything": *MAJ,* p. 225.

334 He found the president: Powell interview.

334 their relationship remained: Administration officials, author interviews.

334 "incredibly quick and focused": State Department official, author interview.

335 exercises in frustration: Armitage interview.

335 "the real business": State Department official, author interview.

335 "just another way": Armitage interview.

335 He was playing: Powell interview.

335 "facing a steeper learning curve": Barbara Slavin and Bill Nichols, "Powell Finds Steep Learning Curve in New Job," *USA Today,* July 19, 2001, p. 8A.

335 "on a short leash": Acel Moore, "Is Powell the Invisible Man in the Bush Administration?" *The Philadelphia Inquirer,* September 11, 2001, p. A23.

335 "it is hard to think": Morton Abramowitz, "So Quiet at the Top," *The Washington Post,* September 11, 2001, p. A27.

335   Karl Rove was said: Woodward, *Bush at War*, p. 14.

336   "wasn't thinking about quitting": Boucher interview.

336   His protective senior staff: State Department officials, author interviews.

336   "I've been struck": Johanna McGeary, "Odd Man Out," *Time*, September 10, 2001.

336   a fairly accurate prognostication: Smullen interview.

336–337 *Time* had eviscerated Rumsfeld: Michael Duffy, "Rumsfeld: Older but Wiser? The Infighter Who Tried to Change the Pentagon Has Failed So Far. Here's Why," *Time*, August 27, 2001, p. 22.

337   "He had had so many years": Wilkerson interview.

337   "The fact of the matter is": Powell interview.

337   "You know, I've been around": State Department officials, author interviews.

CHAPTER SIXTEEN

338   "We're Americans": "Secretary of State On-the-Record Briefing," September 12, 2001, State Department transcript.

338   a possible Bush-Arafat meeting: Janine Zacharia, "Bush-Arafat Meeting Likely This Month," *The Jerusalem Post*, September 9, 2001, p. 1; Jane Perlez, "Bush Might Meet Arafat If Truce Talks Yield Results," *The New York Times*, September 9, 2001, p. 13.

338   At 7:45 a.m.: The account of Powell's breakfast with President Toledo on September 11 is drawn from Powell and Boucher interviews and Roberto Dañino, author interview, February 11, 2004.

340   "A terrible, terrible tragedy": Colin L. Powell, "Statement at the Special General Assembly of the Organization of American States," September 11, 2001, State Department transcript.

341   "He knew from the start": Boucher interview.

341   Alma was about to leave: Alma Powell interview.

341   Annemarie also had: Annemarie and Linda Powell interviews.

342   Richard Clarke sat: Richard A. Clarke, *Against All Enemies: Inside America's War on Terror* (New York: Simon & Schuster, 2004), chap. 1.

343   "Rich, has your building": Ibid.

343   Aboard the secretary of state's plane: Boucher interview.

343   His information was spotty: Colin L. Powell, "Press Briefing on Board Plane en Route Washington D.C.," September 11, 2001, State Department transcript.

343   Powell spent most of the flight alone: Powell interview.

344   "You've got to understand": Boucher interview.

344   they flew up the Potomac: Ibid.

344   al-Qaeda was planning: Clarke, *Against All Enemies*, p. 227.

345   Armitage, representing the State Department: Woodward, *Bush at War*, p. 35.

345   Wolfowitz, in the Pentagon's chair: Clarke, *Against All Enemies*, p. 232.

345   Powell and Armitage would chuckle: Powell interview.

345   "The idea was never": Administration official, author interview.

345   There was no evidence: Clarke, *Against All Enemies*, p. 232.

345   actions Powell could take: "Testimony of Colin L. Powell, Hearing of the National Commission on Terrorist Attacks upon the United States," March 23, 2004, Federal News Service transcript.

346   With little discussion: *Final Report of the National Commission on Terrorist Attacks upon the United States*, July 22, 2004, www.911commission.gov/ (accessed October 27, 2004), p. 213.

347 "our way of life": President's address to the nation, September 11, 2001, White House transcript.

347 Rumsfeld . . . had brought: Clarke, *Against All Enemies,* pp. 23–24; Woodward, *Bush at War,* pp. 32–33.

347 Colin had been unable: Alma Powell interview; Powell interview.

347 For Alma, the Pentagon attack: Alma Powell interview.

348 "a monumental struggle": "Remarks by the President," September 12, 2001, White House transcript.

348 Concerned that Bush would lose: Woodward, *Bush at War,* p. 65.

348 Rumsfeld returned: Ibid., pp. 48–49.

348 After one meeting: Clarke, *Against All Enemies,* p. 32.

349 The neoconservatives in particular: Powell interview.

349 It would be bad policy: Ibid.

349 "snapping Legos together": Ibid.

349 Powell and Armitage decided: Ibid.; Armitage interview.

350 "We didn't show that list": Powell interview.

350 "As one general to another": Woodward, *Bush at War,* p. 59.

350 "no-shit conversation": Richard Armitage, interview with Edward Stourton, BBC Radio, April 10, 2002.

350 Bush had already been up: Press Briefing, September 15, 2001, White House transcript.

351 Bush had already made: Woodward, *Bush at War,* p. 73.

351 Powell reported: Details of the September 15 Camp David meeting are drawn from Woodward, *Bush at War,* chap. 6; Suskind, *The Price of Loyalty,* pp. 186–191; Bob Woodward and Dan Balz, "At Camp David, Advise and Dissent; Bush, Aides Grapple with War Plan," *The Washington Post,* January 31, 2002, p. A1.

352 a 10 to 50 percent chance: Woodward, *Bush at War,* p. 83.

352 Powell spoke first: Ibid., pp. 86–88.

352 Powell thought that Wolfowitz: Woodward and Balz, "At Camp David, Advise and Dissent."

353 Paul O'Neill sat by himself: Suskind, *The Price of Loyalty,* pp. 190–191.

354 "hit the reset button": Bill Keller, "The World According to Powell," *The New York Times Magazine,* November 25, 2001, p. 61.

354 "Most Americans were vulnerable": Boucher interview.

354 The Saudi Arabian leader: Saudi government official, author interview, November 9, 2001.

355 Powell privately questioned: State Department official, author interview.

355 "pure litmus test": Powell interview.

355 "the soul mates": Ibid.

355 On the Middle East: Ibid.

355 It simply wasn't possible: Ibid.

356 "Sharon good, Arafat bad": Ibid.

356 "JINSA crowd": Ibid.

357 "There were a lot of caricatures": State Department official, author interview.

357 "a price to be paid": "President Bush Speaks to the United Nations," November 10, 2001, White House transcript.

357 there were none of the customary: Karen DeYoung, "Bush Urges Coalition to Fulfill Its 'Duties,' " *The Washington Post,* November 11, 2001, p. A1.

358 "whether it might be misread": Administration official, author interview.

358 the Israelis "start[ed] bitching": Powell interview.

358 the president "just wonders": Ibid.
358 "bound forever together": Colin L. Powell, speech at the University of Louisville, November 19, 2001, State Department transcript.
359 After such a lengthy: Powell interview.
359 "Our objective is to convince": "President Discusses War, Humanitarian Efforts," November 19, 2001, White House transcript.
359 "very complimentary": Powell interview.
359 "If Cheney had had his way": State Department official, author interview.
360 had not endeared him: Tom Clancy with General Anthony C. Zinni and Tony Koltz, *Battle Ready* (New York: G. P. Putnam's Sons, 2004), p. 373.
360 Two days after Powell's speech: The account of Zinni's initial trip to Washington and visit to the White House is drawn from author interview with Anthony C. Zinni, December 7, 2003; Powell interview; and author interviews with administration officials.
361 "We're going to go forward": Powell interview.
362 Putin's emotionless, ice-blue stare: Ibid.

CHAPTER SEVENTEEN

364 "Ultimately, a Secretary of State": Henry A. Kissinger, "Condoleezza Rice: A New Panache in Foreign Affairs," *Time*, April 18, 2005, p. 52.
364 more than 80 percent: Polls commissioned in December 2001 by several major news organizations, including CNN, *Time*, ABC News, *The Washington Post*, the Harris Poll, the Gallup Poll, *USA Today* and Fox News, recorded a job approval rating of over 80 percent for President Bush. Results available at www .realclearpolitics.com/NEW POLLS/polls-GWB_JA.html (accessed December 13, 2005).
364 significant progress: Colin L. Powell, "Statement on President Bush's Budget Request for FY 2003," February 5, 2002, State Department transcript.
365 a particularly satisfying trip: Powell interview.
365 Powell received a disturbing call: Ibid.; William H. Taft IV, author interview, October 13, 2005.
365 "You'd better hold on": Powell interview.
365 On Saturday, November 10: Tim Golden, "After Terror, a Secret Rewriting of Military Law," *The New York Times*, October 24, 2004, p. 1.
366 Taft told Powell: Taft interview.
367 A forty-two-page draft memorandum: John Yoo and Robert J. Delabunty memorandum for William J. Haynes II, General Counsel, Department of Defense, "Application of Treaties and Laws to al Qaeda and Taliban Detainees," January 9, 2002. Reprinted in Karen J. Greenberg and Joshua L. Dratel, eds., *The Torture Papers: The Road to Abu Ghraib* (New York: Cambridge University Press, 2005), p. 38.
367 Rumsfeld suggested: Donald Rumsfeld and General Richard Myers, "Department of Defense News Briefing by Secretary Rumsfeld and General Myers," January 11, 2002, Department of Defense transcript.
367 "Both the most important": Memorandum from William H. Taft IV to John C. Yoo, "Your Draft Memorandum of January 9," January 11, 2002. Reprinted at www.newyorker.com/online/content/articles/050214on_onlineonly02 (accessed October 12, 2005).
368 Although he mentioned the disagreement: Taft interview.

368 Yoo replied to Taft's memo: John Yoo and Robert J. Delabunty, letter to William H. Taft IV, January 14, 2002. Reprinted at www.newyorker.com/online/content/articles/050214on_onlineonly02 (accessed October 12, 2005).

368 "In general, the State Department": Bradford Berenson interview, "Frontline: The Torture Question," PBS, October 19, 2005.

368 Rumsfeld issued written instructions: Donald L. Rumsfeld, memorandum to chairman of the Joint Chiefs of Staff, "Status of Taliban and Al Qaeda," January 19, 2002. Reprinted in Greenberg and Dratel, *The Torture Papers,* p. 80.

369 Taft was astounded: Taft interview.

369 "his feeling was": Former State Department official, author interview.

369 Powell urged the president: Powell interview.

369 He didn't like: Ibid.

369 news of his dissent: Rowan Scarborough, "Powell Wants Detainees to Be Declared POWs; Memo Shows Differences with White House," *The Washington Times,* January 26, 2002, p. 1.

370 "unpersuasive": Alberto R. Gonzales, memorandum to the president, "Decision Re Application of the Geneva Convention on Prisoners of War to the Conflict with al Qaeda and the Taliban," January 25, 2002. Reprinted in Greenberg and Dratel, *The Torture Papers,* p. 118; R. Jeffrey Smith and Dan Eggen, "Gonzales Helped Set the Course for Detainees," *The Washington Post,* January 5, 2005, p. A1.

370 "the process was being pushed": Powell interview.

370 Before the day was out: Ibid.

370 Powell prepared his own memo: Colin L. Powell, memorandum to counsel to the president and assistant to the president for national security affairs, "Draft Decision Memorandum for the President on the Applicability of the Geneva Convention to the Conflict in Afghanistan," January 26, 2002. Reprinted in Greenberg and Dratel, *The Torture Papers,* p. 122.

371 On February 7: George W. Bush memorandum for the vice president, et al., "Humane Treatment of al Qaeda and Taliban Detainees," February 7, 2002, p. 134.

371 "I didn't agree with it": Powell interview. On June 29, 2006, in Hamdan v. Rumsfeld, the U.S. Supreme Court struck down Bush's plan to try the Guantánamo detainees before special military commissions. The court ruled the commissions were neither authorized by federal law nor required by military necessity. The majority opinion additionally said that Common Article 3 of the Geneva Conventions, as part of the "law of war," applied to all detainees.

372 the documents were not circulated: Taft interview.

372 the principals examined: Administration official, author interview.

373 Abdullah made the same argument: Jordanian official, author interview, February 1, 2002.

373 "We will not give up hope": Colin L. Powell, remarks with King Abdullah, January 31, 2002, State Department transcript.

373 "Sharon has to take": Alan Sipress, "Powell Criticizes Sharon, Attacks on Palestinians," *The Washington Post,* March 7, 2002, p. A12.

374 Armitage saw an opportunity: State Department official, author interview.

374–75 Bush had privately instructed Rumsfeld: Woodward, *Plan of Attack,* p. 1.

375 "it would look like": Ibid., p. 3.

375 "The Vice President": Ibid., p. 4.

375   "to remove the regime": Tommy Franks, *American Soldier* (New York: Harper-Collins, 2004), pp. 330–331.

376   He did not mention Iraq: George W. Bush and General Tommy Franks, "Remarks by the President and General Tommy Franks," December 28, 2001, White House transcript.

376   Powell felt the exercise was prudent: Powell interview.

376   "Iraq isn't going anywhere": Bill Keller, "The World According to Powell," p. 62.

376   "axis of evil": "President's State of the Union Address," January 29, 2002, White House transcript.

377   "The President is examining": Colin L. Powell, "Hearing of the House International Relations Committee," February 6, 2002, Federal News Service transcript.

377   "It doesn't mean": Richard Wolffe and Gerard Baker, "Powell's New Doctrine," *Financial Times,* February 14, 2002, p. 18.

377   "knows the region well": Barbara Slavin and Susan Page, "Cheney Will Go Abroad to Discuss War on Terror," *USA Today,* February 7, 2002, p. 7A.

377   White House officials made clear: Author notes.

377–78   none of them would publicly declare: Woodward, *Plan of Attack,* p. 111.

378   "peace and stability": George W. Bush, Dick Cheney and Colin L. Powell, "Remarks by the President, the Vice President, and the Secretary of State on the Middle East," March 7, 2002, White House transcript.

378   Rice gave an upbeat report: Dana Milbank and Karen DeYoung, "The Birth of a Balancing Act," *The Washington Post,* April 6, 2002, p. A1.

379   "Don's Christian compassion": Powell interview.

379   "I really need you": Ibid.

379   "a calming presence": Administration official, author interview.

379   "Don didn't want to touch it": Powell interview.

380   "the outlines of a just settlement": George W. Bush, "President to Send Secretary Powell to the Middle East," April 4, 2002, White House transcript.

380   The president had spoken: Author notes.

381   Powell found himself: Powell interview.

381   "no plans to meet": Author notes.

381   It was an idea: U.N. official, author interview.

381   Bush…saw little point: George W. Bush, interview with Trevor MacDonald, April 4, 2002, author notes.

381   "I was going to try": Powell interview.

382   "I may not even have": Colin L. Powell, interview with Tim Russert on *Meet the Press,* NBC, April 7, 2002, State Department transcript.

382   "this was a last chance": The account of Powell's April 7–17, 2002, trip to the Middle East is drawn from author interviews with Zinni, Powell and other administration officials.

383   "fellow general": Powell interview.

383   No one knew: Administration official, author interview.

383   "the views of somebody": Powell interview.

384   "The White House went crazy": Ibid.

384   "I plan to return": Colin L. Powell, "Remarks at David Citadel Hotel," April 17, 2002, State Department transcript.

384   "man of peace": George W. Bush and Colin L. Powell, "President, Secretary Powell Discuss Middle East," April 18, 2002, White House transcript.

384 the president...seemed overwhelmed: Karen DeYoung and Walter Pincus, "Crises Strain Bush Policies; Friends, Foes Find Lack of Coherence in Foreign Affairs," *The Washington Post,* April 21, 2002, p. A1.

385 "in real danger": Ibid.

385 "ham-handed" efforts: Robert Kagan and William Kristol, "The Detour," *The Weekly Standard,* April 8, 2002, p. 9.

385 Karl Rove...warned: DeYoung and Pincus, "Crises Strain Bush Policies."

385 The effort to juggle: The account of Crown Prince Abdullah's visit to Crawford is drawn from author interviews with Powell and Saudi government officials.

387 the speech he gave: George W. Bush, "President Bush Calls for New Palestinian Leadership," June 24, 2002, White House transcript.

387 Powell spent the afternoon: Author notes.

388 "if a tyrant like Saddam Hussein": Richard Perle interview, "Frontline: The War Behind Closed Doors," PBS, February 20, 2003.

388 "I think the JINSA crowd": Powell interview.

CHAPTER EIGHTEEN

389 Nothing else holds: Shultz, *Turmoil and Triumph,* p. 923. Over two days of testimony during the congressional Iran-*contra* hearings in 1987, Shultz spoke of his "sense of estrangement" from the White House staff and said that President Reagan had not informed him of key foreign policy decisions. Some questioners suggested that Shultz had not been tough enough in opposing the arms-for-hostages scheme. "I can't escape the notion that had you opposed this flawed policy and were willing to resign over this policy difference," Representative Henry Hyde (R–Illinois) said, "you could have stopped it dead in its tracks." Resignation, Shultz later wrote in his memoirs, "was not my way...it had been essential for me to stay in there and slug it out."

389 "I understand": The account of Powell's July 26–August 4, 2002, trip to Asia is drawn from the author's notes.

389 a front-page article: Todd S. Purdum, "Embattled, Scrutinized, Powell Soldiers On," *The New York Times,* July 25, 2002, p. 1.

391 The meeting had not been vetted: Administration official, author interview.

391 He had, in fact, discussed: Powell interview.

391 "I'm *supposed* to go out": Ibid.

392 "It was not a happy circumstance": U.N. official, author interview.

393 "he's said many things": Foreign official, author interview.

393 closest overseas counterparts: Foreign officials, author interviews.

393 Armitage fretted: Armitage interview.

394 "The President has good instincts": Wilkerson interview.

394 At Armitage's urging: Armitage interview.

394 In one version: Woodward, *Plan of Attack,* pp. 134–135.

394 "always uneasy": Powell interview.

394–95 Myers...did not seem: Ibid.

395 at Rumsfeld's constant beck and call: Ibid.

396 "the anti-Christ": Ibid.

396 "Where I really got my authority": Ibid.

396 "the right number of troops": Ibid.

396 "Tommy Franks is no rookie": Ibid.

396 "I did not die on my sword": Ibid.

396 In mid-January 2002: Rowan Scarborough, "U.S. Seeks al Qaeda Link to Iraq," *The Washington Times,* January 14, 2002, p. A1.

397 at the White House and the Pentagon: Administration officials, author interviews.

397 Even without a central role: State Department officials, author interviews.

398 The idea had originated: Edward Walker interview on "Frontline: War, Truth and Consequences," PBS, October 9, 2003.

398 "absence of buy-in": State Department official, author interview.

398 "always started on time": Armitage interview.

399 "We knew what we were talking *about*": The account of interagency meetings during the lead-up to the war is drawn from author interviews with several State Department officials.

399 When Richard Haass: Nicholas Lemann, "How It Came to War," *The New Yorker,* March 31, 2003, www.newyorker.com/fact/content/articles/03033ifa_fact (accessed January 16, 2006).

399 Haass reported: Former State Department official, author interview.

399 "My recollection": Armitage interview.

400 "new threats": George W. Bush, "Graduation Speech at West Point," June 1, 2002, White House transcript.

400 "working on nuclear": Dick Cheney, interview on *Meet the Press,* NBC, May 19, 2002, among numerous other allegations concerning Iraq's nuclear weapons program.

400 "no time to lose": Mann, *Rise of the Vulcans,* pp. 334–335.

400 "But the real question here": Chuck Hagel, interview on *Face the Nation,* CBS, August 4, 2002, Federal News Service transcript.

401 Working through his notes: Woodward, *Plan of Attack,* pp. 150–151.

401 "When you hit this thing": Powell interview.

402 "My responsibility that day": *MAJ,* p. 480.

402 Rice thought: Administration official, author interview.

402 "He sure did": Woodward, *Plan of Attack,* p. 152.

403 "get as close": Peter Riddell, *Hug Them Close: Blair, Clinton, Bush and the "Special Relationship"* (London: Politico's, 2003), p. 2.

403 Their first attempt: Ibid., p. 124.

403 It was immediately clear: British official, author interview.

403 Blair had a solid record: For an extended discussion of the roots of Tony Blair's foreign policy, see Riddell, *Hug Them Close.*

404 Blair's doctrine was internationalist: Peter Riddell, "Tony Blair Needs a Hug," *Foreign Policy,* November–December 2003, p. 90.

404 Blair had a deep personal belief: British official, author interview.

404 Bush's insistence: Ibid.

404 By the spring of 2002: A series of classified British government memoranda from this period were leaked in early 2005 to *The Sunday Times* (London), which published transcripts and a series of stories about them throughout the year.

405 "explained to the prime minister": Author notes; Karen DeYoung, "Bush Tells Sharon Israel Must Withdraw," *The Washington Post,* April 6, 2002, p. A1.

405 "You could do this on your own": Christopher Meyer, interview on "Frontline: Blair's War," PBS, April 3, 2003.

405 The British government's political instincts: British official, author interview.

405 "military action was now seen": David Manning, memo to Matthew Rycroft, July 23, 2002, www.timesonline.co.uk/article/0,,2087-1593607,00.html (accessed November 10, 2005).

405 In July, he wrote: Meyer, "Blair's War," PBS.

406 Cheney objected: Woodward, *Plan of Attack*, p. 157.

406 Bush *should* talk about Iraq: Administration official, author interview.

406 The more Bush thought about it: Ibid.

406 "when he was out of town": State Department official, author interview.

406 One sunny afternoon: Llewellyn interview.

407 In the August heat: Karen DeYoung, "For Powell, a Long Path to Victory," *The Washington Post*, November 10, 2002, p. A1.

407 "Attacking Iraq": General Anthony Zinni, "Speech before the Florida Economic Club," August 23, 2002, www.npr.org/programs/morning/zinni.html (accessed November 11, 2005).

407 "The case of Saddam Hussein": Dick Cheney, "Vice President Speaks at VFW 103rd National Convention," August 26, 2002, White House transcript.

407 "This guy is going to make": Zinni interview.

408 No one had warned Powell: Boucher interview.

408 "The President always encourages us": Colin L. Powell, "Interview on BBC Breakfast with Sir David Frost," August 29, 2002 (withheld for broadcast on September 8, 2002), State Department transcript.

408 "pissed at me": Zinni interview.

409 The United States already had: DeYoung, "For Powell, a Long Path to Victory."

409 The next day: Woodward, *Plan of Attack*, p. 167.

409 "necessary to deal with": George W. Bush, "President Discusses Foreign Policy with Congressional Leaders," September 4, 2002, White House transcript.

409 On September 6: Woodward, *Plan of Attack*, pp. 174–175.

409 "What we didn't know": British official, author interview.

410 "This is it": Ibid.

410 The vice president sat in: Ibid.

410 "the *cojones* meeting": Ibid.; Woodward, *Plan of Attack*, p. 178.

410 Powell clashed with Cheney again: Woodward, *Plan of Attack*, pp. 182–183.

410 "Look, there really is": DeYoung, "For Powell, a Long Path to Victory."

411 "No country . . . should reject": Kofi Annan, "Address to U.N. General Assembly," September 12, 2002, www.un.org/News/Press/docs/2002/SGSM8378.doc.htm (accessed January 16, 2006).

411 "wait and listen": U.N. official, author interview.

411 "All the world now faces": George W. Bush, "Speech to the United Nations General Assembly," September 12, 2002, White House transcript.

411 As he neared the punch line: Woodward, *Plan of Attack*, pp. 183–184.

411 The process would be brief: Author notes.

411 Powell made the rounds: Ibid.

412 All were pleased: Adolfo Aguilar Zinser, author interview, December 15, 2003.

412 Even if a decision: Ibid.

412 "We do know": Colin L. Powell, "Secretary's Interview on the Larry King Show," October 9, 2002, State Department transcript.

412 "trying to acquire": Colin L. Powell, "Secretary's Interview on Oprah Winfrey Show," October 22, 2002, State Department transcript.

413 "then the United States": Colin L. Powell, interview with Ellen Ratner of Talk Radio News, October 30, 2002, State Department transcript.

413 the White House Iraq Group: Barton Gellman and Walter Pincus, "Depiction of the Threat Outgrew Supporting Evidence," *The Washington Post*, August 10, 2003, p. A1.

413   A September 8 front-page story: Michael Gordon and Judith Miller, "U.S. Says Hussein Intensifies Quest for A-Bomb Parts," *The New York Times,* September 8, 2002, p. 1.

413   "what you have to have": Dick Cheney, interview on *Meet the Press,* NBC, September 8, 2002, Federal News Service transcript.

413   "only really suited": Gellman and Pincus, "Depiction of Threat Outgrew Supporting Evidence."

413–14   Harry Belafonte...compared Powell: Harry Belafonte interview on *Larry King Live,* CNN, October 15, 2002, CNN transcript. The broadcast included a replay of Belafonte's original comments on October 8.

414   "If Harry had wanted": Colin L. Powell, "Secretary's Interview with Larry King," October 9, 2002, State Department transcript.

414   the idea that two hundred inspectors: Karen DeYoung and Walter Pincus, "U.N. Pressed for Tough Stance on Iraq," *The Washington Post,* October 14, 2002, p. A25.

414   Wolfowitz took the lead: Defense Department official, author interview.

414   Irritation with the ploy: Administration and U.N. officials, author interviews.

415   an interagency group was formed: DeYoung, "For Powell, a Long Path to Victory."

415   "a very powerful constituency": Powell interview.

415   Cheney's attendance: Ibid.

416   In the Bush administration: Administration officials, author interviews.

416   Early suspicions: State Department officials, author interviews.

416   "There was a time": State Department official, author interview.

417   Wolfowitz insisted: Administration officials, author interviews.

417   Powell was not totally displeased: State Department official, author interview.

418   "the art of the possible": British official, author interview.

418   "consider the situation": United Nations Security Council Resolution 1441, November 8, 2002. Available at www.un.int/usa/sres-iraq.htm (accessed November 13, 2005).

418   "reliable as a Volvo": Hans Blix, *Disarming Iraq* (New York: Pantheon Books, 2004), p. 109.

418   Their first session: Ibid., pp. 85–89.

418   they found Bush a stark contrast: Ibid.

419   Rice, who sat in: Administration official, author interview.

419   Rumsfeld's office: Powell interview.

419   But the end stage: Annemarie Powell interview; Berns interview.

419   She worried about his celebrity: Annemarie Powell interview.

420   As Negroponte walked: DeYoung, "For Powell, a Long Path to Victory."

420   "the world must not lapse": George W. Bush, "President's Statement on Security Council Resolution," November 8, 2002, White House transcript.

CHAPTER NINETEEN

421   "Experience proves": Ulysses S. Grant, *Personal Memoirs of U.S. Grant,* vol. 1 (New York: Charles L. Webster & Company, 1885), p. 68.

421   "I'm here to serve": Colin L. Powell, interview with *Paris Match,* December 13, 2004, State Department transcript.

421   Even Blix: Blix, *Disarming Iraq,* p. 108.

422   "we do not have": Central Intelligence Agency, "Unclassified Report to Congress on the Acquisition of Technology Relating to Weapons of Mass Destruction and Advanced Conventional Munitions, 1 January Through 30 June 2000," www.fas.org/irp/threat/bian_feb_2001.htm#4 (accessed May 3, 2005).

422 "Iraq has continued": National Intelligence Council, "Key Judgments, October 2002 National Intelligence Estimate," www.fas.org/irp/cia/product/iraq-wmd .html (accessed May 3, 2005).

422 "active, detailed and growing": Tony Blair, "Prime Minister's Iraq Statement to Parliament," September 24, 2002, www.number-10.gov.uk/output/Page1727.asp (accessed May 3, 2005).

423 "Many Americans have raised": George W. Bush, "Remarks by the President on Iraq," October 7, 2002, White House transcript.

423 A number of U.S. intelligence officials: Karen DeYoung, "Bush Cites Urgent Iraqi Threat," *The Washington Post,* October 8, 2002, p. A1.

423 a State Department "Fact Sheet": Senate Select Committee on Intelligence, "Report on the U.S. Intelligence Community's Prewar Intelligence Assessments on Iraq," July 7, 2004, www.gpoaccess.gov/serialset/creports/iraq.html (accessed February 10, 2005).

423–24 "The world is still waiting": Colin L. Powell, "Press Conference on Iraq Declaration," December 19, 2002, State Department transcript.

424 Wilkerson...had met: Wilkerson interview.

424 "a strong believer": Colin L. Powell, interview on *Face the Nation,* CBS, January 19, 2003. The University of Michigan case, *Grutter v. Bollinger,* was the Supreme Court's first affirmative action ruling in twenty-five years. It involved a white law school applicant who charged that her rejection had been unconstitutional because some African Americans and ethnic minorities with lower overall scores had been admitted to the school. Bush called the law school's admissions policy of giving extra consideration to blacks and minorities a "quota system" that was "fundamentally flawed," and the administration filed a brief in support of the plaintiff. In a 5–4 decision on June 23, 2003, the Court upheld the right of universities to consider race in admissions decisions. Writing for the majority, Justice Sandra Day O'Connor said that the state maintained a "compelling interest" in promoting diversity. In a separate decision, the Court rejected in part the specific admissions system used by the University of Michigan's undergraduate college.

425 "Let's see": George W. Bush, "President Urges Congress to Support Nation's Priorities," July 8, 2002, White House transcript.

425 His remark was widely criticized: Matthew Engel, "Bush Jibe Angers Black Leaders," *The Guardian* (London), July 10, 2002, p. 12.

425 "We know that the president": British official, author interview.

425 "I have to kind of lean back": Colin L. Powell, interview with *The Washington Post,* January 8, 2003, author notes.

426 Military war games: James Fallows, "Blind into Baghdad," *The Atlantic Monthly,* January–February 2004, http://theatlantic.com/issues/2004/01/fallows.htm (accessed June 1, 2004).

426 Franks thought that Powell's: Tommy Franks with Malcolm McConnell, *American Soldier: General Tommy Franks* (New York: Regan Books, 2004), p. 394.

427 Powell thought it would be a stretch: Powell interview.

427 "There was a lot of confusion": State Department official, author interview.

427 Powell's office tried to send: Ibid.

427–28 A few days after Turkey's November 4 election: Administration officials, author interviews.

428 UNMOVIC inspectors could not say: Blix, *Disarming Iraq,* p. 111.

428 Blix privately agreed: Ibid., p. 112.

428 Bush was losing patience: Powell interview.

428 "Cheney thought we had no option": Ibid.

429 "a moment when we all made": Ibid.

429 As Powell remembered: Ibid.

429 "I didn't need his permission": Woodward, *Plan of Attack*, p. 274.

429 "reaching a conclusion": Powell interview.

430 "The president had come": Ibid.

430 "would had to have been made": State Department official, author interview.

430 "flawless rectitude": David McCullough, *Truman*, p. 533.

431 "transparent dodge": Ed Cray, *General of the Army: George C. Marshall, Soldier and Statesman* (New York: Cooper Square Press, 1990; paperback edition, 2000). Citations are to paperback edition, p. 659.

431 "No, gentlemen": Ibid., p. 661.

431 " 'Nobody made me President' ": Colin L. Powell, interview with Peter Slevin of *The Washington Post*, November 10, 2003, State Department transcript.

432 "old Europe": Donald Rumsfeld, press briefing, January 23, 2003, Defense Department transcript.

432 "the Europeans are worried": Administration official, author interview.

432 De Villepin called the Security Council: "Provisional Minutes," United Nations Security Council, January 20, 2003, U.N. transcript.

433 Fischer's remarks startled Powell: Powell interview.

433 "I didn't see it": Ibid.

433 De Villepin was late in arriving: U.N. official, author interview.

433 "Did you hear what Dominique did?": Powell interview.

433 Iraq's WMD program was "frozen": Dominique de Villepin, "Press Conference by Foreign Minister of France," January 20, 2003, U.N. press release; "Nothing Today Justifies War on Iraq: France," Agence France Presse, January 20, 2003.

434 The French position: French official, author interview.

434 "diplomacy was no longer relevant": "War in Iraq: How the Die Was Cast Before Transatlantic Diplomacy Failed," *Financial Times*, May 27, 2003, p. 15.

434 "Essentially, I was still pushing": Powell interview.

434 "The die was cast after that": State Department official, author interview.

434 "ambushed" by the French: Glenn Kessler and Colum Lynch, "France Vows to Block Resolution on Iraq War; U.S. Schedule Put at Risk by U.N. Debate," *The Washington Post*, January 21, 2003, p. A1.

435 "made it more of a story": Powell interview.

435 "The decision to go to war": French official, author interview.

435 "the re-run of a bad movie": George W. Bush, "President Bush Remarks to the Press," January 21, 2003, White House transcript.

435 "cannot be sustained": Senators Joseph Biden and Chuck Hagel, NPR, January 23, 2003.

436 Just before Christmas: Woodward, *Plan of Attack*, pp. 247–250.

436 "new intelligence": Report of the Senate Select Committee on Intelligence.

436 "Libby and 'the boys' ": Armitage interview.

436 The meeting had been "bizarre": Ibid.

437 "a dress-up doll": Boucher interview.

437 "I've been here": Colin L. Powell, "Remarks at the World Economic Forum," January 26, 2003, State Department transcript.

438 "He's a decent guy": R. C. Longworth, "Powell Pleads Case for Attack on Iraq," *Chicago Tribune*, January 27, 2003, p. 1.

438 "pretty fired up": Armitage interview.

438 Blix told the Security Council: Blix, *Disarming Iraq,* pp. 138–141.

439 " 'We've really got to make' ": Powell interview.

439 he was taken aback: Ibid.

439 "Condi, please": Ibid.

440 "We were going out": Wilkerson interview.

441 In addition to proving the case: Ibid.

442 "information that the White House had added": Report of the Senate Select Committee on Intelligence.

442 "This is not going to meet": Wilkerson interview.

442 Late that night: Ibid.

442 Cheney had called: Armitage interview.

442 "Powell said, 'I don't want to' ": Boucher interview.

443 no one from the Defense Department: Powell interview.

443 "totally reliable information": Wilkerson interview.

443 CIA analysts showed: Boucher interview.

443 Wilkerson was worried: Wilkerson interview.

443 a grainy picture: Powell interview.

444 "moving a prohibited vehicle out": Wilkerson interview.

444 "Don't you have a picture": Boucher interview.

444 They spent hours: Powell interview.

444 McLaughlin, who had brought: Boucher interview.

444 "pulled in their experts": Powell interview.

444 No one suggested: Wilkerson interview.

444 "what we really know": Powell interview.

445 It was an area: State Department officials, author interviews.

445 "George would give": Wilkerson interview.

445 "trimming the garbage": Powell interview.

445 "what we were all involved in": Wilkerson interview.

445 "Powell began the process": Administration official, author interview.

446 Brzezinski . . . came away impressed: Brzezinski interview.

446 "I knew he needed me": Alma Powell interview.

446 Powell was as nervous: Wilkerson interview.

447 "you're going to be there": Ibid.

447 make sure that Tenet was waiting: Boucher interview.

448 "this show wasn't for us": Aguilar Zinser interview.

448 "when it comes to U.S. policy": "USA Today/CNN/Gallup Poll," Institute for Public Accuracy press release, February 5, 2003.

448 "I cannot tell you everything": Colin L. Powell, "Remarks to the United Nations Security Council," February 5, 2003, State Department transcript.

449 Al-Douri furiously scribbled notes: Michael Dobbs, "At Council, Political Theater," *The Washington Post,* February 6, 2003, p. A1.

450 The other ministers followed: "Briefing Security Council, U.S. Secretary of State Powell Presents Evidence of Iraq's Failure to Disarm. Several Council Members Call for More Time for Inspections; France Proposes Strengthening Inspection Regime," United Nations Press Release, www.un.org/News/Press/docs/2003/sc7658.doc.htm (accessed April 14, 2005).

450 Much of the world: Sydney J. Freedberg, Jr., and Corine Hegland, "The World Reacts to Powell's Case," *The National Journal* 35, no. 6, February 8, 2003.

450 "[t]here is only one truth": Ibid.

450 A *Newsweek* poll: Richard Wolffe and Daniel Klaidman, *Newsweek,* February 17, 2003, p. 26.

450 Three out of four: Deborah L. Acomb, "Poll Track for February 15, 2003," *The National Journal* 35, no. 7, February 15, 2003.

451 "irrefutable": Unsigned editorial, *The Washington Post,* February 6, 2003, p. 36.

451 "the most powerful case": Unsigned editorial, *The New York Times,* February 6, 2003, p. 38.

451 "I'm not ready": Mary McGrory, "I'm Persuaded," *The Washington Post,* February 6, 2003, p. 37.

451 "a powerful, methodical": Nick Anderson, "Much of the Skepticism Among Lawmakers Appears to Buckle," *Los Angeles Times,* February 5, 2003, p. 15.

451 "I'd like to move": "Hearing of the Senate Foreign Relations Committee," February 6, 2003, Federal News Service transcript.

451 "strong case": Nick Anderson, "Much of the Skepticism Among Lawmakers Appears to Buckle."

452 Those closest to Powell: Alma Powell interview; Linda Powell interview.

452 Wilkerson . . . awoke depressed: Wilkerson interview.

CHAPTER TWENTY

453 "I wish some things": Franks, *American Soldier,* p. 544.

453 Blair knew by January 2003: British officials, author interviews.

454 Blair's own legal team: Attorney General, Lord Goldsmith, memo to the prime minister "on the legality of military action against Iraq," March 7, 2003, http://image.guardian.co.uk/sys-files/Guardian/documents/2005/04/28/legal.pdf (accessed December 17, 2005).

454 Blair was under no illusion: British officials, author interviews.

454 he glared testily: Bush-Blair news conference, author notes, January 31, 2003.

454 "This is a matter of weeks": George W. Bush, news conference with Tony Blair, January 31, 2003, White House transcript.

454 Hans Blix had not: Blix, *Disarming Iraq,* pp. 152–156.

455 After their public showdown: Ibid., p. 182.

455 At Powell's suggestion: Ibid., p. 184.

455 the jostling for a majority: State Department officials, author interviews.

455 a second witch doctor: Ibid.

456 "no choice": Ian Black and Michael White, "Chirac Pledges to Veto New Resolution," *The Guardian* (London), February 18, 2003, p. 4.

456 In the Delegates Lounge: U.N. ambassadors, author interviews.

456 "the moment of truth": Colin L. Powell, State Department briefing, March 17, 2003, State Department transcript.

457 If he had been in charge: Powell interview.

457 Britain's role was "unclear": Donald Rumsfeld, Defense Department briefing, March 11, 2003, Department of Defense transcript.

457 "no doubt": Alan Cowell, "British Dissent over Iraq War Imperils Blair's Future," *The New York Times,* March 12, 2003, p. 1.

457 "I think we could have gotten": Armitage interview.

458 "I think Powell believed": State Department official, author interview.

458 "to get America and Europe working": Karen DeYoung, "At the United Nations, Yet Another Clash Looms over Iraq; U.S. Role in Reconstruction at Issue," *The Washington Post,* March 26, 2003, p. A29.

458 Franks himself was concerned: Franks, *American Soldier,* p. 525.

459 twenty-five times more money and fifty times more troops: James Dobbins et al., *America's Role in Nation-Building: From Germany to Iraq* (Santa Monica, Calif.: RAND, 2003), www.rand.org/pubs/monograph_reports/MR1753/ (accessed November 21, 2005).

459 "everything that could go wrong": State Department official, author interviews.

459 included the possibility: Eric Schmitt and Joel Brinkley, "State Dept. Study Foresaw Trouble Now Plaguing Iraq," October 19, 2003, *The New York Times,* p. 1.

459 In studies conducted during the winter: Conrad C. Crane and W. Andrew Terrill, "Reconstructing Iraq: Insights, Challenges, and Missions for Military Forces in a Post-Conflict Scenario," Strategic Studies Institute, U.S. Army War College, February 2003, www.strategicstudiesinstitute.army.mil/pubs/display.cfm?PubID=182 (accessed November 15, 2005); "Dealing with the Civilian Population in Post-Saddam Iraq," U.S. Marine Corps Warfighting Laboratory, February 6, 2003, www.ceto.quantico.usmc.mil/studies/Post-SaddamIraq.pdf (accessed November 16, 2005).

460 "uncoordinated and faltering": Anthony H. Cordesman, "Planning for a Self-Inflicted Wound: U.S. Policy to Reshape a Post-Saddam Iraq, Revision Three: December 31, 2002," Center for Strategic and International Studies, Washington, D.C.

460 A joint study: Edward P. Djerijian, Frank G. Wisner, Rachel Bronson and Andrew S. Weiss, "Guiding Principles for a U.S. Post-Conflict Policy in Iraq," Council on Foreign Relations, January 2003, www.cfr.org/content/publications/attachments/Post-War_Iraq.pdf (accessed November 14, 2005).

460 "serious planning gaps": Lorne W. Craner, Arthur E. Dewey and Paul E. Simons, memo to Undersecretary Dobriansky, February 7, 2003, National Security Archive, www.gwu.edu/~nsarchiv/NSAEBB/NSAEBB163/iraq-state-03.pdf (accessed September 22, 2005).

460 "several hundred thousand soldiers": Eric Shinseki, "Testimony Before the Senate Armed Services Committee," February 25, 2003, Federal News Service transcript.

460 "wildly off the mark": Paul Wolfowitz, "Testimony Before the House Budget Committee," February 27, 2003, Federal News Service transcript.

461 "big-time vindication": White House official, author interview.

461 "major combat operations": Karen DeYoung, "Bush Proclaims Victory in Iraq; Work on Terror Is Ongoing, President Says," *The Washington Post,* May 2, 2002, p. A1.

461 "cakewalk": Kenneth Adelman, "Cakewalk in Iraq," *The Washington Post,* February 13, 2003, p. 27.

461 American casualties: "Operation Iraqi Freedom U.S. Casualty Status—19 Mar thru 30 Apr 03," Department of Defense, www.defenselink.mil/news/casualty .pdf (accessed December 7, 2005).

462 "a high level": Jay Garner, interview with the BBC, November 26, 2003, www.bbc.co.uk/radio4/today/reports/international/jay_garner_20031126.shtml (accessed February 12, 2004).

462 that meant Cheney: Armitage interview.

462 "intense rivalry": Garner interview, BBC.

462 "What we wondered": State Department official, author interview.

462 "a thoroughly vivid moment": Powell interview.

463 they were not involved: State Department official, author interview.

463 "an elite group of exiles": "The New Iraq," *60 Minutes II*, CBS, April 2, 2003.

463 "we ought to go in": Mark Bowden, "Wolfowitz: The Exit Interviews," *The Atlantic Monthly*, July–August 2005, p. 110.

463 Rumsfeld sent memos: Karen DeYoung, "Role for Exile Leaders Urged; Rumsfeld Proposes Interim Authority in Southern Iraq," *The Washington Post*, April 4, 2003, p. 23.

463 "How stupid could you be?": State Department official, author interview.

463 "bring forth representatives": Colin L. Powell, interview with Pakistan Television, April 10, 2003, State Department transcript.

463 "the nucleus of a temporary Iraq government": Charles J. Hanley, "Iraq Government to be In Place Soon," Associated Press, May 6, 2003.

463 Kofi Annan ... declined: U.N. official, author interview.

464 When the ORHA team finally arrived: Garner interview, BBC.

464 "Assertions that we are already failing": Paul Wolfowitz, "Testimony Before the Senate Foreign Relations Committee," May 22, 2003, Federal News Service transcript.

464 "If everything had been": Administration official, author interview.

465 "the job of running": L. Paul Bremer III, *My Year in Iraq* (New York: Simon & Schuster, 2006), p. 7.

465 "We all knew Jerry": State Department official, author interview.

465 "full authority": Bremer, *My Year in Iraq*, p. 11.

465 "judo approach": State Department official, author interview.

465 State's "hostility" toward: Frum and Perle, *An End to Evil*, p. 38.

466 "full-fledged détente": Ibid., pp. 214–215.

466 "a deliberate and systematic effort": Newt Gingrich, "Transforming the State Department," speech at the American Enterprise Institute, April 22, 2003, www.aei.org/publications/filter.all,pubID.16992/pub_detail.asp (accessed November 8, 2005).

466 "abdicated values and principles": Gingrich interview; Newt Gingrich, "Rogue State Department," *Foreign Policy*, July–August 2003, p. 42.

467 "one of the decisive": Gingrich interview.

467 "condescendingly hostile": Ibid.

467 "There are people who believe": White House official, author interview.

467 "tried to be a good leader": Wilkerson interview.

468 they huddled: Armitage interview.

468 When the defense secretary was invited: Donald Rumsfeld, interview with *Fox News Sunday*, May 4, 2003, Federal News Service transcript.

468 "an able, able diplomat": Ari Fleischer, White House briefing, April 22, 2003, White House transcript.

468 It was "disturbing": Senator Patrick Leahy, "Hearing of the Foreign Operations Subcommittee of the Senate Appropriations Committee," April 30, 2003, Federal News Service transcript.

469 Ever since Thomas Jefferson: Colin L. Powell, "Testimony Before Foreign Operations Subcommittee of the Senate Appropriations Committee," April 30, 2003, Federal News Service transcript.

469 "If he had wanted to": State Department official, author interview.

469 "enormous respect for your character": John Brady Kiesling, resignation letter, February 27, 2003, www.govexec.com/dailyfed/0303/031203kiesling.htm (accessed November 14, 2005).

469 "The feeling in the building": State Department official, author interview.

470 "sophomoric": Steven R. Weisman, "What Rift? Top Aides Deny State Dept.–Pentagon Chasm," *The New York Times,* May 31, 2003, p. 1.

470 "It was the obsession": U.S. ambassador, author interview.

470 "draw the appropriate lesson": Patrick Anidjar, "Rumsfeld Says Syria Aiding Iraqi Regime," Reuters, April 9, 2003.

470 "change the dynamics": White House official, author interview.

471 "on the table": Flynt Leverett, *Inheriting Syria* (Washington, D.C.: Brookings Institution, 2005), pp. 143–144.

471 Tehran sent a message: Guy Dinmore, "U.S. Split over Iranian Bid to Renew Relations," *Financial Times,* March 17, 2004, p. 1; Flynt L. Leverett, "Iran: The Gulf Between Us," *The New York Times,* January 24, 2006, p. 21.

471 Powell publicly suggested: Glenn Kessler, "Powell Backs Iran Protests, but Says Talks Are Possible," *The Washington Post,* June 18, 2003, p. A20; Glenn Kessler, "U.S. and Russia Press Iran on al Qaeda, Weapons; Concerns Mount over Nuclear Facilities, Influence in Iraq; Some at Pentagon Urging Intervention," *The Washington Post,* May 28, 2003, p. A14.

472 "my commitment": "President Bush Remarks at Sharm al Sheik Summit," June 3, 2003, White House transcript.

472 Israel "must deal with the settlements": Mike Allen and Glenn Kessler, "Five Arab Leaders Denounce Violence; Bush Vows to Pursue a Palestinian State," *The Washington Post,* June 4, 2003, p. 1.

472 "He was very tough": Arab official, author interview.

472 "We were not going to," Tamara Lipper and Michael Hirsh, "Stepping into the Fray," *Newsweek,* June 16, 2003, p. 26.

472 "no question about it": Arab official, author interview.

473 he planned to use the opportunity: Powell interview.

473 beginning to "capture": Wilkerson interview.

473 "OSD hard over": Armitage interview.

473 a "visceral" loathing: Woodward, *Bush at War,* p. 340.

473 "pushing an open door": Powell interview.

474 "careful to bring the boss along": Powell interview.

474 "of course": Richard Armitage, "Testimony Before the Senate Foreign Relations Committee," February 4, 2003, Federal News Service transcript; Armitage interview.

474 "I said, 'Look' ": Powell interview.

474 "We had to tell the Chinese": Ibid.

475 Rumsfeld was adamantly opposed: David E. Sanger, "Administration Divided over North Korea," *The New York Times,* April 21, 2003, p. 15.

475 insisted Kelly be prohibited: Pritchard interview.

475 The three-way meeting: Congressional Research Service, "North Korea: A Chronology of Events, October 2002–December 2004," January 24, 2005, Library of Congress.

475 "keep the Chinese in": Powell interview.

475 Bush's eventual agreement: David E. Sanger, "U.S. Said to Shift Approach in Talks with North Korea," *The New York Times,* September 4, 2003, p. 1.

476 "I got my summer buzz": President Bush, remarks to reporters, August 1, 2003, White House transcript.

476 a front-page story: Glenn Kessler, "State Dept. Changes Seen if Bush Reelected; Powell and Armitage Intend to Step Down," *The Washington Post,* August 4, 2003, p. A1.

476   Powell called it "nonsense": Mike Allen, "Powell Calls Resignation Report 'Gossip'; Secretary and Deputy Visit Bush for Talks," *The Washington Post,* August 5, 2003, p. A2.

476   "highly valued members": Scott McClellan, White House briefing, August 4, 2003, White House transcript.

476   The White House had "panicked": Armitage interview.

477   "First things first": President Bush, remarks to reporters, August 6, 2003, White House transcript.

477   "dysfunctional": Armitage interview.

478   Powell himself had raised: Powell interview.

478   "She tries": Ibid.

478   the main impediment: Ibid.

478   "overbearing": Alma Powell interview.

478   "He didn't check it": Powell interview.

478   "Republican former Cabinet secretary": David Ignatius, "A Foreign Policy Out of Focus," *The Washington Post,* September 2, 2003, p. A21.

478   "senior State Department official": Glenn Kessler and Peter Slevin, "Rice Fails to Repair Rifts, Officials Say; Cabinet Rivalries Complicate Her Role," *The Washington Post,* October 12, 2003, p. A1.

478   Rice called Powell: Armitage interview.

479   "I've got eighteen months to go": Llewellyn interview.

479   "all executive, legislative and judicial functions": Bremer, *My Year in Iraq,* p. 13.

479   But Powell was convinced: Powell interview.

479   Bremer repeatedly appealed: Bremer's concerns and exchanges with the Pentagon regarding troop levels are a recurring theme in his book *My Year in Iraq.*

480   "We know where they are": Donald Rumsfeld, interview on *This Week with George Stephanopoulos,* ABC, March 30, 2003.

480   "We found the vans": Colin L. Powell, briefing aboard Air Force One, May 30, 2003, State Department transcript.

481   "We went out there": Powell interview.

481   In the first public breach: Evan Thomas, Richard Wolffe and Michael Isikoff, "(Over)selling the World on War," *Newsweek,* June 9, 2003, p. 24.

481   "reconstituted nuclear weapons": Dick Cheney, interview on *Meet the Press,* NBC, March 16, 2003, Federal News Service transcript.

481   "Although Kay and his team": Colin L. Powell, "What Kay Found," *The Washington Post,* October 7, 2003, State Department transcript.

482   "You're not going to believe": Wilkerson interview.

482   Tenet called: Boucher interview.

482   "our friends up the river": Ibid.

482   "They never walked in here": Powell interview.

482   formal notification from the CIA: Ibid.

483   "I'll tell you what": Colin L. Powell, interview on *The Michael Reagan Radio Show,* December 23, 2003, State Department transcript.

CHAPTER TWENTY-ONE

485   "If I had known": *Paris Match* interview, December 13, 2004.

485   "a long, hard slog": Donald Rumsfeld, memo to General Dick Myers et al., October 16, 2003, reprinted in *USA Today,* May 20, 2005, www.usatoday.com/news/washington/executive/rumsfeld-memo.htm.

486 "Terrorists declared war": George W. Bush, "Remarks at Bush-Cheney 2004 Event," January 8, 2004, White House transcript.

486 "progress"…"challenges": Colin L. Powell press conference, January 8, 2004, State Department transcript.

487 "Partnership is the watchword": Colin Powell, "A Strategy of Partnerships," *Foreign Affairs,* January–February 2004, www.foreignaffairs.org/backissues/decade/2000.

487 "Success doesn't always come": Colin L. Powell, interview with Armstrong Williams.

487 "a lot of probables": Colin L. Powell, press conference, January 8, 2004.

487 the CIA announced: "DCI Announces Duelfer to Succeed Kay as Special Advisor," CIA press release, January 23, 2004.

487–88 Kay told reporters: Walter Pincus and Dana Milbank, "Arms Hunt in Iraq to Get New Focus; Next Chief Named for Effort," *The Washington Post,* January 24, 2004, p. A1.

488 "Who's right?": Colin L. Powell, briefing to reporters, January 24, 2004, State Department transcript.

488 Powell was not surprised: Powell interview.

488 "The fact of the matter is": Ibid.

488 "find out the facts": President Bush, remarks to reporters, January 27, 2004, White House transcript.

488 "it turns out we were all wrong": David Kay, "Testimony Before Senate Armed Services Committee," January 28, 2004, Federal News Service transcript.

489 Cheney began calling: Dana Milbank and Dana Priest, "Bush to Back Probe of Iraq Data, Officials Say; Reported Shift Comes amid Pressure from Hill," *The Washington Post,* February 1, 2001, p. A1.

489 "laid out the construct": Powell interview.

489 He was "absolutely convinced": Colin L. Powell, interview with *The Washington Post,* February 2, 2004, State Department transcript. (The transcript inaccurately places the meeting on February 3.)

490 "the whole White House operation was mad": Powell interview.

490 aides quickly began contacting: Richard W. Stevenson, "Powell and White House Get Together on Iraq War," *The New York Times,* February 4, 2004, p. 11.

490 the "bottom line": Colin L. Powell, remarks at the State Department, February 3, State Department transcript.

490 "coordinated" with the White House: Stevenson, "Powell and the White House Get Together on Iraq War."

490 "anything…that suggests any weakness": Powell interview.

491 "provisional bottom line": George Tenet, "Remarks at Georgetown University," February 5, 2004, Federal News Service transcript.

492 "the first time I heard": Powell interview.

492 "But the question is": Wilkerson interview.

492 "Is everyone else going to apologize?": Powell interview.

492 several Democrats: Colin L. Powell, "Testimony Before the House International Relations Committee," February 11, 2004, Federal News Service transcript.

493 conclusions far more damning: "Report of the Senate Select Committee; Commission on the Intelligence Capabilities of the United States Regarding Weapons of Mass Destruction," March 31, 2005, www.wmd.gov/report/ (accessed September 13, 2005).

494 "This war is going to happen": Ibid. In June 2006, former CIA official Tyler Drumheller told *The Washington Post* that he had reviewed a draft of Powell's U.N. speech in the days before its delivery and raised serious concerns about inclusion of the mobile bioweapons laboratories allegation. He said he had personally informed Director George Tenet and his deputy, John E. McLaughlin, that "Curveball," the Iraqi exile who was the principal source of the charge, was believed to be mentally unstable and a liar and the information should not be used. Assured that the matter would be taken care of, Drumheller said, he was amazed to hear Powell tell the U.N. Security Council that the United States had "first-hand descriptions" of the mobile labs. In response to queries from the *Post*, Tenet and McLaughlin released statements they had made to the Senate Intelligence Committee stating they had no recollection or documentation of the conversations. "Nobody came forward to say there was a series problem with Curveball," Tenet told the committee. McLaughlin said, "If someone had made these doubts clear to me, I would not have permitted the reporting to be used in Secretary Powell's speech." See Joby Warrick, "Warnings on WMD 'Fabricator' Were Ignored, Ex-CIA Aide Says," *The Washington Post*, June 25, 2006, p. A1.

494 "somebody in that room": Boucher interview.

494 A Defense Intelligence Agency memo: Walter Pincus, "Newly Released Data Undercut Prewar Claims; Source Tying Baghdad, Al Qaeda Doubted," *The Washington Post*, November 6, 2005, p. A22.

494 Powell had knowingly compromised: Wilkerson interview.

495 "inferential thinking": Powell interview.

496 "They hate Aristide": David M. Halbfinger, "Kerry Maintains the Administration Is Partly to Blame for the Unrest in Haiti," *The New York Times*, February 25, 2004, p. 20.

496 Aristide's foreign minister: French official, author interview.

496 Aristide's personal security: State Department official, author interview.

497 At 10 p.m. Saturday: Powell interview.

497 "not cutting off all your friendships": Ibid.

497 "Colin Powell is a master": French official, author interview.

498 "Make sure there's no table": Powell interview.

498 each faction was convinced: Glenn Kessler, "U.S. Has a Shifting Script on N. Korea; Administration Split as New Talks Near," *The Washington Post*, December 7, 2003, p. A25.

498 "coordinated" steps: David E. Sanger, "U.S. and 2 Allies Agree on a Plan for North Korea," *The New York Times*, December 8, 2003, p. 1.

498 rejected by Cheney: Glenn Kessler, "Impact from the Shadows, Cheney Wields Power with Few Fingerprints," *The Washington Post*, October 5, 2004, p. A1.

499 unless they were prepared: Powell interview.

499 a telephone call: Armitage interview.

499 Cheney had intervened: Powell interview.

500 When he realized the next morning: Ibid.

500 He later recalled the conversation: Ibid.

500 "the two senior political officials": Ibid.

500 "more than 75 key people": Woodward, *Plan of Attack*, p. x.

501 some people praised Powell: William Safire, "Colin in the Cross-Fire," *The New York Times*, April 28, 2004, p. 21.

501 This time around: Colin L. Powell, "Interview with Associated Press TV," April 19, 2004, State Department transcript.

501 "Americans did this": "Abuse of Iraqi POWs by GIs Probed," *60 Minutes II,* CBS, April 28, 2004, www.cbsnews.com/stories/2004/04/27/60II/main614063 .shtml (accessed January 19, 2005).

502 a lengthy story: Seymour M. Hersh, "Torture at Abu Ghraib," *The New Yorker: Fact,* April 30, 2004, www.newyorker.com/fact/content/?040510fa_fact (accessed January 19, 2005).

502 "Nobody was prepared": Powell interview.

503 "Condi consistently": Administration official, author interview.

503 the State Department had been excluded: Powell and Taft interviews. Documents leaked in 2004 and 2005 demonstrated that specific interrogation methods arguably amounting to torture had been approved by senior officials, including by Rumsfeld.

503 Kallenberger visited Powell: Powell interview.

504 beaten to death: Carlotta Gall, "U.S. Military Investigating Death of Afghan in Custody," *The New York Times,* March 4, 2003, p. 14; "Prisoners 'Killed' at U.S. Base," BBC News, March 6, 2003.

504 "When we heard about that": Taft interview. An Army investigation launched a year later determined that the men had been chained, beaten and deprived of sleep for days. Investigators recommended that criminal charges be brought against twenty-seven officers and soldiers; fifteen eventually were prosecuted. Five of those pleaded guilty to assault and other crimes; the harshest penalty any received was five months in prison. Only one soldier was convicted at trial, although he received no prison sentence. The case against the former military police commander at Bagram was eventually dropped by the Army. See Tim Golden, "Years After 2 Afghans Died, Abuse Case Falters," *The New York Times,* February 13, 2006, p. 1.

504 "the people in the field": Boucher interview.

504 "excessive and disproportionate": "Report of the International Committee of the Red Cross (ICRC) on the Treatment by the Coalition Forces of Prisoners of War and Other Protected Persons by the Geneva Conventions in Iraq During Arrest, Internment and Interrogation," February 2004, www.globalsecurity.org/military/ library/report/2004/icrc_report_iraq_feb2004.htm (accessed February 8, 2006).

504 Powell had repeatedly raised: Powell interview.

504 "We read it in the newspaper": Taft interview.

505 "It was too awful": State Department official, author interview.

505 "You've got to understand": Powell interview.

505 "War's over": Ibid.

505 Powell had persistently maintained: Bremer, *My Year in Iraq,* pp. 209–226.

506 "We are determined": State Department official, author interview.

506 "We were fighting": State Department official, author interview.

507 "the United States will be represented": National Security Presidential Directive 36, www.fas.org/irp/offdocs/nspd/ (accessed February 8, 2006).

507 "among the ugliest negotiations": Administration official, author interview.

507 "wrong war": "Kerry: Wrong War in the Wrong Place," Associated Press, September 7, 2004.

508 conclusions that contradicted: Dana Priest and Walter Pincus, "U.S. 'Almost All Wrong' on Weapons; Report on Iraq Contradicts Bush Administration Claims," *The Washington Post,* October 7, 2004, p. A1.

508 "the sourcing was inaccurate": Colin L. Powell interview, "Meet the Press," NBC News, May 16, 2004.

508   Half of the electorate: www.pollingreport.com/BushJob1.htm (accessed February 27, 2006).

509   "they would have backed down": Wilkerson interview.

509   overestimating their own courage: Congressional sources, author interviews.

509   "It's easy for us": State Department official, author interview.

509   "I couldn't do what he does": Zinni interview.

509   "I don't think he wants to be known": Llewellyn interview.

509   "right man": Carlucci interview.

510   "They needed him to do it": Alma Powell interview.

510   "I never haggled": Cray, *General of the Army,* pp. 144–145.

510   "Colin Powell isn't George Marshall": Slevin interview with Powell, November 10, 2003.

511   He was developing a head cold: Glenn Kessler, the *Washington Post* correspondent aboard Powell's plane, generously provided the author with notes of the January 3–9, 2005, trip.

511   his last trip: As it turned out, Powell made one more journey as secretary of state: a quick turnaround to Ukraine to attend the swearing-in of a new president on January 22–23.

512   he would be missed: Alma Powell interview.

512   "come on [their] television show": Powell interview.

513   "much to be proud of": Colin L. Powell, "Remarks to State Department Employees," January 19, 2005.

EPILOGUE

514   "Leaving is just as natural": *Paris Match,* December 13, 2004.

514   "I'm going to grind through": Powell interview.

516–17 "When you give up command": Ibid.

517   "I can drive myself": Deborah Orin, "Big Wheel Colin Shifts Gears to Inspire Youth of N.Y.," *The New York Post,* November 25, 2005, p. 26.

517   "enough troops for war": Robin Gedye, "Powell Breaks Silence on Rifts, Rumsfeld and 'Old Europe,' " *The Telegraph* (London), February 26, 2005, p. 1.

517   "too loud, too direct": Roger Boyes, "Powell Fury at Being Misled over WMD," *The Times* (London), March 30, 2005, p. 38.

517   "turned out to be such a mess": Colin L. Powell, interview with Barbara Walters, *20/20,* ABC, September 9, 2005.

517   "Our troops need to hear": Colin L. Powell, letter to John McCain, October 5, 2005, Office of General Colin L. Powell, USA (Retired).

518   "What I saw": Lawrence Wilkerson, speech at the New America Foundation, October 19, 2005, www.newamerica.net/index.cfm?pg=event&EveID=520 (accessed December 15, 2005).

518   "I wouldn't characterize it": Colin L. Powell, interview with David Frost, BBC, December 17, 2005, www.bbc.co.uk/print/pressoffice/pressreleases/stories/200512_december/17/powell (accessed March 12, 2006).

518   "He can be the most endearing person": Richard Leiby, "Breaking Ranks; Larry Wilkerson Attacked the Policy on Iraq and Wounded His Friendship with Colin Powell," *The Washington Post,* January 19, 2006, p. C1.

519   They were largely placid events: David E. Sanger, "Bush and Former Cabinet Members Discuss Topic No. 1: Iraq," January 5, 2006, www.nytimes.com (accessed January 5, 2006).

520   "a good public servant": Colin L. Powell, interview with Barbara Walters.

BIBLIOGRAPHY

Much of the material in this book is based on interviews conducted entirely or partially on the records. Additional sources of information both in conversations specifically for the book and in earlier reporting for *The Washington Post*, include many unnamed current and former officials at the State and Defense departments, the White House, the intelligence community and the United Nations, as well as in the Washington diplomatic corps and foreign governments, who spoke on the condition that they not be identified. Some permitted identification of the agency in which they worked; others insisted they be identified only as generic "administration officials." All interviews relied upon were conducted by the author, except as indicated, and are cited in the chapter notes.

BOOKS

Albright, Madeleine. *Madam Secretary.* New York: Miramax Books, 2003.

Atkinson, Rick. *Crusade: The Untold Story of the Persian Gulf War.* New York: Houghton Mifflin Company, 1993.

Azrael, Jeremy R., and Emil A. Payin, eds. *U.S. and Russian Policymaking with Respect to the Use of Force.* Santa Monica, Calif.: Rand Corporation, 1996. www.rand.org/publications/CF/CF129/CF-129.chapter6.html.

Baker, James A., III. *The Politics of Diplomacy.* New York: G. P. Putnam's Sons, 1995.

Basler, Roy B., ed. *The Collected Works of Abraham Lincoln*, vol. 1. New Brunswick, N.J.: Rutgers University Press, 1955.

Bennett, Louise. *Jamaica Labrish*, 10th ed. Kingston: Sangster's Book Stores, 2003.

Binkin, Martin, and Mark J. Eitelberg et al. *Blacks and the Military.* Washington, D.C.: Brookings Institution, 1982.

Blix, Hans. *Disarming Iraq.* New York: Pantheon Books, 2004.

Branch, Taylor. *Pillar of Fire: America in the King Years, 1963–1965.* New York: Simon & Schuster, 1998. Reprinted, New York: Touchstone, 1999.

Bremer, L. Paul, III, with Malcolm McConnell. *My Year in Iraq.* New York: Simon & Schuster, 2006.

Buckley, Gail. *American Patriots: The Story of Blacks in the Military from the Revolution to Desert Storm.* New York: Random House, 2001.

Bush, George H. W., and Brent Scowcroft. *A World Transformed.* New York: Knopf, 1998. Reprinted, New York: Vintage Books, 1999.

Cannon, Lou. *President Reagan: The Role of a Lifetime.* New York: Simon & Schuster, 1991.

Clancy, Tom, with Anthony C. Zinni and Tony Koltz. *Battle Ready.* New York: G. P. Putnam's Sons, 2004.

Clark, Jeffrey J. *Advice and Support: The Final Years, 1965–1973.* Washington, D.C.: United States Army Center of Military History, 1988.

Clarke, Richard A. *Against All Enemies: Inside America's War on Terror.* New York: Simon & Schuster, 2004.

Clausewitz, Carl von. *On War.* Translated by Michael Howard and Peter Paret. Princeton, N.J.: Princeton University Press, 1976.

Clinton, William J. *My Life.* New York: Knopf, 2004.

Collins, James Lawton, Jr. *The Development and Training of the South Vietnamese Army, 1950–1972.* Washington, D.C.: Department of the Army, 1991.

Cook, Marianna. *Fathers and Daughters, in Their Own Words.* San Francisco: Chronicle Books, 1994.

Cray, Ed. *General of the Army: George C. Marshall, Soldier and Statesman.* New York: Cooper Square Press, 1990. Paperback edition, 2000.

Curtain, Philip D. *The Atlantic Slave Trade: A Census.* Madison: University of Wisconsin Press, 1969.

Daalder, Ivo H., and James M. Lindsay. *America Unbound: The Bush Revolution in Foreign Policy.* Washington, D.C.: Brookings Institution, 2003.

Dobbins, James, et al. *America's Role in Nation-Building: From Germany to Iraq.* Santa Monica, Calif.: RAND, 2003. www.rand.org/pubs/monograph_reports/MR1753/.

Dockery, Martin J. *Lost in Translation: Vietnam: A Combat Advisor's Story.* New York: Random House, 2003.

Eskew, Glenn T. *But for Birmingham: The Local and National Movements in the Civil Rights Struggle.* Chapel Hill: University of North Carolina Press, 1997.

Foner, Nancy, ed. *Islands in the City: West Indian Migration to New York.* Berkeley: University of California Press, 2001.

Franks, Tommy, with Malcolm McConnell. *American Soldier: General Tommy Franks.* New York: Regan Books, 2004.

Frum, David, and Richard Perle. *An End to Evil: How to Win the War on Terror.* New York: Random House, 2003.

Gates, Henry Louis, Jr. *Thirteen Ways of Looking at a Black Man.* New York: Random House, 1987. Reprinted, New York: Vintage Books, 1998.

Grant, Ulysses S. *Personal Memoirs of U. S. Grant,* vol. 1. New York: Charles L. Webster & Company, 1885.

Greenberg, Karen J., and Joshua L. Dratel, eds. *The Torture Papers: The Road to Abu Ghraib.* New York: Cambridge University Press, 2005.

Harris, John F. *The Survivor: Bill Clinton in the White House.* New York: Random House, 2005.

Jordan, Vernon. *Vernon Can Read!* New York: Public Affairs, 2001.

Kahin, George M. *Intervention: How America Became Involved in Vietnam.* New York: Knopf, 1986. Reprinted, New York: Doubleday, 1987.

Karnow, Stanley. *Vietnam: A History.* New York: Viking Press, 1983. Reprinted, New York: Penguin Books, 1985.

King, Desmond. *Making Americans: Immigration, Race and the Origins of the Diverse Democracy.* Cambridge, Mass.: Harvard University Press, 2000.

Kitfield, James. *Prodigal Soldiers.* New York: Simon & Schuster, 1995.

Leverett, Flynt. *Inheriting Syria.* Washington, D.C.: Brookings Institution, 2005.

MacGregor, Morris J., Jr. *Integration of the Armed Forces, 1940–1965*. Washington, D.C.: United States Army Center of Military History, 1985. www.army.mil/cmh-pg/books/integration/IAF-fm.htm.

Markusen, Ann, ed. *America's Peace Dividend*. New York: Council on Foreign Relations, 2000. www.ciaonet.org/book/markusen/index.html.

McCullough, David. *Truman*. New York: Simon & Schuster, 1992.

McKay, Claude. *Selected Poems of Claude McKay*. New York: Harcourt, Brace and Co., 1953.

Means, Howard. *Colin Powell: Soldier/Statesman–Statesman/Soldier*. New York: Donald I. Fine, 1992.

Morris, Dick. *Behind the Oval Office*. New York: Random House, 1997.

Moskos, Charles C., and John Sibley Butler. *All That We Can Be: Black Leadership and Racial Integration the Army Way*. New York: Twentieth Century Fund, 1966.

Nalty, Bernard C. *Strength for the Fight: A History of Black Americans in the Military*. New York: Free Press, 1986.

Ott, Major General David Ewing. *Field Artillery, 1954–1973*. Washington, D.C.: Department of the Army, 1975. www.army.mil/cmh-pag/books/Vietnam/FA54-73/fm.htm.

Peterson, Lieutenant General Frank E. *Into the Tiger's Jaw: America's First Black Marine Aviator*. Novato, Calif.: Presidio Press, 1998.

Powell, Colin L., with Joseph E. Persico. *My American Journey*. New York: Random House, 1995. Ballantine paperback edition with afterword, 1996.

Reid, Ira De A. *The Negro Immigrant: His Background, Characteristics and Social Adjustment, 1899–1937*. New York: Columbia University Press, 1939. Reprinted, New York: Arno Press, 1969.

Riddell, Peter. *Hug Them Close: Blair, Clinton, Bush and the "Special Relationship."* London: Politico's, 2003.

Roth, David. *Sacred Honor: Colin Powell; The Inside Account of His Life and Times*. Grand Rapids, Mich.: Zondervan Publishing House, 1993.

Rothkopf, David. *Running the World: The Inside Story of the National Security Council and the Architects of American Power*. New York: Public Affairs, 2005.

Schwarzkopf, General H. Norman. *It Doesn't Take a Hero*. New York: Bantam Books, 1992. Bantam paperback edition, 1993.

Shultz, George P. *Turmoil and Triumph: My Years as Secretary of State*. New York: Charles Scribner's Sons, 1993.

Stephanopoulos, George. *All Too Human*. Boston: Little, Brown and Company, 1999.

Suskind, Ron. *The Price of Loyalty: George W. Bush, the White House, and the Education of Paul O'Neill*. New York: Simon & Schuster, 2004.

Vickerman, Milton. *Crosscurrents: West Indian Immigrants and Race*. New York: Oxford University Press, 1999.

Weinberger, Caspar W. *Fighting for Peace: Seven Critical Years in the Pentagon*. New York: Warner Books, 1990.

Whitman, Christine Todd. *It's My Party Too: The Battle for the Heart of the GOP and the Future of America*. New York: Penguin Group, 2005.

Woodward, Bob. *Bush at War*. New York: Simon & Schuster, 2002.

———. *The Choice*. New York: Simon & Schuster, 1996. Touchstone paperback edition, 2006.

———. *The Commanders*. New York: Simon & Schuster, 1991.

———. *Plan of Attack*. New York: Simon & Schuster, 2004.

JOURNAL ARTICLES AND MANUSCRIPTS

Cordesman, Anthony H. "Planning for a Self-inflicted Wound: U.S. Policy to Reshape a Post-Saddam Iraq." Third Revision. Center for Strategic and International Studies Report (December 2002).

Djerijian, Edward P., et al. "Guiding Principles for a U.S. Post-Conflict Policy in Iraq." Council on Foreign Relations Report (January 2003). www.cfr.org/content/publications/attachments/Post-War_Iraq.pdf.

Domingo, W. A. "The Tropics in New York." *The Survey Graphic: Harlem Number* (March 1925): 650. http://etext.lib.Virginia.edu/harlem.

Gingrich, Newt. "Rogue State Department." *Foreign Policy* (July–August 2003): 42.

Powell, Colin L. "A Strategy of Partnerships." *Foreign Affairs* (January–February 2004).

Riddell, Peter. "Tony Blair Needs a Hug." *Foreign Policy* (November–December 2003): 90.

"Secretary Colin Powell's State Department: An Independent Assessment." Foreign Affairs Council Task Force Report (March 2003).

Terry, Wallace II. "Bringing the War Home." *Black Scholar* (November 1970): page unknown.

CONGRESSIONAL HEARINGS

House Appropriations Subcommittee on Commerce, Justice, State, Judiciary and Related Agencies. "Hearing on the President's Budget Request for Fiscal Year 2005." 108th Congress, 2nd sess., March 3, 2004.

House Armed Services Committee. "Hearing on the President's Budget Request for Fiscal Year 1992." 102nd Congress, 1st sess., February 7, 1991.

House Budget Committee. "Department of Defense Budget Priorities for Fiscal Year 2004." 108th Congress, 1st sess., February 27, 2003.

House International Relations Committee. "Hearing on the President's Budget Request for Fiscal Year 2003." 107th Congress, 2nd sess., February 6, 2002.

———. "Hearing on the President's International Affairs Budget Request for Fiscal Year 2005." 108th Congress, 2nd sess., February 11, 2004.

Senate Appropriations Subcommittee on Foreign Operations. "Hearing on Proposed Budget Estimates for Fiscal Year 2004." 108th Congress, 1st sess., April 30, 2003.

Senate Armed Services Committee. "Confirmation Hearing of Colin Powell to Be Chairman of the Joint Chiefs of Staff." 102nd Congress, 1st sess., September 27, 1991.

———. "Confirmation Hearing of Colin Powell to Be Chairman of the Joint Chiefs of Staff." 102nd Congress, 1st sess., September 30, 1991.

———. "Hearing on the Department of Defense Authorization Act." 108th Congress, 1st sess., February 25, 2003.

———. "Hearing on the Status of Iraqi Weapons of Mass Destruction and Related Programs." 108th Congress, 2nd sess., January 28, 2004.

Senate Foreign Relations Committee. "Confirmation Hearing of Colin Powell to Be Secretary of State." 107th Congress, 1st sess., January 17, 2001.

———. "Hearing on the President's Budget Request for Fiscal Year 2003." 107th Congress, 2nd sess., February 5, 2002.

———. "Hearing on North Korea's Programs to Develop Weapons of Mass Destruction." 108th Congress, 1st sess., February 4, 2003.

———. "Hearing on the President's Budget Request for Fiscal Year 2004." 108th Congress, 1st sess., February 6, 2003.

————. "Hearing on Iraq Stabilization and Reconstruction Efforts." 108th Congress, 1st sess., May 22, 2003.

CONGRESSIONAL REPORTS

Senate Select Committee on Intelligence and House Permanent Select Committee on Intelligence, "Joint Inquiry into Intelligence Community Activities Before and After the Terrorist Attacks of September 11, 2001," prepared December 2002, redacted and released August 2003.

Senate Select Committee on Intelligence, "Report on the U.S. Intelligence Community's Prewar Intelligence Assessments on Iraq," released July 7, 2004.

U.S. MILITARY REPORTS

Brownlee, Romie L., and William J. Mullen. "Changing an Army: An Oral History of General William E. DePuy," United States Military History Institute (Carlisle, Pa.), 1986. carlisle-www.army.mil/usamhi/Sampler/Changing/.

Crane, Conrad C., and W. Andrew Terrill. "Reconstructing Iraq: Insights, Challenges, and Missions for Military Forces in a Post-Conflict Scenario," Strategic Studies Institute, U.S. Army War College, February 2003. www.strategicstudiesinstitute .army.mil/pubs/display.cfm?PubID=182 (accessed November 15, 2005).

"Dealing with the Civilian Population in Post-Saddam Iraq," U.S. Marine Corps Warfighting Laboratory, released February 6, 2003. www.ceto.quantico.usmc.mil/ studies/Post-SaddamIraq.pdf.

Jaffe, Lorna S. "The Development of the Base Force: 1989–1992," Joint History Office, Department of Defense, July 1993. www.dtic.mil/doctrine/jel/history/ baseforc.pdf.

Henderson, Oran K. "Report of Investigation," memorandum to commanding general, Americal Division, April 24, 1968.

"Report of the Department of the Army Review of the Preliminary Investigations of the My Lai Incident" ("Peers Report"), U.S. Department of the Army, released March 14, 1970. www.law.umkc.edu/faculty/projects/ftrials/mylai/findings.html.

Ulmer, Walt and Mike Malone. "Study on Military Professionalism," U.S. Army War College, released June 30, 1970. http://ahecwebopac.carlisle.army.mil:4525/F/ 82YSYT3YD98K461TB351VQFEKQUQMNKCXJ1RRS2U7PED5RE6HP-11560 ?func=full-set-set&set_number=076352&set_entry=000001&format=999.

INDEPENDENT REPORTS

Commission on the Intelligence Capabilities of the United States Regarding Weapons of Mass Destruction, "Report to the President," released March 31, 2005. www.wmd.gov/report/.

International Committee of the Red Cross, "Report on the Treatment by the Coalition Forces of Prisoners of War and Other Protected Persons by the Geneva Conventions in Iraq During Arrest, Internment and Interrogation," February 2004. www .globalsecurity.org/military/library/report/2004/icrc_report_iraq_feb2004.htm.

National Commission on Terrorist Attacks upon the United States, "Final Report of the National Commission on Terrorist Attacks upon the United States," released July 22, 2004. www.911commission.gov/.

Walsh, Lawrence E., "Final Report of the Independent Counsel for Iran/Contra Matters," released August 4, 1993. www.fas.org/irp/offdocs/walsh.

SELECTED GOVERNMENT DOCUMENTS

"Backgrounder on the Morrill Act." State Department report, undated. http://usinfo
.state.gov/usa/infousa/facts/democrac/27.htm.

"Iraq Contingency Planning." State Department memorandum, February 7, 2003.
www.gwu.edu/~nsarchiv/NSAEBB/NSAEBB163/iraq-state-03.pdf.

"Key Judgments, October 2002 National Intelligence Estimate." National Intelligence Council report, declassified July 18, 2003. www.fas.org/irp/cia/product/
iraq-wmd.html.

"National Security Directive 26: U.S. Policy Toward the Persian Gulf." White House
memorandum, October 2, 1989. http://bushlibrary.tamu.edu/research/nsd/NSD/
NSD%2026/0001.pdf (accessed March 31, 2005).

"National Security Presidential Directive 36: United States Government Operations
in Iraq." White House memorandum, May 11, 2004. www.fas.org/irp/offdocs/
nspd/.

"National Security Review 12: Review of National Defense Strategy." White House
memorandum, March 3, 1989. www.fas.org/irp/offdocs/nsr/nsr12.pdf.

"North Korea: A Chronology of Events, October 2002–December 2004." Congressional Research Service Report, January 24, 2005.

"Unclassified Report to Congress on the Acquisition of Technology Relating to
Weapons of Mass Destruction and Advanced Conventional Munitions, 1 January
Through 30 June 2000." CIA report, February 2001. www.fas.org/irp/threat/
bian_feb_2001.htm#4.

"United Nations Security Council Resolution 1441," November 8, 2002. www.un.int/
usa/sres-iraq.htm.

MANUSCRIPT COLLECTIONS

Dwight D. Eisenhower Presidential Library and Museum, Abilene, Kans.

Harry S. Truman Presidential Museum and Library, Independence, Mo.

Historical Manuscripts Collection, U.S. Army Center of Military History, Carlisle, Pa.

Jimmy Carter Library and Museum, Atlanta, Ga.

John F. Kennedy Library and Museum, Boston, Mass.

Modern Military Records Unit, National Archives, College Park, Md.

National Security Archive, George Washington University, Washington, D.C.

National Security Project, Brookings Institution, Washington, D.C.

Papers of General Colin L. Powell (Ret.). Special Collections, National Defense University Library, Fort Lesley J. McNair, Washington, D.C.

The Pentagon Papers, Gravel Edition. www.mtholyoke.edu/acad/intrel/pentagon/
pent1.html.

Ronald Reagan Presidential Library, Simi Valley, Calif.

PUBLIC REMARKS

Blair, Tony. "Prime Minister's Iraq Statement to Parliament," September 24, 2002,
London, U.K. British Government transcript.

Buchanan, Patrick. "Remarks to the 1992 Republican National Convention," August
17, 1992, Houston, Tex.

Bush, George H. W. "Remarks to Reporters," August 5, 1990, Washington, D.C. White
House transcript.

———. "Remarks at a Photo Opportunity with Agriculture Leaders," May 2, 1991,
Washington, D.C. White House transcript.

————. "Remarks in the Rose Garden," May 23, 1991, Washington, D.C. White House transcript.

————. "Address to the Nation," May 1, 1992, Washington, D.C. White House transcript.

Bush, George W. "Remarks at a San Antonio News Conference," September 24, 1997, San Antonio, Texas.

————. "A Distinctly American Internationalism," November 19, 1999, Washington, D.C. Federal News Service transcript.

————. "Press Conference at the National Press Club," May 23, 2000, Washington, D.C. Federal News Service transcript.

————. "Presidential Debate at Wake Forest University," October 12, 2000, Winston-Salem, N.C. Federal News Service transcript.

————. "Announcement of Colin Powell's Nomination for Secretary of State," December 16, 2000, Crawford, Tex. Federal News Service transcript.

————. "Press Conference with Mexican President Vicente Fox," February 16, 2001. White House transcript.

————. "Remarks with President Kim Dae Jung of South Korea," March 7, 2001, Washington, D.C. White House transcript.

————. "Remarks by the President in Photo Opportunity with the National Security Team," September 12, 2001, Washington, D.C. White House transcript.

————. "President Bush Speaks to the United Nations," November 10, 2001, New York, New York. White House transcript.

————. "President Discusses War, Humanitarian Efforts," November 19, 2001, Washington, D.C. White House transcript.

————. "Remarks by the President and General Tommy Franks," December 28, 2001, Washington, D.C. White House transcript.

————. "President's State of the Union Address," January 29, 2002, Washington, D.C. White House transcript.

————. "Remarks by the President, the Vice President, and the Secretary of State on the Middle East," March 7, 2002, Washington, D.C. White House transcript.

————. "President to Send Secretary Powell to the Middle East," April 4, 2002, Washington, D.C. White House transcript.

————. "President, Secretary Powell Discuss Middle East," April 18, 2002, Washington, D.C. White House transcript.

————. "President Bush Delivers Graduation Speech at West Point," June 1, 2002, West Point, New York. White House transcript.

————. "President Bush Calls for New Palestinian Leadership," June 24, 2002, Washington, D.C. White House transcript.

————. "President Urges Congress to Support Nation's Priorities," July 8, 2002, Washington, D.C. White House transcript.

————. "President Discusses Foreign Policy with Congressional Leaders," September 4, 2002, Washington, D.C. White House transcript.

————. "Remarks by the President in Address to the United Nations General Assembly," September 12, 2002, New York, New York. White House transcript.

————. "Remarks by the President on Iraq," October 7, 2002, Cincinnati, Ohio. White House transcript.

————. "President's Statement on Security Council Resolution," November 8, 2002, Washington, D.C. White House transcript.

————. "President Meets with Leading Economists," January 21, 2003, Washington, D.C. White House transcript.

————. "President Bush Meets with Prime Minister Blair," January 31, 2003, London, England. White House transcript.

————. "Remarks by the President at Multilateral Meeting with Arab Leaders," June 3, 2003, Sharm el-Sheikh, Egypt. White House transcript.

————. "President Discusses Economy, North Korea with Cabinet," August 1, 2003, Washington, D.C. White House transcript.

————. "President Bush and Secretary Powell Meet in Crawford," August 6, 2003, Crawford, Tex. White House transcript.

————. "Remarks by the President at Bush-Cheney 2004 Reception," January 8, 2004, Washington, D.C. White House transcript.

————. "President Bush Welcomes President Kwasniewski to White House," January 27, 2004, Washington, D.C. White House transcript.

————. "President Holds Press Conference," November 4, 2004, Washington, D.C. White House transcript.

Cheney, Richard B. "Remarks at the National Press Club," May 20, 1992, Washington, D.C. Federal News Service transcript.

————. "Vice President Speaks at VFW 103rd National Convention," August 26, 2002, Nashville, Tenn. White House transcript.

Clinton, William J. "Remarks at Retirement Ceremony for General Colin L. Powell," September 30, 1993, Washington, D.C. Federal News Service transcript.

Eisenhower, Dwight D. "Remarks at the Governors' Conference," August 4, 1953, Seattle, Wash. Eisenhower Library.

Fleischer, Ari. "White House Press Briefing," September 15, 2001, Washington, D.C. White House transcript.

————. "White House Press Briefing," April 22, 2003, Washington, D.C. White House transcript.

Gingrich, Newt. "Transforming the State Department," April 22, 2003, Washington, D.C. American Enterprise Institute transcript.

Jefferson, Thomas. "First Inaugural Address," March 4, 1801, Washington, D.C.

Kennedy, John F. "Commencement Address at Yale University," June 11, 1962, New Haven, Connecticut.

McClellan, Scott. "Press Briefing by Scott McClellan," August 4, 2003, Washington, D.C. White House transcript.

————. "Press Briefing by Scott McClellan," November 15, 2004, Washington, D.C. White House transcript.

Nixon, Richard M. "Speech to the Nation," November 3, 1969, Washington, D.C.

Powell, Colin L. "National Security Challenges in the '90s: The Future Ain't What It Used to Be," May 16, 1989, Carlisle, Pa. Powell Papers.

————. "Address at the National Defense University," December 13, 1989, Washington, D.C. Powell papers.

————. "National Defense University Distinguished Lecture Program," November 30, 1990, Washington, D.C. Powell Papers.

————. "Remarks at Vietnam Veterans Memorial," May 27, 1991, Washington, D.C. Federal News Service transcript.

————. "Remarks to the National Press Club," September 23, 1993, Washington, D.C. Powell Papers.

————. "Remarks at Retirement Ceremony," September 30, 1993, Washington, D.C. Federal News Service transcript.

————. "Remarks at the Republican National Convention," August 12, 1996, San Diego, California. Federal News Service transcript.

———. "Remarks at the Republican National Convention," July 31, 2000, Philadelphia, Pennsylvania. Federal News Service transcript.

———. "Secretary Powell Greets State Department Employees," January 22, 2001, Washington, D.C. State Department transcript.

———. "Town Hall Meeting," January 25, 2001, Washington, D.C. State Department transcript.

———. "Press Conference at the United Nations," February 14, 2001, New York, New York. State Department transcript.

———. "Press Appearance with Swedish Foreign Minister Anna Lindh," March 6, 2001, Washington, D.C. State Department transcript.

———. "Remarks on Meeting Between President Bush and South Korean President Kim Dae Jung," March 17, 2001, Washington, D.C. Federal News Service transcript.

———. "Statement at the Special General Assembly of the Organization of American States," September 11, 2001, Lima, Peru. State Department transcript.

———. "Press Briefing on Board Plane en Route Washington D.C.," September 11, 2001.

———. "Secretary of State on-the-Record Briefing," September 12, 2001, Washington, D.C. State Department transcript.

———. "Speech at the University of Louisville," November 19, 2001, Louisville, Kentucky. State Department transcript.

———. "Remarks with King Abdullah of Jordan," January 31, 2002, Washington, D.C. State Department transcript.

———. "Remarks at David Citadel Hotel," April 17, 2002, Jerusalem, Israel. State Department transcript.

———. "Press Conference on Iraq Declaration," December 19, 2002, Washington, D.C. State Department transcript.

———. "Remarks at the World Economic Forum," January 26, 2003, Davos, Switzerland. State Department transcript.

———. "Remarks to the United Nations Security Council," February 5, 2003, New York. State Department transcript.

———. "State Department Briefing," March 17, 2003, Washington, D.C. State Department transcript.

———. "Press Briefing Aboard Air Force One," May 30, 2003. State Department transcript.

———. "Secretary Powell's Press Conference," January 8, 2004, Washington, D.C. State Department transcript.

———. "Briefing to Reporters," January 24, 2004, Washington, D.C. State Department transcript.

———. "Remarks After His Meeting with United Nations Secretary General Kofi Annan," February 3, 2004, Washington, D.C. State Department transcript.

———. "Remarks at the Brookhaven Boys and Girls Club," October 2, 2004, Atlanta, Georgia. State Department transcript.

———. "On-the-Record Briefing," November 15, 2004, Washington, D.C. State Department transcript.

———. "Remarks to the National War College," September 19, 2005, Washington, D.C. Author notes.

Rumsfeld, Donald L. "Department of Defense News Briefing by Secretary Rumsfeld and General Myers," January 11, 2002, Washington, D.C. Department of Defense transcript.

————. "Defense Department Briefing," March 11, 2003, Washington, D.C. Department of Defense transcript.

Tenet, George. "Remarks at Georgetown University," February 5, 2004, Washington, D.C. Federal News Service transcript.

Weinberger, Caspar W. "The Uses of Military Power," November 28, 1984, Washington, D.C.

Zinni, Anthony. "Speech Before the Florida Economic Club," August 23, 2002, Tallahassee, Florida.

PRINT AND BROADCAST MEDIA

Newspapers: *The Atlanta Journal-Constitution, Austin American-Statesman, The Boston Globe, The Boston Herald, Chicago Tribune, Financial Times* (London), *The Guardian* (London), *The Houston Chronicle, The Jerusalem Post, The Lakeland Ledger, Los Angeles Times, Michigan Chronicle, Modesto Bee, The New York Times, Newsday* (New York), *The Philadelphia Inquirer, The Plain Dealer* (Cleveland), *San Antonio Express-News, The San Francisco Chronicle, The Times* (London), *USA Today, The Wall Street Journal, The Washington Post, The Washington Times, Women's Wear Daily.*

Magazines: *The Atlantic Monthly, Commentary, The Crisis, Ebony, Ladies' Home Journal, Los Angeles Times Magazine, The Nation, The National Interest, The National Journal, Newsweek, The New American, The New Republic, The New York Times Magazine, The New Yorker, Newsday Magazine, Parade, Time, U.S. News & World Report, The Weekly Standard, The Washington Post Magazine.*

News Agencies: Agence France Presse, The Associated Press, BBC News, Federal News Service, Reuters, United Press International.

Television/Radio Programs: ABC (*20/20, ABC News, Good Morning America, Nightline, This Week*); BBC (BBC Radio, *Breakfast with Sir David Frost*); CBS (*60 Minutes II, CBS News, Face the Nation*); CNN (*Larry King Live, Late Edition*); Fox (*Fox News Sunday*); *The Oprah Winfrey Show; The Michael Reagan Radio Show;* NBC (*Meet the Press, Today*); NPR; Pakistan Television; PBS (*Frontline, The NewsHour with Jim Lehrer, Talking with Sir David Frost*); Talk Radio News; TV One (*Armstrong Williams*).

INDEX

PHOTOGRAPHIC CREDITS

All illustrations not listed here are courtesy of the Colin L. Powell Papers, National Defense University.

AP Images: Cheney and Powell in Saudi Arabia; Chicago parade; Republican Presidential Convention; Bush with advisers at Camp David; NATO summit in Prague; U.N. Security Council; News conference with Security Council members; Former secretaries of defense and state at White House

George Bush Presidential Library: Powell appointed chairman of Joint Chiefs of Staff; Powell briefs Bush on Operation Desert Storm; Powell and Bush on phone calls

Department of the Army: Helicopter crash in S. Vietnam; Powell with troops at Fort Campbell; Powell and Rumsfeld at Fort Campbell

Department of Defense: Powell's retirement ceremony

Courtesy Bruce Llewellyn: Young Luther and Nessa Powell

Courtesy Gene Norman: Young Powell on his bicycle

Ronald Reagan Library: Reagan appoints Powell national security adviser; Powell and Reagan at Reagan's ranch

The Washington Post/Dudley M. Brooks: Powell with Alma

The Washington Post/Frank Johnston: Cheney and Powell on White House South Lawn

The Washington Post/Rich Lipski: Card, Rice, and Powell in Oval Office

The Washington Post/Gerald Martineau: Powell and Clinton; Washington, D.C. Boys and Girls Club; Powell saying good-bye to State Dept. employees

The White House: Powell briefs Reagan and Baker; Powell family outside Oval Office; Bush and Powell in a lighthearted moment; Bush, Powell, and Armitage in Texas

A NOTE ABOUT THE AUTHOR

Karen DeYoung is an associate editor at *The Washington Post,* where she has held a number of editing positions and served as a foreign policy reporter in Washington and a correspondent abroad. She is the recipient of numerous awards for foreign correspondence and for diplomatic and explanatory journalism, including the 2002 Pulitzer Prize given to the *Post* for national coverage of the war on terrorism. A graduate of the University of Florida, she lives in Washington, D.C.

A NOTE ON THE TYPE

This book was set in Bodoni, a typeface named after Giambattista Bodoni (1740–1813), the celebrated printer and type designer of Parma. The Bodoni types of today were designed not as faithful reproductions of any one of the Bodoni fonts but rather as a composite, modern version of the Bodoni manner. Bodoni's innovations in type style included a greater degree of contrast in the thick and thin elements of the letters and a sharper and more angular finish of details.

Composed by North Market Street Graphics,
Lancaster, Pennsylvania
Printed and bound by R. R. Donnelley & Sons,
Harrisonburg, Virginia
Designed by Wesley Gott